Encyclopedia of Archaeology

The Great Archaeologists

Encyclopedia of Archaeology

The Great Archaeologists

Volume I

Edited by Tim Murray

ABC-CLIO

Santa Barbara, California
Denver, Colorado
Oxford, England

A Cataloging-in-Publication Data record is available from the Library of Congress.

ISBN 1-57607-199-5
05 04 03 02 01 00 99   10 9 8 7 6 5 4 3 2 1

ABC-CLIO, Inc.
130 Cremona Drive, P.O. Box 1911
Santa Barbara, California 93116–1911

This book is printed on acid-free paper ∞ .

Manufactured in the United States of America

Advisory Board

Contents

Alphabetical List of Entries, xi

Preface and Acknowledgments, xiii

Introduction, xv

The Contributors, xix

The Great Archaeologists
Volume I

William Camden (1551–1623), *Graham Parry, 1*

John Aubrey (1626–1697), *Graham Parry, 15*

Edward Lhwyd (1660–1709), *Graham Parry, 27*

William Stukeley (1687–1765), *Graham Parry, 39*

Johann Joachim Winckelmann (1717–1768), *Max Kunze, 51*

Sven Nilsson (1787–1883), *Johan Hegardt, 65*

Daniel Wilson (1816–1892), *Bruce G. Trigger, 79*

Gabriel de Mortillet (1821–1898), *Nathalie Richard, 93*

Heinrich Schliemann (1822–1890), *Leo Klejn, 109*

Augustus Pitt Rivers (1827–1900), *Mark Bowden, 127*

Frederic Ward Putnam (1839–1915), *Curtis Hinsley, 141*

Gustaf Oscar Augustin Montelius (1843–1921), *Bo Gräslund, 155*

Nikodim Pavlovich Kondakov (1844–1925), *Leo Klejn, 165*

William Henry Holmes (1846–1933), *David J. Meltzer, 175*

Sophus Otto Müller (1846–1934), *Marie Louise Stig Sørenson, 193*

Sir Arthur Evans (1851–1941), *Tim Murray, 211*

Sir William Matthews Flinders Petrie (1853–1942), *Margaret S. Drower, 221*

Gustaf Kossinna (1858–1931), *Leo Klejn, 233*

Vasiliy Alekeyevich Gorodcov (1860–1945), *Leo Klejn, 247*

Marcellin Boule (1861–1942), *Nathalie Richard, 263*

Joseph Déchelette (1862–1914), *Laurent Olivier, 275*

Howard Carter (1874–1939), *Tim Murray, 289*

Abbé Henri Breuil (1877–1961), *Claudine Cohen, 301*

Sylvanus Griswold Morley (1883–1948), *Douglas R. Givens, 313*

Manuel Gamio (1883–1960), *Roberto Cobean and Alba Guadalupe Mastache Flores, 325*

Albert Egges van Giffen (1884–1973), *H. T. Waterbolk, 335*

Alfred Vincent Kidder (1885–1963), *Douglas R. Givens, 357*

Sir Mortimer Wheeler (1890–1976), *Barry Cunliffe, 371*

Vere Gordon Childe (1892–1957), *Bruce G. Trigger, 385*

Dorothy Garrod (1892–1968), *Sir Grahame Clark, 401*

William Duncan Strong (1899–1962), *Richard B. Woodbury, 413*

Jorge R. Acosta (1904?–1975), *Roberto Cobean and Alba Guadalupe Mastache Flores, 425*

Pei Wenzhong (1904–1982), *John W. Olsen, 441*

James Bennett Griffin (1905–1997), *Stephen Williams, 451*

Volume II

Christopher Hawkes (1905–1992), *Christopher Evans, 461*

Kathleen Mary Kenyon (1906–1978), *Thomas Holland, 481*

Robert John Braidwood (b. 1907), *Patty-Jo Watson, 495*

Sir Grahame Clark (1907–1995), *Peter Rowley-Conwy, 507*

Eric Higgs (1908–1976), *Geoff Bailey, 531*

Aleksei Pavlovich Okladnikov (b. 1908), *Ruslan S. Vasilevsky, 567*

Hasmukh D. Sankalia (1908–1989), *K. Paddayya, 581*

Su Bingqi (1909–1997), *Lothar von Falkenhausen, 591*

Xia Nai (1910–1985), *Lothar von Falkenhausen, 601*

Stuart Piggott (1910–1996), *Niall Sharples, 615*

James Alfred Ford (1911–1968), *James B. Griffin, 635*

André Leroi-Gourhan (1911–1986), *Anick Coudart, 653*

Irving Benjamin Rouse (b. 1913), *Robert C. Dunnell, 665*

Walter W. Taylor (1913–1997), *Jonathan E. Reyman, 681*

Gordon Randolph Willey (b. 1913), *Robert Preucel, 701*

Charles McBurney (1914–1979), *John Gowlett, 713*

Charles Thurstan Shaw (b. 1914), *Graham Connah, 727*

J. Desmond Clark (b. 1916), *Fred Wendorf,* 743

François Bordes (1919–1981), *Lewis Binford (with Nancy Medaris Stone),* 759

Mats P. Malmer (b. 1921), *Marie Louise Stig Sørenson,* 775

Robert McCormick Adams (b. 1926), *Norman Yoffee,* 791

Lewis Binford (b. 1929), *Clive Gamble,* 811

Roger Curtis Green (b. 1932), *Janet Davidson,* 835

David Clarke (b. 1938–1976), *Roland Fletcher,* 855

Epilogue: The Art of Archaeological Biography, Tim Murray, *869*

Glossary, 885

Index, 895

Alphabetical List of Entries

Acosta, Jorge R., *425*

Adams, Robert McCormick, *791*

Aubrey, John, *15*

Binford, Lewis, *811*

Bordes, François, *759*

Boule, Marcellin, *263*

Braidwood, Robert John, *495*

Breuil, Abbé Henri, *301*

Camden, William, *1*

Carter, Howard, *289*

Childe, Vere Gordon, *385*

Clark, Sir Grahame, *507*

Clark, J. Desmond, *743*

Clarke, David, *855*

Déchelette, Joseph, *275*

Evans, Sir Arthur, *211*

Ford, James Alfred, *635*

Gamio, Manuel, *325*

Garrod, Dorothy, *401*

Gorodcov, Vasiliy Alekeyevich, *247*

Green, Roger Curtis, *835*

Griffin, James Bennett, *451*

Hawkes, Christopher, *461*

Higgs, Eric, *531*

Holmes, William Henry, *175*

Kenyon, Kathleen Mary, *481*

Kidder, Alfred Vincent, *357*

Kondakov, Nikodim Pavlovich, *165*

Kossinna, Gustaf, *233*

Leroi-Gourhan, André, *653*

Lhwyd, Edward, *27*

Malmer, Mats P., *775*

McBurney, Charles, *713*

Montelius, Gustaf Oscar Augustin, *155*

Morley, Sylvanus Griswold, *313*

Mortillet, Gabriel de, *93*

Müller, Sophus Otto, *193*

Nilsson, Sven, *65*

Okladnikov, Aleksei Pavlovich, *567*

Pei Wenzhong, *441*

Petrie, Sir William Matthews Flinders, *221*

Piggott, Stuart, *615*

Pitt Rivers, Augustus, *127*

Putnam, Frederic Ward, *141*

Rouse, Irving Benjamin, *665*

Sankalia, Hasmukh D., *581*

Schliemann, Heinrich, *109*

Shaw, Charles Thurstan, *727*

Strong, William Duncan, *413*

Stukeley, William, *39*

Su Bingqi, *591*

Taylor, Walter W., *681*

Van Giffen, Albert Egges, *335*

Wheeler, Sir Mortimer, *371*

Winckelmann, Johann Joachim, *51*

Willey, Gordon Randolph, *701*

Wilson, Daniel, *79*

Xia Nai, *601*

Preface and Acknowledgments

This project has had a long gestation. After what seem to be thousands of letters, faxes, phone calls, and electronic messages to (and from) archaeologists all over the world, it is something of a shock to contemplate such a large and diverse book. There were times when I doubted whether we would ever complete the project, but the fact that it has finally happened is, in large measure, due to the hard work and commitment of the authors whose work makes up this rich diversity. They, rightly, deserve the most acknowledgment for their industry and their patience.

I gave very few instructions about the way in which each author was to tackle their subject (the most detailed instructions were contained in the style sheet), as I was (and remain) firmly of the view that in the current state of research into the history of archaeology the last thing we need are formulas to be applied to this most introspective of activities. Each of the authors approached their subject in ways that suited them best, and there is an interesting sample of approaches that either consciously or unconsciously mirror biography writing in other sciences. It was also my desire that I would use only the lightest of editorial touches to retain this sense of diversity and polyvocality and, for most of the essays, I was able to do this. That I was able to do so is largely due to the care taken by the authors and by their translators. Of these, Dr. Judith Braid (Déchelette, Mortillet, and Boule), Sergei Bunaev (Okladnikov), Cynthia Hood (Breuil), and Steven Lindberg (Winckelmann) deserve special mention.

My work as editor began when I was a Visiting Fellow of Clare Hall, Cambridge, and I am particularly grateful to the Wenner-Gren Foundation for Anthropological Research (through the award of the Richard Carley Hunt Fellowship) for making it possible to work in such a marvelous environment. This is one of those unintended by-products of teaching-free time! The office staff of Clare Hall, particularly Elizabeth Ramsden, made the job of communicating with hundreds of scholars on four continents less difficult than it otherwise might have been. The vast bulk of this project was supported by the Department of Archaeology at

La Trobe University. Not only have two long periods of research leave at the University of Cambridge and the Université de Paris 1 Panthéon-Sorbonne made it possible to begin and then to complete the project, the two departmental secretaries, Stella Bromilow and Ros Allen, spent many hours scanning text, translating arcane word-processing software, and transmitting faxes.

I was particularly fortunate in having Kristi Ward from ABC-CLIO contact me in search of a book about the history of archaeology at a time when I needed an understanding publisher. It is a simple statement of the truth that there would be no book without her. I was also very lucky to have Susan McRory from ABC-CLIO's Denver office managing the production of the book. Given the scale of the project and the schedule for production, she deserves more than a sincere thank you. The completion of this book was greatly aided by the award of an Australian Research Council and French Ministry of Higher Education and Research Fellowship, which allowed me to take leave from teaching and administration and go to Paris. La Trobe University also very generously funded the appointment of a research assistant, Susan Bridekirk, who was able to make a really effective contribution in the closing stages of the project. I am very grateful to them all.

As usual, my family have borne the brunt of this book since its inception, and I dedicate it to them as a token of compensation. I would be lost without them.

Tim Murray
Melbourne, Australia
1999

Introduction

It has often been observed that during the nineteenth century archaeology became a preeminently popular science because of its potent cocktail of mystery, patient investigation, direct physical contact with the relics of ages past, and of course, the lure of foreign parts. Little has changed since then, as new civilizations have been unearthed, languages have been deciphered, and the antiquity of human life on earth has been extended to almost unimaginable depths. Archaeology has touched and continues to touch everybody, and although much of it has become highly technical and arcane, the central elements of our quest for an understanding of the history of human beings have remained largely intact. In the late twentieth century archaeologists might be a little more wary about claiming an ability to reconstruct the past, or indeed to be in a position to pronounce definitively on the question of when human beings became properly human, but there remains a core of belief that only archaeology can reveal the evidence of the whole human story from prehistoric to historical times.

From our present vantage point claims about the ability of archaeology to make such a fundamental contribution to humanity seem self-evidently true, but a significant element of the history of archaeology is the story of how people were persuaded that archaeological sites and their contexts (as well the material remains of human lives) could yield important historical and anthropological information. Naturally the forms of that information and the various theories and perspectives that have underwritten its production and dissemination have changed, but the desire to make the past meaningful to the present has remained. But making meanings has had (and continues to have) significant consequences.

During the course of the last three hundred years archaeology has evolved to become a potent tool for both creating and destroying histories, identities, and even nations. Archaeologists have demonstrated their power to support and to oppose prevailing ideologies, government policies, and popular movements. There are many examples of the power of archaeology to do good, to enhance our self-understanding, to more clearly comprehend the extraordinary capacity of human beings to change, to adapt, and to overcome challenges from all quarters. However, there are also very many examples of the potential of archaeology to cause harm, whether it is employed in spurious racial and ethnic histories that are then used to justify the domination of one group over another, or whether it is used to undermine the viability of indigenous views of the histories of colonized peoples. Thus another significant lesson from the history of archaeology is that the knowledge which it produces is embedded in the culture and society of its time and that this is never value neutral.

If we allow that archaeological knowledge has such significance and such potential consequences, then we should also allow those who are most affected to understand how it is (and by whom it is) produced. The primary purpose of this book is to contribute to that understanding through reflections by practicing archaeologists on the lives and work of their forebears, colleagues, and teachers. There are many fine histories of archaeology, the two most intellectually satisfying and comprehensive being Bruce Trigger's *A History of Archaeological Thought* (Cambridge: Cambridge University Press, 1989) and Alain Schnapp's *The Discovery of the Past* (London: British Museum Press, 1996), but in that context the texture of individual action is necessarily sacrificed for more general discussion.

Similarly, there are a number of excellent biographies and autobiographies of archaeologists, but these have tended to focus on those with the very highest public profile outside archaeology. There is absolutely nothing wrong in this—indeed, archaeologists such as Mortimer Wheeler, Gordon Childe, Flinders Petrie, and Augustus Pitt Rivers are found in this book too—but the goal of broadening our understanding of archaeology would not be furthered by focusing only on the famous (or in the case of Heinrich Schliemann, the infamous). Far better is to explore the lives of those, who despite playing a significant role in the development of world archaeology, were largely unknown outside the discipline.

It will come as no surprise that the selection of the subjects and their biographers was a challenging process. From the start I accepted that the criteria for inclusion (that the subject had made a major contribution to the development of archaeology as a discipline) would mean that we were likely to produce a volume with a lot of dead white males. It is well understood that opportunities for women to excel in archaeology (as in many other fields) have been restricted until recent decades. It is also understood that many archaeologists (both women and men) have done fine work that does not yield the kind of recognition that applies to the subjects in this book. It is one of the most encouraging developments in the history of archaeology that our attention has begun to draw away from a focus on the "great" archaeologist to an exploration of the personal and institutional fabric of the discipline, which provides the context in which great discoveries or fundamental methodological and theoretical advances can be made. A recent collection of essays, *Excavating Women: A History of Women in European Archaeology,* edited by Margarita Diaz Andreu and Marie Louise Stig Sørensen (London and New York: Routledge, 1998) is a good example of this more broadly conceived disciplinary history.

Thus there can be no doubt that public understanding of the institutions and processes of archaeology is important. However, we also need to acknowledge that the most direct point of contact between people and archaeology is the work of archaeologists whose discoveries and ideas have the power to transform our ideas about ourselves. The subjects of the biographies in this book have made fundamental contributions of this kind, even though many of them are unknown outside archaeology. When this book was being planned I took advice from my editorial board: K.-C. Chang (Harvard University), Douglas Givens (Peabody Museum, Harvard University), Leo Klejn (European University, St. Petersburg), Colin Renfrew (University of Cambridge), Alain Schnapp (Université de Paris 1 Panthéon-Sorbonne) and Bruce Trigger (McGill University). Their wisdom (and their networks) was crucial, and it was supplemented by many others, particularly Martin Millett, Richard Bradley, Clive Gamble, Steve Shennan, Jim Allen, Michael Hunter, Klaus Randsborg, Richard J. Pearson, Gina Barnes, Gordon Willey, and Ralph Solecki.

Greatness, like just about everything else, is a subject archaeologists find it very easy to argue about, and there was by no means universal agreement about the list of potential subjects. This is wholly appropriate. The fifty-eight biographies presented here are the survivors of a list of over eighty who were regarded as having met the criterion. I expect that many readers will find a number of omissions to be puzzling (for example, no Leonard Woolley, no Gertrude Bell, no Margaret Murray, no Gertrude Caton Thompson, no Louis Leakey, no Glyn Isaac), and for some the annoying consequence of a cultural, disciplinary, or gender bias. But while I cannot claim sufficient wisdom to be aware of all my biases, the very great majority of those missing are absent because of the inevitable limitations of time and space.

But having said this, it seems to me that it is far more profitable to focus on what we can learn from what is in the book than to spend too much time wringing our hands about what is not. This book of archaeological biographies, written by practicing archaeologists—many of the authors themselves being eminent in the field—is a unique window on the evolution of the discipline of archaeology. Perhaps of equal importance, the biographies also allow us to observe the evolution of the archaeologist—part scientist, part humanities scholar, part fieldworker, and in some cases seemingly part magician. It is a rare privilege.

The Contributors

GEOFF BAILEY is professor of archaeology at the University of Newcastle, England. A noted field archaeologist with strong research interests in the archaeology of Australia and of Paleolithic Europe, Bailey has also made important contributions to the development of archaeological theory.

LEWIS BINFORD is professor of archaeology at Southern Methodist University, Dallas. Widely regarded as being the most influential prehistoric archaeologist of the last fifty years, Binford is most famous for groundbreaking studies in both archaeological method and theory.

MARK BOWDEN is the author of a major study on General Pitt Rivers.

SIR GRAHAME CLARK was one of the most significant archaeologists of the twentieth century. Based at the University of Cambridge, England, Clark made major contributions to the archaeology of the European Mesolithic and was one of the creators of the concept of world prehistory.

ROBERTO COBEAN works at the Instituto Nacional de Antropología e Historia (INAH) in Mexico City.

CLAUDINE COHEN researches the history of French archaeology and paleontology and works at the École des Hautes Études en Sciences Sociales, Paris.

GRAHAM CONNAH is emeritus professor of archaeology at the University of New England in Australia. Connah is best known for his research into African archaeology (particularly of later periods), but he has also played a significant role in the development of historical archaeology in Australia.

ANICK COUDART conducts archaeological and ethnological research under the auspices of the Centre National de la Recherche Scientifique (CNRS) and is based in Paris. A student of Leroi-Gourhan, Coudart has most recently done fieldwork in Papua New Guinea.

BARRY CUNLIFFE is professor of archaeology at Oxford University. His research interests include the archaeology of Roman Britain.

JANET DAVIDSON works at the National Museum of New Zealand. Her research focus is on Oceanic archaeology.

MARGARET S. DROWER has published the standard biography of Flinders Petrie. She has had a long association with the Egypt Exploration Society in London.

ROBERT C. DUNNELL is emeritus professor of anthropology at the University of Washington, Seattle. He is best known for his writings on theoretical archaeology and the history of archaeology in North America.

CHRISTOPHER EVANS is director of the Cambridge Archaeology Unit of the University of Cambridge, England. He is an influential historian of English archaeology, as well as being a noted field archaeologist.

ROLAND FLETCHER teaches prehistoric archaeology at the University of Sydney, Australia. He is the author of many works on spatial archaeology and has a strong interest in theoretical archaeology.

CLIVE GAMBLE is professor of archaeology at the University of Southampton, England. He is best known for his work on the archaeology of global settlement by fully modern human beings and the Paleolithic of Europe.

DOUGLAS R. GIVENS, a research associate of the Peabody Museum at Harvard University, is a historian of archaeology in North America.

JOHN GOWLETT teaches archaeology at the University of Liverpool. His research interests include the Paleolithic, early hominid studies, and paleoanthropology.

BO GRÄSLUND is professor of archaeology at the University of Uppsala, Sweden. He is a noted historian of archaeology in Scandinavia.

JAMES B. GRIFFIN is most famous through his long association with the Department of Anthropology at the University of Michigan. Griffin was widely regarded as one of the most significant North American archaeologists of the postwar period.

JOHAN HEGARDT teaches archaeology at the University of Uppsala, Sweden.

CURTIS HINSLEY is professor of history at the University of Northern Arizona, Flagstaff. He has published widely in the history of archaeology in the southwestern United States.

THOMAS HOLLAND works at the Oriental Institute, University of Chicago, and is a specialist in the archaeology of the Levant.

LEO KLEJN is currently on the staff of the European University at St. Petersburg, Russia. He is one of the most significant archaeologists of his generation in Russia; he has a strong international reputation in theoretical archaeology.

MAX KUNZE is a noted Winckelmann scholar and works at the Winckelmann Institute in Berlin, Germany.

ALBA GUADALUPE MASTACHE FLORES works at the Instituto Nacional de Antropología e Historia (INAH) in Mexico City.

DAVID J. MELTZER is professor of archaeology at Southern Methodist University, Dallas. His research interests include the Paleoindians of North America, the peopling of the Americas, and the history of archaeology in North America.

TIM MURRAY is professor of archaeology at La Trobe University, Melbourne, Australia. His major research interests are in the history and philosophy of archaeology and in theoretical archaeology.

LAURENT OLIVIER is a specialist in European Iron Age archaeology and works at the Museé des Antiquités Nationales in Saint Germain-en-Laye, France.

JOHN W. OLSEN is professor of anthropology at the University of Arizona. His major research interest is in Old World prehistory, particularly that of China and Central Asia.

K. PADDAYA teaches archaeology at the Deccan College, Pune, India. His major research interests are in the history and theory of archaeology.

GRAHAM PARRY is professor of English at the University of York, England. His major research interests are in the relationships between literature and the visual arts and in the history of antiquarianism.

ROBERT PREUCEL teaches in the Department of Anthropology, University of Pennsylvania, and holds a curatorial position at the university's Museum of Archaeology and Anthropology. His research interests include North American archaeology and archaeological method and theory.

JONATHAN E. REYMAN works at the Illinois State Museum and has published widely on the history of archaeology in North America.

NATHALIE RICHARD of the University of Rennes, France, is a historian of French archaeology.

PETER ROWLEY-CONWY teaches archaeology at the University of Durham, England. His major research is in the European Mesolithic and in the archaeology of animals, particularly the analysis of faunal assemblages from archaeological sites.

NIALL SHARPLES teaches archaeology at the University of Cardiff, Wales. He has research interests in the history of archaeological thought and conducts field research into the archaeology of Neolithic England.

MARIE LOUISE STIG SØRENSON teaches archaeology at the University of

Cambridge, England. Her research specialties are in European Iron Age archaeology, gender studies in archaeology, and the history of archaeology.

BRUCE G. TRIGGER is professor of anthropology at McGill University, Toronto, Canada. He is a noted historian of archaeology and has published a biography of Gordon Childe.

RUSLAN S. VASILEVSKY works at the Institute of Archaeology and Ethnology, Siberian Branch of the Russian Academy of Sciences, in Novosibirsk.

LOTHAR VON FALKENHAUSEN is a professor in the Department of Art History at the University of California, Los Angeles (UCLA). His research focuses on Chinese art.

H. T. WATERBOLK is a noted Dutch archaeologist who taught at the University of Groningen, the Netherlands, before his retirement.

PATTY-JO WATSON is professor of anthropology at Washington University, St. Louis. Her major research interests are in archaeological method and theory and in the archaeology of food production in Western Asia and in North America.

FRED WENDORF is professor of anthropology at Southern Methodist University, Dallas. He has had a distinguished career in the archaeology of the American Southwest and North Africa. His research interests include Paleolithic archaeology and the origins of agriculture.

STEPHEN WILLIAMS taught the archaeology of North America at Harvard University, Cambridge, Massachusetts.

RICHARD B. WOODBURY taught anthropology at the University of Massachusetts, Amherst.

NORMAN YOFFEE is a professor in the Department of Near Eastern Studies and the University Museum of Anthropology at the University of Michigan. Yoffee has written widely on the rise and collapse of ancient civilizations (particularly that of ancient Mesopotamia) and on archaeological theory.

Encyclopedia of Archaeology

The Great Archaeologists

Graham Parry

William Camden   1551–1623

Oxford classics scholar, genealogist, numismatist, etymologist, topographer,
Jacobean political scientist, and schoolteacher, William Camden was an example
of the English Renaissance person. The first scholar to record the rich history of
British antiquity and to publish in English, he linked English antiquaries and
humanist scholars with their contemporary European counterparts.

Effectively the founder of antiquarian studies in England through his
immensely influential book *Britannia,* William Camden was able to
bring an exceptionally wide range of skills to the elucidation of the remote past of his country. Well read in Greek and Roman literature, he
was familiar with all the references to Britain in the ancient historians,
geographers, and poets. He was an eminent topographer and had a pronounced interest in coins and inscriptions. As a herald, he was expert in
genealogies and the history of significant families and knowledgeable
about the offices and ceremonies of state. He became the historian of his
own age, writing an important account of the reigns of Elizabeth and
James, so that by the end of his own life he was not only the master of
British antiquity but also the interpreter of the modern political scene.

Camden was born in 1551 in London, the son of a painter. He attended St. Paul's School, where he received an excellent classical training, then proceeded to Oxford, where he was a student at Broadgate
Hall, later known as Pembroke College. About 1575 he became a master
at Westminster School and remained there for the rest of his life. At Oxford, the lure of antiquities inspired his frequent excursions to inspect
castles, earthworks, and ruins of all kinds. He was fortunate to be encouraged in these pursuits by Sir Philip Sidney and Fulke Greville, aristocratic men of letters and sympathetic sponsors who believed his passion for antiquities might be made to serve a patriotic cause: that is,
through the illumination of English history, the English people could better appreciate the nature and merits of their own country. So Camden began to keep notes of his observations and antiquarian discoveries, but
nothing came of these collections until he met the Flemish geographer
Abraham Ortelius in 1577. Ortelius was the modern Ptolemy, eager to
learn the topography of all countries and to turn that knowledge into
maps. His reputation had been solidly established by his atlas of the
world, entitled *Theatrum Orbis Terrarum,* published in 1570, and by his

A portrait medallion of William Camden. (© Copyright the British Museum)

Synonymia Geographia in 1578. He now planned to produce a series of maps of the ancient world, and he pressed Camden to turn his notes into a topographical account of Roman Britain that would identify and comment on the Roman sites. From these plans emerged *Britannia,* written in Latin and published in 1586.

The initial intention of the book was to describe Britain as a province of the Roman Empire and to search out those places mentioned in the works of Julius Caesar, Cornelius Tacitus, Ptolemy, and the surviving itinerary lists of antiquity. Camden particularly hoped to identify place-names from three important collections. The most notable of these was known as the Antonine Itinerary, a third-century A.D. record of routes across the Roman Empire. Fifteen itineraries in Britain were described, with the names of settlements and the distances between them. Ptolemy had given many lists of place-names and geographical features in Britain in his *Geography,* written in the mid-second century. Then there was the Notitia Provinciarum, or Notitia Dignitatum, an administrative register of offices and ranks throughout the late Roman Empire of the third century A.D., which included a section on Britain. Together, these documents furnished a large number of place-names for Roman Britain, but they also raised many questions. So many Roman settlements had disappeared, while others had developed into new towns, often with new names. Camden was well qualified to unravel these antiquarian puzzles. As a result of his travels around the country, he was probably more familiar with historic places than any other Englishman of his time, and he fortified his reading of all the ancient texts that had a bearing on Britain with a rudimentary knowledge of etymology. His purpose, he wrote, was "to restore Britain to its Antiquities, and its Antiquities to Britain, to renew the memory of what was old, illustrate what was obscure, and settle what was doubtful, and to recover some certainty in our affairs."

In the end, the book that appeared in 1586 was not primarily a reconstruction of Roman Britain. As Camden organized his material, he became increasingly curious about the native people subdued by the Romans. Who were the Britons? Where had they come from? What were their beliefs and customs and their forms of government? Camden was the first scholar to try to reconstruct the society of the ancient Britons in any detail. The prevailing view of British antiquity had previously been derived from the ingenious inventions of Geoffrey of Monmouth's *History of the Kings of Britain,* written in the mid-twelfth century. According to his chronicle, Britain had been settled by the Trojan Prince Brutus and his followers, who, after many years of wandering, had come to the land of Albion, where they defeated the few giants remaining from the most ancient days (including Gogmagog) and founded as their principal city Troynovant, or New Troy, which became London. The name of the land became Brutayne or Britain, after the Trojan hero. From Brutus descended a line of kings, including Locrine, Camber, Lear, and Cymbeline (who was ruling at the time of the birth of Christ). King Arthur was a late flowering of this ancient stock. This account, known as the "British History," was widely accepted, even as late as the seventeenth century. It satisfied the almost universal desire for known and illustrious origins; it associated Britain with an ancient high culture and with the epic story of the fall of Troy; and it gave Britain an antiquity comparable to that of Rome. The British History had been challenged in the reign of Henry VIII by the Italian scholar Polydore Vergil, who settled in England and wrote its first objective history, the *Anglica Historia* (1534). Polydore could find no credible records to support the Trojan legends or the Arthurian stories, but he was much reviled for his honesty. The British History, though shaken, stood firm.

Camden would have nothing to do with the British History. He announced that nowhere in the classical histories could he discover any reference to Brutus or to a Trojan expedition to the north. Proclaiming his allegiance to documented history, he composed a picture of a barbarian society as it appeared at the time of the Roman conquest. His primary sources were Julius Caesar and Tacitus, but he augmented his portrayal with material from Pliny, Strabo, and indeed any classical source that mentioned Britain. He took full advantage of the existence of a wide range of well-edited classical texts, the product of a century of humanist scholarship. Camden was persuaded that the people who occupied Britain at the time of the Roman invasions were closely related to the Gauls, whom he was able to identify as a Celtic people. Through classical writings, he traced the Celts back to Armenia and Asia Minor. Inevitably for a sixteenth-century scholar, he was obliged to place the Celts within the biblical record, and he adopted the fairly conventional view that they were descended from Gomer, son of Japhet, whose offspring populated the west after the dispersion of the nations from the Tower of Babel. Camden, however, did not get excessively entangled in biblical antecedents.

To riddle out problems of origins and relationships, Camden employed etymology. This strategy was valued but unreliable, since it lacked rules and was vulnerable to exploitation by less scrupulous exponents. Already proficient in Greek and Latin, he learned Welsh, the surviving form of the ancient British language. His competency in Welsh is unknown, though JOHN AUBREY noted that "he kept a Welsh servant to improve him in that language." Camden also studied Anglo-Saxon. From this knowledge base, he explored the meaning of the name "Britain" through its etymology, and the effort proved rewarding. He deduced from the numerous variants of "Britannia" that appeared in the Greek and Roman writers, and especially from Procopius's use of "Britia" as a name for the island, that the ancient inhabitants called themselves Brits or Briths. Noting that the word *brith* in Welsh means "painted" or "colored," he extrapolated that the natives called themselves by this name because they painted themselves in striking colors, a distinguishing habit reported in almost all the early Roman allusions to the British people. Camden proceeded to make another discovery along the same lines that also had a credible ring to it: he perceived

> that in the names of almost all the ancient Britons, there appears some intimation of a Color, which without doubt arose from this custom of painting. The red color is by the Britons called "coch" or "goch," which word I fancy lies concealed in these names, Cogidunus, Argentocoxus, Segonax; the black color they call "du," of which methinks there is some appearance in Mandubratius, Cartismandua, Togodumnus, Bunduica, Cogidunus.

And so on with white and blue (*glas,* as in King Cuniglas), yellow, gold, scarlet, and green. The enigmatic names of the ancient British leaders suddenly sprang to parti-colored life as Camden's etymological imagination touched them.

Camden's enterprise of drawing together all known references to ancient Britain allowed him to form a composite and credible picture of a primitive society. The Britons tended to live in woods defended by banks and ditches. They kept cattle and domestic animals and grew corn, but their agriculture was very limited. They were ruled by numerous kings and princes, but their government was weak and prone to division. Warfare was endemic. In fighting, their leaders used chariots and relied on a strong infantry. Their weapons were spears, swords, and shields, and they did not use armor. They decorated their bodies with colored images of beasts and deliberately scarred their limbs. Their religion was "a dismal and confused heap of superstition" presided over by Druids. In sanctuaries of oak groves, human sacrifices occurred. The Druids preserved some kind of ancestral wisdom, the nature of which Camden did not speculate on. The Britons had primitive boats made of wooden frames covered with leather, which still survives as the coracle. They also had a coinage, suggesting a developed form of internal and external trade. This picture, now familiar through the classical historians, was a novelty in late Elizabethan England.

Camden was particularly attentive to the coinage of the Britons in the first century B.C. In successive editions of the *Britannia,* he enlarged the section devoted to the subject, so that by 1607, when he published his final revision, he was able to illustrate eighteen specimens. John Leland, the Tudor antiquary who toured England in the 1530s and 1540s, had denied that British coinage existed at the time of the Roman invasion. Camden was the first scholar to establish its existence convincingly. He not only recognized a number of British coins but also identified the mints at Verulamium and Camulodunum and the names of the princes, such as Cunobelin and Comius, for whom they were issued. He guessed from inscriptions that some of the coins might have been minted as tribute money to the Romans. He noted too the frequency with which horses appeared on the coins, as if a horse cult might have had a significant place among the Britons. His examples were taken from the collection of his friend Sir Robert Cotton, who also furnished John Speed with specimens to illustrate his *History of Britain* in 1611. Camden also gave the fullest account yet published of Roman coins pertaining to Britain—those struck there as well as those relating to events in Roman-British history.

Camden was clearly fascinated by the distinctive character of the ancient Britons. As he described how the Romans occupied, civilized, and incorporated the country into their empire, he was motivated by patriotic sentiment to uphold the honor of these ancestral people. After an account of the military occupation, he reminded his readers of the many Roman poets who were moved to write about Britain because the country stirred their imagination by its exotic remoteness and by the bravery of its inhabitants. He took care to emphasize details that gave the impression that the greatest emperors and generals were preoccupied with the matter of Britain. He depicted the growth of civility occurring under Roman rule as a long process that eventually entitled the Britons to participate fully in the mature civilization of antiquity—an issue of some importance to seventeenth-century readers of Camden, for it meant that modern Britain was a legitimate heir of classical culture and imperial values.

To round out his picture of ancient Britain, Camden had to pronounce on the origins of the Picts and the Scots. Etymology rather than ethnology came to his aid. He rejected the venerable Bede's eighth-century opinion that the Picts had come from Scythia, preferring to believe that they were related to the tribes of northern Britain and differed from them only in their independence from Roman rule, which consigned them as a result to a continued state of barbarism. Like the Britons, the Picts received their name from their custom of painting their skins, a custom that lingered on far longer in Caledonia than in Roman Britain. As for the Scots who occupied Ireland at the time of the Roman invasion of Britain, Camden was prepared to entertain a Scythian provenance. A chorus of chroniclers and historians, going back at least to the Saxon Gildas in the sixth century, emphasized the etymological probability that "Scoti" and "Scythae" were linked. Scythia in the Middle Ages and the Renaissance referred to a loosely defined territory to the north and east of Greece and did in fact include the region around the Black Sea that was the heartland of the Celts, who during the first millennium B.C. spread westward into parts of Europe, including Gaul, Britain, and the Iberian peninsula. The old traditions of a Scythian origin for the Scots thus had some plausibility, even to the extent that those accounts, as passed on by the chronicler Nennius in the late eighth century, had the Scots migrating from Iberia to an uninhabited Ireland. Yet the similarity between "Scoti" and "Scythae" was purely coincidental. Camden's only means of probing the darkness of time beyond the moments lit by the ancient historians was by the lamp of etymology, which, as a false science, distorted more than illuminated. He was right to think of language as an important clue to origins, but he had little understanding of the language groups of Europe and Asia and little grasp of the process of linguistic change. He, like his contemporaries, could only make assumptions based on similarity of sound. His frustration at the endless etymological speculation about national origins—endless because there were no known rules to the game—spilled over in his discussion of the Scots. After summarizing a score of scholarly guesses, he exclaimed: "If all this gives no light into the original of the Scots, [my readers] must apply themselves for it elsewhere, for I am perfectly in the dark in this point; and have followed the truth (which has still fled from me) with much labour to no purpose."

A similar etymological mist hung over the Saxons when Camden sought to trace their derivation. He decided to focus on their name, rather than their language, artifacts, or remains, as the principal clue to their origins. First there was the approach eponymous: Did they take their name from their leader in migration, one Saxo? Then there was the approach characterful: did the name derive from the Latin epithet for their stony (*saxea*) temperament? Perhaps their use of curved swords known as "saxa" had a particular relevance. Were they related to the ancient tribes of the Saci or the Sassones of Asia? Intelligent guesswork was Camden's best hope, but he admitted that most inquiries into origins were profoundly frustrating.

The early editions of *Britannia* were not enthusiastic about the Saxons, who, being a harsh and alien race, were less agreeable in Camden's imagination than the Britons or the Romans. By 1607, however, when the last revised edition appeared, he had grown more sympathetic, and the account of the Saxons had been noticeably enlarged. His changed attitude owed much to his improved familiarity with the Anglo-Saxon language, which in turn had been encouraged by friendships with William Lambarde, who had been taught by Laurence Nowell, the principal figure in the Elizabethan revival of Anglo-Saxon, and with Sir Robert Cotton. He came to recognize that for all their initial barbarism, the Saxons had been the people who had contributed most decisively to the formation of the English identity by means of language and religion. The shift to a more positive attitude toward the Saxons is evident in a passage in *Remains Concerning Britain,* the collection of essays published in 1605 that complement the material in *Britannia.* "This warlike, victorious, stiff, stout and rigorous Nation, after it had as it were taken root here for about one hundred and sixty years, and spread its branches far and wide, being mellowed and mollified by the mildness of the soil and sweet air, was prepared in fulness of time for our regeneration in Christ." Indeed, the remarkable receptivity of the Saxons to Christianity deeply impressed Camden and did much to offset his initial prejudice against the race for their origins among the barbaric German tribes. The broad, indelible impression the Saxons made on the history, society, and landscape of Britain was revealed in the profusely detailed description of individual counties that filled most of *Britannia.*

The relating of history to landscape was the permanent achievement of *Britannia.* The body of the book took the form of "perambulation" through the counties of Britain, with Camden offering a many-layered account of each particular region. He described the physical character of each county, noting the salient features and relating them whenever possible to the British landmarks mentioned in Ptolemy's *Geography.* He also attempted to associate place-names in the Antonine Itinerary with existing towns or with sites where there was evidence of Roman settlement. He remarked on the occasions when a place had been the scene of memorable events, both historical and legendary. Camden relentlessly plied his etymological skills to try to extract meaning from old names. Consider, for example, his presentation of the Cornish town Lostwithiel:

> More within the land, upon the same river Fowey, the *Uzella* of Ptolemy is seated; and has not yet quite lost its name, being called at this day *Lestuthiell,* from its situation. For it was upon a high hill, where is *Lestormin,* an ancient castle; though now 'tis removed

into the valley. Now *Uchel* in British signifies the same *high* and *lofty;* from whence *Uxellodunum* of Gaul is so termed, because the town being built upon a mountain has a steep rugged ascent every way. This in the British History is called *Pen-Uchel coit,* a high mountain in a wood, by which some will have *Exeter* meant. But the situation assigned to it by Ptolemy, and the name it has to this day, do sufficiently evince it to have been the ancient *Uzella.* Now it is a little town and not at all populous; for the channel of the river Fowey, which in the last age used to carry the tide up to the very town, and bring vessels of burthen, is now so stopped up by the sands coming from the lead-mines that it is too shallow for barges. However, 'tis the County-town.

Camden's express intention in writing the *Britannia* was "to restore antiquity to Britain," and he was indeed able to fill the landscape with historical associations as he traced on the present scene the lingering remains of the remote past and evoked incidents that had once occurred there. The land was rich in history, and Camden was for the first time making this richness geographically explicit and accessible. The ancient British tribal divisions shaped his method of inquiry, for Camden discoursed on the counties as they came within the old tribal areas, beginning with the Danmonii, whose territory was present-day Cornwall and Devon. Serving as background was the only way the Britons received attention in the topographical part of the book, for Camden did not recognize any earthworks or field monuments as the work of the Britons and only attributed a few artifacts to them. (He noted, for example, the discovery of "brass-weapons"—bronze spearheads, axes, and swords—in old mine-workings and associated them with the ancient Britons; however, he did not illustrate them.) For Camden, the Britons remained an honored but largely invisible presence in the land.

In fact, neither did the Romans feature very prominently in the county descriptions. Although the germ of *Britannia* was the elucidation of the Antonine Itinerary, and the primary intention was to describe Britain as a Roman province, in practice Camden had relatively little to say about the Roman dimension, beyond identifying place-names. It was of course difficult to link the British landscape with specific historical incidents in Roman times, for few such incidents were recorded. For the most part, however, Camden did not show much curiosity about Roman remains, and he did not attempt to envisage the layout or appearance of a town or military site; he did not try to revive in the imagination the walls, villas, temples, baths, or barracks, whose stones lay tumbled about. He was usually content to establish that, for example, Ilkley was Olicana in Ptolemy, and then to move on. Even in his reference to the

An engraving of Stonehenge taken from the 1600 edition of Camden's Britannia. (© Copyright the British Museum)

A Saxa quæ vocantur Corselstones pondere..............
altitudine 24 pedes, latitudine ped.... ambitu.10.:
B Saxa quæ vocantur Coronets. 6.vel. 7. teviturant..)
C Locus ubi ossa humana effodiuntur..)

Antonine Itinerary, Camden lacked a sufficiently clear sense of the routes taken by the Roman roads, so he followed instead the courses of rivers, describing the towns and villages on their banks.

The one category of Roman remains that arrested his attention was inscriptions. These he recorded wherever he found them, and from them he could deduce the presence of certain legions, with their places of origin and the names of their officers and sometimes of their men, as well as the existence of temples to various deities, Roman and Romano-British. In many cases he was able to associate an inscription with an imperial reign. The 1607 edition of *Britannia* contained what was effectively a full inventory of the Roman inscriptions known at that time.

Camden did have a rudimentary archaeological sense, however, as was evident in the antiquarian tour he made to Hadrian's Wall with his friend Robert Cotton in 1600. There they searched for inscriptions, altars, and coins—anything that might help to identify forts and settlements or throw light on the times of occupation, the resident religious cults, and the legions that manned the wall. This was a purposeful topographical inspection, which yielded a number of inscribed stones and other artifacts, most of which were sent back to Cotton's house in Conington, Huntingdonshire. Although no formal excavations took place, this search for Roman antiquities along the wall was possibly the first serious archaeological exercise carried out in Britain, and it is notable for its recognition that objects as well as texts had a place in antiquarian inquiry. The expedition clarified Camden's understanding of the defensive settlements along the wall and gave him a pleasurable sense of being closer to the Romans here than anywhere else in the country. The consequence of this journey was that in the 1607 edition of *Britannia,* the descriptions of Cumberland, Westmorland, and Northumberland contained an unusually rich gathering of newfound inscriptions, which were printed and in some cases illustrated, making these sections of the book especially informative about the Roman history of Britain. Camden's limitations as an interpreter of ancient finds was shown by his reluctance to use them to illustrate Roman life on the frontier. He did not try to speculate about the implications of his discoveries; he was content to record them and leave them to a later generation to interpret. As he wrote in his preface, "Somewhat must be left for the labours of other men. Another age, a new race of men, will produce somewhat new successively. 'Tis enough for me to have broken the ice; and I have gained my ends if I have set others about the same work, whether it be to write more, or amend what I have written."

Camden's growing familiarity with Saxon England, the result of his extensive reading in chronicles and ecclesiastical documents, was manifested in the steady growth of information relating to Saxon history in the successive editions of *Britannia.* By 1607 he was able to depict Saxon activities all across the country with unprecedented comprehensiveness, giving many references to settlement patterns, military campaigns, the foundation of churches and monasteries, and ecclesiastical history. He derived his material from Gildas's sixth-century chronicle on the state of Britain after the departure of the Romans, from Bede's *Ecclesiastical History,* Asser's *Life of Alfred,* and the Anglo-Saxon Chronicle, all of which were in print by 1600. He was able to consult the wealth of Saxon manuscripts, many of them relating to ecclesiastical life, that Robert Cotton had collected for his remarkable library. Camden related this plentiful historical detail to the topography of England in a way that brought the past of each county vividly to life.

Camden made a number of field trips in order to gather information for his work. His principal antiquarian tours were: 1578, Norfolk and Suffolk; 1582, Yorkshire; 1589, Devon; 1590, Wales; 1596, Salisbury and Wells; 1600, Carlisle and Hadrian's Wall. In compiling *Britannia,* he depended heavily on regional correspondents for the transmission of local detail. Nonetheless, Camden himself had seen more of Britain at first hand than any previous observer, with the exception of John Leland, whose antiquarian notes were accessible, though still unpublished, in Camden's time.

To a modern reader, Camden's inability to recognize any pre-Roman remains is remarkable. Despite his interest in the ancient Britons as professed in the historical introduction to *Britannia,* he seemed unaware that physical traces of their presence survived. Barrows, tumuli, earthworks, and stone monuments were all attributed to the Romans, Saxons, or Danes. He offered no judgment of his own on the builders or purpose of Stonehenge and contented himself with retelling its traditions and legends. Indeed, it is doubtful if he ever visited that monument, so brief was his account of it. As for Silbury Hill, the great Neolithic mound in north Wiltshire, he suggested it might be a Roman or Saxon boundary marker. In like manner, the Rollright Stone Circle in Oxfordshire was deemed to be a Danish monument, a conclusion encouraged by the similarity of the name with Rollo, the Danish warlord who was known to have been active in England. (So much for the promptings of etymology. It would not be until the last third of the seventeenth century that John Aubrey would recognize stone monuments and barrows as the work of the ancient Britons.)

Editions of *Britannia* were published in 1586, 1587, 1590, 1594, 1600, and 1607. The English translation by Philemon Holland of the 1607 edition appeared in 1610, with a further printing in 1637. An edition was published in Frankfurt in 1590. County maps by Christopher Saxton and John Norden accompanied the editions from 1607 onward. The appearance of *Britannia* in 1586 might well have prompted the formation of the Society of Antiquaries, which began to meet in that year. It certainly encouraged the growth of antiquarian studies in provincial centers by stimulating local curiosity about the regional past.

Camden published several other works of an antiquarian or historical nature. *Remains Concerning Britain* (1605) was an important collection of essays on topics associated with *Britannia,* though it seems to have been designed for a more popular audience than the greater work. The essays, written in English, had strong patriotic overtones and were aimed at enticing the more general reader toward the study of antiquities. Among the contents were essays on English names, collections of proverbs, epigrams, anagrams, rebuses, specimens of medieval Latin verse by English writers, and an anthology of English epitaphs. There was a certain overlap with *Britannia,* since some chapters were merely English synopses of the sections in *Britannia* dealing with the character of the island, the first inhabitants, and the languages of Britain. This last essay was notable for first advancing in English the view that the extensive family of Germanic languages, to which Saxon belonged, might be part of an even larger group, which we now call Indo-European. Camden derived this concept from the French scholar Joseph Scaliger, and he furnished linguistic examples to illustrate the possibility of a broad interconnection, though he was not prepared to endorse the idea outright. Camden's admiration for all things Anglo-Saxon shone brightly in the *Remains.* To demonstrate how deeply indebted the English language was to the Anglo-Saxon tongue, he provided his readers with extensive glossaries and etymologies. The book as a whole was a significant step in the advance of Anglo-Saxon studies, and it enjoyed popular success, with six editions appearing before the Civil War.

Camden had a notable reputation as a historian, based on his *Annals of Queen Elizabeth* (1615, in Latin; 1625, English translation). This complex political history adopted a Tacitean approach, echoing, as the title suggested, Tacitus's *Annales.* Camden was encouraged to undertake this work by James I, who wished to see a vindication of his mother, Mary Queen of Scots, set in the context of Elizabethan politics. Camden had broad access to state papers (many of which he had been given by Lord Burleigh, Elizabeth's senior minister and Camden's patron, to whom *Britannia* had been dedicated), and to letters, council records, and parliamentary diaries. The *Annals* effectively constitutes the first English history based fully on primary sources. A sequel dealing with James's reign was projected but never completed. To encourage historical studies in England, Camden founded a chair in Civil History at Oxford in 1622.

Among his other publications were a collection of Saxon and Norman chronicles, *Anglica, Normannicaa Veteribus Scripta* (Frankfurt 1602); a collection of epitaphs from Westminster Abbey (1600); and a Greek grammar (1595). He engaged, reluctantly, in a controversy with Ralph Brooke, the York herald, in the 1590s over the imputation of genealogical errors in the 1594 edition of *Britannia,* but otherwise his career was unruffled. He enjoyed the friendship of a wide circle of European humanist scholars, and his correspondents included Ortelius, Lipsius,

Hondius, Gruter, Isaac Casaubon, Peiresc, Hotman, and de Thou. Largely through his contacts, English antiquaries of the Jacobean Age were linked to their European counterparts. Camden was a respected herald, being Clarenceux King-of-Arms from 1597 until his death in 1623. He is buried in Westminster Abbey.

References
Primary
Camden, William. 1695. *Britannia*. Ed. E. Gibson. Reprinted Newton Abbot, UK, 1971.

———. 1984. *Remains Concerning Britain*. Ed. R. D. Dunn. Toronto.

Secondary
Kendrick, Thomas Downing. 1950. *British Antiquity*. Reprinted 1970. London: Methuen.

Mendyk, S. G. 1989. *Speculum Britanniae: Regional Study, Antiquarianism and Science in Britain to 1700*. Toronto: University of Toronto Press.

Parry, Graham. 1995. *The Trophies of Time: English Antiquarians of the Seventeenth-century*. Oxford and New York: Oxford University Press.

Piggott, Stuart. 1976. "William Camden and the Britannia." In Stuart Piggott, *Ruins in a Landscape*. Edinburgh: Edinburgh University Press.

Smith, T. 1695. "Life of Camden." Trans. from the Latin by E. Gibson. In *Britannia*. Ed. E. Gibson. Reprinted Newton Abbot, UK, 1971.

Trevor-Roper, Hugh. 1985. "Queen Elizabeth's First Historian." In Hugh Trevor-Roper, *Renaissance Essays 1460–1620*. London: Secker and Warburg.

Graham Parry

John Aubrey 1626–1697

Author of the first archaeological treatise in English, John Aubrey was the first scholar to engage in serious fieldwork to understand pre-Roman megaliths and to reconstruct the character of the ancient British societies that built them. By doing this Aubrey moved antiquarian studies toward archaeological practice.

I was inclined by my Genius from my childhood to the love of Antiquities, and my fate dropt me in a country most suitable for such enquiries," wrote Aubrey in his manuscript of *Monumenta Britannica*. That "most suitable" country was Wiltshire, where Neolithic remains abound. The son of a prominent member of the local gentry, Aubrey was born in the hamlet of Easton Pierse near Malmesbury in 1626. The family fortunes had been raised by his grandfather, a successful Elizabethan lawyer. Aubrey was educated for a while by the same schoolmaster who had taught Thomas Hobbes, and this coincidence was the basis for a long friendship between the two scholars. In 1642 he went up to Trinity College, Oxford, but his residence there was soon interrupted by the outbreak of the Civil War. He returned again for two years at the end of 1646, when he "enjoyed the greatest felicity of my life, for ingeniose youths, like rosebuds, imbibe the morning dew." At Oxford he was able to indulge fully his passion for learning and his insatiable curiosity for all things old. When he left, his life became a succession of misfortunes, which included the sale of his estates, lawsuits, bankruptcy, and eventual homelessness. For decades, as he pursued antiquarian learning, he could afford only temporary lodgings and was sustained by the goodwill of friends. He died in 1697 and was buried in the Church of St. Mary Magdalene, Oxford.

Sociable, idiosyncratic, infinitely curious, and swept along by enthusiasm, Aubrey was continually making observations, but he never organized or published them. He was an engaging, somewhat wistful figure, whose modes of inquiry and contributions to knowledge have been valued more during the last thirty years than during the previous three hundred. He was among the first to conduct serious fieldwork to elucidate the enigma of ancient stone monuments, and the first to attribute these monuments to the tribal societies of pre-Roman Britain. He attempted to reconstruct imaginatively something of the character of those societies and developed a respectable sense of the functioning

John Aubrey. (From John Britton's Memoir of Aubrey, *published in 1841)*

communities of ancient Britons in the area now called Wessex. He believed that more could be known about the past by the study of objects than by the reading of books. He understood, in a limited way, the advantages of excavation, and he had an advanced appreciation of the comparative method—that is, making deductions by considering together similar objects or classes of objects. His improved practice owed something to his membership in the Royal Society but much more to his own imagination and intuition. More than any other figure of his time, he exemplified how antiquarian studies could move toward archaeological practice and how a methodological approach to data could replace mere accumulation of facts accompanied by speculation.

The formative influence on Aubrey's early career was William Dugdale's *Antiquities of Warwickshire* (1656), which inspired him to begin a similar survey of Wiltshire. Dugdale's great volume contained a history of the shire and a parish-by-parish account of church monuments and their inscriptions, local worthies, old established families (with details of their histories and coats of arms), notable buildings, and unusual landscape features. As Aubrey began to collect material toward his survey, he was inclined to pay attention to topics that were fashionable in the protoscientific circle at Oxford in the 1650s—Baconian topics such as the economics of agriculture, soil types, crops, mineral resources, and medicinal springs. This work he entitled *The Natural History of Wiltshire*. In 1659 he became involved in a similar project, organized by a group of local gentlemen, to describe the same county, but they soon lost interest, leaving Aubrey to persevere with what he called variously his "Wiltshire Collections" or his "Wiltshire Antiquities." So, with two Wiltshire enterprises under way, he was heavily committed to regional studies.

Most of the material he collected for his "Wiltshire Antiquities" could be classified as local history. He went through the parish churches, recording inscriptions and coats of arms and relating them to the gentry of the district. He extracted information from old charters and from monastic documents, which enabled him to describe the pattern of land ownership in Wiltshire over the centuries. He reconstructed the history of significant towns, recorded the notable events associated with them, and made observations on the more memorable buildings of the county. His compilations were, for the most part, fairly conventional, in the tradition of Dugdale's work on Warwickshire.

The unconventional material in his collections related to ancient stone monuments and earthworks, to which he was powerfully attracted. His familiarity with Wiltshire had made him aware of the large number of standing stones, tumuli, and barrows scattered across the county, and his imagination was stirred by his attempts to guess the origin and purpose of these monuments. Stonehenge had always fascinated him, but he himself discovered the even larger Neolithic monumental complex at Avebury in 1649, when he was out hunting and suddenly found himself among the stones. The nucleus of Avebury was already known as an ancient site, for it was described in WILLIAM CAMDEN's *Britannia* of 1610 as "an old Camp with a fair trench," with "four gaps as gates, in which stand huge stones as jambs." Aubrey was the first to recognize the full extent of the monument and to appreciate that it was not a camp but some kind of ceremonial site, the scheme of which had been obscured by the growth of the village on the spot. He identified the circle of megaliths for the first time as a manmade construction. Struck by the similarity between his own name and that of the monument, he almost came to look upon the site as a personal possession, and he returned many times to map the complex and reflect on its significance. He taught himself the use of surveying instruments and employed a plane table to make accurate measurements. He traced the bank and fosse, proving to his satisfaction that it was not part of a defensive system. He identified the first section of the great avenue and suspected it had a ceremonial function. Noting depressions in the earth, he tried to imagine what had caused them and to guess where missing stones must have been. He was able to reconstruct a secondary circle of stones within the greater circle. He tried also to locate the complex within the landscape, by noting the old approach roads, now not visible, and the relationship of Avebury to Silbury Hill and to neighboring barrows. What he saw at Avebury helped to clarify the monumental pattern at Stonehenge: there he was able to detect, by analogy with Avebury, a circle of postholes inside the bank, where he thought smaller stones had once been. These are now called the Aubrey-holes, in his honor.

As his passion for the explication of ancient monuments grew, he removed most of his notes relating to them from his collection of "Wiltshire Antiquities" and began a new manuscript devoted entirely to investigation of fieldworks, which he entitled *Monumenta Britannica*. Royal curiosity may have also motivated him. In 1663 Charles II heard of Aubrey's claim that Avebury "did as much exceed Stonehenge as a cathedral does a parish church." The king asked him to write a description of the site, "and the Duke of York commanded me to give an account of the old Camps and Barrows on the Plains." This new compilation developed into the most original and enterprising study of British prehistoric remains in the seventeenth century. Aubrey was the first person to seriously assert that these remains—stone circles, barrows, hill-forts—were the work of the ancient Britons. Previously, learned opinion had assigned them variously to the Romans, the Saxons, or the Danes. Inigo Jones, in his *Stoneheng Restored* (1655), published after his death by his nephew John Webb, had attempted to prove that the standing stones were the weather-beaten remains of a Roman temple, a claim he justified largely from the geometry of the monument's ground plan. The more general consensus was that Stonehenge and the mounds and barrows nearby dated from early Saxon times. The dating of field monuments of all kinds was further confused by the opinions of the Danish scholar Olaf Worm. His book *Danicorum Monumentorum Libri Sex* (1643), the first systematic survey of the field monuments of Denmark, had attributed most stone monuments and tumuli in Denmark to the Danes of the fourth century and after. In his view, tumuli were the graves of military leaders, or warriors killed in battle; barrows were mass graves for soldiers; stone circles were places of assembly for the election of kings and leaders and for legislative purposes. Since the Danes had invaded and settled a large part of England in the ninth century, there was some attempt to associate large field monuments with the Danes, especially by the physician and antiquary Walter Charleton. His *Chorea Gigantum* (1663), literally, the "Giants' Dance," presented Stonehenge as a place of regional assembly erected by the Danes.

Aubrey's belief that stone monuments were raised by the ancient Britons was thus a conceptual breakthrough. By observation and by information from correspondents, he gathered details of stone circles, megaliths, barrows, tumuli, hill-forts, camps, ramparts, and ditches from all over the British Isles, and it gradually became clear to him that a common primitive culture had once covered the whole region. Moreover, since their monuments lay in so many places beyond the perimeter of Roman, Saxon, or Danish occupation, they must antedate any of those settlements. "These Antiquities are so exceeding old, that no books do reach them; so that there is no way to retrieve them but by comparative antiquity, which I have writ upon the spot from the Monuments themselves." The accepted view was that the British inhabitants of the island before Caesar had no technological skills or social organization capable of raising great structures. Aubrey tried to reconstruct the British tribal societies that had flourished in Wiltshire and the southwest, partly from information delivered by Julius Caesar and Cornelius Tacitus, partly by comparison with what he had heard of primitive life in Virginia. He included these credible imaginings of ancient British society in his manuscript of *The Natural History of Wiltshire*.

In compiling *Monumenta Britannica,* Aubrey was assembling the first book in English that can be seriously regarded as an archaeological treatise. His concern was principally with the field monuments themselves. He described them in great detail, measured them, and often provided competent sketches as illustrations; he looked closely at the material remains of a vanished culture, made comparisons with similar structures to determine that there were definite categories of monuments, and tried by observation and reflection to deduce the function of stone circles, standing stones, mounds, and earthworks. Although he included quotations from classical and modern authors and noted local legends concerning ancient sites, he gave priority to the material remains. In order to retrieve the meaning of monuments that dated back before the time of written records, Aubrey recognized that he must study the stones, not books. "I do here attempt to work out [their purpose] after a kind of algebraical method, by comparing those that I have seen one with another, and reducing them to a kind of Æquation, so to make the stones give evidence for themselves."

Besides Avebury and Stonehenge, Aubrey left valuable observations of the Stanton Drew stone circle in Somerset, the Rollright Stones in Oxfordshire, the Boscawen-Un Stone Circle in Cornwall, and various standing stones and monumental groups in Dorset. On the basis of information from correspondents, he was able to describe in detail the complex known as the Devil's Arrows in Yorkshire and the main Cumbrian field monuments—King Arthur's Round Table, the Mayburgh Circle, the

An aerial view of Stonehenge. (© Aerofilms Ltd.)

Keswick Circle, and Long Meg and Her Daughters. In later years Aubrey added descriptions of Welsh, Irish, and Scottish Neolithic remains, as friends furnished him with competent information. Because so many of these monuments have been altered or destroyed over the centuries since Aubrey wrote, his accounts preserve an invaluable record of them as they stood when they first attracted the eyes of intelligent observers.

Aubrey concluded that stone circles were ceremonial sites and that standing stones marked places of ritual significance. He considered the circles to be temples and became persuaded that they were in fact temples of the Druids. Accordingly, he titled the section in his book dealing with these monuments "Templa Druidum." He was strengthened in his opinions by etymological clues: stone monuments were found at both Stanton Drew and Kerig y Drudion in Wales, and both names seemed to indicate a druidic connection. He ignored the fact that references to the Druids in Greek and Roman writings always associated them with groves and trees, particularly oaks, and never with standing stones. Aubrey could not conceive that various cultures might have flourished in prehistoric Britain. Like most of his contemporaries, he thought only of a single nation of ancient Britons occupying the country before the Romans came. The long vistas of time in which prehistoric cultures emerged and then faded were closed to him. Today, the stone circles he investigated are assigned to the late Neolithic period of the third to the mid-second millennium B.C.; since the Druids were the priests of the Celts, who did not reach Britain until the fourth or third century B.C., there is little likelihood that monuments such as Stonehenge and Avebury were druidic sanctuaries (even though popular imagination continues to see them in this light).

After a protracted discussion of Druids and Bards (tribal singers), illustrated from ancient sources and with input from his friends and correspondents, Aubrey moved on in the second section of *Monumenta Britannica* to a discussion of "camps," under which he included all kinds of earthworks, hill-forts, enclosures, fosses, and embankments. His views on these remains were not as insightful as his observations about stone monuments. He was inclined to believe that most barrows and earthworks dated from the time of the Roman invasions. Shape seemed to be the primary basis for attributions: circular earthworks were likely to be either British or Danish, the irregular ditches and ramparts were probably British, the rectangular ones Roman. Barrows were the mass graves of Britons slain by the Romans. Aubrey did not engage in any excavations, and he was willing to accept as adequate proof of a Roman burial the fact that an urn had been found within a tumulus, reflecting the view common to that age that all urn burials were from the Roman period.

He was also disposed to believe that all earthworks had been made in the millennium between the first century B.C. and circa A.D. 900. Over the years Aubrey gathered details of hundreds of "camps" situated throughout mainland Britain, often making outline drawings and measurements.

A further section of *Monumenta Britannica* was devoted to notes on Roman remains in Britain, based on Aubrey's own investigations or on reports from correspondents. Besides familiar details of Verulamium, York, Colchester, Chester, and other well-known sites, there was a wealth of information about Roman discoveries in London, many of them the result of the rebuilding of the city after the Great Fire of 1666. Aubrey's friend Christopher Wren provided much of this information, since he had often uncovered Roman remains when laying the foundations for his new churches and civic buildings. Included were accounts of roadways, temple foundations, mosaic pavements, portions of frescoed walls, and grave goods. The wooden wharfside of the Thames in Roman times was discovered, lying about one hundred feet beyond the seventeenth-century river line. Aubrey recorded the location of every find, but he made no illustrations, and most of the smaller objects he described drifted into private collections and eventually disappeared. All told, Aubrey's pages of poorly arranged and miscellaneous notes about Roman antiquities did not contribute significantly to the body of knowledge about Roman Britain. Rather, they form a sad record of how much was found and then casually lost.

The most rewarding result of Aubrey's considerable familiarity with Roman Britain was the map he drew of the southwest region, showing the Roman and British settlements, camps, and hill-forts and the roads and tracks connecting them. The map illustrated the overlay of Roman authority on the British tribes as well as the coexistence of two sturdy peoples. The dense concentration of settlements and earthworks in the region of Malmesbury, Salisbury, and the Welsh marches indicated how populous the land had been—and also how extensive Aubrey's understanding was of the archaeology of ancient Britain. Modern towns were marked on the map to emphasize the continuing pattern of habitation from antiquity.

With the exception of this map, the second section of *Monumenta Britannica* contained little material of lasting value, but by assembling notes on so many different kinds of earthwork, Aubrey conveyed the impression of intense and enduring activity over the whole of the country in its early history. Clearly a great deal was happening, even if the sparing comments of Roman and Saxon writers made it seem otherwise. Aubrey left no doubt that early Britain had experienced a very eventful history. His was a chronicle not of glamorous Trojans or Greeks, nor of legendary kings or Arthurian heroes, but of nameless people who had warred across the country and marked the hills and plains and river valleys with their presence. Aubrey could not penetrate through the shadows to the lives of these people, but his work aroused an expectation that more might eventually be known as learning progressed. As he remarked in his introduction to *Monumenta Britannica,* "This Inquiry I must confess is a groping in the Dark: but although I have not brought it into a clear light, yet I can affirm, that I have brought it from an utter darkness to a thin Mist."

Physical remains were not the only survivals of antiquity that fascinated Aubrey. He became convinced that popular customs and ceremonies might be a tenuous link between the present and the vanished societies of the ancient world. Continually recording odd customs and old wives' tales, he eventually gathered enough information to make a manuscript collection that he called "Remains of Gentilisme and Judaisme." It was his contention that "the Britons imbibed their Gentilisme from the Romans, and as the British language is crept into corners, *sc.* Wales and Cornwall, so the remains of Gentilisme are still kept there, which customes (no doubt) were anciently all over Britaine and Gaule: but the Inundation of the Goths drove it out together with the language." He was not entirely convinced by this thesis, asking parenthetically why it was, "the British Language being utterly lost in England, that so many Roman Customes should yet remain?" Nevertheless, he liked to think in terms of persistence, because there were so many similarities between surviving customs and practices described by Roman authors, especially by Ovid in his *Fasti,* or calendar of festivals, and by Pliny in his *Natural History.* Judaism was viewed as another source of pre-Christian customs that spread into England, though Aubrey did not explain the process by which it was introduced. His assumption was that "in the infancy of the Christian Religion it was expedient to plough (as they say) with the heifer of the Gentiles: that is, to insinuate with them, and let them continue and use their old Ethnick Festivalls, which they new-named with Christian names." His method generally was to note a custom and then to seek a Roman source in order to establish continuity with the remote past. Some linkages were more credible than others, and his tracing of English harvest ceremonies back to Roman practices was very plausible.

Aubrey gathered together an extraordinarily rich range of rural customs and superstitions. Some were familiar, such as church-ales (ales or beers brewed and served by the church), which he traced to the love feasts of the early church, to Roman convivia, and to Greek and Hebrew feasts after sacrifice; many were unfamiliar, such as sin eating, in which a poor man symbolically eats the sins of the deceased, a practice Aubrey related to the scapegoat of the Old Testament. Although Aubrey tried to organize his material into categories—festivals, marriages, funerals, omens, divination, oaths, etc.—its miscellanea virtually defied classification, and personal anecdotes mingled promiscuously with objective reporting. He was conscious that many survivals were relics of ancient belief, the "flotsam from the lost religions of the ancient world," but his assumption that they descended from Roman customs introduced into Britain by conquest was too restrictive (though completely within the scope of knowledge at the time). Today such beliefs and customs would be considered the remnants of a universal common culture that prevailed all over Europe in immemorial times and was concerned less with religion than with the prevention of misfortune, the courting of good luck, and the ensuring of fertility.

Aubrey's eagerness to record country customs was given an edge by his realization that the Civil War and the Puritan ascendancy had undercut or outlawed many of them, which were consequently fading in his own lifetime. He was also anxious to note superstitions and old wives' tales, not knowing what blurred memory of ancient beliefs or events lay concealed in them but conscious that they retained something of value. "I know that some will nauseate these old fables, but I do profess to regard them as the most considerable pieces of Antiquity that I collect: and that they are to be registered for posterity, to let them understand the encroachment of Ignorance on Mankind." His instinct to collect the old fables and customs was well founded, though he hardly knew what to do with them. He was unwittingly the pioneer of folklore studies, and in showing this curiosity for nonwritten, ahistorical material, he was centuries ahead of scholarship and fashion and was thus unappreciated in his own time. He lent the manuscript of "Remains of Gentilisme" to the Oxford antiquary White Kennett (later bishop of Peterborough), who began to make his own collection of folklore material, the unpublished "History of Custom." Aubrey's manuscript was eventually published in 1881, at a time when folklore studies were flourishing.

Aubrey seems to have regarded the course of human history as settled ages punctuated by catastrophe. He entertained an affection for the sturdy primitive Britons but welcomed the Roman invasion as the imposition of a higher culture. The Saxon invasions were generally referred to as a "deluge" of barbarism, and the Danes were worse. He had no respect for anything Saxon, a people "who lived sluttishly in poor houses where they ate a great deal of beef and mutton, and drank good ale in a brown mazard; and their very Kings were but a sort of Farmers." He scarcely believed that the Saxons could build with stone, and he did not share the favorable seventeenth-century estimate of their Christian culture. He wrote little about the Normans, but he had a characteristic antiquarian fondness for the Middle Ages, which he tended to imagine as a time of splendid building when learning was cultivated in hospitable monasteries across the length and the breadth of the land. Meanwhile, outside, the barons were endlessly embroiled—though Aubrey regarded these conflicts as high-spirited exercises that kept the nation fit. Then came the orgy of destruction that was the Reformation. Aubrey nowhere recorded any satisfaction at the emergence of Protestantism: the benefits of reformed religion did not compensate for the cost in ruined buildings, dispersed libraries, and vandalized art. In his own lifetime, the Civil War, which he was inclined to see as another upsurge of radical protestation against a cultivated conservative establishment, had had a devastating effect on the whole inheritance from the past—buildings, works of religious and secular art, customs, beliefs, ownership of land, and family lineage. Even the landscape had been changed, with woods and trees cut down and fortifications raised. "When I was a boy, before the Civil Warres," was the opening to Aubrey's observations, as if he were the survivor of a lost civilization. Images of shipwreck recurred in his writings: everywhere was scattered wreckage, far more than a single man could reclaim. Still, he was not deterred.

Not only was Aubrey conscious of times of dramatic alteration in society, but he was also aware of continuous change occurring over long periods of relatively settled government. He made many notes on various aspects of medieval art and society that charted the gradual evolution of form and style. Aubrey was the first to trace the development of Norman and Gothic architecture by the changing shape of the arch and fenestration. He included his "Chronologia Architectonica" in the fourth part of *Monumenta Britannica,* which contained over fifty drawings and referred to over eighty buildings in ten counties. From this material, Aubrey tried to characterize the styles prevalent in different reigns and so devise a chronology for postconquest architecture. Oxford and London provided the majority of the examples, for Aubrey found details of the building record easier to come by in those places. He was careful to give examples for which a clear date could be established, and the comparative method helped to confirm his sense of the succession of styles and ornamental detail. Long before Thomas Rickman formulated his account of the phases of Gothic in 1817, Aubrey offered a sound basis for a guide to medieval architecture (and beyond, for he also recorded the progress of Italianate design from the time of Edward VI). It was never published.

Along similar lines Aubrey compiled a history of costume that he called "Chronologia Vestiaria," based on examples culled from tombs, stained glass, and illuminated manuscripts, and he left many notes about the introduction of new fashions in earlier generations. He began a record of the way the shape of shields on tombs changed over the centuries, his "Chronologia Aspidologica," a matter of some interest to an age absorbed with heraldry. Of greater value was his study of handwriting styles from Saxon times to the seventeenth century, one of the first systematic accounts made in England on the subject of paleography.

John Aubrey was elected a member of the Royal Society in 1663. Soon afterwards he presented a paper on Avebury, the first occasion on which an antiquarian subject was discussed at the society. In fact, since no similar paper had been offered to the Society of Antiquaries earlier in the century, Aubrey was effectively the first to present a true archaeological paper in England. He provided a measured plan, offered a discussion of the monument in relation to other artifacts, made deductions from the structure, and did not force preconceptions on his material. Informed observation was paramount. In this he differed from Walter Charleton's presentation of Avebury at the same meeting, for although Charleton also submitted a measured plan, his discourse was influenced by his conviction, derived from books, that all stone circles were Danish in origin. After the presentations and discussion, the members asked Aubrey and his Wiltshire friend James Long to investigate further and to excavate around and below a great triangular stone. The dig did not take place, but the pattern that had begun forming—of observation and comparison leading to a hypothesis to be strengthened by systematic excavation—marked the beginning of recognizably modern methods of field archaeology.

At bottom, however, Aubrey was not in sympathy with the principles of mensuration, quantification, and verification advocated by the Royal Society, preferring instead anecdotal evidence, ingenious insight, and the pleasures of exotic information. As the naturalist John Ray reprimanded him in 1691, "I think that you are a little too inclinable to credit strange relations." His wandering life after his bankruptcy in 1671 and the gradual dispersion of his private library thereafter affected his ability to work consistently; the perennial disorder of his manuscript collections grew worse. All he ever brought to publication were his *Miscellanies* in 1695: an assortment of papers, gathered over many years, on paranormal phenomena, coincidence, portents, and dreams, which he described in his preface as "the Oeconomia of the Invisible World." In the last phase of his life he became closely associated with the younger generation of antiquaries then emerging in Oxford, men such as Arthur Charlett, White Kennett, Thomas Tanner, and Edmund Gibson. The benefits of Aubrey's work began to appear in public as his papers were consulted by those scholars whom Gibson recruited to revise and enlarge

William Camden's *Britannia* in the 1690s. Thomas Tanner incorporated many of Aubrey's views about the functions and ancient British origin of stone monuments into his contributions to the county of Wiltshire. Later, WILLIAM STUKELEY, the eighteenth-century antiquary, would make use of Aubrey's remarks on Stonehenge, Avebury, and stone circles to develop his own elaborate theories concerning the origin and function of such field monuments.

After 1667, Aubrey collaborated for many years with Anthony Wood, the Oxford antiquary, in accumulating biographical details of notable Englishmen and of Oxford writers in particular. Many of Aubrey's gleanings went into Wood's monumental biographical register, *Athenae Oxonienses* (1691 and 1692). Aubrey's own collection of biographical sketches, with their extraordinarily vivid touches and memorable anecdotes, have become the chief vehicle of his fame in the twentieth century, under the title of *Brief Lives*. Aubrey wrote several other works, all of which remained in manuscript during his lifetime. His *Perambulation of Surrey,* an account of the topography and antiquities of that county, was published in 1718. He completed a treatise on education in 1684; the *Wiltshire Collections* appeared in 1682. *The Natural History of Wiltshire* was edited by the Wiltshire antiquary John Britton and published in 1847; *Monumenta Britannica* has never been printed in its entirety, the confused and overwritten condition of the manuscript being the main obstacle to its publication. However, an incomplete photographic facsimile with partial transcription of the text appeared in 1980. Almost all of Aubrey's manuscripts are in the Bodleian Library, Oxford.

References
Primary

Aubrey, John. 1898. *Brief Lives.* Ed. Andrew Clark. 2 vols. Oxford: Clarendon.

———. 1980. *Brief Lives.* Ed. O. Lawson Dick. London: Secker and Warburg.

———. 1980. *Monumenta Britannica.* Ed. J. Fowles and R. Legg. Boston: Little, Brown.

———. 1980. *The Natural History of Wiltshire.* Newton Abbot, UK.

———. 1980. *Three Prose Works.* Ed. J. Buchanan-Brown. Fontwell, UK: Centaur Press.

Secondary

Hunter, M. 1975. *John Aubrey and the Realm of Learning.* London: Science History Publications.

Parry, Graham. 1995. *The Trophies of Time: English Antiquarians of the Seventeenth-century.* Oxford and New York: Oxford University Press.

Powell, Anthony. 1963. *John Aubrey and His Friends.* London: Mercury.

Ucko, Peter J., M. Hunter, A. J. Clark, and A. David. 1991. *Avebury Reconsidered from the 1660s to the 1990s.* London: Unwin Hyman.

Graham Parry

Edward Lhwyd *1660–1709*

Recording the hitherto unexplored barrows, tumuli, earthworks, metalwork, and artifacts of prehistoric Britain, Edward Lhwyd was the first to use these material remains to argue for a high degree of social organization and technical skills in pre-Roman British societies.

Edward Lhwyd, or Lhuyd, was the outstanding Celtic scholar of the late seventeenth century, a talented antiquarian, and a notable paleontologist and botanist. He was born near Oswestry in 1660 into a well-established Welsh family. In 1682 he entered Oxford's Jesus College, the traditional home of Welsh students at that university, and he remained there until 1687. As a student he became friendly with Dr. Robert Plot, the antiquary and natural philosopher who had been appointed first keeper of the new Ashmolean Museum in 1683, and before long Lhwyd became his assistant. Plot had a particular interest in fossils and shells, which he communicated to Lhwyd, who also showed a genius for botany. Since the mission of the Ashmolean in its early days was to advance understanding of the natural world, Lhwyd's talents fit tidily into Plot's scheme of research. With Plot's encouragement, he began compiling a catalog of shells in the Ashmolean, developing in the process considerable skills in taxonomy. During his vacations, he also began to collect plants in the region of Mount Snowdon in Wales, sending back specimens to the Physic Garden at Oxford and keeping minute descriptions of their particulars. Lhwyd was the first to recognize "that the mountains of Britain have a distinct Alpine flora and fauna of their own." Plot introduced Lhwyd to the naturalists Martin Lister and John Ray, both of whom readily printed material gathered by Lhwyd in their own works of classification. Lister's great compilation of shells, *Historia Conchyliorum* (1685, 1687, 1691), was illustrated with over a thousand copper engravings and contained contributions on shells and fossils from Lhwyd; Ray's book on British plants, *Synopsis Methodica Stirpium Britannicarum* (1689–1690), listed forty new varieties that Lhwyd had discovered in Wales.

In the late 1680s, Lhwyd became increasingly drawn to the study of fossils, or "formed stones" as he called them. He was convinced they were the petrified remains of organisms that had died long ago, not sports of nature or stones that grew in the earth in the shape of living

*Edward Lhwyd.
(Copyright Griffith
Institute)*

forms, as Plot was inclined to believe. Like Robert Hooke, the eminent Oxford scientist, he considered fossils to be evidence of cataclysmic changes in the earth's surface in earlier times, though he neither speculated about the length of time in which such changes might have occurred nor openly challenged the conventional views of world history that assumed a Creation some four thousand years before the birth of Christ. Lhwyd made significant advances in identifying and classifying an unprecedented range of fossils, and in 1691 he published his description of those in the Ashmolean collections as *Lithophylacii Britannici Ichnographia*. That same year, he succeeded Plot as keeper of the museum. In archaeological annals, Lhwyd is noteworthy for making the distinction between fossils and flint implements such as arrowheads and axe-heads. Nehemiah Grew's Catalogue of the Museum of the Royal Society (1681) had grouped such stone implements together with fossils as another variety of "formed stone" and had considered them as natural in origin. Lhwyd recognized prehistoric stone tools and weapons as manmade artifacts attributable to the ancient Britons.

It did not take long for Lhwyd's interests to broaden from fossils and stone implements to British antiquity in general, and this intellectual shift was encouraged by his acquaintance with JOHN AUBREY at Oxford and with Aubrey's friend Edmund Wild. These two men awakened his curiosity about ancient British remains discoverable both above and below ground. From Aubrey in particular he learned the conceptual habit of using these remains, whether arrowheads or stone circles, as evidence from which deductions could be made about the nature and perhaps even the development of the primitive inhabitants of Britain. Lhwyd came to form a remarkably advanced understanding of prehistoric British culture. Possessing a skeptical temper, he was not overly influenced by religious preconceptions, and so he did not feel the need to fetch the original inhabitants of Britain from Babel or the biblical lands, as was common in seventeenth-century antiquarian thought; nor did he seem to believe in the brief biblical chronology suggested for the earth. On the other hand, he did not entertain a very complex prehistory for Britain; he assumed that a Celtic race had occupied the islands at an unknown time in the past, had spread into all parts, and had developed a fairly uniform culture that was well established by the time of the Roman invasion.

The Ashmolean Museum, after an engraving by Michael Burghers. (Reprinted from R. T. Gunther, Early Science in Oxford, Vol. 4, 1925)

Lhwyd was given an opportunity to elaborate his antiquarian opinions when he was recruited in 1693 to be a contributor to Edmund Gibson's revised edition of WILLIAM CAMDEN's *Britannia*. This new edition, eventually published in 1695, was the first attempt to update Camden's great volume of topographical history, which had first been published in 1586 and revised by the author through successive editions until 1607. Translated into English in 1610, it had been out of print since 1637. By the end of the century Gibson, a young scholar of Queen's College, Oxford, who had already proven his abilities with editions of Roman and Anglo-Saxon works, launched the ambitious project for a thorough revision of the *Britannia* that would also incorporate the advances of modern scholarship in Camden's subject matter. He gave the 1607 edition the status of a classical text, having it freshly translated and insisting on its integrity as an important document that could not be altered. At the end of the entry for each county, each new contributor was entitled to make his own additions, to summarize the recent improvements in knowledge relating to that region, and to add notes on places and monuments that Camden had overlooked. Gibson recruited an impressive team of contributors, noted for its intellectual accomplishments and for the prevalence of young scholars. At first Lhwyd was given the care of three Welsh counties, but soon he was in charge of the whole principality. He immediately proposed to make an antiquarian tour to cover the ground in person and gather material, and he spent the summer of 1693 traveling purposefully around Wales.

Without a doubt, Lhwyd's "Additions" to the Welsh counties were outstanding: indeed, they transformed this section of *Britannia* from a rather inadequate sketch of unfamiliar terrain to the most rewarding part of the new volume. Camden did not know Wales, and his grasp of the Welsh language had been uncertain. (Welsh was assumed to be the surviving form of the Celtic language of the British people encountered by the Romans—an assumption that still persists today.) Camden had been primarily interested in trying to associate existing place-names in Wales with stations on the Antonine Itinerary and locating the tribal areas mentioned in Ptolemy's *Geography*. Lhwyd, in contrast, spoke Welsh and was both long familiar with the central counties of Wales and avidly curious about his homeland. He supplemented his own knowledge by sending out questionnaires about antiquities and local customs to gentlemen, clergy, and schoolmasters in areas he could not visit. The consequence of all this research was that Lhwyd's "Additions" were usually longer than Camden's original entries and were stocked with valuable information, vividly presented.

Like most seventeenth-century antiquaries, Lhwyd was inclined to use etymology to riddle out the traces of primitive meaning in place-names and topographical terms. Given his sound knowledge of Welsh, and his firm common sense, he was more successful than his predecessors in an area too often overrun by fanciful speculation. For example, he remarked of the River Wye:

> The British name of this river is Wysk, which word seems a derivative of Gwy or Wy. At present it is not significative in the British: but is still preserved in the Irish tongue, and is their common word for water. There were formerly in Britain many rivers of this name, which may now be distinguished in England by these shadows of it, *Ex, Ox, Ux, Ouse, Esk,* etc.

Confronting the mysterious pyramidal heaps of stones found on many Welsh mountains, some of considerable size, Lhwyd explicated the meaning of the word *kairn,* noted that cairns were still built up over the graves of malefactors and suicides in his own time, suggested that this custom was formerly widely observed and not restricted to outcasts, quoted from Virgil how cairns marked honorable places of burial in Roman times, insisted that the practice of accumulating stones over a grave was far older and more widespread than the Roman Empire (for cairns occur in Ireland and Scotland), and speculated that the huge cairns on

Plinlimmon—"a hundred cart-load of stones"—were the pre-Christian funeral monuments of tribal chieftains. Lhwyd's was a spacious, imaginative mind, and he used language, literature, customs, and fieldwork to interpret a practice that has persisted over thousands of years.

Lhwyd made an important methodological advance in his Welsh "Additions" by his simple but significant way of presenting information about material remains. He provided extremely specific details of structures or objects, indicating their dimensions and condition, describing what was found with or near them and at what depth, and noting who had possession of removable items. So, for example, he gave a minute account of a tessellated pavement found in 1689 in the garden of a Mr. Francis Ridley, near Monmouth; he recorded the size of the tesserae, the materials and colors, and the pattern and the images in the decoration. He was particular in his description of coins, giving details of the emperors' heads. He looked closely at Roman bricks found at Caerleon bearing a legionary hallmark, "not inscribed but stamped with some instrument," which suggested the presence of an army brickworks there. He gave a specific account of Roman copper ingots and described a number of Roman brooches and how they fastened. This kind of information has enduring value and allows later generations of antiquarians and archaeologists to make use of centuries-old material. When Lhwyd did not understand what he was saw, such as a peculiar layout of stones or an inscription of meaningless letters or symbols, he nonetheless described it accurately and even illustrated it, in the hope that a later scholar would make use of it.

Lhwyd's most important strides were made in the field of British antiquities, and his contribution to *Britannia* demonstrated that the scale of British remains was far greater than had yet been imagined. Monoliths, triliths, stone circles, stone enclosures of various forms, horizontal stones, cairns, barrows, tumuli, and earthworks were presented as the remains of a complex and technically proficient society that had flourished in the British Isles before the Romans and may have formed part of a wider prehistoric culture extending across Europe: "I think it probable, should we make diligent enquiry, that there may be Monuments of this kind still extant in the less frequented places of Germany, France and Spain; if not also in Italy." His own "diligent inquiry" had located many such sites, hitherto unnoticed and often in the last stages of disintegration. In Gower, for instance, at the Kevn Bryn circle, the great stone in the center

> is much diminished as having five tuns or more broke off it to make mill-stones. I guess the stone originally to have been between 25 and 30 tuns in weight. The carriage, rearing and placing of this massy rock is plainly an effect of human industry and art;

but the pulleys and levers, the force and skill by which 'twas done, are not so easily imagined.

He was fully persuaded that these stone monuments were the work of the ancient Britons and erected long before the Roman occupation. Their rudeness conveyed an evident antiquity, from a time when iron was not yet in use. He had no reason to believe that the Saxons or Danes built these piles, for their number and magnitude indicated they were the work of stable communities: "Such vast perennial memorials seem rather to be the work of a people settled in their own country, than of such roving pirates."

Lhwyd had read Aubrey's "Templa Druidum" from the manuscript of *Monumenta Britannica,* as his notes several times acknowledged, and he concurred with Aubrey's attribution of these stone complexes to the ancient Britons. He agreed too that many were sacred sites. But Lhwyd was his own man and arrived at his conclusions independently, by observation and reflection. Though he kept an open mind about the possibility, he did not readily associate the Druids with these sanctuaries, as Aubrey had done. Roman sources, after all, made the Druids priests of woods and groves. Lhwyd turned to a Celtic source rather than only classical ones for clues to the function of the stone circles, and he cited an early account of the life of St. Patrick to telling effect. Under consideration was the great circle called Y Gromlech in Pembrokeshire (which had an eighteen-foot monolith at its center and "a piece broken off, about ten foot long and five in breadth, which seems more than twenty oxen can draw"); he noted that

> Irish historians call one of their chiefest idols *Cromcruach,* which remained till St. Patrick's time in the plain of Moy-sleuct in Brefin. This Idol is described to have been *auro et argento caelatum,* and said to be attended with twelve other Idols much less, all of brass, placed about him. *Cromcruach,* at the approach of St. Patrick, fell to the ground, and the lesser Idols sunk into the earth up to their necks.

Lhwyd wondered if the story incorporated a memory of stone circles still in active use in historical times as "a place of idolatrous worship." Perhaps the standing stones *were* the idols, worshipped as gods—certainly a fresh interpretation of the function of standing stones. He reinforced his belief with information supplied to John Aubrey by the Scottish antiquary Dr. James Garden of Aberdeen, included in *Monumenta Britannica,* which tended to the same conclusion.

Lhwyd had much in common with Aubrey: a fascination with the ancient Britons, a fondness for natural history, a highly observant eye, and an uncommon receptivity to the cross-fertilization of ideas. Though both had speculative imaginations, Lhwyd was more methodical and disciplined. For example, Lhwyd was willing, on etymological grounds, to follow Aubrey in believing that the stones at Kerig y Drudion in Denbighshire were associated with druidic ceremonies. He conceived of the Druids as a working priesthood spread across the Celtic world but certainly not possessed of any mysterious powers. However, he believed that superstitions associated with druidic practices might still linger on in Wales, and in a remarkable flight of imagination that Aubrey would have applauded, he suggested in his account of Denbighshire that a surviving curiosity of Welsh folklore might preserve "a relic of the Druids' doctrine." There was a widespread belief that around midsummer's eve, snakes gathered in companies and, by communal hissing, created a kind of bubble that then encircled one of the snakes and hardened into a ring as it passed off the tail. These snake-rings, as they were known in Welsh, were glass or earthen amulets and were deemed to bring fortune and prosperity to their owner. Lhwyd reported seeing "at several places about twenty or thirty." He then recalled Pliny's account of the magical snake egg, created by "the spittle and secretion of angry snakes" and used by the Druids to ensure good fortune, and he proposed that, given their similarity in folklore, the snake-rings prized by the Welsh (which in his opinion were actually Roman beads) may have been a vestige of druidic religion. Who is to say he was wrong?

In his extensive contributions, Lhwyd did more than any of his predecessors to enlarge understanding of the societies that inhabited the land before the Romans. Instead of being overly dependent on classical sources, with their fairly repetitive information based on limited contact, he formed a picture from material remains supplemented by folklore and the classical reports. He drew attention to the high degree of social organization and technical prowess needed to erect the great stone complexes. He made it clear, too, that the Britons had considerable metalworking skills. In particular, he noted the discovery of several caches of weapons, axe-heads, bolts, daggers, and swords, and though he erred in calling them brass when they were obviously bronze, he gave them a British rather than Roman provenance. He linked them to similar finds described in Robert Plot's *Staffordshire* and provided illustrations of an axe-head, dagger, and hasp that enabled later scholars to correct their identification as Bronze Age implements. As the following comments demonstrate, even an open-minded antiquarian like Lhwyd had considerable difficulty circumventing the idea that the Romans were the sole exponents of civilization in the lands of northern Europe:

For my own part, I must confess, that for a long time I suspected these instruments Roman, supposing them too artificial to have been made by the Britains before the Romans civilized them; and that they were not swords, etc. but intended for some other uses. But seeing they had gold and silver coins before that time (as all Antiquaries allow) and that 'tis scarce questionable but that the golden Torquis described in the last County was theirs; and also that Pliny tells us the Druids cut down their Mistletoe with golden sickles: I know but they might have more arts than we commonly allow them, and therefore must suspend my judgement.

Lhwyd illustrated some of the gold and silver coins of the ancient Britons that bore no signs of any Roman influence, and from them he deduced the existence of a moderately developed economic system. The long disquisition on torques in Merionethshire paid tribute to the elaborate goldwork of the Britons. As he investigated the etymology of the word *torc,* he found analogies in languages, such as Irish, that were not in contact with Rome, which emboldened him to think that perhaps the Latin language absorbed words from older languages, such as the Celtic group, and was not always in a position of linguistic hegemony over its subject nations.

Nor ought any one to think it absurd, that I thus endeavour to derive Latin words from the Welsh, seeing there are hundreds of words in that language, that agree in sound and signification with the Latin, which yet could not be borrowed from the Roman, for that the Irish retain the same, who must have been a colony of the Britains, long before the Roman conquest.

Not the least of Lhwyd's achievements in the "Additions" to *Britannia* was his creation of a cultural space in which the society and productions of the ancient Britons could be admired as something different from and independent of classical civilization, which had hitherto overshadowed all contiguous cultures. All things Celtic attracted Lhwyd. He was possibly the first to recognize the characteristic patterns of braided interlace and knotwork as features of a culture that he could trace throughout Wales, northern England, Scotland, and Ireland. He was unclear about the identity of this culture, as about the significance of the decoration, but he was struck by the frequency with which these designs occurred on early Christian monuments and sculpture, and he left an account of the style for the benefit of others who might make something of it. He described the "certain endless knots" of a cross in Pembrokeshire and provided an accurate illustration of the "chequered carving" on a monument in Flintshire. He linked his discoveries with similar examples depicted by Robert Plot in his

Staffordshire (though he disagreed with Plot's contention that they were of Danish origin) and with the Bewcastle cross in Cumberland.

Lhwyd's research for *Britannia* inspired him to undertake a work that would bring together his knowledge of Celtic languages and ancient British antiquities and his interest in natural history. In 1695, encouraged by a group of Welsh gentry, he issued a proposal for his *Natural History and Antiquities of Wales* together with an *Archaeologia Britannica* that would be a comprehensive historical, geographical, and philological account of Wales. He planned to establish the affinities between the Welsh/British language and the Irish, Scottish, Cornish, and Breton tongues, which would lay the groundwork for a study that would inquire into the existence of a common culture prevalent in these regions in pre-Roman times. He issued a questionnaire, "Parochial Queries," to gather information about his proposed topics from knowledgeable people all over Wales, and he then set about his travels, for he believed above all in the importance of personal inspection of sites of interest. For four years he toured intensively, going as far afield as the Scottish islands, Ireland, Cornwall, and Brittany and making collections. In 1707 he published his *Glossography,* the first part of the projected *Archaeologia Britannica* and a work that confirmed Lhwyd's preeminence as a Celtic philologist. However, the other parts of his scheme failed to appear. The composite cultural survey of Welsh antiquities, customs, traditions, and folklore, which would have complemented the linguistic material and thrown light on the mentality of Celtic peoples, including the Britons, proved too difficult to compile. Nor could Lhwyd order his notes on all the monuments in Wales presumed to be British and raised no later than the Roman conquest. His details of Roman and later monuments in Wales remained in manuscript, as did his lists of inscriptions, his observations on ancient British coins and camps and burial places, and his extensive collections relating to the natural history of the region.

The *Glossography* is a substantial folio and in itself represents a remarkable achievement of comparative philology. Lhwyd demonstrated the relationship between the Celtic languages surviving in western Europe by extensive word-lists, with etymological observations and indications of shifts of meaning in cognate words. He included a Welsh dictionary, an Irish dictionary, and a Cornish grammar. By showing the similarities between Breton and Cornish and Welsh, he was able to make some progress in reconstructing the ancient Gallic language spoken in Gaul in Roman times. The prodigious philological learning that underpinned this book still strikes the reader with awe, and its publication by the university press at Oxford left no doubt that Lhwyd was a master of Celtic studies without peer.

Lhwyd's travels during the years 1697–1701 were an impressive testimony to the thoroughness of his research. He made the first antiquarian tour of the Highlands and Islands of Scotland, including Iona, and these Scottish journeys were well documented in his letters. He constantly took notes on the language spoken by the common people, remarking on differences in pronunciation and word use according to locality. He visited Scottish antiquaries wherever he could, calling for instance on Sir Robert Sibbald in Edinburgh, the author of most of the additions concerning Scotland in the 1695 *Britannia*. He collected Gaelic manuscripts (thirty-nine of which are now in the library of Trinity College, Dublin). He conversed extensively with gentlemen and clergy about local customs, and his notes testified to his increasing interest in Celtic folklore. An account of the questionnaire that Lhwyd submitted to his Scottish antiquarian acquaintances reveals the scope of his inquiries. He asked correspondents to provide the local dialect equivalent of words relating to natural history and domestic life taken from John Ray's *Dictionariolum Trilingue* (1675), an English-Latin-Greek vocabulary. Then he requested details of towns, villages, and geographical features within a ten- to twenty-mile radius, seeking suggestions as to the meaning of local place-names. He sought information about barrows, burial chambers, standing stones, and inscribed stones. He asked for an account of amulets and charms prized by the people of the neighborhood, with specimens if possible, and for examples of coins and ancient brass utensils found locally. Flint arrowheads (known as "elf-bolts," from the belief that they were shot by fairies or witches to injure people and cattle) were a particular topic of interest, along with other artificial and natural stones (prehistoric implements and fossils). Lhwyd requested information on local games and customs, on Christian names and titles, on local poets and their works, and on any writers who had flourished in the region in past centuries.

Unfortunately, much of the vast store of information that Lhwyd accumulated by means of his travels and his questionnaires was lost. After the compilation of the *Glossography*, his health failed, and he was never able to organize his collections for the second part of *Archaeologia Britannica*, the proposed great compendium of the Celtic culture of western Britain. He died in 1709, and his papers, being in a confused state, were dispersed, and many were later destroyed by fire. Because of the *Glossography*'s narrow linguistic appeal, and because it stood alone rather than in company with the volume on Celtic studies that should have crowned Lhwyd's career, his reputation is circumscribed. Yet his work for the *Britannia* of 1695 remains a lasting record of his exceptional powers as an interpreter of prehistoric remains and proves his worth as an incomparable topographer and local historian. His philological research in charting the relationships of the Celtic languages of the British Isles and Brittany, and preserving many of their features, effectively laid the foundation for all later study of these languages.

References
Primary
Camden, William. 1695. *Britannia.* Reprinted Newton Abbot, UK, 1971.

Lhuyd, Edward. 1707. *Archaeologia Britannica, Vol. 1 Glossography.* Reprinted Oxford: Scolar Press, 1981.

Secondary
Campbell, J. L., and D. Thomson. 1963. *Edward Lhuyd in the Scottish Highlands 1699–1700.* Oxford: Clarendon.

Emery, F. 1958. "Edward Lhuyd and the 1695 Britannia." In *Antiquity.*

———. 1971. *Edward Lhuyd 1660–1709.* Cardiff.

Gunther, R. T., ed. 1945. "The Life and Letters of Edward Lhuyd." In *Early Science in Oxford,* vol. 14. London: Dawsons of Pall Mall.

Parry, Graham. 1995. *The Trophies of Time: English Antiquarians of the Seventeenth-century.* Oxford and New York: Oxford University Press.

Piggott, Stuart. 1976. *Ruins in a Landscape.* Edinburgh: Edinburgh University Press.

Graham Parry

William Stukeley   1687–1765

Best known for his superb draftsmanship, detailed surveying and recording of
Stonehenge and Avebury in the eighteenth century before their wholesale
desecration, William Stukeley was a fieldwork pioneer. His geographical and
topographical methods of relating monuments to landscape and comparative
studies of the structural similarities and common features of many stone circle
groups convinced him that these were ancient temples.

William Stukeley can be regarded as the last of the great English antiquarians and the first of the reliable archaeologists. He was born in 1687 at Holbeach in Lincolnshire, the son of a country lawyer. He went up to Corpus Christi College, Cambridge, in 1704, where he began to experience those emotions characteristic of the developing antiquary: "I frequently took a walk to sigh over the ruins of Barnwell Abbey, and made a draught of it, and used to cut pieces of the yew trees there into tobacco stoppers, lamenting the destruction of so noble monuments of the piety and magnificence of our ancestors." In 1709 he moved to London to train as a doctor; he later practiced in Boston, Lincolnshire. From 1710 until 1725 he undertook an annual antiquarian tour on horseback to different parts of England, in order to view churches, abbeys, remarkable buildings and gardens, and sites of historic interest. A competent draftsman, he made many drawings on these tours, and the fruits of his observations were published in 1724 in a well-illustrated volume, *Itinerarium Curiosum* [List of Curiosities].

Stukeley returned to London in 1717 and became the secretary of the newly revived Society of Antiquaries, which had lapsed for over a hundred years after its closure by James I in 1607. At this time, Stukeley's close friends included Roger Gale (the son of the scholarly dean of York, Thomas Gale), Thomas Herbert (eighth earl of Pembroke), Lord Winchelsea, Humphrey Wanley, and the virtuoso Richard Mead. Stukeley became a fellow of the Royal Society in 1718. Apparently dissatisfied with the indifference of the Society of Antiquaries to Roman Britain, Stukeley founded the eccentric Society of Roman Knights in 1722. "The business of this Society is to search for and illustrate the Roman Monuments in the Britannic Isles," ran Stukeley's opening address, which urged the members to seek out and describe "camps, temples, walls, amphitheaters, monuments, roads, inscriptions, coins, buildings and

A self-portrait of William Stukeley. (Copyright Bodleian Library)

whatever has a Roman stamp on them." Members adopted the names of Celtic figures associated with the Roman conquest of Britain, so Lord Winchelsea was Cingetorix, Roger Gale was Venutius, his brother Samuel was Cunobelin, and Stukeley himself chose the name of Chyndonax. The society took the unusual step of admitting women as members: the aristocrat Lady Hertford was Bonduca, and Miss Gale was Cartismandua, queen of the Brigantes. The group's gatherings tended to be sociable rather than productive of new insights concerning the Romans in Britain.

Stukeley had already shown an aptitude for preserving the past with his enterprising action over the remarkable structure in Scotland known as Arthur's O'on, or Arthur's Oven. This enigmatic stone building, circular and domed, stood by the river Carron near Falkirk and seems to have been an authentic Roman construction, possibly a temple or shrine. It was surely the northernmost Roman monument and was exceptionally well preserved. Stukeley asked his friend Andrews Jelfe, an architect and builder who was sent to that part of Scotland to supervise repairs to fortifications, to conduct a survey of Arthur's O'on and record it in drawings. This Jelfe did, and Stukeley published an illustrated description of the monument in 1720, based on Jelfe's reports. The account proved invaluable, for in 1743 the building was demolished by its owner, who used the stone to repair a dam.

Stukeley's most enduring achievements were not in Roman studies but in prehistoric antiquities, the result of his fieldwork with megalithic monuments. As early as 1710 he had been puzzled by the Rollright Stones in Oxfordshire. In 1716 he visited Stonehenge, and his fascination with this monument was shared by his friend Lord Pembroke, whose estates lay nearby. Together they frequently inspected the site, measured it, and discussed the possible origin and function of the prodigious stones. After Roger Gale lent Stukeley a transcription of JOHN AUBREY's manuscript of *Monumenta Britannica* that his father had made, Stukeley's curiosity about stone circles was intensified by Aubrey's research and by his suggestion that they were temples associated with the Druids. In 1719, in company with the Gale brothers, he set off to inspect Avebury, the site that Aubrey had discovered and recognized in 1649 as a great ceremonial complex extending over a wide area. For the next few years, Stukeley applied himself to elucidating the many problems raised by megalithic monuments, effectively advancing the work that Aubrey had begun. He laboriously gathered notes on circles and allied monuments all over the British Isles and undertook intensive fieldwork on the two major sites of Stonehenge and Avebury. His work at Avebury was especially valuable, because at the very time that Stukeley grew interested in the monument, the local landowner had begun its wanton destruction, breaking up the great stones for building materials and lime. Without Stukeley's meticulous record of the location of every stone and his perceptive tracing of depressions and contours, current knowledge of the monument would be greatly reduced.

Stukeley had an exceptionally observant eye, and he was able to add considerably to Aubrey's assessment of the site. He recognized, for instance, that the extent of the monument was much larger than Aubrey had indicated. From 1719 to 1724, he made plans and drawings of the full spread of the stone circles inside the great bank and ditch. Following the long avenue flanked by standing stones, he detected its terminus in the village of West Kennet, marked by a small double circle of standing stones. This last circle was destroyed in the 1720s, soon after Stukeley's survey, but its existence was verified by the excavations of 1930. He also traced the line of another, less-defined avenue leading westward from Avebury.

Similarly intensive fieldwork was carried out at Stonehenge over the same period. Here again Stukeley's ability to observe a large complex plan where others saw only a monument served him well. In 1721 he was able to identify the avenue that leads from the entrance to Stonehenge, passing by the Heel Stone toward the river Avon. Unlike the avenue at Avebury, which was marked with stones, this one consisted of two parallel ditches with the earth between them slightly raised to form a discernible pathway. During his investigations of 1723, he also recognized that there was an extremely long earthwork enclosure to the north, which could be associated with the monument. He named this enclosure the Cursus and speculated that it might have been a prehistoric racecourse or hippodrome, where races of ritual significance took place and "games, feasts, exercises and sports" were held on ceremonial occasions. The name has stuck, and the Stonehenge Cursus can now be seen as a member of a large group of such enclosures widely distributed in Britain and of Late Neolithic date.

Stukeley was also the first to notice the significance of the orientation of Stonehenge. He remarked in his book *Stonehenge* (1740) that in the avenue's direction he had discovered "answers to the principal line of the whole work, the north-east, whereabouts the sun rises, when the days are longest." This suggestion, that the monument's astronomical

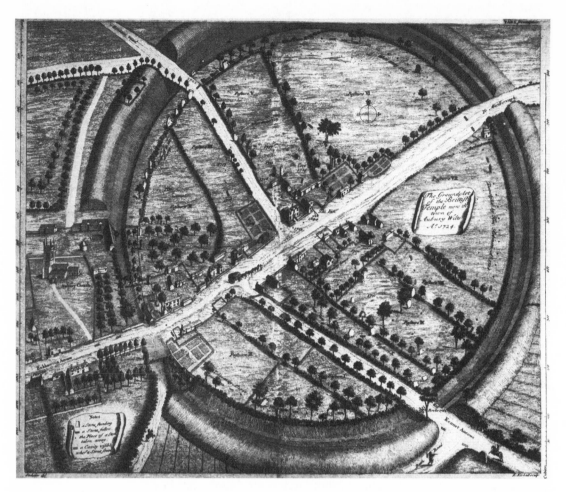

Stukeley's plan of Avebury, 1724. (Reprinted from Isobel Foster Smith, Windmill Hill & Avebury, *1965)*

bearing points to sunrise at the summer solstice, has colored thinking about Stonehenge ever since Stukeley put it into print.

In the course of his detailed, accurate surveying of the site, Stukeley came to believe that it might be possible to deduce an ancient unit of measurement used by the builders to determine the disposition of the stones. Such an exercise could help confirm or deny the claim that Stonehenge was a Roman temple, an idea advanced in *Stoneheng Restored* (1655), a posthumous work by Inigo Jones brought out by his nephew, the architect John Webb. Stukeley determined, by means of Roman bricks from Verulamium, that a Roman foot was eleven and a half English inches, but he could not make this measure fit the scheme of Stonehenge. Instead, he concluded that the operative unit of measurement there was twenty and four-fifths inches, which he deemed to be the same as an Egyptian cubit. He later gave this unit the more evocative name of the "Druid's cubit." Deducing ancient standards of measurement was a trend of the age, and even Isaac Newton busied himself with estimating the "Sacred Cubit of the Jews" from descriptions of antique structures, including the Great Pyramid.

In addition to the survey of the whole area of Stonehenge during the years 1721–1724, Stukeley and his friend the earl of Pembroke engaged in some limited excavations within the stone circle, from which they learned that the monoliths had been levered into holes in the solid chalk floor of the plain and then packed in with flints for complete stability. (Their work at Stonehenge concluded with a banquet and a dance upon one of the lintels.) In some of the nearby barrows, they carried out admirable cross-sectional digs, carefully cutting down through the neat, deliberate layers across the whole diameter of the barrow and noting the composition of each phase. They minutely documented all the finds, identified the bones of animals, and left undisturbed the human remains, having noted the orientation of burial. They were also careful to leave *in situ* the urns of cremation burials. They ascertained that these tumuli were not mass graves of fallen warriors, as was the commonly held belief, but single graves of men and women of high importance in their society. These were the best executed and best recorded excavations to date in England.

The question of who had raised Stonehenge and Avebury and the barrows had to be answered. In the early 1720s Stukeley was inclined to describe all of these antiquities as Celtic and attribute them to the ancient Britons whom the Romans had encountered in the first century B.C., though he believed they were erected several centuries earlier than the Roman conquest. (He suggested a date of 460 B.C. for Stonehenge, which he arrived at by computations based on cyclic variations of magnetic north over the centuries.) He was convinced that the barrows on the Wiltshire plains were made by the same people who built the stone circles. By 1723 he was getting ready to publish the results of his investigations into stone circles and henge monuments in a volume to be called "The History of the Temples of the Ancient Celts," but he desisted. The work was left in manuscript (of which versions exist in the Bodleian and Cardiff Public Library), probably because he decided to devote his energies to the publication of *Itinerarium Curiosum,* the record of his antiquarian tours. Had it been published, this work on Celtic temples would have been the outstanding archaeological book of its time. His own fieldwork at Stonehenge and Avebury would have formed the basis, together with his notes on the Rollright Stones, the Stanton Drew Circle, Kit's Coty, and other southern stone structures. These he had intended to supplement with Aubrey's observations on stone circles preserved in the manuscript of *Monumenta Britannica,* and EDWARD LHWYD's information regarding stone monuments in Wales, also in manuscripts to which he had access. He also took advantage of the substantial information about stone circles in the British Isles, available in the 1695 edition of WILLIAM CAMDEN's *Britannia.* Stukeley made a persuasive case in his manuscript for the pre-Roman origin of all stone circles and henges and also for barrows (citing evidence of Roman roads cutting through barrows to establish the prior existence of the latter). From Aubrey he derived the belief that stone circles were ancient temples, and he was able to enumerate various common features that he had identified: they usually had "an area or plane before or around 'em," and they were set near rivers or streams and were approached by means of an avenue made of stones or raised earth. The circles themselves might be single or double and might contain an altar stone, or what he called a "cove" or sanctum, made usually of three standing stones. He noted the similarity between these close-clustered uprights and the stone remains of chamber tombs, and he remarked on the frequency with which barrows and burials occurred near stone circles, wondering if "the burials gave first occasion to the temples?" The problems of erecting megaliths exercised him, and he was able to make some insightful suggestions about the possibility of moving great stones on rollers, or sledges, and envisaged ways in which they could be raised and levered into position.

Stukeley completed and published the account of his various antiquarian journeys, *Itinerarium Curiosum,* in 1724. This volume contains a great deal of intelligent archaeological observation, especially in the sections dealing with southwestern England. In particular, his remarks about the different functions and classes of earthworks—hill-forts, barrows, and dykes—were quite sophisticated. Although overly inclined to assign a Roman origin to some major earthworks, such as Maiden Castle, he did consider many to be the work of the pre-Roman British tribes or of the Belgae, a significant advance in dating at a time when the Saxons and Danes were so often held to be the principal reshapers of the landscape. The quality of his observations can be judged from his remark that barrows were often situated on what is known as a "false crest" and appeared to stand on the skyline when viewed from the valley below, where the village associated with the barrow probably lay. "I observe the barrows upon Hakpen Hill (in Wiltshire) and others are set with great art not upon the very highest part of the hills but upon so much of the declivity or edge as that they make appearance as above to those in the valley."

Stukeley also seems to have been the first to recognize ancient field systems, the outlines of which, as defined by margins of stones cleared from the site, he noted on a number of occasions. For example, at Cranborne Chase, "I frequently observed on the sides of hills long divisions very strait crossing one another with all kinds of angle: they look like the baulks or meres of plow'd lands, and are really made of flint o'ergrown with turf; they are too small for plow'd lands, unless of the most ancient Britons, who dealt little that way." They were indeed the remains of prehistoric field systems, and *Itinerarium Curiosum* contains the first description of their characteristic outlines.

Stukeley's understanding of the remote past was fostered by his imaginative sense of the extent of time. Unlike all his predecessors, except Aubrey and Edward Lhwyd, he was prepared to believe that there had been a long and eventful occupation of Britain in prehistoric times and that the marks of the vanished societies of ancient Britain lay everywhere across the land. Discounting the legendary history of Britain detailed by Geoffrey of Monmouth, the commonly held view of antiquity in the seventeenth century was that the Britons who lived in the island before the coming of the Romans had left no traces of their presence. Stukeley disagreed. STUART PIGGOTT, his foremost interpreter, has highlighted the basic archaeological principles that enabled Stukeley to be open to deeper perspectives into the past. The first was his willingness to accept that there was a long pre-Roman period over which field antiquities could have been distributed. Then there was his recognition that various prehistoric societies had probably occupied the southern part of Britain by invasion or immigration from the continent, so that it was not necessary to think of the pre-Roman occupants of the island as one uniform group labeled "British." He wrote, for example, in *Itinerarium Curiosum* that "the incredible number of barrows that overspread this country from the sea-side to North Wiltshire persuades me a great people inhabited here before the Belgae." (He was inclined to think there had been a large migration from Spain.) The third important feature of Stukeley's achievement was, in Piggott's words, "the application of the geographical and topographical method to the study of a group of related structures [such as linear earthworks or henge monuments] in order to interpret them as a coherent whole in the light of such historical knowledge as was available."

Behind all of Stukeley's best work was sharp observation coupled with an ability to interpret intelligently what he saw. Not surprisingly, he was one of the first to notice the phenomenon of crop marks. Piggott quotes a letter of 1719 to Roger Gale in which Stukeley detected the underlying presence of the remains of the Roman town at Great Chesterford in Essex by patterns in the cornfield. He saw "the most charming sight that can be imagined": "the perfect vestigia of a temple as easily discernible in the corn as upon paper. The people say, let the year come as it will, this place is ever visible, and that it has been so ever since the memory of man, and fancy the fairies dancing there causes the appearance." Several similar accounts appeared in *Itinerarium Curiosum*.

Stukeley's skills as a field archaeologist were at their peak in the early 1720s, when he was surveying and excavating at Avebury and

Stonehenge and writing up his antiquarian tours. Thereafter, speculation and theory began to prevail over acuity. In particular, his obsession with druidic lore distorted his ability to evaluate British antiquity. He had long been attracted to the Druids and their mysteries, as was evident in the name he adopted as his nom de guerre for the Society of Roman Knights. He had read a published report by the French antiquary Guenebault, which described the discovery at Dijon in 1598 of a glass cinerary urn contained within a stone cylinder and inscribed in Greek with the name of a priest, Chyndonax. The account concluded by suggesting that Chyndonax was probably a Druid. Stukeley appropriated the name for himself, and over the years he wove an elaborate fantasy around the Druids. He believed they had come to Gaul and Britain in the train of the Phoenicians, whom he regarded as the early settlers of those northern countries. In this matter, Stukeley was following the opinions of the French antiquarian Samuel Bochart, expressed in his *Geographia Sacra* (1646), and of Bochart's English follower Aylett Sammes in *Britannia Antiqua Illustrata* (1676). Both of these writers argued for the Phoenician colonization of Iberia, Gaul, and Britain. Stukeley became convinced that the Druids preserved a knowledge of the religion of the patriarchs: the revelation given by God to Adam and transmitted down through the Adamite generations until the time of Abraham. This knowledge consisted, *inter alia,* of the essential goodness of the Supreme Being, his plans for humanity, his preferred forms of worship, and the moral law he had laid down for Adam and his successors. It also included an understanding of the secrets of nature and the operations of the natural world. The Druids had become the conservators of this ancient wisdom after the Flood. (Stukeley accepted as evidence on this point the writings of Berosus, later revealed as a late fifteenth-century forgery.) In time the Druids spread westward with the migration of the Phoenicians and eventually became the priesthood of the Celts. In Stukeley's view, the Druids had grasped the mystery of the Trinity and were awaiting a Messiah. So, in establishing themselves in Britain, they brought with them "Abraham's religion" and the knowledge of the one true God. It became a point of principle with Stukeley that the stone circles throughout the British Isles, and most notably at Stonehenge and Avebury, were the temples of the Druids and therefore the tangible remains of Druid culture. Like Aubrey, Stukeley was willing to associate Druids with stone circles without any supporting evidence and despite the fact that all references to Druids in the ancient histories situated them in woods and groves of oak trees. (As modern archaeologists discovered, phases of the construction of Stonehenge extended from late Neolithic times until the early Bronze Age; since the Druids as a Celtic priesthood probably did not appear in Britain until the fourth century B.C., the connection between the monument's origins and the Druids is highly unlikely.)

Stukeley familiarized himself with the great variety of druidical lore contained in English and continental books published in the seventeenth century, and his fascination with the subject found full expression in *Stonehenge* (1740) and *Abury* (1743). These two works were transformations of his original 1724 project on the history of the temples of the ancient Celts, now overrun with speculations about the Druids. The books contain much valuable archaeological reporting of his surveys and excavations, but their druidic embroidery caused them to be received with some scorn and devalued the important information they preserved. *Stonehenge* and *Abury,* like *Itinerarium Curiosum,* are notable for their excellent illustrations by Stukeley himself and by his friend the engraver Gerard Vandergucht.

In 1726 Stukeley moved from London to Lincolnshire, where he married. In 1729 he took holy orders and became the vicar of All Saints, Stamford. His archaeological days were over. He made his last tour in 1725 with Roger Gale; they visited the Lake District, inspected the Keswick stone circle and the stone complex known as Long Meg, and then went on to Hadrian's Wall and to Durham and Yorkshire. Along the wall he and Gale recorded inscriptions and made drawings of the forts and camps. He regretted that there was no adequate account of Roman Britain, although in fact John Horsley was then in the process of compiling his great work *Britannia Romana* (1732). Stukeley may have given up fieldwork at this stage, but he continued with antiquarian pursuits that did not require firsthand observation of sites. He developed an interest in ancient British coinage. He founded an antiquarian society in Stamford that failed to flourish, and he helped to establish an Egyptian society in London, whose members were supposed to have traveled to the eastern Mediterranean or Egypt (Stukeley himself had not). This club brought him into contact with the Duke of Montagu, whose friendship he enjoyed and who encouraged him to develop a taste for the Gothic and to indulge in the fashionable cult of sentimentality. He busied himself preparing *Stonehenge* and *Abury* for the press and outlined a grand history of patriarchal Christianity, which would help to strengthen the case for Christianity and the Church of England in particular against the criticism of rationalists and skeptics. This work was never written.

In the 1740s Stukeley was enmeshed in one of the great forgeries of the age. He was approached by an Englishman living in Copenhagen, one Captain Charles Bertram, who claimed to have turned up a manuscript description of Roman Britain written in the fourteenth century by a monk at Westminster named Richard and apparently based on the report of a Roman officer of the later empire. An itinerary and a map accompanied this narrative, and the whole provided a remarkably detailed picture of Britain in the third or fourth century. Richard's work consisted of a geographical introduction, followed by an ethnographical account of the ancient British, their customs and religion, and the role of the Druids. There were sections on the economy of Britain and on the administrative structure of the island under the Romans, with accounts of the tribal divisions and the towns and military stations. The itinerary was on the model of the Antonine Itinerary but included many more names, and the map gave the position of about 250 towns. The work concluded with a description of the islands around the coast of Britain. Altogether, the manuscript was guaranteed to excite any antiquary. Bertram, however, had ingeniously fabricated the "De Situ Britanniae" from a wide variety of existing sources, ancient and modern. He sent Stukeley specimens of the text in facsimile handwriting to gain his approval, and Stukeley cautiously indicated that he thought the discovery was genuine. After much investigative correspondence, he identified Richard of Cirencester, a known historian who had been a monk at Westminster Abbey, as the likely author. Stukeley managed to get Bertram elected as a member of the Society of Antiquaries, and in 1756 the account of Richard of Cirencester was printed in Copenhagen along with texts of Saxon chroniclers Gildas and Nennius, under the title *Britannicarum Gentium Historiae Antiquae Scriptores Tres.* For nearly a century the work was a prime source for Roman Britain; Edward Gibbon used it, although expressing reservations, as did the antiquaries Richard Gough and Colt Hoare. "De Situ Britanniae" was finally exposed as a forgery when the full resources of textual criticism were brought to bear on it by German and English scholars in the mid-nineteenth century.

In the 1750s Stukeley's own interest in Roman Britain focused on the figure of Carausius, the naval commander who proclaimed himself emperor of Britain in A.D. 287. Successfully defying Rome until he was admitted into partnership in the empire in 290, he was assassinated three years later. His short reign is notable for its numerous coinage. Stukeley compiled a *History of Carausius,* which was published in 1757, and two volumes of *The Medallic History of Carausius* (1757 and 1759). He attempted to identify the British mints of the late third century with moderate success. However, his numismatic skills were shown in a poor light when he entered into a controversy over the significance of a Carausian coin with a reverse of a female bust and the inscription "ORIUNA." Although he had not seen the coin firsthand, Stukeley argued at some length that Oriuna was the wife of Carausius; it was eventually discovered that the lettering on the coin in fact read "FORTUNA."

From 1747 until his death in 1765, Stukeley was rector of St. George's, Bloomsbury, and was able to play an active though not greatly respected part in the London antiquarian scene. His long fascination with Druids, with whom he felt some strange ancestral infinity, percolated into the literary consciousness of the mid-eighteenth century. In the poems of Gray, Mason, Collins, and later William Blake, the depiction of the Druids owed much to Stukeley: they are the preservers of an ancient wisdom, which derived from humanity's first age; the guardians of true religion practiced in Britain in primitive times; the defenders of native British liberty against Roman oppression. They had a magical appeal to the eighteenth-century imagination as antiquarian, romantic, and patriotic figures.

Stukeley's enduring contribution to archaeology was undoubtedly the fieldwork he carried out in Wiltshire in the earlier part of his life. Accurate measurement, precise draftsmanship, intelligent understanding of the relationship of monuments to landscape, and an ability to make rewarding comparisons with similar sites and structures—all these qualities made him a pioneer of field archaeology. His misfortune was to have no collaborators of comparable skill. He was virtually the last of the Restoration antiquarians to be interested in the British past, and he did not train or attract any followers who could develop or extend his own excellent work in the field. But twentieth-century archaeologists, especially those working on Stonehenge and Avebury, have found invaluable his record of the sites as they stood in the early eighteenth century.

References
Primary
Stukeley, William. 1724. *Itinerarium Curiosum.*
———. 1740. *Stonehenge.*
———. 1743. *Abury.*
Secondary
Piggott, Stuart. 1985. *William Stukeley: An Eighteenth-Century Antiquary.* London: Thames and Hudson.

Max Kunze

Johann Joachim Winckelmann   *1717–1768*

Translated from the German by Stephen Lindberg

Regarded as the founder of art history and classical archaeology, Johann Joachim Winckelmann developed a methodology and systematic organization of artistic styles and influences to explain the meaning and history of classical works of art. His writings had immense influence on the artistic and intellectual development of eighteenth-century Europe.

Johann Joachim Winckelmann's work has long been a topic of interest in a variety of disciplines. To classical archaeologists he is a *heros ktistes,* a "hero founder"; to art historians he is one of the first to have pursued scholarly study of the arts of Mediterranean antiquity; and in German-language literature he is considered an originator of scholarly prose. His exploration of Greek art remains among the most stimulating and influential conceptions in the humanities in the latter half of the eighteenth century. In 1764 his major work, *Geschichte der Kunst des Alterthums* [History of the Art of Antiquity], was published in Dresden. It examined especially Greek and Roman art but also considered the arts of the Egyptians, the Persians and Phoenicians, and the Etruscans and their neighbors, all from the perspective of history, culture, aesthetics, and art theory. His work and influence radiated outward from Rome, his home after 1755, back to the rest of Europe and took hold of the artistic and intellectual worlds in Germany, France, and England.

Our view of Winckelmann's character is based on an appreciation of the unusual path of his life: rising from modest circumstances in a small Prussian town to become a European authority in matters of art and antiquity. The son of an impoverished cobbler, he was born on 9 December 1717 in the town of Stendal in the Brandenburg Mark (eastern Germany), where he attended the Latin grammar school. He sang in the boys' choir, which he directed for a time, and was the reader for the school principal, who was nearly blind. The principal obtained an allowance for him from a private source to enable him to stay in Berlin for several months in the winter of 1735–1736. Winckelmann, having no other means, worked as a private teacher in order to attend the gymnasium

Johann Joachim Winckelmann. (Copyright National Swedish Art Museum)

(secondary school) in the Cölln section of Berlin. There, from the philologist Christian Tobias Damm, he acquired his first knowledge of ancient Greek and of Homer's epics. On his departure from the school, someone noted beneath his name in the yearbook that he was "homo vagus et inconstans" (a vague and inconstant man). The years that followed brought a restless search for information and knowledge. A brief period in the gymnasium in Salzwedel was followed in 1737 by two years spent at the University of Halle studying theology—a standard requirement for those aspiring to an office in the Prussian state service and the only course of study that received financial assistance from both the state and the church. Winckelmann also completed courses in Hebrew, Greek, history, and law and may have come in contact with Johann Heinrich Schulze, a highly educated man who used his collection of ancient coins as a tool in his teaching of history.

Winckelmann had long sustained an interest in medicine and mathematics, and thus his further studies brought him to Jena in 1741, where he took courses in these subjects for a year. After a period as a private, live-in tutor in the Brandenburg Mark and in Magdeburg, he finally found a position in 1743 as assistant principal in Seehausen. Winckelmann spent nearly five years at this post, engaged in excruciating conflicts with the authorities of the school and the church. He later remembered Seehausen with bitterness, as a time when he had to teach the ABCs "to children with scabby heads." "I have sampled many things," he recalled, "but nothing has surpassed my servitude in Seehausen. When I sometimes think back on my schooling, it amazes me that I could budge my neck under that weight." The years spent in seclusion with the works of Greek and Latin authors, insofar as he could obtain editions of them, made him familiar with antiquity, and the ancient world of art came alive for the first time in engravings he was able to borrow or view.

In 1748 he found a new position as the librarian of the collection of Imperial Count Heinrich von Bünau, a former diplomat whose home was in Nöthnitz near Dresden. In addition to working on the catalog in the fields of history and law, Winckelmann was also given the task by his new employer, who had what was then the preeminent library in Germany, of doing preliminary work on the Ottonian emperors for a published history of the empire. His own reading extended beyond the ancient writers to include those of the English and French Renaissance, particularly historical and political authors. With growing interest he studied theoreticians of the fine arts (Chambray, Fébelien, de Piles, Richardson, and Dubos). In one of the manuscripts written during his years in Nöthnitz, titled *Gedanken vom mündlichen Vortrag der neueren allgemeinen Geschichte* [Thoughts on the Oral Presentation of Modern General History], Winckelmann observed that political history could not be reduced to accounts of rulers and battles and that historical writing had to be augmented by the "famous discoveries of nature and art." He was thus anticipating ideas of his later works, which emphasized the context of art in history and brought aspects of cultural history into play.

Winckelmann was increasingly fascinated by Dresden, with its art collections and its creative and scholarly community. In 1754 he gave up his position as librarian in Nöthnitz to live in Dresden among artists and art lovers. He stayed initially with the painter and sketch artist Adam Friedrich Oeser, who was Winckelmann's age. Stimulated by discussions with Oeser about art, impressed by visits to Dresden's Gemäldegalerie—its collection of ancient sculpture, though barely accessible at the time, and the collection of casts—and based on his knowledge of the Greek world as conveyed in classical literature, Winckelmann produced his programmatic first work, *Gedanken über die Nachahmung der griechischen Wercke in der Mahlerey und Bildhauer-Kunst* [Reflections on the Imitation of Greek Works in Painting and Sculpture], which caused something of a sensation and laid the foundation for its author's fame. He presented an image of ancient Greece in which art could flourish freely because both its creators and patrons lived in prosperity and freedom in a democratically founded state. This account was accompanied by enthusiastic descriptions of artworks from antiquity, such as the famous Laocoön group and the so-called Herculanean Women of Dresden. The memorable and thrilling depiction of ancient Greece with its political freedom and thriving art was deliberately conceived as a reproof to his own time, where Winckelmann found a relationship between creative decline and the dependence of contemporary artists on an absolutist court and its patronage. Based on the supremacy of Greek art, he developed his famous theory of imitation, in which he justified the necessity of imitating the beauty of nature and the ideal beauty of Greek statues, with their "noble simplicity and tranquil stature of expression and pose." One had to return to these origins, since "the good taste that is increasingly spreading through the world first began to form under the Greek sky."

The descriptive text of this comprehensive attempt to penetrate the essence of Greek art derived largely from Winckelmann's knowledge and interpretation of the written traditions of antiquity and less on the living experience of classical art. Since the sixteenth century, the unspoken subtext of every humanistic interpretation was Horace's dictum, *ut pictora poesis* (a poetic picture), with its demand that literary description and representation in the fine arts be harmonized. Winckelmann saw his ideal artist as the *pictor eruditus* of Renaissance tradition. Later, in Rome, he supplemented this with the idea of a new type of scholar and art connoisseur, who performed the actual creative work and served as a bridge between the owner of ancient works of art and the artist (whose role became that of a restorer of antiquities).

The success of this maiden work began to arouse hopes of a trip to Italy. As a Protestant in a Catholic princely residence, it seemed to him that Rome, his new objective, would be accessible only if he converted from Protestantism to the Catholic faith, which he did in June 1754. With a stipend from the Saxon court, he arrived in Rome in November 1755. It was a stroke of luck that soon thereafter he met the painter Anton Raphael Mengs, who introduced him to Rome and was the same kind of stimulating companion that Oeser had been in Dresden. "Without Mengs," Winckelmann wrote, "I may as well have been in a desert, since I wouldn't have been provided with an address. I don't even drink coffee except with him, and I even have my books and papers in his room."

As he encountered classical sculptures in Roman collections, Winckelmann quickly replaced his original plan of expanding his Dresden book with the idea of a more comprehensive work on the "taste of Greek artists." Classical statues, which Winckelmann had until then known mostly from engravings, proved to be far more complex than he had assumed. Winckelmann turned his attention especially to questions concerning the sculptures' true state of preservation, the restorations that had been made in arbitrary fashion by later artists, and their consequent misinterpretation. A still-unpublished draft called "Von den Vergehungen der Scribenten über die Ergäntzungen" ["On the Assaults of the Hack Writers on Restorations," in Winckelmann's literary remains in Paris, vol. 57, 19–26] was written during this early residence in Rome. He began to undertake a survey of the artworks in Roman palazzi and villas, noting their condition and delving into their iconic references. At the same time he endeavored to give thorough descriptions of each of the famous statues in the Belvedere Court of the Vatican, with the goal of developing a language and descriptive technique that would be adequate to a work of art and would evoke its essence. His now-famous descriptions of the Laocoön group and the torso (or Apollo) of Belvedere decisively influenced scholarly prose in German. Several years later, specific accounts, such as that of the Apollo of Belvedere, enriched with literary and mythological images were published, and in revised form later found their way into *Geschichte der Kunst des Alterthums*. By making the observer part of the act of viewing the artwork and by giving expression to his personal enthusiasm for the sensuous natural beauty of male statues, Winckelmann introduced a new perspective on classical art. For him, the ideal male figure in sculpture was distinguished by its stature and tranquility but also by a sublimated eroticism.

The thirteen years Winckelmann spent in Rome were marked by tireless activity and an unrelenting search for knowledge about antiquity and for new classical works. The contemporary German philosopher Johann Gottfried Herder credited him with cutting a path "in the forest of some 70,000 statues and busts that are found in Rome, in this still-overgrown forest of misleading footprints, full of the screaming voices of advice-filled interpreters, deceptive artists, and ignorant antiquarians." From his survey it became clear that the countless works of antiquity could not be analyzed by means of better or more comprehensive works of engravings; after all, in 1719 the Benedictine priest Monfaucon published twelve volumes with 40,000 illustrations on 1,200 plates, to be followed by five supplementary volumes. Rather, what was required was a system of organization based on the insight that the art of the ancients could be understood as developing in historical context. In investigating the "style of peoples, ages, and artists" and defining the origin, growth, change, and decline of the art of particular peoples, it became possible for Winckelmann to classify each artwork according to its formal and thematic design. This historicization of art found expression in the very title of his major work, *Geschichte der Kunst des Alterthums,* which was published in 1764 and brought him to the zenith of his fame.

Predecessors like the Comte de Caylus (*Receuil d'antiquités égyptiennes, étrusques, grecques, et romaines,* vols. 1–7, Paris 1752–1759) had attempted through encyclopedic scholarship to bring all known Mediterranean cultures within the history of art. Winckelmann's contribution was his presentation of these cultures within their own history and artistic development. It was an approach that lent itself conceptually to the formulation of national styles, even though his actual work was based on a limited set of objects and relied more on written sources than on surviving works. Nevertheless, he had attempted to outline the artistic style of the Egyptians, the Phoenicians, the Persians and the Parthians, the Etruscans, and the Italians. Without a doubt, Greek art stood at the center of his *Geschichte der Kunst des Alterthums,* and he discussed it in two distinctive parts of his book: according to its essence and according to "the external circumstances" of its historical development. Building from classical theories of art (particularly L. A. Florus but also Quintillian, Pliny, and Cicero) and Renaissance theory (the philologist J. C. Scalinger's postulate of a sequence of four styles for literature), Winckelmann proposed, with explicit reference to Scalinger, an analogous series of four styles within Greek art: the older style (*stilo primitivo*), the high style, the fine style, and the style of the imitators. He tried to describe the levels of development and changes and to illustrate them with specific works. Sculpture was clearly the focus of this effort, but in accordance with the art theory that had prevailed since the Renaissance, a separate chapter was devoted to painting. Since, with few exceptions, the monumental paintings of the Greeks have not survived to the present day, his view that painted vessels previously considered Etruscan were in fact of Greek or southern Italian/Greek origin gains particular significance. These vase paintings with their inexhaustible reservoir of themes and motifs would become a new source for archaeologists with the first great publications by Giovanni Battista Passeri (*Picturae Etruscorum in Vasculis,* 1767–1775) and Winckelmann's friend Pierre-François Hugue d'Hancarville, who presented the vases of the Hamilton collection. This was a collection of artifacts recently unearthed from Pompeii by Sir William Hamilton, collector of Roman antiquities and English diplomat at the Court of Naples. Winckelmann was aware that there were few notable works on which to base a definition of the early style of Greek art and that the images on coins would have to serve as a pale substitute. It also became increasingly clear to him from observing many existing replicas of lost Greek statues that Greek art could for the most part only be reconstructed from Roman copies. This was an insight to which the painter Anton Raphael Mengs had clearly contributed.

After his arrival in Rome, Winckelmann had managed to retain his personal independence for almost two years without a position. Only in 1757, when the Seven Years' War threatened to cut off his stipend from Saxony, did he become the librarian of the Papal Cancelleria in the service of a former nuncio and confidant of the Saxon court, papal secretary Alberigo Achinto. After Achinto's death a year later, he became the librarian and adviser of the influential Cardinal Alessandro Albani. Freedom was for Winckelmann not simply a precious, private good; it was the true driving force and prerequisite for the arts of the present as well as the past. In addition to nature, climate, and education, he emphasized in his *Geschichte der Kunst des Alterthums* that freedom had initiated the flowering of Greek art: "In the design of the constitution and government of Greece it is freedom that is the most distinguished reason for the superiority of its art. Freedom had always had its place in Greece, even alongside the thrones of the kings, who ruled paternally, before the enlightenment of reason allowed them to taste the sweetness of complete freedom." This appeal to freedom continued to be a criterion in analyzing specific works of art and the context of their origin. No doubt because of his fundamentally republican and democratic disposition, Winckelmann's works were repeatedly published in new translations in prerevolutionary France and during the French Revolution as proof of the artistic benefits of democracy.

Winckelmann continually improved and rewrote his *Geschichte der Kunst des Alterthums.* For this reason the dramatist Johann Wolfgang von Goethe called it "a living work for the living," praise that also recognized its protean and cumulative level of knowledge. Even in his final major work, the *Monumenti Antichi Inediti* [Unpublished Ancient Monuments, 1767], Winckelmann summarized the key ideas of his art history in *Trattato preliminare del'arte disegno e delle bellezze* [Preliminary Treatise on Design and Beauty], thereby introducing fresh viewpoints into the discipline.

Constantly seeking to expand and deepen his knowledge of classical works in Rome, its vicinity, and in Italy generally, he made his first journey to Naples, Portici, Herculaneum, and Pompeii in 1758, to be followed by two more such trips. During these journeys he also visited the temple in Paestum and saw the physical evidence of Greek architecture for the first time. Four years later he published the result of this contact with Greek architecture in his *Anmerkungen über die Baukunst der Alten* [Remarks on the Architecture of the Ancients], in which he lauded the "three wondrous Dorian temples" of Paestum and thereby helped to return to European consciousness these oldest yet forgotten structures of the Greeks—and thus their art in southern Italy and Sicily. In 1759 Winckelmann had first directed his attention to the architecture of the Greeks, using the temples of Agrigento as his subject matter. The resultant essay declared that the great authority of the Roman architect Vitruvius did not resolve the problem of the origins of architecture; only by personally studying the monuments could one clarify questions concerning their distinctiveness and the history of their development. Yet the real problem was the lack of comprehensive sketches of the architectural ruins or drawings of their recreation. Winckelmann was never able to build on this first effort to hypothesize about Greek architecture.

The discoveries at Herculaneum were of particular interest at the court in Dresden, since three statues of vestal virgins in the Dresden collection were from the area around Vesuvius. Winckelmann was given the task of reporting on the new findings. In letters to Gian Lodovico Bianconi in Dresden (the so-called *Relazzioni*) and in two pieces, *Sendschreiben von den herculanischen Entdeckungen* [Open Letter on the Discoveries at Herculaneum, 1762] and *Nachrichten von den neuesten herculanischen Entdeckungen* [Reports on the Newest Discoveries at Herculaneum, 1764], Winckelmann described such discoveries as the theater of Herculaneum and the streets of Pompeii, thereby awakening general interest in the excavations. He also reported extensively on the Roman wall paintings and objects of everyday life, since "all of their forms [are] founded on principles of good taste." In his writings on the historical and topographical situation of the city buried by Vesuvius and in his discussions of the ancient literary sources, he was attentive to the functions of the newly discovered objects and the artistic and aesthetic aspects of Roman crafts. Winckelmann foresaw the subsequent influence of Roman tools, vessels, mosaics, and jewelry: "The imitation of them could introduce an entirely new taste, and lead us away from the artificial back to nature, wherein we can later discover the art." Already by the 1760s, after the publication of "*Antichità die Ercolano esposte*" (Naples 1757ff.), the "Pompeiian style" of classical archaeology had been established.

Winckelmann spent just over a year in Florence during 1758–1759, painstakingly examining more than 3,000 ancient engraved gems in the collection of the late Philipp von Stosch. In 1760 he published an extensive catalog with descriptions of the engraved stones (*Description des pierres gravées du feu Baron de Stosch*). He introduced two significant methodological points into archaeology through his careful study of the rich world of images on these gems. First, he achieved a hermeneutic breakthrough by using Greek rather than Roman mythology and history to explain the themes and images represented. This insight would be explored further with great consequence in his later major works. Second, in the chapter on the Etruscans he formulated important aspects of the distinctiveness of the Etruscan style and the succession of styles, and he established periods, which he then connected to Etruscan history and mythology in *Geschichte der Kunst des Alterthums*. One of the crucial conclusions he drew from his method of analyzing style was that the most fruitful and distinct phase of Etruscan art occurred as early as the sixth century and the first half of the fifth century B.C., before Greek influence began to obscure uniquely Etruscan elements. This view was vigorously contested by his contemporaries as well as his successors (such as the Göttingen scholar Christian G. Heyne).

With this catalog Winckelmann earned his first public recognition. On 29 August 1760 he was unanimously elected to the Etrusca Accademia of Cortona. Further honors followed, such as membership in the Royal Society of London and the Academy of San Luca in Rome and his formal appointment as *scrittorat* of the Vatican library. Positions as *antiquario della camera apostolica* and president of Antiquities of Rome (1764), which were obtained through his patron Albani, were important steps in his career. Then his life was abruptly cut short. While on a trip to Germany, Winckelmann was murdered on 8 June 1768 at an inn in Trieste by a cook named Franceso Arcangeli.

Winckelmann was perhaps best known among the European public interested in the arts and antiquity through his essays in the series *Bibliothek der schönen Wissenschaften und der freyen Künste* [Library of the Humanities and the Free Arts]; these included *Erinnerung über die Betrachtung der Werke der Kunst* [Recollection on the Viewing Works of Art, 1759] and *Von der Grazie in Werken der Kunst* [On Grace in Works of Art, 1759]). Separately published was *Abhandlung von der Fähigkeiten der*

Empfindung des Schönen in der Kunst, und dem Unterrichte in derselben [Treatise on the Ability to Perceive the Beautiful in Art and How to Teach It, 1763]. His final work, the two volumes of *Monumenti Antichi Inediti,* which was published in Rome in 1767, was aimed more at artists and scholars. Winckelmann, who had adopted Rome as his own, wrote this work in Italian and chose to address himself to the world of Italian scholars because he viewed Rome rather than Paris as the true intellectual center of Europe. Using previously unpublished artworks from different genres that were interesting for their figurative representation—most of which were selected from the collection of his patron Alessandro Albani—he sought to demonstrate his archaeological and interpretive methodology for unlocking meanings within works of antiquity as well as determining their style and their period of origin. This treatment of unpublished works of antiquity opened up a new strategy in archaeology, producing the large museum catalogs and investigations of corpora in the nineteenth and twentieth centuries, which attempted to organize existing works of antiquity systematically according to genre or theme.

If Winckelmann had also hoped *Monumenti Antichi Inediti* would supply classical models to inspire contemporary artists, the "archaeological" phase of European classicism came the closest to fulfilling that hope. Jacques-Louis David, for example, turned to Winckelmann's edition for the middle figure in his painting *Leonidas at the Thermopylae*. With another work, his *Versuch einer Allegorie, besonders für die Kunst* [Essay on Allegory, Especially for Art, 1766], Winckelmann tried to provide memorable classical themes as stimulation to artists for their own works and to offer examples of allegories already used in antiquity, particularly from Greek mythology. These efforts to directly influence the art of his time had less impact than he hoped. Still, it was the discovery of the imagery and beauty of Greek art, as given its first comprehensive exposure in *Geschichte der Kunst des Alterthums,* that continued to be influential and that became the breeding ground for European classicism.

Nevertheless, despite the number and frequency of translations of his major work, *Geschichte der Kunst des Alterthums* into French and Italian, his writings were increasingly ignored, a development already apparent in the generation that followed him. Goethe, for example, wrote this bon mot about Winckelmann: "One doesn't learn anything when one reads him, but one becomes something." This view is found today among some archaeologists and art historians, who consider his work unreadable because it is hopelessly dated. What is often forgotten is that many scholarly methods still in use are derived from the precepts Winckelmann established, which for generations determined the paths that scholarship would take.

There are several reasons for the distance between today's readers and *Geschichte der Kunst des Alterthums* and the rest of Winckelmann's corpus. First, the available editions are uninspiring, having been issued for the most part without any archaeological commentary or illustrations; this fact doubtless has had an impact on its poor reception. Even for the educated reader in Germany in the nineteenth and twentieth centuries, Winckelmann's major book became less and less intelligible because most of the classical works mentioned or treated at length—in some cases, with whole chapters—were virtually unknown or at least very difficult to access, much less view adequately. The writer Johann Jakob Wilhelm Heinse traveled through Italy from 1780 to 1782 with *Geschichte der Kunst des Alterthums* in hand, and he was able to experience as Winckelmann had the antiquities in the great collections in Florence, Rome, and Naples. However, after Napoleon began plundering the collections of classical art in Italy, the works that Winckelmann had described, treated, or interpreted—the foundations of his history of art—were increasingly forgotten or considered lost after changing hands so often. Since none of the editions indicated the current whereabouts of the antiquities Winckelmann had discussed, it was nearly impossible for the reader to supplement the text with personal observations. For nonarchaeologists, the number of recognizable antiquities was reduced to a handful of statues, famous because they were frequently copied. The descriptive litanies that Winckelmann had devoted to the Laocoön and the Apollo of Belvedere became the subject of German studies: Winckelmann the writer was praised for his achievement in scholarly prose, of which he was—as later became clear—the founder. Indeed, he is sometimes regarded as the writer "who revealed new paths to modern poetry" (Elida Maria Szarota, 1973).

That Winckelmann's work increasingly achieved more literary than archaeological relevance is also related to his own personality and his view of classical art. One characteristic of his writings was the palpable enthusiasm with which he approached his subjects. This was as true of his eloquent descriptions of classical statues as it was of the appealing if somewhat utopian image of ancient Greece that he sketched in the *Sendschreiben* and that he always returned to, in modified form, in his later works. Contemporaries and successors, archaeologists and art lovers have all been drawn to his rhetoric and have been guided to a new understanding of classical art. Despite his zeal, however, he always maintained the sobriety one expects of a scholar. His precise observation, his painstaking engagement with artworks and written sources, his knowledge of the arguments of his predecessors and contemporaries—these characteristics are apparent from his published works and from the numerous unpublished excerpts and notes in his literary remains. The seemingly paradoxical principles of scholarship and enthusiasm were also decisive in his aesthetic, which combined normativeness—a sense of constancy of cultural norms and values—with a historical consciousness. Enthusiasm, not indifferent erudition, was always the most important trait when dealing with antiquities, as Winckelmann said, "Those who have become familiar with antiquities only through scholarship have never learned anything else about them."

References
Primary

Becker, W. G., ed. 1800. "Gedanken vom mündlichen Vortrag der neueren allgemeinen Geschichte (1754–55)." Published from Winckelmann's literary remains in *Erholungen*. Leipzig.

Eiselein, J., ed. 1825–1929. *Johann Winckelmanns sämtliche Werke: Einzige vollständige Ausgabe,* vols. 1–12. Donaueschingen.

Fernow, C. L., H. Meyer, and J. Schulze. eds. 1808–1820. *Winckelmanns Werke,* vols. 1–8. Dresden: Weimar Edition.

Kunze, Max. 1967–1984. *Winckelmann-Bibliographie.* Series 4. Berlin: Winckelmann-Gesellschaft Stendal.

Rehm, W., ed. 1952–1957. *Johann Joachim Winckelmann, Briefe,* vols. 1–4. Berlin.

Ruppert, H. 1942. *Winckelmann-Bibliographie: Verzeichnis der Veröffentlichungen von und über Winckelmann.* Berlin: Winckelmann-Gesellschaft Stendal.

———. 1942–1955. *Ergänzungen zur Winckelmann-Bibliographie.* Berlin: Winckelmann-Gesellschaft Stendal.

———. 1955–1956. *Winckelmann-Bibliographie.* Series 3. Berlin: Winckelmann-Gesellschaft Stendal.

Winkelmann, Johann Joachim. 1755. *Gedanken über die Nachahmung der Griechischen Wercke in der Mahlerey und Bildhauer-Kunst.*

———. 1759. *Erinnerung über die Betrachtung der Werke der Kunst.* In *Bibliothek der schönen Wissenschaften* (hereafter BSW), vol. 5, 1: 1–13.

———. 1759. *Von der Grazie in Werken der Kunst.* In BSW, vol. 5, 1: 13–23.

———. 1762. *Sendschreiben von den Herculanischen Entdeckungen.* Dresden.

———. 1763. *Abhandlung von der Fähigkeit der Empfindung des Schönen in der Kunst, und dem Unterrichte in derselben.* Dresden.

———. 1764. *Geschichte der Kunst des Alterthums.* Dresden. (2d ed., Vienna 1776).

———. 1764. *Nachrichten von den Herculanischen Entdeckungen.* Dresden.

———. 1766. *Versuch einer Allegorie, besonders für die Kunst.* Dresden.

———. 1767. *Monumenti Antichi Inediti.* Vols. 1–2. Rome. In I: (xv-xxiv) *Prefazione.*—I-CII *Trattato preliminare dell'arte del disegno degli antichi popoli.*

———. 1767. *Anmerkungen über die Geschichte der Kunst des Alterthums.* Dresden.

English Translations of Winckelmann's Works

Winkelmann, Johann Joachim. 1765. *Reflections on the Painting and Sculpture of the Greeks: With Instructions for the Connoisseur, and an Essay on Grace in Works of Art*. Trans. Henry Fusseli. London: A. Millar.

———. 1849–1873. *The History of Ancient Art*. Trans. G. Henry Lodge. Boston: J. R. Osgood.

———. 1972. *Writings on Art*. Ed. David Irwin. London: Phaidon.

———. 1987. *Reflections on the Imitation of Greek Works in Painting and Sculpture*. Trans. Elfriede Heyer and Roger C. Norton. La Salle, IL: Open Court.

Johan Hegardt

Sven Nilsson 1787–1883

Translated from the Swedish by Laura Wrang

One of Sweden's most important researchers, a pioneer in quaternary geology and glacial theory, Sven Nilsson helped to develop the three-age system and to establish the complexity of prehistory. He used natural science and comparative ethnography as archaeological methods, and he gave artifacts a broader interpretive base by studying their function and manufacture.

Sven Nilsson was one of the founders of Swedish archaeology, but he is surprisingly little known within his country. His anonymity is due to his versatility and to the consequent difficulty of surveying his scientific oeuvre. Yet he was a powerful, dynamic person and a hard-working, enthusiastic researcher. His extensive correspondence and diaries reveal his intellectual curiosity, which drew him into very different fields throughout his long life; he was, in fact, a pioneer in Swedish zoology and geology. Well known in his own time, his network of contacts was wide, and he opened his home to Swedish and foreign scientists (Regnéll 1983a). Even so, the results of his life's work are not easily summarized. The best approach may be roundabout: by examining Nilsson's scientific-theoretical points of departure, which were fairly constant, we may come to understand and appreciate his thinking and his achievements.

Sven Nilsson was born on 8 March 1787, the youngest in a family of six children. His parents taught him to read and write, and his home had an atmosphere of warm religious devotion and piety. His father told him legends and sagas, which fostered an interest in ethnology and antiquarian research and prompted his work *Skandinaviska Nordens Ur-invånare*. Since his parents were farmers, Nilsson came in contact with nature at an early age and acquired knowledge of plants and animals. These themes—religion, righteousness, stories, and nature—formed the bases of Nilsson's scientific production. Add to this the influence of the Enlightenment and Romanticism, and Sven Nilsson was a modern nineteenth-century man.

In 1806 Nilsson enrolled at Lund University with the highest recommendations. His intention was to become a priest, a common goal for a country student. He took a degree in theology and then, in 1809, a degree in philology. He studied Greek, Latin, aesthetics, and history.

Sven Nilsson, by
Carl Peter Lehman.
(© Swedish Portrait
Archives / Stockholm)

Although his interest in classical studies waned in later life, he maintained an aptitude for languages and was always able to express himself freely in Latin, French, English, and German. He received his bachelor's degree in 1811, with the highest marks in natural history as well as in theoretical and practical philosophy. Nilsson was then offered an associate professorship in theology, which he declined. (Later, in 1835, he took a degree in clerical and pastoral theology, although primarily for economic reasons [Regnéll 1983a, 12–13]). Despite turning away from the priesthood, Nilsson's religion continued to affect his scientific thinking. Among his favorite poems was the famous work of the Swedish Enlightenment, which expressed the hope of a new age, when the sciences would constitute a societal norm. The deep spiritualism of the poem also spoke to Nilsson and illustrated that there was no necessary contradiction between scientific pursuits and religious sentiments.

The Natural Sciences in General and Zoology

In 1812 Nilsson was offered an assistantship at Lund's natural history cabinet, or pre-museum institution, as well as an associate professorship in natural history. To qualify for these posts he wrote an obligatory dissertation on mammalogy. Even then Nilsson's academic career was by no means fixed. He continued his studies in zoology but also pursued studies in geology and anatomy (Regnéll 1983a, 12–14). In 1816 he was given a teaching position in economy, and in 1818 he took a degree in medicine. However, he was primarily concerned during this period with the natural science collections. Before 1812 two professors had assumed responsibility for them. One instructed in mathematics, physics, and astronomy, while the other taught zoology, botany, mineralogy, chemistry, and economy. The collections were kept in curio cabinets, where the objects were mixed without distinction. In 1788 it was decided to divide the materials into three separate departments: curios and artifacts, ancient and ethnographic finds, and objects of nature. The problem of lack of space was solved by the construction of new buildings in 1800. A donation considerably improved the museum's holdings, adding 17,000 inventory numbers, including a complete subfossil bison. Nilsson was responsible for classifying the donation, and through this work he came in contact with subfossil remains from peat bogs and the subfossil research (Löwegren 1983, 87–89).

In September 1828 the first international conference for naturalists was held in Berlin. Nilsson had been elected to the Royal Swedish Academy of Sciences in 1812, and through state funds he was able to participate in the conference. At the meeting, Nilsson worked with the secretary of the royal academy to draw up plans for the academy's transformation into the Swedish Museum of National History. The two men gathered ideas by visiting various institutes. As with Lund, the donation of a significant collection formed the basis of the museum's rebirth, and Nilsson again served as a driving force. In November 1828 he asked for leave from his curator's position in Lund to take over the care of the Stockholm collections. He installed a new type of cabinet from drawings made in Berlin, and he was the first in the country to use arsenic to protect the items. One of the museum's goals was to obtain a complete collection of Scandinavian fauna. The acquisition of animals increased after the formation of the Swedish Hunters Association in 1830, which had Nilsson's encouragement as a means of gathering specimens for the museum. Regardless, Nilsson soon left Stockholm. He did not feel at home there, and he had received an offer from Lund University to become acting professor with the promise of a professor's salary when it became permanent—which it did in 1832. He also missed his research, since most of his time at the Stockholm museum was spent in organizational tasks (Löwegren 1983, 104–114).

After Nilsson was made professor at Lund University in 1832, its natural science museum became the center for Swedish zoology, and a period of intensive zoological research began. In his inaugural lecture Nilsson emphasized that education in zoology should include the history of the subject. In line with his religious schooling, he noted that Moses had divided the animals into different categories and that Solomon had spoken of mammals, birds, reptiles, and fish. However, it was Aristotle and the Greeks who gave zoology its actual scientific basis. Nilsson's thinking was greatly influenced by Aristotle's method, which he regarded as anatomical, physiological, psychological, and comparative—a never-ending source of practical knowledge. The Swedish scientist's focus on psychology underpinned his later interest in the social structure and living conditions of Stone Age people. He advocated "comparative psychology" even for animals, contending that animals were sensitive creatures with a "thinking" soul and that they should not be studied as dead objects. Therefore, animal behavior should be investigated from all possible angles.

In Nilsson's view all natural-scientific research rested ultimately on careful comparisons, which made collecting decisive for the development of the sciences. Comparisons, however, were not the goal of science but its foundation. As he wrote in the late 1860s, his comparative method coincided with the need to clarify facts; after clarification, logical deduction could be used to reach reasonable conclusions. In the early nineteenth century, geology and ethnography were subjected to criticism for being based on hypotheses and guesswork. Nilsson dismissed this view and considered the critics to be ignorant of the premises of the disciplines and therefore incapable of judging the conclusions. The natural sciences came under fire for materialism, but Nilsson believed that a materialistic emphasis could lead to greater prosperity for all if it helped to increase the knowledge of natural resources and their availability. He also disagreed with the religious critique of the discipline. In his view the natural scientist realized that everything was adapted to a specific purpose and that there was a permanent order ruled by unchangeable laws. Since the natural scientist was forced to look beyond the physical and transitory to the nonphysical and eternal, it was impossible not to see the traces of an almighty Creator. Such a science could not lead to harmful materialism.

Nilsson's engagement with contemporary debates over science revealed his remarkably accumulative and systematic mind. At the same time, his thinking was characterized by a rich imagination, making him a successful combination of historian and naturalist. He had a radical view of education and proposed a structure based on logic and experience as in natural science. He saw similarities between the natural sciences and the grammatical rules of philology as well as the logic of geometry, and he favored natural-science instruction in both lower and higher schools. His allegiance to the natural sciences placed him in opposition to the conservatism of the times, which saw a connection between scientific advances and the revolutions that were sweeping Europe. Instead, Nilsson advocated a pacifist view of science, which made peace the basis of scientific progress, since the researcher was a witness to succession without violent restructuring. The natural scientist was thus neither stationary nor revolutionary but rather the calm and self-assured man of progress.

Nilsson became a central figure within nineteenth-century Swedish zoology, and through his forty-year career as a university teacher, as well as his ability to popularize his scientific interests in lectures and publications, he exercised an influence that lasted well beyond that time. In 1836 Nilsson formed the Zoological Hunters Society for the purpose of promoting zoological knowledge and the development of hunting. Fascinated with birds since his youth, he was finally able to pursue ornithological studies through his position at Lund. Moreover, as society members gave accounts, among other things, of the presence of prehistoric tools of stone and animal bones in their hunting districts, the collections of sub-fossil bones increased. Because of his contacts with hunters and landowners, Nilsson received information about finds and their locations. He visited many during his numerous travels in Scania (southern Sweden), and he made valuable observations at the sites and participated in excavations (Löwegren 1983, 120). This overlapping of interests was typical for Nilsson and underscores the importance of integrating his different areas of activity.

Geology

Although the botanist Linnaeus had made significant contributions to mineralogy and paleontology in his *Systema Naturae,* Nilsson confronted a dearth of relevant geological literature in his early years. To overcome this problem he studied mineralogy in Copenhagen in the spring of 1815. He had a lifelong affinity for geology and paleontology, giving private tutoring and public lectures on these subjects up to 1852 (Regnéll 1983b, 24). Nilsson's geological studies were related to the development of European geology overall and were influenced by the work of Lamarck and Charles Lyell, but his greatest source of inspiration was the French naturalist and paleontologist Baron Georges Cuvier.

Nilsson sought to find firm ground for his ideas, even those concerning the development of the earth. The eternal source of power worked according to laws, and the first basic law of matter was the force of attraction. The original composition of elements was gaseous. The earth, ever since its creation as a ball of steam, had been gradually solidifying. These ideas originated from Buffon's work *Époques de la nature* (1778). Nilsson also regarded Cuvier as the high priest of natural science, and he therefore asserted that all created things go through a determined process and then decay (Regnéll 1983b, 32–35).

For Nilsson, geology was the science that described the transformation of the earth. Only changes that had occurred on or near the surface could be the object of the geological study. Through a process that had gone on for millennia, the earth had inscribed its own history, and it was the geologist's task to seek out and correctly interpret these physical documents, to reveal observable facts as well as explain the causes behind the changes. No absolute dating was possible, but geology could give the relative age.

Nilsson's method was to study processes in present time and then draw conclusions about earlier occurrences, an approach that echoed Lyell's principle of uniformitarianism (Regnéll 1983b, 39). Like all other natural sciences, geology was based on observations of phenomena and therefore was comparative. Science should avoid metaphysical conclusions, and theories should only give postulates. Only pure experience could be regarded as decisive (Regnéll 1983b, 38–39).

Paleontology

Through zoology, Sven Nilsson directed research toward fossils, which indicated that earth history was an ongoing process. As early as 1820 he had commented on the reality of development (Regnéll 1983b, 41), drawing from the theory behind Cuvier's zoological system (1812). Cuvier was convinced of a divine intervention in organic life and that the entire animal kingdom had developed from four fundamental concepts. In a lecture in 1826 Nilsson discussed the diversification of the animal kingdom against the background of Cuvier's system. One of the main ideas was that the development of each family was reflected in the development of individuals—that ontogeny recapitulates phylogeny—in the sense that both processes begin simply and become more complicated, a view that he later applied to his sociocultural evolutionary scheme. Nilsson was among the first in Sweden to express the view that species had developed and died out through an inability to adapt to climatic changes; he asserted this seven years before the publication of Charles Darwin's *The Origin of Species* (1859).

Nilsson noted that the distribution of animal species was often very limited, and in line with his method of drawing conclusions about the past on the basis of the present, this observation helped him in the development of certain theories. He was the first in Sweden to assert that glacial periods had occurred in the Scandinavian peninsula, during which time the earlier flora and fauna had died out. He was also the first to consider the question of the migration routes of the animals, and he concluded that migration had occurred from the south and northeast. Thus there had to have been a tongue of land that linked southern Sweden with Denmark and Germany. The question of land elevation was a recurrent theme for naturalists, historians, and theologians, as scientific evidence that disproved the biblical account of creation was contentious. These speculations were connected with the dawning realization that many phenomena in Scandinavia should be interpreted as glacial in nature. Nilsson realized that it was the land that moved and not the body of water that subsided or rose. He also correctly contended that land elevation had ceased in the southernmost parts of the country and had been replaced by a reverse movement. An earlier land bridge, by which both animals and plants had reached Sweden, had since sunk below the surface of the sea.

An understanding of the processes by which the inland ice shaped the landscape of the Scandinavian countries gradually developed in the nineteenth century. Nilsson was one of the pioneers of this embryonic discipline of quaternary geology, but his role in the introduction of glacial theory to Sweden has been overlooked. Geology, zoology, and archaeology were linked together in Nilsson's scientific pursuits (Regnéll 1983b, 65–74). For example, calcareous tuff and peat bogs gave indications of extinct plant and animal species, such as the auroch. Displayed in the zoological museum at Lund University was (and is) an auroch that had been killed by a Stone Age hunter, showing that extinct animal species had lived during the same time as humans. Nilsson himself had extracted the animal from a peat bog. Thus late-quaternary research was able to create a picture of the environment and living conditions of Stone Age people.

The almost circular shell of the brachiopod Ancistrocrania tuberculata *set in a piece of Danian chalk, studied by Nilsson. (Corbis)*

Scandinavian Fauna

For Sven Nilsson, natural-science research had a connection with cultural history. Linnaeus had integrated humans—*Homo sapiens*—into his investigations, and when Nilsson included a chapter on the history of hunting and fishing in his *Skandinavisk Fauna,* it was in accordance with that scientific tradition. The first edition of *Skandinavisk Fauna*'s initial volume appeared in 1820. Intended as a handbook for hunters and zoologists, it dealt with mammals. The second volume, *Foglarna* (1824), dealt with birds, and the third and fourth volumes, *Amfibierna* (1842) and *Fiskarna* (1852–1855), with amphibians and fish respectively. The volumes were reprinted several times but have never been translated.

Skandinavisk Fauna became a standard text for hunters, zoologists, and nature lovers and was the first summary of the higher animals of Sweden and Norway. Through this work zoology received the same attention as botany had during Linnaeus's time. The reliability of the work is admirable. Nilsson broke with the Linnaean tradition and applied geological, geographical, and economic perspectives to his investigation. In the second edition of *Foglarna* (1835), the chapter on the history of hunting and fishing was actually Nilsson's first outline of a cultural-evolutionary overview.

During this time there were two widely accepted cultural-historical theories. One maintained that human culture was a product of the

highest human nobility and wisdom. The other asserted that human beings originally had existed at the lowest level of animal savagery and crudity. Nilsson upheld the latter and interpreted this to mean that individual peoples had successively developed to a nobler state. In *Foglarna*,
Nilsson devised two parallel chronologies, one based on weapons and
the other on economy. The former was divided into three periods, beginning with the earliest history and the absence of metals. The second
period covered the time up to the introduction of firearms technology—the late Middle Ages. Then firearms technology had its own
chronology. The economic chronology was based on the axiom of successive progress and was divided into three developmental stages: the
savage, the nomad, and the agriculturalist. None of these chronologies
was archaeological in any real sense. However, the cultural-historical
section of the book attracted the attention of antiquarian circles, and in
1836 it was published in Danish and Norwegian.

Beginning in 1831 the Dane Christian Jürgensen Thomsen had published a number of works that discussed the three-age system—the idea
that human culture evolved from the Stone Age, to the Bronze Age, and
then to the Iron Age. At Lund University, Bror Emil Hildebrand had already arranged the archaeological collections after Thomsen's scheme as
early as 1830. In Stockholm at the time, Nilsson was not aware of this.
When he returned to Lund, he devoted his time to *Skandinavisk Fauna*
and zoological instruction. Thomsen and Nilsson were therefore equally
surprised when in 1836 they came in contact with each other's works.
They soon became friends and corresponded regularly.

Nilsson's cultural-historical development scheme was therefore not
a social-economic variant of Thomsen's three-age system but an independently formulated model of cultural development. His version, however, gave the three-age system the cultural-historical shape that was
missing in Thomsen's chronology, enabling further investigations. Nilsson's interest in cultural development consequently had its point of departure in questions other than the purely antiquarian, and his archaeological work began in earnest after 1840.

The Savage, the Nomad, and the Agriculturalist

Savages were described as the original primitive humans, who cared for
their offspring instinctively and took one day at a time, like animals. Such
people could only have been hunters or fishers. Eventually savages became nomads through increased experience. For example, hunters took
care of a calf after they had killed its mother and in this way accumulated
a herd. At the start the nomadic economy was mixed, consisting of both
hunting and the care of livestock, but it subsequently developed into

sedentary pastoralism. The shepherds built sheds for themselves and their livestock and stored food in barns. Thereafter began a period of clearance by burning. The first "plough" was a hoe. Eventually the nomads became agriculturalists and developed a more well-defined social structure. Nilsson believed he could identify these three stages in the source material. For him it was clear that the earliest peoples were savages, since they did not know the use of metals in toolmaking. This was confirmed through ethnographic analogies.

Nilsson also noted that anyone who had struck flint for flintlock guns knew the difficulties of making stone tools. Mastering the technique of creating a flint knife must have required practice since childhood. Nilsson was also certain that a cutting edge could only be obtained by striking the flint, not through polishing. Further, he pointed out that the stones used in flint knapping were common among the collections. He was the first Swede to identify the function of the knapping-stone. Burned clay pots showed that the savages had cooked meat, which exposed a paradox in Nilsson's thinking. How primitive could the savages be if they had made complicated tools and clay pots and had cooked meat? Nilsson's description of the variety of artifacts did not always match his theoretical reasoning. Nonetheless, the first inhabitants of Sweden had been identified, and it was now a matter of postulating when they had lived in Sweden. Here Nilsson made use of his geological knowledge to argue that only a relative chronology could be determined. This was probably the first time the relationship between relative and absolute dating was explicitly expressed within Swedish archaeology.

In Nilsson's scheme four different peoples with different customs and religions had reached the country and suppressed the earlier groups or peacefully assimilated with them. From the travel accounts of the Greek geographer Pytheas, he could chronologically distinguish the two earlier peoples from the two later. About 3,000 years must therefore have passed since the savages inhabited the country. Folktales and other accounts that were popular among the peasantry in southern Sweden were important for Nilsson's discussions. But ethnological analogies and historical sources were not entirely reliable, since it was difficult to distinguish between fact and fantasy. Thus it was necessary to return to reality—to the archaeological remains. These were easier to understand. However, the artifacts should be interpreted as functional objects and examined to determine how they were used and by whom. Tracing the past through present-day observations was the method Nilsson practiced within natural science, and he employed it in cultural-historical research as well. Ethnographical, ethnological, and historical analogies, systematic empiricism, and a concern with establishing relative chronologies formed the bases of Nilsson's archaeology. His discussion in *Foglarna* is thus the first outline of modern Swedish archaeology.

The Stone Age

After *Foglarna* Nilsson devoted more of his time to archaeology, and between the years 1838 and 1843 the Stone Age volume of *Skandinaviska Nordens Ur-invånare* was published in pamphlets. It was here that he first used the term *prehistory*. A second edition was printed in 1866. This edition was revised and equipped with an appendix as well as a sixth chapter that treated the oriental origin of the Bronze Age culture of Sweden. (Since this edition is published in German, French, and English, there is no need to discuss it in detail here.)

Two important points should be emphasized, however. First, even in the first edition he added a fourth stage to his development scheme from 1835, namely, the agriculturalist with a written language and coinage, as well as a division of labor among the members of society. Second, his development model constituted a whole, in which the development of human culture was not only regarded as material but also as spiritual and intellectual. For Nilsson the material comprised the visible part of the process, yet it was the nonmaterial development that was potent and important. In a real sense progress was thus the development of the nonmaterial, the spiritual and the intellectual. This mode of thinking was closely related to German romanticism, with its highly influential ideas about the mind striving toward greater freedom. Nilsson translated a natural-science approach, which he himself believed Cuvier had developed, into a complex, humanistic method.

Nilsson's model of cultural development was therefore both material/empirical and spiritual/metaphysical, although development could only be measured empirically, namely, through technological change. By viewing development in this way, Nilsson could collect the traces of past cultures, compare them with similar ones that still existed, and thereby seek knowledge of past conditions by reference to present-day ones. This comparative ethnography, or comparative ethnographic archaeology as he also called it, was not a new idea, but Nilsson was the first to apply this thinking to cultural history. The scheme played a decisive role in the foundation of modern anthropology by E. B. Tylor and L. H. Morgan. In its connection with Hegelian philosophy, it also held some importance for Friedrich Engels and Karl Marx. OSCAR MONTELIUS, who criticized Nilsson in other contexts, believed that the cultural-evolutionary scheme was of high quality and that Nilsson, through his comparative method, had elevated antiquarian research to a science. Nilsson was aware that his work was pioneering. His conclusions were highly respected in Sweden and were regarded as correction to the speculative and poetic display of Scandinavian ancient history.

However, Nilsson eventually began to lose prestige within the archaeological establishment, mainly because his attempts to determine the origin of the Swedish Bronze Age led to chronological misjudgments. He questioned, for example, Danish archaeologist J. J. Worsaae's division of the Stone Age into two parts. Nilsson was never an archaeologist in an antiquarian sense. Through his broad knowledge, he composed a picture of prehistory that was more complex than was usual within the confines of general archaeology. But it was chronology that would form the core of late-nineteenth-century archaeology in Scandinavia, not socioeconomic theories.

The Bronze Age

At an early stage Nilsson had come in contact with Bronze Age remains through his participation in several excavations. He believed that there was a sharp break between the Stone Age and the Bronze Age. Therefore, he dismissed the idea that people in the Stone Age, after they had increased their knowledge through experience, had begun to use bronze objects. For him the primitive Stone Age culture was incapable of development, and the bronze objects were so distinctive that they must be the evidence of a new migration into Sweden. In Nilsson's account this new culture brought agriculture and suppressed the Stone Age hunters and fishermen. Only by presuming that the knowledge had been obtained from the same place could one explain the similarities among the bronze weapons found in different European countries. The knowledge must therefore have reached Scandinavia from countries in the south.

He thus linked the Scandinavian Bronze Age with an immigrating Phoenician tribe. The suggestion met with wide criticism, and Nilsson defended himself by claiming that common sense and logical inference proved his case. In the 1870s this resulted in an intense debate between Oscar Montelius and Sven Nilsson—in spite of Nilsson's great age. Montelius, who had achieved fame for his dating of the Scandinavian Bronze Age, wrote in 1884 that archaeologists had made many mistakes by trying to answer questions about migrations, cultural stages, and cultural development—exactly the kind of issues Nilsson had addressed. This episode laid the foundation for Nilsson's somewhat tarnished reputation. Afterwards, research was directed more toward chronological questions and particularly toward the typological method that Montelius originated. Even so, it should be remembered that Nilsson contributed to the division of the Bronze Age into two parts.

Archaeological Achievements

Nilsson began to collect artifacts during the 1820s. These collections were carefully classified and systematized, and they formed the basis of his chapter on the history of hunting and fishing. The collections also included some ethnographic objects. Through extensive travels, purchases, and excavations he increased his holdings. The result of thirty years' work encompassed about 3,000 inventory numbers. In 1851 he sold the collection to the historical museum at Lund University. At this time Nilsson was deeply involved in his archaeological activity and had started a new collection (Stjernquist 1983, 157–165). Nilsson advocated a relatively free right to collect artifacts, and he participated in an extensive debate on this during the 1860s. He claimed that with stricter state regulation, much would be hidden away or destroyed, but a freer right to collect would mean that more artifacts would eventually reach the institutes (Stjernquist 1983, 166–167).

Through excavations Nilsson came in contact with archaeological fieldwork at an early stage. As early as 1819 he took part in an excavation in which he was entrusted with the osteological examinations, natural enough in view of his zoological knowledge. The passage grave that was excavated was assumed to be from the Stone Age before the use of metals, and it indicates that during the 1820s some researchers were already speaking in terms of a three-age system. Nilsson was not directing the fieldwork, however, and his contributions as a field archaeologist are thus linked with the investigations of Stone Age passage graves and Bronze Age barrows. Consequently, he realized the importance of more comprehensive knowledge with which to interpret the past. As a field archaeologist Nilsson was careful and systematic (Stjernquist 1983, 168–169).

Within Bronze Age research, Nilsson carried out, among other things, a restoration of the monumental Early Bronze Age cairn at Kivik, which is famous for its carved rock slabs. He became interested in rock carvings, and he was among the first to date the carvings to the Bronze Age (Stjernquist 1983, 175–176). Gradually he intensified his research on the Bronze Age. The Bronze Age volume of *Skandinaviska Nordens Urinvånare* was the first to be translated into a foreign language—German—even though it was completed long after the first edition of the Stone Age volume. With regard to the analysis of artifacts, particularly those from the Stone Age, Nilsson's primary interest was in understanding the functional-technical problems of their use and manufacture. In the course of his research he clarified how flint tools were made, both through the use of experiments as well as through ethnographical and ethnological analogies. Nilsson's contributions as an archaeologist helped to confirm and develop the three-age system. He showed how Stone Age societies had probably lived and demonstrated that the three-age system applied to Sweden as well as Denmark.

Conclusion

From the perspective of both science and history, Sven Nilsson is one of Sweden's most important researchers. His contributions within archaeology, geology, and zoology should not be underestimated. Nilsson continually presented and explained his scientific-theoretical points of departure. Because of this, and because of his broad basic education and untiring will to research new areas and problems, he remains an excellent example for researchers today.

Acknowledgments

Professor Bo Gräslund, for his advice, and Laura Wrang, who translated the Swedish text.

References
Primary archival material
Lunds universitetsbibliotek (The Library of Lund University).
Primary
Nilsson. Sven. 1835. *Skandinavisk Fauna. En handbok för jägare och zoologer. Foglarna.* Ny omarbetad upplaga. Lund.

————. 1838–1843. *Skandinaviska Nordens Ur-invånare, ett försök i komparativa ethnografien och ett bidrag till menniskoslägtets utvecklings historia. Bd. 1. Stenåldern. Innehållande en beskrifning öfver de vilda urfolkens redskap, hus, grifter och lefnadssätt m.m. samt utkast till beskrifning över en i forntiden hit inflyttad kimbrisk koloni.* Lund.

————. 1848. "On the Changes in the Fauna of Sweden." Report of the Seventeenth Meeting of the British Association for the Advancement of Science. Notices and Abstracts of Communications at the Oxford Meeting, June 1847, p. 79. London.

————. 1848. "On the Primitive Inhabitants of Scandinavia." Report of the Seventeenth Meeting of the British Association for the Advancement of Science, Oxford, June 1847, pp. 31–32. London.

————. 1866. "Stonehenge. An Attempt to Explain the Above Monument." By Professor S. Nilsson, etc., etc. Read June 13th, 1865. *Transactions of the Ethnological Society of London,* n.s., 4: 244–263.

————. 1868. *The Primitive Inhabitants of Scandinavia. An Essay on Comparative Ethnography, and a Contribution to the History of the Development of Mankind: Containing a Description of the Implements, Dwellings, Tombs and Mode of Living of the Savages in the North of Europe during the Stone Age.* 3d ed., with an introduction by J. Lubbock. London.

Secondary

Löwegren, Yngve. 1983. "Sven Nilsson, zoologen." In Regnéll, G., ed. *Sven Nilsson*. En lärd i 1800-talets Lund. Studier utgivna av Kungl. Fysiografiska Sällskapet i Lund. Lund.

Regnéll, G. 1983a. "Av stubbotan rot." In Regnéll, G., ed. *Sven Nilsson*. En lärd i 1800-talets Lund. Studier utgivna av Kungl. Fysiografiska Sällskapet i Lund. Lund.

————. 1983b. "Zoologen och arkeologen som var geolog." In Regnéll, G., ed. *Sven Nilsson*. En lärd i 1800-talets Lund. Studier utgivna av Kungl. Fysiografiska Sällskapet i Lund. Lund.

Stjernquist, B. 1983. "Sven Nilsson, som banbrytare i svensk arkeologi." In Regnéll, G., ed. *Sven Nilsson*. En lärd i 1800-talets Lund. Studier utgivna av Kungl. Fysiografiska Sällskapet i Lund. Lund.

Bruce G. Trigger

Daniel Wilson   *1816–1892*

Artist, administrator, anthropologist, and archaeologist with a formidable range of talents, Daniel Wilson is most widely known as the first English speaker to apply the Danish approach to prehistoric archaeology outside Scandinavia. Hence he may be regarded as the first prehistoric archaeologist, as distinguished from antiquarian, in the United Kingdom.

Artist and Antiquarian

Wilson was born into a middle-class Edinburgh family. His father, Archibald, was a tea, and later wine, merchant but was not very successful. His mother, Jane Aitken, the daughter of a prosperous land surveyor from Greenock, encouraged the intellectual development of her children. At an early age, Daniel and his younger brother George, who was to become Regius professor of technology at the University of Edinburgh, developed a strong interest in history and natural science. After attending the Edinburgh High School, Wilson apprenticed with the Edinburgh steel engraver William Miller. During this period he also attended various lectures at the University of Edinburgh, although he did not attempt to earn a degree. In 1837, Wilson moved to London where he made a living as an engraver and popular writer. He worked with the English artist J. M. W. Turner, engraving the latter's *Departure of Regulus*. He also married Margaret Mackay, the daughter of a Glasgow businessman and friend of the Wilson family. In 1842, he returned to Edinburgh and opened an artist's supplies and print shop, which he operated until 1848. He continued to support himself with his writings, which included *Oliver Cromwell and the Protectorate* (1848).

Wilson's first major antiquarian project was his *Memorials of Edinburgh in the Olden Times* (1848). Inspired by the historical romanticism of Sir Walter Scott, Wilson had long deplored the destruction of the buildings of Old Edinburgh in the course of urban renewal. He made pencil drawings of these old structures and began to record what could be observed in the course of their demolition. In 1846, he identified St. Margaret's Chapel, a stone structure in the castle dating from the time of Malcolm III. In *Memorials of Edinburgh* Wilson published a large number of his most interesting sketches accompanied by a rambling account of the history of the city.

Daniel Wilson.
(Copyright National
Galleries of
Scotland)

Wilson's Scottish antiquarian interests continued into his later years. In 1878, he published *Reminiscences of Old Edinburgh,* which recounted the history of the city and his youthful memories of it. While his training as an artist was never again to be as central to his work, his later archaeological publications were invariably praised for the quality of their illustrations.

Memorials of Edinburgh established Wilson's reputation as a leading Scottish antiquarian. Already in 1846, with the support of the publisher Robert Chambers, Wilson was elected a member of the Society of Antiquaries of Scotland, and the following year he became an honorary secretary of the society. Over the next few years, Chambers and Wilson worked to transform the society into a significant research institution.

Archaeologist

Wilson's conversion from antiquarian into prehistoric archaeologist resulted from his involvement in a project to turn the collections of the Society of Antiquaries into a modern national archaeological museum for Scotland. Scottish antiquaries had long and close relations with their Scandinavian counterparts. Hence it is not surprising that the model they selected for reorganizing their collections was the three-age system (Stone, Bronze, and Iron Ages) devised by Christian Thomsen for the National Museum of Antiquity, which he had opened in Copenhagen in 1819. Wilson not only studied collections of artifacts but visited sites and corresponded with people throughout Scotland. The result was a new display modeled on Thomsen's principles, as well as a catalog that constituted a first step toward Wilson's *Archaeology and Prehistoric Annals of Scotland* (1851, rev. ed. 1863). This book was the first comprehensive treatment of the Scottish past relating primarily to material culture and the first comprehensive study of prehistoric archaeology published in the English language. Like Thomsen's work, Wilson's was based on the investigation of museum collections and the field study of prehistoric monuments rather than on systematic excavations.

Implicit in Wilson's treatment of prehistory was an acceptance of cultural evolution that did not exclude diffusion and migration as factors helping to bring about cultural change. This view was rooted in the French Enlightenment philosophy, which was as familiar and acceptable to reform-minded individuals in Scotland as it had been in Thomsen's Denmark. Wilson divided his book into four sections, assigned to the periods of Stone (Primeval), Bronze (Archaic), and Iron (Teutonic) and to the Christian era. Within each section, chapters were devoted to different topics: tombs, fortifications, dwellings, weapons, vessels, ornaments, art, religion, and domestic life. In the sections dealing with more recent times, historical information increasingly supplemented the record of material culture. While Wilson applied the Thomsen-Worsaae chronology of Danish prehistory to Scottish data, there is no evidence that he clearly understood the seriational principles upon which Thomsen had based his chronology.

Wilson's approach was not entirely evolutionary. He observed that artifacts from Scotland differed in shape and decoration from those of corresponding periods in Denmark, especially during the Iron Age. Wilson also examined prehistoric skulls, the varying shapes of which suggested the presence of different people in Scotland before the arrival of the Celts. He regretted that many scholars rated philology ahead of physical anthropology as a means of tracing historical connections among human groups. Yet Wilson accepted the biblical assertion that all human groups shared a common ancestry and agreed with the monogenists that all human groups were behaviorally very similar.

Like the Scandinavian archaeologists, Wilson adhered to a biblical chronology that suggested human beings had been created only about 6,000 years ago. By a curious coincidence, the three regions of Europe where prehistoric archaeology was to develop before the 1860s—Scandinavia, Scotland, and Switzerland—had all been heavily glaciated during the last ice age; hence the length of the archaeological record of human presence in these regions was—and remains—close to that of the traditional biblical chronology. Wilson also accepted the biblical account of early human history, which, like many other exponents of Enlightenment philosophy, he squared with ideas of cultural evolution by maintaining that, as human groups had moved away from their point of creation in the Middle East, they had lost their knowledge of metallurgy, which they had to recover in the course of later cultural development. In spite of these limitations, Wilson presented the first account of Scottish prehistory—from the arrival of its first human inhabitants to the dawn of history—that was actually based on a chronological ordering of archaeological data.

The Archaeology and Prehistoric Annals of Scotland was distinguished by its careful organization and elegant, if by today's tastes rather florid, literary style. One of Wilson's major intellectual achievements was to distinguish between history and prehistory, not merely as time periods but as different approaches to studying the past. Others may or may not have used the term *prehistory* to denote the period of human existence before written records, but Wilson played a pioneering role in delineating the special characteristics of prehistory as a discipline. Because he had worked as a popularizing historian and then as an antiquarian, he was well equipped to understand the contrast between studying the past with and without the aid of written documents. He objected strongly to the traditional antiquarian practice of labeling any archaeological assemblage that appeared rude or barbarous as native, druidical, or British, as if such an attribution explained what had been found. He believed that his craniometric analyses had demonstrated the movements of peoples in prehistoric as well as historical times. Hence it was unrealistic to attribute all prehistoric artifacts to the ancestors of peoples whose occupation of particular regions in the early historical period was recorded. The study of prehistory had both historical and evolutionary dimensions. It involved working out movements of peoples in prehistoric times as well as tracing the general ways in which technology, social organization, and religion had grown more complex. Although Wilson believed that many innovations had come from the Middle East, which he regarded as the cradle of humanity, he thought that ironworking might have been invented in Scandinavia. There is no indication that he regarded the study of prehistory as in any way inferior to that of history—only as different.

Wilson viewed every artifact as the embodiment of its maker's knowledge, skill, and taste and believed that by studying the archaeological record it was possible to learn something about the habits, thoughts, and beliefs of specific prehistoric groups. Tools provided information about prehistoric economies, the remains of dwellings about social organization, and burials about religious beliefs. Wilson suggested that it might be possible to determine something about the status of women in different parts of Europe in prehistoric times by comparing the amount of luxury goods buried with each sex. The results of such studies would not be a traditional history recounting the words and deeds of individuals but an account of cultural changes that had occurred in prehistoric times. The objectives of prehistoric archaeology were thus the same kinds of knowledge that philosophers and ethnologists sought by employing Dugald Steward's "conjectural history," a speculation about what the past must have been like. Yet only prehistoric archaeology offered a means to study directly the history of humanity before the earliest written records. Wilson might not have invented the methods of prehistory, but in *The Archaeology and Prehistoric Annals of Scotland* he made a major contribution toward defining the goals of a new discipline in a form that would remain relevant into the twentieth century.

Although Wilson received an honorary LL.D. from the University of St. Andrews in recognition of his great achievement, he was not able to obtain an academic position in Scotland. In 1853, with the support of Lord Elgin, governor of the United Provinces of Canada and a fellow member of the Society of Antiquaries of Scotland, Wilson was appointed to the chair of history and English literature at University College, Toronto, at an annual salary of £350. Although Wilson settled in Toronto with his wife and two daughters, he never ceased to regret his separation from the friends, scholarly life, and libraries of Edinburgh. He applied unsuccessfully for the chair of history at St. Andrews in 1861 and that of English literature at the University of Edinburgh in 1863. There is no evidence that he continued to seek other posts in Scotland. In 1855, he declined the principalship of McGill College in Montreal, at an annual salary of £500, apparently because he judged the academic milieu in Toronto to be more promising.

Wilson quickly became one of the leading figures in higher education in Canada in the latter half of the nineteenth century. Originally a Baptist and then an evangelical Anglican, he detested the sectarianism he encountered in Ontario and championed a nondenominational system of higher education, in which people from different religious backgrounds could mingle and learn to cooperate. He also supported, in opposition to the Oxford-Cambridge model, the Scottish approach to higher education as the best for Canada, because it offered a broader range of subjects, including options that would prepare students for particular professions.

Wilson greatly enjoyed teaching English literature. He played a major role in introducing literary book reviewing to Ontario, and he published two significant books on literary subjects: *Chatterton: A Biographical Study* (1869), which documented the life of the chief poet of the eighteenth-century "Gothic" literary revival, and *Caliban* (1873), a study of the supernatural creatures in William Shakespeare's plays. Wilson was less fond of teaching history and in these courses tended to concentrate on earlier periods, including prehistoric ones. In 1857, he began to teach a course on "Ancient and Modern Ethnology," which is widely believed to have been the first course dealing exclusively with anthropology to be taught in a university anywhere in the world. He continued to teach this course annually for the rest of his life, and after 1882, his title at the University of Toronto changed to professor of history and ethnology.

Anthropologist

When he came to Canada, Wilson wished to become a Canadian antiquary. He began to collect artifacts for a Canadian museum that he proposed to establish, and in the summer of 1855, he visited the prehistoric copper mines along the south shore of Lake Superior. The following summer he traveled to the prehistoric earthworks in the Ohio Valley and over the years examined various archaeological sites in southern Ontario. Yet he published no formal accounts of these investigations and did not gather a major collection of local artifacts. Even his informal archaeological fieldwork dwindled in the 1860s. The systematic study of Ontario prehistory was left to David Boyle, who built the archaeological collections of the Ontario Provincial Museum and became Canada's first salaried archaeologist in 1887.

Wilson's abandonment of Ontario archaeology was the consequence of expanding interests that were to transform him from an archaeologist into an ethnologist. Already in the first edition of *The Archaeology and Prehistoric Annals of Scotland,* Wilson had exhibited an interest in the prehistoric cultures of the Mississippi Valley, Mexico, and Central America. After he moved to Toronto, Wilson discovered in the New World a laboratory for the study of European prehistory. He encountered Indians who were living exactly as he imagined prehistoric Scots had, European frontier settlers who appeared to be regressing to the lifestyles of their Iron Age ancestors, and Africans, taken involuntarily from a distant continent, who were being forced to adapt to an alien geographical and social environment under the worst possible conditions. Like the eighteenth-century philosopher and historian William Robertson, author of *The History of America* (1777), Wilson hoped to learn something about the "essential characteristics" of human beings by comparing indigenous cultural development in the Old and New Worlds and by examining the movements of peoples and clashes of cultures that had been occurring in the Western Hemisphere since the time of Christopher Columbus. The findings of this research were published in 1862 in *Prehistoric Man: Researches into the Origin of Civilization in the Old and New World* (2d ed. 1865; 3d ed. 1876). He performed much of the research for this book by visiting libraries, archaeological and ethnological collections, and scholars in Washington, D.C., Philadelphia, New York, Boston, and Albany. He also obtained information from travelers, Indian agents, and missionaries across Canada and by visiting Indian bands in southern Ontario and Quebec (which also involved measuring the natives' heads).

Prehistoric Man was based on the assumption, shared with Robertson and other Scottish Enlightenment philosophers, that there had been little, if any, direct contact between the Old and the New Worlds after the initial settlement of the Americas and that the parallel development of civilization in the two hemispheres resulted from common human instincts. Wilson believed that, in addition to reason and moral sense, these instincts included specific propensities for religion, language, tool-making, the construction of buildings, art, the use of fire, and even boat building. Every human being thus possessed the basic drives and abilities that could be used to construct cultures of varying degrees of complexity. These ideas were derived from Scottish Common Sense philosophy, which had been popular in Edinburgh in his youth and was to remain popular in North American academic circles throughout most of the nineteenth century.

Wilson was especially anxious to refute the American anatomist Samuel Morton's claim that the American Indians represented a uniform and separately created species of human beings. Like most devout Christians, Wilson was a monogenist who believed that all human beings were descended from common ancestors, with physical differences representing reversible adaptations to specific natural environments. Wilson amassed craniometric evidence of considerable variation both between and within American Indian populations. This led him to abandon his earlier belief that human crania, because of its slow evolution, provided reliable indicators of racial and ethnic identity. Wilson believed that the American Indians were an amalgam of groups who had come to the New World across the Pacific and Atlantic Oceans as well by traversing the Bering Strait. In postulating transoceanic migrations, he was following the American ethnologist Alexander Bradford, who in 1841 had linked the high civilizations of Mesoamerica with southern Asia by way of Polynesia. Still older were the speculations of Constantine Rafinesque about the population of the New World. Wilson thus believed that the earliest humans to arrive in the New World included peoples culturally advanced enough to sail across oceans. Yet he maintained that, because they were few in number, had not brought any domesticated plants and animals with them, and quickly dispersed in their new home, they would have lost whatever skills they initially possessed. Hence they had to start again at a primitive level and create the civilizations of the New World in isolation from those of the Old World. Consequently, the civilizations found in these two hemispheres provided independent evidence concerning the innate abilities of human beings.

Wilson concluded, like many contemporary American scholars, that William Prescott in the mid-nineteenth century had grossly exaggerated the cultural achievements of the Aztecs and Incas. Yet he believed that these peoples had reached the level of the earliest civilizations in Egypt and the Middle East and suggested that, given more time to develop, they might have equaled, or excelled, the achievements of western Europeans. Wilson maintained that civilizations developed first in mild climates and judged the Maya of Central America to have been the most advanced aboriginal civilization of the Americas. He pinpointed Peru as a center for the development of metallurgy but did not believe either the Incan or the Aztec civilization was very old. Wilson argued that, because of the easy conditions under which tropical civilizations arose, they tended toward despotism, pomp, and sensuous display rather than promoting the moral and mental progress of ordinary people. More progressive civilizations developed only later and in harsher climates; so far, they had evolved only in the Old World. Had they continued in isolation, peoples such as the Micmacs and Iroquois might have become the French and English of the New World. This sort of environmental speculation constituted typical Enlightenment explanations of cultural diversity.

Wilson rejected the long-standing view that degeneration was an overall pattern in human history, although, like many Enlightenment evolutionists, he appeared to accept the traditional claim that agriculture, animal husbandry, and metallurgy were aspects of earliest cultures. For Wilson, degeneration was something that frequently happened to human societies. The Stone Age represented less a primary stage in cultural development than a base level to which human societies from time to time declined and from which they then had to reascend.

Wilson did not confuse inherent ability with cultural development. He pointed out that, under especially propitious circumstances, the Anglo-Saxons, Hungarians, and Arabs had evolved from barbarism to civilization in only a few generations. He also argued that aggressiveness probably did more to facilitate such a transition than docility. Hence cannibalism and human sacrifice were not evidence of an inability to become civilized. Like all nineteenth-century anthropologists, he believed that cultural progress occurred more quickly when individual human beings had the leisure to use their intellects to devise ways to control their environment more effectively. Because they provided more leisure and healthier living conditions for more people, more advanced societies fostered still-faster cultural development. While he maintained that human nature could not be permanently altered, either by the natural environment or by cultural progress, intellectual development and even brain function could be affected in the short term, and for better or worse, by environmental factors such as climatic conditions, social class, diet, education, and state of health.

Wilson also observed that, when peoples at very different levels of cultural development encountered one another, it almost always resulted in the rapid degeneration and collapse of the less-evolved society and the integration of its surviving members into the more advanced one. He viewed this process of cultural and biological mixing as one of the most important ways in which cultural progress came about. Wilson believed that all races were temporary and that new ones came into existence as a result of interbreeding between existing ones. He looked forward to the creation of a new North American people in whom the blood and cultural achievements of Indians and blacks as well as Europeans would become inextricably mixed. As he reminded readers, it was agreed that throughout British history progress had resulted from new peoples entering the country and mingling with its inhabitants. Wilson cited the Métis of western Canada (who were descended from white fathers and Indian mothers) and the Haitians as examples of the beneficial results of racial and cultural blending. In his opinion, only primitive peoples were likely to be "pure-blooded." Wilson's view contrasted with the widely held opinion that native peoples were unalterably inferior to Europeans and therefore were doomed to total extinction as European settlement spread across North America.

Wilson greatly admired Charles Darwin's scholarship and welcomed Darwin's studies of variation within species as support for monogenesis. Yet, although Wilson was a longtime friend of the Lamarckian evolutionist Robert Chambers, in 1862 he saw no reason to accept the idea of biological evolution, especially as it applied to human origins. He continued to insist on the fixity of human nature, while maintaining that human societies could be perfected by increasing knowledge—or could lapse as a result of moral failures into barbarism. Later, he conceded the antiquity of human beings and the likelihood that the human body had evolved from that of an apelike higher primate. He also removed all references to a biblical chronology from the third edition of *Prehistoric Man* (1876). In evaluating Wilson's cold response to evolutionist claims, it must be remembered that, before Eugene Dubois discovered the remains of *Pithecanthropus erectus* in Java in the 1890s, there was no fossil evidence of hominids whose cranial capacity was not as large as that of modern peoples.

Although Wilson slowly became reconciled to the idea of humans being physically descended from other animals, he continued to object to what he perceived as the materialist Darwinian assumption that human beings were little different from apes. For Wilson, the possession of reason and an innate moral sense clearly differentiated human beings from all other animals. He insisted that the transition between apes and humans must have been instantaneous. Contrary to the views of most nineteenth-century evolutionists, he contended that there was no significant difference in intellectual potential between human groups that were culturally most and least advanced, while there was an unbridgeable moral and intellectual gulf between the most advanced apes and all human be-ings. Wilson's acceptance of an evolutionary explanation of human ori-gins remained belated and heavily qualified. In matters relating to bio-logical evolution and its relevance for the origins of culture, Wilson was, from 1859 on, a reluctant follower, not a leader.

Later Work

After 1876, there is little evidence of change in Wilson's anthropologi-cal or archaeological ideas. He continued to teach and to write papers, many of which were published in the *Transactions* of the Royal Society of Canada, which had been founded in 1882. Even these essays addressed topics and refined and qualified ideas that he had advanced at an earlier stage in his career. Some of the best of these papers were revised and published as *The Lost Atlantis and Other Ethnographic Studies* (1892). A novel interest of this period was why most people were right-handed; Wilson himself had been born left-handed and taught himself to be am-bidextrous. After considering evidence from many fields and carrying out experiments using University of Toronto undergraduates, Wilson concluded that handedness was a hereditary phenomenon related to which hemisphere of the brain developed earlier. This work, his last, was titled *The Right Hand: Left Handedness* (1891).

While anthropology remained Wilson's favorite avocation, there was a marked decline in the quantity and originality of his research after the publication of *Prehistoric Man* in 1862. The enthusiasm motivating his extensive work for that book might have risen from a hope that if he ri-valed William Robertson's researches into New World prehistory, he might secure an academic post in Scotland. As it became clear that he was destined to remain in Canada, an increasing amount of Wilson's time was devoted to university administration and academic politics. He had already demonstrated considerable talent in this field. In 1860, he, rather than the president of University College, defended the college's privileges before a select committee of the Canadian assembly. Wilson became the president of University College in 1882 and was president of the University of Toronto, of which University College was a part, from 1887 until his death in 1892.

Wilson's later years were marked by increasing disagreements with younger colleagues. He opposed with some success the development of a specialized science curriculum, which he believed would undermine the moral basis of education. He was also criticized for not advocating the appointment to academic positions of enough native-born Canadians or even exclusively Toronto graduates. He earned lasting censure for his opposition to admitting women as students to University College, which was brought about by an Order in Council of the Antra government in 1884. Wilson did not oppose the education of women but preferred the establishment of separate colleges for them, modeled on Vassar and Smith in the United States. Many colleagues concluded that Wilson had ceased to be in touch with the times. Yet when the University College building was gutted by fire in 1890, he acted immediately to keep the college functioning and repair the damage.

Throughout his life, Wilson remained a talented landscape painter, often producing as many as five watercolors a day during his summer vacations. He was also involved in a wide variety of civic activities, which included being a founder of the Protestant Episcopal Divinity School in Toronto, president of the Toronto Young Men's Christian Association, and founder of a Newsboy's Lodging and Industrial Home for street urchins.

Accomplishments

The Archaeology and Prehistoric Annals of Scotland was the first work outside Scandinavia to apply in a substantial fashion the Danish approach to prehistoric archaeology—the three-age system and excavated sites, museum collections, ethnographic observations, and oral history. Hence Wilson may be regarded as the first prehistoric archaeologist, as distinguished from antiquarian, in the United Kingdom. Growing interest in Scandinavian archaeology was evident among members of the Society of Antiquaries of Scotland before Wilson began his work and is indicated on a more general scale by the translations of Thomsen's *Guidebook to Scandinavian Antiquity* (1848) and *Primeval Antiquities of Denmark* (1849) into English. Yet, even if Wilson did not fully understand the ideas underlying Thomsen's primitive seriation, his work was not a slavish imitation of his Scandinavian mentors. Wilson drew attention to the major stylistic differences between Danish and Scottish antiquities. He also documented more precisely than had ever been done before the explanatory potential of prehistoric archaeology and how it differed from traditional political history. These accomplishments are considerably more important than the much-debated question of whether Wilson was the first person to employ the term *prehistory* (or its equivalent in some other language).

The Prehistoric Annals of Scotland was widely read, and a second edition appeared in 1863, into which Wilson incorporated many ethnographic observations that he had made in the New World. The eminent English historian Henry Hallam praised the edition as the most scientific treatment of "primitive history" ever written, and his review helped Wilson secure his appointment at University College. Despite the seeming interest of English antiquarians in the writings of Thomsen and Worsaae, Wilson's work did not have a strong impact on the practice of antiquarianism in England in the 1850s. His proposal that the prehistoric collections of the British Museum should be reorganized according to the three-age system went unheeded. The adoption of a more scientific approach to prehistoric archaeology in England was to be associated with the development of Paleolithic archaeology in the 1860s, and Wilson's adherence to a biblical chronology made his work of little interest to these scientists.

After he moved to Canada, Wilson's interest in archaeology declined, although he did write the article on archaeology for the ninth edition of the *Encyclopedia Britannica* (1878). Despite his early intentions, Wilson personally contributed very little to the development of archaeology in Ontario, and in later years he did not attempt to maintain close contacts with those who did. Nor was Wilson long remembered by archaeologists either in North America or in Scotland. By the end of the nineteenth century, his archaeological work seems to have been scarcely remembered in Scotland. Joseph Anderson, whose culture-historical approach to archaeology was very different from Wilson's, made few references to him, and in his syntheses of Scottish prehistory V. GORDON CHILDE appears not to have been aware of him.

Wilson's anthropological writings seem to have sold well and to have been read in North America, Britain, and Germany. Even so, apart from favorable mentions of his craniometric research, his name rarely appears in modern histories of anthropology. In recent years, Wilson's advocacy of integrating aboriginal peoples into North American society has been interpreted as indicating that he was an apologist for Euro-Canadian expansion. Yet Wilson rejected the racism that was commonly directed against Indians and blacks in North America during the nineteenth century. He also rejected the efforts of Darwinian-inspired anthropologists to exaggerate the intellectual differences among various human groups and to narrow the gap between the most "primitive" human beings and the great apes. These attitudes make Wilson's views on racial matters seem far more modern than those of Lubbock, Morgan, and many other anthropologists of the late nineteenth century. No one appreciated at that time how long human evolution had taken and thus how great was the separation between all living apes and humans. Consequently, while Wilson was right about human nature, he erred in his rejection of human evolution—just as Darwinians (apart from Alfred Russell Wallace) were right about evolution but wrong in the racist views that they constructed to support their conclusions.

Throughout his life, Wilson continued to be guided by the religious beliefs, the cultural evolutionism of the Enlightenment, and the Common Sense philosophy with which he had become familiar in the Edinburgh of his youth. In historical terms, his anthropological ideas must be judged to have been, not ahead of his time, but behind it. By refusing to embrace the concept of human evolution in 1862, he doomed his own work to irrelevance in the opinion of Lubbock and other "progressive" evolutionists. Although modern archaeologists and anthropologists may admire Wilson's refusal to subscribe to the racism inherent in nineteenth-century social Darwinism, they must also understand how and why Wilson forfeited a leading role in the development of anthropology in the late nineteenth century. His slow and half-hearted acceptance of biological evolution in the years that followed did nothing to restore his position.

Might Wilson have accomplished more had he stuck to archaeology? This question ignores the fact that he also wrote books in the field of English literature and was the administrator of a major university. Studies of Wilson's life have tended to emphasize some of his interests while ignoring others. Only when his life is viewed as a whole does it become clear how much this largely self-taught and multifaceted scholar accomplished. From that perspective, the extent of Wilson's contributions to the early development of prehistoric archaeology appears even more remarkable.

References
Primary
Wilson, Daniel. 1851. *The Archaeology and Prehistoric Annals of Scotland.* London: Macmillan.

————.1862. *Prehistoric Man: Researches into the Origin of Civilisation in the Old and New World,* 2 vols. London: Macmillan.

————.1863. *The Prehistoric Annals of Scotland.* London: Macmillan.

Secondary
Berger, Carl. 1983. *Science, God, and Nature in Victorian Canada.* Toronto: University of Toronto Press.

————. *1990.* "Wilson, Sir Daniel." *Dictionary of Canadian Biography* 12: 1109–1114.

Chippindale, C. 1988. "The Invention of Words for the Idea of 'Prehistory.'" *Proceedings of the Prehistoric Society* 54: 303–324.

Clermont, N., and P. E. L. Smith. 1990. "Prehistoric, Prehistory, Prehistorian . . . Who Invented the Terms?" *Antiquity* 64: 97–102.

Cole, D. 1973. "The Origins of Canadian Anthropology, 1850–1910." *Journal of Canadian Studies* 8: 33–45.

Langton, H. H. 1901. "Sir Daniel Wilson." *Review of Historical Publications Relating to Canada* 5: 199–217.

Marinell, A. 1981. "'A Fine, Genial, Hearty Band': David Laing, Daniel Wilson and Scottish Archaeology." In *The Scottish Antiquarian Tradition,* ed. A. S. Bell. Edinburgh: J. Donald.

McCardle, B. E. 1980. "The Life and Anthropological Works of Daniel Wilson (1816–1892)." M.A. thesis, Department of Anthropology, University of Toronto.

McKillop, A. B. 1987. *A Disciplined Intelligence: Critical Inquiry and Canadian Thought in the Victorian Era*. Montreal: McGill–Queens University Press.

Trigger, Bruce G. 1992. "Daniel Wilson and the Scottish Enlightenment." *Proceedings of the Society of Antiquaries of Scotland* 122: 55–75.

Nathalie Richard

Gabriel de Mortillet   *1821–1898*

Translated from the French by Judith Braid

One of the founders of prehistory in France and Europe, Gabriel de Mortillet developed a classification of stone tool technology that has remained standard until the present day. The establishment of the first national museum of prehistory in the world and the first international conference on prehistory were due to Mortillet's immense influence.

*From the Petit Séminaire to the Musée
des Antiquités Nationales*

Louis Laurent Marie Gabriel de Mortillet (born 29 August 1821 at Meilan, Isère, died 25 September 1898 at Saint-Germain-en-Laye, Yvelines). Under the influence of his mother, Adélaïde de Montélégier, an ardent Catholic and monarchist, he entered the Petit Séminaire in Grenoble as a boy. However, he proved a rebellious pupil and soon left; the only mark his stay in Grenoble made on him was a deep-seated anticlericalism that colored his later career. In 1839 he was sent to Paris to prepare for the entrance examination for the Ecole Centrale, which he passed in 1841. From then until 1846 he studied engineering and took a keener interest in geology and conchology (the study of shells), taking courses at the Musée National d'Histoire Naturelle. After his studies he decided to stay on in Paris and threw himself into politics on the side of the democrats opposing the monarchy of Louis Philippe. He wrote for the Socialist press under Proudhon *(Le peuple),* Flocon *(La réforme),* and Leroux *(La revue indépendante).* Caught up in the revolutionary events of 1848, he criticized in several pamphlets the conservative turn of the Second Republic after the departure of the king and was sentenced for violation of the press laws. He took refuge in Savoy, his native province, which was still part of the kingdom of Piedmont-Sardinia.

At this point his scientific career really began. Given the task of cataloging the geological collections at the museum in Geneva in 1852, he was invited to be in charge of the museum at Annecy in 1854. He spent three years sorting and cataloging the geological treasures of Savoy, hoping to publish a map of the region, but the project had to be abandoned when the province was annexed by France; only the preface was completed. From 1858 to 1863 Mortillet worked in Italy for the Lombard-Venetian Railway Company. He began his first research into prehistory. Intrigued by the discovery of Neolithic settlements exposed when the water level in the Swiss lakes dropped during the winter of 1853–1854, he thought that the Italian lakes must contain similar remains. He published his first articles on the subject in 1859 and 1860, just as discussions in France were leading to the recognition of the work of Jacques Boucher de Perthes, a mid-nineteenth-century French antiquary who had discovered very old artifacts in the gravels of the River Somme that were associated with the remains of extinct animals. In 1863, he began a project with the Swiss archaeologist Desor and the Italian archaeologist Stoppani that led to the discovery of several settlements in Lake Varese.

Under the liberalization of the Second Empire, Mortillet, by now an experienced prehistorian, was able to leave Italy in 1864 and settle in Paris. He had firsthand knowledge of Swiss and Italian research, and French prehistory would benefit considerably from his international connections at a later date. From 1864 to 1868 his income came from the prehistory review he had founded, *Les matériaux pour l'histoire positive et philosophique de l'homme,* before he became conservator at the Musée des Antiquités Nationales at Saint-Germain-en-Laye in 1868. He held this post until 1889, and it was during his years at the museum at Saint-Germain that he did most of his work. His theories, expressed in scientific journals of the time, are summarized in several basic works, of which the most important are *Le préhistorique* (1883), *Les origines de la chasse, de la pêche et de l'agriculture* (1889), and his last work, *La formation de la nation française* (1899). The scope of his work, coupled with his professional activity, makes Gabriel de Mortillet one of the main founders of prehistory in France and in Europe.

The Scientist and the Politician

It would be impossible to understand Gabriel de Mortillet's scholarly work without taking into account certain underlying philosophical attitudes, which he expressed in both the political and scientific spheres. There is no mystery about his political allegiance, as Mortillet played a significant role in the Republican camp from 1846. At that time he was deeply imbued with democratic ideals and supported popular education, which would make universal suffrage possible. Hence he concentrated his efforts on popularizing both political and scientific ideas. His biographers note his contributions to the scientific column of *L'almanach populaire* after 1846. During his stay in Italy he was asked to edit the "review of scientific progress" for the paper *L'Italie.* In 1848 he veered more

sharply toward popular indoctrination and founded a bureau for democratic and social propaganda, which enabled him to put out a series of
pamphlets under the title *Politique et socialisme à la portée de tous* (1849).
Eleven installments in all were published, dealing with topical themes,
such as the red flag (no. 1), the right to work (no. 4), religion (no. 6),
and socialist theories inspired by Proudhon (nos. 7, 10, and 11). The
twelfth brochure, entitled *La guillotine,* accused the conservative Republican government of reverting to the methods of the Terror. That,
combined with his involvement in the June Days of 1848, earned him
political condemnation and forced him into exile in 1849.

On his return to France under the Second Empire, Mortillet was
cautious in his resumption of politics. He waited until the Third Republic was safely established before he made public his position, which was
in any case fairly moderate. He was no longer a Socialist but a Radical,
and it was as the latter that he was elected mayor of Saint-Germain-en-
Laye in 1882, then deputy for Seine-et-Oise in 1885. His political career
was short-lived, for he was defeated in the 1888 municipal elections and
did not stand for office in the legislative elections of 1889.

Mortillet's political activity, although modest in scale, nevertheless
corresponded to certain basic philosophical beliefs, which, in their turn,
influenced his scientific attitudes. The main ideas can be grouped under
the single heading of materialism. From 1880 onward, Mortillet was
one of the prime movers of a group of scientists, mostly anthropologists,
who called themselves "scientific materialists." This title, which has no
connection with the Marxist term, referred to a radical materialism that
had its origins in eighteenth-century French philosophy and probably in
nineteenth-century German materialism. (Mortillet's meeting with
Karl Vogt in Geneva in 1852 may have marked the genesis of this influence.) One can trace the essentials of this extreme materialism in
L'homme, a review that Mortillet founded and ran between 1884 and
1887. The chief editor and his materialist colleagues, such as the physi-
ologists Fauvelle and Collineau, the folklorist Paul Sébillot, and the prehistorians Philippe Salmon and Adrien de Mortillet, outlined a theory
that stressed above all the physico-chemical unity of the world. The unity
of a universe entirely ruled by the laws of physics and chemistry was
matched by a corresponding unity of knowledge. Only science could explore this exclusively material world and only by copying the inductive
methods of physics and chemistry. Any other means of knowledge,
whether philosophical or metaphysical, counted as superstition. This
materialism opposed with equal vehemence religion on the one hand
and positivism on the other, which stood accused, in its reluctance never
to question first principles, of playing at metaphysics. Louis Pasteur,

who seemed to embody best the synthesis of Catholic faith and positivism, became a favorite target for *L'homme,* as did Victor Cousin and his disciples, who dominated philosophy at the Sorbonne.

Mortillet's extremist stance in philosophy determined his attitude in politics and in science. In the political domain his materialism led to an uncompromising anticlericalism. He was one of the instigators of the Libre Pensée (free thought) movement, so influential in the Third Republic, when politician Jules Ferry was battling for free state school education. In several texts Mortillet pitted true knowledge, represented by science, against the obscurantism of religion. Seeing religious faith as a "Method of Tradition, forcing us to look backwards, fatally retrograde," he took up the defense of "reason, or the Method of Observation, allowing us to study freely what surrounds us and [favoring] progress" (1896, 1). He systematically denounced the Catholic Church for making its own interpretations of scientific data, castigating its "strenuous efforts to monopolize science" (1887, 609). In his pages one can see the epistemological battle for the separation of science and religion changing into a political struggle for the separation of church and state. This was why Mortillet was with the Radicals in the fight for state education, maintaining that it was "an absolutely basic principle to have no religious interference in the schools" ("Mathias Duval," 1886, 28). His support for state schooling went hand-in-hand with his commitment to the popular dissemination of knowledge. In 1849 he had made "free education on the widest scale" an essential requirement for effective democracy. Consequently, when he founded *Matériaux* he fixed its subscription very low. After 1870 and the trauma of the defeat by Prussia, the argument for the spread of knowledge took on a nationalist tinge. France's honor had to be restored by educating for vengeance. Mortillet found himself in the ranks of l'Association Française pour l'Avancement des Sciences, established in 1872 with the motto "Pour la science et pour la patrie" (for science and for the fatherland). This confidence in the powers of science appeared also as a commitment in favor of colonization; the argument is reminiscent of that inspiring the French government's policies for Africa and Asia.

Mortillet's adherence to materialism held implications for his scientific ideas as well as his politics. His belief in the material unity of the universe implied the unity of the laws of a physical or chemical nature that governed it. For Mortillet, the only law for the scientist studying life was the law of evolution. In the nineteenth century the synthesis between prehistory and the theory of evolution did not take place instantaneously, despite the coincidence that the year 1859 saw both the publication of *The Origin of Species* by Charles Darwin and the first debates on the antiquity of human beings at the Académie des Sciences. In fact, it seemed initially as if the supporters of fossil man tried to keep the two issues separate. Thus in 1863, when the Moulin-Quignon jaw—the first human remains thought to be Paleolithic—was discovered and discussed, its main advocates claimed that it represented a human type within the limits of modern variations and that, far from proving the hypotheses of Lamarck and Darwin, it contradicted them.

Mortillet was responsible for bringing together the two issues and went so far as to turn prehistory into a laboratory for applied transformism (the evolution of human beings). Given the unity of a materialist universe, Mortillet defended the existence of a single law ruling the living world and secularizing its history. This universal law was the law of progress. But there must be agreement on the precise meaning of the word *progress*. Mortillet had no doubts: it meant evolution, encompassing both biology and culture, which made it reminiscent of Herbert Spencer's idea of evolution. On the strictly biological level, Mortillet inclined toward the neo-Lamarckians, insisting more specifically on the influence of environment on living creatures. However, on this point he was rather ambiguous, since he did not seem to perceive any fundamental distinction between the transformism of French naturalism and Darwin's ideas. He even seemed to think that the basis of Lamarck's system, the principle of the adaptation of form to needs, contained in essence all the developments specified later by Darwin. This vision of progress, at once geological, biological, and cultural, revealed a Mortillet who was more of a Spencerian than a Lamarckian or a Darwinian. Moreover, because progress obeyed the strict determinism of the transformation of the environment, it had to be completely linear. The cultural sphere was not independent, and Mortillet was unable to conceive of parallel developments or "tree-models" in the evolution of material cultures. Here, for example, is his sketch of the cultural genealogy of the Paleolithic:

> During the Chellean, man had only a very crude hand-hammer. This instrument was more of a weapon than a tool. It was no use for cutting open an animal or skinning it. Man had to go naked. This was no great hardship, for he lived in a warm period. In the Acheulian the temperature dropped. Man felt the need of clothing. He improved the hand-hammer to make it both a weapon and a tool for skinning his prey. As the cold increased, skins simply cut from animals were not sufficient. Then he created Mousterian tools. The scraper for cleaning and softening the skins, the chopper for cutting them and the point for making holes. During the intense cold of the Magdalenian there existed a whole range of stone and bone tools for making clothing which was needed more and more (1897a, 22–23).

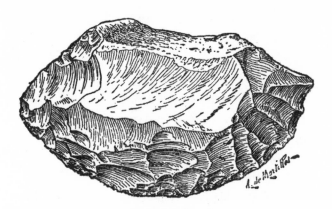

A Mousterian scraper in flint. (Reprinted from Gabriel de Mortillet, La formation de la nation française, *1897)*

Mortillet's materialism fed into a theory of evolution that influenced all his scientific explanations. His belief in the interpretative power of an evolutionist archaeology was reinforced by a more naive kind of materialism, revealed in his contention that all human activity left behind material traces. He went so far as to affirm that "just as geology has shown us fossil drops of rain, so prehistoric studies have shown us fossil souls" (1875, 120). The implication was that tools and artifacts manifested intelligence and the ability to reason, to appreciate things aesthetically, and to observe. It can be argued that the whole of Mortillet's theoretical work in prehistory sprang directly from his epistemological optimism in the power of archaeology and his belief in a global, strictly linear evolution.

Mortillet, Prehistory, and Evolution

The major contribution made by this French scholar to the science of prehistory in the nineteenth century lay in the classification of stone objects that he drew up between 1869 and 1872. Here he set out a division of tool technology into categories whose denominations have remained standard until the present day.

The impetus for the project began in 1867, when he was part of the organizing committee for the Stone Age hall in the "History of Work" section of the Exposition Universelle. Under the presidency of Edouard Lartet, this committee mounted an exhibition that was extremely successful in bringing prehistory to the notice of a wider public. Yet Mortillet reacted against Edouard Lartet's classification scheme. In 1861 Lartet, using as his criteria the transformation of fauna from one archaeological stage to another, had identified four epochs in the Paleolithic: the age of the great cave-bear, the age of the elephant (or mammoth) and rhinoceros, the age of the reindeer, and the age of the aurochs. Mortillet did not agree with this chronology, and he was able to pursue his own lights when he was asked in 1868 to organize the Stone Age galleries at the Musée des Antiquités Nationales.

Mortillet felt that the paleontological data "was not sharp enough to make such clear, neat divisions" as Lartet had posed. He preferred to "abandon basing divisions on fauna" and instead to "appeal to the archaeological method" (1872, 433). Thus he proposed a classification "based on the products of human industry" (1869, 553), in which the classes of objects were designated, as in the geological model, according to the name of an eponymous site. These classes, named Acheulean, Mousterian, Solutrean, Magdalenian, and Robenhausian, were consistent with the law of technical progress, which followed refinements in the working of flint and gradual developments in bone toolmaking. However, this strict law of progress had several consequences. The first was that Mortillet was unable to fit the Aurignacian into his scheme. In 1869, using typological criteria, he had placed the Aurignacian epoch between the Solutrean and the Magdalenian, because bone tools appeared in it. This chronology was contradicted by an examination of lithic toolmaking, which seemed to regress from fine Solutrean blades to Aurignacian objects. And so, rather than admit the complex processes of tool evolution, Mortillet preferred to eliminate the Aurignacian from his final classification scheme in 1872.

The very rigidity of the evolutionary schema underlying the classification plan gave it universal validity. Since it was solely determined by changes in environment and by biological change that saw the growth of human faculties, Paleolithic culture had to develop in an autochthonous manner. And if in France "toolmaking progress developed in a normal, regular manner, without any appreciable outside influences" (1897a, 22), the universal law of progress implied that the Paleolithic stages occurred in the same order elsewhere. Hence the classes defined by Mortillet were exactly equivalent to epochs.

Mortillet's classification was thus a universal and natural chronology (based on natural laws). For a while it precluded any ideas of parallel or treelike evolution and any cross-cultural influences. A few nineteenth-century prehistorians questioned it—for instance, E. Dupont in Belgium and MARCELLIN BOULE and Salomon Reinach in France—but it was not seriously disputed until the beginning of the twentieth century. In 1907 work on the Aurignacian by HENRI BREUIL started the demolition of the edifice, whose great merit (and great flaw) lay in its simplicity. The author attacked his rival, stating "the neatness of a simplistic system" was "incapable of picking out from diverse facts those which will give rise to more objective and accurate views of reality." He maintained that "it is neither by a perfectly uniform and smooth development, nor by facile explanations of successive migrations that such complex questions can be resolved." For his own part, he believed that he had proved, thanks to the Aurignacian, that "the evolution of Western peoples is not as simple as has been thought; outside influences must undoubtedly have modified its course many times" (Breuil 1907, 47). Mortillet's construction collapsed. Yet from his legacy there remained still the idea of a classificatory system that was in part a chronology and denominations that have been preserved down to the present day.

TEMPS.				AGES.	PÉRIODES.	ÉPOQUES.
ACTUELS.		HISTORIQUES.		DU FER.	Mérovingienne.	WABENIENNE, Franque, Burgonde, Germanique.
					Romaine.	CHAMPDOLIENNE, Décadence Romaine.
						LUGDUNIENNE, Beau-temps Romain.
		PROTOHISTORIQUES.			Étrusque, Galatienne.	MARNIENNE, Gauloise, 3° Lacustre.
						HALLSTATTIENNE, des Tumulus, 1re du Fer.
				DU BRONZE.	Bohémienne.	LARNAUDIENNE, 2° Lacustre en majeure partie.
						MORGIENNE, 2° Lacustre partie, des Dolmens partie.
GÉOLOGIQUES.	QUATERNAIRES.	PRÉHISTORIQUES.		DE LA PIERRE.	Néolithique, Pierre polie.	ROBENHAUSIENNE, 1re Lacustre, des Dolmens majeure partie, de l'Aurochs partie.
					Paléolithique, Pierre taillée.	MAGDALÉNIENNE, des Cavernes en majeure partie, du Renne en presque totalité.
						SOLUTRÉENNE, partie du Renne et du Mammouth.
						MOUSTÉRIENNE, du Mammouth majeure partie.
						CHELLÉENNE, Acheuléenne, du Grand Ours, de l'Éléphant antique.
	TERTIAIRES.				Éolithique, Pierre éclatée.	OTTAÏENNE, Tortonienne.
						THENAISIENNE, Aquitanienne.

Nineteenth-century prehistory was much preoccupied by another debate, that of man's Tertiary ancestor, and here again Mortillet's evolutionist beliefs had a crucial influence. The naturalists Darwin and Haeckel were the first to tackle the question, but it soon stirred the interest of paleoanthropologists. The human fossil remains found in the nineteenth century—the Neanderthal calotte, the la Naulette mandible, and the skeletons of Cro-Magnon and Baoussé-Roussé—were discussed with reference to theories of evolution. It soon became clear that some of these remains had features that were distinct from modern human types. Some naturalists maintained that these were pathological features, but there were many who saw paleoanthropology as an excellent testing ground for transformism.

In this general context there emerged the debate over the existence of an intelligent human ancestor in the Tertiary period. The controversy was provoked by the discovery of incised bones and apparently worked flints in Tertiary soils. Most of these findings were quickly contested, but those of Abbé Bourgeois, who found flints in the Pliocene deposits of Saint-Prest (Loir-et-Cher) in 1867, seemed authentic to Mortillet and many of his contemporaries. However, they could not agree on the question of the maker of the flint. In the absence of any remains of human bones, they could merely speculate on the answer. For some who were skeptical of transformism, the intelligent being of the Tertiary had to be human, created by God in the beginning. This notion had its leading supporter in Armand de Quatrefages, professor at the Musée National d'Histoire Naturelle. It was not shared by Gabriel de Mortillet who, faithful to his strict concept of evolution, deduced from the flints the existence of a transitional creature between man and ape. The variation in fauna since the Tertiary period led him to think that the human species as it was today could not have been the same then. The flints of Thenay implied "the existence at this time of an intelligent being who preceded man and who must be seen as his precursor" (1873, 613). He wasted no time in giving a more precise description. This creature was the missing link between man and ape and so was awarded the name *anthropopithecus* (1878, 825). Mortillet's transformist beliefs thus enabled him to deduce, unaided by any empirical evidence, the appearance of the flint toolmaker of Thenay. For Mortillet this theoretical invention had all the credentials of truth. In his inflexible system he saw the anthropopithecus not as a "simple hypothesis" but rather as "a logical deduction, drawn from the direct observation of the facts" (1873, 613).

Thus an imaginary creature, the anthropopithecus, made its entry into nineteenth-century prehistoric scholarship. In his book, *Le préhistorique,* Mortillet devoted a great many pages to it. In fact, as a result of the three sites he considered utterly reliable, he went so far as to make out three species of anthropopitheci, distinguished both by culture and by geological epoch. To the *Anthropopithecus bourgeoisii* of Thenay, named after its finder, must be added the *Anthropopithecus ramesii,* whose remains had been discovered by Rames at Puy-Courny in Cantal in 1877, and the *Anthropopithecus ribeiroii,* excavated by Ribeiro at Otta in Portugal in 1871. The whole question of the anthropopithecus lost some of its topicality in the 1880s, when no new convincing sites were discovered. But Mortillet's position remained unwavering and had subscribers until 1894, when the debate on man's ancestors took a new direction with the discovery in Java of the *Pithecanthropus erectus* by Eugene Dubois. The appearance of these actual bones belied the theory of the anthropopithecus as the perfect link, for only the skull cap looked really primitive, while the teeth and the femur were like those of modern man. So the pithecanthropus replaced the anthropopithecus, destroying the concept of evolution promulgated by Mortillet and suggesting that the transformation of species was neither as linear nor as simple as the French prehistorian had thought.

Mortillet's philosophical beliefs had a strong impact on a third sphere, namely, the debate about prehistoric art and religion. He was absolutely certain that Paleolithic peoples were primitive, removed from modern people not just in time but because, as savages, they stood on a lower rung of the ladder of biological and cultural development. However, discoveries of art objects and funeral practices inevitably raised a few problems for a priori ideas about primitive beings. In 1864 Edouard Lartet and Henry Christy, those tireless explorers of the Vézère valley, published an account of the "engraved and sculpted objects of prehistoric times." They included several pieces, striking in their beauty, and stressed the difficulty of accepting these objects as "going back to such early times, given that these works of art do not sit well with the state of uncouth barbarism which we attribute to these aboriginal peoples" (Lartet and Christy 1864, 34). To answer this crucial objection, they suggested an interpretation of the art as a playful imitation of nature. Mortillet became one of the main supporters of this idea and composed lengthy descriptions of imitative works, praising their "very naive, but very authentic style" (1879, 233). He insisted particularly on the absence of any sense of composition, because that demonstrated the limitations of an artist who was incapable of "reflection or foresight" (1883, 420). In *Le préhistorique* he summarized his criticism in a phrase often cited—"the childhood of art is very far from being child art" (1883, 416). By this he meant that Magdalenian art was not a clumsy sketch done by an artist whose mind was comparable to that of a modern child, but rather that this art was perfect for its time and its naiveté reproduced the limits of its creator's mental faculties. The outcome of this debate for Mortillet was that Magdalenian art proved the barbarity of primitive man. He refused to see any symbolic value in it and denied the existence of anything abstract.

For several decades these notions of prehistoric art held sway, until they were undermined by various new discoveries, especially those concerning ritual Paleolithic funeral practices. The whole issue was revived in earnest when Louis Lartet, Edouard's son, discovered the burial sites at Cro-Magnon in 1868. He claimed that the human skeletons covered with ochre and wearing marine shell necklaces dated from early times. But Mortillet rejected this interpretation. In *Le préhistorique* in 1883 he maintained that the tools found in the cave were certainly Paleolithic but that the skeletons had been placed there in the Neolithic. He concluded that there was no proof at all of the existence of ritual burial practices in the Paleolithic. The debate took a further twist when human bones were found in the caves of Baoussé-Roussé, near Menton, in 1886. Despite Mortillet's skepticism, most of the prehistorians, with Emile Cartailhac at their head, eventually accepted the theory of prehistoric ritual cults, thus breaking down the equating of primitive with barbarian.

The link was abandoned for good when Paleolithic cave art was recognized. At first, the traces of this art seemed so incompatible with the prevailing views of Paleolithic man that the evidence was simply discounted. Such was the case of the caves at Altamira, where the Spaniard Marcelino de Sautuola discovered polychrome frescoes in 1878. In France the reaction was one of disbelief and silence. In fact only Emile Harlé, a paleontologist from Bordeaux, published an account of the discovery in *Les Matériaux* in 1881. He asserted that the frescoes must be recent, arguing that the techniques used to produce them were too skilled to be those of a Paleolithic artist. Mortillet, like his colleagues, adopted the same skeptical position and did not mention Altamira in *Le préhistorique*. Similarly, when Léopold Chiron, a teacher from the Ardèche, had written to him in 1879 to tell him about engravings discovered on the walls of the cave at Chabot, Mortillet had not even bothered to reply. Rock art, whose beauty, complexity, and frequent location in galleries deep below the earth's surface denoted a purpose other than imitation, remained totally ignored, for it was simply impossible to conceive of in a philosophical system of linear evolution and Paleolithic savages. The art was only really discovered (or rediscovered) at the end of the nineteenth century, when Emile Rivière presented a paper to the Académie des Sciences on the cave of la Mouthe. The general discussion on that occasion led to the conversion of the academic community. Mortillet, suffering from cataracts and semiretired from scientific life, did not take part. In his last article, however, written in 1898, he confessed that his beliefs had been swayed by the engravings of Pair-non-Pair, though he still maintained that its art was naive and refused to comment on the other finds.

Gabriel de Mortillet's death coincided with the collapse of the philosophical and ideological beliefs underlying his scientific thinking, not only on classification and man's earliest ancestor but also on art. Yet concluding on this note of ruin should not obscure the very significant role of his thought in the founding of prehistory in France. In key academic positions for half a century, Mortillet was both a great theoretician and the leader of a school. A controlling influence, he helped to train, through his writing and his teaching, a large proportion of the French prehistorians of the second generation.

The Founding of Prehistory

Traditionally, Jacques Boucher de Perthes is seen as the father of French prehistory, but the title should by rights be shared equally with Mortillet, whose ideas had a clearer influence on contemporary scholars and whose professional work helped to turn prehistory into a separate scientific discipline. He instigated the professional structure of the discipline, which for a time was called "palethnology" before it changed to "prehistory." In 1864 he founded a specialist journal, the first in Europe, under the title of *Matériaux pour l'histoire positive et philosophique de l'homme*. It was continued by the archaeologists Emile Cartailhac and Eugène Trutat in 1869 under a slightly different title and was published until 1888. Then it merged with the *Revue d'anthropologie* and the *Revue d'ethnographie* and took the name *Anthropologie*. For a while prehistory was without any specific review, but in 1904 it regained a specialist publication with the *Bulletins de la Société Préhistorique de France*.

Matériaux was launched with an obvious specialist aim. According to its outline of contents, it was to deal with "everything connected with the origin, the development, and the primitive history of man" (*Matériaux* 1864–1865, I:5). This definition corresponded originally to a field of research that was much broader than the scope of prehistory today, since it included human biology, geology, anthropology, and sometimes classical archaeology. The question of boundaries did not prevent *Matériaux* from defining a new discipline and providing it with an instrument of dialogue and dissemination. The precise circulation of the review is not easy to calculate, but the list of subscribers in 1870–1871 names 250 recipients, mostly from the provinces. Moreover, the total number of authors who had contributed to the review was 600, which gives sufficient proof that the publication was a real means of dialogue between scholars. The disappearance of *Matériaux* showed that its readership was too small to ensure its survival and, above all, that the public did not differentiate between it and journals on anthropology in general. The situation would be quite different with twentieth-century prehistorical publications.

Beside *Matériaux* there were other official channels that allowed the voice of prehistory to be heard in the nineteenth century. The Musée des Antiquités Nationales at Saint-Germain-en-Laye became, after its opening in 1867, a center for exhibitions and research. In 1862 Napoleon III decided to create a museum that would display the research on the conquest of the Gauls that he himself had carried out. The initial project was widened further with the inclusion of a collection of polished stone presented by the king of Denmark and the series of worked stone that Boucher de Perthes gave the emperor. When the museum finally opened, it was no longer merely Gallo-Roman but included a variety of national antiquities. By this date it already had more than twenty-five hundred prehistoric items that had to be classified. To carry out this task, Gabriel de Mortillet was named as conservator in 1868. He held this post for over twenty years and made the museum a showcase for his theoretical ideas. He cataloged the collections so as to prove the validity of his chronological classification scheme. The museum also had a specialist library, and the catalog drawn up in 1889 listed more than 7,500 entries. That the museum was a place of both exhibits and research was shown by its schedule, which divided the week into days open to the public and days reserved for study.

Equipped with a national museum and a journal, prehistory also had an international organization, which was due largely to Mortillet's initiative. In 1865 the Société Italienne des Sciences Naturelles instigated an international conference on prehistory. Mortillet was invited and was asked to give the opening address, in which he called for the creation of an international organization. The motion was put to a vote and carried unanimously. The first International Conference on Prehistoric Anthropology and Archaeology was held in Neuchâtel in 1866. It was followed by thirteen more meetings at varying intervals, with the last taking place in 1913 in Geneva. Mortillet played a vital role in these conferences, giving numerous papers and serving as a member of the permanent organizing committee. His influence determined the part that France played in the conferences, for Paris was the only European city in which the conference met more than once (in 1867, 1892, and 1906) and French was until 1913 the official language for the publication of the proceedings.

Although it was well organized, French prehistory was only partially institutionalized. Mortillet's activity did not extend to the formation of a national specialist society. Perhaps he thought that the international conference was adequate or preferable. Whatever the reason, he did not suggest another organization. When he was invited in 1893 to chair the first provincial specialist group, the Société Normande d'Études Préhistoriques, he did not seize the chance to propose a motion for a national society. Only after Mortillet's death would one appear.

Despite its professional trappings, the teaching of prehistory in nineteenth-century France left much to be desired. There were only isolated courses, sometimes free, sometimes included in the official curricula. Mortillet himself contributed to this fragmentation. He ran the prehistoric anthropology course at the Ecole d'Anthropologie, which was founded in 1876 with grants from the municipal and general councils of Paris and was awarded official recognition in 1889. Yet this establishment remained outside the university. Since it could not confer the state-recognized diploma, it could not help to train professional academics in prehistory. Although Mortillet was very concerned with education for the future, he apparently did not fight for the creation of a university degree course in prehistory.

Despite the incomplete institutionalization of prehistory in the nineteenth century, one should not regard its structure as a failure. Mortillet, working on all fronts simultaneously, managed to make his science a largely autonomous discipline, enjoying wide dissemination to a provincial audience and an unparalleled popularity in the last decades of the century.

References
Primary

Mortillet, G. de. 1849. *Politique et socialisme à la portée de tous.* Paris: Propagande Démocratique et Sociale, 12 pamphlets collected in 7 volumes.

————. 1869. "Essai d'une classification des cavernes et des stations sous abri, fondée sur les produits de l'industrie humaine." *Comptes rendus hebdomadaires des séances de l'Académie des Sciences* 58: 553–555.

————. 1872. "Classification des diverses périodes de l'age de la pierre." *Revue d'anthropologie* 1: 432–437.

————. 1873. "Le précurseur de l'homme." *Association Française pour l'Avancement des Sciences Lyon*: 607–613.

————. 1875. "Les études préhistoriques devant l'orthodoxie." *Revue d'anthropologie* 4: 116–129.

————. 1878. "La descendance de l'homme." *Association Française pour l'Avancement des Sciences Paris*: 823–825.

————. 1879 "Sur l'origine des animaux domestiques." *Matériaux,* 2d series, 10: 227–234.

————. 1883. *Le préhistorique, antiquité de l'homme.* Paris: C. Reinwald.

————. 1887. "L'église et la science." *L'homme* 4: 609–614.

————. 1889. *Les origines de la chasse, de la pêche et de l'agriculture.* Paris: Lecrosnier.

————. 1896. "La foi et la raison dans l'étude des sciences." *Revue de l'Ecole d'Anthropologie* 6: 1–14.

————. 1897a. "L'évolution quaternaire de la pierre." *Revue de l'Ecole d'Anthropologie* 7: 18–26.

————. 1897b. *La formation de la nation française, textes, linguistique, palethnologie, anthropologie.* Paris: F. Alcan.

Secondary

Breuil, Henri. 1907. *La question aurignacienne: Etude critique de stratigraphie comparée.* Paris: Vigot Frères.

Gran-Aymerich, E., and J. Gran-Aymerich. 1984. "Les grands archéologues: G. de Mortillet." *Archéologia*: 197.

Hublin, J. J. 1989. "Les paradoxes de l'anticléricalisme, le cas d'un mandarin." *Science et vie* 166: 150–153.

Junghans, G. 1987. *G. de Mortillet (1821–1898). Eine Biographie: Materiellen zur Darstellung seiner Ideen und Beitrage zur Erforschung von Ursprung und Geschichte des Menschen.* Bonn: Habelt.

Lartet, E., and H. Christy. 1864. *Cavernes du Périgord. Objets gravés et sculptés des temps préhistoriques.* Paris: Librairie Académique, Didier et Cie.

———. 1886. "Mathias Duval et le dîner du matérialisme scientifique." *L'homme* 3: 25–28.

Reinach, S. 1899. *Gabriel de Mortillet.* Nogent-le Rotrou, Impr. Daupeley-Gouverneur, extract from *Revue historique.*

Richard, N. 1989. "La revue *L'homme* de Gabriel de Mortillet, anthropologie et politique au début de la troisième république." *Bulletins et mémoires de la Société D'Anthropologie de Paris,* n. s., 1, 3–4: 231–257.

———. 1989. "Le temps transformiste de G. de Mortillet." In *Le temps de la préhistoire,* Société Préhistorique Française, Archéologia, Dijon, 1: 10–11.

———. 1991. "L'anthropopithèque de Gabriel de Mortillet: Le débat sur l'ancêtre de l'homme au XIXe siècle." *Les nouvelles de l'archéologie* 44: 23–29.

Leo Klejn

Heinrich Schliemann   *1822–1890*

Treasure hunter, popularizer, and fraud, Heinrich Schliemann was hardly a model archaeologist. However, the fabulous Bronze Age sites that he dug up endowed archaeology with a popularity and fascination among the general public that it maintains to this day. Schliemann's enormous contribution to archaeology is as contentious as ever.

Heinrich Schliemann is the most famous of all archaeologists. He excavated Homer's Ilios and the legendary towns of ancient Greece—Mycenae, Orchomenos, Tiryns. A romantic myth, woven by Schliemann himself, surrounds his well-known life story. He first sketched a fair account of his autobiography in his book *Ithaka* (1869), but by the time he wrote the preface of *Ilios* (1881), he had moved to deliberate fantasy. The majority of authors who took Schliemann as their subject (e.g., Seiffert 1913; Payne 1959; Ludwig 1969) represented him as a grasping gold-digger, as did most reporters during his lifetime. To disprove these accounts, his widow, Sofia Schliemann, authorized Alfred Bruckner (Schliemann 1892) to supplement her husband's legend with additional information from other works; this expanded "autobiography" became the standard description of Schliemann's life, with a ninth edition appearing in 1961. Ernst Meyer, who was Schliemann's most reliable biographer (1936; 1969), and Heinrich A. Stoll, the author of a novel about Schliemann (1957), both accepted the myth. A small volume by Russian author D. N. Egorov (1923) was probably the most perspicacious analysis until recently, when a critical biography, based on intensive documentary research, was written by W. Calder and D. A. Trail (1986).

Schliemann himself left a huge literary heritage—10 books, 150 volumes of diary manuscripts, and 60,000 letters in twenty languages. Only a small portion of letters have been published (two volumes edited by Meyer [1953, 1958] and one by Stoll [1958]). Articles about Schliemann are extraordinarily numerous. The bibliography compiled in 1974 by G. Korres in Greece lists about 2,300 publications. Thus, despite an abundance of documentary material, the public has given unquestioning credence to the Schliemann myth for over a century.

According to the myth, Schliemann, the son of an impoverished pastor, received as a boy a Christmas gift from his father—a book about

Heinrich Schliemann. (Reprinted from Ward Briggs, ed., Classical Scholarship: A Biographical Encyclopedia, *1990)*

the fall of Troy. Struck by the pictures of its conflagration, he promised his father that when he grew up, he would excavate the ancient city. He also made the same pledge to Minna, a neighbor's daughter whom he loved at that time. They dreamed of excavating Troy together. The rest of his life was devoted to accumulating enough money to make good his pledge.

As the story goes, Heinrich knocked about the world, worked hard, and sacrificed for the sake of his dream. Meanwhile, Minna married someone else. It took forty years, but Heinrich amassed millions, went to Turkey, found and excavated Troy, and proved the reality of Homer's stories to scholarly skeptics. The self-taught amateur disgraced the academic professionals. He discovered the ancient fortress, the hoard of King Priam, and the adornments of the beautiful Helen on the hill Hissarlik. He dismissed his thieving workers in order to keep the precious artifacts from being pillaged. He married a beautiful Greek woman, Sofia, and they valiantly continued the excavation together. On a momentous day, the pair brushed the dirt from gold vessels and a diadem. Sofia wrapped the great treasure in her shawl and secreted them in the cabin where they lived.

Not all of the story is fiction, for the Iliad certainly existed, and there was a picture book of Troy. As a boy, Schliemann had a playmate named Minna, and he corresponded with her even in old age. Sofia was also real, as was Schliemann's fortune, which enabled him to undertake excavations at Ilios. And he did indeed find gold within its walls. However, at the beginning of the nineteenth century, a provincial German boy could not guess that the remains of Troy were underground and would require excavation. At that time, only Pompeii and Herculaneum had been uncovered. Schliemann's life was not shaped by his desire to study ancient towns—indeed, he was middle-aged before he became interested in it. The decision to excavate was made even later. Finally, far from being a self-taught "amateur," he had attended the Sorbonne.

It is difficult to say whether he found the great treasure while excavating or whether the individual precious objects had been found at different times and had been set aside for secret and illegal removal from Turkey. The objects were not mentioned in his diaries. From their correspondence, we know that his wife was not with him at the time. The town that he excavated was not Troy but classical Ilios, as proven by the inscriptions on stones found at the site. The town was apparently from the same period as the Trojan War and had the same powerful walls and topography attributed to Troy. However, Hittite sources referred to another and different town. Indeed, it is not absolutely certain that the Trojan War actually occurred, despite Schliemann's conviction that it had. The fact remains that although he did not find what he expected to find, it was a discovery of great moment. This makes his real story much more interesting than the mythical life he so successfully created.

On 6 January 1822, in the small village of Ankershagen (Mecklenburg, North Germany), a son was born to Ernst Schliemann, a minister. The boy was named Johann Ludwig Julius, or simply Julius, but several years later when his elder brother Heinrich died, Julius was renamed in his memory. Although he claimed an early passion for archaeology, his sister remembered that becoming a sailor was his childhood dream. He even carved, "Heinrich Schliemann, Matros" (sailor), on a wicket in the garden of their house. His mother died when he was nine, and after his father was prosecuted for debt, the boy was sent to live at Kalkhorst (near Lubeck) with his uncle, who was also a pastor. Health and financial problems disrupted his schooling, and he spent five and a half years as a shopkeeper's apprentice. His character, his view of the world, and his understanding of human relations were formed in that little store. One day he hurt his back lifting a heavy barrel and had to quit his position. Moving to Hamburg, he found employment on a ship headed for Venezuela; thus he realized his youthful ambition of becoming a sailor. In December 1841 the brig was wrecked near Holland, but the crew was safely brought to shore. Schliemann remained in Holland, worked as a postman, and began to study languages on his own—English, French, Dutch, and Greek. His command over languages proved advantageous, and by 1844 the twenty-two-year-old Schliemann had a well-paid job as a correspondent in the large commercial firm of Schroders. The firm traded with Russia, so Schliemann quickly began learning this language. According to legend, he mastered an archaic form of the language. His spoken Russian employed old-fashioned expressions, but even with these idiosyncrasies, he was able to make personal contact with Russian businessmen. In January 1841 Schliemann was sent to Petersburg as the firm's agent. The following year, he opened his own business in Russia, which was based on the resale of indigo, and registered himself as a merchant in Petersburg.

Meanwhile, the gold rush in the western United States had enticed his younger brother Ludwig to California, where he disappeared. In 1849 Heinrich Schliemann went to save his brother for the sake of his sisters, but he also used the opportunity to make some quick money in California. By opening a change office (a gold to money conversion service) near the goldfields, he was able to double his fortune in one year. Nevertheless, he came back to Russia, preferring the stability of Nicholas I's regime to the wild west. Schliemann considered himself quite Russian and often referred in his diary to "my beloved Russia." Upon his return he registered as a merchant in Narva, a small town near the western frontier, since his goods were passing through that border.

In 1852 he married Ekaterina Lyzhina. He told his relatives that she was eighteen years old and that theirs was a love-match, but in truth she was twenty-six and had consented to marry Schliemann only after much persuasion and for the sake of his money. She had three of his children— a son and two daughters. During the Crimean War Schliemann was involved in smuggling munitions into Russia, particularly saltpeter and sulfur for powder and lead for bullets. He made enormous profits.

In the late 1850s Schliemann experienced some shocks that forced him to question the direction of his life. A fire swept through his storehouse in Memel, destroying a considerable part of his capital. A commercial crisis in 1857 also affected his financial security. Although Schliemann weathered the financial storms, he began to think that wealth was too transitory and insecure to be the sum total of one's life. He turned his mind to scholarly activity and traveling, and to fame.

The epoch of great archaeological discoveries had already begun. The excavation of Nineveh and its ruins (1848, 1849) had made the Englishman Austen Henry Layard famous, and at age thirty-one, he was granted an honorary doctorate by Oxford University and became chancellor of the University of Aberdeen. Sir Henry Rawlinson discovered and deciphered the Behistun inscription in Persia and was granted a doctorate and noble rank. Auguste Mariette, who excavated the Serapeum (a major Pharaonic site) and the Sphinx in Egypt, was given the title of Bey by the Turkish sultan. Fame could also be had at home. In Russia, scholarly travels to Siberia, the Urals, and the Volga basin had been the primary means of acquiring geographic, ethnographic, and archaeological knowledge in the eighteenth century and the first half of the nineteenth century. In these new journeys scholars traveled to the Crimea and to New Russia (Novorossia) and the books about such journeys were tremendously popular.

By 1856 Schliemann's fortune had risen to one million talers (approximately equivalent to rubles at that time), and the first signs that he wished to change the way he lived his life began to appear in his letters and diaries. He thought of giving commerce up and concerning himself with science. He began to study Latin and Greek, and through this he formed a friendship with instructors from the university and the high schools. It was Schliemann's first entry into an academic community. A variety of new goals surfaced in his diary notes: making long journeys to distant places, from Greece to Brazil; studying languages, philosophy, archaeology, and Homer; obtaining his own estate in the country; living in a university town in Germany. Troy was not mentioned.

In 1859 Schliemann left Russia to travel extensively. His route did not accord with his later claim that he was seeking Troy, given the fact that he visited Scandinavia, Germany, Italy, Egypt, Palestine, Syria, Greece, and the Cyclades. He began to doubt his decision to make a fresh start. A lawsuit over property recalled him to Russia, and he returned to the commercial world with a vengeance. Soon he doubled his fortune to more than 2 million talers. He left Petersburg to travel again, but this time his itinerary was transglobal: Africa, India, Java, China, Japan, and the United States. His first published work (impressions of his voyage) subsequently appeared in a Petersburg magazine. In 1866 he returned briefly to Russia to travel in the south. The following year, he published a travel book about his visit to China and Japan.

Then, at the age of forty-four, Schliemann became a student at the Sorbonne in Paris. He was later to claim that during this time he "gave himself up to archaeology," but documents and letters testify that he exaggerated. He studied the humanities in general—French poetry of the sixteenth century, Arabic language and poetry, Greek philosophy and literature, Petrarch and his travels, Egyptian archaeology and philology. While in the thick of his studies in 1868 Schliemann decided to visit the places in Greece and Turkey mentioned by Homer. He took the same route as Odysseus—to Corfu, Cephalonia, and Italy, then to Peloponnese, Mycenae, Turkey, and the straits where Troy was said to be. He even made small excavations in Ithaca, which indicates that Ithaca, not Troy, was the focus of his attention. This voyage differed from his earlier travels in that he now had the benefit of a university education; moreover, the sites of Homer's Greece were obscure and mysterious and seemed to intrigue him and to demand further investigation.

By the late 1850s, the discussions about the authenticity and unity of Homer's poems, which had begun at the end of the eighteenth century, were in full swing. Some scholars upheld the unity of the text, while others admitted large interpolations or believed that Homer contributed the kernel of an idea developed by later singers. Another viewpoint was that Homer's poem was a collection of songs about separate heroes, making Homer a compiler. The authenticity of the events represented in the poem also had a mixed reception. Those who contended for the gradual or piecemeal development of the text would naturally regard many details as invented, but proponents of the unity of the poem also disagreed about authenticity. A single author could resort to fiction as easily as many.

Schliemann did not accept with enthusiasm everything he heard at the university. Some convictions formed earlier were already unchangeable, and he used his new knowledge to support these deeply rooted ideas. In particular, he had an unshakable faith in the sacred reality of Homer and accepted no criticism of the text. Schliemann's next book, *Ithaka, Peloponnes, and Troy,* was written immediately after his Odyssean voyage and was published in 1868 in both French and German. Dr. R. Hercher of Berlin University had visited Ithaca two years before Schliemann and strongly doubted the reality of the events related by Homer. He declared that anybody "who wants to fix Homer's Ithaka with maps and plans" would end in a muddle. In his book Schliemann intended to do just that, but his minimal excavations had yielded no indisputable evidence. Even so, Schliemann rejected the conclusions of almost all his predecessors concerning the location of Troy—that it was the modern Balli Dag. Schliemann was persuaded that it was at Hissarlik. He also reinterpreted Greek historian Pausanius regarding the graves of Agamemnon and his retinue in Mycenae, arguing that they were situated not outside the citadel but inside. In *Ithaka* Schliemann wrote with aplomb about "mistakes of all the archaeologists."

Schliemann expected the book to cause a sensation and a storm of objections. But its effect was more modest. He submitted the book as a thesis to the University of Rostock in his native Mecklenburg, and while the review board was unimpressed by his discussions about the location of Troy, they awarded him his doctorate.

By this time, Schliemann's Russian wife did not want to live with him but would not agree to divorce him. In 1869, he went to the United States (he had recently gained American citizenship), where divorces were simpler. Then a Russian friend, the Greek Orthodox archbishop Theolekletos Vimpos, found the perfect new bride for Schliemann. She was young, beautiful, and Greek, she adored Homer, and she was Vimpos's relative. Out of this eccentric mésalliance developed a successful marriage. Sofia Kastriotis (Engastromenos) became the companion and comrade of her elderly, ambitious, and energetic husband.

In 1870 Schliemann arrived at Hissarlik, the small Turkish village that he had been persuaded by Frank Calvers during his earlier trip to the region was the location of Homer's Troy. In 1871 he began the first archaeological season under incredibly difficult conditions. He had to suffer cold winds, malaria, thieves, and corrupt local officials. Yet even more annoying was the unpleasant discovery that while inside the hill he found a great many antiquities, such as stone axes and clay crocks, he did not find any bronze armor from Homer's heroes. Schliemann was reduced to despair. He had already declared publicly that he had found Troy, but there was no evidence to support his claim. Schliemann stubbornly pressed on, digging deeper into the hill day after day, month after month. He returned to Hissarlik the next year, engaged hundreds of laborers, and continued to excavate. After 1872 he shifted his strategy from the complete removal of the hill to a more conservative approach of cutting through the hill with a wide trench from the north to the south. It was a crude undertaking, as everything in the upper layers was pulled out without first making a detailed record, drawings, or analysis. Schliemann was looking for the subsoil, since he believed that the Trojan War had occurred at the start of European history. Therefore the palace of Priam had to lie deep below the surface.

In July 1872 he came upon a huge wall of large stones. Schliemann was ecstatic—here at last was the Trojan wall! The next year, "Priam's hoard," or "the great Trojan treasure," was found at the very end of the season. The romantic legend put into circulation by Schliemann (he and Sofia working alone to prevent thievery, Sofia hiding the treasure with her shawl, and so on) was connected to this discovery. Yet the event was not marked in his diaries, and the dates and the location of the find differed in the few accounts of it that exist. Schliemann's bodyguard and assistant Nikolaus Yannakis later published his evidence (confirmed by Schliemann's own correspondence) that Sofia was not in Hissarlik then. In Yannakis's version, it was he, not Sofia, who was with Schliemann when the discovery was made.

It seems clear today that the objects were found in several different places and that they were assembled by Schliemann in order to conceal them from the Turks and remove them from Turkey without notifying the government. Schliemann's permit initially stated that one-half of the excavated objects were to be left in Turkey. This was subsequently changed to a total prohibition against exporting any cultural material from the site. Schliemann, an experienced smuggler, took everything. Officials in Athens began proceedings against him, and the court returned a guilty verdict, but the sentence was only a small fine. Schliemann paid the fine five times over and with this gesture mollified the Turkish government.

Schliemann now used his hoard as proof to support his claim that he had just uncovered Homer's Troy. This being achieved, he declared that he was abandoning the project *auf immer* (forever). What he did not realize then was that the objects found were a thousand years more ancient than the supposed date of the Trojan War (the thirteenth century B.C.)

and that, in getting to them, he had destroyed buildings from the time glorified by Homer. Soon he was obliged to write: "Because of my former erroneous idea that Troy was to stand on the subsoil, in 1871 and 1872, to my regret I destroyed the considerable part of the city, as I broke unmercifully all the buildings of the upper layers" *(The Trojan Antiquities, 1874, 309)*. This book on the Trojan excavations was published in three versions—German, French, and English—with 218 photos and an atlas in quarto. Schliemann changed the location of Homer's city from the subsoil to the burnt layer, which was the third from the bottom according to his numbering of the layers. (In fact, the burnt city turned out to be part of the second layer from the bottom.)

The Trojan Antiquities contained other admissions. Schliemann confessed that Troy was apparently not as large as Homer had depicted. "It grieves me extremely, of course, to give such small dimensions; I would like to make them a thousand times larger, but the truth must be first of all. Homer was an epic poet, he wasn't a historian, and that's quite natural that he exaggerated everything in his poetic license." With this statement Schliemann moved away from being an amateur to becoming a scholar, although he had much further to go and still frequently retreated to unscientific analysis and tactics. In 1876 Schliemann visited the Olympia excavations being carried out by Ernst Curtius, where the most up-to-date excavation methods were being developed and applied. According to one source, Schliemann looked at the site, grimaced, and said: "These gentlemen do everything the wrong way round. They take away layer by layer. In such manner they will waste time and money infinitely. One needs to dig deep down straight away, then one will find." Objects were his primary aim, and he thought nothing of stratigraphy.

Blunders from the first campaign continued to come to light. In 1877, at the exhibition of Trojan finds in London, one observer noted pick damage to three vases found near Priam's hoard. He asked Schliemann, "How could you allow working with a pick at such an important place?" Schliemann replied: "My navvies always excavated with a pick when the soil was hard, and at the moment I might be absent from the place." Recollecting this dialogue, Schliemann added: "The answer was true, but . . .I realized that I had committed a foolish slip." But Schliemann could learn from his mistakes as well as from his colleagues. His biographer Egorov remarked that due to that episode, Schliemann experienced the important difference "between the most fervent personal initiative and the collective experience characteristic for men of science" (1923, 86).

After his Trojan discoveries, Schliemann felt compelled to test his mettle at Mycenae, the other city "full of gold." He had already announced

Schliemann's excavations at the Acropolis of Mycenae. (Corbis-Bettmann)

several years earlier his revision of the traditional account of Mycenae by Pausanius, and in 1876 that intuition guided Schliemann to select a site for excavation within the citadel. (It turned out later that the most ancient graves were in fact outside the citadel.) Schliemann's trenches soon produced graves and grave obelisks from within a stone circle edging the royal burial vault. The graves were packed with gold. More than one hundred pounds of artifacts, including masks, diadems, goblets, and ornaments, were recovered. The other objects were a match for the artifacts: gold, gem encrusted bronze swords, silver perfume bottles, and painted earthenware vessels. Unfortunately, many mistakes were made here as well. Schliemann did not keep diaries and field notes. Only Panagions Stamatakis, an official appointed by the Greek Antiquities Preservation Service as sentinel, kept brief records despite Schliemann's resistance. Stamatakis objected to Schliemann's approach of destroying more recent monuments in order to reach the older ones, and he insisted on stabilizing them. Even so, obelisks were removed from their places marking specific graves before their precise location had been documented.

Schliemann believed that he had found the graves of Agamemnon and his retinue, and he ceased excavation when the number of skeletons recovered equaled the number of heroes from Mycenae mentioned by Homer. After Schliemann's departure, Stamatakis excavated one more grave and thus undermined this theory. The graves proved to be about three centuries older than the period traditionally established for

Agamemnon and the Trojan War. But Schliemann never admitted this. Repeated questions about whether the gold mask really belonged to Agamemnon drew his derisive response: "Who else would be in that grave?" Schliemann's version of the undertaking, *Mycenae* (1878), was produced in three languages and was written in a more scholarly style than *The Trojan Antiquities*. There were, for example, few emotional asides about how the reality of the excavation did not correspond to the poetry of Homer.

In 1878 he visited Ithaca again, this time as an experienced archaeologist, but he found neither the palace of Odysseus nor Laertes' fields. In fact, he failed to see anything of great antiquity and subsequently abandoned the idea of further excavation on the island. In July he applied to return to Hissarlik. Too many errors had been made during his excavations there, and he intended to rectify these with new, more methodical and systematic excavations and to place the artifacts at the disposal of the archaeological community. (He had paid the "debt" resulting from the stolen treasures to the Turkish government.) Emile Burnouf, a well-known French archaeologist, worked with him at Hissarlik, and their two-year campaign produced a book, *Ilios: The City and Country of Trojans,* published in 1881. Schliemann included an appendix of archaeological essays by archaeologists Rudolf Virchow, J. P. Mahaffy, and A. H. Sayce, which discussed a wide range of topics. Though he returned to Troy at the head of a large team, Schliemann was determined to conduct the excavations personally and keep the glory for himself. At a dinner party one evening, he gave a toast that expressed his philosophy: To the proverb "shared joy is double joy, shared grief is half-a-grief," he added, "shared work is not work." In reality he needed as much help as he could get.

Contacts with Rudolf Virchow, the leading authority in German prehistoric archaeology, were especially significant for Schliemann. They had first become acquainted in 1875, during discussions over the vessels with faces (in Schliemann's view, images of owl-eyed Athena) found at Hissarlik. Virchow's studies of the face-urns of Pomerania led him to interpret the Trojan vessels as analogous funeral urns. As they corresponded they became friends.

In 1879 Virchow arrived at Hissarlik and remained with Schliemann for a month, though they stayed in contact after that. From Virchow, Schliemann learned to report results in a systematic manner, to exercise prudence, and to limit his conclusions to a few and well-supported ones. Virchow's archaeological principles were based on his anthropological premises; in brief, he was committed to the stability of all forms of life and to the denial of the evolutionary origin of species. Hence, despite his beneficial influence on Schliemann, he also gave Schliemann some erroneous ideas.

During this second Hissarlik excavation, Schliemann became especially perturbed by criticism from journalists and some archaeologists. He was particularly offended by his depiction as a lucky gold-digger, a man only incidentally involved in scholarly pursuits. In response, he constructed his mythical autobiography, which endowed him with a romantic aura and ascribed to him an inborn passion and respect for the discovery of the past.

In 1880 Schliemann transferred his activity back to Greece again—to Orchomenos, where the legendary King Minias and the Minyan people had lived. Homer had described only three cities as abundant in gold: Troy, Mycenae, and Orchomenos. Schliemann's reasons for digging at Orchomenos are clear enough, but there was another incentive. Before beginning the project, he again visited Olympia, where Wilhelm Dorpfeld, a young architect and a secretary at the German Archaeological Institute in Athens, took Schliemann around the site, causing him to realize how useful an architect could be during the excavation of an ancient city whose conglomeration of walls had been built at different times. However, Orchomenos did not justify his hopes, for the so-called tomb of Minias had been robbed long ago. As it turned out, however, Schliemann's luck still held. He discovered a new type of pottery in Orchomenos, which he named Minian ware. Many scholars now associate this pottery with the first appearance of the ancestors of the Greeks in Greece.

In 1882 Schliemann began the third season of excavations in Hissarlik. This time he was joined by his new assistant Dorpfeld, who quickly sorted out the stratigraphy of the walls and when they had been built. He rectified Schliemann's mistake with the burnt layer, attributing it to the second rather than third layer from the bottom. Dorpfeld also discovered a continuation of the city in a valley outside the walls, restoring for Schliemann the idea of a "large Troy" and the citadel as "Pergamus." All this was published in the book *Troia* (1884).

In 1884 Schliemann was back excavating in Greece again. Over the next two years he dug at Tiryns, the home of Heracles and Diomedes. Tiryns represented the same culture as neighboring Mycenae but was much better preserved, and the purpose of these excavations was not the discovery of treasure but the development of a clearer picture of Mycenaean culture. "The new world begins here," Schliemann proclaimed, and the plan of the powerful fortress-palace, with its towers, frescos, and pillars, was published in the book *Tiryns* (1885).

In subsequent years Schliemann reflected less on the rehabilitation and confirmation of Homer and more on the civilization that came to light through Homer's epic. There was even the possibility of several civilizations, as the influence of other cultures became apparent in the

Greek world. Something alien to Greek simplicity was revealed in the gorgeous splendor of gold articles, some other tradition was present in the methods of embalming, the chimerical pictures, and fresco painting. For Schliemann it was the influence of the Orient. He traveled to Egypt to see the museums and monuments and searched for Phoenician settlements. Driven by tremendous intuition, Schliemann traveled to Crete and even tried to organize excavations in Knossos! It is an irony in the history of archaeology that the owners of the land asked an exorbitant price, and on that occasion the merchant Schliemann silenced the scholarly Schliemann. The bargain was not resolved, and it was left to Sir ARTHUR EVANS to discover Cretan civilization.

In 1890 a heated argument drew Schliemann back to Hissarlik. Since 1883 a retired captain named Tim Ernst Botticher, amateur archaeologist, had been publishing essays critical of the identification of Hissarlik with Troy. He asserted that, according to available materials, Troy was not a city but a necropolis where the dead had been cremated. He accused Schliemann of intentionally destroying and concealing evidence that would contradict his conclusions. At first Schliemann responded curtly, but Botticher continued his attacks and found other problems with analyses by Schliemann and Dorpfeld. For example the position of the original fortress could not have been on the hill, since the hill was made up of a succession of settlements, but on the plain. Scholars who were already dubious about Schliemann's archaeological competency began to think that Botticher might be right.

In 1889, Schliemann, now sixty-five years old, rushed to Paris to the Anthropological Congress, at which Botticher was giving a paper. Schliemann spoke at the congress and invited Botticher, and anybody who wished, to visit Hissarlik at his expense for a special investigation of the disputed places. The visit took place in December but Botticher did not admit that Schliemann was correct. Schliemann then scheduled a bigger conference for March 1890 and, with Dorpfeld, began excavating at Hissarlik. Archaeologists came from England, France, Germany, and the United States at the appointed time, and concluded that Schliemann was right. In conjunction with the conference, Schliemann had arranged with his Leipzig publisher, Brockhaus, to produce a well-illustrated book in which the results of all the Hissarlik excavations would be surveyed in a scholarly but popular manner by a reputable independent specialist. Virchow advised them to enlist a young but already experienced German archaeologist, Carl Schuchhardt, who knew the classical and prehistoric archaeology of Europe. The result was the book *Schliemann's Excavations at Troy* (1891).

Schliemann continued excavating until the end of July. Then he

Schliemann presents his findings to a packed hall. (Library of Congress)

traveled to Germany for surgery to removed bony growths from the auditory canals in his ears. Further visits to medical specialists in Halle and Paris continued the treatment, but on Christmas Day 1890 he collapsed on a street in Naples and died the next day. Before he had completely healed, he had caught a cold, and the inflammation spread quickly to his brain. He fell unconscious and died in a hotel soon after, on 26 December 1890.

All of high society, including the king of Greece, was present at his burial in Athens. A bust of Homer was placed at the head of the gravesite. The Schliemann children, bearing the Homeric names Andromache and Agamemnon, stood by his coffin. The words *To the hero Schliemann* were inscribed in Greek on the sublime tombstone. An international man, he was born German, made his fortune and his home in Russia for about twenty years, studied in France, had an American passport, was a honorary doctor of Oxford University—but he idolized and lived in Greece and died in Italy.

The fate of the Trojan Collection was the result of Schliemann's will. During his life, the final destination of the collection had changed from year to year. At first Schliemann intended to return the artifacts to Greece, but he resented the Greek Archaeological Society. Schliemann then decided to build a museum in his native Mecklenburg and to house the collection there. But in 1872 he changed his mind because the duke of Mecklenburg had not answered his letter outlining the offer. Schliemann considered transferring the collection to Italy in exchange for the right to excavate in Sicily, but he dropped this plan and decided to sell the collection to the British Museum. British officials hesitated—the prospect of a quarrel with Turkey, which was involved in litigation with Schliemann at the time, gave them cold feet. So he toyed with the idea of having the Louvre purchase the artifacts. When it was apparent that the French were in no hurry to accept the proposal, Schliemann's friends, particularly Virchow, persuaded him to consider Germany as the collection's final resting place.

At the same time Schliemann was secretly in contact with Russian officials. He agreed to sell his collection to the Hermitage museum in Petersburg for half its worth, "for I have made my fortune in Russia." Another reason for the largesse was that he wanted to excavate in Kolchis, on the Black Sea in Russia, where the Argonauts had found the golden fleece. But the Czar disapproved of the Hermitage discussions. Schliemann's civil divorce in the United States was not recognized in Russia; thus, according to the Orthodox Church, he was a bigamist and a criminal in Russia. With these negotiations at a dead end, Schliemann agreed to Virchow's recommendation and in 1881 made out his will transferring the Trojan Collection to the "German people" forever.

Toward the end of World War II part of the Trojan collection perished, and Priam's hoard vanished. There were many conjectures about its fate—that soldiers had ransacked it, or fire had destroyed it, or it had been transported to the United States. Fifty years later, the hoard was found in Moscow where it had been taken by Soviet troops. Whether or not the treasures will be returned to Germany is a matter of debate. One group contends that the artifacts are compensation for Russian losses during the war, while another counters that its removal was not registered officially as reparations.

Opinions about Schliemann's importance to archaeology differ widely. One position is that he laid down "the foundations of the correct archaeological method" (Casson 1939, 221). Others believe that he was "the utter antagonist of any scientific method and had not the slightest idea that such method and the worked out technique existed at all" (Michaelis 1908, 217). Many thought him mad, others though him a treasure-hunter.

Schliemann can be accused of many faults: arrogant naiveté, in that he began excavating without any training or experience; precipitate identifications; a lack of historical awareness; fanaticism; improvidence in destroying "unimportant" layers; and a general carelessness about organizing and preserving a record of his excavations. What compounds this judgment is that his endeavors occurred after Fiorelli's careful excavation of Pompeii, after Newton's work at Halicarnassus, and at the same time Ernst Curtius was brilliantly excavating Olympia. The Achaeans did not destroy Troy; Schliemann did.

While admitting these defects, there are two extenuating points. First, despite these models of excellent excavation technique, the vast majority of archaeologists had operated much the same way that Schliemann did. At this stage in the development of archaeology, there were not many places where the novice could receive training in the skills of proper excavation. Schliemann had attended the Sorbonne, consulted with Frank Calvert and Emile Burnouf, visited Olympia many times, and enlisted skilled collaborators. The second point is thus related to the first: Schliemann was not unaware of advances and often tried to gain insight from his errors. His successor at Hissarlik, Carl Blegen, remarked that Schliemann "learned by his own mistakes, and he succeeded very much in that" (1963, 26–27).

Schliemann did not understand the stratigraphy at Hissarlik, but then no one did until Blegen's work in the twentieth century. Moreover, since at that time Homeric antiquities were thought to mark the beginning of classical archaeology, it was unlikely that any archaeologist could have conceived of any prehistoric culture and therefore accurately interpreted the significance of the site. Schliemann erred in his identification of the shaft graves at Mycenae, believing them to be linked to Agamemnon and his followers, but more experienced professional scholars made even more shocking blunders, such as declaring the gold of Mycenae as Byzantine or from the Huns.

After enumerating Schliemann's flaws, it is necessary to recognize his merits. First and foremost, he discovered the Trojan and Mycenaean civilizations at Ilios, Mycenae, Orchomenos, and Tiryns. Before this scholars doubted their existence, and the unearthing of that world was indeed one of the great moments of archaeology. Because of it, Homer's epic poetry and mythology became sources of historical information. Schliemann enriched Greek history by bringing another two thousand years into the historic record, and his findings linked classical, oriental, and prehistoric archaeologies in a new way. His excavations were the first to be conducted on a very complex site, and he, together with Dorpfeld, developed and introduced into field methodology the conception of a building level as the architectural frame of a cultural layer. And, long before archaeologist WILLIAM FLINDERS PETRIE, Schliemann began to determine the age of structures according to the kind of ceramics found at the same level. This was not new to prehistoric archaeology, but Schliemann was the first to employ it in the classical field.

Finally, Schliemann brought an enormous amount of public attention to archaeology and raised the profile of the discipline through his discoveries, his publications, and his extraordinary success.

References
Primary
Schliemann, Heinrich. 1869. *Ithaka. Peloponnese and Troy.* Leipzig.

———. 1874. *Trojanische Alterthumer.* Leipzig: Brockhaus (in English, *Troy and Its Remains.* London: John Murray, 1875); attached: *Atlas Tojanischer Alterthumer.* Leipzig: Brockhaus, 1874.

———. 1878. *Mycenae. A Narrative of Researches and Discoveries at Mycenae and Tiryns.* London: John Murray.

———. 1881. *Ilios. The City and Country of Trojans.* New York: Harrers and Brothers.

———. 1881. *Orchomenos.* Leipzig: Brockhaus.

———. 1884. *Troja.* London: John Murray.

———. 1886. *Tiryns.* New York: Chas. Scribner's Sons, 1885; London: John Murray.

———. 1890. *Bericht über die Ausgrabungen in Troja im Jahre 1890.* Leipzig: Brockhaus.

———. 1892. *Heinrich Schliemann Selbstbiographie, bis zu seinem Tode vervollstandigt.* Ed. S. Schliemann and Alfred Bruckner. Leipzig: Brockhaus.

———. 1936. *Briefe von Heinrich Schliemann.* Ed. Ernst Meyer. Berlin–Leipzig: Walter de Gruyter.

———. 1953, 1958. *Heinrich Schliemann—Briefwechsel,* 2 vols. Ed. Ernst Meyer. Berlin: Mann.

Secondary
Calder, William M., III, and David A. Traill. 1986. *Myth, Scandal and History: The Heinrich Schliemann Controversy and a First Edition of the Mycenaean Diary.* Detroit: Wayne State University Press.

Casson, Stanley. 1939. *The Discovery of Man: The Story of an Inquiry into Human Origins.* New York: Harper.

Dorpfeld, Wilhelm. 1902. *Troja und Ilion*. Vols. 1–2. Athens: Beck und Barth.

Meyer, Ernst. 1969. *Heinrich Schliemann, Kaufmann und Forscher*. Gottingen: Musterschmidt.

Michaelis, A. 1908. *A Century of Archaeological Discoveries*. Trans. B. Kahnweiler. London: John Murray.

Schuchhardt, C. 1891. *Schliemann's Excavations. An Archaeological and Historical Study*. London: Brockhaus.

Traill, David. 1995. *Schliemann of Troy: Treasure or Deceit*. New York: St. Martin's.

Biographical Documentary Novels

Egorov, D. N. 1923. *Genrikh Shliman*. St. Petersburg: Brokgauz-Efron.

Ludwig, E. 1969. *Schliemann, Kaufmann und Forscher*. Gottingen: Musterschmidt.

Payne, Robert. 1959. *The Gold of Troy*. London: Hale.

Poole, Lynn, and Gray Poole. 1966. *One Passion, Two Loves*. New York: Crowell.

Seiffert, O. 1913. *Heinrich Schliemann, der Schatzgraber*. Berlin: H. Pactel.

Stoll, Heinrich A. 1957. *Der Traum von Troja. Lebensroman Heinrich Schliemanns*. Leipzig: List.

Mark Bowden

Augustus Pitt Rivers   *1827–1900*

Described as "the first scientific British archaeologist," Augustus Pitt Rivers argued that the whole context of an excavation, from potsherds and animal bones to soil, was all archaeological evidence. He is remembered for his great excavation techniques and his typologies for field monuments and portable artifacts. Pitt Rivers promoted the establishment of a sound chronology for British archaeology and worked tirelessly to preserve the historic field monuments of Britain.

Augustus Henry Lane Fox Pitt Rivers was the second son of a Yorkshire gentleman, William Lane Fox, and a Scottish noblewoman, Lady Caroline Douglas. He took the name Pitt Rivers on inheriting the estate, but not the title, of his cousin Horace Pitt, sixth Baron Rivers, in 1880. This inheritance came to him through the early deaths of his elder brother and several other intervening heirs.

Born on the Lane Fox estate at Bramham near Wetherby, West Yorkshire, Fox spent much of his childhood in London, especially after the death of his father in 1832. After a short period at the Royal Military Academy, Sandhurst, he was commissioned into the Third Battalion of the Grenadier Guards in 1845. The no-doubt tedious round of ceremonial duties in London and Windsor, with rest periods at Winchester or Chichester, was broken only by the Chartist riots of 1848, during which the Third Battalion guarded the royal palaces and the magazine in Hyde Park. Now a captain, Fox was to find more intellectual stimulation with his appointment in 1851 to the committee of inquiry into the adoption of a new rifle for the infantry. That year was significant for Fox. It was the year of the Great Exhibition, that remarkable stimulus to late-nineteenth-century science. It also seems to have been, coincidentally or not, the year when Fox began his ethnographic collection of weapons, armor, locks, keys, and other implements.

In 1853, after a long courtship, Fox married Alice Stanley, daughter of Sir Edward Stanley, second Baron Alderley. Although it was originally a love match, both Fox and his bride were to be bitterly disappointed by married life. In later years, they lived under the same roof but were effectively estranged.

Meanwhile, Fox had been appointed as an instructor at the British Army's School of Musketry at Hythe, but the opening of the Crimean

Augustus Pitt Rivers. (Copyright Pitt Rivers Museum, University of Oxford)

War in 1854 brought overseas service, first as instructor of musketry for the Guards Brigade at Malta and subsequently at Scutari. As deputy assistant quartermaster general of the Second Division, he participated in the invasion of the Crimea and the Battle of the Alma. Shortly after the start of the Siege of Sebastopol, he was invalided home. After another spell at Malta, where his first son was born, he was censured by a senior officer over the methods he had employed for musketry instruction. His name was cleared, and in 1861 he was posted to Canada as musketry instructor to the Guards Brigade stationed there during the American Civil War.

In the following year he became assistant quartermaster general at Cork, southern Ireland, where he was to remain until 1866. He was fascinated by the prehistoric circular forts, or raths, of Ireland, and these monuments were the first objects of his antiquarian fieldwork. He surveyed several of them and, with local antiquarian Richard Caulfield, undertook some rather unscientific digging at one or two of these sites. He also surveyed promontory forts and ogham stones and even noted some medieval antiquities at this time.

These pursuits must be viewed in the light of other developments in Fox's life. His marriage into the Stanley family brought him into contact with the intellectual elite of the day. The Lane Foxes, though interested in agricultural improvements, can hardly be described as a cerebral family, but in the Stanley household Fox met Herbert Spencer, John Stuart Mill, and a host of leading scientists and social scientists. It was under the stimulus of this distinguished company that Fox read *The Origin of Species* as soon as it was published in 1859 and became a convert to Darwinism, a transition no doubt promoted by his acquaintance with two other leading lights, Sir John Lubbock, antiquarian, and Thomas Henry Huxley, philosopher and politician, whom he met on joining the Ethnological Society of London in 1861.

The Darwinian theory of evolution gave point to Fox's ethnographic collection, and over the following decade he developed his own theory of the "Evolution of Culture," a system that came to fruition with a number of lectures published throughout the late 1860s and early 1870s. The theory, simply stated, was that human cultural development is directly analogous to natural evolution; summed up in one phrase,

"History is but another term for evolution" (Fox 1875, 498). The theory of the evolution of culture, which was part and parcel of Herbert Spencer's "universal process" and, more particularly, "social Darwinism," dominated Fox's anthropological and archaeological work until the end of his life.

In 1874 Fox's collection, now amounting to some 14,000 pieces, was placed on loan in the Bethnal Green branch of the South Kensington Museum, now the British Museum of Natural History. No longer merely a gentleman's private cabinet of curiosities, it was now a tool for the education of the public: "The knowledge of the facts of evolution, and of the processes of gradual development, is the one great knowledge that we have to inculcate, and this knowledge can be taught by museums, provided that they are arranged in such a manner that those who run may read. The working classes have but little time for study" (Fox 1891, 116).

Fox had been elected a fellow of the Society of Antiquaries of London in 1864, and when he returned from Ireland to England in 1867, he began his archaeological fieldwork in earnest. Among the most significant episodes over the next thirteen years were his surveys and excavations in Yorkshire with the great barrow digger Canon William Greenwell; his surveys and excavations on the hill-forts and flint mines of the Sussex Downs; field walking in Oxfordshire and Wiltshire; discoveries of Paleolithic implements and animal bones in the drift gravels of the Thames valley; and barrow excavations at Guildford, where he was stationed from 1874 until 1877, and at Brighton. He also traveled abroad at this time, undertaking archaeological fieldwork in France and Denmark. A notable feature of the catalog of his fieldwork is that, unlike his contemporaries, he devoted a relatively small proportion of time to funerary monuments. This decision reflected his belief that the excavation of settlement sites would yield more valuable socioeconomic evidence: "Our knowledge of prehistoric and early people is derived chiefly from their funeral deposits, and for all we know of their mode of life they might as well have been born dead" (Fox 1892, xii).

Fox had joined the Anthropological Society in 1865 and become honorary secretary of the Ethnological Society in 1868. In the same year he was general secretary of the International Archaeological Congress that met at Norwich and London. In 1871 he played a key role in the amalgamation of the "ethnologicals" and "anthropologicals" to form the Anthropological Institute; he was later to serve as its president. He became a vice-president of the Society of Antiquaries in 1871 and was elected Fellow of the Royal Society in 1876. The breadth of experience that he had gained by 1880 was remarkable, and so too was the breadth of his acquaintance in the archaeological world. He knew and worked with Albert Way, director of the Society of Antiquaries, and William Owen Stanley (both relations of his wife); Sir John Evans, the numismatist and author of the classics *Ancient Stone Implements* and *Ancient Bronze Implements;* Augustus Franks of the British Museum; and the anatomist George Rolleston of Oxford University. Finally, he was to meet the great archaeologist WILLIAM FLINDERS PETRIE, by chance, in Egypt.

In 1880 Fox inherited Lord Rivers's estates in Dorset and Wiltshire and took the name Pitt Rivers. He celebrated his good fortune by taking a holiday in Egypt, but he left the Nile steamer halfway through the trip and went searching, successfully, for Paleolithic remains in the drift gravel of the Valley of the Kings. It was one of his most remarkable and controversial discoveries. Certain geologists refused to accept that the chert flakes he had found were the result of human agency. Pitt Rivers, however, anticipating such skepticism and having characteristically forearmed himself with the statements of reliable witnesses to the finding, retaliated with incontrovertible arguments.

For the remaining twenty years of his life, Pitt Rivers's archaeological work was divided between a notable series of excavations in Cranborne Chase, mostly on his own property, and his official duties as the first inspector of ancient monuments. Lubbock's Ancient Monuments Act of 1882 provided for the appointment of an inspector to effect the legislation. Pitt Rivers, now a wealthy and respected archaeologist, was perhaps the obvious choice for the post, especially since placating irate landowners was one of the inspector's principal tasks. Another main duty was surveying the monuments on the act's original schedule and any others brought under government protection. Between 1883 and 1889 Pitt Rivers undertook seven journeys of inspection, primarily in highland Britain, surveying and sketching the monuments in his remit. The act was far from satisfactory, however, due to its inherent limitations, and in 1890 Pitt Rivers gave up the small salary attached to the office; he continued in an honorary capacity, but in practice the administration of the Act virtually ceased.

The excavations in Cranborne Chase were undertaken by Pitt Rivers with a number of assistant supervisors and draftsmen and laborers from the estate. Among the sites were the Neolithic Wor Barrow; several round barrows and Bronze Age enclosures, such as South Lodge; the hill-fort of Winkelbury; the Romano-British settlements of Woodcutts and Rotherley; the linear ditches Bokerley Dyke and, outside the chase in north Wiltshire, Wansdyke; and the medieval King John's House, Tollard Royal. Several exercises in experimental archaeology were also carried out. Accounts of all the excavations, with the exception of the

Excavation of the ditch of South Lodge Camp, Cranborne Chase. Charles Flower and Herbert Toms (in suits) are on the left. (From Mark Bowden, Pitt Rivers, *1991)*

Roman building at Iwerne, were published (Pitt Rivers 1887; 1888; 1890; 1892; 1898).

The ethnographic collection that had been on loan to Bethnal Green was given to Oxford University in 1884 to form the Pitt Rivers Museum. The general founded another museum at Farnham in Cranborne Chase, in which were displayed finds from his excavations, elaborate models of the sites themselves, and his continually growing collection of ethnographic objects. To make this somewhat remote museum attractive to the public, Pitt Rivers laid out the Larmer Pleasure Grounds, with lawns, picnic bowers, and an open-air theater; there were sporting events, a private band, dances, and "other inducements" to bring in the local people (Pitt Rivers 1891, 119). Through all this effort can be seen his theory of the evolution of culture with its stress on gradual change, a strong conservative message to the agricultural laborers of the district.

Pitt Rivers dabbled in politics but without success. He was cynical about party politicians: "This is an age of science and we should listen to the voice of scientific men. They see the affairs of the world from a higher standpoint than political men who are merely wire-pullers and self-interested partisans" (Pitt Rivers Papers). Though brought up in an ultrareactionary family, in practice Pitt Rivers was fairly tolerant of most shades of contemporary political thought, with one notable exception: he hated political and social radicals.

The general expended much effort on the fashionable study of physical anthropology, especially in regard to the attempt, now known to be fruitless, to isolate races through craniometry. His racism and right-wing attitudes have been much discussed by recent authorities who have often failed to see the man in the context of his times. That his views now appear so extreme is largely a reflection of the enormous social and political changes that have occurred since his day. His lifetime witnessed such events as the extermination of traditional Tasmanian society (1830–1870), the brutal suppression of the Jamaican mutiny (1865), and the atrocities in the Congo Free State (1886 onward). In Britain itself, in areas well known to Pitt Rivers, the plight of the Irish in time of famine and of the Highland Scots under some of the worst excesses of the Highland clearances (1851–1854) were glaringly apparent. Yet these events provoked little outcry, even from the liberal intelligentsia of the day. The general's outlook was, in many respects, as liberal as that of his close colleagues and as liable to crumble in face of the perceived dangers of extending democracy to the "ignorant masses." He cannot be regarded as an amiable man, however. There is a hard, cynical edge to his temperament, very different in tone from the warm humor of his colleague Sir John Evans. His acrimonious family relationships also stand in marked contrast to the affectionate Evans household. Moreover, the general treated his tenants and dependents with a lack of sympathy that, while perhaps typical of the Victorian landowner, reflects no credit on him as an individual.

With his retirement from active soldiering in 1882, the general's main business was the management of his estate. He and his wife had mutually agreed to live in silence, and he had quarreled with nearly all his children. So he built roads, planted trees, dug ponds, bred experimental farm animals, shot game birds, ignored tradesmen's bills, and evicted tenants. The general died on 4 May 1900 and continued to assert his independence by having himself cremated.

General Augustus Pitt Rivers has undoubtedly been one of the most influential of British archaeologists. However, his influence has fluctuated and changed its character throughout the hundred years since his death.

Standards of fieldwork and excavation were generally at a very low ebb in the first twenty or thirty years of the twentieth century, though a handful of archaeologists working at the local level, such as Pitt Rivers's one time assistant Herbert Toms, were doing work of some quality. Pitt Rivers himself was almost forgotten. Of significant national figures in British archaeology at this time only a few, among them Francis Haverfield, Heywood Sumner, Harold St. George Gray, and Arthur Bulleid, seem to have attempted to adhere to the general's precepts. Haverfield was an indefatigable researcher into the history of the Roman frontier in northern England, and though the results of his exertions were often inconclusive, the recording of his excavations was of a higher order than that of many of his successors in that field. Sumner was an artist-turned-archaeologist who devoted much time to surveying the earthworks of Cranborne Chase and the New Forest in south England; he also excavated a number of Roman sites, consciously trying to emulate the standards set by the general, who was something of a hero to him. Bulleid had been excavating the lake villages of Somerset for some years with considerable skill and was to continue this project throughout the first half of the twentieth century in collaboration with St. George Gray, who had been one of the general's assistants in Cranborne Chase. St. George Gray was a prolific excavator to the end of his life, digging notably at Maumbury Rings, Arbor Low, and Avebury. He maintained Pitt Rivers's standards but never attempted to improve on them and frequently failed to publish, omissions that were to earn him scathing criticism from archaeologist MORTIMER WHEELER in later years.

As early as 1934, Pitt Rivers was recognized as "the first scientific British archaeologist" (Clark 1934, 414), but it was Wheeler who resurrected the general by claiming discipleship and writing extensively in praise of his excavation techniques (1954, 13, 25–29). Wheeler's near-contemporaries CHRISTOPHER HAWKES and STUART PIGGOTT found similar merit in the general's work, gaining inspiration from his typological theory and reinterpreting a number of his sites from the Farnham Museum collection and archives (e.g., Hawkes et al. 1947).

Pitt Rivers's place in archaeological history was thereby assured, but he remained a shadowy figure until the late 1970s. The situation changed with the publication of the first full biography (Thompson 1977), based largely on a study of the Pitt Rivers Papers in the Salisbury Museum and the general's notebooks from his inspectorship, which were deposited in the Public Record Office. Moreover, a major archaeological project on the prehistory of Cranborne Chase was undertaken (Barrett et al. 1992a, 1992b) that included the re-excavation of the general's sites at South Lodge and Barrow Pleck. One of the directors of the project seized the opportunity to make a dramatic reinterpretation of Pitt Rivers's significance (Bradley 1983), arguing that he was not merely a good archaeological technician but that his work possessed a strong theoretical basis. The museum at Farnham had been closed to the public since 1966, and in 1975 the archaeological collections had been taken over by the Salisbury and South Wiltshire Museum. In 1983, the museum opened a new gallery devoted to the general, which led in turn to the publication of another biographical study (Bowden 1991). Meanwhile, Pitt Rivers's contribution to ethnography and anthropology was also being studied (e.g., Chapman 1985). The history of ancient monuments legislation became a subject of wide interest, perhaps in part because of the creation of the Historic Buildings and Monuments Commission (HBMC) in 1984, and the general's role as first inspector of ancient monuments was re-examined by a number of scholars (e.g., Chippindale 1983; Murray 1989).

Pitt Rivers's fame has therefore rested at different times on his abilities as an excavator, a builder of typologies, and a theorist. He should perhaps also be assessed as an administrator, as one who bridged the gap between anthropology and archaeology, and as an educator.

Following Ian Hodder (1986, 120) we may suggest that just as it is the idea of context that divides the modern archaeologist from the treasure hunter, so it was the idea of context that in the past divided the archaeologist from the antiquarian. Given this proposition, and it is an attractive one, very few people in the nineteenth century can be called archaeologists, but Pitt Rivers numbers among them. The Rev. James Joyce, excavator of Silchester, might, on these grounds, have some right to be called the first British archaeologist; it was in his address in 1867 to the Society of Antiquaries of London that the idea of context was first fully expounded. Pitt Rivers almost certainly heard that lecture. At any rate he became a strong advocate for the precise recording of contextual information. The following exemplifies his meticulous method:

> My assistant, Mr. James, was watching the digging at the time, and he noticed the discolouration of the white chalk rubble, caused by the rust from the iron objects. The knife and the nail were then picked up. I myself saw the find within a few minutes of the discovery, and investigated the circumstances on the spot with great care. There can be no doubt whatever that these objects lay upon the surface of the ground, before the rampart was thrown over them (1892, 254–255).

Pitt Rivers was undoubtedly one of the finest excavators of his generation. At his best, at Bokerley Dyke and Wansdyke, his care in recording information in plan and section drawings rivals modern practice (e.g., 1892, pl. CCXVI). Yet he was inconsistent. The Wansdyke excavations were undertaken between 1889 and 1891, but though he continued to excavate for another six years, he never again achieved the same standards. Indeed there seems to have been a marked decline in his recording techniques. Contextual precision was sacrificed to generalized measurements. This is partly a reflection of his physical digging method, which was always by "spit" (measured excavation units of known and regular extent) rather than by stratigraphic layer. It is possible that he overcame the drawbacks of this method in his Bokerley Dyke and Wansdyke excavations only through the efforts of one of the assistants he was employing at this time, Claude Gray, brother of Harold St. George Gray. This hypothesis, however, remains to be proven. The general's worsening health and disappointment over the failure of the Ancient Monuments Act may have been additional factors in the decline of his fieldwork.

In the evidence that he chose to record, Pitt Rivers was far in advance of his contemporaries. He kept most, and published some, of the potsherds and animal bones that others usually discarded:

> Tedious as it may appear to some, to dwell on the discovery of odds and ends that have, no doubt, been thrown away by their owners as rubbish yet it is by the study of such trivial details, that Archaeology is mainly dependant for determining the date of earthworks. The value of relics, viewed as evidence, may on this account be said to be in an inverse ratio to their intrinsic value (1892, ix).

However, the general had other technical weaknesses besides inconsistency. He was not a very good field archaeologist, using that term in its strict sense. He preferred to employ contour surveys to record the topography of sites, impressed by the apparent objectivity of this method and by its vital role in three-dimensional model making, but he failed to realize that a contour survey cannot be read as a conventional hachured survey (a straightline survey that cuts across contours) can. He was not adept at seeing relationships between earthworks, and perhaps not even particularly good at seeing the earthworks themselves. Sir Richard Colt Hoare had observed, by analysis of the surface indications, that the Brown's Barn Entrenchment was overlain by Wansdyke. Pitt Rivers was apparently unable to appreciate Colt Hoare's reasoning and was forced to excavate in order to investigate this relationship (1892,

261). At South Lodge the general recognized a single lynchet, or a closure (1888, pl. LXXX), but Herbert Toms noted that this was only one element of an extensive field system (which he returned to survey after the general's death) (Toms 1925).

The theory of the evolution of culture, like the Spencerian thought on which it was based, has not found wide acceptance. Darwin himself rejected "social Darwinism" and especially its political notion that evolution was to be equated with progress. Thomas Henry Huxley rejected the gradualism of Darwin's theory, but it was fundamental to Pitt Rivers. As he wrote, "If in the whole face of nature there is undoubted evidence of any especial fiat of creation having operated capriciously, or in any other manner than by gradual evolution and development, my principles are false" (1868, 436). The general held to this doctrine tenaciously because it was the basis of his own political message:

> For good or for evil we have thought proper to place power in the hands of the masses. The masses are ignorant, and knowledge is swamped by ignorance. The knowledge they lack is the knowledge of history. This lays them open to the designs of demagogues and agitators, who strive to make them break with the past, and seek the remedies for existing evils, or the means of future progress, in drastic changes that have not the sanction of experience. The law that Nature makes no jumps, can be taught by the history of mechanical contrivances, in such a way as at least to make men cautious how they listen to scatter-brained revolutionary suggestions (1891, 115–116).

His position, however, was false. Darwinian evolution proceeds by the selection of random genetic adaptations while cultural change proceeds by the direct transmission of learning. Cultural change can therefore take place within, as well as across, generations. Natural evolution and social change are simply not two parts of the same process. This refutation of the central premise of Pitt Rivers's thought does not imply a total rejection of his archaeological work, practical or theoretical. If he was wrong about the mechanism by which sequences are created, he was not wrong about the sequences themselves. Archaeology in the late nineteenth century was a chronological science desperately seeking a chronology. A number of British archaeologists were making strides toward a resolution of this problem, such as Evans in the field of prehistoric implements, but Pitt Rivers probably did more than nearly anyone in his generation to promote the establishment of a sound chronology for British archaeology. This he achieved by his work behind the scenes in the Royal Archaeological Institute, a major scientific society, and similar bodies and, more particularly, by the creation of typologies for field monuments as well as portable artifacts.

It has become customary to argue that Pitt Rivers's success as an administrator stemmed from his military background. However, anything less efficient than the British army of the mid-nineteenth century (except in trivial matters of parade-ground precision) can hardly be imagined. It is more plausible to suggest that Pitt Rivers's undoubted personal efficiency and capacity for hard work were personal qualities that flourished despite his military training.

Archaeology and anthropology were seen largely as two aspects of the same science in the later nineteenth century. It was only when anthropology began to develop its own fieldwork and lost its interest in material culture that the two disciplines drifted apart. There was nothing unusual, therefore, in Pitt Rivers's use of an ethnographic parallel, culled from his travels in the Hebrides, to explain the longitudinal boring of sheep bones to form bobbins on Iron Age and Romano-British sites in Cranborne Chase (1888, 173). With his background as "a voracious and omnivorous collector" (Gray 1905, xxxi), however, the general was particularly well placed to capitalize on such comparisons, and his overriding interest in the theory of cultural evolution ensured that he made full use of these opportunities. The linkage of archaeology and anthropology, which was such a significant part of his work, was therefore stimulated by his theoretical position: archaeology and anthropology were inseparable elements in the system of cultural evolution.

Public education was the general's ultimate goal. He had very strong views on museum design and believed that existing museums confused their distinct roles in research and education (1891). He also felt that most museum displays were simply tedious:

> A carefully-made model, to scale, of any earthwork or building, in which a discovery has been made, is a much more interesting object in a collection, than the now familiar series of stone and bronze axes, spears, swords and urns, with which nearly all our Museums are supplied in such abundance, and with such unvarying uniformity, that they almost pall upon the visitor in search of something new (1892, xii).

How far his own museums were successful in his lifetime it is impossible to say; there is no evidence as to whether or not the many visitors were convinced by the theory of cultural evolution. In the twentieth century that is no longer the criterion. What is certain is that Farnham Museum is still remembered with immense affection by those who visited it and that the Pitt Rivers Museum in Oxford continues to inspire and delight a numerous and varied public. Schoolchildren, novelists, poets, musicians, products designers, and natural historians have found as much stimulus in its crowded galleries as have archaeologists and ethnographers.

Pitt Rivers was the beneficiary of good fortune. His inheritance of a large part of Cranborne Chase in 1880 was a stroke of the greatest luck, as he himself and many others have noted, but he was also fortunate in that he entered the world of archaeology at a most auspicious time for the discipline. In the late 1850s and early 1860s the discoveries of Boucher de Perthes in France and others in Paleolithic archaeology had placed the subject firmly in the limelight. The implications of the finding of human debris in drift gravels had an immediate impact on the scientific world, especially in light of the controversy over Darwin's theory. The general was able to make his own significant contribution to this major scientific debate and simultaneously to benefit from the growing body of anthropological knowledge and from the first syntheses of European prehistory by J. J. Worsaae and Sir John Lubbock. At the same time the work of the few competent excavators, such as the Rev. James Joyce and Robert Mortimer, was creating an atmosphere in which Pitt Rivers could establish high standards of scientific investigation and reasonably suggest that they should be the norm. He was also present at, and instrumental in, the first faltering steps of the preservation movement, a movement led by people as diverse as John Lubbock, his son-in-law, and such an unlikely bedfellow as the artist William Morris. Finally, he was at the forefront of the upsurge of interest in museology and public education. It is entirely fitting that his name is permanently linked with one of the greatest, and most eccentric, of Britain's museums.

References
Primary
Pitt Rivers, Augustus H.L.F. 1868. "Primitive Warfare, Part 2." *Journal of the Royal United Services Institution* 12: 399–439.

———. 1875. "On the Evolution of Culture." *Proceedings of the Royal Institute of Great Britain* 7: 496–514.

———. 1887. *Excavations in Cranborne Chase,* vol. 1. Privately printed.

———. 1888. *Excavations in Cranborne Chase,* vol. 2. Privately printed.

———. 1890. *King John's House, Tollard Royal.* Privately printed.

———. 1891. "Typological Museums." *Journal of the Society of Arts* 40: 115–122.

———. 1892. *Excavations in Cranborne Chase,* vol. 3. Privately printed.

———. 1898. *Excavations in Cranborne Chase,* vol. 4. Privately printed.

The Pitt Rivers Papers. Salisbury and South Wiltshire Museum.

PRO work 39/1–16. Pitt Rivers' Inspectorate Field Notebooks. Public Record Office, Kew.

Secondary

Barrett, John C., Richard Bradley, and Martin Green. 1992. *Landscape, Monuments and Society: The Prehistory of Cranborne Chase.* Cambridge: Cambridge University Press.

Barrett, John C., Richard J. Bradley, and M. Hall. 1992. *Papers on the Prehistoric Archaeology of Cranborne Chase.* Oxford: Oxbow Monograph 11.

Bowden, Mark C. B. 1991. *Pitt Rivers: The Life and Archaeological Work of Lieutenant-General Augustus Henry Lane Fox Pitt Rivers, DCL, FRS, FSA.* Cambridge: Cambridge University Press.

Bradley, R. J. 1983. "Archaeology, Evolution and the Public Good: The Intellectual Development of General Pitt Rivers." *Archaeological Journal* 140: 1–9.

Chapman, W. R. 1985. "Arranging Ethnology: A.H.L.F. Pitt Rivers and the Typological Tradition." In *Objects and Others: Essays on Museums and Material Culture,* ed. G. W. Stocking. Madison: University of Wisconsin Press.

Chippindale, C. 1983. "The Making of the First Ancient Monuments Act, 1882, and Its Administration under General Pitt Rivers." *Journal of the British Archaeological Association* 136: 1–55.

Clark, G. 1934. "Archaeology and the State." *Antiquity* 8: 414–428.

Gray, Harold St. George. 1905. *Index to Excavations in Cranborne Chase and King John's House, Tollard Royal, With a Memoir of General Pitt Rivers and Bibliography of His Published Works.* Taunton. Privately printed.

Hawkes, C. F. C., et al. 1947. "Britons, Romans and Saxons round Salisbury and in Cranborne Chase." *Archaeological Journal* 104: 27–81.

Hodder, Ian. 1986. *Reading the Past.* Cambridge: Cambridge University Press.

Murray, Tim. 1989. "The History, Philosophy and Sociology of Archaeology: The Case of the Ancient Monuments Protection Act (1882)." In *Critical Traditions in Contemporary Archaeology: Essays in the Philosophy, History and Socio-Politics of Archaeology,* ed. V. Pinsky and A. Wylie. Cambridge: Cambridge University Press.

Thompson, M. W. 1977. *General Pitt Rivers: Evolution and Archaeology in the Nineteenth Century.* Bradford-on-Avon, UK: Moonraker Press.

Toms, H. 1925. "Bronze Age, or Earlier, Lynchets." *Proceedings of the Dorset Natural History and Archaeology Field Club* 46: 89–100.

Wheeler, R. E. M. 1954. *Archaeology from the Earth.* London: Penguin Books.

Curtis Hinsley

Frederic Ward Putnam   1839–1915

Curator and professor at the Peabody Museum and then founding professor of archaeology at Cambridge, Chicago, New York, and Berkeley, Putnam was the institutional builder of American archaeology. Respected as the first systematic and scientific archaeologist in North America, he never had the time to publish his excavations.

Like many generations of his family before him, Frederic Putnam was born and raised in Salem, Massachusetts. His ancestors on both sides were early emigrants from England; the earliest American ancestor, John Putnam, settled in Salem in 1640. The Putnams had a long association with Harvard: Frederic's father, grandfather, and great-grandfather had all graduated from Harvard College. The family of his mother, Elizabeth Appleton, had similarly long connection with both New England and Harvard. As a boy Putnam was privately tutored and assisted his father in horticultural work, but it was Henry Wheatland, curator at the Essex Institute in Salem, whom he considered his "father in science": "I joined in all his schemes with the enthusiasm and hope of youth. [To] him, with the consent of my parents, am I indebted for my instruction under Agassiz, Wyman, and Gray" (Putnam 1893a). His initial work in natural history involved birds and fishes, and his first publication, through the Essex Institute when he was sixteen, was a catalog of the fishes of Essex County. The same year he chanced to show Louis Agassiz through the local collections, after which Agassiz invited him to come study and serve as assistant in the formative years of the Museum of Comparative Zoology at Harvard.

Putnam spent the next eight years (1856–1864) studying with Agassiz, Jeffries Wyman, and Asa Gray, until Agassiz's students revolted against his teaching. Putnam, as leader, was sent home to Salem, Wheatland, and the Essex Institute (Lurie 1960; Dexter 1965). As superintendent of the institute he was joined by Edward S. Morse, A. S. Packard, and Alpheus Hyatt (all former Agassiz students); he founded the Salem Press and edited the *American Naturalist* in these years as well. In 1868 the philanthropist George Peabody, having endowed museums at Harvard and Yale, bestowed on his home county of Essex an endowment to found a scientific society in Salem. Putnam became director of the new Peabody Academy of Science, where he remained until his appointment

Frederic Ward Putnam. (Copyright Peabody Museum, Harvard University)

at the Peabody Museum in Cambridge in 1874 (Morse 1915).

Putnam's first love was ichthyology. Anxious to establish a reputation independently of Agassiz, he gave most of his attention in the Salem years to fishes. But as his excursions to shell mounds (the first one in 1856), caves, and burial sites became more frequent, Putnam's interests drifted steadily toward archaeology. The clear shift occurred around 1874; after this point Putnam interested himself in natural history mainly out of financial need. (He had married Adelaide Martha Edmands of Cambridge in 1864, and they now had two daughters and a son.) But the training in natural history was indelible and fundamentally determined Putnam's philosophy and methods in archaeology. As his biographer Alfred Tozzer later observed, "During his whole career Putnam was a natural historian in the old-fashioned, but best sense of the word" (Tozzer 1935). Putnam told Lewis Henry Morgan in 1880 that the transition from zoology to anthropology seemed natural:

> Now if I am no longer a zoologist, I claim that my zoological studies, & methods I obtained during the 8 years I was a pupil & assistant with Prof. Wyman, both in human and general anatomy have prepared me for my archaeological & ethnological research in a better manner than if I had gone directly to these later studies without that previous zoological knowledge, and therefore while I am no longer a student in zoology I am *one in anthropology* (Putnam 1880).

On the death of Jeffries Wyman in 1874, Asa Gray agreed to serve for one year as temporary curator of the Peabody Museum of Archaeology and Ethnology with the understanding that Putnam, in whom he had a confidence not shared by others at Harvard, be hired to accession the collections gathered under Wyman's beloved but rather lethargic hand. The arrangement was intended, too, to test Putnam's competence, for it was reported that Harvard president Charles W. Eliot doubted Putnam's "literary sufficiency" (Salisbury 1875). Putnam, it seems, already possessed an identity that would shadow him throughout his life. The source of it lay in three facts of his early career: that he had been enrolled, under Agassiz, in the Lawrence Scientific School rather than the standard Harvard College curriculum; that he had figured prominently in the student revolt against the revered Agassiz; and that, despite the years of study under Agassiz and others, he had left the scientific school without a degree. The consequent suspicion among his Harvard colleagues that Putnam lacked a certain breadth of training and depth in philosophy, as parochial as it may seem today, drove and directed him for years. It instilled in him both a determination and a sometimes maddening caution, evident during his long, piecemeal construction of archaeology and anthropology at Harvard and elsewhere. Circumspection marked his advice to his son Eben in 1890: "Still you must court criticism in every way. Try to make your first production as perfect as possible that it may bear the stamp of careful study and great authority, and thus secure credit for what you may do in the future. No other work that you will ever write will need the care of this your first" (Putnam 1890).

A few years later, on leaving Chicago in disgust at the ambitious, avaricious approach to anthropology of the new Field Museum, he addressed himself to Edward E. Ayer, the midwestern nouveau riche lumber magnate who directed that institution, with an unmistakably Boston conservatism:

> We are living in an age of great accomplishments, and the tendency is to grow too fast and not always with certainty to ultimate results. A scientific and educational institution cannot be pushed in many ways to advantage. It must have a healthy, steady growth, and everything connected with it should be prospective. Therefore, far-reaching plans should be made so that the next generation will honor their predecessors (Putnam 1893b).

At such rare times Putnam expressed his own deepest insecurities. As late as 1898, after Putnam had spent two decades as Peabody curator and one as Peabody professor, and when he was approaching sixty years of age, President Eliot still felt it appropriate and necessary to ask him to explain his lack of an academic degree. Putnam reviewed his entire education, closing with some defensiveness:

> It is simply one of those cases where one omits to do in youth what would have proved advantageous later. However, I had a perfect and thorough training under Agassiz, Wyman, and Gray, and it has been my pride in manhood to be able to say that I was their student, and to know that they were pleased to acknowledge me as such. The thorough methods of research that I learned during those eight years have given me power in my later undertakings; and it is such methods that I have endeavored to teach to others (Putnam 1898).

In 1875 Putnam, as the new curator of the Peabody Museum, assembled the nucleus of a staff: Lucien Carr, who served as assistant curator without pay until 1894; and Jennie Smith, who served for forty years in numerous clerical capacities until Putnam's death in 1915. This pivotal trio was augmented by a succession of men and women who volunteered to work for Putnam as long as their own finances and interests permitted. For instance, Cordelia A. Studley, who had been a medical student, cared for the osteological collections from 1882 until 1887; she left because she could no longer afford to work without pay. Others similarly came and went. Beyond the core staff and the volunteer student assistants, a third group orbited around Putnam. With the exception of Alice Fletcher (see below), these were all men, and most were engaged in archaeology rather than ethnology. As Wheatland and Agassiz had for him, Putnam functioned variously as mentor, critic, occasional financial source, and doorkeeper to the ambitions of these men; consequently, relationships with him (and thus with the museum) were ambivalent and sometimes intensely personal, a common state of affairs in the all-male, often claustrophobic, competitive, and grateful/resentful world of nineteenth-century American science (Noble 1992). These individuals were Putnam's first "students," his correspondence school in archaeology that functioned simultaneously as a collecting arm for the Peabody Museum. Some served only briefly, others for decades; some never visited the museum or saw their collections installed, others begged to spend a few days with Putnam or Carr in Cambridge. Some worked for little money and less recognition, whereas others craved fame and position in science, possibly at the Peabody itself. All looked to Putnam for guidance and encouragement.

Consider but one example of the "correspondence school." Putnam inherited from Wyman the labors and loyalty of Henry Gillman of Detroit. A gentleman-naturalist who gathered together a 2,000-specimen herbarium as well as private mineralogical and archaeological collections from the shores of Lake Superior, Gillman had begun sending bones and artifacts from burial mounds in 1873. To Putnam he shipped Ojibwa material culture accompanied by his own, rather idiosyncratic commentary: "I enclose a list of the things with the Indian names as closely as I could obtain them. The canoe is capable of carrying three persons with their equipment, & is just such as is now used by the Indians of the Great Lakes. I think Mr. Longfellow would like to see this embodiment of his admirable description in 'Hiawatha'" (Gillman 1876).

Putnam considered Gillman a dedicated and intelligent contributor. But as the national economic depression deepened in the late 1870s, Gillman found both business and politics in Michigan unprofitable. He sold his collections and moved to Florida, proposing to continue with shell-mound archaeology. Struggling now with a citrus business, he informed Putnam that he could no longer work without remuneration. Consequently his scientific avocation stalled. Returning to Michigan in 1882, he undertook a month-long excavation near Lake Huron, but now Putnam found the results unsatisfactory: "The present exploration has not given us anything of special interest for exhibition but if Mr. G. has made a *thorough* exploration of each mound & sends us *all* that was obtained *as well as* carefully prepared *notes,* the exploration will be an important one" (Putnam 1882; emphasis in original).

Putnam's terms of emphasis, which began to appear more frequently in the 1880s, are telling. Thoroughness in excavation, notation, sketching, and photography of sites—these were becoming his new hallmarks and standard, which he reiterated to all his workers henceforth. The fascinating but undocumented finds of the recent past had been superseded by systematic and meticulous recording. Unfortunately, Gillman no longer measured up, and he never submitted the prescribed report.

As Putnam pursued the mysterious Moundbuilders through the 1870s and 1880s, he looked, among other places, into stone graves in Tennessee. Here he enlisted the aid of Edwin Curtis, a poorly educated, humble, honest worker who followed Putnam's instructions as closely as possible, reported faithfully, and shipped his treasures reliably, all at minimal cost. He rarely offered his own opinions and was content to hear Putnam's. Partly for these reasons, Putnam considered him an ideal fieldworker, but for lack of funds he lost Curtis's services in 1878. And so it went. In this period Putnam supervised the field activities of a wide variety of such enthusiastic but untrained correspondents: Earl Flint in Nicaragua; E. B. Andrews in Ohio; Paul Schumacher and Edward Palmer in California. In most cases the collaboration was short-term, but there were two exceptions: Charles C. Abbott in New Jersey and Charles Metz in Ohio.

The most enduring and tempestuous relationship began in the 1870s with Charles Abbott, who was convinced that he had discovered in the gravel beds near his home in Trenton evidence that humans had existed in North America prior to the last ice age. For twenty-five years Abbott sent tons of stone artifacts to the Peabody Museum, where the "Abbott Collection" occupied (and still occupies) several cases. Through correspondence Putnam constantly instructed and corrected, encouraged and reproved his rambunctious friend. They exchanged hundreds of letters and many visits to the Cambridge museum and the Abbott family homestead. Sadly, the attention only increased Abbott's dependence, and when his sole opportunity for a career position in archaeology appeared, at the new University Museum in Philadelphia in 1889, the years of loyal service left him ill prepared to become an independent professional archaeologist. "*You* made it possible for me to become an archaeologist," he told Putnam, "and every jot and tittle of *ideas* as well as specimens, rightfully belongs and certainly shall go to the Peabody Museum" (Abbott 1889). After his dismissal in 1892, their relationship deteriorated rapidly, as Putnam's cautious approach to the question of the antiquity of humans in North America frustrated and ultimately infuriated him. He accused Putnam of withdrawing support, protecting his own reputation, and distancing himself from the Trenton evidence at the cost of scientific truth:

> Years ago, when I was toiling in the field and building up the collection I gathered, you did not keep so close-mouthed, and I fail to see that there is more reason for it now. Leave to the Angel Gabriel the trumpeting of the truth as to paleolithic man; the facts and the end of the world coming together. Such is your admirable plan (Abbott 1889).

There was a painful barb of truth in Abbott's words. While Putnam's hesitation was due in part to his respect for the unresolved questions about New Jersey geology in the 1890s, it was also true that under the embryonic professional conditions of the time, men such as Abbott required above all someone to vouch for their characters, since they lacked academic credentials or firm institutional standing. Referring to another of Putnam's fieldworkers, Ernest Volk, Thomas Wilson of the Smithsonian put his finger squarely on Putnam's dilemma. "Who is Volk, anyhow?" was the critical point, he reminded Putnam:

> The argument in the whole affair depends largely upon his reputation and character for truth and honesty. While it was all well enough to compliment the men who furnished the money by which this discovery is made, I think it would have been wiser for us to have given expression to our belief in Volk's honesty and integrity, and thus our acceptance of his discovery as genuine (Wilson 1900).

Given his own sense of marginality and the dubious stature (as he still saw it in 1900) of museum archaeology, Putnam found it more congenial to praise the patrons of Peabody science than to commit himself publicly to men like Abbott and Volk. Devoting his career to the cautious building of a legacy, he never lost the sense of precariousness and vulnerability.

After 1880, however, it was in Ohio rather than New Jersey that Putnam believed the prehistory of North America would be revealed.

With the faithful aid of Charles L. Metz, a physician in Madisonville, Ohio, Putnam tested his methods and staked his reputation amid the artificial mounds in the rolling hills of the Ohio River valley (Dexter 1977). In 1878 Metz had discovered prehistoric Madisonville Cemetery and set up a local society to promote regional archaeology. He and a coworker, Charles F. Low, published their findings in the *Journal of the Cincinnati Society of Natural History;* in 1880 Putnam began joint explorations at the cemetery and extended them over the next decade to Port Ancient, the Turner Group, and other sites in the valley of the Little Miami River. The long collaboration was professionally and personally fruitful. Through summertime fieldwork and wintertime letters of instruction, Putnam taught Metz how to clear a site; to "dig and trench" through a mound; to photograph and note relative positions of artifacts and skeletal remains in situ; to handle a working crew; to avoid competitors, curiosity seekers, and especially journalists; and to write up his field notes. The happiest and (in terms of fieldwork) most productive days of Putnam's career were spent here, encamped in the river valleys of southern Ohio in the humid summer months of the 1880s with his family, Metz, and Low. Here, too, in conjunction with Metz, Putnam established his reputation as the first systematic archaeologist in North America, the man best suited to train the next generation. "No man ought to be allowed to push spade or pickaxe into a western mound or earth-work except as at least disciple to the system of research of Professor F. W. Putnam," wrote Frank Hamilton Cushing in 1886 (Cushing 1886). Fifty years later Alfred Tozzer seconded the assessment: Under Putnam, "for almost the first time, methods of exact measurements coupled with topographical maps, sections, and other scientifically determined data were employed in American archaeology" (Dexter 1982).

By 1885 Putnam felt that the Ohio work had convincingly demonstrated the significance of the region for American prehistory, "the importance of conducting explorations in a thorough and systematic manner," and "the great advance which had taken place during the last few years in American archaeology, which was at last being studied in a way due to its importance, by a few earnest workers pursuing the investigation with all the methods of science" (American Antiquarian Society 1887, 10). Putnam's phrases warrant attention, for they expressed the elements of "science" as Putnam was attempting to establish it at the time: the exclusiveness and seriousness suggested by "a few earnest workers"; the deliberate purpose, rather than serendipitous or curious backyard discovery, inherent in "pursuing an investigation"; the rigor and defined contour of investigation implied by such words as "thorough," "systematic," and "methods." Year after year Putnam habitually employed

these terms, announcing in his reports with increasing confidence that "at last" method had arrived in American archaeology. Through his "correspondence school," not through classroom teaching, and notably with Metz, Putnam was dispelling, as he said, the popular image of archaeology as a playground for men of "rashness" and "haste" in judgment and replacing it with a model of "caution" and "moderation" (American Antiquarian Society 1885, 22).

Putnam was also breaking new ground for women in anthropology, against entrenched institutional resistance. In addition to Jennie Smith and Cordelia Studley, he hired Alice E. Putnam in 1886 and, a few years later, Frances Mead, who served as museum assistant until his death. He vigorously encouraged Zelia Nuttall's work on Mexican codices, and Sara Yorke Stevenson considered him her mentor, though he could give her no financial or direct institutional support. In 1893 he wrote: "Several of my best students are women, who have become widely known by their thorough and important works and publications; and this I consider as high an honor as could be accorded to me" (Dexter 1978, 5). Given the male lineage of American science with which Putnam was so strongly identified—just as Wheatland was Putnam's "father" in science, so Franz Boas wrote of himself in the 1890s as Putnam's "son"—such relationships with women were, not surprisingly, idiosyncratic and somewhat experimental.

The telling case was that of Alice Fletcher. In 1880 Fletcher began visiting the Peabody Museum, with Putnam's encouragement, to familiarize herself with his work. From this time she viewed him as her paternal adviser in anthropology, although she was in fact a year older than he. Throughout her years of work with Omaha, Winnebago, Nez Perce, and other tribes in the 1880s, she worked unceasingly and devotedly for Putnam. When Fletcher received, as a result of personal friendship, a lifetime fellowship from Mary Copley Thaw of Pittsburgh, Putnam was deeply pleased, while the Peabody trustees, who accepted it on Fletcher's behalf, were unenthusiastic. Among her friends there was gala celebration; there was no public recognition whatsoever in Cambridge (Mark 1988). Fletcher's status rose steadily in American anthropology in the 1890s and after the turn of the century. Still, when Boas organized a Festschrift for Putnam's seventieth birthday in 1909, Fletcher was asked to contribute to the volume but was excluded from the males-only dinner. "I'm glad to know why I was left out of the dinner," Fletcher responded to Putnam's apology. "I forgot I was a woman. I only remembered I was a friend and a student" (Dexter 1978, 6).

After several years of delay because of the opposition of Alexander Agassiz, Putnam became Peabody professor as well as curator in 1887. Yet Putnam still offered no curricular instruction at any level; the professorship amounted to continuing the hands-on tutoring and correspondence that had been Putnam's own experience and with which he was most comfortable. Then, in the fall of 1890, George A. Dorsey and John G. Owens forced the issue by enrolling themselves for graduate work with Putnam, despite the absence of a formal program. The Harvard faculty responded by creating the necessary Department of Archaeology and Ethnology. Dorsey received the first doctorate in 1894, taught briefly with Putnam, then moved to the Field Museum in Chicago in 1896. Owens's promising future was cut short in 1893 by his death from fever at the Mayan city of Copán in Honduras, but his brief career demonstrates well the dominance of field experience over the classroom in Putnam's early teaching at Harvard.

Owens had met Jesse Walter Fewkes, a zoologist trained by Louis Agassiz, at a Harvard summer school on marine biology in 1889. Fewkes, who was about to succeed Cushing as director of the Hemenway Southwestern Archaeological Expedition, asked Owens to assist him for the summer of 1890. After a season at Zuñi pueblo, Owens enrolled with Putnam. He stayed in Cambridge for three winter months, then left for a second season with Fewkes in the Southwest, this time at Hopi. The extent of Owens's formal instruction during the winter in Cambridge is not clear, but it could hardly have been thorough. He presented papers at local gatherings, studied advanced geology, worked on the Abbott Collection, and read materials on the Southwest. At the end of the summer of 1891, he came back to Harvard, for one month. He wrote up some Hopi material and prepared to leave for Copán as a member of the first Peabody expedition to Central America. He also spent a few days (according to his letters) "tak[ing] some special lessons in Anthropometry under Dr. Boas of Clark University" (Owens 1891), an early example of the collaboration between Boas and Putnam's Harvard department that was common until the first World War. With the exception of a few weeks the following summer and three weeks in the fall of 1892 (largely spent in preparing for Honduras again), Owens had no more time with Putnam or the museum. During his three years enrolled at Harvard, he worked at Zuñi, Hopi, and Copán and set up an anthropology exhibit with Fewkes in Spain. There was hardly a moment for classroom or laboratory instruction.

Nor did Putnam have the time to provide it. In 1891 he began an association with the World's Columbian Exposition, the Chicago World's Fair of 1893, that lasted four years, divided his attention and his energy between Cambridge and Chicago, and left him demoralized and exhausted. Chicago was not a happy experience for Putnam. He had high hopes of simultaneously making substantive advances in anthropology, especially that of the Western Hemisphere, and bringing its lessons to the American public in striking ways, but his efforts bogged down in seemingly endless frustrations. For two years he and Boas, who served as his chief assistant at the fair, supervised archaeological and anthropological work throughout the hemisphere including, significantly, further work at Turner and Hopewell in Ohio. The collections, photographs, and data poured in from the Southwest, the Great Plains, Yucatán, Peru, Alaska. They had more than fifty workers in the field. But from the moment of his arrival in Chicago, the fair's directors seemed to place every conceivable obstacle in Putnam's way and were much more concerned with the commercial exhibits than the scientific efforts. Putnam's promised space in the Anthropological Building was reduced by more than 60 percent. He had to move his office nine times in eight months. In the end, the Anthropology Building was not ready for visitors until one month after the fair had opened (Hinsley 1991; Dexter 1969).

Still, due to Putnam's direction at Chicago, the general public confronted, for the first time in the United States, anthropological questions and subject matter, however confusedly, partially, and ethnocentrically presented and received. It was at the Chicago fair that Mayan architecture first came to North American public attention, for instance. The subsequent interests of a number of wealthy patrons of anthropology and archaeology were directly traceable to the stimulus of Putnam's efforts at the exposition. In addition, their experiences at Chicago forged a strong bond between Putnam and Boas, as did their joint rejection by the Chicagoans in the transitional period between the end of the fair and the establishment of the Field Museum (1894–1895).

For his part, Putnam left Chicago feeling that "after squeezing all the juice out of me they threw me aside as a used up orange" (Putnam 1894). Putnam then entered the final distinctive phase of his career: no longer active fieldworker or struggling young archaeologist, he now became (between 1895 and 1909) the most powerful institution builder in American anthropology.

While always retaining his positions at Harvard and the Peabody, in 1894 Putnam began a decade of work at the American Museum of Natural History in New York as well. Here he served as part-time chair and curator of the Department of Anthropology (he suggested the name, instead of "archaeology and ethnology"), set the agenda for the department, edited its publications, and, most important, brought Franz Boas with him as head of ethnology and somatology. His permanent staff and field assistants included Marshall Saville, Ales Hrdlicka, Alfred Kroeber, Roland Dixon, John Swanton, Adolphe Bandelier, and Carl Lumholtz, anthropologists, archaeologists, and physical anthropologists who were later to become leaders in their fields. During Putnam's tenure Boas carried out the Jesup North Pacific Expedition (1897); Putnam also arranged Boas's initial position in anthropology at Columbia University (Dexter 1966b, 1976).

In 1901 Putnam began discussions with Phoebe Apperson Hearst and Benjamin I. Wheeler, president of the University of California, regarding the establishment of a department and museum of anthropology in Berkeley. Two years later he became professor of anthropology in the new department, resigning from the American Museum in 1904 and dividing his time between California and Harvard. Just as Boas had aided him in Chicago and New York, Putnam now brought Alfred Kroeber to effectively head the new department/museum complex and to direct the Ethnological and Archaeological Survey of California that was immediately founded in 1903. Putnam's presence and activities also stimulated the formation of anthropological societies on the Pacific Coast (Dexter 1966a). He remained in his positions in Berkeley and Cambridge until ill health forced his retirement in 1909.

Frances Mead's thorough bibliography of Putnam's work (1909) lists more than 400 publications, not including many institutional annual reports; but with few exceptions, these are rarely more than five pages in length, and many are only a few paragraphs. Putnam's natural history training emphasized brief contributions of observation and description, which was the dominant style of presentation in his early environment and remained his preferred genre. The single exception was the volume on archaeology that he edited and largely wrote while serving with the Wheeler Survey of the western territories in the late 1870s (Putnam

1879). The excavations in Ohio were clearly intended to be his life's work in archaeology. In 1897, when they were working together in New York, Boas had urged his mentor to publish the Hopewell materials:

> I really think that your important discovery makes it a duty to you to bring the subject before the public at the earliest possible time. I wish I could find words to express strongly enough my feeling on this point. It is in your power to advance our knowledge of American Anthropology immensely, and I think you ought to find a way to spare time enough to do so (Dexter 1982, 28).

As late as 1909 Putnam was still promising Metz that he would write up nearly thirty years of notes for their "final report." By that time, understandably, Putnam's energies were rapidly failing; the complete description and interpretation of the Turner and Hopewell sites would fall to the next generation.

It is most significant that Putnam never found the "spare time." He was (and is) celebrated as the preeminent builder of institutions within American archaeology, an honor he deserves for his unflagging work at Cambridge, Chicago, New York, and Berkeley. At the same time, Putnam's theoretical positions were extremely conservative and, in some instances, outdated or under question in his own lifetime. The caution engendered by early marginality and struggle eventually added to his credit as one committed to laying solid foundations, but the same conservatism led to a notable reluctance to venture far from his close methods of observation. His was a hands-on science, an archaeology of strained eyes and dirty fingernails.

References
Primary
Abbott, Charles C. 1889. Letter to F. W. Putnam, May 22. F. W. Putnam Papers, Harvard University Archives, Cambridge, MA.

American Antiquarian Society. 1885. *Proceedings for 1883–1885.* Worcester, MA.

———. 1887. *Proceedings for 1885–1887.* Worcester, MA.

Cushing, F. H. 1886. Letter to Alpheus Hyatt, January 20. Peabody Museum Papers, Harvard University Archives, Cambridge, MA.

Gillman, Henry. 1876. Letter to F. W. Putnam, October 6. Peabody Museum Archives, Harvard University, Cambridge, MA.

Owens, J. G. 1891. Letter to Deborah Stratton, October 25. John Owens Papers. Peabody Museum Archives, Harvard University, Cambridge, MA.

Putnam, Frederic Ward. 1879. *Archaeology.* Report of the U.S. Geographical Surveys West of the 100th Meridian (Wheeler Survey). Vol. 7. Washington, DC: Government Printing Office.

———. 1880. Letter to Lewis Henry Morgan, April 8. L. H. Morgan Papers, Rush Rhees Library, University of Rochester, Rochester, NY.

———. 1882. Letter to Stephen Salisbury, September 4. Salisbury Family
Papers, American Antiquarian Society, Worcester, MA.

———. 1890. Letter to Eben Putnam, February 25. F. W. Putnam
Papers, General Correspondence. Harvard University Archives,
Cambridge, MA.

———. 1893a. Letter, April 17. *Historical Collections of the Essex Institute*
30: 186–189.

———. 1893b. Letter to Edward E. Ayer, December 31. F. W. Putnam
Papers, Harvard University Archives, Cambridge, MA.

———. 1894. Letter to Samuel A. Crawford, March 7. Franz Boas
Papers, American Philosophical Society, Philadelphia.

———. 1898. Letter to Charles W. Eliot, June 22. C. W. Eliot Papers,
Harvard University Archives, Cambridge, MA.

Salisbury, S. 1875. Letter to Robert C. Winthrop, February 12. Salisbury
Family Papers, American Antiquarian Society, Worcester, MA.

Wilson, T. 1900. Letter to F. W. Putnam, January 3. F. W. Putnam Papers,
Harvard University Archives, Cambridge, MA.

Secondary

Benjamin, M. 1898. "Frederic Ward Putnam." *Scientific American* 79, 9:
131.

Boas, Franz, ed. 1909. *Putnam Anniversary Volume. Anthropological Essays
Presented to Frederic Ward Putnam in Honor of His 70th Birthday, April 16,
1909, by His Friends and Associate*s. Cedar Rapids, IA: Torch Press.

———. 1915. "Frederic Ward Putnam." *Science,* n.s. 42, 1080 (10
September): 330–332.

Dexter, R. W. 1965. "The 'Salem Secession' of Agassiz Zoologists." *Essex
Institute Historical Collections* 101, 1: 27–39.

———. 1966a. " Contributions of Frederic Ward Putnam to the
Development of Anthropology in California." *Science Education* 50, 4:
314–318.

———. 1966b. "Frederic Ward Putnam and the Development of
Museums of Natural History and Anthropology in the United States."
Curator 9, 2: 151–155.

———. 1966c. "Putnam's Problems Popularizing Anthropology." *American
Scientist* 54, 3: 315–332.

———. 1976. The Role of F. W. Putnam in Developing Anthropology at
the American Museum of Natural History. *Curator* 19, 4: 303–310.

———. 1977. "Contributions of Cincinnati-Area Physicians to Ohio
Archaeology in the 19th Century." *Ohio State Medical Journal:* 409–411.

———. 1978. "Guess Who's Not Coming to Dinner: Frederick Ward
Putnam and the Support of Women in Anthropology." *History of
Anthropology Newsletter* 5, 1.

———. 1982. "The Putnam-Metz Correspondence on Mound
Explorations in Ohio." *Ohio Archaeologist* 32, 4: 24–28.

Dixon, R. B. 1915. "Frederic Ward Putnam." *Harvard Graduates Magazine*
24: 305–308.

Dorsey, G. A. 1896. "History of the Study of Anthropology at Harvard
University." *Denison Quarterly* 4, 2: 77–97.

Hinsley, Curtis M. 1991. "The World as Marketplace: Commodification of the Exotic at the World's Fair Exposition, Chicago, 1893." In *Exhibiting Cultures: The Poetics and Politics of Museum Display,* ed. Ivan Karp and Steven D. Lavine. Washington, DC: Smithsonian Institution Press.

Kroeber, Alfred L. 1915. "Frederic Ward Putnam." *American Anthropologist* 17: 712–718.

Lurie, Edward. 1960. *Louis Agassiz: A Life in Science.* Chicago: University of Chicago

Mark, Joan. 1988. *A Stranger in Her Native Land: Alice Fletcher and the American Indians.* Lincoln: University of Nebraska Press.

Mead, Frances H. 1909. *Bibliography of Frederic Ward Putnam.* Reprinted from the Putnam Anniversary Volume: 601–627. Cedar Rapids, IA: Torch Press.

Morse, E. S. 1915. "Frederick Ward Putnam, 1839–1915: An Appreciation." *Historical Collections of the Essex Institute* 52: 3–8.

Noble, David F. 1992. *A World without Women: The Christian Clerical Culture of Western Science.* New York: Alfred A. Knopf.

Peabody, C. 1915. "Frederic Ward Putnam." *Journal of American Folklore* 28: 302–306.

Tozzer, Alfred M. 1935. "Frederic Ward Putnam, 1839–1915." *National Academy Biographical Memoirs* 16: 125–138.

Bo Gräslund

Gustaf Oscar Augustin
Montelius
1843–1921

No other single researcher has done as much to develop traditional archaeological dating methods as Oscar Montelius. Montelius's prehistoric chronology was based on the systematic organization of a wide variety of data types for relative chronology and the systematic use of cross-dating for the purpose of establishing absolute and relative dating.

S wedish archaeologist Gustaf Oscar Augustin Montelius was born in Stockholm on 9 September 1843 and died there on 4 November 1921. His family belonged to well-established administrative and ecclesiastical circles. Montelius began his studies at Uppsala University in 1861, first studying natural science but soon switching to the humanities, particularly history and the Scandinavian languages. In 1869, he received a Ph.D. in history with a thesis in archaeology (which was not an independent university discipline in Sweden until 1913).

By 1863, Montelius was employed on a part-time basis at the Museum of National Antiquities in Stockholm. He moved to permanent status in 1868, first as junior and then, in 1880, as senior executive officer. Between 1907 and 1913, he was state antiquarian and the head of the Central Board of Antiquities and the Museum of National Antiquities. He received an honorary professorship in 1888, but he was never attached to a particular university. In 1907, he was offered a chair in archaeology in Berlin, but he declined. Montelius was a fellow of the Swedish Academy (and a member of its Nobel Prize committee) and the Royal Academy of Letters, History, and Antiquities. He held membership as well in foreign scientific societies and in a large number of other organizations, and during his life he was charged with numerous commissions.

When Montelius began as a prehistorian in the mid-1860s, knowledge of chronological details in European archaeology was almost non-existent. In spite of a long research tradition, Scandinavian archaeology had not yet advanced beyond a division of the Stone Age into an earlier (Mesolithic) and a later (Neolithic) phase, a similar division of the Bronze Age into two stages, and a division of the Iron Age into three periods. In most other parts of Europe, prehistoric research had not even reached

Oscar Montelius.
(Uppsala University
Library)

that level of chronological understanding. Consequently, archaeologists were limited in their ability to interpret prehistoric life and society in any depth. Montelius clearly recognized this problem, and throughout his career as an archaeologist he was engaged in creating reliable time scales for prehistoric Europe. No other single researcher did so much to develop traditional archaeological dating methods as Montelius. Largely because of his efforts and methodological examples, prehistoric archaeology in northern Europe by the end of the century had access to a fairly detailed and reliable chronology, both in relative and absolute terms. In fact, Montelius's work left its mark on the development of prehistoric chronology in other parts of Europe as well as the Near East.

Bronze Age Chronology

Montelius's doctoral dissertation of 1869, "Från jernåldern" [From the Iron Age], was fairly descriptive, but it included an excellent discussion of the emergence of the Iron Age in northern Europe. His interest had already been caught by the problem of Bronze Age chronology. Ten years earlier, the famous Danish archaeologist J. J. A. Worsaae had divided Bronze Age graves into one earlier group characterized by inhumations under barrows and one later group with cremations in secondary positions or under flat ground. Montelius moved a step further by postulating a general division of Bronze Age artifacts into one earlier and one later phase.

From the beginning, Montelius realized that the only way to create something like a reliable chronology for the Bronze Age was to systematically collect data from a large geographical area and from essentially all kinds of archaeological sources. He embarked on this task with singular energy and purpose. Thanks to generous scholarships, he was able to undertake comprehensive travels in Europe. In 1876, 1877, and 1879 he visited most of the important museums, collections, and scholars in Europe, and he familiarized himself with practically all of the vital Bronze Age material, which at that time was mostly unpublished. Such wide-ranging research was a prerequisite of his overall evaluation of the Bronze Age in Europe.

Although he worked intermittently at numerous other tasks, Montelius seems to have been almost obsessed by the problem of Bronze Age chronology, particularly as it related to Scandinavia. The long road toward his final synthesis was lined with some twenty greater and minor publications, including a number of papers that he presented at the international archaeological congresses in Copenhagen (1869 and 1873), in Bologna (1871), in Stockholm (1874), and in Budapest (1876). Among some of the more comprehensive works were "Bronsåldern i norra och mellersta Sverige" [The Bronze Age in North and Central Sweden] (1872–1873) and "Spännen från bronsåldern" [Brooches of the Bronze Age] (1880–1882). However, none of these works foretold his definitive and unifying synthesis, which was published in 1885 in a monograph in Swedish entitled *Tidsbestämning inom bronsåldern med särskildt afseende på Skandinavien* [Dating in the Bronze Age with Special Reference to Scandinavia]; an abbreviated edition in English appeared in 1986.

In this book, Montelius divided the Bronze Age in Scandinavia and northern Germany into six main periods. Even today, this division is so well established that is often regarded as self-evident. But we should recall that before Montelius's books appeared, there was hardly any appreciation of the chronology of the Bronze Age in any European country. Montelius's most prominent colleagues, brilliant scholars like his own superior Hans Hildebrand, the Dane SOPHUS MÜLLER, and the Norwegian Ingjald Undset, had even expressed doubts about the possibilities of distinguishing two separate phases of the age. And at the end of the 1870s, authoritative German archaeologists were still questioning the very existence of a Bronze Age.

However, the criticism that had initially been directed toward Montelius's project was silenced when *Tidsbestämning* appeared. The documentation and argumentation of the book were so convincing and so extensive that Montelius's critics quickly capitulated. His chronological system for the Bronze Age with the six subperiods rapidly won wide approval in scientific circles.

In *Tidsbestämning,* Montelius also presented an absolute dating of the Bronze Age, something that until then had been almost completely obscure. Through cross-dating and comparing a limited number of closed finds from northern, central, and southern Europe and the Near East that contained artifacts of different geographical origin, Montelius was able to synchronize the subperiods of the Nordic Bronze Age with historically datable events in the eastern Mediterranean and the Near East. In this way, he succeeded in bracketing the period of the Nordic Bronze Age from about 1500 B.C. (at the latest) to about 500 B.C.

Montelius's Bronze Age chronology of 1885 has been repeatedly reinforced by new discoveries. For example, the magnificent burial site at Håga outside Uppsala proved to be a type find for his Bronze Age period four. When Montelius visited the excavation in 1904, he could be heard muttering contentedly to himself: "Well, they seem to have read my *Tidsbestämning*." This book is probably the only broad-ranging chronological work from that time, from any country, that has in all essentials retained its credibility to the present. The same is true for his absolute datings. Only a few years after the publication of *Tidsbestämning*, Montelius suggested that the beginning of the Nordic Bronze Age ought to be pushed even further back in time, to around 1800 B.C. His theory was considered unreasonable by the majority of the scientific community, and Montelius was barely in his grave when it was abandoned. In the 1970s, calibrated radiocarbon dating confirmed his postulate.

The enduring significance of Montelius's Bronze Age chronology is a reflection of its basis in sound scientific method. Montelius developed and refined an old Scandinavian tradition of grounding archaeological interpretation on data gained through the systematic observation of reliable find contexts—on the observation of what was generally found and not found together at sites. *Tidsbestämning* is, in fact, the first example of the methodical organization of a great number of find data for the creation of a relative chronology. It also stands out as the first example of the systematic use of cross-dating for the purpose of establishing absolute and relative datings. Regardless, Montelius's methodological masterpiece, which was published only in Swedish, has remained essentially unknown outside Scandinavia; paradoxically, his great international reputation rests mainly on later works published in German, English, and French, which have not had the same lasting authority.

Stone and Bronze Age Chronology

In 1891 Montelius published a monograph in German, *Zur Chronologie der jüngeren Steinzeit in Skandinavien* [The Chronology of the Neolithic in Scandinavia], in which he sketched three main divisions for the Late Stone Age. Each was characterized by one of the three primary megalithic grave types: dolmens, passage graves, and stone cists. Closed artifact finds were scarce, but they were still numerous enough to allow Montelius, with some intuitive input, to draw up the absolute temporal framework for the Neolithic period. He hypothesized, again by means of cross-dating, its beginnings at around 3000 B.C. Although at the time this starting point was considered much too early, radiocarbon dating more than two generations later revealed that it was actually not early enough. Montelius next turned to the chronological problems of the Iron Age. In 1895–1897 he published *Den nordiska jernålderns kronologi* [The Chronology of the Nordic Iron Age], where he again brought order to a previously muddled chronological scene.

Dolmen at Håga, on the island of Orust. (Reprinted from Oscar Montelius, Civilizations of Sweden, 1969)

European Chronology

Montelius's cross-dating studies in *Tidsbestämning* eventually led to the first modern overview of the chronological relationships of the Bronze Age for the whole area between northern Italy and Scandinavia. His goal was to develop a chronology for the period 2500 B.C.–500 B.C. for much of Europe, the Mediterranean, and the Near East. He presented condensed chronological overviews for the Bronze Age in various areas, such as Egypt, France, and the British Isles. In 1903, he summarized his views on the chronology and the cultural relationships of the Copper Age and the earliest Bronze Age in northern Europe in a comprehensive, influential work in German entitled *Die Chronologie der ältesten Bronzezeit in Norddeutschland und Skandinavien* [The Chronology of the Earliest Bronze Age in Northern Germany and Scandinavia]. Here, he also examined archaeological data that demonstrated cultural contacts between the northern countries and the eastern Mediterranean area.

During the later part of his career, Montelius devoted his attention to the study of northern and central Italy, areas that were important for the evaluation of the Bronze Age north of the Alps, and to the preclassical period in Italy, Greece, and the Near East. From 1895 to 1910 he produced a magnificent five-volume corpus in French, *La civilisation primitive en Italie depuis l'introduction des métaux* [The Primitive Civilizations of Italy before the Introduction of Metals]. His chronological synthesis was published in 1896 in *Preclassical Chronology in Greece and Italy*. In 1912, two richly illustrated volumes, *Die vorklassische Chronologie Italiens* [The Preclassical

Chronology of Italy], presented a twelve-part division of the Stone and Bronze Ages in Italy. A corresponding work for Greece, *La Grèce préclassique* [Preclassical Greece], was published posthumously in 1924. Two additional significant works were: *Die Bronzezeit im Orient und Griechenland* [The Bronze Age of the Near East and Greece], published in 1892, and *Die älteren Kulturperioden im Orient und Europa* [The Oldest Periods of Civilization in the Near East and Europe] from 1916–1923.

The Typological Method

Montelius's name has been closely associated with the so-called typological method of dating in archaeology. It was developed jointly with Hans Hildebrand at the beginning of the 1870s. The method involves the ordering of artifact types according to their characteristics, such as form, decoration, and size, in a relative time sequence based on degrees of similarity and dissimilarity. Montelius's Bronze Age chronology has often been regarded as the first successful application of the typological method, but this is incorrect. There is no real typological analysis in *Tidsbestämning*, which, in all essentials, is based on observations of the closed finds and other find-contexts.

The misapprehension of Montelius as the great typologist (Hildebrand was that to a much larger degree) primarily results from Montelius's own rather unclear theoretical writings, in works such as *Den förhistoriske fornforskarens metod och material* [The Methods and Material of Prehistoric Archaeology] from 1884 and two often-cited works, *Typologien eller utvecklingsläran tillämpad på det mänskliga arbetet* [Typology, or The Theory of Evolution Applied on Human Production] from 1899 and "Die typologische Methode" [The Typological Method] from 1903. Montelius gave the impression that he worked in two stages: First, he made a wholly independent typological analysis, and then he used the find-contexts to check the results. However, there is no doubt that in practice, he worked the opposite way. Like Hildebrand, Montelius also proposed an analogy between cultural development and biological evolution. But a closer examination of Montelius's work and of the development of archaeology during the years when the typological method was being established suggests that the Darwinian theory of evolution was hardly an incitement to typology as a method for dating. It was instead used as a powerful tool of instructive comparison whose main aim was to legitimize the young science of archaeology.

Montelius as a Scholar

As a prehistorian, Montelius did not have a theoretical bent. He was primarily an empiricist, but he was also, for his time, an unusually conscientious methodologist. His strength lay in his supreme ability to collect information, to systematize, digest, and generalize great quantities of archaeological data, and to present his results in a clear and convincing way. He utilized his knowledge of details to illuminate broad questions, but he did not allow a single part to overshadow the whole. In all that he undertook, whether practical work or research, his keen ability to separate the unimportant from the important was evident. Considering his enormous production, it is also striking, seen from a modern perspective, how few serious scientific misjudgments he made. This primarily reflects his in-depth knowledge of the archaeological material, his focus on the overall find-contexts, and his steady methodological skills, which did not exclude a certain intuitive judgment when data was scanty.

Given his systematic nature, energy, and curiosity, it is remarkable that Montelius did not become a prominent excavator. Though he carried out many smaller digs, he never engaged in larger excavations, and he often failed to produce sufficient excavation reports and publications for those excavations he did undertake.

Aside from his chronologies, Montelius was also interested in issues of prehistoric culture. He was an energetic advocate of the opinion that prehistoric Europe was closely tied together by distribution networks through which cultural diffusion took place, mainly in the direction from the eastern Mediterranean to northwestern Europe. He rejected the contemporary supposition that marked changes in the archaeological material were the result of migrations; instead, he maintained that, according to the archaeological sources, Scandinavia had been characterized by population continuity since the Neolithic period. Montelius also held to his opinion that cultural diffusion from the south to the north took place more quickly than was generally believed at that time.

Montelius was an energetic popularizer of his science. He continuously made public presentations of the collections at the Museum of National Antiquities, and he gave innumerable lectures, even touring Europe and the United States. Many of his scientific works were edited for consumption by the general public, including a substantial number of monographs and some fifty articles. In these popularized publications, he placed less emphasis on the chronological problems that engaged him so much as a researcher and discussed instead general cultural and social perspectives, expressing himself not in scientific jargon but in a simple, clear, and easy style.

Montelius as a Person

Through his scientific accomplishments and his personal qualities, Montelius became a central figure in European archaeology. Many of his works were published in major European languages. His correspondence was enormous, he was a great traveler (and was often accompanied by his wife), and he was an esteemed guest and lecturer at museums and universities all over Europe. His extensive international network of contacts was no doubt facilitated by his proficiency in both written and spoken German, French, Italian, and English.

Montelius's character seems to have been rather straightforward and uncomplicated. Though certainly relishing his position as an international authority, his vanity was balanced by a cheerful and conciliatory temperament and a sense of humor that kept him from taking himself or his science too seriously. Quick to laugh and joke, he was a social person to whom others were attracted, and he possessed an inexhaustible fund of anecdotes. In contrast to his openness about everyday things, however, his deeper personal feelings were kept private. By nature cooperative, he sought to defray confrontation, and he appeared in many situations as an equalizing and unifying presence. In discussing his own scientific ideas he was sure and pertinent. Since he himself was sensitive to criticism, he tended to be markedly generous in his judgments of others.

As a rule, Montelius lectured without notes, speaking with great elegance in a powerful, melodious voice. He had a stately and robust figure. He was a hard worker, blessed with good health that lasted until the last days of his life. Politically Montelius was a liberal. Through his wife, he became interested in women's rights and supported the fight for female suffrage, and he was also heavily involved in the Scandinavian movement and in inter-Nordic cultural circles (a movement that was concerned with preserving and enhancing Scandinavian culture).

Oscar Montelius lived all his life in Stockholm, in the same house in which he was born. In 1871 he married Agda Reuterskiöld; they had no children. Montelius died in Stockholm at the age of seventy-eight.

References
Primary
Oscar Montelius's published works comprise 408 items. A complete bibliography, except for a few posthumously edited works, appeared in G. Ekholm, *Bibliographia Monteliana* (Uppsala, 1922).

Montelius's private archives are located in the Antiquarian-Topographical Archives in Stockholm.

A selection of works in non-Swedish languages follows.

Montelius, G. O. A. 1885. *Dating in the Bronze Age with Special Reference to Scandinavia*. With an introduction by Bo Gräslund. Stockholm, 1986. Condensed translation of the Swedish *Tidsbestämning inom bronsåldern, med särskildt afseende på Skandinavien*. Stockholm.

———. 1888. *The Civilisation of Sweden in Heathen Times*. London.

———. 1890. "L'age du bronze en Egypte." *L'anthropologie*.

———. 1895, 1904, 1910, and 1923. *La civilisation primitive en Italie depuis l'introduction des métaux*, vols. 1–4. Stockholm: Imprimerie royale; Berlin: A. Asher

———. 1895. *Les temps préhistorique en Suède et dans les autres pays scandinaves*. Paris.

———. 1898. Die Bronzezeit im Orient und Griechenland. *Archiv für Anthropologie* 25: 1898.

———. 1899. *Der Orient und Europa*. Stockholm.

———. 1900. Die Bronzezeit im Orient und Griechenland. *Archiv für Anthropologie* 26: 1900.

———. 1902. *La chronologie préhistorique en France et en d'autres pays celtiques*. Compte rendu, Congrès International d'Anthropologie et d'Archaéologie Préhistorique. Paris.

———. 1903. *Die typologische Methode. Die älteren Kulturperioden im Orient und Europa, I, Die Methode*. Stockholm.

———. 1906. *Kulturgeschichte Schwedens von den ältesten Zeiten bis zum elften Jahrhundert nach Christus*. Leipzig.

———. 1907. "Les debuts de l'age de fer." *Annales, 20e Congrès archéologique et historique de Belgique*, 1907. Gand.

———. 1907. "Les relations entre la France et l'Italie à l'age du bronze." *Compte-rendus, Association Français pour l'Avancement des Sciences*, 35, Reims, 1907; Paris, 1908.

———. 1908. "The Chronology of the British Bronze Age." *Archaeologia* 16: 1908.

———. 1912. *Die vorklassische Chronologie Italiens*. Vols. 1–2. Stockholm.

———. 1916–1923. *Die älteren Kulturperioden im Orient und Europa*.

———. 1924. *La Grèce préclassique*. Stockholm.

Leo Klejn

Nikodim Pavlovich Kondakov   *1844–1925*

A scholar of the history, development, and influences of Byzantine art, Kondakov was one of the founders of Russian archaeology and Russian art history. He died in exile, and his influence on Russian archaeologists and their discipline in Russia today is only now being acknowledged.

An outstanding Russian archaeologist and an art historian, a specialist in Byzantine history, the founder of the far-flung Novorossiysk-Petersburg school of archaeology, Kondakov was born in the village of Khalan, in the province of Kursk. His father was a freed serf and the steward of the estate of Prince Trubetskoys. He grew rich and sent his son to study at secondary school in Moscow in 1855. In 1861, the year that serfdom was abolished, Kondakov entered the University of Moscow to study with the prominent Slavic historian and philologist Fedor Ivanovich Buslayev (1818–1897). Buslayev was one of the pioneers of comparative linguistics in Russia and was known for his investigations of Russian mythology and symbolism. He was interested in the interaction of cultures and developed the idea of "wandering motifs"—motifs that appear in the art of different groups—in folkloric studies. The interests of this teacher were passed on to his disciple Kondakov.

However, Buslayev was skeptical of the growing discipline of prehistoric archaeology, primarily because it was founded on evolutionary principles and he could not accept Darwinism. In 1873 he published the article "Guesses and Dreams about Primordial Mankind" in "Rossiyskiy Vestnik" (*The Russian Herald*), in which he jeered at the ideas of evolutionists:

> Some beast made arms of forepaws, began to grind stones and discovered by chance the secret [of] how to get fire by friction and drilling, then became an expert, a shaman and a priest after being a lame cripple. . . . The reader sees himself to what extent all that playing at a primitive man is far from the precise method of positive sciences.

Kondakov, in consideration of the strength of his teacher's opinions, chose a later, less controversial period for his own studies—one

Nikodim Pavlovich Kondakov. (Courtesy of Dr. R. Munchaev, Director, Institute of Archaeology, Russian Academy of Sciences)

that was elucidated in annals and chronicles and that involved plenty of beautiful objects.

Buslayev believed that Slavic heathenism was very peculiar, in that it was forgotten in ancient Russian art, which, he insisted, had developed from ancient Christian and Byzantine art. These ideas strongly influenced Kondakov as well as Buslayev's other pupils who worked in this field, such as A. N. Afanasyev (1826–1871), who became famous for his three-volume work *Poetical Views of Slavs on Nature* (1865–1869), which is still read; A. A. Kotliarevskiy (1837–1881), known to Slavic archaeologists for his work *About Funeral Customs of Slavs;* A. N. Veselovskiy (1838–1903), a widely known historian of literature, master of comparative analysis, and the author of *Historical Poetics;* and Vsevolod Fedorovich Miller (1848–1913), the founder of the historical school of Russian folkloric studies and a prominent investigator of the relationship between Scythians, Sarmatians, and Ossetians.

Kondakov graduated in 1866 and became a teacher at the same secondary school where he had been a student and his first publications appeared. After traveling abroad to study classical monuments, he was appointed in 1871 to the professorial chair of the theory and history of art at the Novorossiysk University in Odessa, one of Russia's preeminent universities. Odessa had an old archaeological museum and the Odessa Archaeological Society, which had existed since 1839. Fedor Ivanovich Uspenskiy, who was to become an academician (member of an imperial academy of eminent academics) and the leading figure in Russian Byzantine history, also worked at the university. In Kondakov's inaugural lecture, "The Discipline of Classical Archaeology and the Theory of Arts," he described classical archaeology in the spirit of JOHANN JOACHIM WINCKELMANN, as connected primarily with art. This tradition was very popular in both Russia and Germany. The essence of Kondakov's lecture was that art theory could attain scholarly status if it used the facts of art history and classical archaeology.

Scholars in Odessa were actively studying the local classical monuments of the Northern Black Sea littoral region, and Kondakov immediately joined them in that work. In 1876–1878 he took part in the excavation of the necropolis of ancient Nimphaeum in Kerch (the Crimea), where members of both the Greek and Scythian aristocracy were buried. In the opinion of later Russian archaeologists, the Nimphaeum in Kerch was excavated, researched, and recorded in three years in more detail than any other necropolis in the classical world, including the classical centers of Athens, Pergamon, Miletus, and Rome, where excavations had been going on for centuries. This work proved to be of great assistance and inspiration to Kondakov in his subsequent work on Byzantine art.

From 1873 Kondakov traveled regularly to study antiquities: in 1873 to Georgia, in 1875–1876 to the main cities of Europe (Vienna, Paris, London, and so on), and their museums and libraries, in 1881 to the Sinai, and in 1884 to Constantinople. At the end of each journey Kondakov would produce a monumental work of summary and synthesis, and piece by piece the history of Byzantine art was described and published in *The Ancient Architecture of Georgia* (1876) and in *Byzantine Churches and Monuments of Constantinople* (1884). In 1875–1876 Kondakov published his doctoral thesis as *The History of Byzantine Art and the Iconography on the Miniatures of Greek Manuscripts.* This work won the Gold Medal of the Russian Archaeological Society, and as a result, in addition to receiving his doctoral degree, Kondakov was appointed to the influential Emperor's Archaeological Commission, whose three members were in charge of all archaeological activity in Russia.

In his thesis Kondakov argued that Byzantine art was not stagnant; it had developed and transformed. In the style of Winckelmann, Kondakov described how each period had its own iconography and its own stylistic representation of a given image. Byzantine artists did not aim at representation of the truth of nature; rather they were concerned with describing devotion to God and with the expression of definite spiritual values. Byzantine art was theological art and every detail was the symbol of a spiritual value. Kondakov's approach was to describe art as a process independent of society. "A monument must be elucidated by itself, according to its historical attributes," Kondakov wrote later (*Byzantine Enamels* 1892).

Kondakov saw the scholar's task as placing material in a historical order using comparative analysis, dating the item and then elucidating its relation to the more general artistic processes of its epoch. Thus the history of art did not undertake historical analysis of content—that was the business of the archaeology of art. Kondakov insisted that scholars had to separate the form from the content of art history. He considered that the analysis of content (mode of life, political conditions, and the like) was the business of classical archaeology and that form was the least studied aspect of the material.

In his work the young scholar laid out concrete methods of formal analysis. These comprised a comparative method, or "the method of objective comparison of forms," and, more often, an iconographic method, with "the iconographic type" as its principal. Vladimir Nikolayevich Lazarev, a disciple of Kondakov, explained that "Byzantine art was not an art of individual masters and artists . . . the typical approach to reality, presented in canonical, ideal forms predominated in it invariably . . . types, once worked out, lasted with extraordinary steadiness in Byzantine art, they underwent only insignificant and chiefly gradual changes in the process of development" (Lazarev 1925, 7).

There was a high degree of standardization in Byzantine art. Each image had obligatory attributes and peculiarities, and it was not difficult to make them out. The difficulty was with revealing changes in them. Kondakov investigated the movement of forms and their changes, tracing traditions, influences, and decadence in the material. He grouped works of ancient art according to their themes and plots. The basic pivot of the method was the concept of amendments: researchers tried to identify copies and their relationship to the original; copies formed the amendment. Kondakov's iconographic method was concerned not with describing diffused stylistic correlations, but with establishing the exact dependence of copies on the original. It analyzed Byzantine art by exposing genetic lines of copying and tracing the influences and adaptations in the development of the iconographic.

Thus the conception of the type entered Russian archaeology a decade before the appearance of OSCAR MONTELIUS's work, albeit in another context. Montelius established the development and evolution of type from initial forms to daughter forms, and Kondakov established the relation of the original to its copies. In Russian archaeological literature Kondakov was often accused of extreme formalism, although common sense would indicate that it is necessary to study forms in order to comprehend content. Source criticism studies are often similarly charged with embodying only source criticism rather than historical character. Kondakov went too far in stressing formal analysis: the description of types is itself an interpretation of content. Kondakov founded a school of specialist Byzantine archaeology at Novorossiysk University, and he gave his students not only an interest in Byzantine art but also the skills to study it via his iconographic method.

In 1888 Kondakov, now forty-four, was given the chair of art history at Petersburg University, along with the position of principal curator of medieval antiquities at the Imperial Hermitage Museum. In 1889 he became an academician. Two of his pupils moved with him from Odessa: D. V. Aynalov (1862–1938), who became a well-known historian of art and was the author of *Hellenistic Principles of Byzantine Art;* and

Boris Vladimirovich Farmakovskiy (1870–1928), the future head of Soviet classical archaeology and one of the founders of the Russian Academy of the History of Material Culture.

Kondakov arrived in Petersburg during a fierce conflict between Petersburg and Moscow archaeologists. The Imperial Archaeological Commission, under its chairman archaeologist Count A. A. Bobrinskiy, monopolized permissions to excavate. The Moscow Archaeological Society, with Countess Praskovia Sergeevna Uvarova at its head, began a campaign against Bobrinskiy. A group of Petersburg archaeologists, including Kondakov, left the Moscow Archaeological Society in solidarity with the Archaeological Commission. Kondakov had not been in touch with the Moscow archaeologists for ten years, which was much longer than his new colleagues in Petersburg, but he was a man of principle and an extraordinarily loyal man.

From 1889, Kondakov and his friend Ivan Ivanovich Tolstoy, a future academician, began a monumental multivolume work in both Russian and French entitled *Russian Antiquities in Monuments of Art*. It was conceived "to represent . . . the development of ancient Russian art in exact pictures of artistic monuments of Russian antiquity and olden times." The first two volumes were published in 1889: Volume I, "Classical Antiquities of South Russia," and Volume II, "Scythian and Sarmatian Antiquities." Six volumes were published in all (1889–1899).

Kondakov continued his work on Russian archaeology and in 1898 he published a new synthesis: *Russian Hoards. A Study of Antiquities of the Period of the Grand Dukes.* Using formal stylistic analysis, Kondakov considered "research of burial mound antiquities, hoards and others first of all in the aspect of their style, typical form of subjects, its historical changes" to be his main task (*Russian Hoards,* p. 10). Thus the iconographic typology was transformed imperceptibly by Kondakov himself into the archaeological typology, i.e., into a stylistic version of the functional category of things. The book became a series, and successive volumes were published in Soviet times.

Kondakov continued to travel extensively—in 1888 he visited Spain, in 1889 the Caucasus, in 1891 Syria and Palestine, and in 1898 the Slavic countries. The research and conclusions of these journeys were published at the beginning of the twentieth century, with the result that Byzantine art could be described as a complex of monuments that stretched from Constantinople in Asia Minor and the Near East to the Balkan Peninsula, from the Caucasus to Italy, and from Egypt to Russia. For Kondakov, Byzantine art was the result of three different cultural and aesthetic traditions. The first was from Hellenism, and the second from Greek-Oriental Asia Minor, the Levant, and Egypt. The third great influence was from the nomads from the steppes of the Black and Caspian Seas to Central Asia and South Siberia. The second tradition was the greatest influence on Slavic art: "Cultures of the Russian and Slavic-Balkan South were apparently made up in the general condition of influence from basic Greek-Oriental culture, and we must explain the supremacy of the Oriental element in our and Balkan decoration just by that fact, not by influence of Central Asia and Persia" (Kondakov 1909, 59).

Many of Kondakov's new students in Petersburg went on to greater things—Yakov Ivanovich Smirnov (1869–1918) became famous because of his studies of Sassanid silver; Sergey Aleksandrovich Zhebelev

(1867–1941) later became the head of Soviet historian-classicists, wrote the first Russian introduction to archaeology and died of starvation during the siege of Leningrad; Boris Andreyevich Turayev became the head of Russian Egyptology and was the teacher of Vasiliy Vasilyevich Struve, who would later become the head of Soviet Oriental studies. All four became Academicians, but Kondakov considered his best pupil to be Yakov Smirnov, although another, Mikhail Ivanovich Rostovtsev (1870–1952), became the most famous. He was an expert on Scythian archaeology and a historian of Hellenism and of Roman economic relations; he emigrated to the United States in 1920 to take up a teaching position at the University of Wisconsin.

Another archaeologist, Vladimir Nikolayevich Lazarev (1897–1976), thirty years younger than all of them, spent most of his life analyzing Kondakov's creative work. Good students were attracted to and inspired by Kondakov because of his extensive knowledge and the novelty of his ideas, but perhaps also because of his teaching abilities, gained during his years as a secondary school teacher. Kondakov wrote loquaciously, and his style was almost banal and languid. His pupils stuck together and were called "fact-admirers"—not that they all kept to the empirical method, but their particular attention to form and formalism resulted in their nickname. All of Kondakov's disciples were noted for their phenomenal erudition and for their fundamental synthesizing studies. If Kondakov had done little except educate his famous disciples, that alone would have been enough to immortalize his name in the discipline of archaeology. But he made other significant contributions, first in Odessa and then in Petersburg. His work deeply impressed his pupils, and this is especially evident in the creative work of Rostovtsev and Farmakovskiy.

The end of the nineteenth century was a prolific period in Russian archaeology. In 1899 two important Russian archaeological landmarks were published. The first of these—A. A. Spitsyn's *The Settling of Ancient Russian Tribes According to Archaeological Data*—determined the boundaries of annalistic Russian tribes. This important work can be compared with the analogous work of GUSTAF KOSSINNA but it appeared earlier. The second significant work—*Russian Prehistoric Ceramics* by VASILIY ALEKEYE- VICH GORODCOV—developed the basic principles for the formal analysis of ceramics and any archaeological material, becoming the basis of all the typological work by Russian archaeologists. The influence of these principles spread to the Americas with the translation of Gorodcov's work into English.

In 1899 Kondakov gave the lecture "On Scholarly Tasks of the History of Ancient Russian Art" at the Society of Amateurs of Ancient Written Language and Art, stating that ancient Russian art represented "an original artistic type, a large-scale historic phenomenon formed due to the work of the Great Russian people with the help of quite a number of foreign and oriental peoples." Kondakov ascertained that the origins of Russian art lay in its relation to Byzantine art and the influence of the Orient and the world of nomads. Nomadic influences, from the Scythians to the Tartars, were as significant as the influences of settled peoples. The "barbarians," such as the Persians, he said, were just as important to study as the Romans. In this matter Kondakov anticipated a later "Eurasianist" perspective. Zhebelev described Kondakov's lecture as "a war-cry for Russian archaeology."

Kondakov proved that the influence of Byzantine art on Russian art was not constricting and necrotizing, but particularly fruitful. One can argue that surely both tendencies existed and that what hampered the development of Russian art in some areas also enriched and stimulated it in others. At the time these ideas were fresh. According to Kondakov, Russian masters did not merely copy Byzantine forms, they also used them creatively, drawing upon previous original Russian art, with its own local roots. The mixing of one's own (local) and another's forms could result in the creation of something new. These ideas were alien to diffusionism, and I have suggested elsewhere that this significant new current of ideas should be called "combinationism." The French historian Gabriel de Tarde considered that innovations are only "combinations of previous images" and that one may describe an invention as "a logical copulation." At the beginning of the twentieth century Leo Frobenius, who likened cultures to living organisms, talked about the crossing or pairing (*Paarung*) of cultures. Later, in 1911–1920, the British ethnographer W. H. R. Rivers took the idea further. According to Rivers, material objects and their types may spread in the course of contact, but language, religion, and social structures interact, on the whole, only during the amalgamation of peoples. The results of this amalgamation resemble, not a mechanical mixture (as argued by the German ethnologist Fritz Graebner), but a chemical alloy, with new properties.

Kondakov began to work with these ideas and they were taken further by his pupils Rostovtsev and Farmakovskiy. Rostovtsev used the example of the Bosporus and Scythia, where Iranian elements combined with local Greek elements. Farmakovskiy considered the results of the combination of the Ionic with the Oriental in the archaic Scythian culture of the Caucasus. Academician Ivan Ivanovich Tolstoy (who was the teacher of Vladimir Yakovlevich Propp, an outstanding specialist in folklore and the founder of Russian semiotics) and the famous artistic and literary critic Vladimir Vasilyevich Stasov, who discovered the sepulchral vault in the Pantikapaeum necropolis in 1872, were Kondakov's long-term friends. Meanwhile Kondakov himself took more and more interest in icons and in 1911 published his important work in this area: *Iconography of Our Lady. Connections of Greek and Russian Icon-painting with Italian Painting of the Early Renaissance* (later the two-volume *Iconography of Our Lady* [1914–1915]).

The reign of Tsar Nicolas I in the nineteenth century is still remembered in Russia as a time when the government sought to redefine Russia and Russian culture as an expression of the Orthodox East as distinct from the cultural traditions of the West. Byzantium was the prototype for the contemporary Russian Empire, in that it unified Europe and Asia and was the source of Orthodoxy and the pattern for autocracy. In 1841 a royal edict ordered architects to keep "the semblance of ancient Byzantine architecture" in mind when building churches.

However, this meant that liberal intellectuals and revolutionaries identified Byzantine influence with dominant dogmatic principles and with the maintenance of traditions of autocracy and Orthodoxy. For such intellectuals Kondakov's work was justification for, and praise of, the conservative foundations of Russian society. Kondakov was indeed a conservative, closely connected with monarchist and church circles. He was also the imperial court's expert on icon-painting. The son of an ex-serf, he was now readily admitted to the palace of Tsar Nicolas II. In 1916, during the First World War, he received the Legion of Honor from the French government.

Kondakov was seventy-three and in the Crimea when the Revolution began. During the Civil War (1918–1920) he lived in Odessa in territory occupied mainly by antirevolutionary and anticommunist White Russians and by supporting troops of the European powers. When that outpost of the counterrevolution fell at the end of 1919, Kondakov left with a crowd of emigrants on a French steamer bound for Constantinople. From there he traveled to Sofia in Bulgaria, where he lived for a year. Poor working conditions caused him to move in 1921 to Prague in Czechoslovakia, where his Russian and foreign pupils organized the Seminarium Kondakovianum under his leadership. This was transformed into the Kondakov Institute after his death in 1925. The institute was very important in the development of Czechoslovak Byzantine art criticism and Slav philology and history. It was also well known for the work of the outstanding Czech archaeologist and Slav historian Lubor Niderle (1865–1944). When the Germans occupied Czechoslovakia, the institute moved to Belgrade, in Yugoslavia, where it was destroyed in 1941 during a German air raid.

After Kondakov's death Lazarev published a booklet dedicated to the memory of his teacher. But Kondakov was completely ignored by the

Soviet Union, because he was a specialist in the art of the Russian Orthodox church and he was a White Russian émigré. His numerous pupils, and the pupils of his pupils, have occupied leading positions in Soviet academe. D. V. Aynalov, B. V. Farmakovskiy, B. A. Turayev, V. N. Lazarev, V. V. Struve are some examples. He is now recognized as a founder of Russian archaeology and well regarded for his contributions to the discipline as an erudite thinker, generator of ideas, great scholar, and great teacher.

References
Primary

Kondakov, Nikodim Pavlovich. 1875–1876. *Istoriya vizantiyskogo iskusstva i ikonografia po miniatyuram grecheskikh rukopisey* [History of Byzantine Art and Iconography after Miniatures of Greek Manuscripts].

———. 1875–1876. *Nauka klassicheskoy arkheologii i teorii iskusstv* [The Science of Classical Archaeology and Theory of Arts].

———. 1889–1899. *Russkie drevnostti v pamyatnikakh iskusstva* [Russian Antiquities in Monuments and Art]. Vols. 1–6. St. Petersburg (in cooperation with I. I. Tolstoy).

———. 1892. *Vizantiiskoi emali* [Byzantine Enamels]. St. Petersburg.

———. 1898. *Russkie klady. Issledovanie drevnostey velikoknyazheskogo perioda* [Russian Hoards. A Study of Ancient Grand Dukes Period]. St. Petersburg.

———. 1899. *O nauchnykh zadachakh istorii drevnerusskogo iskusstva* [On the Scholarly Tasks of History of Ancient Russian Art]. Pamyatniki Drevney Pis'mennosti, 132.

———. 1909. *Macedonia.* St. Petersburg.

———. 1911. *Ikonografiya Bogomateri. Svyazi grecheskoy i russkoy ikonopisi s italyanskoy zhivopis'yu rahhego Vozrozhdeniya* [Iconography of Our Lady. Connections of Greek and Russian Icon Painting with the Italian Painting of the Early Renaissance].

———. 1914–1915. *Ikonografia Bogomateri* [Iconography of Our Lady]. Vols. 1–2. St. Petersburg.

Secondary

Lazarev, Vladimir Nikolayevich. 1925. *Nikodim Pavlovich Kondakov (1844–1925).* Moscow.

David J. Meltzer

William Henry Holmes   1846–1933

William Henry Holmes's great knowledge of ceramic and lithic technologies, his pioneering studies of the American Paleolithic, and his interdisciplinary approach to archaeology make him one of the precursors of the "New Archaeology."

William Henry Holmes was the preeminent figure in American archaeology in the decades around the turn of the century. His status was partly rooted in achievement: Holmes pioneered new arenas in the study of material culture, particularly ceramic and lithic technology; he spearheaded the highly successful rout of the "American Paleolithic" (the claim that prehistory in the Americas began, as it did in Europe, in Pleistocene times and was marked by artifacts similar to those of the European Paleolithic); he took a scientific and "philosophical approach" (Mason 1886, 818), which was valued not so much for its content—a bridge across disciplines to link a venerable method with the fashionable (evolutionary) theory of his day—but for existing at all when much of archaeology was methodologically soft and theoryless; he was, as a result, a precursor of what was hailed as the "New Archaeology." In part, however, Holmes's status was rooted in office: he was a key figure in Washington, D.C., science, when the capital's museums and research bureaus were at the center of American science. But when that center shifted into the expanding university system, changing with it the theoretical compass of American anthropology, Holmes's prominence diminished—to the point that his work virtually disappeared from archaeological sight. Only lately has there been renewed interest and appreciation of his contributions (e.g., Johnson 1993; Meltzer and Dunnell 1992).

Holmes was born and raised in pre–Civil War, rural Ohio but was of "small account on the [family] farm," spending his time hunting, fishing, sketching, and painting, while his older brothers assumed the "heavier burdens" (WHH/RR 1:12). In school he earned a teaching certificate, but after beginning that career he found the "teacher's life so unattractive" that he decided to take up art instead. Failing in several attempts to get artistic instruction, he resigned himself to teaching and, with a $200 advance from his father, left for Salem, Massachusetts, to take courses "in a teacher's school of high grade." He never got there. Before he left Ohio, a chance meeting with a War Department clerk from Washington inspired Holmes to visit that city to seek instruction in art.

*William Henry
Holmes.
(Smithsonian
Institution photo no.
PORT 45-A-1)*

Holmes arrived in Washington the spring of 1871 and enrolled in the classes of the painter Theodore Kaufmann, quietly "relegat[ing] to the scrap heap" the idea of a teaching career (WHH/RR 1:24–25). Mary Henry, daughter of Joseph Henry, secretary of the Smithsonian Institution, was also in Kaufmann's class and told Holmes about the Smithsonian. He went there to sketch, and on his first visit in April 1871 he was barely inside when he stopped to draw two mounted birds. A passing naturalist glanced at the sketches and then invited Holmes to the up-stairs research areas to see the illustrations in a volume on hummingbirds.

There Holmes met several resident scientists, one of whom (the paleontologist Fielding Meek) hired Holmes on the spot to draw fossils and do other artistic piecework. Holmes's skills sharpened, and a year later he was appointed artist on Ferdinand V. Hayden's United States Geological and Geographical Survey of the Territories—one of four federally sponsored, competing geological surveys that were fore-runners of the present United States Geological Survey (USGS).

Holmes went west that summer of 1872 to Yellowstone, Wyoming, and from then on his professional life always inextricably mixed science and art and, though it took many paths, never strayed too far or too long from government service. By the time he retired sixty years later, he had served as an artist and geologist for the Hayden survey and the USGS (1872–1889); he had risen from illustrator and honorary curator of aboriginal pottery at the Smithsonian Institution's United States National Museum (USNM) to its head curator of anthropology (1882–1894, 1897–1920); he had been an archaeologist with the Smithsonian's Bureau of American Ethnology (BAE) and succeeded its founder, John Wesley Powell, as its chief (1889–1894, 1902–1909); and in the last half of his career (1906–1932) he had served as curator and ultimately director of the National Gallery of Art. The only interruption from steady Washington employ was three years in Chicago (1894–1897), where he was curator of anthropology in the newly formed Field Museum of Natural History and professor of archaeologic and graphic geology at the University of Chicago. (For further biographical details, see Hough 1933; Mark 1980, 131–163; Meltzer and Dunnell 1992, x–xxv; Nelson 1980; Swanton 1937.)

Holmes's interest in archaeology was kindled in 1875 when he was placed in charge of the Hayden party responsible for surveying the San Juan Valley of New Mexico, Arizona, and Colorado (Holmes 1878b). As he described it, "This region was the home of the ancient cliff-dwellers [Anasazi] and I examined and reported on the remarkable ruins encountered at nearly every turn, thus making [my] entry into the fascinating realm of archaeology" (WHH/RR 1:30). Although he spent the next fourteen years nominally employed as a geologist, increasing amounts of his time were devoted to "the study of primitive art in its various branches" (WHH/RR 1:33). These were years in which Powell was the director of both the USGS and BAE (an unusual arrangement that lasted from 1881 to 1894), and he paid little heed to the bureaucratic fences between the two agencies: their administrative and (to a degree) scientific staffs were interchangeable (Rabbitt 1980, 59). It was individual freedom and genius that was important to Powell, and each person was expected to find and fulfill theirs (Hinsley 1981, 152).

Holmes found his in archaeology. In the early 1880s, the USNM began receiving large collections from throughout North America, and especially from the BAE's mound survey in the eastern United States (under Cyrus Thomas) and its ethnographic and archaeological fieldwork in the American Southwest. Although Holmes's duty was merely to catalog and illustrate those materials, he soon went far beyond that—with Powell's wholehearted approval (e.g., Powell 1884, xxvii; 1891, xxv). By decade's end, Holmes had produced major descriptive and analytical reports on shell work (Holmes 1883), textiles (Holmes 1888), and ceramics (Holmes 1886a, 1886b, 1886c) and had begun the studies of quarrying and stone tool technology that would forge his lasting reputation (Holmes 1890b, 1890c, 1890d, 1893b).

Holmes's interest in and talent for analyzing material culture was attributed to his having "learned to think as the Indian thinks" (McGee in Powell 1897, xcv), but that claim says more about the BAE's self-promoting ideal of scientific populism—in which the education valued was rooted in hard-won field and ethnographic experience (Pyne 1980, 114)—than about Holmes's actual background. Over his career, including long field stints in the West, Holmes "had singularly few contacts with the living Indians." Even kindly John Swanton, who wrote Holmes's biographical memoir for the National Academy of Sciences, admitted that Holmes's studies of material culture "lacked the control which might have been supplied by direct observations of native artisans" (Swanton 1937, 236; also Mark 1980, 157).

But that was of little consequence to Holmes, who felt that "if savages learned it others can learn it" (Holmes 1897, 151). He compensated for his minimal ethnographic experience and observation by carefully

Holmes is the first person on the right in this photo of Camp Study, Colorado. (Corbis)

reading the accounts of those with that expertise; by sending out colleagues, such as BAE ethnographer James Mooney, with questionnaires to record native manufacturing techniques (Holmes 1903a, 53); by meticulously studying the Smithsonian's extensive artifact collections, as well as collections offered by private individuals (including J. D. McGuire, Clarence B. Moore, and Warren K. Moorehead) and even those housed at other museums and institutions (e.g., Holmes 1884); and by experimentally replicating ceramic and stone artifacts (Holmes 1903a, 73). He had to abandon his efforts at reproducing stone tools when he permanently disabled his left arm while "attempting to flake a bowlder of very large size" (Holmes 1897, 61).

Holmes's comprehensive studies of ceramics illuminates his scientific character, including his ability to overcome a lack of direct ethnographic study. Most distinctive was his extraordinary artistic talent, for the majority of the illustrations that accompany his works were his own. He possessed a careful eye for sorting and grouping slight variation in form and design, insisted on rigorous classification, and was intensely interested in technology (what he termed the study of "technic evolution"; Holmes 1903a, 48). His ceramic studies culminated in the massive "Aboriginal Pottery of the Eastern United States" (Holmes 1903a), which was initially intended as a supplement to Thomas's mound survey report (Thomas 1894). It soon became an independent concern, a part of Powell's never-realized series "covering the whole range of native arts and industries" (Holmes 1903a, 15).

"Aboriginal Pottery of the Eastern United States" is an archaeological milestone, illustrating and discussing pottery from the High Plains to the Atlantic and the Gulf of Mexico to lower Canada (Griffin 1981, 51). It was a work that attempted to put into practice a set of theoretical constructs, largely invented by Holmes (e.g., Holmes 1886b, 1890a) and intended to subsume the understanding of the evolution of ceramic technology under a set of principles derived from "laws of nature." This was part of his own ultimate goal of understanding "the development of the features illustrating the various branches of human progress from the point of view of evolution" (Holmes to Walcott, 28 January 1897, WHH/RR 7:150). In this, his work bore a strong resemblance to contemporary material culture studies in the Old World (e.g., Pitt Rivers 1875), although Holmes's inspiration derived not from that source but from the American evolutionist Lewis Henry Morgan (Morgan 1877; see Holmes 1909).

Holmes adopted Morgan's general scheme, freely using the stage terms of savagery, barbarism, and civilization (e.g., Holmes 1903a, 18; 1905, 552). Still, he realized those categories worked only at the large scale and were not precisely defined nuggets of empirical reality; the difficulty he saw in wholly separating the phenomena of one stage from another attested to that (Holmes 1892a, 248–249). So evolution was best viewed in the particular arts, each changing at its own pace (Holmes 1903a: 22).

For Holmes, the archaeological manifestation of evolutionary change was obvious enough: "In a general way the vessels of primitive people will be simple in form, while those of more advanced races will be more varied and highly specialised" (Holmes 1886b, 444). Driving that movement along the "pathways of progress" was human volition: "The desires of the mind constitute the motive power, the force that induces all progress in art" (Holmes 1890a, 139)—subject, of course, to certain rules, or "modification by environment" (Holmes 1886b, 458), and historical context. So, for example, the earliest vessel form was derived from the shape of extant nonceramic vessels, and that degree of copying was a "law [which] holds good in an inverse ratio to culture" (Holmes 1886b, 446). Material culture was both dependent on and indicative of "the kind and grade of culture of the people acquiring the art," as well as the "resources of the country" (Holmes 1886b, 444).

In practice, Holmes learned that matters were not so straightforward. As he painstakingly detailed and illustrated the material, color, form, size, decoration, and use of thousands of ceramic vessels from areas across eastern North America (e.g., Holmes 1903a, 80–201), the similarities and differences he saw did not strictly follow his progressive expectations and in fact were often at odds with it: "It may be questioned whether degree of simplicity is a valuable index of age" (Holmes 1903a, 24). Holmes could only conclude that this class of material culture— and North American prehistory generally—did not display appreciable time depth. Yet that conclusion was not new to Holmes; he first reached it a decade earlier, in his assault on the American Paleolithic.

Of his many contributions to the field, the one Holmes singled out above all others was his laying to rest the American Paleolithic. He would come to identify the period from 1889 to 1894, when he actively campaigned against the theory, as "one of the most important periods of my career in the field of science, and one of the most important, per-haps, in the history of American archaeological research" (WHH/RR 1:35). However, Swanton was not so sure: "Men seldom attain perma-nent fame for their negative accomplishments, and Holmes's contribu-tion here did little more than shorten the pathway of his contemporaries and save them some useless and wasteful meanderings" (Swanton 1937, 237). But Swanton underestimated the nature of Holmes's legacy. The "negative accomplishment" was merely the end result of positive re-search: Holmes's pioneering and highly productive study of stone tool technology, based largely on original and innovative field research on prehistoric stone quarries. Although most of his work concentrated on the Piney Branch and Dumbarton Heights quarries in the Washington area, Holmes soon took every opportunity to examine other quarries (e.g., Holmes 1891, 1894a, 1900, 1901, 1903b).

At the quarries Holmes came to understand, as few had before him, the "life history" of a stone tool. Unlike his peers who arranged artifacts by static categories of form and supposed function (e.g., Abbott 1881), Holmes viewed artifacts as part of a technological and functional process, "of manufacture, rejection, elaboration, transportation, storage [in caches], specialisation, and use." Further, as he envisioned it, there was a bottleneck through which the entire process flowed. Manufacturing, he argued, was aimed at the production of "leaf-shaped blades" (or blanks), and it was those blades that were then used on the spot or taken from the quarry for use or to be modified into other tool forms (Holmes 1897, 58; as Johnson [1993, 152] emphasizes, Holmes recognized that stone tool production was not the only activity at a quarry site [cf. Bryan 1950]). In retrospect, the details of Holmes's vision of technology proved simplistic, but in general his approach and the dynamic view of bifacial reduction strategies (a means of making stone tools by removing material from both sides of a flake) he formulated remain viable today (Johnson 1993, 152).

Given this view of technology, Holmes realized that artifact forms might be found representing any point along the process. Yet he estimated that less than half of the products were ultimately used or even finished (Holmes 1897, 143). He further saw that the character of those artifacts varied along several dimensions, dependent on the nature and amount of raw material: the distance to its sources (Holmes 1897, 138), the means by which it was acquired, and the degree of reworking required. Thus, Holmes early distinguished between "native stone" and "exotic" stone and curated and expedient artifacts (the latter he referred to as "extemporised" tools [Holmes 1897, 90]). He also contrasted direct procurement and indirect (through exchange), suggesting that indirect might be recognized archaeologically by "careful comparison of the forms of implements"—or style, in modern parlance (Holmes 1897, 140).

Most important for the pressing question of human antiquity in the Americas, Holmes observed that the half of the products of the manufacturing process that were unfinished were often morphologically distinct, so much so that the unwary—and here he had proponents of the American Paleolithic in mind—might easily misconstrue them as finished, apparently primitive artifacts (e.g., Holmes 1894b, 137; 1897, 53): "It has been repeatedly stated that the gravel finds of the eastern United States closely resemble well-established European types of Paleolithic implements. The critical observer will find, however, that this resemblance is superficial, and that they have a very much closer analogy with the rude quarry-shop rejects of America; and the latter are not really implements" (Holmes 1892b, 296).

The reason for that resemblance, Holmes believed—explicitly following the then-popular notion that ontogeny recapitulates phylogeny (Gould 1977)—was that the stages in the production of a stone tool, from cobble to finished product, mirrored the long evolution of stone toolmaking (Holmes 1890c, 23; 1897, 61). The artifacts of "a people of high culture doing their rudest work" (e.g., fashioning blanks at the quarry) will "pass through like changes of form and reach closely identical results [as] a people of low culture grade doing their best work" (Holmes 1894b, 137). The way to differentiate artifacts that appeared primitive because they were unfinished rejects of recent manufacture as opposed to those that were primitive because they were ancient was by examining indications of specialization, signs of use, and context (Holmes 1892b, 296; 1894b, 124).

Ultimately, Holmes argued, the age of any purported American Paleolithic artifact would have to be independently confirmed by geological evidence (Holmes 1892b, 296–297): "the separation of a single specimen from the main body of flaked stone art in America, save upon purely geologic evidence, is wholly unwarranted" (Holmes 1892b, 296). Here he brought to bear his own considerable geological skills. Over several years, he systematically examined all the leading American Paleolithic sites to determine whether the artifact-yielding deposits were Pleistocene in age or younger (e.g., Holmes 1893a, 1893e, 1893f). That determination was complicated by the question of whether artifacts were in primary or secondary context. Holmes was particularly concerned with this issue because he believed it was necessary to assume at the outset that artifacts found deep in Pleistocene deposits had entered there long after they formed, either as a result of slumping, bioturbation (the movement of materials in sites due to biological action), or the other natural agencies that carry modern artifacts down into ancient deposits (e.g., Holmes 1893a, 24–25; 1893e, 161): "Talus deposits form exceedingly treacherous records for the would be chronologists. They are the reef upon which more than one palaeolithic adventurer has been wrecked" (Holmes 1893a, 27).

There was, additionally, the question of whether the precise age of the enclosing deposits could be ascertained. To help resolve this problem, Holmes allied himself with "the foremost geologists" of the country, including the University of Chicago's Thomas C. Chamberlin, then also head of the USGS Glacial Division. Together they showed that the gravels and/or loess in which finds of purported Paleolithic artifacts were made were not Pleistocene in age but rather were Pleistocene debris reworked in later, recent times. This removed the crucial geological underpinnings of the American Paleolithic.

The assault by Holmes and his colleagues on the American Paleolithic triggered a firestorm of controversy, which quickly spread from the archaeological issues that sparked it into a broad dispute over geological issues and the appropriate conduct of science. The Paleolithic quarrel even turned on the proper role and relationship between federal and nonfederal scientific research (see Meltzer 1983, 1991). In doing so, the dispute tapped the discontent of its age, occurring as it did around the economic panic of 1893 and coinciding with the agrarian-based Populist movement. The increasing intervention of the federal government in local affairs that had national import (such as labor strikes) spawned widespread suspicion and distrust of federal aggrandizement (Weibe 1967, 97). It was in this context, in fact, that Powell's administration of both the BAE and USGS came under close scrutiny in and out of Congress, and he was ultimately forced to resign as USGS director (Rabbitt 1980, 191–236).

In the end, however, Holmes and the BAE's archaeology triumphed. After 1900, few new discoveries of American Paleolithic artifacts were reported (cf. Winchell 1913). Powell, though not entirely objective, proclaimed that Holmes had "revolutionized" American archaeology (Powell to Holmes, 8 June 1894, WHH/RR 5:138). A committee of his peers agreed, awarding him first place in the 1898 Loubat Prize competition—given to the best work in anthropology or archaeology in the preceding five years—for his "Stone Implements of the Potomac-Chesapeake Tidewater Province" (1897), which detailed his quarry and stone tool studies. And in 1905 he was elected to the National Academy of Sciences. It was an honor W. H. Dall reported would have come sooner, were it not "for circumstances which you had no responsibility for, and which should have no weight" (Dall to Holmes, 20 April 1905, WHH/RR 9:136). The circumstances are lost to history, but at the time the academy's only anthropologists were Franz Boas (Columbia University) and Frederic Ward Putnam (Harvard University). Boas, who rejected evolution, had a radically different vision of anthropology than Holmes did, and he also harbored resentment that went back a decade, when Holmes had received the Field Museum curatorship that a young and precariously employed Boas desperately wanted. Two years earlier, Holmes had been appointed Powell's successor, though Boas had sponsored W. J. McGee for the post. The tension between Boas and Holmes was kept below the surface in an outwardly civil relationship that was critical at a time when the young discipline of anthropology could ill afford open warfare between its two major figures. Two decades later, however, their mutual animosity would publicly explode.

Holmes ascribed his election to the national academy to the "geological work in the Survey of the Territories, and to the leading part taken by me in the archaeological researches of the period" (WHH/RR 9:135). He may have overemphasized his relatively limited geological contributions, the best-known products of which were his majestic and startlingly accurate geological panoramas, especially those published in the folio atlas accompanying Dutton's "Tertiary History of the Grand Canyon" (Dutton 1882), and the fact that he came close to formulating the concept of a laccolith (Holmes 1878a). Yet that background was important for what it meant to his success against the American Paleolithic and the inspiration it provided for his archaeological approach and method, which was strictly uniformitarian (e.g., Holmes 1886b, 443). In common with Powell, Thomas, McGee, and the other geologists-turned-anthropologists of the BAE (Hinsley 1981, 159; Meltzer 1983, 13–15), Holmes began with the material remains of historic groups and traced them backward "gradually and without sensible break" to their prehistoric ancestors (Powell 1890, 500). This was the method that in the twentieth century would be independently rediscovered and codified as the "direct historical approach" (Steward 1942).

In applying his archaeological uniformitarianism, Holmes was well aware that "a few generations, or at most a few centuries, close the definite record of tribal history; beyond this the field of archaeological research extends indefinitely" (Holmes 1913, 566–567; 1903a, 21–22). Nor did his method become a fetish, as it had for his colleague Cyrus Thomas, whom Clarence Moore once accused of trying too hard to prove as post-Columbian everything that was aboriginal. He was in danger, wrote Moore, of losing sight of the fact that "Columbus did not bring the Indians over here" (Moore to Holmes, 13 December 1910, WHH/SIA). Even so, Holmes felt that without the historic record the archaeologist would "find himself groping in the dark" (Holmes 1913, 567). In the end he always found that "no other race than the Indian in his historic character and condition need be conjured up" (Holmes 1893a, 27) to account for the archaeological remains of America (including the alleged Paleolithic artifacts). In many instances he paid little heed to his own warnings about the problems of linking archaeological remains with specific peoples, and correlated those remains with specific ethnographic and linguistic groups (e.g., Holmes 1897, 134–135; 1903a, 81, 130, 150).

Naturally, then, Holmes's detailed studies of material culture were organized along geographical lines and into culture areas, not temporal units (e.g., Holmes 1903a, 20–23; 1914; 1919, 148–149, fig. 41), for it was along the axis of space rather than time that material culture was at least ethnographically comprehensible. To a degree (dependent on how much time was represented), Holmes's geographically circumscribed units—for example, his Middle Mississippi Valley ceramic group—remain viable today. Ironically, although Holmes was sensitive to spatial variation and was acutely aware "of the importance of provenience and association in an archaeological context" (Griffin 1981, 51), there is little of that information in many of his major works (e.g., Holmes 1903a). That deficiency is at least partly attributable to his heavy reliance on museum collections, which at that time were not precisely documented.

Archaeologists in Holmes's day, anthropologist Alfred Kroeber later remarked, had "no sense of time whatever," and he was mostly correct (1940, 2). Time—or, more correctly, deep time—was largely invisible to Holmes. This was so partly because of his staunch rejection of an American Paleolithic, the epochal scale at which he perceived evolutionary change, and the dearth of chronological techniques. Equally significant was the absence of tangible evidence of evolutionary progress, the axis along which change occurred and the scale by which it was measured. However much Holmes had difficulty seeing progress in the small details, he clearly believed in it writ large. In those days, evolution could be little else, as even one lifetime would plainly show. At the

Philadelphia Centennial Exposition in 1876, where Holmes helped organize the Hayden survey exhibits on the southwestern pueblo ruins, the amazing power of steam was celebrated. At the World's Columbian Exhibition in 1893, where Holmes directed the BAE and USNM's exhibits, the steam that had driven the engines and machinery of the American industrial age was already outmoded, soon to be replaced by the power of electricity. The message was not lost on Holmes, nor few others living in the economically and politically turbulent 1890s; they shared a belief that industrial societies were moving toward a rosy future (Weibe 1967, 140–141), which Holmes called "enlightened" and thereby added another stage to Morgan's tripartite scheme (Holmes 1905, 552).

That hope of enlightenment provided the basis for the progressive movement in the United States in the first decade of new century, which viewed the human condition as improvable through national action, social reform, universal education, and the application of science. It is perhaps no coincidence that in all his years among the Washington elite, Holmes only served on two presidential inaugural committees: for Theodore Roosevelt in 1905 and Woodrow Wilson in 1913. Though one was a Republican and the other a Democrat, both presidents were (at least at their inaugurals) icons of the orderly, scientific progressivism that Holmes himself so strongly believed in and embodied.

Symptomatic of progressivism was the emergence of professional classes, including a host of new and refurbished sciences. With professionalism came the inevitable boundary marking, intended to keep the emergent corps free of the taint of amateurism. Those boundaries were established in several ways, one of which was rhetorical. Holmes himself engaged in vigorous polemics about the proper conduct of science (e.g., Holmes 1892a, 1893c, 1917), which he saw as a commitment to empirical observation and scientific measurement, a strong sense of order and method, and the subsumption of the empirical phenomena under general laws. Anything else was the "old archaeology" (Holmes 1893d, 135). Lines were also drawn with the formation of societies, and dozens, including the American Anthropological Association, sprang to life in the decades around the turn of the century (Stocking 1960; Weibe 1967, 121). Finally, and perhaps ultimately most important, membership in the professions became the privilege of university-certified practitioners.

Like all others of his generation, Holmes was self-taught in archaeology, but by the time he retired, it was nearly impossible to become a professional archaeologist by that route. In the first decades of the twentieth century, many of the major university programs in anthropology were established and already producing professionally trained anthropologists and archaeologists (Darnell 1969). As Boas and others clearly recognized, the future of anthropology was in those universities, not in museums (Stocking 1974, 284). While Holmes perhaps saw those portents just as clearly, he was unable to influence the molding of the next generation because, as he joked, "few die and none resign in the Government service" (Holmes to G. Stanley Hall, 25 April 1905, quoted in Noelke 1974, 313).

Moreover, the intellectual character of university training was indelibly shaped by Boas and not by Holmes and his museum colleagues. Though invited to an initial meeting at Columbia University to plan the "objects and methods" of teaching anthropology, members of the museum community were not subsequently appointed to the permanent committee on the subject (Darnell 1969; Meltzer 1985, 256). That in itself is not surprising, since Boas had an expansive vision of anthropology, one in which language, thought, customs, and ideas were paramount and material objects—the focus of traditional museum anthropology—played a less significant role (Hinsley 1981, 251). Academic anthropology required "men of quite different training and bent of mind" than those in museums (Boas to Carl Schurz, 12 August 1903, FB/APS). In saying this, Boas had Holmes squarely in his sights. While he admired Holmes's "thorough appreciation of visual objects," he believed his "interest in that part of anthropology that deals with ideas alone is slight" (Boas to Alexander Graham Bell, as regent of the Smithsonian, 7 August 1903, FB/APS). Boas's harsh indictment was naturally colored by his disdain for cultural evolution and was made in the heat of his very public campaign (Boas 1902a, 1902b) to prevent Holmes's appointment as Powell's successor (Hinsley 1981, 265–270). But the observation was not entirely without merit. Holmes was at his best in dealing with material culture.

Indeed, because Holmes was a museum scholar, one segment of his professional life remains poorly known—namely, the classification of collections and the exhibits he created, arranged, and displayed. He believed "the classification and installation of these collections is probably the most important single achievement of my archaeological career," and certainly it tapped his superb organizational skills (Swanton 1937, 237). Moreover, in an age when exhibitions and world's fairs were regular events, much of Holmes's time was devoted to organizing and supervising the government's exhibits on archaeology and anthropology. The list includes the 1876 Centennial and expositions in New Orleans (1883–1884), Louisville (1884), Cincinnati (1888), Chicago (1893), Omaha (1898), Buffalo and Charleston (1902), St. Louis (1904), Hampton Roads (1907), and Seattle (1909).

His efforts at such relatively anonymous tasks, coupled with the rise of anthropology in the universities, helps explain Holmes's disappearance from archaeological sight. But there is more to it than that; there were also the changes that were taking place within archaeology and anthropology. In the early decades of this century Boas and his students came to dominate the field, and in the process they utterly rejected the theoretical foundation of the BAE program and literally dropped its work from histories of anthropology (e.g., Boas 1904). Holmes and the Washington anthropologists, their disciplinary hegemony slipping away, tried to regain control in December 1919. That month in the *Nation* Boas attacked four unnamed anthropologists for using their professional cover to spy for the federal government. Holmes's long simmering resentment toward Boas and his "Prussian control of Anthropology" (Holmes, 24 December 1919, HBC/NAA) boiled over in a fit of patriotic indignation. In Washington he oversaw Boas's dismissal from his position as honorary philologist in the BAE, orchestrated his censure at the annual meeting of the American Anthropological Association, and engineered the pressure on Boas to resign from the National Research Council (Stocking 1968, 292). The attack was swift and sure, but the victory was fleeting: within the year, Holmes had resigned from anthropology to devote his last years to the National Gallery of Art, while Boas remained firmly entrenched in the discipline. Holmes saved one final salvo for proponents of a deep human antiquity in the Americas (Holmes 1925).

In 1919 Holmes published his last major work in archaeology, part one of his planned two-volume *Handbook of Aboriginal American Antiquities* (Holmes 1919). Though the second volume on ceramics was never finished, this first volume, on lithic technology, won Holmes another Loubat Prize (second place this time). But like his effort to stem the Boasian tide, its influence would not last. American archaeology, newly armed with stratigraphy and seriation and soon to have with the Folsom discoveries (early Stone Age artifact discovered in 1927 and associated with the earliest inhabitants of the United States) a deep prehistory that reached at least back to the latest Pleistocene, redirected its attention to chronology (Kidder 1936). Out of that culture history emerged, and with its preoccupation with time, Holmes's *Handbook,* guided by the spirit of the BAE program and organized by culture areas, was largely irrelevant (Guthe 1952).

Nonetheless, that *Handbook* reflects well on what Holmes had accomplished over his career, revealing as it does his well-honed understanding of artifacts and their materials, technology, and variation. It was that feel for material culture, and his efforts to embed it within a larger, theoretically and scientifically grounded understanding of prehistory, that distinguished Holmes's work from his contemporaries and helped set the stage for modern American archaeology.

Note

Archival material is cited using the following acronyms:

FB/APS—Franz Boas Papers, American Philosophical Society, Philadelphia, PA.

HBC/NAA—Henry B. Collins Papers, National Anthropological Archives, Smithsonian Institution, Washington, DC.

WHH/SIA—William Henry Holmes Papers (Record Group 7084), Smithsonian Institution Archives, Washington, DC.

WHH/RR—William Henry Holmes, Random Records of a Lifetime, National Museum of American Art, Smithsonian Institution, Washington, DC.

References

Primary

Holmes, William Henry. 1878a. "Report on the Ancient Ruins of Southwestern Colorado, Examined during the Summers of 1875 and 1876." *Tenth Annual Report, U.S. Geological and Geographical Survey of the Territories, 1876:* 383–408.

———. 1878b. "Report on the Geology of the Sierra Abajo and West San Miguel Mountains." *Tenth Annual Report, U.S. Geological and Geographical Survey of the Territories, 1876:* 187–195.

———. 1883. "Art in Shell of the Ancient Americans." *Second Annual Report, Bureau of Ethnology, 1880–1881:* 179–305. Washington, DC.

———. 1884. "Ancient Pottery of the Mississippi Valley, a Study of the Collection of the Davenport Academy of Sciences." *Davenport Academy of Sciences, Proceedings* 4: 123–196.

———. 1886a. "Ancient Pottery of the Mississippi Valley." *Fourth Annual Report, Bureau of Ethnology, 1882–1883:* 361–436. Washington, DC.

———. 1886b. "Origin and Development of Form in Ceramic Art." *Fourth Annual Report, Bureau of Ethnology, 1882–1883:* 437–465.

———. 1886c. "Pottery of the Ancient Pueblos." *Fourth Annual Report, Bureau of Ethnology, 1882–1883:* 257–360. Washington, DC.

———. 1888. "A Study of the Textile Art in Its Relation to the Development of Form and Ornament." *Sixth Annual Report, Bureau of Ethnology, 1884–1885:* 189–252. Washington, DC.

———. 1890a. "On the Evolution of Ornament, an American Lesson." *American Anthropologist* 3: 137–146.

———. 1890b. "Excavations in an Ancient Soapstone Quarry in the District of Columbia." *American Anthropologist* 3: 321–330.

———. 1890c. "A Quarry Workshop of the Flaked-stone Implement Makers in the District of Columbia." *American Anthropologist* 3:1–26.

———. 1890d. "Recent Work in the Quarry Workshops of the District of Columbia." *American Anthropologist* 3: 224–225.

———. 1891. "Aboriginal Novaculite Quarries in Garland County, Arkansas." *American Anthropologist* 4: 49–58.

———. 1892a. "Evolution of the Aesthetic." *Proceedings, Forty-first Meeting, American Association for the Advancement of Science, Rochester, 1892:* 239–255.

———. 1892b. "Modern Quarry Refuse and the Palaeolithic Theory." *Science* 20: 295–297.

———. 1893a. "Are There Traces of Man in the Trenton Gravels?" *Journal of Geology* 1: 15–37.

———. 1893b. "Distribution of Stone Implements in the Tidewater Country." *American Anthropologist* 6:1–14.

———. 1893c. "Gravel Man and Palaeolithic Culture: A Preliminary Word." *Science* 21: 29–30.

———. 1893d. "A Question of Evidence." *Science* 21: 135–136.

———. 1893e. "Traces of Glacial Man in Ohio." *Journal of Geology* 1: 147–163.

———. 1893f. "Vestiges of Early Man in Minnesota." *American Geologist* 11: 219–240.

———. 1894a. "An Ancient Quarry in Indian Territory." *Bureau of Ethnology Bulletin* 21.

———. 1894b. "Natural History of Flaked Stone Implements." *Memoirs, International Congress of Anthropology, Chicago, 1894:* 120–139.

———. 1897. "Stone Implements of the Potomac-Chesapeake Tidewater Province." *Fifteenth Annual Report, Bureau of Ethnology, 1893–1894:* 13–152. Washington, DC.

———. 1900. Obsidian Mines of Hidalgo, Mexico. *American Anthropologist* 2: 405–416.

———. 1901. "Aboriginal Copper Mines of Isle Royale, Lake Superior." *American Anthropologist* 3: 684–696.

———. 1903a. "Aboriginal Pottery of the Eastern United States." *Twentieth Annual Report, Bureau of American Ethnology, 1898–1899:* 1–201. Washington, DC.

———. 1903b. "Traces of Aboriginal Operations in an Iron Mine near Leslie, Missouri." *American Anthropologist* 5: 503–507.

———. 1905. "Contributions of American Archaeology to Human History." *Smithsonian Institution Annual Report for 1904:* 551–558. Washington, DC.

———. 1909. "Biographical Memoir of Lewis Henry Morgan, 1818–1881." *Biographical Memoirs of the National Academy of Sciences* 6: 219–239.

———. 1913. "The Relations of Archaeology to Anthropology." *American Anthropologist* 15: 566–567.

———. 1914. "Areas of American Culture Characterization Tentatively Outlined as an Aid in the Study of the Antiquities." *American Anthropologist* 16: 413–446.

———. 1917. "The Place of Archaeology in Human History." *Proceedings of the Nineteenth International Congress of the Americanists.* Washington, DC.

———. 1919. "Handbook of Aboriginal American Antiquities. Part I." *Bureau of American Ethnology Bulletin* 60.

———. 1925. "The Antiquity Phantom in American Archaeology." *Science* 62: 256–258.

Steward, J. 1942. "The Direct Historical Approach in Archaeology." *American Antiquity* 7: 337–343.

Secondary

Abbot, Charles C. 1881. *Primitive Industry.* Salem, MA: G. Bates.

Boas, Franz. 1902a. "The Bureau of Ethnology." *Science* 16: 676–677.

———. 1902b. "The Smithsonian Institution and Its Affiliated Bureaus." *Science* 16: 801–803.

———. 1904. "The History of Anthropology." In *Congress of Arts and Science.* Ed. H. J. Rogers. 5: 468–482.

———. 1919. "Scientists as Spies." *Nation* 109: 797.

Bryan, K. 1950. "Flint Quarries; The Source of Tools and at the Same Time the Factories of the American Indian." *Peabody Museum of American Archaeology and Ethnology, Papers* 17(3).

Darnell, R. 1969. "The Development of American Anthropology 1879–1920: From the Bureau of American Ethnology to Franz Boas." Ph.D. dissertation, University of Pennsylvania.

Dutton, C. 1882. "Tertiary History of the Grand Canon District with Atlas." United States Geological Survey, Monograph ll.

Gould, Stephen J. 1977. *Ontogeny and Phylogeny.* Cambridge, MA: Harvard University Press.

Griffin, J. B. 1981. "The Acquisition of a Little-known Pottery Haul from the Lower Mississippi Valley." *Geoscience and Man* 22:51–55.

Guthe, C. 1952. "Twenty-five Years of Archaeology in the Eastern United States." In *Archaeology of Eastern United States.* Ed. J. B. Griffin. Chicago: University of Chicago Press.

Hinsley, Curtis M. 1981. *Savages and Scientists. The Smithsonian Institution and the Development of American Anthropology 1846–1910.* Washington, DC: Smithsonian Institution Press.

Hough, W. 1933. "William Henry Holmes." *American Anthropologist* 35: 752–764.

Johnson, J. K. 1993. "North American Biface Production Trajectory Modelling in Historic Perspective." *Plains Anthropologist* 38: 151–162.

Kidder, Alfred V. 1936. "Speculations on New World Prehistory." In *Essays in Anthropology.* Ed. R. Lowie. Berkeley: University of California Press.

Kroeber, Alfred L. 1940. "The Work of John R. Swanton." In *Essays in Historical Anthropology in North America.* Smithsonian Miscellaneous Collections 100.

Mark, J. 1980. *Four Anthropologists: An American Science in Its Early Years.* New York: Science History Publications.

Mason, O. T. 1886. "Anthropology." In *Annual Report of the Smithsonian Institution for 1885:* 815–870. Washington, DC.

Meltzer, David J. 1983. "The Antiquity of Man and the Development of American Archaeology." *Advances in Archaeological Method and Theory* 6: 1–51.

———. 1985. "North American Archaeology and Archaeologists, 1879–1934." *American Antiquity* 50: 249–260.

———. 1991. "On 'Paradigms' and 'Paradigm Bias' in Controversies over Human Antiquity in America." In *The First Americans: Search and Research.* Ed. T. Dillehay and D. Meltzer. Boca Raton, FL: CRC Press.

Meltzer, David J., and R. C. Dunnell. 1992. "Introduction." In *The*

Archaeology of William Henry Holmes. Ed. D. J. Meltzer and R. C. Dunnell. Washington, DC: Smithsonian Institution Press.

Morgan, L. H. 1877. *Ancient Society.* New York: World Publishing.

Nelson, C. 1980. "William Henry Holmes: Beginning a Career in Art and Science." *Records of the Columbia Historical Society* 50: 252–278.

Noelke, V. 1974. "The Origin and Early History of the BAE, 1879–1910." Ph.D. dissertation, University of Texas, Austin.

Pitt Rivers, A.H.L.F. 1875. "On the Evolution of Culture." *Royal Institution of Great Britain, Proceedings* 7: 496–520.

Powell, John Wesley. 1884. "Report of the Director." *Third Annual Report, Bureau of Ethnology, 1881–1882*: xiii-lxxiv. Washington, DC.

———. 1890. "Prehistoric Man in America." *Forum* 8: 489–503.

———. 1891. "Report of the Director." *Eighth Annual Report, Bureau of Ethnology, 1886–1887*: xxvii-xxxvi. Washington, DC.

———. 1897. "Report of the Director." *Fifteenth Annual Report, Bureau of Ethnology, 1893–1894*: xvii-cxxi. Washington, DC.

Pyne, S. 1980. *Grove Karl Gilbert: A Great Engine of Research*. Austin: University of Texas Press.

Rabbitt, M. 1980. *Minerals, Lands, and Geology for the Common Defence and General Welfare, Volume 2, 1879–1904*. Washington, DC: Government Printing Office.

Stocking, George W. 1960. "Franz Boas and the Founding of the American Anthropological Association." *American Anthropologist* 62: 1–17.

———. 1968. *Race, Culture and Evolution*. New York: Free Press.

———. 1974. *A Franz Boas Reader: The Shaping of American Anthropology, 1883–1911*. Chicago: University of Chicago Press.

Swanton, John. 1937. "Biographical Memoir of William Henry Holmes, 184–1933." *Biographical Memoirs of the National Academy of Sciences* 17: 223–252.

Thomas, Cyrus. 1894. "Report of the Mound Explorations of the Bureau of Ethnology." *Twelfth Annual Report, Bureau of Ethnology, 1890–1891*. Washington, DC.

Weibe, Robert H. 1967. *The Search for Order, 1877–1920*. New York: Hill and Wang.

Winchell, N. 1913. *The Weathering of Aboriginal Stone Artifacts*. St. Paul: Minnesota Historical Society.

Marie Louise Stig Sørensen

Sophus Otto Müller   *1846–1934*

One of the key figures in the nineteenth-century development of the methods and theories of archaeology, Sophus Müller also made substantial contributions to the understanding of Danish prehistory and to the establishment of the Danish National Museum.

Personal and Academic History

Sophus Otto Müller was born in 1846 in Copenhagen, Denmark, and lived there until his death eighty-eight years later. His mother was of noble birth, and his father, Councillor of State C. L. Müller, was employed at the royal collections in Copenhagen as a numismatist and museum director. Thus Müller grew up, and remained throughout his life, in the academic, upper-middle-class milieu of Copenhagen. This was the same circle in which archaeology had originated, and from early on, Müller had a close connection with archaeology and the collections of antiquities. It was a conservative environment, influenced philosophically by positivism and late romanticism.

Müller enrolled in 1864 at Copenhagen University, where he studied classics and attended the lectures given by the archaeologist J. J. A. Worsaae (Jensen 1988a, 46). He also attended the lectures of the famous and influential literary critic Georg Brandes and read the English geologist Charles Lyell, who further inspired his interest in archaeology (Mackeprang 1934). Müller passed the qualifying philological-historical exams in 1871 and worked for a short time as a teacher (Mackeprang 1934, 6). During the 1870s he gradually became more closely associated with the collections in Copenhagen and with Worsaae, the curator of the Royal Museum of Nordic Antiquities (renamed the National Museum after 1892). In 1871, Müller traveled on the continent with Worsaae, visiting museums in Germany, Austria, and Switzerland.

His first major publication, a dissertation titled "En Tidsadskillelse mellem Fundene fra den aeldre Jernalder i Danmark" [A Chronological Division of the Finds from the Older Iron Age in Denmark], was presented in the journal *Aarbøger* [Yearbook] in 1874. This fine piece of work contained a clear and logical argument and extensive use of data (see, e.g., Gräslund 1974). Two years later, he published another major chronological thesis, proposing that the Danish Bronze Age should be divided into a western and an eastern group. During these years he continued his study

Sophus Müller. (The Royal Library, Copenhagen)

trips to the major museums and collections in central, western, and northern Europe. When he ended his continental travels in 1878, he found employment as a scientific assistant to his father in the department of numismatics (which was now housed in the same building as the archaeological collection). He kept in contact with Worsaae and his group and participated in the regular visits made by the archaeological staff to parishes throughout the country to collect information on prehistoric monuments and finds (Kristiansen 1985, 15). Müller also started an archaeological journal, *Nordisk Tidskrift* [Nordic Journal], which was produced in Stockholm until 1885, when OSCAR MONTELIUS rejected his article on archaeological methods (Müller 1884, 162, n. 1). In 1880 Müller received a Danish doctoral degree for a very innovative dissertation about animal ornamentation in Scandinavia.

Müller became curator at the Royal Museum in 1885, and in 1892, when the museum was reorganized as the National Museum, he became codirector with responsibility for the prehistoric collections, the antiquities (i.e., the classical) department, and the ethnographic collection. He remained at the National Museum until his retirement in 1921. Museum administration and related activities became just as much his concern as academic research. Although the administrative changes occurring during Müller's lifetime are too complex to cover here, suffice it to say that he was at the center of Danish antiquities throughout his career (Mackeprang 1934; Klindt-Jensen 1975; Kristiansen 1985; Sorensen 1996). During his tenure, the National Museum assumed all the main tasks arising from archaeology's emergence as a discipline: publications, preparation of finds for exhibition or storage, excavations, inspections, conservation, and the training of the next generation of archaeologists. The teaching of archaeology disappeared from the university and was taken over by the National Museum (Klindt-Jensen 1975, 84, 87).

Thus, in addition to his academic works, Müller was an active administrator. He also had extensive excavation experience, and the context of the finds always played a paramount role in his analysis and interpretations. He was at times a publicist (e.g., Müller 1897 and 1907), but because of his authoritarian and somewhat aristocratic personality, he was less comfortable with this than his predecessor Worsaae had been. He was also well traveled; in addition to his earlier excursions, he went on his honeymoon to Turkey, Russia, and Greece, where he saw the Mycenaean finds excavated two years earlier by HEINRICH SCHLIEMANN (Jensen 1988a, 51). He was therefore familiar with much of the prehistoric material then known and housed in the main European museums and collections. From 1881 he was secretary of the Royal Nordic Antiquaries Society, and he was also editor of its journal, *Aarbøger for Nordisk Oldkyndighed og Historie* [Yearbook for Nordic Archaeology]. In sum, he effectively dictated and controlled Danish archaeology during this period.

Sophus Müller is one of the key figures in the nineteenth-century development of the methods and theories of archaeology. His dispute with Montelius (Müller 1876, 1884) about typology has been characterized as the first methodological debate on such issues (Gräslund 1974, 16). It serves as an extremely interesting and insightful illustration of the early split between an essentially objective and subjective methodology and how that affected the discipline. Müller also defined several significant cultural sequences in Danish prehistory and laid the solid foundation for future studies. His works include various illustrated manuals in which the different types of artifacts were clearly ordered, beautifully illustrated, and briefly described, such as the volumes of *Ordning af Danmarks Oldsager* [Arrangement of Denmark's Prehistoric Objects] (1888–1895). Much of this work still constitutes the backbone of the discipline in Denmark, and researchers actively draw upon it. Müller can be credited with establishing the fundamental themes of Danish archaeology: "The wide-ranging research and penetrating analysis of Müller, and not least his profound respect for source material, seem to me to have perpetuated a certain tradition in Denmark" (Becker 1989, 119).

Context of Archaeological and Administrative Activities
Müller's natural conservatism was strengthened by his social network among the Copenhagen intelligentsia. However, as Worsaae's heir, he took over a museum that was national-liberal in its aims and purpose and romantic in its origins. All of these influences shaped Müller's views on the national and educational role of archaeology. Regarding the nature of archaeological inquiry, however, Müller from the first displayed an independent mind and a willingness to diverge from all previous archaeology. He was intellectually far ahead of most of his peers in archaeology, even though he was politically (and personally) conservative. This tension—between being on the one hand an intellectual visionary and on the other dominant and autocratic—caused some interesting and long-lasting conflicts that affected the structural organization of Danish archaeology.

When Müller became involved with archaeology, it had only recently become established as a profession, and its members worked for either the National Museum or the new provincial museums. Others in archaeology were either wealthy private collectors or illegal looters of barrows. The archaeological circle was small, yet because it was an international discipline, Müller would soon become part of a large discursive network that met regularly and exchanged opinions and knowledge through private letters, debates, and published articles. For example, as early as 1871 Müller participated in the Fifth International Archaeology Congress in Bologna, Italy, where fellow archaeologists Montelius and Hans Hildebrand discussed typologies. At the university, there was close cooperation with other disciplines, and Müller collaborated with natural scientists and communicated, and sometimes worked, with historians (e.g., Müller and Neergaard 1903). Moreover, the intellectual community in which Müller lived, and the extended one that he met on his European travels, was engaged during the last decades of the nineteenth century in lively discussions about the nature of knowledge and a new scientific epistemology, relative positivism. The concern with understanding the essential differences and similarities between cultural studies and the natural sciences was particularly interesting for archaeology, since its subject matter overlapped such distinctions.

The beginning of Müller's academic life in 1864 coincided with Denmark's devastating defeat by Germany, which resulted in the loss of Schleswig-Holstein (Jensen 1988a, 46). This was a traumatic national event that influenced Danish cultural life in many ways. That it also affected Müller deeply may be indicated by two aspects of his archaeological work. First, it could explain his emotional acceptance of the nationalistic reasons for archaeology that Worsaae so strongly argued for and that Müller, despite the changing epistemological framework, supported (e.g., Müller 1907). Second, it is probably the reason for his very strong anti-German sentiments. This caused him to give special attention to the "old Danish regions" in Germany (Müller 1897). It also swayed his cultural interpretations—for example, when he argued that Danish prehistoric development was clearly at a level above the neighboring regions of Germany and Sweden, or when he stated that Schleswig-Holstein shared the same culture and was populated by the same people as Denmark. It may also have confirmed his desire to locate the origins of cultural evolution in the Mediterranean area, and it is clearly seen in his critique of GUSTAF KOSSINNA's 1911 theory, which argued that Schleswig-Holstein was the Indo-Germanic homeland (Müller 1914, 279, n. 1, 335ff). However, as Jensen (1988a, 1988b) has argued, he was also clearly influenced by the development of territorial claims being argued for through German archaeology. This was possible partly due to the fact that Müller's interest was in cultural history rather than in the object per se. Despite these contemporary political factors—and despite his own recognition that the researcher's selection of data is never absolutely objective—Müller's interpretations were based primarily on his analysis of the data.

During Müller's long employment at the National Museum, Denmark underwent substantial social and political changes, which had an impact on archaeology's development as a "national discipline" (Kristiansen 1985; Sorensen 1996). The tensions surrounding the role of archaeology in the late nineteenth and early twentieth century had two clear sources, both of which were linked to Müller's career and how he exercised his power. Archaeology was still a relatively young subject, and it had been established and formed by the self-same people whose positions and privileges were now either disappearing or being transformed. Archaeology had also been made public as a basis for creating communal pride and identification, but that simultaneously entailed public access. Gradually, archaeology assumed responsibilities and duties that superseded its former endorsement of individual pursuits and personal interests. Instead, different groups began to claim rights to the antiquities, and as the past acquired value, its traces became potential commodities.

Thus, the upper-class intelligentsia found themselves and their spheres of influence caught in a changing world; in parallel fashion, new pressures were exerted on archaeology and its resources. Müller accepted and emphasized archaeology as a preeminent national subject, and his grand synthesis *Vor Oldtid* [Our Prehistory] (1897) was marketed as such (Jensen 1988b). However, he never accepted that its nationalization made archaeology a democratic discipline. His autocracy (some even referred to him as a despot) increasingly grated against the spirit of the times. He acknowledged in his writings the close link between archaeology and the populace: "Now it is behind a harrow and a plough, working in the bogs or gravel pits, that we find the friends of the museum and prehistoric research" (1907, 50). Yet not his nature but his approach to the archaeological record may have forced Müller to adopt this attitude, since he depended on positive collaboration with the people of the land in order to secure knowledge about the find-contexts, which he regarded as important as the object.

Shortly after Worsaae's death in 1885, Müller supported the move to reorganize the royal collections, and he is often criticized for his role in the centralization—intellectually and administratively—that beset Danish archaeology after Worsaae (e.g., Kristiansen 1985). He won (and, according to some, even sought) a confrontation with the provincial museums, and after 1887 all scientific and administrative activities were conducted by the National Museum. Müller saw the provincial museums as subservient to the needs of the National Museum—they should not hinder its collection of artifacts or its prehistoric research. For Müller the National Museum was the parent of all other museums and the natural center of research—and therefore "it must have all the rare and scientifically significant finds" (1907, 49). Consequently, while the National Museum grew and developed, the regional museums declined. In practice, archaeological activities were carried out by only three groups: the staff of the National Museum, the private collectors, and the looters, who began their devastation of the barrows (Kristiansen 1985, 16f). It has been argued that Müller did not appreciate the need for better legal protection of the monuments, so he instead invested his resources in "a ruthless, systematic fight against the looting by means of proclamation, newsbills and public meetings conducted by the poet Skoldborg" (Kristiansen 1985, 16–17). In the 1918 debates about a monuments protection law, he was vocal in his opposition. He reasoned that such legislation would be difficult to enforce or would be less effective than the voluntary scheduling (the public reporting of sites and monuments in a "schedule"), and it would damage the good relations that existed with the public (Mackeprang 1934, 10f).

The Nature of Knowledge

What distinguished Müller from most of his contemporaries was his precise and clear view of the nature of archaeology and the production of archaeological knowledge. He is commonly characterized as a positivist, and he was arguably the one who introduced an explicitly positivistic philosophy to Danish archaeology. Regardless, it is important to stress that Müller was basically a synthesizer and that he rejected empirical studies as an end in themselves. Thus he was a positivist in terms of emphasizing repeated observations as the basis for knowledge formulation, but he did not accept that objects "speak" for themselves. In his popular account of the history of the National Museum, Müller (1907) carefully detailed how archaeologists reached their understanding of objects. He explained that the nature and function of an object cannot be determined solely by its similarity with other known items, and he outlined instead several stages of knowledge generation. First, many similar objects were compared to the single item; second, the objects were studied in their contexts; third, the arrangement of the objects within their contexts was investigated; fourth, comparison with other countries established which objects and practices were imports and which were locally produced, thus formulating an absolute chronology; and finally, ethnographic case studies were consulted to suggest the production and use of artifacts. Müller then added that these stages were the crafts and tools of the discipline, and they must be supplemented with the *art* of asking the right questions. Such art came partly from experience and partly from a person's natural skills and talents (1907, 39). The objects could be explained when all these lines of inquiries were combined. The practical implications, as Müller saw them, of these principles were: first, that the National Museum needed to continuously expand its collection; second, that more informative find-contexts were essential; and, third, that excavations should therefore only be conducted by professional archaeologists (1907, 30ff).

Müller presented observation and comparison as analytical tools and asserted that contexts—whether find-contexts or contexts in terms of like objects or within world cultures—were the framework for analysis. Both elements were intellectual innovations to archaeology, and their intelligent and logical formulation made the departure from previous practices even more obvious. Montelius in particular represented the contemporary trends in science, and Müller's divergence was apparent in his critique of the "Swedish typology" (Müller 1884). Müller rejected empirical studies because they could never reach beyond the limitations of the objects—a fatal flaw, since the aim of archaeology was "to find normal truths, not the truth about this single vessel or sword, but about all the objects of the same form" (Müller 1884, 165).

Müller stressed that as methods, typologies could establish assumptions, but they could not produce scientifically verifiable hypotheses (Müller 1884, 170ff). He argued that observation combined with induction was the proper way to formulate scientific results (ibid., 172, 174; 1897, 691). Ideal archaeological praxis consisted of comprehensive observation and extensive comparison, although this should not be considered the only approach (ibid., 181). He described the inductive method as follows:

> When a certain condition is often observed, we deduce, that this is a rule, and when it has been repeated in a large number of instances, one assumes, that it is always so. . . . That which brings us to this conclusion is our belief in there being order and regularity in life, otherwise we could conclude nothing" (ibid., 185).

He also stated that the proposition of general regularities must be accepted with some reservation, given the continuous changeability of human life. For Müller, the conclusions scientists reached were only approximately secure, a premise that ran counter to the laws of natural science (ibid., 185ff). However, he added a subtle point in arguing that the type-concept in fact expresses a certain regularity, which can be described as "that most persistent in evolution, the unchangeable in that which is changing" (ibid., 186f). Müller also emphasized experience as the basis for knowledge and comparison between experiences as the basis of general laws. This may suggest the influence of the philosopher John Stuart Mill specifically and of positivism generally (ibid., 168ff). It is also consistent with Müller's acknowledgment of the subjective element in knowledge generation, and it may explain why he gave such preference to induction over deduction. The latter was vulnerable to subjective interventions, since "no scholar can suppress the knowledge about the finds-context that he already has" (ibid., 177).

For Müller, archaeological practice should aim to propose regularities based on comparisons and induction, with the limitations of both being sought through further observations. A suggested regularity was always only an approximation (ibid., 187). Based on these regularities, it was also possible to deduce hypotheses that could supplement the observed relationships and be tested by them. Thus, while emphasizing and giving primacy to the inductive aspects of the research processes, Müller also acknowledged the role of deduction and the interrelations between the two principles. To understand the kind of positivism found in Müller's work, it is important to appreciate that human agency was acknowledged both in the interpretive process (the natural talent) and as an influence on how data were perceived.

Another interesting element of Müller's positivism was that he did not consider archaeology to be a science, although he allowed that the natural sciences had substantial contributions to make to archaeology. Nor was archaeology a historic discipline. The independence of archaeology—both regarding its subject matter, its methods, and its theory—was one of Müller's themes (e,g., Müller 1897, 1, 689). The aim of archaeological work was to reach interpretation, and the knowledge generated arose primarily from the objects, the monuments, and the landscape.

Methodology: The Evidence of Find-Contexts
Based on his strong belief that pure typologies were merely thought-experiments (since no one could erase preexisting knowledge about a closed find [Müller 1884, 177]), Müller engaged during the last decades of the nineteenth century in an intense discussion with Montelius about the "Swedish method," which he called "the typological method" (Gräslund 1974; Müller 1884, 165). The resulting debate greatly influenced subsequent developments in classification

Müller heard Montelius's and Hildebrand's views on typology in 1871, and his own chronological publications from the 1870s clearly had in mind Hildebrand's work on fibulae typology. It was not typology as such that Müller rejected but rather its use as a methodology that presumed and explained regularity in the development of types. At the heart of the dispute, then, was the linkage between typology, evolution, and chronology. Müller's critique was most forcefully expressed in a long article titled "A Minor Contribution to the Prehistoric Archaeology's Methods" (1884). Here he maintained that it was not possible to undertake a typological grouping of artifacts before considering their finds-contexts, because, again, prior knowledge about the finds-contexts could not be suppressed and would affect the typology (1884, 175–176). He accepted and strongly emphasized that a subjective element pervaded all classification (Müller 1884, 165, 168ff, 173, 175ff, 186). He further stressed that the mechanisms regulating similarity and dissimilarity in humanly created artifacts were different from those involving natural phenomena (Müller 1884, 186). Culture and nature were not the same sort of subject matter, Müller wrote; since they were not regulated by similar kinds of laws, it was not possible to analyze them by the same methods. Müller did not accept that changes were due to an internal typological evolution; instead, they were caused by external factors. He also focused on the finds—that is, on the combination of objects—rather than on an object itself as the basis for knowledge. In the summary of Klindt-Jensen, Müller "opposed the idea of evolution by law. To look for this kind of consistency, he stressed, was to forget the freedom of action, however limited by time and space, fixed rules and the tendency to imitate which man enjoyed" (1975, 93).

Müller and Cultural History
Over the years, Müller made chronological subdivisions of all the main prehistoric periods in Denmark and vigorously defended the results against both international and local critique. His chronologies were based on studies of artifacts, "combined with studies of their distribution, the burial practices which they associate with and the objects they are found with" (Müller 1874, 347). Müller used and argued for this approach in his earliest publication. In modern terminology, the proposed chronological schemes were based on typology in combination with chorology, finds combinations, and mortuary studies. Some of his ideas were extraordinarily well conceived, such as the chronological division of the material from the Roman Iron Age (1874), which became the foundation of all later subdivision of the Roman Iron Age in Denmark. Others contained basic misunderstandings, such as the 1876 geographical division of the material from the Bronze Age. He did eventually accept Montelius's

division of the Bronze Age, and he even added his own refinements, though these were never fully adopted. His lasting contributions to Bronze Age studies were: his division of the material into categories, such as graves and hoards; his attention toward the distinct objects found in men's and women's graves; and his settlement studies.

Müller's research was significantly different from that of previous archaeologists, and he brought many new insights, as well as new analytical procedures, into both chronology and cultural history. Müller believed that the originality of his work, represented, for example, in his ability to propose correspondence between form-groups and chronology, was attributable to the use of "the evidential contribution of the finds themselves" [*Fundenes vidnesbyrd*], with "finds" here referring to finds-contexts rather than single objects (Müller 1874, 341). This is evidence of his early and explicit rejection of the tradition of using literary sources for interpretation and his emphasis instead on archaeological data, the finds themselves, and interpretations based on objects and their contexts.

Müller also defined, partly through excavation campaigns, new archaeological cultures, such as the Single Grave Culture (a local variant of the Corded Ware Culture) in Jutland. He used the evidence of stratigraphy to propose a chronological scheme for the culture in terms of the level of interments: lower graves, ground-level graves, and upper graves (1898). This chronology is still employed today. Müller also introduced large-scale topographic studies and regional surveys (e.g., 1904; 1911; 1912; 1913; 1914), which were made possible by the systematic collection of data and demonstrated Müller's ability to work with an abundance of data. He possessed a real empathy with the setting of monuments within a landscape; in one famous study, for example, he suggested that Neolithic and Bronze Age settlements would be located close to the contemporary road and track systems, which in turn would be indicated by the distribution of barrows (1904).

The material from the main prehistoric periods of Denmark was presented in large pictorial "atlases" that Müller produced between 1888 and 1895. The high-quality illustrations are one reason the volumes continue to be extremely useful. In 1889 he also founded the monograph series *Nordiske Fortidsminder* [Nordic Prehistoric Memorials] to publish detailed accounts of particularly important finds and scientific investigations, such as the Gundestrup cauldron, the sun chariot from Trundholm, and the excavation of the Jellinge graves. He published studies of particular artifact types, such as Bronze Age necklaces, and he produced during his later years an extensive discussion of art from different prehistoric periods (1918, 1921, 1933)

Passage grave at Mejls, Jutland, with its covering mound removed. (From Grahame Clark, Archaeology and Society, *1965)*

Throughout his academic life Müller emphasized the importance of the Mediterranean area for the cultural development of northern Europe. His was an evolutionary perspective: "Together they [the different departments at the National Museum] make a whole, since our culture is merely a link in the whole of Europe's evolution and further again in the large world-family's evolution" (1907, 111). While ethnographic studies could be used to explain the function of archaeological objects and to demonstrate the evolution of cultures, the world of antiquity was needed to explain the impetus for change. His early training in the classics probably fostered this conviction, but his attitude was strengthened by his visit to Greece and his inspection of the Mycenaean finds (Jensen 1988a). It was also implicit in his understanding of the difference between culture and nature, which was expressed, for example, in his comments on art and civilization (e.g., 1880). In his view, these two dimensions were so intertwined that naturalistic art, in contrast to pure ornamentation, could only be created in highly developed cultures. He clearly saw art as both an important reflection of the cultural level of a society and the finest achievements of prehistoric people. Moreover, his studies in this area were "informed by a warm feeling for art and sensitivity toward visual patterns" (Klindt-Jensen 1975, 96).

Müller perceived cultural development in terms of evolutionism and diffusion. When he referred to transitions between periods, however, he emphasized finds and finds-combinations rather than typology, because change occurred at a larger social scale than the object itself. He ascribed the reasons for shifts in the combinations of finds to "smooth movement" (though exactly what he meant by this was not entirely clear) or to special factors such as migration or disruption of trade routes. Regardless, a certain amount—smaller or larger—of finds-contexts had to contain objects from both periods in order to demonstrate a transition between them. He also predicted that when sufficient materials became available, transitional blocks would give way to ordered periods, in which every finds-context had an assigned place (Müller 1874, 380).

Practical Tasks: Excavations, Museums, Management
Müller and his team of hand-picked assistants developed new and systematic techniques of excavation (which were used until the 1930s) and standards for monuments protection (Kristiansen 1985, 16). Barrows were, for example, studied by means of a quadrangular sector in the center, and settlements were excavated in strata of 20-centimeter spits within sectors of one square meter (Becker 1989, 123). The artifacts were measured and plotted in their respective positions. Müller also introduced the extensive use of photography for recording purposes. Following logically upon his emphasis on finds-contexts, Müller insisted on professional excavations, for "it is not merely the prehistoric objects, that we are digging after, but rather all the understanding of the past which lies covered in silt and turf, in clay and gravel" (1907, 57). He pointed out that the professional conduct of the discovery of the Single Grave Culture barrows had resulted in very thorough findings, including the faint traces of wooden coffins, the shadows of the body, and the complex stratigraphies within the burial mounds. Beginning in 1893 the government provided an excavation grant to the National Museum, and during the following decade, the accession of finds soared (and thereafter stabilized).

At the close of the nineteenth century, agricultural reforms and the domestication of the remaining wilderness were drastically changing the face of the land. The heightened awareness of the rapid destruction of potential archaeological remains gave excavations an added urgency. Several significant finds were made during this period, such as the Gundestrup cauldron and the sun chariot from Trundholm. Müller initiated close cross-disciplinary collaborations, especially with the natural sciences. An example was the work of the Second Kitchen Midden Commission whose team included archaeologists, a geologist, a zoologist, an osteologist, and a botanist. Müller's publication on rubbish heaps from the Stone Age (Madsen 1900) also illustrated his partnership with other disciplines.

For Müller, however, protection was preferable to excavation. Archaeological resources were irreplaceable, so he believed that, whenever possible, their investigation should wait for future generations. Scheduling increased dramatically under Müller: Of the 4,665 scheduled monuments that were located on privately owned land in 1906, 70 percent had been scheduled since 1890 (Müller 1907, 69). The fact that the scheduling was voluntary indicated to Müller that both rich and poor shared a communal and strongly felt reverence for the past. Müller faced another huge managerial task in the monitoring of all the prehistoric monuments in the country, which Worsaae had begun in 1873. This involved describing the extant monuments and collecting particulars about those that had disappeared. All information was mapped and accompanied by illustrations, and the resultant data sets soon became a source for new types of spatial analysis (e.g., Müller 1909).

Müller also introduced innovations in the presentation of museum collections to the public. He reorganized the collections in his charge according to what were then very modern principles, such as providing explanatory texts and grouping by theme and region. He continued to stress that a museum was an academic institution concerned with the education of the people. Consequently, recreations or reconstructions were unacceptable because they were inherently false. He recognized the important cultural-political role of the National Museum, and he emphasized its accessibility, since the only prerequisite for benefiting was the ability to see. Its purpose was "that every one can learn the entire development of our folk-life in the easiest possible manner" (1907, 10). He believed strongly in the self-evident communicative power of the objects themselves. "What more lends special value to the museum: the impact of what we see there is so strong, it penetrates us so deeply, because it is the very object of the past. . . . Pale and colourless is that which can be spoken and written in comparison with the artefact itself" (1907, 11). In Müller's view, although the gap between scholars and laypeople was evident in all academic disciplines, the distance was less in archaeology, because the two groups had the museum as a shared meeting ground. Müller was director of several collections within the National Museum, but he clearly placed the Danish prehistoric collections first. The others served as the basis for comparisons or for specialist studies (1907, 107), though he appreciated that together they formed a unique totality (ibid., 110–111).

Müller's Contribution to European Archaeology
Müller's significant contribution was to synthesize the data sources and methods of archaeology into a comprehensive archaeological method

(the word *theory* was not used then). His approach was intelligent, sharp, and logical, and his critique of the typological method played no small role in qualifying its initially abstract and reified formulation. Even Montelius, for example, acknowledged that the study of finds-combinations must happen in tandem with the study of the internal connections between types (Gräslund 1974, 197–198; Klindt-Jensen 1975). Müller's general cultural-historical contributions to European prehistory have not had a lasting impact, nor were they very influential in his own time. However, his studies of Danish prehistory and his methodological insights were, and are, extremely significant. The objective, natural-science orientation found in Montelius's studies apparently won the day, but Müller's works ensured that this approach to archaeology never achieved the status of the only right and true method. The subtlety of Müller's arguments and the subjectivity of scientific knowledge, which he so courageously pointed out, became embedded in the understanding of the prehistoric archaeology of northern and central Europe. In this way Müller helped define the intellectual scope of modern archaeology.

Through his involvement in discussions about the nature of archaeological inquiry—what are the limits of knowledge of the past and how do archaeologists arrive at their conclusions?—Müller contributed substantially to the formation of a discipline that was independent from both history and literature. He had a vital role in revealing the informative value of finds-combination and for introducing an explicitly archaeological notion of source criticism. Müller's lucid understanding of the diverse potential of archaeological data, and his ability to put into practice his theoretical constructs, made him one of the founders of the modern discipline of archaeology. Jensen very appropriately described Müller's contribution in terms of "the modern" breakthrough in archaeology (1988a).

Müller's Character

A critical biography of Müller does not as yet exist, but because he was a key figure in an extremely important and dynamic phase of the discipline's history, he is routinely mentioned in various historiographical works. Subtle and not-so-subtle comments are often made about his personality, which has frequently been characterized as arrogant and authoritarian, dominant and dictatorial. The early editions of the official Danish biographical lexicon (*Dansk Biografisk Handleksikon*) contained the following entry: "[He] was not a modern civil service type and probably did not want to be. . . . [he] established his objectives and pursued that which he considered the right issues with a strong and steady hand without any consideration" (1923, 691). In the third edition (1982), J.

Brondsted, himself a director of the National Museum, painted a similar picture:

> Müller was an intellectual aristocrat. In his personality was a touch of haughtiness, his sarcasm was feared, and he gained enemies. But he was first and foremost a man of uncommonly sterling character, who saw his goals clearly and pursued them swiftly and energetically. He was a born archaeologist, an eminent observer and with the finest intuition for the prehistoric objects. . . . In the then so young discipline . . . it is hardly possible to measure what distortions and harms could have happened without a leader of Müller's fibre and calibre (Brondsted 1982).

There is little doubt that Müller's personality had an impact on the still-strong centralized structures of Danish archaeology. His character also introduces another factor into the analysis of the relationship between the National Museum and the general population, including tensions among different sociopolitical groups. Even so, there is a tendency in the literature to fix on Müller's personal attributes, and the negative developments they encouraged, and thus to neglect an intellectual assessment and appreciation of Müller (see also Jensen 1988a). The 1884 article that was spurred by Montelius's typological initiatives remains one of the most interesting and stimulating papers in Danish archaeology. It presented and argued for an archaeology that would be logical, coherent, based on data, and yet totally humanistic and interpretative. It acknowledged the influence of the researcher on the subject matter in a surprisingly modern way, while still affirming the power of observation.

References
Primary
Müller, Sophus Otto. 1874. "En Tidsadskillelse mellem Fundene fra den aeldre Jernalder i Danmark." *Aarbøger for Nordisk Oldkyndighed og Historie*: 335–392.

———. 1876. "Bronzealderens Perioder." *Aarbøger for Nordisk Oldkyndighed og Historie*: 185–312.

———. 1880. "Dyreornamentikken i Norden, dens Oprindelse, udvikling og For hold til samtidige stilarter." *Aarbøger for Nordisk Oldkyndighed og Historie*: 185–405.

———. 1884. "Mindre Bidrag til den forhistoriske Archaeologis methode." *Aarbøger for Nordisk Oldkyndighed og Historie*: 161–216.

———. 1888–1895. *Ordning af Danmarks oldsager*. Vols. 1–3. Copenhagen.

———. 1897. *Vor Oldtid*. Copenhagen: Det Nordiske Forlag.

———. 1898. "De jydske Enketgrave fra Stenalderen efter nyeste undersøgelser." *Aarbøger for Nordisk Oldkyndighed og Historie*: 157–282.

————. 1904. "Vei og Bygd i Sten-og bronzealderen." *Aarbøger for Nordisk Oldkyndighed og Historie:* 1–64.

————. 1907. *Nationalmuseet. Hundrede aar efter Grundleggelsen.* Copenhagen: Folkeoplysningens Fremme.

————. 1909. "Bronzealderens Begyndelse og a ldre udvikling I Danmark, efter de nyeste Fund." *Aarbøger for Nordisk Oldkyndighed og Historie:* 1–119.

————. 1911. "Vendsyssel-studier I, II." *Aarbøger for Nordisk Oldkyndighed og Historie:* 233–275; 276–320.

————. 1912. "Vendsyssel-studier III." *Aarbøger for Nordisk Oldkyndighed og Historie:* 83–142.

————. 1913. "Sonderjyllands Stenalder." *Aarbøger for Nordisk Oldkyndighed og Historie:* 169–322.

————. 1914. "Sonderjyllands Bronzealder." *Aarbøger for Nordisk Oldkyndighed og Historie:* 195–348.

————. 1918. *Oldtidens Kunst i Danmark.* I, Stenalderens Kunst. Copenhagen: C. A. Reitzel.

————. 1919. "Bopladsfund fra Broncealderen." *Aarbøger for Nordisk Oldkyndighed og Historie:* 31–105.

————. 1921. *Oldtidens Kunst i Danmark.* II, Bronzealderens Kunst. Copenhagen: C. A. Reitzel.

————. 1933. *Oldtidens Kunst i Danmark.* III, Jernalderens Kunst, forromersk og romersk tid. Copenhagen: C. A. Reitzel.

Müller, Sophus Otto, and C. Neergaard. 1903. *Dannevirke.* Nordiske Fortidsminder, Vol. 1. Copenhagen.

Secondary

Becker, C. J. 1989. Chapter 8. In *The Pastmasters: Eleven Modern Pioneers of Archaeology.* Ed. Glyn Daniel and Christopher Chippindale. London: Thames and Hudson.

Brondsted, J. 1923. *Dansk Biografisk Handleksikon.* Copenhagen: Nordisk Forlag.

————. 1982. *Dansk Biografisk Handleksikon.* 3d ed. Copenhagen: Nordisk Forlag.

Gräslund, Bo. 1974. *Relativ datering. Om kronologisk metod i nordisk arkeologi.* Tor 16. English revised version, 1987. *The Birth of Prehistoric Chronology: Dating Methods and Dating Systems in Nineteenth-Century Scandinavian Archaeology.* Cambridge: Cambridge University Press.

Jensen, J. 1988a. "Sophus Müller og det moderne gennembrud i dansk arkaeologi." In *Festskrift til Olaf Olsen pa 60-ars dagen den 7. Juni 1988.* Ed. A. Andersen et al. Copenhagen: Det Kongelige Nordiske Oldskriftselskab.

————. 1988b. "Ur-europeeren." In *Europas Opdagelse. Historien om en ide.* Ed. H. Boll-Johansen and M. Harbsmeier. Copenhagen: Christian Ejlers.

Klindt-Jensen, O. 1975. *A History of Scandinavian Archaeology.* London: Thames and Hudson.

Kristiansen, K. 1985. "A Short History of Danish Archaeology—An Analytical Perspective." In *Archaeological Formation Processes. The*

Representativity of Archaeological Remains from Danish Prehistory. Ed. K.
Kristiansen. Copenhagen: Nationalmuseet.

Mackeprang, M. 1934. "Mindeord om Sophus Müller." *Aarbøger for Nordisk
Oldkyndighed og Historie:* 3–21.

Madsen, A. P., et al. 1900. *Affaldsdynger fra stenalderen i Danmark.*
Copenhagen: Reitzel.

Sorensen, M. L. S. 1996. "The Fall of a Nation, the Birth of a Subject:
The National Use of Archaeology in Nineteenth Century Denmark."
In *Archaeology and Nationalism.* Ed. T. Champion and M. Diaz-Andreu.
London: University of London Press.

Tim Murray

Sir Arthur Evans   *1851–1941*

*Arthur Evans had already made significant contributions to both classsical
and Romano-British archaeology before he began to excavate the Palace of
Minos on Crete, one of the most famous archaeological sites in the world.
Evans's excavations and analysis established the scope and influence of
Bronze Age Minoan civilization.*

Arthur John Evans was born on 8 July 1851 at Nash Mills, Hemel
Hempstead, Hertfordshire. He was the eldest son of Sir John
Evans, whose great distinction was as a geologist and antiquary, pastimes
he indulged in when not working for the paper manufacturer John Dick-
inson. Sir John Evans was extremely well-connected in British scientific
circles. Not only was he a fellow of the Royal Society but he counted
among his close friends Sir John Lubbock (later, Lord Avebury), Hugh
Falconer, Alfred Tylor, Augustus Pitt Rivers, and Joseph Prestwich—
all leaders in the effort to firmly establish the scientific credentials of
prehistoric archaeology in Britain. Archaeologists were frequent visitors
to Nash Mills, including the great Oscar Montelius, and it is easy to
suppose that such a background fostered the young Evans's own mania
for collecting. A story is told that at the age of fifteen, while visiting the
Somme Gravels with his father, Arthur found a hand-axe—which may
have marked the high point of his interest in the Paleolithic! Arthur lost
his mother when he was six, and that blow may have been the root cause
of his reserve in personal relationships. Nonetheless, he was very close
to his father, both as a son and a fellow scientist, and there seems to have
been what Sir John Linton Myres described as a "generous rivalry" between the two. Indeed, Arthur Evans had a lot of catching-up to do before he could shake his nickname as "little Evans, son of John the Great."

Evans had a conventional upper-middle-class education, finishing
his schooling at Harrow. Here he excelled in natural history, modern languages, and classical Greek. Myres, his close friend and colleague,
painted a charming portrait of a precocious young man displaying
"marked individuality in many directions; hampered at games by his eye-
sight—the only athletic feat he admitted was 'jumping at conclusions' in
a general information paper—but physically active, of 'disarming and engaging simplicity,' instinctively 'rebellious against conventions,' with 'an
amused disdain of consequences,' and reacting violently to disturbance.

He had keen literary sense, and vital relish for the best English poetry, especially Elizabethan, and a deep love of music, which he retained through life" (Myres 1941b, 324).

In October 1870 Evans left Harrow for Brasenose College, Oxford, and gained first-class honors in modern history in 1874 (not without some drama, according to Fitton [1995, 119]). Evans left Oxford for Göttingen, where he studied for a year. There is little doubt that Evans, who was possessed of independent means, was somewhat less focused on his studies than his father had been. Evans loved to travel, particularly with his wife, Margaret Freeman, whom he married in 1878.

Before his marriage he traveled to Bosnia, Herzegovina, Finland, and Lapland, and his letters, sent from the Balkans to the *Manchester Guardian,* were reprinted in 1876. This publication was followed by his fascinating *Illyrian Letters* (1878), written from his house, Casa San Lazzaro, in Ragusa, now called Dubrovnik. Evans lived in Ragusa from 1877 to 1882, and as he pursued independent research on the history and antiquities of the southern Slavic peoples, he became a vocal advocate of Illyrian independence from the Austro-Hungarian Empire. Evans's outspoken support for the Crivoscian insurrection in 1882 resulted in his imprisonment by the Austrian authorities and his eventual deportation as persona non grata. His expulsion from his "Balkan paradise," in the words of his sister Joan, led to more wandering and independent study.

In 1883 Evans and his wife left for an extended tour of Greece, which gave him the chance to visit the sites of HEINRICH SCHLIEMANN's excavations and to meet the great man in Athens. Fitton has argued that Evans was initially more interested in prehistoric archaeology than in the archaeology of the classical world, but the experience of seeing the remains of the preclassical Mycenaean civilization fired his interest in the archaeology of that period (Fitton 1995, 120).

Evans returned to Oxford to take up the post of keeper of the Ashmolean Museum, then in a sorry state. Over the next decade Evans not only reversed the slide but, by virtue of gifts of Egyptian antiquities from Sir WILLIAM FLINDERS PETRIE and a number of very generous bequests (particularly from Drury Fortnum), restored the collections and saw them housed in a new building. Given his previous propensity for travel, and his strong tendency to tread his own path, one can only surmise that Evans learned the virtue of patience and the skill of packing as much as possible into his regular travels. There were also upheavals in his personal life, none greater than the untimely death of Margaret Evans in March 1893.

Evans's biographers identify 1894 as a year of crisis in his professional life as well, because early in that year he visited Crete for the first time. Myres observed a watershed in Evans's research, with the period before 1894 being taken up with classical archaeology (particularly numismatic studies) and Romano-British archaeology (with notable excavations in a Roman villa at Frilford and a late Celtic urnfield at Aylesford). After 1894, the bulk of his formidable output would be related to the archaeology of Crete. However, there is no doubt that his interest in Cretan archaeology was the result of his interest in the nature and extent of oriental influences on the cultures of early Europe. Evans had noted the existence of what he considered to be Mycenaean writing on stones and gems collected from all over the Aegean. Myres further fired his enthusiasm by bringing back seal-stones from Crete and by his attempts to persuade Evans to dig on the Kephala Hill at Knossos and to continue the promising early excavations that local antiquarian Minos Kalokairinos began in 1878.

In March 1894 Evans toured the central and eastern districts of Crete collecting engraved gems and examining symbols that we now associate with linear script on vessels, on figurines, and on early walls. He was to return in 1895 and 1896. During this time he successfully negotiated the purchase of one quarter of Kephala Hill from its Turkish owners. He was not to acquire the rest until 1899, when the Turks were driven from Crete, an uprising that Evans staunchly supported in much the same manner as he had championed the earlier cause of the Illyrians. Once again Evans blasted into print in the *Manchester Guardian,* and in this case, his advocacy paid handsome dividends. In 1900 the new government granted him permission to excavate the site.

Evans and his colleague D. G. Hogarth swung into action. A Cretan Exploration Fund was established, a link with the British School at Athens was forged, and money was raised from Evans's private resources. Digging began in earnest in the same year. In the first season the general plan of the palace was delineated, and the excavation of the "Throne Room" and "Magazines" was begun. Among the spectacular finds were the first of the marvelous frescoes, traded items from Egypt and Babylon, and a large number of tablets covered with linear script. Evans went on to identify three different scripts: pictographic, Linear A, and Linear B, only the last of which has been translated (and not until after Evans's death). The palace was an extremely large and highly complex site presenting formidable problems of excavation and conservation.

There can be no doubt that Evans leaned heavily on the expedition architect Theodore Fyfe and the pottery expert Duncan Mackenzie, but it is also true that his early geological and stratigraphic training with his father was of enormous benefit. By the end of the first season Evans was confident that he had uncovered a Bronze Age palace of startling architecture and a compelling assemblage of artifacts. Links with other parts of the Mediterranean world, established through a number of these artifacts, allowed Evans to date the site as a whole. For Evans, Minoan civilization was a part of a chain that connected southwest Asia and Egypt. A major step in establishing the internal chronology of the site was taken in 1903 when the *Journal of Hellenic Studies* published Mackenzie's study of the pottery of Knossos, spanning the period from 2000 B.C. to roughly 1400 B.C.

Intensive excavation of the site continued for the next eight years, largely financed by Evans's private fortune. During the same period the success at Knossos sparked a rush of excavations funded by the Italians (at Phaestos), the Americans (at Gournia), the French (at Mallia), and of course the British School at Athens at the sites of Psychro, Praesos, Palaikastro, and Zakro. All of this frenetic activity was taking place against an equally frenetic political background, as Crete moved toward formal incorporation into the Greek kingdom in 1909.

Of equal importance to his excavations were Evans's self-funded efforts to restore the Palace of Minos. These attracted criticism on the grounds of accuracy (though subsequent work clearly indicated that there were few inaccuracies) and later came under fire as the ethic of conservation supplanted that of restoration. In his defense, Evans was certainly strongly influenced by the desire to make the site comprehensible to others, but he was also responding (in a way that seemed practical) to the immediate problems raised by the need to stabilize the recently excavated fabric of the palace. Of course, the nature of Evans's vision of Minoan civilization was a product of the man himself and, appropriately, is the subject of continuing debate. Few could disagree with Joan Evans's assessment of the meaning of Knossos to her half-brother:

> Time and Chance had made him the discoverer of a new civilization, and he had to make it intelligible to other men. Fortunately it was exactly to his taste: set in beautiful Mediterranean country, aristocratic and humane in feeling; creating an art brilliant in color and unusual in form, that drew inspiration from the flowers and birds and creatures that he loved. It provided him with enigmas to solve and oracles to interpret, and opened a new world for eye and mind to dwell in: a world that served to isolate him from the present in which he found no real place (quoted in Fitton 1995, 137).

Time and chance also brought Evans great honors, apart from the congratulatory check for £500 from his father on the announcement of his discovery. Shortly after the first season, Evans was made a fellow of the Royal Society (1901) and was awarded honorary degrees at Edinburgh and Dublin (1901) and a host of diplomas from foreign societies. Although large-scale excavation of the site was completed by 1908, work was still going on at Knossos in 1931. Throughout this period regular publication by Evans and Mackenzie in the *Journal of the Hellenic Society* and the *Annual of the British School at Athens* presented the Evans view of Minoan history and the reasons for the collapse of Minoan civilization. The complex subject of the Minoan scripts was undertaken separately and published (from 1909) in the three-volume *Scripta Minoa*.

*Minoan Palace ruins
at Knossos. (Corbis)*

In 1921 Evans's most enduring legacy, *The Palace of Minos at Knossos,*
began to appear. The second volume followed in 1928, the third in 1930,
and the fourth in 1936. In his biography of Evans, Myres conveyed
something of the scale of his achievement: "Throughout its 3000 pages
the vast work reads like a saga; there is always the great design, within
which each topic and digression has its place; and occasions are found
for correcting and supplementing earlier statements. And as in all his
work, Evans let loose his facile pen, now and then, in passages of literary eloquence" (1941a, 953).

Evans resigned his keepership in 1908 and devoted his energies to
the Hellenic Society and to the British schools in Athens and Rome. In
1909 he received the gold medal from the Royal Institute of British Architects (for his restoration work at Knossos), and he was knighted in
1911. He also held the presidencies of the Hellenic and Numismatic societies during this period. During the Great War, Evans served as president of the Society of Antiquaries of London (1914–1919) and of the
British Association for the Advancement of Science (1916–1919). Evans
attended (at his own expense) the Versailles Peace Conference as a representative of the southern Slavs and continued his public support of the
British Institute in Egypt and the British School at Jerusalem. Still loyal
to his Balkan friends, Evans tried to persuade British Foreign Secretary
Arthur Balfour that an independent Yugoslavia was a possibility. Success

was never complete and was a long time coming, but the Treaty of Rapallo (1922) established the boundaries of this new country. His half-sister Joan put his case eloquently: "The frontiers might not be those he had dreamed of, but Evans had lived to see the country of his adoption a free sovereign State. By his researches into her past, his activities for her present and his faith in her future, he had repaid his debt to the romantic beauty of Illyria" (Evans 1943, 372).

In 1922 Evans began negotiations to transfer all of his freehold property in Crete (including his house overlooking the Palace of Minos) to the British School at Athens. In 1926 Evans was made an honorary citizen of Herakleion. Throughout the 1920s and into the 1930s, as he continued to work on the next volumes of *The Palace of Minos at Knossos,* honorary degrees, lectureships, medals, awards, addresses, and all other forms of recognition made Evans the most honored archaeologist of his generation. In 1936 he was awarded the Copley Medal of the Royal Society, to add to gold medals from the Royal Swedish Academy and the Society of Antiquaries.

In 1938, at the age of eighty-seven, Evans's health began to fail, although he continued to travel until the outbreak of the Second World War. According to Joan Evans, his personal history added a poignancy to his opposition to appeasement:

> In 1940 Time and Chance brought the war to every part of Europe that he loved. Albania was a base for an Italian attack on Greece; Jugo-Slavia nobly wrecked every hope of prosperity and happiness by resisting Germany single-handed; Greece was invaded and conquered. Every stage that every army marched was to him familiar ground; every township that fell was known and loved. On May 20 the Germans invaded Crete; ten days later the English left the island in their hands. For the last time Evans was stirred to real anger. The British withdrawal seemed to him to be a betrayal not only of Greece but also of the historic past. Yet he knew that his anger was to no avail (Evans 1943, 395).

Evans was active to the last, but he died at his house near Oxford in July 1941. All of his biographers concur that he was a person of prodigious gifts who drew on family wealth and the extraordinary learning and talent of his father. An accomplished draftsman, numismatist, collector, and excavator, Evans's artistic tastes were matched by his deductive flair. Certainly his development of the chronology of Knossos was a *tour de force,* but perhaps his most enduring characteristic was his combination of a devotion to the archaeological pasts of the countries he loved with a strong desire to see their contemporary advancement. On the occasion of being made an honorary citizen of Herakleion his reply (in Greek) made this connection explicit:

> We know now that the old traditions were true. We have before our eyes a wondrous spectacle—the resurgence, namely, of a civilization as twice as old as that of Hellas. It is true that on the old Palace site what we see are only the ruins of ruins, but the whole is inspired with Minos's spirit of order and organization and the free and natural art of the great architect Daedalos. The spectacle, indeed, that we have here before us is assuredly of worldwide significance. Compared with it how small is any individual contribution! So far indeed, as the explorer may have attained success, it has been as the humble instrument, inspired and guided by a greater Power (quoted in Evans 1943, 392).

There can be no doubt that Evans was accorded due honor and appreciation in his lifetime and that he possessed great talent and ardent principles. Evans was also a person of passion, as his colleague and friend Myres observed in his obituary to the Royal Society of London. Describing his genius for friendship as well as his devotion to scholarship, Myres tempered a recounting of Evans's honors with a celebration of his unconventional side as well:

> His innate devotion to individual freedom and political justice brought him into close relation with men of conflicting nationalities and creeds, and gave him access to regions and communities that have been visited by few. His interest in the Southern Slavs and the Cretan Greeks began while they were still under the Turk, and he had the satisfaction of witnessing their liberation; it was appropriate that the Yugoslav Kingdom and its Academy were represented at his memorial service in Oxford (1941a, 960).

References
Primary
Evans, Arthur J. 1878. *Illyrian Letters*. London: Longmans.
———. 1896. "The Eastern Question in Anthropology." *Proceedings of the British Association for the Advancement of Science*: 906–922.
———. 1921–1936. *The Palace of Minos at Knossos*. 4 vols. London: Macmillan.
Secondary
Brown, Ann Cynthia. 1983. *Arthur Evans and the Palace of Minos*. Oxford: Ashmolean Museum.
———. 1993. *Before Knossos: Arthur Evans' Travels in the Balkans and Crete*. Oxford: University of Oxford, Ashmolean Museum.
Evans, Joan. 1943. *Time and Chance. The Story of Arthur Evans and His Forebears*. London: Longmans.

Fitton, J. Lesley. 1995. *The Discovery of the Greek Bronze Age.* London: British Museum Press.

Myres, J. L. 1941a. "Arthur John Evans." *Obituary Notices of Fellows of the Royal Society,* no. 10: 941–968.

———. 1941b. "Sir Arthur Evans." *Proceedings of the British Academy* 27: 323–355.

———. 1959. "Sir Arthur John Evans." *Dictionary of National Biography 1941–1950.* Oxford: Oxford University Press.

Margaret S. Drower

Sir William Matthews Flinders Petrie   1853–1942

Responsible for the first scientific excavation of Egyptian antiquities, Flinders Petrie made contributions to our knowledge of dynastic Egypt that are equaled only by those he made to Egyptian prehistory. For him the pottery and domestic objects, the tools and implements of everyday use, the details of the past lives of ordinary people, were more fascinating and revealed more about the past than monuments and inscriptions. First Professor of Egyptology in Britain, Petrie was a great innovator in archaeological technique and method, particularly in the field of relative chronology.

Born in Charlton, Kent, in 1853, William Matthews Flinders was the only child of William and Anne Petrie. His mother was the daughter of the explorer Captain Matthew Flinders, who had charted the coasts of Australia in the *Investigator* between 1803 and 1805. Born shortly before her father's premature death, Anne Flinders had been educated by her mother and aunt and showed remarkable scholarly gifts, teaching herself Latin, Greek, and Hebrew, writing poetry, and, under a pseudonym, publishing several books on mythological and biblical subjects. William Petrie, whom she married in 1851, was a civil engineer and had several inventions to his credit, including an improved form of theodolite and a powerful electric light bulb. As a youth, Flinders suffered from asthma and bronchitis and was kept home from school; his mother taught him French, history, and music, while his father instructed him in mathematics and science. In the latter subjects he showed remarkable precocity, and he seemed to possess a natural aptitude for figures and an extraordinary visual memory. Francis Galton, in his *Enquiries into the Human Faculty,* described him as a mathematical phenomenon who could work out sums by means of an imaginary sliding scale that "he set in the desired way and then read off mentally." Later, those who worked with Petrie in the field also testified to the extraordinary facility he had in remembering where he had seen a certain shape or pattern, perhaps twenty years earlier.

Flinders began collecting Greek and Roman coins, and by the age of fifteen he was commissioned by the British Museum to purchase coins for them from antique shops and country sales. In 1870 the family

moved to Bromley in Kent. No pressure was put on the young Flinders to train for a career or to earn his own living. Instead, he would go off for a week or so at a time to the West Country to triangulate and measure earthworks and plot ancient buildings, staying in cottages or inns and living off buns and apples. The result of these solo expeditions was a series of plans, later deposited in the British Museum, and a book, *Inductive Metrology* (1877). In this volume, Petrie sought to determine the standard of measurement used by the different ancient civilizations by compiling accurate records of the dimensions of doors, windows, statues, and other artifacts from each society and finding the units of which they were likely to have been multiples. Many hundreds of his measurements were made at the British Museum, starting with the Egyptian collection, where he must have spent many hours with notebook and tape measure. In 1877, he and his father surveyed Stonehenge, using a measuring chain of Flinders's own devising; the resulting plans were the most accurate to that date.

During the late 1870s, Petrie's father, a deeply religious man, became interested in the ideas of an old friend, Scottish royal astronomer Piazzi Smyth, concerning the Great Pyramid at Giza. The theory was that this pyramid, unlike all others, had been built under divine inspiration, and its dimensions, if rendered in terms of a hypothetical unit of measurement that Smyth called the "pyramid inch," could be the interpretative key to the whole past and future of humanity. Flinders, though tempted at first to believe some of this, felt that more accurate measurements were needed—and who better to obtain them than he and his father? In 1880, Flinders Petrie went to Egypt, taking with him specially made instruments for his survey; his father procrastinated and never joined him.

Petrie lived in a rock tomb on the Giza plateau and, with an Arab assistant, spent two seasons triangulating the whole pyramid field and minutely investigating the interior plan of the Great Pyramid. His meticulously accurate measurements did not confirm Smyth's theories—in fact, they showed that there was no such thing as a pyramid inch. In the second season, he took a few weeks to travel with friends up the Nile, and the journey confirmed his resolve to try to rescue the Egyptian antiquities that were everywhere being pillaged by treasure hunters and by clumsy or careless excavators who destroyed more than they removed.

"Egypt was like a house on fire," he wrote later, "so rapid was the destruction going on. My duty was that of a salvage man: to get all I could quickly gathered in." At this point he was fortunate to encounter a remarkable woman, Amelia Blandford Edwards, to whom he largely owed his subsequent career. Edwards was a novelist who had fallen in love with Egypt on a long winter cruise. Her book *A Thousand Miles up the Nile* had become a best-seller. Distressed at the plundering of tombs and temples and anxious that proper archaeological work should be carried out, she and her friend Stuart Poole of the British Museum procured the help of other influential individuals and founded in 1882 the Egypt Exploration Fund. Their first excavator, the Swiss Edouard Naville, was a philologist whose main concern was the recovery of inscriptions. He excavated a site in the eastern delta that was believed to be Pithom, one of the cities said to have been built by the Israelites in captivity; the project generated great interest in England and the United States and brought more subscribers to the fund. Their next target was Tanis, which many thought was the other "store city" mentioned in the Book of Exodus. However, Naville was too busy to undertake the excavation. Poole and Edwards, having read Petrie's publication of his results in *Pyramids and Temples of Gizeh* (1883), were greatly impressed by his ability and decided to send him to Tanis to work under the direction of Gaston Maspero, the director of antiquities. Maspero was only too glad to give this eager young man, whose work he already admired, a free hand in the field, merely stipulating that he should report what he had found and that the Bulak Museum in Cairo would assume possession of whatever it wanted.

This was the beginning of scientific excavation in Egypt. Tanis, a huge site, had already been ransacked, and the area was strewn with blocks and limbs of statuary. Working almost without shelter until the timbers arrived for a roof, Petrie dispensed with the usual contractor and overseers and chose his own diggers from the surrounding villages. In charge of a force of over two hundred men and children, Petrie insisted on personally supervising their work and paying them himself. In the second year, joined by F. Ll. Griffith by means of a student grant, he excavated Naucratis, a Greek emporium that he had located by tracing the provenance of a broken figurine bought from a Giza dealer. When he walked over the mound, it was, he said later, "like walking through the smashings of the Museum vase rooms." The discovery of a dedicatory inscription bearing the words "City of Naucratis" confirmed his identification. Similar good fortune enabled him to locate Daphnae at Tell el Defenneh. His energy during these Nile Delta explorations was remarkable: he would think nothing of covering thirty or forty miles in a day and managed to carry on even in the fierce heat of June. From the first, his interest was not so much in the inscribed stones that engrossed Naville but in the pottery and domestic objects, the everyday tools and implements, even if they were broken. In Tanis, not far from the great temple, he uncovered the ruins of Roman houses and dated them by the coins found there. A number of important papyruses were carefully removed, as well as large quantities of pottery, lamps, iron implements, and bronze furniture fittings, "a key whereby to settle the age of a large part of the Roman remains so abundantly found over the whole of Egypt." In Tell el Defenneh, the discovery of a complete range of pottery from the Saite period was as great a prize as the Greek wares. It was a new era in Egyptian archaeology.

Conflicts soon developed with the Egypt Exploration Fund (EEF). Petrie found Poole and other leaders to be dilatory and extravagant, whereas he was always in a hurry and practiced extreme economy. For their part, they considered him very difficult. In spite of Amelia Edwards's efforts at reconciliation, his resignation—temporarily at least—ended his relationship with the fund. Later he was to work with—and break with—the fund many times. Considering the poor communications at the time, the differences between conditions in the field and the congenial circumstances in London, where decisions were made, not to mention the strong personalities and opinions involved, it's a wonder that the EEF and Petrie accomplished as much as they did. For the next few years Petrie was on his own and without financial support, but Edwards again came to the rescue. Two of her friends, both wealthy men, agreed to finance his excavations. They formed a syndicate, with Petrie digging and the three of them sharing the finds—for in those days the museum authorities in Cairo were lax in their division of the spoils with excavators.

From 1887 to 1890, Petrie worked in the Fayyum, in Lower Egypt, and these years were among the most rewarding and certainly the most arduous and dangerous of his life. The entrances to the great brick pyramids of the Middle Kingdom at Hawara and Illahun had eluded discovery in modern times; Petrie succeeded in finding the burial chambers at both sites. At Hawara he tunneled through the brickwork until he reached the empty sarcophagus room. To explore the pyramid's passages, he had to wriggle and slide through the mud in places, feeling for the edge of the stone with his toes or wading up to his neck in water. It was appallingly hot, and most of the time he had no one to assist him. The huge complex south of the Hawara pyramid had already been identified as the Labyrinth that Greek authors had made famous. Petrie examined the scanty remains and decided that it must have been the largest temple ever built in Egypt. The richest prizes from the first season came from a Roman cemetery near Hawara, which day after day offered up splendid mummy (sarcophagus) portraits, about sixty in all. Those that Petrie was allowed to bring home to England created a sensation when they were exhibited in the Egyptian Hall in Piccadilly, for they added a new chapter to the history of portrait painting. In the second season at Illahun, Petrie was able to make an almost complete town plan of houses and streets. He also assembled a substantial collection of domestic artifacts, including pottery, tools, toys, baskets, toilet items, and objects in wood, leather, and papyrus—the material remains that illuminated the lifestyle of a community of laborers and craftsmen four thousand years ago.

In 1890 while Petrie was working in the Fayyum, the Palestine Exploration Fund prevailed upon him to undertake an excavation for them. He chose Tell el Hesy in the Shephelah, in modern-day Israel, which he believed to be the site of ancient Israelite city of Lachish. Working unassisted in the heat of summer, he cut a section through the high mound at a point where erosion had already laid bare successive layers of ancient occupation, and he carefully recorded the pottery in each level. He provided an absolute date for some wares, because he had found their match in a dynastic context in Egypt. "Once settle the pottery," he wrote, "and the key is in our hands for all future explorations. A single glance at a mound of ruins, even without dismounting, will show as much to anyone who knows the style of pottery as weeks of work may reveal to a beginner." Because this was a novel concept in Palestinian excavations, Petrie is usually regarded as the father of biblical archaeology. Though pressed by the fund to continue his work in Palestine, Petrie felt the call of "home" and decided to return to Egypt.

In 1892, as Petrie was uncovering the Egyptian royal city of Tell el Amarna, he heard of the death of Amelia Edwards. In her will she endowed a chair of Egyptology at University College in London and expressed her wishes that Flinders Petrie should be the first Edwards Professor. This gave Petrie, a self-taught archaeologist without academic qualifications, the academic status he had never had; this position was a recognition of his brilliance in the field and his legitimacy as an archaeologist and teacher. Out of his small stipend he paid an assistant, Francis Griffiths, to teach hieroglyphics and Coptic at the college. Under the terms of his appointment, he was to go to Egypt every winter and train students to excavate. Since few could make the trip at their own expense, Petrie started a fund, the Egyptian Research Account. In 1905, after his final break with the Egypt Exploration Fund, the research account was renamed the British School of Archaeology in Egypt. Among those who subsequently owed their training to "the Prof" in the college and on the excavation field were the archaeologists J. B. Quibell, Percy Newberry, D. G. Hogarth, HOWARD CARTER,

Somers Clarke, E. Mackay, Randall MacIver, A. Weigall, G. Wainwright, R. Engelbach, Guy Brunton, Gertrude Caton Thompson, J. L. Starkey, and Lancaster Harding.

Quibell, the first to receive a student grant, went with Petrie to Coptos in 1894. Among their discoveries were several remarkable pieces of statuary that Petrie confidently dated to a period before the Pyramid Age (3000–2500 B.C.). The following year they dug nearby at a huge cemetery at Negada, opening thousands of graves whose contents were a puzzle to Petrie. His initial conclusion was improbable: they must be the remains of illiterate barbarians who invaded the Nile Valley at some time of weakness during the dynastic period. The obvious solution, that these were the predynastic Amratian inhabitants of Egypt of 4000 B.C., before written history, seems not to have occurred to him. He subsequently discovered his mistake through continuing excavations in the same area, which uncovered more predynastic material. Several years later he was able to arrange the contents of these prehistoric burials in some sort of chronological order by an ingenious process that he called "sequence dating." This involved shuffling nearly a thousand tomb-record cards until he found the most likely sequence of evolving shapes and decorations. Now called seriation, the technique made Petrie one of the originators of the statistical method. His classification into Amratian, Gerzean, and Semainian (Negada I and II according to German terminology) is in the main still accepted by prehistorians today. In later years, at Badari in Upper Egypt, he and Guy Brunton found an even earlier phase preceding the Amratian, the Badarian (4500 B.C.).

Excavating in western Thebes in the following winter (1895–1896), a number of important sculptures and inscriptions were found, including a stela of the Pharaoh Merenptah that celebrated a victory over the people of Israel—the only mention of this biblical story in hieroglyphic sources. This discovery was front-page news in England.

In 1897 Petrie married Hilda Urlin, and theirs was a long and devoted partnership. Except when their son and daughter were very small, she was out in the field with him every season, even traveling with him by camel to Sinai, the most taxing of all his expeditions. She helped him with the drawing and recording of objects, paid the workers, doctored their injuries, and prepared the excavation reports. Above all she was in charge of fund-raising: she wrote hundreds of letters to friends, acquaintances, and strangers, and in later years she gave lectures to publicize her husband's work. The spartan life in a Petrie camp generated many amusing stories that circulated among their students and fellow Egyptologists. Their frugality arose partly from a chronic shortage of funds but also because both were indifferent to creature comforts. The expedition house was usually a series of small mud-brick huts with sand floors, each furnished with a bed made of palm fronds, suspended planks for shelves, wooden boxes for tables, and a tin basin; a rush mat suspended over the doorway at night was rolled up during the day. At mealtime, tins of jam, meat, or sardines were passed around, to be eaten with the native bread. Students who survived this regimen were rewarded by Petrie's instruction: Petrie was always on the lookout for talent, and his students were given responsibility and encouraged to publish on their own.

Petrie's greatest contribution to the history of Egypt was the revelation of its earliest phases. Textbooks had always begun with the pyramid builders, and the historian Manetho's first dynasties were regarded as semimythical. Petrie's careful reexcavation of the early royal necropolis at Abydos, which had been ransacked during previous digs, recovered the funerary monuments of the rulers of the first two dynasties. In the mining areas of Sinai during the winter of 1905, he found a Middle Kingdom (2040–1780 B.C.) temple with many inscriptions, some of them in a hitherto unknown script that was later identified as the first Semitic alphabet. Beginning in 1906, his excavations were financed by subscribers to the British School of Archaeology in Egypt (of which Hilda was the secretary) and included the Lower Egyptian sites of Tell el Yehudiyeh, Giza, Rifa, Qurna, Meydum and Hawara (both for the second time), Tarkhan, Lahun, Heliopolis, and, over a number of seasons, Memphis, a huge site that was under water for much of the year.

Petrie's energy was remarkable, and his whole life was concentrated on his work. His season in the field usually began in November and lasted until March or April. On his way back to England, he usually stopped in Greece, Italy, or France to visit museums, confer with fellow archaeologists, and give a presentation or two. Arriving in London in May, he lectured at University College on his latest finds and then repeated his lecture at every opportunity, seeking support for his work and enrolling new subscribers. Meanwhile, he prepared his excavation report on the season's work, with the book usually going to press in August for fall publication. In June or July there was the annual exhibition of his finds at University College. Petrie wrote the catalogs himself and enlisted the help of his wife and students to guide visitors and explain the exhibits. He attended almost every annual meeting of the British Association for the Advancement of Science and usually presented a paper and presided over a session. From 1914 onward he edited his own journal *Ancient Egypt,* which came out four times a year and often contained an article by him. (A popular book aimed toward the general public on some aspect of Egyptian civilization would take him a week or so to write.) In October Petrie would give a course of lectures at the college for his students, and

then leaving them in the care of his assistant Margaret Murray, he was off
for another season in the field. If he and his wife took a summer break,
it occurred during the school holidays, whereupon they and the children
would examine earthworks in England or Wales. In 1917 they surveyed
the White Horse at Uffington; in 1918 they mapped the Cerne Giant;
and in the summer of 1922, Petrie and his son, John, made a cutting in
the flank of Silbury Hill, which established that the mound was manmade and pre-Roman.

The war years from 1914 to 1918 were perforce spent in England.
Petrie busied himself with the arrangement of the museum at University
College, which contained the fruits of his researches. The nucleus of
small antiquities that he and Amelia Edwards had assembled in the 1880s
had been augmented every year by objects he had found or had bought
from dealers—pieces chosen more for their use in teaching than for
their artistic value. This large collection now served as the basis for a series of comprehensive catalogs of numbered types, which are still used
by archaeologists to describe their finds. Tools and Weapons, Scarabs and
Cylinders, Weights and Measures—the list is extensive, though the series
was never completed.

In 1919, now sixty-six years old, Petrie returned to Egypt, only to
find that new government restrictions discouraged excavators, especially those who depended on a generous division of the finds in order
to satisfy patrons. In 1926, after a few seasons digging in the Fayyum, at

Abydos, and at Qau, he decided to focus his efforts on Palestine, now under British mandate. The sites he chose were great tells—the possible remnants of fortresses—on the line of the Wady Ghazzeh (Wady Besor), a natural frontier that the Egyptians probably would have occupied when they set out to conquer the land they called Retenu. Tell Jemmeh, Tell el Fara, and Tell el Ajjul were formidable sites to tackle. Moreover, Petrie's unfamiliarity with the advances in stratigraphical method that were now regularly used by archaeologists in Palestine detracted from the value of his findings. After the season of 1934 at Ajjul, his work was brought to an end by the Department of Antiquities of Palestine on the grounds that his records were not submitted in a suitable form. By then he had already retired (as of 1933) from the chair at University College and, on doctor's advice, had taken up permanent residence in Jerusalem. Unable to obtain a permit to dig in Syria, the Petries undertook work for two seasons on a mound near El Arish, over the Egyptian border. Finally, in 1939, Petrie admitted that his digging days were over. He died in a hospital in Jerusalem on 29 July 1942 and was buried on Mount Zion.

Petrie's life had been one of total dedication to archaeology. Austerity was his creed, and when in England, he had no time for theaters or concerts, though he loved music, played the piano well, and read musical scores for pleasure. He never indulged in novels or sports and would not allow a telephone or a wireless set in the house—such distractions were a waste of time. He had few close friends, and little time to devote to them. His life was one of constant travel; he reckoned he had crossed the Mediterranean eighty times, and rare was the occasion when he was not wretchedly seasick. Many universities gave him honorary degrees. He was a Fellow of both the Royal Society and the British Academy, and in 1923 he was knighted "for services to Egypt." He had little tolerance for those with whom he disagreed, on archaeological or any other subjects. He was a patron of the National Society of Non-Smokers; he wrote a pamphlet on the evils of socialism and penned letters to the London *Times* about public education and the design of hospitals; he disapproved of jazz, alcohol, and modern sculpture. His life was punctuated by a series of feuds, all of them professional. His greatest battles were with the officials of the Egyptian Antiquities Service. Because the directors in the early days were usually French, Petrie was convinced they were Anglophobic and bent on frustrating his applications for permits to dig. He learned to put the concession he wanted third or fourth on his list of priorities, knowing that he would not be awarded his first choice; however, he was always refused the Saqqara pyramid no matter where it was on the list. In 1886 Wallis Budge of the Department of Oriental Antiquities at the British Museum rejected as "rubbish" a complete set of pottery that Petrie had brought back. Although Petrie had initially intended for the British Museum to have his best finds, a coolness developed between the two parties. The museum was never a subscriber to his digs, and most of his finest objects went to Manchester, to the Ashmolean Museum in Oxford, and to the University [of Pennsylvania] Museum in Philadelphia, which had donated generously to his expeditions.

As a field archaeologist, Petrie regarded himself as the natural enemy of philologists and armchair theorists. His slight knowledge of hieroglyphics sometimes caused him to make mistakes in copying, and his lack of philological training could lead to ingenious but improbable conclusions. Nevertheless, he totally rejected the "diffusionist" theories of his colleague Grafton Elliot Smith at University College, who developed an extreme version of the idea that all civilizations came from the Nile Valley. Unable to read German easily, he had little regard for his German colleagues, particularly after disagreements erupted over the outmoded and impossibly long chronology for Egyptian history to which he clung throughout his life. Those who dug with Petrie concurred that he had an almost uncanny flair for identification. In the Fayyum in 1888, he found among his pottery heaps a few alien shards, some of them polychrome; he guessed at once that they must be Aegean. Middle Minoan Kamares ware had not yet been found on Crete, and Knossos and Phaestos had not yet been excavated, so the Greek pottery experts poured scorn on his suggestion. Later, the Mycenaean wares that Petrie found at El Amarna helped to define a chronology for the Aegean Bronze Age.

Flinders Petrie is sometimes regarded as the inventor of modern archaeological method, but this is not altogether true. During his early days in England, he had met General AUGUSTUS PITT RIVERS and had admired his careful recording of the pottery found on his excavations. In the 1870s, HEINRICH SCHLIEMANN was also drawing and recording what he had uncovered at Hissarlik. Petrie probably discussed excavation technique with both of them. Yet after Schliemann had visited Petrie in Hawara in 1888, he expressed disbelief at Petrie's claim that he could tell the date of any piece of pottery he picked up. Petrie's own principles of fieldwork were expressed in *Methods and Aims in Archaeology,* published in 1904. He insisted on constant supervision of his workers, rising at dawn to be the first on site to blow the starting whistle. When a find was made, he inspected the spot and either cleared it himself or assigned a skilled workman to it. He chose his own people and inaugurated the reliance on the Quftis, diggers who initially came from the village of Quft, where he had dug in 1894, and whom he trained. These men in turn trained their sons and nephews, and a second generation of professional excavators grew up; their descendants are still employed today by some archaeologists in Egypt. Petrie also began the *bakhshish* (tipping) system on his digs, which rewarded the finder on the spot and thus avoided the problem other excavators faced of having finds removed from the dig and sold to dealers. Many techniques now in common use on excavations were originated by Petrie. His knowledge of chemistry enabled him to preserve delicate objects in the field, and he used paraffin wax to fix the order of beads in a necklace or the position of loose fragments as they came out of the ground. He was a skilled photographer and built cameras to take whatever sort of picture he needed. He developed his own photographs on the spot in camp, so that poor shots could be retaken.

Modern archaeologists may shudder to think of the rapidity with which he went through site after site and the amount he left undone in each. He was seldom more than one season in each place, and he often tackled several sites in a single stretch. In the early years, he was motivated by a sense of desperate urgency concerning the need to rescue from destruction what was under threat. As the situation improved, and his own trainees became inspectors of antiquities, his choice of location was influenced by a desire to find answers to unsolved problems. He insisted on the prompt publication of his finds, and his record there has never been equaled. However, the haste produced imperfections—of which he was well aware. Not everything he found during the season appeared in publication, and not everything mentioned in the text was illustrated, so he was charged with selective and inadequate presentation. But the records preserved in the Petrie Museum at University College include registers, distribution lists, and tomb cards and are still being studied today. Excavators who hoard their material year after year, until they can solve every question, might consider instead Petrie's legacy in the resources of the volumes at the British School of Archaeology in Egypt.

Petrie's most important work was done before 1910, but those who learned from him perfected his techniques. There is little mention of stratification in his Egyptian reports, but he must be judged in the context of his time. His monuments in archaeology are the Petrie Museum at the University of London, one of the finest teaching collections in the world, and, to a certain extent, the Institute of Archaeology, which he helped to found as a home for his Palestinian pottery. With good reason had his workers once dubbed him "father of pots."

References
Primary
Petrie was responsible for over a hundred books and more than a thousand articles and reviews. An excellent guide to these may be found in my biography of Petrie, cited below.

Secondary

Drower, Margaret S. 1985. *Flinders Petrie: A Life in Archaeology.* London: Gollancz.

Glanville, S. R. K. 1942. "Flinders Petrie. The Scientific Classification of Archaeological Material." *Proceedings of the Royal Institution* 32: 344 ff.

Janssen, R. M. 1992. *The First Hundred Years: Egyptology at University College London 1892–1992.* Printed in the College.

Smith, S. 1942. *Proceedings of the British Academy* 28: 307 ff.

Uphill, Eric P. 1972. "A Bibliography of Sir William Matthew Flinders Petrie (1853–1942)." *Journal of Near Eastern Studies* 31 (October): 356 ff.

Woolley, Leonard. 1941–1950. "Flinders Petrie." In *Dictionary of National Biography.* Oxford: Oxford University Press.

Leo Klejn

Gustaf Kossinna 1858–1931

Considered to be the precursor of Nazi archaeology because of his obsession with German and Indo-European homelands and peoples, Gustaf Kossinna was one of the most famous archaeologists of Central Europe. Although many of his ideas changed the practice of archaeology, with the exception of V. Gordon Childe, he influenced few archaeologists in the anglophone world.

Kossinna was an outstanding German archaeologist who specialized in prehistoric archaeology and was the founder of the "residence archaeology school" (Siedlungsarchaologie). He was a contradictory figure. Although he taught many prominent archaeologists, he very rarely attended excavations. A man of extraordinary erudition, an incomparable connoisseur of a huge range of archaeological material, he was a militant amateur in the discipline. He is considered, with some justification, to be the precursor of Nazi archaeology. However, it was not his conception but rather that of his opponent Carl Schuchhardt that became the official archaeological line in Hitler's Germany. Kossinna's method of settlement archaeology was implemented in the Soviet Union after World War II. His rather dull hagiographical biography was written in Nazi Germany, but his person and activity are described vividly, sensibly, and critically in *Eifurrung in die Vorgeschichte* [Introduction to Prehistory] by H.-J. Eggers (1959), and some of the early episodes with Alfred Gotze and Schuchhardt are discussed in detail in that book.

Gustaf Kossinna was born in 1858 in Tilsit, formerly East Prussia. His father was a secondary school teacher; his mother descended from the gentry. A small and sickly child, Kossinna absorbed the humanistic and pedantic culture of German teachers, mastering Latin and literature, playing the piano, and working hard. This culture—impregnated with German nationalism, with national enthusiasm and missionary hopes—was the direct result of the politics of the time, when Prussia was the leader of German unification.

Kossinna consecutively attended the Universities of Göttingen, Leipzig, Berlin, and Strasbourg. In Berlin he attended lectures in classical and German philology, history, and geography. Lectures by K.Mullenhof on German and Indo-European linguistics (the latter was called Indo-German then) especially fascinated him. The problem of the location of the original Indo-German homeland (Urheimat) was to preoccupy him

Gustaf Kossinna. (Reprinted from Ward Briggs, ed., Classical Scholarship: A Biographical Encyclopedia, *1990)*

for his entire life. He defended his thesis in 1881 in Strasbourg on the purely linguistic subject "Ancient Upper-Frankian Written Monuments." He then became a librarian and from 1892 worked in the library of the University of Berlin.

Thoughts about the original German homeland, about the roots of the German language and its ancient vocabulary, sparked his interest in the material culture of ancient Germans. During the 1880s Kossinna started to read archaeological literature, beginning with the archaeology of East Prussia. His fellow-countryman O. Tischler divided the ancient culture of East Prussia into several branches, explaining the division as the product of tribal differences. Kossina was quickly persuaded of Tischler's view, attaching great importance to it, because it seemed to provide much more solid evidence than that of more ancient writers or the works of contemporary historians.

These interests brought Kossinna into contact with the Berlin Anthropological Society, founded in 1869 by Rudolf Virchow and Adolf Bastian. Virchow had been at the head of German prehistoric archaeology for thirty years and had made important archaeological discoveries, being particularly interested in the locations of various peoples in ancient times and in their archaeological remains. He was the first person to correctly describe the Earthen-forts (Burgwallen) pottery with linear-wavy decoration as Slavic ware and the earlier urnfields as German burials. Kossinna had much in common with Virchow and his circle.

Kossinna accepted Virchow's notion that the laws of culture might mirror those of biology. From this he then developed the idea of the stability of ethnic characteristics and, through this, the possibility of identifying ancient peoples, such as Slavs and Germans, from their contemporary descendants. Virchow made much of the laws of biology in the Anthropological Society: children must resemble their parents, parents must resemble their children, with the medium of transmission being the cell. It was not a huge leap to transfer this idea from biology to culture, developing ideas about the transmission of cultural tradition, succession, and continuity.

Kossinna regularly attended society meetings with Alfred Gotze, who lived near him. Gotze was one of the first to be academically trained in prehistoric archaeology, and on Virchow's recommendation

he had participated in the excavations at Troy after HEINRICH SCHLIE-
MANN's death. In the upper layers of the excavation there he had found
ceramics with protuberances (Buckelkeramik) of the Lausitz type, characteristic of urnfields of Poland and Germany. He had seen such ceramics in many of the museums along the Danube River as well. Gotze believed that such a broad distribution of this type of ceramic had to be the
result of a people who were widely known in ancient times. Herodotus
had described the Thracians as the most numerous people in Europe, and
so Gotze linked Lausitz ware with Thracian ceramics, although he never
published this observation. Nevertheless, Gotze's idea proved to be of
use to Kossinna, who proceeded from the assumption that since Lausitz
ware was not made by Germans, Germans belonged to some other culture in the Bronze Age—but which one precisely?

He found the answer to this question in the work of the Swedish archaeologist, OSCAR MONTELIUS, the "king of archaeology," as Kossinna
called him. After he had established the evolution of archaeological
types, Montelius verified each evolutionary line with other evidence, investigating combinations of artifacts from parallel lines in assemblages.
Montelius had used this method to define relative chronology when
there was no stratigraphy available. However, Montelius had also used
the method to retrace cultural evolution in southern Scandinavia (Denmark, Sweden, Norway), concluding that there had been continuous
cultural development from the Bronze Age through the early Iron Age
until historical times. In Montelius's view one and the same population
had lived there all that time without displacement.

This conclusion had far greater significance for Kossinna than it had
for Montelius. If Germans had lived in Northern Europe since the
Bronze Age then they must have migrated elsewhere. In 1895 Kossinna
gave the paper "Prehistoric Spreading of Germans in Germany" at the
annual meeting of the Anthropological Society (it was published in
1896), arguing that particular types of burials and material culture could
be found from the beginning of history in all those places where literary
sources said that Germans had lived. But Kossinna also argued that material culture was a more precise indicator of the boundaries of the territory of the early Germany than the literary sources. For Kossinna,
Montelius's conclusions supported his view that Germans had lived in
the north of Germany and in southern Scandinavia in prehistoric times
and that prehistoric German territories and boundaries could be determined by excavating prehistoric cultures.

In 1902 the Austrian archaeologist M. Much published *The Homeland of Indo-Germans in the Light of Prehistoric Archaeology*. Using the vocabulary of pre- and early Indo-European languages, Much argued from

corresponding archaeological evidence that northern Europe was not only the original homeland of Germans, but also the homeland of all the Indo-Europeans. Kossinna had located the original "Indo-German" homeland on the Middle and the Lower Danube. After studying Much's theory, he decided to search more deeply for the roots of German culture. If Germans had lived in northern Europe since time immemorial, it was quite possible that Germans had been there even before they had become separate from the "fore people" (Urvolk). Hence northern Europe had been occupied by the Indo-Europeans too.

Kossinna attacked Much, accusing him of plagiarism. In the polemic "Indo-German Question Solved Archaeologically" (1902) he expressed his indignation: "M. Much in his new book . . . now has climbed up my shoulders and explained the original homeland of Germans, that I had identified, as the homeland of Indo-Germans too, corresponding to my old conviction that both those regions coincided originally. In his book he contrived to hush up my paper, so famous in its time, as well as my name" (1902, 161–162). Much ignored Kossinna and the matter died away.

Virchow died in 1904, and Kossinna succeeded him to the chair of prehistory at Berlin University as an extraordinary professor, that is, he was still being paid a librarian's pension. Kossinna did not regard the new appointment as an unexpected and fortunate gift. On the contrary, he was indignant: why had the honor come so late and in such a humiliating form (Eggers 1959)? Kossinna had to wait for sixteen years before being paid as a professor, and he was never appointed professor on the staff.

In 1905 "Ornamented Iron Spear-heads as an Indication of Eastern Germans" appeared. In Eggers's opinion, this paper proved to be Kossinna's best work. Although linguists had divided ancient German tribes into eastern and western groups, the classical authors had said nothing about this division. Kossinna argued that the archaeological record of the region clearly demonstrated such a division, which he felt gave further support to his claim for the superiority of archaeology over other forms of evidence.

Such certainty is characteristic of Kossinna's general approach to the problem. Even the title simplifies the principle by asserting the possibility of identifying cultures by one category of artifact and one identifying attribute. Kossinna was a romantic, a believer in "the national spirit," which saw national particularities in every detailed manifestation of national culture. From this perspective any material culture component can be seen to have a particular national aspect and may be an identifying (or uniting) attribute. Kossinna's opponents later described his principle ironically by the motto "one people, one pot" ("ein Volk, ein Topf"). Kossinna vigorously denied this emphasis on single traits, but in fact the 1905 paper is the only time when he employed a broader perspective.

Kossinna was surrounded by his pupils at the university and, inspired by their enthusiastic and youthfully uncritical attitudes, he lost the ability to deal with criticism from his colleagues. The least objection to his work would cause irritation and fury. To avoid any criticism he tried to occupy key positions in German archaeology, but Carl Shuchhardt stood in his way.

Schuchhardt had been born in Hanover a year later than Kossinna. An experienced archaeologist, he had worked with Schliemann and Humann and, as the head of the museum in Hanover, had participated in many excavations. In 1908 the post of the director of the archaeological department of the Berlin Museum fell vacant. Kossinna considered himself to be the only possible candidate for the post, which he would hold along with his university position. To his great disappointment Schuchhardt was appointed instead. Schuchhardt began to excavate the Romerschanze settlement near Potsdam, close to the residence of the kaiser, who frequently visited the excavations. At this site Schuchhardt was able to reconstitute wooden constructions on the basis of small pits left by posts (postmolds), an important innovation in field archaeology. Schuchhardt recollected later that Kossinna visited the site with one of his disciples but gained little from the experience: "I saw then: observations in the field are not Kossinna's business."

Nevertheless, when Schuchhardt founded the journal *Prähistorische Zeitschrift* in 1909, he initially wanted Kossinna to be his co-editor. Kossinna's inclusion was opposed by Schuchhardt's colleagues, and Kossinna was infuriated by his exclusion. He left the Berlin Anthropological Society and founded his own organization, the German Society of Prehistory (Deutsche Gesellschaft der Vorgeschichte). He also began to edit his own journal *Mannus* (the name of the ancient German mythic ancestor). In the second volume of *Mannus* Kossinna included an article by F. Knocke attacking Schuchhardt's personality.

In the Potsdam excavation report published in his journal, Schuchhardt argued that the settlement, with Lausitz ceramics, was German. Kossinna at first responded to this argument acrimoniously in *his* journal and then decided that it was time to settle accounts with others who also dared to doubt his conclusions; other scholars were expressing their skepticism about his theories. For example, Eduard Meyer, the head of the school of historian-classicists, had declared that Kossinna's method made it possible to prove cultural continuity in any country. This point was also made by rebel disciples working in Slavic countries, as well as by his foreign opponents, who were able to demonstrate the origin of Indo-Europeans in their countries as well. The competent Austrian archaeologist Moriz Hornes was ready "to take that oversimplified identification of pots with peoples as a parody if the author was not wholly serious." The well-known linguist Otto Schrader noted that Kossinna's migrations were quite unsubstantiated and the method itself had no empirical grounds.

Kossinna devoted the first sections of his methodological work *The Origins of the Germans, and the Method of "Residence Archaeology"* (1911) to squaring accounts with his critics. Pretending to be humble at first, he could, he said, ignore "the sceptical talk of dilletanti," but, he said, his disciples induced him to speak "in the interest of scholarship and the influence of 'the new trend' in prehistory."

He had to be polite to Eduard Meyer, "the king in the world of ancient history," arguing that he was simply narrow-minded, "he is excommunicated everywhere" and "he was denied a correct opinion," when the point concerns "questions that are decisive from the highest cultural-historic point of view." Two other critics were declared to be simple compilers. He threatened Schrader by saying that a special manuscript attacking him already lay on the writing table waiting for the time when Schrader forced him to publish it. For the third opponent—Moriz Hornes—prehistory "does not come easy . . . he has not the least talent for it . . . nevertheless he feels the urge to raise his voice again and again . . . exercises in biting jeer and bitter spite" (1911, 8–13). Kossinna had his own style of polemics. The point of debate was not to seek the truth together. It was not even to drive his opponent into a corner and to hurt his pride. Kossinna was satisfied only when he had bludgeoned and trampled his enemies.

As to the foundations of "the residence method," three lines of inquiry were formulated in *The Origin of the Germans:*

> 1. the ethnic interpretation of archaeological "cultural provinces" (Kossinna did not use the term "cultures")
> 2. the possibility of retracing ethnic continuity on the basis of archaeological data
> 3. the idea of explaining the spreading of culture by means of migrations

The first thesis is formulated in the famous phrase: "Clearly outlined archaeological cultural provinces (Kulturprovinzen) always coincide with certain peoples or tribal communities (Volker oder Volkerstammen)" (1911, 3). Put more directly: "My equation: a cultural group = a people" (1911, 9). "Our principle: territories of cultures are territories of peoples" (1911, 4). These statements explain the significance of mapping cultural areas, but at the same time the central elements of the theses were not developed. Kossinna attempted to prove them by examples, but it is known that using this method one can prove whatever one likes. The first of the cited theses was presented in more detail by Erich Blume, Kossinna's favorite disciple, but this was done by logical reasoning, not by the generalization from facts.

Blume called the method "ethnographic," following terminology used in Kossinna's seminars at that time. Kossinna sometimes called his approach "ethnographic prehistory" or "prehistoric ethnology," but with the subtitle "the residence archaeology method" (Methode der Siedlungsarchaologie). "Siedlungsarchaologie" is often translated into other languages (and even translates in German) as "settlement archaeology," but Kossinna was not interested in settlements. His migrationism can be translated as "expansion archaeology," or "the archaeology of spreading." In Germany Kossinna was regarded as an autochthonist: supporting the primacy of continuity, of an age-long habitation of the same territory of Germans by Germans. The word "Siedlung" has many meanings in German. Kossinna studied habitation places so that residence places or territories (Siedlungskunde) provided a central point, allowing the archaeologist to relate material finds to real groups of people in real territories (1911, 8). The only map published in the book was called "Regions of Residence (Siedlungsgebiete) of Germans, Celts and Karpodaces."

The term *residence archaeology* has since become the official name of the so-called new trend in German archaeology. In the same year (1911) at the annual meeting of his society in Koblenz, Kossinna gave a paper on his book *German Prehistory, an Extraordinarily National Science* (published in 1912), signifying a new stage in the development of his doctrine. In the introduction he wrote: "Our current inspiration stemming from hereditary German art has nothing in common with an exaltation from bare feeling, but it rests on the deep, reliable and indestructibly stable foundation of mighty developed historico-natural knowledge." But these were just words—"exaltation" and "bare feeling"!

The book was written with a passion and inspiration that attempted to disguise the weakness of its many arguments. A single fanatical idea is present in all the chapters—that, despite the opinions of classical writers and contemporary classicists, early Germans and their ancestors, the Fore-Indo-Germans, were not barbarians. On the contrary, they were of a higher degree of culture than all others, and they pioneered a whole range of cultural achievements. They were the first to domesticate horses, and they, not the Phoenicians, invented the alphabet; they also invented bronze. The titles of the sections—"Superiority of German artistic taste . . . Grandeur of German spiral ornamentation"—clearly indicate the tone of the volume.

In 1912, with war with the French imminent, Kossinna concluded that Germans were "such people . . . [who] cannot be called barbarians, even if the Romans did it and, more, properly speaking, Romanic successors of Romans, and with special partiality the French, despite their own real barbarism. . . . We were good drinkers since prehistoric times, but we drink not continuously . . . first we do our duty . . . Germans did and must do so always. . . . Only a thorough, manful, mighty people could conquer the world at the end of the Roman times."

While Germans are extolled without restraint in Kossinna's book, other peoples were belittled. The Celts have "villain-barbarian deformed" faces; as for the Dacians, "it is not worth saying [anything] about the meanness of that national type in comparison with Germans." One of Kossinna's disciples, Josef Kostrzewsky, later a patriarch of Polish archaeology, remembered: "When the culture of early-medieval Slavs was considered at the prehistoric seminar at the University of Berlin, and it was in my presence and the presence of a second Slav, the Bulgarian Chilingirov, Professor Kossinna expressed himself like this: well, and now we shall discuss the Slav culture, more precisely—the absence of Slavic culture." Only Indo-Germans and their direct and purest descendants, contemporary Germans, were bearers of culture, and everything that Germans can be is a product of their Germanness and has been there all along. For Kossinna the purpose (and the significance) of archaeology lay in its role of connecting this German past to the German present and the German future; this is why archaeology was of vital importance for the nation.

Kossinna declared that the great German mission—"the mission of world historic importance" required new methodological principles, such as

1. dividing peoples into "Kulturvolker" and "Naturvolker," active and passive, higher and lower, based on the priority of Northern Europe
2. stating that national differences are invariable and permanent
3. granting prehistoric archaeology great political influence

In 1912 Kossinna's favorite disciple, Erich Blume, was murdered by his wife, and Kossinna explained in his obituary for Blume that she was a non-German type, with the "even repellent features of quite a degenerate hybrid." The obituary was more about Kossinna than Blume: "He learned from me to recognise the value of German spirit . . . he also heard . . . from me about the noble appearance of German physical type."

There were more practical conclusions to the 1912 book. Kossinna asked, "How long will German prehistory still be ignored by the first representatives of German scholarship—by Germanists of the Berlin Academy?" The academicians were stirred into action—they elected Carl Shuchhardt as the academy's representative of German prehistory!

After this great shock, yet another blow for Kossinna followed on May 16, 1913. On the land of a brass factory near Eberswalde in the environs of Berlin, workers found a large earthenware vessel that contained eight gold-chased cups, torques, bracelets, and other items with a total weight of 2.5 kilograms of gold. The owner of the factory presented the hoard to the kaiser, who asked his close acquaintance, Schuchhardt, to publish it. Kossinna found this very difficult to accept, given that the find was an example of the culture of "his" ancient Germans. "This event," he wrote, "appeared to me as a nod from the ancient German God of Sky and Sun, in order that I should not tire in my diligence to enlighten German people about everything that is great in ancient German heritage." He took a photographer to the brass factory and examined and photographed everything. He looked through Schuchhardt's completed catalog and found "lots of mistakes" natural for "the layman." Then Kossinna hastily published a small book about the hoard, with photographs and his own catalog. "Those who read this small book will perhaps be amazed anew and ask themselves, how are we to explain that Germans created something which was the most excellent in all of Europe?"

Carl Schuchhardt replied with an angry review of "this small book" in his journal. Citing Kossinna's words about the nod of ancient German god he wrote: "So he determined. Yet not a word about the owner's permission for publication." He added that, despite dissatisfaction with his, Schuchhardt's, catalog, Kossinna had nevertheless taken data about weights from it, again without permission. He also made fun of Kossinna's pompous chatter about the excellence of ancient German decoration, concluding that Kossinna's book was "superficial and unattractive hack-work."

A split in German prehistoric archaeology became inevitable—on one side, Schuchhardt, the Roman-German Commission of the German Archaeological Institute, the Berlin Anthropological Society, the Berlin Academy, and the journal *Prahistorische Zeitschrift,* and on the other side, Kossinna, Berlin University, the German Society of Prehistory, and the journal *Mannus.* Schuchhardt's supporters were influential in the west of Germany, Kossinna's in the east.

Kossinna acclaimed the outbreak of World War I as the fulfillment of the original "destiny" of the German people. In 1915, when the Lotzen prehistoric cemetery was found during military operations in the Masur woods in East Prussia, Field Marshal Hindenburg called in Kossinna to examine it. Kossinna arrived and reported immediately that ancient Germans were buried there—on territory now populated by Poles. The site was excavated for over six months (but not by Kossinna), with Hindenburg visiting every week or fortnight.

Kossinna took the German defeat in 1918 very hard, but he did not become inactive. When discussions about the transfer of "the Danzig corridor" to Poland began at the Versailles Peace Conference, Kossinna immediately wrote the book *Eastern Mark: The Native Land of Germans* (1919). In it he argued very strongly against the creation of the corridor, which might mean a sea exit for Poland, but also meant the disconnection of East Prussia from Germany. Kossinna sent the manuscript of the book to participants at the Versailles Conference, but it had little impact.

However, in this book Kossinna had developed not only his general approach but also some new arguments in support of it. For Kossinna the rights of a people to a territory were determined and measured by the duration of their residence on that territory, and the descendants of former possessors, even of those from very ancient times, had the right to drive present inhabitants away. Thus Kossinna believed that archaeology could be a means of arguing territorial claims and in so doing become a weapon of interstate geopolitics and a potential rationale for extended international and national conflicts.

Kossinna made primordial archaeology "extraordinarily national," very political, and imbued it with a sense of his own grandeur. He published an article in 1920 in *Mannus* with the extraordinary title "The Triumphant Intrusion of My Scholarly Views as a Result of My Scholarly Method," commemorating the twenty-fifth anniversary of his first seminar. In 1924 Kossinna gave a paper in Berlin that became the book *Origin and Expansion of Germans in Prehistoric and Early Historic Times,* published in two parts in 1927–1928. This book contained the final developments of Kossinna's doctrine, completing links between "residence archaeology" and racial theory. Books on race theory by the Frenchman Comte Joseph Gobineau and the Englishman Houston Stewart Chamberlain, although popular in Germany during the nineteenth century, were crudely amateurish. At the beginning of the twentieth century the anthropologist Hans Gunther delineated five races in prehistoric Europe and granted them different psychological capacities in pseudo-scientific form. Following in his footsteps, Kossinna continued the argument that the northern race was more valuable in biological respects, because among the German people there was only 60 percent Nordic blood and only 6–8 percent of the people were of pure northern type. Gunther's version of race theory was incorporated into the dogma of "residence archaeology," and the correlation of culture with a nation, and of cultural succession with racial inheritance, allowed Kossinna to get past any obstacle created by a lack of evidence for his theories.

Expounding the essence of his method, Kossinna wrote:

> If it is necessary to ascertain the origin of Germans, it is possible to do this in . . . a very simple way that I have invented. One needs to begin with the earliest histories of areas in question where Germans are spread and to trace their boundaries backwards century after century . . . until we come to the beginning or to an obstacle we cannot overcome. The only discipline that allows such uninterrupted advancement backward is prehistoric archaeology (1927–1928, 3).

Leaving aside Kossinna's appropriation of Montelius's discoveries as his own, we need to identify the obstacles to reconstruction. Tracing cultural succession in the north of Europe into remote ages with the retrospective method, Kossinna could only get to the second period of the Bronze Age, when tradition suddenly stopped, barring any furthur exploration of the Neolithic. He called the people of the Bronze Age the "first Germans in Germany." Kossinna now saw the possibility of overcoming this interruption by turning to anthropology for help. The new formulation allowed cultures to be different but part of the same race.

Thus Kossinna began his investigation of the Neolithic Indo-German fore people, which he was now able to connect with all the places Indo-Europeans subsequently had been and where history testified to their presence. But these Indo-European cultures do not look like the continuation of the early Neolithic culture of northern Europe. To overcome this problem Kossinna introduced one more change to his method: his earlier stipulation about the necessity of identifying ethnicity with an entire cultural complex was given up entirely. Now one could trace the centrifugal expansion of North-German culture by tracing the expansion of any single particle of that culture, be it a ceramic or an axe type or a burial custom. Kossinna did not prove this theoretical principle; indeed he did not even formulate it. Nevertheless he used it often, especially in this last book.

In *The Origin and Expansion of Germans* Kossinna reconstructed fourteen aggressive raids of Nordic Indo-Germans, naming these raids according to their ordinal numbers: "Der erste Indogermanenzug . . . Der zweite Indogermanenzug," "Die erste Kolonne macschiert . . . Die zweite Kolonne marschiert . . ." somewhat like in the military dispositions of the Prussian General Staff. Every raid was identified according to the movement of any identifying attribute, for example, several of the first raids according to collar flasks, the sixth and the tenth raids according to globular amphorae. One line of movement could be traced according to several objects, changing one another in consecutive order. For example, movement to the south is traced by globular amphorae on the first stage and by battle-axes on the second stage. It was a problem-free reconstruction because the raiders would move obediently and wherever necessary.

With the publication of this book Kossinna considered his life's aim fulfilled. He gave his farewell lecture and left the chair to Max Ebert, who, although he sometimes attended Kossinna's seminars, was a pupil and friend of Schuchhardt's. In 1931 Kossinna's disciples and admirers arranged the festive celebration of the fiftieth anniversary of his doctoral thesis. He died in December of the same year.

Kossinna had many famous pupils. Four of his early students are particularly well known: Hans Hahne, Erich Blume, Max Ebert, and Albert Kikebusch. After them came Ernst Wahle, Walter Schulz, Martin Jahn, and the Pole Josef Kostrzewsky. Herbert Kuhn and the Spaniard Bosch-Gimpera attended seminars in the first postwar years. In the later years of Kossinna's passion for race theory and the fourteen Indo-German raids, students such as Reinert Stampfuss, Lechler, Hummel, and Hammer gathered around him. While few of these ever became famous scholars, many of them made their mark in politics.

When Hitler came to power, the "extraordinarily national" archaeology of Kossinna was mobilized in the service of Nazism. The two societies of archaeologists were united under the name State Union of German Prehistory (Reichsbund der Deutschen Vorgeschichte). Kossinna's pupil Hans Reinert, with the title of Reichsleiter, was placed at its head, and all land managers (Landsleiters) were made subordinate to him. Kossinna's books were reissued many times. The struggle between Schuchhardt and Kossinna was seen as a rivalry between moderate and more respectable nationalism on the one hand and extreme nationalism on the other. Criticism of Kossinna's views was voiced outside Germany, particularly by Polish and Czech archaeologists. Soviet archaeologists opposed the theory of migration too, although their objections were founded on an adherence to the theory of stages, which Soviet dogma demanded. Nonetheless, in the 1950s and 1960s Soviet archaeologists began to use Kossinna's methods, albeit substituting Slavs for Germans.

More specific criticisms were voiced inside Germany. As early as 1941 Ernst Wahle, one of Kossinna's pupils, produced a scathing analysis of some of the methodological underpinnings of Kossinna's general doctrine. In the article "Toward the Ethnic Interpretation of Archaeological Cultural Provinces," Wahle rejected the argument that archaeological cultures are coincident with ethnic groups. After the war he became one of the leaders of archaeological thought in the German Federal Republic. His influence, and the fact that Kossinna's school did not attract followers, meant that Kossinna's dreams were never realized, and West German archaeology took another path. In the German Democratic Republic, Kossinna's disciples and the representatives of Schuchhardt's approach accepted the framework of Marxist archaeology. Thus Kossinna's theories were not elaborated on there either.

However, archaeologists in Eastern Europe continued to use Kossinna's method while rejecting him and his interests. In Germany, both West and East, Kossinna seemed to have vanished into thin air. At the end of the 1950s, articles in German periodicals and books began to appear raising the same questions, and archaeologists became engaged once again with Kossinna's heritage—contradictory, odious, and tempting.

When estimating the importance of Kossinna in the history of archaeology a well-known postwar German archaeologist, H.-J. Eggers, wrote: "For many of his adherents, his name sounds as the name of Montelius. Nevertheless we ought to abstain from putting them on the same level" (1959). Montelius had enough balance and self-awareness to see his mistakes and to eliminate them. And if today, for example, "the typological method" is strictly forbidden by some researchers because some successors of the great Swedish master used that method incorrectly, Montelius is not to blame. Kossinna is another matter. His method of "ethnic interpretation" is severely criticized now, and he is to blame for this. His disciples repeated many of the defects of their teacher.

Kossinna was not a true scholar at all, especially at the end of his life. He developed in the direction of gross dilettantism, giving up the demands of strict methodology and freeing himself from self-criticism, or indeed criticism of any kind. Nevertheless, he is an important figure in archaeology, the complete expression of an important trend in the development of German culture.

The question is how did such a militant dilettante become an important figure in his discipline? There are specific reasons such as the "spirit of the time" and the German situation, but there are more general reasons as well. Kossinna did see and express some of the really vital questions about the possibilities, uses, and developments of archaeology. The ethnic determination of cultures, the possibility of genetic connections with cultures, culturogenesis (the origin of a certain culture), the connection of culturogenesis with the origin of peoples and their languages—all these questions were brought to archaeology by Kossinna.

Unfortunately, the passions that provoked Kossinna's archaeology are again abroad in the world. There is renewed pressure to correlate cultures with ethnic groups. A serious analysis of Kossinna's heritage is necessary not only to solve the problems he raised, but also to avoid repeating his dangerous blunders.

References
Primary
Kossinna, G. 1896. "Die vorgeschichtliche Ausbreitung der Germanen in Deutschland." *Zeitschrift des Vereins für Volkskunde* 6, 1: 1–14.

———. 1902. "Die indogermanische Frage archaologisch beantwortet." *Zeitschrift für Ethnologie* 34: 161–222.

———. 1905. "Die verzierte Eisenlanzenspitzen alls Kennzeichen der Ostgermanen." *Zeitschrift für Ethnologie* 37.

———. 1911. *Die Herkunft der Germanen. Zur Methode der Siedlungsarchaologie.* Wurzburg.

———. 1912. *Die deutsche Vorgeschichte eine gerz vorragend nationale Wissenschaft* (Mannus-Bibliothek 9). Wurzburg.

———. 1927–1928. *Ursprung und Verbreitung der Germanen in vor- und fruhgeschichtliche Zeit.* Wurzburg.

Secondary
Eggers, Hans-Jurgen. 1959. *Einfuhrung in die Vorgeschichte.* Munich: Piper.

Hachmann, Rolf. 1970. *Die Gothen und Skandinavien.* Berlin.

Klejn, Leo S. 1974. "Kossinna in Abstand von vierzig Jahren." *Jahresschrift für mitteldeutsche Vorgeschichte* 58: 7–55.

Stampfuss, Rudolf. 1935. *Gustaf Kossinna. Ein Leben für die deutsche Vorgeschichte.* Leipzig.

Leo Klejn

Vasiliy Alekeyevich Gorodcov

1860–1945

This ex-seminarian and army officer wrote the Russian textbooks on archaeological methodology and excavation techniques. Vasiliy Alekeyevich Gorodcov virtually created Russian prehistory through his excavations of burial mounds and his use of ceramic types to distinguish and map Pit, Timber, and Catacomb grave cultures.

Gorodcov was an outstanding Russian archaeologist who was the founder and head of the extensive Moscow school of archaeology. He belonged to one of the very lowest strata of nineteenth-century Russian society, *raznochinetzes* (intellectuals who do not belong to the gentry).

A son of a village sexton, V. Dubrovki of the Riazan Province, Gorodcov studied at the Riazan theological seminary because his father wanted him to become a priest. Because of conflict with the bishop, he left the seminary for military school, serving as an officer from 1880 until 1906. He was an atypical officer, reading books on the natural sciences, especially on Darwinism, even when sitting on his horse. But it was John Lubbock's *Prehistoric Times,* edited in 1876 by D. N. Anuchin in Russian translation, that really caught his attention and began his interest in archaeology.

Residents of the towns where his military unit was stationed often saw the lone officer horseman dismounting and searching the ground for flints and shards. After eating meat, he kept the bones so as to be able to identify domestic animals from their bones in archaeological sites. Gorodcov began to travel to undertake archaeological surveys.

In 1887, while attending the Seventh Archaeological Congress in Yaroslavl, Gorodcov reported on some Neolithic settlements he had found. This congress was notable for the establishment of a new section of activity devoted to church antiquities, but this hardly appealed to the former priest. Gorodcov was interested in and inspired by the naturalist historians who had begun to create prehistoric archaeology, namely, the geographer and anthropologist D. N. Anuchin and the geologist Inostrantsev. In 1890 at the Eighth Congress in Moscow, Anuchin gave his conceptual paper "About Cultural Influences on the Prehistoric Ground

Vasiliy Gorodcov.
(Courtesy of
Dr. R. Munchaev,
Director, Institute of
Archaeology, Russian
Academy of Sciences)

of Russia," establishing the need to create archaeological maps of Russia. Gorodcov was to build on the theses of Anuchin's paper and began the archaeological mapping of Neolithic settlements of the Oka River. In 1891 he conducted his first independent excavations in the dunes there.

Gorodcov became a member of the Riazan scholarly archives committee, and at the end of the century he was a member of the Yaroslavl scholarly archives committee. These changes in membership were the results of an army transfer to the Volga-Oka region, an area rich in archaeological monuments from all epochs. Gorodcov received practical archaeological training through these provincial committees, which were local centers for the collection of archaeological information in Russia at that time.

In 1899, aged 39 and still an army officer, Gorodcov attended the Eleventh Archaeological Congress in Kiev, presenting the important theoretical and methodical analysis "Russian Prehistoric Ceramics" (published in Transactions of the Congress, 1902). This was Gorodcov's attempt to create a universal classification system for the description of earthenware vessels. The system used material from sites of the Russian forest Neolithic, but it could be applied to material from other regions and epochs. Gorodcov divided all the material into groups, sections, and ranks. The successive steps of the classification were established uniformly beforehand, and it was one and the same for all applications: division according to substances first, then according to forms, then according to decoration, and so on. Gorodcov's classificatory scheme was absolute, canonical, and even more rigorous than the Linnaean system. Gorodcov, writing about it later said that

> at the end of the 19th century, studying botany and zoology, I arrived at the notion that studying archaeological material monuments with the natural-historical method of Linnaeus was possible; I adhered to the idea in my work *Russian Prehistoric Ceramics*. . . . where the Latin terminology was conducted by analogy with the natural-historical method, but unfortunately the editorial staff, confused by such unexpected innovation, did not make way for it (1927, 3).

What Gorodcov was talking about was the application of binary Latin designations (as in plant and animal genera and species) to archaeology. "Types" for Gorodcov were formulated as strictly limited cells of classification, as distinct from OSCAR MONTELIUS, whose types had no strict boundaries. Gorodcov's types were not types strictly speaking (it's impossible to talk about the degree of typicalness here), but formal-logical classes. Montelius's types were developed to allow us to trace the evolution of things (more exactly, evolution of standards, development of ideals), but the types (classes) of Gorodcov were designed primarily to allow us to identify distinct cultures. It was no mere chance that the first version of his classification was the elaboration for fragmentary Neolithic ceramics. While one cannot trace evolutional ranges by using it, it is quite possible to define the territorial and chronological boundaries of groups, as well as contacts and influences. This was a classification system more suited to diffusionists than evolutionists.

Gorodcov was then transferred to the southern Russian Empire, and he began to excavate burial mounds in the Donets River basin. In 1901 he organized excavations in the Izium district of Kharkov Province as part of preparations for the Twelfth Archaeological Congress, to take place in Kharkov. With the small staff of one student and one priest-amateur, he excavated dozens of burial mounds, containing hundreds of burials. In 1903 there were similar excavations in the Bakhmut district of the Yekaterinoslav Province, before the Thirteenth Archaeological Congress in Yekaterinoslav. In 1905 and 1907, in the monumental *Transactions of the Twelfth and Thirteenth Archaeological Congresses,* he published the full reports of all of these excavations, which were a model for their time. The results of the investigations, with summary tables for the distribution of grave materials as well as drawings and photographs, were incorporated into the full reports.

However, Gorodcov's excavations using his systems revealed somewhat meager, plain, and, it seemed, monotonous material. Well-known archaeologists D. Y. Samokvasov, N. E. Brandenburg, and A. A. Bobrinskiy (chairman of the Archaeological Committee) had excavated many steppe burial mounds before him, and there were many burials in each burial mound. Skeletons lay in different poses, with different objects, at different depths, but they were mostly flexed, with their bones often painted red. It was thought that the deceased had been powdered with paint (or ochre), and when the flesh decayed, the paint accumulated on the bones. Iron objects were found with extended skeletons, but there were only copper (or bronze) and stone objects found near flexed skeletons. So "flexed and painted skeletons" were thought to date from the Stone Age or Bronze Age and were perceived pretty much as an amorphous mass.

In 1910 the Russian archaeologist A. A. Spitsyn published a summary of these finds—*Burial Mounds with Contracted and Painted Skeletons*.

N. I. Veselovskiy, a member of the Archaeological Committee, had excavated steppe burial mounds, searching for Scythians and Sarmatians and their gold artifacts, for the Imperial Hermitage Museum. If he came upon flexed and painted skeletons, the probability of Scythian burials was remote, as the Scythians did not bury their dead this way, and he would usually stop the excavation. Other archaeologists had also tried to elucidate this amorphous skeletal mass, by classifying it according to region, to availability, to lack of metal objects, and so on, but with little success. In every case the rest of the material from each excavation did not correlate with these divisions.

Gorodcov, however, had an excellent foreign example to use as a basis for a solution to the problem of mound burial classification. In Denmark, between 1893 and 1894, many burial mounds with several burials in each had been excavated by SOPHUS MÜLLER, a first-class typologist and well-known diffusionist. Müller had summarized this research in 1898 in the paper "Nordische Altertumer," which was read with great interest in Russia. Gorodcov's principle of grave assemblage distribution was very similar to Müller's classification. The latter divided burials into subsoil graves (Undergrave), ground graves (Bundgrave) and upper graves (Overgrave), with correlated artifacts and materials according to that division.

Gorodcov's initial classification was subsoil graves, ground graves, and embankment graves. Then he divided ground graves according to types of arrangement—Pit graves (in a simple pit), Catacomb graves (in a side chamber, dug by undermining from a pit), and Timber graves (in a low timbered frame arranged in the pit). Material, particularly ceramics, was well distributed according to those types of graves: in Pits, round-bottomed vessels; in Catacombs, flat-bottomed beakers with magnificent decoration; and in Timber graves, flat-bottomed pots and vessels with sharp ridges, very sparsely decorated. Patterns similar to those in Timber graves occurred in burials in embankments; hence, according to Gorodcov, they belonged to the same culture.

Stratigraphical observations showed that an initial burial in each mound was always a single one, usually a Pit grave, and then a burial mound was erected over an initial burial. Then other Pit graves were placed into the preexisting burial mound, then Catacomb graves occurred (sometimes the burial mound was made higher because of these), and lastly Timber graves and graves in embankments. Thus, the stratigraphy correlated well with initially chosen types of graves too.

In his reports Gorodcov had discussed "Pit, Catacomb and Timber types of graves," although he remarked that each of them belonged to a special group of population. However, in his manual (1908 and 1910) and in the work "Culture of the Bronze Age in Central Russia" (1916) he talked about "Pit-grave, Catacomb and Timber-grave cultures." Thus these famous cultures of the third to second millennia B.C. made their first appearance in Russian archaeological literature. Many archaeologists began to connect Indo-European origins with the Pit-grave culture, others (more reasonably) ascribed them to Aryan forepeople (ancestors of Iranians and Indo-Aryans) instead. The Timber-grave culture was connected with the first Iranians (and all the Iranians, including Sythian ancestors). The Catacomb culture remained a mystery for a long time until some archaeologists (including myself) connected it with Indo-Aryan origins, that is, with the Aryans of the Rigveda. Gorodcov's analysis transformed the entire understanding of pre-Scythian burial mounds to a discernibly higher level at one stroke—from an amorphous state of skeletal material to a system of cultures, from antiquarianism to twentieth-century archaeology. In the Izium and the Bakhmut reports Gorodcov investigated the rarer extended burials of the Iron Age—burials of late nomads, such as the Turks (Pechenegs, Polovetses, etc.), with whom he linked "stone women" in some burial mounds.

In 1903, the year of the Bakhmut excavations, Gorodcov became a supernumerary (unpaid extra) worker at the Moscow Historical Museum. In 1906, when he retired from the army after twenty-five years' service, he took the post of senior curator at the museum, and in 1907 the 47-year-old began to teach archaeology at the Moscow Archaeological Institute, which trained archivists.

In 1908 he published the first part of his lecture course, *Prehistoric Archaeology,* and in 1910 the second part, *Everyday Archaeology,* appeared. The title of the second part can be explained by the difficulty of translating the Russian word *byt,* meaning daily life, household economy, family relations, and the like. It had a broader meaning at that time, which included the state system, morals, and customs—in other words, culture (the word "kultura" was not in common use in Russia then). By calling historical archaeology (i.e., classical and medieval archaeology), which followed prehistoric archaeology, "everyday archaeology," Gorodcov emphasized that it did not include art and that it differed from classical archaeology. It was not connected with political history, the history of events and heroes, because it could reconstruct only the history of structures and of groups of people. The history of culture differed from the archaeological studies of earlier scholars who focused on the traces of individual events and concrete figures (such as the helmet of Prince Yaroslav, the crown of Monomakh, the sword of Dovmont, traces of the battle in the Kulikovskoye field).

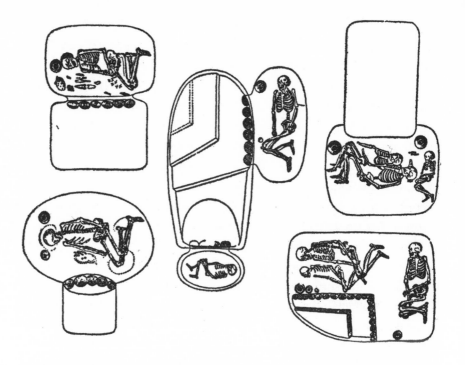

Catacomb burial from South Russia. (Reprinted from A. L. Mongait, Archaeology in the USSR, *1970)*

In *Prehistoric Archaeology* general principles of archaeological research were elucidated and cultures were described in their successive epochs. Principles of classification, worked out earlier for ceramics, were extended to all archaeological material. Types were united into sections, sections into groups, and all according to a strict sequence of criteria at each step. Some criteria were seen in forms, others in substance, still others in functional purposes. Gorodcov treated archaeology as a discipline within the complex of natural sciences, between anthropology (as a science of human beings in general) and ethnology (a discipline concerned with living peoples). This approach exposed a succession of epochs in the material, following GABRIEL DE MORTILLET, with the change of terminology to make it similar to geological terminology (the hierarchy of time categories: era—epoch—period—time). On that basis, during the period of Soviet archaeology, it was obligatory to consider Gorodcov as an evolutionist. There was an also another reason for this. Evolutionism was the most respected of all pre-Marxist currents in Soviet scholarship (although, of course, it was criticized as a bourgeois doctrine, too), so the identification of Gorodcov as an evolutionist raised his status and hence the status of his pupils who were still active.

This identification of Gorodcov as an evolutionist is erroneous. Evolutionists in archaeology considered themselves to be naturalists and clung to contacts with geology, with palaeontology, and in part with physical anthropology (e.g., the Darwinian doctrine of anthropogenesis).

Other approaches to archaeology were notable for their special emphasis on natural disciplines, for example, geographical determinism that chose connections mostly with geography, or biological determinism that emphasized the doctrine of races in its connections with physical anthropology. As I have already mentioned, it was biological and geological systematization in the natural sciences that most impressed Gorodcov and not the doctrine about development. In *Everyday Archaeology* he preferred to call periodization just "chronological classification." Archaeological material, except in cases of direct stratigraphy, appeared to archaeologists at first as a mixture that had to be ordered by classification and then examined to ascertain what classifying divisions had chronological significance.

As for Mortillet's scheme of epochs, who didn't use it in the beginning of the twentieth century? At this time it was generally accepted as fact. Both Uvarov in his *The Stone Age* and Veselovskiy in his teaching course arranged Paleolithic material according to the same scheme. Did this make them evolutionists as well? Abbé Henri Breuil accepted it at the beginning of his work—but one can't regard him as an evolutionist. Therefore it is necessary to judge Gorodcov by his other work. In particular, when he formulated the "general laws" underlying "chronological classification," he suggested a list that would allow for the incorporation of factors such as migration and diffusion, factors alien to evolutionists, into the conception as well.

This is even clearer in *Everyday Archaeology,* in which Gorodcov included "the geographical theory" of Lev Ilyich Mechnikov because he was sympathetic to it. Lev Mechnikov—the elder brother of the well-known biologist, a polyglot and a revolutionary, an officer of Garibaldi's "Thousand"—had settled in Switzerland, where he held the chair of comparative geography and statistics at the University of Lausanne. His work *Civilization and Great Historical Rivers. Geographical Theory of Development of Up-to-date Societies,* published posthumously, became the classic example of geographical determinism in the history of culture. Mechnikov opposed racial theory, and Marxists liked him for this. Mechnikov divided the history of humankind into three periods according to the leading components of geographical environment: the Ancient Ages— the river period; the Middle Ages—the Mediterranean period; the Modern Ages—the ocean period. Four great civilizations, washed by great rivers—the Nile, the Tigris-Euphrates, the Indus-Ganges, the Yangtse–Hwang Ho—constituted the Ancient Ages.

Starting with the influence of the geographical environment, Gorodcov looked at the materials of the ancient "Sumero-Akkadian," Egyptian, and Aegean civilizations. However, he transfered his interest from the origins of those civilizations to their influence on the rest of the world. Gorodcov accorded the Sumerian civilization the highest importance, a theory similar to that of Lord Raglan's Sumerocentrism. He described the spread of "cultural influences" in the steppe zone of Eastern Europe in the following way:

> The most ancient of them went from Mesopotamia and partially from Asia Minor via the Caucasus, from where it spread over the steppe forming a fan-shaped pattern and penetrated far into the depths of the forests. The Central Asian current was the second one, it covered the eastern part of the forests up to the Kama river and all the steppe with the new layer of monuments. At last, the Siberian current followed as the third one and being intersected with the Central Asian current, it formed something in the way of a cultural hearth, but the development of that hearth should be attributed already to the Iron epoch.

Gorodcov included several Iron Age cultures of Russia—the Catacomb culture (wide Mediterranean connections), the Fatyanovo culture (west European connections), the Kobanian culture (before Halstatt), and the Yenisey culture—in the common system according to the network of influences and contact connections. He incorporated Tripolye culture into the wide belt of early agricultural societies, spread across Asia to the Danube River basin, rejecting the autochthonous view that connected Tripolye culture with the Slavs through the Scythians.

It is quite clear that Gorodcov was basically a diffusionist, and as many diffusionists do, he assigned a role for migrations:

> The Pit-grave people spread as a wide flow in South Russia, capturing all the region of the lower reaches of Volga, the Don and the Dnieper rivers. . . . The people, who buried their corpses in catacombs, appeared later. . . . The Timber-grave people, who occupied vast area to the North from the sources of the Donets and the Don rivers and to the West—up to the banks of Dnieper and probably further, appeared still later (1910, 151–152).

But it was diffusion that united these materials into a system:

> The definition of cultural currents and influences was the most important task for the times under study. . . . At the time of bronze implements . . . Egypt and Iran, more correctly, Central Asia began to have quite independent cultural hearths. The union of these points formed undoubtedly the cultural basis of the time

of bronze implements. Each of the three named hearths aspired to send the rays of its cultural influences everywhere. . . . Cultural rays, originating from various hearths, crossed each other here and there, forming ranges of new cultural hearths, some of them had time to rise in paramount importance by the end of the time: . . . Asia Minor and Phoenicia, . . . India, China and Siberia (the Yenisey river). One more new range of hearths appeared under the cultural influence of all those hearths . . . on banks of the Kama river . . ., the Hungarian hearth, that influenced North German and Scandinavian cultures in its turn (1910, 160–161).

Gorodcov subsequently considered and described Scythian and Sarmatian antiquities and their eastern connections, the contrary movements of Goths, and the great migration of peoples. He paid much attention to the monuments of late nomads—Turks and Pechenegs, Turks and Polovetses—and to the archaeology of Ugro-Finnish nationalities. It is said that Gorodcov's work resembles the later (and broader in geographical respect, but more geographically limited) work of that other diffusionist, V. GORDON CHILDE—his *The Dawn of European Civilization* (1925) also had a huge influence on Russian archaeology.

Gorodcov's *Prehistoric Archaeology* was reissued during Soviet times (1923), but a planned reissuing of *Everyday Archaeology* did not eventuate. Nevertheless, Gorodcov's published courses served as basic manuals and reference books for decades more; the short manual *Introduction to Archaeology,* written by Gorodcov's disciple A. V. Arcikhovskiy and similar to Gorodcov's books, did not replace them until 1940. Gorodcov had more than one hundred publications by the time of the revolution, including works that were mostly theoretical in form. The basic concepts of archaeology, especially ideas on the problem of classification, were stated in them.

The scope of Gorodcov's fieldwork was extraordinarily wide. He excavated all types of sites, from the Palaeolithic to the Middle Ages, and created the Russian textbook on excavation methods. In addition he undertook extensive survey work within Russia, especially of Bronze Age cultural sites, trying to arrange his work chronologically and to consider connections between different cultural groups and their genetic relations. He was the systematizer of Russia's archaeological riches, and he wanted archaeology to become a system of knowledge, a strict discipline.

To Russia, Gorodcov was Sophus Müller, JOSEPH DÉCHELETTE, and the young Childe rolled into in one, and for all of that he was neither a professor nor even a university graduate. A university education was obligatory for a professorship in Russia. Gorodcov was not noble, and he had no strong academic or scholarly connections. However, the Russian Revolution, which occurred when he was 58, changed Gorodcov's fortunes. In 1919 he became professor at Moscow University for the first time, and four years later became the head of the Archaeological Department of the Russian Association of Scientific Research Institutes of Social Sciences (RANIION). People's Commissar of Public Education A. V. Lunacharskiy was the head of the whole association. The thirty-fifth anniversary of the beginning of Gorodcov's scholarly activity was celebrated that year at the Historical Museum, and one of halls of the museum was named after him. In 1923 his course *Prehistoric Archaeology* was reissued under a new title—*Archaeology. Vol. I. The Stone Age.* The sections on classification and about laws of existence of archaeological phenomena were included with small alterations in the booklet *Typological Method,* published in 1927 in Riazan, the capital of his native province.

In this last publication rigorous classification was taken to its limit and the scheme assumed completed, canonical form:

> All material archaeological remains are divided in categories, then categories are divided in groups, groups—in sections and sections—in types. Purpose of types is the principle of division (principium divisionis) in categories, substance of types is the principle of division in groups, form peculiar to several types is the principle of division in sections, form peculiar to one type is the principle of division in types (1927, 6).

If we take arrowheads as an example: category—arrowheads; group—copper arrowheads; section (according to the form from the shaft side)—socketed arrowheads; type (according to the form of the point part)—three-edged arrowheads. Gorodcov wanted to construct natural classifications like those of Linnaeus, but he felt that his "types" were not determined realistically: "Only types that include objects founded or punched in one mould (Typos) of the same substance, meet that determination quite well. A collection of such objects gives ideal pure types" (1927, 8). Ideal pure types are not usual in archaeological material at all. Thus an artificial classification has its advantages—in a systematization of material for the sake of search, identification, differentiation. And, of course, it must be strict, common, universal.

Gorodcov's scheme quickly became the standard for archaeological classification in the Soviet Union. In 1930 his pupil A. V. Arcikhovskiy classified the temporal rings of Viatiches as well as other things according to that scheme (category—bracelets; group—copper bracelets; section—twisted bracelets; type—triple bracelet) in his "Burial Mounds of

Viatiches." The term *category* began to stand everywhere for a group of things chosen according to functional purposes. In 1927 in the United States at the First Pecos Conference, binary terminology and the principles of Linnaeus were discussed, and in 1933 Gorodcov's Riazan booklet was translated into English and published in the United States. In 1939 Clyde Kluckhohn remarked that "methods of classifying pottery wares on the basis of highly technical and rather precisely defined operations have been elaborated. But I am aware of but a single paper (by a Russian!) where there has been even a tentative and fumbling consideration of the implications of the typological method" (Kluckhohn 1939, 338). One can see the influence of Gorodcov's ideas in the classifications of IRVING ROUSE (1960), R. Bartra (1964), and A. Garcia Kook (1967).

As to "the implications of the typological method," Kluckhohn overlooked the circumstance that V. F. Gening noticed correctly in his *Essays of History of Soviet Archaeology*. The archaeological laws outlined by Gorodcov in his booklet as the basis of "the typological method" are not connected with the method in the text. The laws stand alone, as does the method. But neither Kluckhohn, nor Gening, nor Lebedev (in his "History of Home Archaeology") took any notice that Gorodcov's "typological method" had little in common with the typological method of Montelius, and it would be better not to use the same names so as to avoid confusion. Gorodcov's method was not aimed at defining relative chronology according to the evolution of standards of things manufactured (as with Montelius), but simply a typology and, even more exactly, a classification.

Gorodcov was therefore interested not so much in using classification to date objects, as WILLIAM FLINDERS PETRIE had done, but rather in establishing the relationship of objects found in archaeological sites to each other. His laws really dealt with correlations between things, including genealogic correlations, but not with classification per se. Gorodcov wanted to introduce a theoretical basis for his classification, and for the chosen succession of steps (why function was first, then substance, and so on.), and he searched for that basis in regular "correlations between industrial phenomena" (*Archaeology* 1: 8). Despite much hard thinking he could not find the logical connection. But the laws themselves are interesting. Gorodcov listed six laws in 1923, five in 1927, and four in 1933, which he finally called "principles." Here is the most complete list:

> 1. The law of causality reads that an earlier monument is the reason for any similar monument, i.e., each type has its prototype.
> 2. The law of evolution dictates the development from simplest forms to more complex forms, but evolution is supposed to be treelike, not unilinear.

3. The law of inertia asserts that people aspire "to retain all the forms of culture for as long time as possible in the shape inherited from preceding generations."

4. The law of borrowings "explains likeness of phenomena by their communication from one nationality to another one."

5. With the law of chance occurrences Gorodcov tried to explain by a common source those things that were formerly explained by availability of "deeply hidden reason."

6. The law of struggle of material creatures for existence explains the survival of the more "fit" phenomenon among phenomena with the same function.

The first law rejected absolute innovations, the second describes the direction of evolution, the third, the fourth, and the fifth reflect and ground diffusionist interpretations, and the sixth deals with different versions of development (i.e., not unilinear evolution here, too). Only the first law is acceptable both to evolutionists and diffusionists; the rest of the laws are undoubtedly diffusionist. These laws, on the whole, elucidate the life of ancient material culture as the object of investigation. These are not laws of archaeology as a discipline, but some principles according to which the peculiarities of its objects were formed. In 1923 Gorodcov unified his "chronological classification" with the whole scheme of classification. He began to mark out *eras* according to availability of industry; *periods,* according to the substance of leading types of implements; *epochs,* according to the leading processing methods; *times,* according to morphological changes of leading types (Gorodcov 1926).

A very active and united school of archaeology formed around Gorodcov during his teaching at Moscow University and at the RANIION. Artemiy Vladimirovich Arcikhovskiy (1902–1978), Aleksandr Yakovlevich Briusov (1885–1966), Aleksey Petrovich Smirnov (1899–1974), Sergey Nikolayevich Kiselev (1905–1962), Yevgeniy Ignatyevich Krupnov (born 1904), Maria Yevgenyevna Foss (1899–1953), Boris Aleksandrovich Rybakov (born in 1908)—all were leading Moscow archaeologists, leaders of Soviet archaeology and its branches.

Young postgraduates and pupils of Gorodcov also studied at the sociological seminar of academician (member of the Academy of Sciences) V. M. Friche, an old Bolshevik and a propagandist of Marxism. From 1923 seminars were held on the incorporation of Marxism into archaeology and the sociological consideration of archaeological materials. Arcikhovskiy, for example, gave the paper "The Sociological Importance of Evolution of Agricultural Implements." Gorodcov's ideas were seen to be of use in this process of incorporation. For example, in *Archaeology* he wrote that "implements of labour always played one of the important parts in the development of human culture. Their perfection promoted augmentation of material values and then development of spiritual forces" (1923, 147–148). But while Gorodcov declared archaeology's independence, his disciples wanted to make it Marxist. Gorodcov did adapt to new trends and to the demands of Soviet Marxist ideology, trying to master Marxist ideas and interests, as seen in his article "Significance of Studying the Ancient Techniques in Archaeology."

The Paleoethnological School of B. S. Zhukov, formed around the chair of anthropology at Moscow University, was considered by Gorodcov's pupils to be their major opponent (future outstanding Soviet archaeologists S. P. Tolstov, O. N. Bader, M. V. Voyevodskiy, A. V. Zbruyeva, and others were based there). "The Palaeoethnologists" stuck to geographical determinism, took a great interest in the ethnic side of culture, and considered archaeology to be merely a branch of ethnology turned to the past. Zhukov criticized Gorodcov's "chronological classification" for artificially cutting chronological borders, which they felt led to the separation of cultures of the same type. Zhukov himself considered all cultures with bronze implements but without iron implements, irrespective of their chronology, to belong to the Bronze Age. But Gorodcov thought that it was more important to unite all the simultaneous cultures in one period because of their contact relations—an approach that reflected his diffusionist interests. In Gorodcov's scheme, cultures without metal could be classified in the Bronze Age, if metal already existed at another place, even a distant one. The cultural influences that spread from there bound the entire period into a single entity.

Young scholars from both schools initiated a public debate in 1929. Arcikhovskiy read a paper on behalf of three young archaeologists (Arcikhovskiy, Briusov, and Kiselev), explaining a new "method of ascent," reconstructing the structure of a society from its implements using Marxist laws. The necessity of using ethnographic data and even written sources was presented with such conviction that archaeology became an independent fundamental discipline equal with history; it could study historical process itself. Arcikhovskiy, Rybakov, and the entire school of Gorodcov retained this conviction even after giving up the "the method of ascent." Arcikhovskiy later expressed their credo in his legendary phrase "archaeology is history armed with a spade."

This concept was inspired by Yuriy Vladimirovich Gotye (1889–1943), Arcikhovskiy's and Rybakov's second university teacher. Gotye considered archaeology to be independent and history and archaeology to be related branches of Russian knowledge (*Essays on History of Material Culture of Eastern Europe* [1925]). Gorodcov conceived of archaeology as a fundamental discipline, not simply as source criticism. He wrote: "Archaeology is the discipline about events, accompanying the life of extinct generations of mankind, so far as those events were expressed in material creations" (1923, 5). The public debate was considered sufficiently important to be reported by the press. However, the resolution of the debate was subsumed by the politics of the real world.

The year 1929 was that of "the great break" in the life of the Soviet Union, according to Stalin. It was the year of complete collectivization in agriculture, with peasants being removed by force to Siberia, and of savage repression of the church. Struggles within the Communist Party were aggravated by Stalin's grasping individual power and removing real and possible rivals. The atmosphere in the social sciences was very tense, with the ideologization of science gathering distinct momentum. Societies of local amateur antiquarians were being persecuted because they produced bourgeois knowledge.

Zhukov was arrested and his school broken up, and Gorodcov's pupils were criticized as well. Archaeological leaders from Leningrad declared that "Marxist archaeology" was a nonsense, and as archaeology did not correspond with Marxism it was liable to liquidation. Their argument was that objects are not independent, they are nothing without people and society, hence, they are not worthy of a special discipline. Formalism and making a fetish of things are characteristics of bourgeois scholarship. The history of material culture, as an object of research, is necessary, but not archaeology, which was distinctive because of the kinds of data it employed. But this new approach was called into question too. One suggestion was to divide disciplines according to successive social-economic formations, regardless of the kind of data being considered.

Three "innovative archaeologists," the main participants of the public debate, issued the penitential article "The Emergence, Development and Disappearance of Marxist Archaeology" (1930). In the same year Leningrad archaeologist V. I. Ravdonikas published the large work *For Marxist History of Material Culture,* in which he pounced not only upon Arcikhovskiy but also upon Gorodcov, calling "the so-called venerable scholar" typically bourgeois. He spoke ironically of Gorodcov's pretensions to the superiority of working out the theory for the typological method (deliberately taking no notice of fact that the question was in the theory of classification, but not in the typological method): "Thus, it turned out that before V. A. Gorodcov European science made its way gropingly; Mortillets and Monteliuses 'tried' to practise incomplete experiments and did not have time to be grown up enough for a scientific theory, and only he, V. A. Gorodcov, made mankind happy with such theory" (p. 43).

Gorodcov was dismissed from all his posts. Amid arrests, dismissals, raging public criticism and self-criticism, a crowd of Gorodcov's pupils coming out of a lecture hall saw his portrait on the wall and tore it down and trampled it. More recently, A. A. Formozov asked older pupils about this episode: one said that he could not recollect it, another that he had not taken part, a third that the reprisal with the portrait had taken place but it had been deserved; only one said that he was ashamed and regretted it. The storm blew over in several years. In 1934 Gorodcov and some other outstanding archaeologists were awarded the degree of Doctor without defense of a thesis (the Doctor's degree in Russia is a stage higher than a Ph.D.).

In 1935, at the age of 75, Gorodcov published the article "Social and Economic System of Ancient Inhabitants of the Timonovka Palaeolithic Dwelling-site" (*Soviet Ethnography* 3). The article continues the series of sociological interpretations published by his pupils in 1923–1927 and shows that even at this late stage in his life he was improving his fieldwork methods and learning from his students. Gorodcov joined the Bolshevik party late in life and managed to avoid arrest even during the terrible year of 1937. He was a very old man during World War II and died in the year of the victory, 1945.

As for his pupils, Arcikhovskiy became professor at Moscow University and was the editor of *Soviet Archaeology* for many years; the academician Rybakov was at the head of all of Soviet archaeology for thirty years and was the director of the Institute of Archaeology of the Academy of Sciences; Kiselev and Krupnov were his deputy directors. Arcikhovskiy had a large following; Krupnov had many pupils—specialists in the archaeology of the Caucasus; Rybakov had his disciples—specialists in the history and philology of the Slavs. But it was easier for them to create their schools because they followed the standard academic paths. For Gorodcov to establish his large school, he had to create a system of archaeology in Russia, and in so doing he created himself.

References
Primary
Gorodcov, V. A. 1902. "Russkaya doistoricheskaya keramika" [Russian Prehistoric Ceramics]. Trudy XI Arkheologicheskogos'yezda.

———. 1905. "Resultaty arkheologicheskikh issledovaniy . . . (Izyumskiy uezd)" [The Results of Archaeological Explorations . . . (Izyum District)]. Trudy XII Arkheologicheskogos'yezda, I.

———. 1907. "Resultaty arkheologicheskikh issledovaniy . . . (Bakhmutskiy uezd)" [The Results of Archaeological Explorations . . . (Bakhmut District)]. Trudy XIII Arkheologicheskogos'yezda, I.

————. 1908. *Pervobytnaya arkheologiya* [Prehistoric Archaeology]. Moscow.

————. 1910. *Bytovaya arkheologiya* [Everyday Archaeology]. Moscow.

————. 1916. "Kultury bronzovoy epokhi v Sredney Rossii" [Cultures of the Bronze Age in Central Russia]. Otchet Istoricheskogo Museya za 1914, 121–226. Moscow.

————. 1923. *Archaeology. Vol. I. The Stone Age.* (Reissue of *Pervobytnaya archeologiya,* 1910.)

————. 1926. Letter to the editorial staff of *New East* 13–14: 464.

————. 1927. *Typological Method.* Riazan.

————. 1930. "Significance of Studying the Ancient Techniques in Archaeology." *Transactions of the Archaeological Section of the Institute of Archaeology and Art Criticism* (RANIION) 5.

————. 1933. "The Typological Method in Archaeology." *American Anthropologist,* n.s., 35, 21: 95–102.

————. 1935. "Social and Economic System of Ancient Inhabitants of the Timonovka Palaeolithic Dwelling-site." *Soviet Ethnography* 3.

Secondary

Bryusov, A. Ya. 1960. "V. A. Gorodcov." Trudy Gos. Istoricheskogo Muzeya, 37. Moscow.

Bryusov, A. Ya., ed. 1985. "K 125-letiyu so dnya rozhdeniya V. A. Gorodcova" [To the 125th Anniversary of V. A. Gorodcov]. *Sovetskaya Arkheologiya* 4.

Friche, V. M. 1928. "V. A. Gorodcov." *Trudy sekcii arkheologii Instituta arheologii i iskusstvoznaniya RANIION* 4.

Kluckhohn, Clyde. 1939. "The Place of Theory in Anthropological Studies." *Philosophy of Science* 6: 328–344.

Ravdonikas, V. I. 1930. "Za marksistskuju materainoj kulturny" [For Marxist History of Material Culture]. *IGAIMK* 7, 3–4.

Nathalie Richard

Marcellin Boule 1861–1942

Translated from the French by Judith Braid

Using paleontology and paleoanthropology Marcellin Boule revitalized the
study of prehistory in France through his theories about human evolution. His
work elevated human paleontology to the rank of a true science, capable of
establishing chronological answers to the questions of prehistory.

Marcellin Boule (born 1 January 1861 at Montsalvy, Cantal, died 4
July 1942 at Montsalvy) was introduced to the natural sciences in
his youth by the local pharmacist at Aurillac, Jean-Baptiste Rames, who
was himself an amateur geologist. Rames helped him follow his vocation
as a scientist, and though his family background was fairly modest, Boule
was able to continue his schooling until he had earned a doctorate. He
studied first in Toulouse and took degrees in natural sciences and geology. In 1886 he was awarded a scholarship and went to Paris. Armed
with a recommendation from Rames, he met Ferdinand Fouqué, the geologist at the Collège de France who introduced him to petrography,
and also Albert Gaudry, whose major work, *Les enchaînements du monde*
animal, had made a particular impact on the young Boule. He graduated
in 1887 and then taught geology at the Faculty of Science in Clermont-
Ferrand. He returned to the Museum d'Histoire Naturelle in Paris,
where he spent the rest of his scientific career. Taken on first as a trainee,
he became in 1892 assistant to Gaudry, who held the chair of paleontology. Once he had finished his doctoral thesis in 1894, he became
Gaudry's assistant at the museum and made his mark through his organization of the paleontology gallery, which was opened in 1898. For this
work Boule received the award of Chevalier de la Légion d'Honneur. In
1903, Boule succeeded his teacher to the chair of paleontology, a post
he would hold until his retirement in 1936.

His professional position was strengthened still further by his appointment as director of the Institut de Paléontologie Humaine in Paris.
The first organization for specialized research in the field, the institute
was founded in 1914 by Prince Albert I of Monaco and inaugurated in
1920. Boule also edited several major publications in the fields of paleontology and prehistory. With R. Verneau he was the editor of the review *L'anthropologie* from its inception in 1893 until 1930. He founded

Marcellin Boule.
(Copyright Frank
Spencer)

the *Annales de paléontologie* in 1906 and in 1920 the *Archives de l'Institut de Paléontologie Humaine.*

Marcellin Boule was considered the unrivaled leader of French paleontology in the first third of the twentieth century. During his career he received numerous scientific honors; won prizes once from the Société de Géologie and twice from the Institut; was awarded the Huxley medal by the Royal Institute of Anthropology of Great Britain and Ireland and the Wollaston medal by the Geological Society of London; and was made Commandeur de la Légion d'Honneur in 1935. He taught or inspired many French paleontologists, including Teilhard de Chardin, who shifted to paleontology on his advice; J. Piveteau, with whom he wrote a work on fossils in 1935; and H. Vallois, who brought out a new edition of Boule's *Les hommes fossiles* in 1946.

Two major works stand out from his prolific output. The first is the study of the La Chapelle-aux-Saints skeleton, in which Boule was able to explain his ideas on paleontology by proposing an original identification and reconstruction of Neanderthal man (Boule 1913). The second is his book *Les hommes fossiles,* which summarized his thinking for the general public and enjoyed a huge success. The first edition in 1921 was sold out in a year and was followed by a second edition in 1923 as well as by an English translation. This second edition was supplemented and reissued by Vallois in 1946. Boule also produced numerous scientific articles, many published in journals that he edited, textbooks for secondary schools, and popular works, such as the *Guides du touriste, du naturaliste et de l'archéologue*. The guidebooks were usually written in collaboration, and he assumed responsibility for the geological and paleontological sections. By 1942 there were eight volumes in print, of which the first dealt with Cantal, his native region.

The variety of works written by Boule serves to confirm, if any proof were needed, that the fame and influence of the paleontologist went far beyond the narrow confines of his profession as scientist. Boule did not make use of his intellectual popularity to bolster a political career. He went so far as to denounce the way some of his colleagues mixed politics and science, condemning, for example, GABRIEL DE MORTILLET for using prehistory as an anticlerical and rational socialist weapon. He himself tried to stay neutral in the clerical/anticlerical debates in French politics and some of his scientific collaborators, such as Abbé HENRI BREUIL and the Jesuit Teilhard de Chardin, were men of the church. Although he intervened very rarely in the political arena, he defended himself in 1908 against the criticism of the clerical party, which was provoked by his analysis of Neanderthal man. His counterattack in *Le matin* on 27 December posed the famous question, "Is it better to be descended from a fallen angel or a perfected monkey?" His other forays into politics were confined to a handful of nationalist anti-German texts written during the First World War, such as the article on "La guerre" that appeared in *L'anthropologie* in 1914.

Boule kept politics at arm's length because he saw his life's work as exclusively scientific. It seemed to him that "science is one of the main sources of happiness" and that "its service demands much selflessness and many sacrifices" (quoted in Hammond 1937, 611). So he devoted his life to a cause that was purely scientific, namely, to make paleontology into a separate science. As he maintained in 1902, "paleontology must not be content to serve as a handmaid to Geology, or to be, as it were, a science which complements Zoology"; it "must be autonomous" (*Titres et travaux* 1902, ii).

Yet the beginnings of this commitment to paleontology were complex, because Boule hesitated at length between the study of fossils and the study of rocks. Influenced by Rames, he leaned at first toward geology, and his doctoral thesis was in this field. Although "naturally drawn to the study of the mountains of his native region" (ibid., i), he still familiarized himself with paleontology. During his time in Toulouse, he met the prehistorian and cave art specialist Emile Cartailhac, who introduced him to paleoanthropology and prehistory. In 1884 he published an article on flint pits in the review *Les matériaux pour l'histoire naturelle et primitive de l'homme.* In Paris, his mentor Albert Gaudry influenced the direction of his paleontological work. Boule chose to direct his career to the study of fossils, setting for himself a research goal of completing Gaudry's work by examining, not the links between genuses, but the relations between species. Several of his first pieces dealt with tracing back the history of such species as horses, bears, and rhinos.

Boule's zeal for paleontology was accompanied from the first by an awareness of the particular importance of human paleontology, to which he devoted most of his work. In his view, only paleontology was able to "reconstitute the successive phases of creation." And paleoanthropology, the only true "historical science" (*Titres et travaux* 1902, ii), was an absolutely indispensable discipline for the study of humankind's earliest existence. It alone could rejuvenate prehistoric archaeology, whose atrophy Boule noted in the 1880s. He felt that prehistorians had confined themselves for some time to "pure archaeology," while geologists had turned away from recent scientific developments. The young scholar, "struck by the drawbacks in the present state of affairs," decided therefore "to pose again the questions of human paleontology, mostly through [drawing on] stratigraphy" (ibid., 63).

Thus the function of paleoanthropology was to revitalize prehistory by giving it the historical or diachronic dimension that it had lacked so far. This was the basic principle of Marcellin Boule's archaeological thinking and was first broached in 1888 in an "Essai de paléontologie stratigraphique de l'homme," in which he put forward a chronology of the Paleolithic based on the periodicity of glacial phenomena. Archaeology was subordinated to the geological and paleontological analysis of the deposits. This original conception of prehistory was developed at greater length in *Les hommes fossiles.* There Boule reaffirmed that manufactured objects, which served as a basis for drawing up a classification, reflected only "the intellectual and moral aspects of the oldest human societies." But paleontology, "by helping us to understand better the main anatomical features of our distant ancestors, is alone able to shed some light on their origins, their zoological links, their physical evolution, that is to say on the genealogical history of hominids" (1921, ix). Paleontological analysis would therefore dominate the work.

Seen in the context of late-nineteenth-century prehistory, Boule's contribution was extremely innovative. By synthesizing the data of Quaternary geology with that of paleontology and archaeology, Boule was implicitly taking a stand against another method of studying prehistory—that of Gabriel de Mortillet, whose classification system, based exclusively on items of human manufacture, held sway at that time. Boule refused to regard flints as sufficient criteria for chronological mapping and contended they only achieved that status once they were assimilated into the more fundamental data of geology and paleontology. He rejected Mortillet's linkage of biological and technical progress. Although techniques certainly did reflect the intellectual and moral evolution of societies, only bones could show the history of the species. The two processes occasionally coincided but remained distinct, and it was vital not to extrapolate too hastily from the improvements in techniques to overall progress. Boule thought that manufacturing classifications "could only have a local character, since different industries could be, even today, contemporaneous in different territories" (1921, 46). So only biological progress could serve as a marker for a general chronology.

It is clear, then, that Boule participated in the renewal of prehistory that took place at the end of the nineteenth century and that was expressed in another form in the works of Henri Breuil, his colleague at the Institut de Paléontologie Humaine. During the 1937 jubilee organized by the Museum d'Histoire Naturelle, Breuil acknowledged Boule's contribution in raising human paleontology to the rank of a true science, capable of establishing chronological conclusions in questions of prehistory.

Boule's Paleontological Model

According to Boule, only biological progress was valid in any general sense; technical developments merely allowed, at best, the clarification of the evolving local facies. But this claim did not imply that biological progress was linear. All of Boule's work in paleontology attempted to prove the opposite, and so it presented a contrast, on this point as on many others, to the transformist ideas of Mortillet and his followers at the Ecole d'Anthropologie.

Boule perceived a single law in paleontology, which led him to assert that "the development of creatures did not occur as simply as might have been thought at the dawn of science." In fact, "uni linear series appear to us to be more and more rare; [and] if they do exist, it is extremely difficult to locate them or to pursue them very far." On the other hand, it was easy to compare "each group of similar creatures . . . to a tree or a bush with differing degrees of density, each branch of which is either a genus or a species or a race" (1913, 249–250). Using this model, it followed that present forms represented only a few branches, since many branches had died out or produced "doubly fossilized" species, which were very old in geological terms and had no descendants. The model of the tree, which Boule preferred to that of the line, was the result of his extreme caution regarding interpretations. He refused to draw conclusions about descent from morphological similarities, even though it seemed plausible on occasion. Instead, he favored the idea of simple kinship, with similarity between morphological traits showing that individuals belonged to two branches of the same tree.

This theory was set out first in the work on animal species that Boule undertook at the start of his career, sometimes in collaboration with his teacher Gaudry. For instance, he used the rich paleontological sequences excavated from the Ice Age Gargas cave in the Hautes Pyrénées to reconstitute the evolution of species of bears since the Oligocene. The reconstruction of different evolutionary paths was depicted in several concurrent tables, each in the form of a tree whose branches were ordered in different ways according to the evolutionary possibilities (Boule and Gaudry 1892). However, Boule felt restrained by his association with Gaudry, since he had chosen to build a career well away from the violent arguments that shook the scientific community after the publication of Charles Darwin's *Origin of Species*. It was not until after his mentor had retired that Boule tackled the question of human evolution. The study of La Chapelle-aux-Saints man, undertaken between 1911 and 1913, was a crucial step in his thinking on paleontology. Here he maintained that "the human group was no exception" (1913, 250) in the animal world and revealed his ambition to examine different human evolutionary directions from the perspective of a paleontologist. He would apply to human beings the same analytical techniques that had been applied to animal species, describing first their zoological traits before making comparisons with neighboring species.

The La Chapelle-aux-Saints man was an ideal candidate for this type of purely scientific analysis. The skeleton, discovered in 1908 by the Bouyssonie brothers, who were priests in southwestern France, in the Bonneval cave, had the great advantage of being almost complete. Unlike the fragments discovered earlier, the remains comprised one intact half of the skull and face, the vertebrae, and the limbs, which allowed a complete diagnosis of the Neanderthal type. The French paleontologist was thus able to produce a monograph of over two hundred pages, which remained the definitive text until the Second World War. It was only after 1950 that scientists dared to question the conclusions put forward by Marcellin Boule in 1913.

Boule proposed an analysis that was striking for the absolute rigor of its scientific style as well as for its preconceptions. The rigor was evident in every line of the very detailed descriptions of the skeletal bones, which were accompanied by numerous illustrations (most of them reproduced in the book *Les hommes fossiles*) and by systematic comparisons with bones belonging either to anthropoid apes or to modern human beings. Though dimensions were also given, they did not constitute the vital part of the text. Boule opposed the prevailing taste for anthropometry and was suspicious that the abuse of figures created "the very real danger of giving the illusion of a mathematical precision which Nature . . . cannot accommodate" (1913, 5).

The meticulous description, however, was underwritten by an obvious ideological bias. For Boule's ultimate objective was to prove that the evolution of the hominids followed the same treelike model that characterized all the other groups in the animal kingdom. It was therefore inevitable that some branches of the human evolutionary tree had become extinct. Neanderthal man, whose primitive characteristics had been known since the middle of the nineteenth century, seemed to Boule an excellent specimen of a branch from which *Homo sapiens* did not descend. Thus his entire description was intended to distance La Chapelle-aux-Saints man from modern man and to place him clearly outside the limits of the present-day variations in the human species. Given this "alienation," the conclusion was inescapable that the distance between the Neanderthal type and the modern type was too great for evolution to have occurred in the relatively short space of time between the Lower Paleolithic and modern times. Boule's bias resulted in some errors of interpretation, especially in his description of the posture of La Chapelle-aux-Saints man. Although he briefly noted signs of osteoarthritis, Boule looked at the alignment of the vertebrae and decided that the spinal column's curvatures were different from those of a modern person and that Neanderthal man's gait, though bipedal, was stooped and slouched. Swayed by his preconceptions, Boule ignored the possibility that the deformation of the vertebrae might have been the result of the osteoarthritis. (In the early 1950s, French paleontologist and geologist Camille Arambourg, who suffered from the same disease, had an X-ray made of his own neck, thereby overturning Boule's interpretation and establishing Neanderthal man's perfect bipedal gait.)

In addition to the errors that were revealed after 1950, Boule's monograph employed language in its descriptions that, though not necessarily inaccurate, seemed to evoke in the reader a sense of the "otherness" of La Chapelle-aux-Saints man. Certain passages overemphasized the brutishness of Neanderthal man. So, for example, his face had "a bestial appearance because of the *absence* of forehead, the *huge* volume of the supraorbital arches, *enormous* round orbits, a *very* broad nose, and above all *massive* maxillae" (1913, 79; italics added). Notwithstanding this biased rhetoric, Boule offered the following description of the Neanderthal type. His body was short but heavily built. His head, which was enormous, had a low-vaulted skull and an animal face. From the spinal column and the bones of the limbs could be deduced a bipedal posture that was less perfect than that of modern men. The features of the braincase

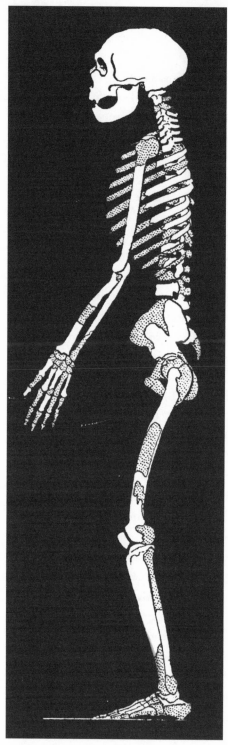

Skeleton of fossil man from La Chapelle-aux-Saints, reconstructed from side view. About one-fifteenth of natural size. (Reprinted from Marcellin Boule, Fossil Men: Elements of Human Palaeontology, 1923)

were primitive, especially in the relatively reduced size of the frontal lobes, which anthropologists since the nineteenth century had regarded as the seat of the intelligence. Boule believed that his morphological account was further substantiated by the archaeological data, since Mousterian (Middle Paleolithic) toolmaking seemed to him among the most rudimentary. Thus "the uniformity, simplicity and coarseness of his stone tools, the likely absence of any concerns of a moral or aesthetic order go well together with the brutish appearance of this powerful heavy body . . . in which simple vegetative or animal functions predominate over cerebral ones" (1921, 238).

So it was that Neanderthal man, while presenting in many respects a morphological link between humankind and the great apes, was not situated halfway between the two. His intellectual faculties placed him clearly on the side of the animals. Yet soon after this half-beast, the people of the Cro-Magnon type appeared, who seemed to be ancestors of certain modern races. In Boule's view, the only possible conclusion was that the two types coexisted, because the alternative would admit of "a change so great and so sudden as to be absurd" (1921, 243). His hypothesis seemed to be confirmed by the discovery in 1872 at Grimaldi cave in the south of France of Cro-Magnon skeletal material in Mousterian soils. Boule was therefore able to exclude Neanderthal man from humankind's lineage

and to define him instead as a side branch. Coinciding with the Mousterian culture in its last stages, Neanderthal became extinct in the Aurignacian, from which only the *Homo sapiens* branch survived, leading from
Cro-Magnon to modern man. La Chapelle-aux-Saints man marked the
first stage of a paleontological synthesis in which Boule believed deeply.
In the organization of its species or varieties, the hominid group appeared
identical to the other animal groups. All conformed to the tree model.

Naturally enough, Boule believed he could reconstruct humankind's whole biological development from his basic hypothesis that
there had existed during the Mousterian two parallel human types, one
of which had no descendants. His book *Les hommes fossiles* (1921) presented this full history, as he conceived it, which was strictly in line with
the tree model of evolution. The work opened with remarks on the fossil primates. Boule admitted that this information was necessary for a
better understanding of the morphological features of humankind's most
distant ancestors, but he deplored the paucity of these discoveries and
the fragmentary nature of the data. As a result, there was simply not
enough evidence to identify the actual shift from ape to human being. At
best, the data allowed speculation on the pithecoid branches, which were
distinct from human origins and so confirmed a treelike evolutionary
pattern. In the next chapter, the description of the famous Java Pithecanthropus followed the same preconceived logic. Boule upheld the view
put forward by Dutch paleontologist Eugene Dubois, who had discovered the remains in 1891 and who claimed that his Pithecanthropus was
the oldest fossil hominid known at that date. Boule described the excavated remains and concluded that if only the skull and the teeth were
studied, one could believe it was an apelike creature. However, the femur
suggested human characteristics, and Boule contended this discrepancy
meant that there was no direct connection between the Pithecanthropus
and humans. On the contrary, it proved the existence of a parallel branch
for the Java type. So Boule drew two genealogical trees that matched this
hypothesis. The first—the least likely in his opinion—made the
Pithecanthropus into a branch that diverged from the *Homo* group after
the latter separated from the anthropoid apes. The second, which he preferred, depicted the Pithecanthropus splitting off from the branch of anthropoid apes but not from that of humans. In the second case, the Java
femur would mark the partly converging evolution of humankind on one
side and a branch of the large anthropoid apes on the other. Afterward
the Pithecanthropus would have died out, and *Homo sapiens* "alone would
have reached the finishing post of this race for progress" (1921, 110). The
scenario here was exactly the same as the one Boule proposed in 1913 to
describe the parallel evolution of Neanderthal man and *Homo sapiens*.

Equally influenced by his theory of 1913 was his interpretation of the earliest fossil men of the Lower Paleolithic. Indeed, it was among these remains that Boule tried to find additional proof of the existence of two branches in the Mousterian. The Mauer mandible—a large, broken human jawbone with small teeth and receding chin, which was recovered in 1907 by workmen in a sandpit at Mauer in southern Germany—provided the first significant element. This Pleistocene fragment seemed to possess striking similarities with Neanderthal man. In his eagerness to convince his readers, Boule discarded his cautious precepts about the need to distinguish between resemblance and descent and declared instead that there was a "fairly close link" between *Homo heidelbergensis,* defined by the mandible, and *Homo neanderthalensis* (1921, 157). He believed he had discovered the ancestor of Neanderthal man, whose existence he had predicted in 1913 when he made La Chapelle-aux-Saints man the last of an ancient lineage. But he still had to find a likely candidate to be a progenitor of Cro-Magnon and *Homo sapiens.* The elusive fossil man was slow to reveal himself, but Boule thought he had found him in the Piltdown man, whose skeletal remains were discovered in Sussex, England, in 1912–1915. Thrilled to be able to bolster his theory, Boule once again abandoned the caution that had been his guide on other occasions. Because the Piltdown remains fitted into his system so neatly, he largely overlooked the controversy that from the outset had cast doubt on the authenticity of the bones found by Charles Dawson, Grafton Elliot Smith, and Arthur Smith Woodward.

Boule never believed that the Piltdown discovery was a hoax. The skull, although certainly contemporaneous with the Mauer mandible, seemed to him much closer to that of *Homo sapiens* than of Neanderthal man. As for the Piltdown jaw, there were significant differences with the modern human jaw as well as with the Mauer one. Yet it was very close to the jaw of a chimpanzee. Although he rejected the interpretation of Woodward and Dawson—that the two sets of fossil remains belonged to the same primitive hominid, *Homo dawsonii*—Boule nevertheless concluded that two distinct species had coexisted at Piltdown. The one, to which the skull belonged, was part of the ancestry of *Homo sapiens.* The other, represented by the jaw, constituted a group of hominids that differed both from *Homo heidelbergensis* (the ancestor of *Homo neanderthalensis*) and from the ancestor of *Homo sapiens.* Thus Boule turned the Piltdown discoveries into a keystone to support his own reconstruction of the biological history of man, by confirming that several types of hominids coexisted in the West during the Lower and Middle Paleolithic.

Having established these antecedents, Boule continued his biological history by lifting almost word for word the theory from his 1913 monograph concerning Neanderthal man and inserting it into the relevant chapter of *Les hommes fossiles*. Only in the following chapter of the work, when humankind began to move toward the Upper Paleolithic, did his account become any less complicated. In the "âge du renne" a single type survived, the last stage in the physical evolution of human beings. With the triumph of *Homo sapiens* Boule ended his work.

A reading of *Les hommes fossiles* shows clearly that Boule's paleoanthropological ideas had crystallized by 1913. His later writings had but a single aim: to make more credible a system that reconstructed human biological history on the model of a tree of evolution, stressing, in the final analysis, the unique and superior position of *Homo sapiens* as the culmination of that history. By way of conclusion, we may observe that despite his devotion to science as a secular pursuit, Boule was not able to free himself from the prevailing theological wisdom concerning humanity's superior position in creation.

References
Primary
Boule, Marcellin. 1888–1889. "Essai de paléontologie stratigraphique de l'homme." *L'anthropologie,* 3d s., 3, 4.

———. 1892. *Les oubliettes de Gargas, Matériaux pour l'histoire des temps quaternaires.* In collaboration with A. Gaudry. Paris, 4th part.

———. 1911–1913. "L'homme fossile de La Chapelle-aux-Saints." From *Annales de paléontologie* 6 (1911); 7 (1912); 8 (1913). Paris: Masson.

———. 1914. "La guerre." *L'anthropologie* 25: 575–580.

———. 1921. *Les hommes fossiles, eléments de paléontologie humaine.* Paris: Masson. 2d ed., 1923; 3d ed. H. Vallois, 1946; English translation, 1923. *Fossil Men,* Edinburgh: Oliver & Boyd.

Boule, Marcellin, and J. Piveteau. 1935. *Les fossiles, eléments de paléontologie.* Paris: Masson.

Secondary
Albarello, Bruno. 1987. *L'affaire de l'homme de la Chapelle-aux-Saints.* Les Monédières, Treignac.

Gruber, J. 1970. "Boule, Marcellin." In *Dictionary of Scientific Biography.* Ed. C.G. Gillespie. New York: Charles Scribner's Sons.

Hammond, M. 1937. "Jubilé de Marcellin Boule." *L'anthropologie* 47: 583–648.

———. 1982. "The Expulsion of the Neanderthals from Human Ancestry: Marcellin Boule and the Social Context of Scientific Research." *Social Studies of Science* 12: 256–275.

Vallois, H. 1902. *Titres et travaux scientifiques de M. Marcellin Boule.* Paris: Masson.

———. 1937. "Jubilé de M. Marcellin Boule." *L'anthropologie* 47: 635–648.

———. 1941–1946. "Marcellin Boule." *L'anthropologie* 50: 203–210.

Laurent Olivier

Joseph Déchelette   *1862–1914*

Translated from the French by Judith Braid

Self-taught scholar and ex-businessman, Joseph Déchelette was one of the first professional, full-time archaeologists in France. Despite his short archaeological career Déchelette is known as "the father of French protohistory" (the period between prehistory and classical archaeology). Déchelette was a master typologist, and he used his organizational skills and deep knowledge of the Bronze and Iron Age archaeological records to develop the basis of a new prehistory of Europe.

A Volunteer in the No Man's Land of French Archaeology

> *Ja, auch Dich haben sie schon genau so belagen so wie sie es mit uns heute immer noch tun; und Du hast ihnen alles gegeben: Deine Kraft, Deine Jugend, Dein Leben.*
>
> —*"Es ist an die Zeit," German popular song of the First World War*

It was October. The roads were waterlogged, deeply rutted by the constant traffic, trampled by thousands of panting men and beasts. Day and night they pressed on, staring at the swaying backs ahead of them, their sodden boots sliding in the skid marks of the men in front. They were marching in a great blue wave to the far horizon, lulled by the crunch of the nails on the road, the rasp of iron on stone, and the rubbing of their wet sleeves, swinging by their sides. Without a word, absorbed in their thoughts, neither happy nor sad, they pressed on.

How far away the summer was now, and how the past, the simple everyday things, seemed unreal, gone forever! You could get used to anything, even the ceaseless pounding of the artillery that lit up the night sky with an orange glare like the throbbing of an enormous blast-furnace. Strangely, it was the horses that succumbed first; they rolled their eyes in terror and keeled over into the ditches, legs in the air. Sometimes you could hear the distant musket as a horse was shot in its huge bony head and the convoy moved off. October was ushering in the winter; the men were getting used to the war.

They had not realized that they were like the horses. Like them they ate standing up, all in a line in the rain, obeyed orders uncomplainingly, and waited patiently until it was time to sleep, to arrive, to set off again.

Joseph Déchelette was 52. He had left Lyon a few days before and

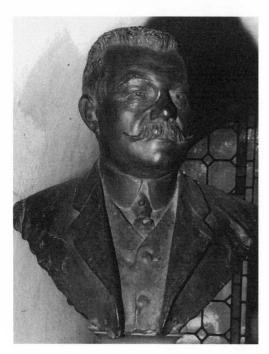

Joseph Déchelette.
(© Photo. M.A.N.
de Saint-Germain-
en-Laye, Musée des
Antiquités
Nationales)

found himself now in the uniform of a captain of reserve with the others on the Aisne front. Assigned to the 298th Infantry Regiment, he had been put in charge of a company of men, who, like him, were natives of Roanne in the Loire. "He was a boss out of uniform, so of course they had to make him a captain," they explained.

All of them treated him with deference and respect in which there was a trace of incomprehension. Although he had been under no military obligation, he had arranged to be included in active service, to oppose what he considered to be unwarranted aggression by the German Empire. Although he could have spent the rest of the war as an instructor at Fort La Motte, he too had volunteered to go to the front with his company. Nobody had bothered to ask them whether they wanted to go or not.

The last few days had transformed him, he felt a surge of youthful energy out in the field. Each new day spent here was of crucial importance for the outcome of the war and would figure in the history books. For the last fifteen years he had lived quietly in retirement, concerned only with intellectual problems, visiting all the museums in Europe, going to all the conferences, reading all the books. But now he was where the fate of the world was being decided, where history was being made, at the very heart of events. And he was surrounded by his soldiers. These humble people who would never have dared knock at his office door, let alone mount the steps to his house in Roanne, were all round him, calling him Captain, talking to him, their heads bent over their clumsy fingers as they rolled a cigarette, of the homes and the wives they missed and the children they were worried about. The same stories, or rather, as he was discovering, parts of the same history to which he also belonged. He had totally underestimated this aspect of the problem in his archaeological research. He was becoming aware of another aspect of humanity. As a researcher, he had let humanity be confined to the artificiality of inventories of pottery, ornaments, or weapons and to the aridity of descriptions of soil layers or groups of remains. Of course, these objects were the only things we had with which to interpret long-lost societies, but they came down to us incomplete, after several thousand years of transformation, products of a process outside our control. Strictly speaking, they were merely objects; the subject remained the people who had made them, used them, and discarded them. People, not events, wrote history, a history that was shaped by the place where one was born, whose meaning did not change.

The order to attack came suddenly on the Saturday morning, when the men were resting after the harsh rigors of the previous day. They set off. First there was a long concealed section through the zigzag trenches that led to the front lines. Redoubts, glacis, counterscarps, terms straight out of seventeenth-century military treatises appeared afresh in the era of electricity. They watched other men run by, flattening themselves against the earth walls or sand bags, giving them a friendly tap on their knapsack or a word of encouragement "That's it, lads!" The floor of the trench was slippery and waterlogged, but they were still protected inside French lines. At about three in the afternoon they climbed the last berm and suddenly found themselves in open ground, dizzy, in a meadow that sloped down toward the German lines. The German trenches were there, quite close, at the side, and they could see the Germans moving around inside.

"What the hell are they doing?" shrilled a voice behind him. For a moment nothing happened, then, once the first two sections had gone over, the shooting began. "They're attacking from the side!" shouted Captain Déchelette. "We must advance or they'll shoot us down like rabbits!"

They ran to a field of beetroot and dived into the broad leaves. They could hear the characteristic boom of the first shells falling round them. The ground shook beneath them, and they shut their eyes while stones and earth rained down. You just had to wait for it to pass and hope it wouldn't get you. They had been there for a quarter of an hour when Corporal Delorme heard an almost inaudible voice calling him.

"Is it you, Sir?" He crawled over to Déchelette and found him lying on his side, his knapsack upside down by his head, motionless. "I've been hit!" he said again. There was no blood, no visible wound, but Captain Déchelette had been hit full in the chest by a jagged splinter of shell.

"Don't worry, Sir, you'll be all right." said Delorme, as if to reassure himself. "These shells won't last long. Our men will send help. They've probably left already. You'll soon see, they'll take you behind the lines to a lovely white hospital full of little nurses to look after you. Don't you worry."

"Now we must pray." said Déchelette. The corporal gave him the last drops of his ration of rum and threw away the little flask, which all of them had drained before leaving. Evening was drawing on. "I'm cold," said the captain, who was shivering. Delorme covered him with his cape and sat beside him.

Déchelette had difficulty speaking. He said that he felt now that he had not much longer to live, and made Delorme promise to write to his brother Victor to tell him the news, and asked him to try not to forget him after he had gone. He talked about his wife, whom he had married late in life, when he was over forty, of her sweet nature, her intelligence, and how much he regretted the way it had all turned out.

The pounding of the artillery grew twice as fierce, like a storm. Delorme began to weep bitterly about his life, over so soon, the misery of ending up in a field of beetroot, so far from home, the wretchedness of getting killed, in the dark, by people who did not know you and who could not even see what they were shooting at, about the sheer bloody stupidity of war, which made people kill one another who had not wanted to be there in the first place. "We must lay down our lives," murmured the captain.

Déchelette was brought back that night, carried on two rifles, with Delorme limping behind. In the morning he was taken to safety behind the lines, to a nearby village in which the regiment had set up its headquarters, an anonymous village, like hundreds of others ravaged by the war, inhabited by shadows stealthily foraging in the ruins. He was laid in a burnt-out barn. He could see the sky through the charred beams and asked for a priest. The major came to see him and said with a sad smile that he could do nothing much for him, except help him bear the pain. The lieutenant-colonel paid him a visit and assured him that his sacrifice had not been in vain: they had managed to hold on to the 300 meter strip into which they had advanced. His men stood round him in silence.

He remembered the lonely Sunday afternoons at the Marist College at Saint Chamond and the massive silhouette of his father. He remembered that he had been a brilliant pupil. He remembered that he had been eight years old when the Franco-Prussian War broke out in 1870, and that he had done his military service at Saint Etienne. He remembered all the family, gathered round the table, though he himself had had no children. He remembered his wedding suit in 1905 and his gold pince-nez. He remembered his uncle Bulliot, who used to take him out digging with him to Mont Beuvray. He remembered the magic power of the Gallic town of Bibracte, buried in the forest, frozen, summer and winter, in the icy clouds of the Morvan, as if under a spell. He remembered the procession of huge gnarled trees and the rich smell of the earth full of sherds. He remembered as well the hut that he had built and the table covered with the day's finds, lit up by the sun coming in through the window. He remembered the book he had written on his five years of excavations at Mont Beuvray.

He remembered that he loved paintings. He remembered his career in industry, which had opened up for him a world of travel and unexpected contacts. He remembered too that he could speak English and German, could read Italian and Spanish, and that in recent years he had learned Czech and Portuguese. He remembered that he had been awarded the Légion d'Honneur. He remembered that he had been given an honorary doctorate by the University of Freiburg, its medieval streets paved with pebbles from the Rhine, and the delicate green of the paintings of Cranach and Holbein the Younger in the dim recesses of Notre Dame Cathedral. He remembered his friends who were still there in Germany. He remembered as well the Danube, so narrow that one could step over it, the Danube that led to the East after crossing all the empires of Europe.

He remembered holidays in Saône et Loire, when he was a schoolboy, the cool romanesque churches, and the fabulous illustrations in books by Arcisse de Caumont. He remembered one of his first articles in 1889, which was called "Le château de Montrenard et ses seigneurs," and his radical change of course around the age of thirty, after he had devoted himself for so long to medieval and Renaissance art. He remembered that he had been director of the Museum in Roanne for twenty-two years and on the board of the local branch of the Banque de France. He remembered too that he had been a correspondent of the Institut de France and the Société des Antiquaires, a member of the Comité des Travaux Historiques, a divisional inspector of the Société Française d'Archéologie, conservator of the Antiquités et Objets d'Art du Département de la Loire, member of the Commission Départementale des Monuments Historiques, entrusted by the Ministère de l'Instruction Publique et des Beaux-Arts with the cataloging of the churches in and around Roanne and the prehistoric sites in Auvergne and Burgundy, foreign member of the Academies of Madrid and Stockholm, contributing member of the Deutsches Institut and the Archaeological Societies of London, Edinburgh, Dublin, Copenhagen Brussels, Prague, and Hamburg, as well as of other things that he could not recall clearly.

He remembered the looming shape of the Coliseum in the evening light, the dark little streets by the Campo dei Fiori, a glass of wine, the Theatre of Marcellus like warm bread; he remembered the silvery Tiber lapping the antique piers of the bridge to the Isola Sacra. He remembered the towns of the north, the incredible profusion of museums, and collecting for the *Revue archéologique* all that was known about Celtic archaeology in Italy.

He remembered Madrid, the Marquis of Cerralbo, his panama hat, the amazing excavations he carried out in his Iberian cemeteries. He remembered how he had let himself be drawn into research on the

Entrance to a burial chamber discovered in 1873 in Briteiros (Iberia) measuring over 9 feet high and 9 feet wide. Through the hole at the bottom, offerings could be made to the dead. (Society of Antiquaries)

archaeology of Spain, which had proved so time-consuming, and that had helped to make sense of this mass of disparate data. He remembered Monsieur Chevarondin, who had taken him under his wing when he was still quite young and who, when he died, had left him all his books on history and archaeology. He remembered his library, at home in Roanne, where he had kept almost everything that had been published in the last twenty years, and the heady smell of the books. He remembered the sudden insight he had had on reading Dragendorff's work on Samian ware, his desire to translate it into French and his subsequent embarking on a book in which he postulated a new archaeology of Gallo-Roman pottery.

He remembered the baroque glories of Bohemia, the Charles Bridge in the snow, and the streets leading up to the castle in Prague. He remembered his friend Pic on the steps of the museum, which dominated Wenceslas Square, where the heart of the old Czech nation is buried. He remembered the excavation of the oppidum of Stradonice, and the report on it that he had translated, because it broadened people's horizons, made them abandon their parochialism, and would reveal the existence of a genuine Celtic civilization from one end of Europe to the other, and not mere waves of barbarian invasions. He remembered Picard, the publisher, in his back shop, surrounded by reams of fresh paper, and the *Manuel d'archéologie,* which was to be the first of its kind and have a unique approach from prehistory to the Gallo-Roman period. He remembered that now it would not be finished. It was a pity because all the bibliography was ready, filed on thousands of slips.

He remembered the noisy cafes, the buzz of conversations and the clatter of cups, the women's eyes shining, the spark of ideas. He remembered those who had contributed so much: OSCAR MONTELIUS, Salomon Reinach, Camille Jullian. He remembered how he had wanted to broaden people's viewpoints, which always seemed to be confined to what was narrow, local, what one could possess and so believed one understood. He remembered that he had wanted to bring a breath of fresh air to these disciplines, which, although they were just born, were already falling into divisions of castes, groups, and bureaucracies and stifling what they did not understand, what they could not control, what seemed threatening: innovation, ideas. He remembered that he had thought he could succeed by showing the prehistorians the new outlook that would come from introducing historical problems, and showing the historians what they could learn from the methodology of prehistory.

He remembered that what he hated most of all was mediocrity and cowardice. He remembered that he lived at 22 Rue de la Prefecture at Roanne in the Loire. He remembered almost everything.

Captain Déchelette died shortly before one in the afternoon of Sunday, 4 October 1914. His men made him a coffin from some planks they found in the abandoned houses nearby and buried him in an orchard, behind which there were already several officers buried. On his grave his soldiers laid flowers that they had found in neighboring gardens.

At the meeting of the Société Préhistorique de France on 22 October 1914 the president, Monsieur Taté, sent best wishes to the members of the society who were on active service and announced the death of Monsieur Joseph Déchelette, the distinguished member from Roanne, as well as that of Commander Audéoud, also killed at the front. The newspapers carried good news: "The Germans have stopped fleeing!" Maurice Barrès wrote in the *Echo de Paris,* "A mood of joy reigns in the trenches! You know it from the papers and the letters from your sons, husbands and brothers." It was certainly not the right place or time to undertake a critical study of Déchelette's work, but still one had to recognize that his scholarship, although immense, was basically classical and not strictly prehistorical, in other words based on geology and natural sciences. In fact, he had excavated surprisingly little, and what he had done was basically only around Roanne.

In any case, his famous *Manual,* although inaccurate in many details, was a very fine piece of work by this modest provincial scholar. Then they went on to condemn German barbarity for burning Rheims cathedral, razing the Museum of Archaeology, and attempting to bomb Notre Dame. It was decided unanimously to expel from the Société Préhistorique de France all the members of German or Austro-Hungarian nationality. Then Monsieur Bossavy exhibited a polished axe-head discovered in the foundations of a house at Le Pecq, a piece of grooved sandstone that had come from a newly discovered cave with rock carvings in Seine et Marne, and an experiment at photography, using reflections from a mirror with three faces, which might prove very useful for reproducing certain artifacts, particularly vases, and finally a magnificent flint blade from le Grand Pressigny, in the famous hoard at Barroux (Indre et Loire). Monsieur Hue continued the interesting paper that he had begun at the July meeting on the submerged forests of the beach at Luc-sur-Mer, and at six the meeting ended and everyone went for a drink.

On 20 November 1914 the official statistics recorded a total of 58,167 officers and men killed and wounded. Back in the villages people used a more basic way of reckoning, working out that there were already four times more dead in the first three months of fighting than there had been in the whole of the Franco-Prussian War. But they were still a long way from the 30 million victims that the 1914–1918 war would cost. Slowly the twentieth century was beginning to take shape in a gigantic mortar, in which tens of millions of hands, feet, brains, were crushed together, hundreds of tons of bones pounded with hundreds of thousands of hectoliters of blood, mixed with an unknown quantity of deadly weaponry produced by all the factories in the world working overtime. It would be a harsh century, which would owe nothing to the provincial nineteenth century. It would be the century of the triumph of the masses, the taming of men and the perversion of nature, a truly modern century.

In his huge empty house an old man, now almost blind, had started painting again. His wife Adèle was dead, his son Jean had died in hospital, and his other son Michel had been killed in the war. He had replied to his dealer, who was pestering him with questions, "All you need to know is that I am working on a vast project, which is the only way I can stop thinking about what is happening now." The canvas was enormous, endless, and on it he would concentrate everything he had learnt about life and would capture the ephemeral essence of the reflections of light on water. Hokusai had said, "By the time I was fifty, I had turned out countless drawings, but everything I produced before I was seventy was worthless. It was when I was about seventy-three that I first began to understand the true structure of Nature. When I am a hundred and ten, every detail in my work, be it a dot or a line, will be alive." An elderly neighbor, who walked with a stick, used to come and see him often and had urged him as strongly as he could to start painting again. This was Clémenceau. He knew that in this universal cataclysm, in which what was not reduced to rubble would be severed from its meaning, there was one man who had to bequeath France's heritage to future generations: something beautiful, something simple, something living. And that is why he had said, "You must paint these 'Waterlilies,' Monet."

Déchelette's death left a gap that has yet to be filled. Even so, it must be stated clearly that the First World War did not put an end to some sort of "golden age" of French archaeology, embodied in Déchelette and others. Indeed, the discipline had not yet acquired an identity, let alone reached a golden age. It was still caught between archaeology and prehistory, between the historical approach and the natural sciences. Déchelette's work is a special case, because it was isolated and doomed to extinction, like its author, having no direct issue. In many ways it illustrates the basic difficulty that French archaeological research has confronted all along in its development as an autonomous intellectual field, which has prevented it from equipping itself with the structures needed to take up its rightful place as a major contributor to the study of humankind.

Déchelette has to be considered one of the first professional archaeologists, not because he was paid by an institution to conduct his work, but because his social and financial situation allowed him to devote himself full-time to research on a European scale. His career was relatively brief (roughly fifteen years between 1899, when he retired from business, until 1914), but in the space of those few years, he managed to accumulate an extraordinary mass of data, from the prehistoric era to late Antiquity. Above all, he acquired an encyclopedic knowledge that enabled him to tackle problems from a synthetic perspective. When the publisher Picard, on the advice of the archaeologist Salomon Reinach, proposed a manual of national archaeology, Déchelette was the obvious person to do it.

His situation, however, was never an easy one. Déchelette was a self-taught scholar and never belonged to the academic elite or shared its exclusive focus on classical archaeology. It was this elite that held sway in Paris and had powerful connections in the government. On the other hand, he was, both socially and intellectually, above the level of local scholars and amateurs, who were limited to their arrondissement or even their canton. He had to forge his own way, and his success in the field of protohistoric archaeology was no accident. Déchelette was forced to advance into the no-man's-land between history and prehistory, and he discovered what innovations were possible at the frontier where different disciplines meet. This boundary, or rather this rift, ran through the whole history of French archaeology and had social, political, and ideological ramifications. On the right was a conservative middle class, which had made its money in trade and industry and now was eager for public recognition. As the academies of the ancien régime had been emptied by the revolution, these nouveaux riches citizens had filled the vacancies and tried to adopt the values and traditions of the past. Their opposite number was the unruly little group of prehistorians and anthropologists—freethinkers and supporters, like GABRIEL DE MORTILLET, of the republican and radical left. These people proclaimed the triumph of science over all other beliefs and saw themselves as the intellectual heirs of the eighteenth-century scientists and philosophers, the Encyclopédistes. The full import of Déchelette's attempt to open up the disciplines of prehistory and classical archaeology to one another must be seen in this perspective; its significance was not solely academic, for it mirrored his social movement between the provinces and the Parisian intelligentsia.

Déchelette's career coincided with a time of crucial change in French archaeology. In the last quarter of the nineteenth century, the learned societies lost their central role in French archaeology. With new discoveries and the progress of research, archaeology became a field of specialists and required a higher level of professional competence. Excavations were costly and now took weeks, if not months. Funds had to be raised, workers had to be hired, and the finds had to be published at regular intervals and made available to researchers in museums, not housed in private collections. Meanwhile, there was the growing recognition that archaeological sites were not inexhaustible, so for their own protection, their excavation had to be documented and regulated.

Only the state could assume this responsibility, which meant that archaeological remains had to be declared part of the national heritage. Sweden had already introduced a law along these lines, and the debate began in France around 1900. It was not resolved, for the archaeological community was divided. Beginning in 1876 with the Congrès International d'Anthropologie et d'Archéologie Préhistoriques, there had been great hopes for a new science of prehistory based on the combined methods and insights of geology, anthropology, and ethnology. However, no common ground could be found, so the idea faded. The academic world resisted the intrusion of archaeology as a marginal area outside its control; its humble discoveries seemed unworthy to share museum space with masterpieces. The state chose not to become involved, and the local amateurs, anxious to retain their prerogatives, declared with one voice that private property must not be touched and that restrictive legislation would simply dry up the fund of goodwill so crucial to research. At this juncture, then, French archaeology missed its opportunity to claim a legal framework that would have given it a structural basis for respectability, like a monuments protection act. The need to implement such legislation would have created administrative structures and the whole apparatus of an established discipline. (The position with regard to historical monuments was quite different: acquiescence came easily, and a law was passed in 1913.) Since archaeology as a discipline was not recognized, it could not benefit from specialist teaching in universities. In his inaugural lecture for the chair of national history and antiquity at the College de France in 1907, Camille Jullian declared that "the study of flints and bronzes predating written records also has the right to be called history." But there was little advocates could do given the total absence of political will.

Déchelette, faced with a fragmented discipline in which archaeological remains were interpreted in isolation, tried to gather together scattered records, to connect disparate data, and to define a relevant method that would work for all the periods covered by archaeology. This was the aim of the *Manuel*. Like ANDRÉ LEROI-GOURHAN fifty years after him, Déchelette recognized that archaeological remains were not just mere material evidence whose function allowed access to the past from which they sprang. Déchelette understood the complexity of artifacts whose meaning must be expressed structurally. While Leroi-Gourhan concentrated on the dynamic aspect of the problem, particularly through the study of prehistoric floors, Déchelette was one of the first to examine empirically the structural nature of archaeological matter.

Déchelette proposed using technology as the key to reading structure. For an interpretation to be accurate, it must be corroborated at the level of the material itself (or of the text, if one prefers) by a locally coherent organization (the coherence of the text), linked to a general order (the order common to all texts). Déchelette wanted to exploit the coherence of synchronicity (determined by the association of elements one with another, since they had been laid down at the same time in "closed finds" like tombs or treasures, left undisturbed), as well as the general order of time (characterized by the succession of ensembles or combinations of ensembles that had evolved one from another).

His 1904 publication *Les vases céramiques ornés de la Gaule romaine* probably gave the best account of his method. The analysis of decorative techniques coupled with the identification of categories of vases clarified the apparent chaos of the shards and indicated the existence of a series of workshops ranked in time and space. It was thus possible to discern the general development of the ceramic industry in the Gallo-Roman era, which coincided with a gradual shift in the centers of production from northern Italy to the banks of the Rhine. On a more detailed level, the study of the decorative motifs and the stamped forms allowed archaeologists to identify each workshop by the individual output of its potters. In turn, researchers could then trace how techniques and decorative themes were transmitted from workshop to workshop, or even from potter to potter. The next step could be an analysis of the changes in the iconographic repertory, thereby moving from a techno-chronological study of the archaeological materials to questions of economic history or historical anthropology.

If the approach was applied on a wider scale, scattered protohistorical archaeological remains could be ordered in a pattern of coherent evolution, the stages of which could be dated with reasonable accuracy. Here Déchelette pursued the line begun by his Swedish mentor, Oscar Montelius, whose general chronology of the Bronze Age established a subdivision into five phases according to the stylistic and morphological developments in archaeological materials. The synchronisms obtained by the discoveries at Mycenae and Troy, dated historically, enabled this series of evolutionary sequences to be anchored for the first time in an absolute chronology, instead of in a relative succession of ages or periods. Déchelette applied Montelius's framework to the French Bronze Age and in 1906 substituted a four-phase chronology for the bipartite system of Mortillet, who had merely distinguished an ancient era from a more recent one. It is interesting that both Déchelette and Mortillet turned to the eastern Mediterranean to find the chronological reference points for continental Europe, which consequently drew them into other questions—in particular, understanding Mediterranean influences on the origins of European civilizations and how ideas and concepts were exchanged in prehistoric times.

The evolution of a techno-typological method, which adapted Lamarck's transformism to the domain of archaeology, and the trend in the new research toward sociology and psychology initiated the emergence of another conception of history. History, or rather the processes of historical development as they were grasped through the medium of archaeology, could not be determined just by a series of events. Instead, history was produced by constant interaction between societies and their natural and human environment. Using this perspective, Déchelette found himself inevitably opposed to the representation of protohistory that was increasingly adopted in Germany, and he posited the idea of waves of invasions from central and eastern Europe, or the invasion of France by German tribes. Referring to the transition to the Iron Age, Déchelette wrote, "It is totally unnecessary to assume that a foreign invasion must be responsible for the appearance of the new metal in Gaul. . . . Its widespread use . . . at least in the initial stages . . . cannot be attributed to hypotheses of an ethnographical nature . . . but rather to geographical and economic considerations" (*Manuel* 2:548–549).

However, the methodological program for racial archaeology—for the affirmation of Germanic superiority—was already apparent in 1911 in GUSTAF KOSSINNA's major work on German prehistory, which he called "a science of the highest national interest." In the field of protohistory, German diffusionism (the assumption that important discoveries are made only once and then diffuse to other places by means of trade, exchange, or conquest) would dominate until the 1960s. The collapse of any viable alternative is perhaps attributable to the failure of French archaeology to reach a level of organizational maturity. By contrast, institutes proliferated in countries (like Germany) where archaeology was another weapon in the ideological arsenal of the state.

Joseph Déchelette, the father of French protohistory, was not a creative genius. Rather he was a conscientious worker, who applied himself as enthusiastically to his archaeological pursuits in his retirement as he had done to his career in manufacturing. Again, a comparison with another great French archaeologist of the twentieth century, André Leroi-Gourhan, is illustrative: they both had the same self-taught start in the subject, the same interest in connections between disciplines, but also the same isolation. Archaeology was never really important in France because it remained outside the areas debated by the intelligentsia and because, unlike sociology or economics, its voice was too weak to have a significant political impact. A history of archaeology seen from the crucial perspective of how knowledge is used in the perpetuation of social and political elites has yet to be written.

Regardless, the ideas fermenting in Déchelette's work are striking in their richness and vigor and, in some ways, prefigure the *nouvelle histoire* developed by the Annales School. They share a global perspective and a concept of total history in which subjects intersect, and both are open to the study of landscapes, economics, mentalities, and representations. In 1953, in his *Combats pour l'Histoire*, Lucien Febvre defined history as follows: "It is the scientific study of the different activities and different creations of men of long ago, captured at that date, in the context of societies which were extremely diverse and yet comparable one with another . . . activities and creations] with which they covered the surface of the earth and the succession of ages." Such a historical perspective might well have been adopted by Déchelette as his own.

References
Primary
Déchelette, Joseph. 1902. "Montefortino et Ornavesso, étude sur la civilisation des gaulois cisalpins." *Revue archéologique,* 3d s., 40, 1: 245–283.

———. 1903. "L'archéologie préhistorique et les fouilles de Carthage." *L'anthropologie* 14: 661–675.

———. 1904. *Les fouilles du Mont Beuvray de 1897 à 1901. Compte-rendu suivi de l'inventaire général des monnaies recueillies au Beuvray et au Hradischt de Stradonic, étude d'archéologie comparée, avec un plan.* Paris et Autun.

————. 1904. *Les vases céramiques ornés de la Gaule romaine* (*Narbonnaise, Aquitaine et Lyonnaise*). 2 vols. Paris.

————. 1906. "Les sépultures de l'Age du Bronze en France." *L'anthropologie* 17: 321–342.

————. 1908–1909. "Essai sur la chronologie préhistorique de la péninsule ibérique." *Revue archéologique,* 1908, 4th s., 12: 219–265, 390–405; 1909, 4th s., 13: 15–38.

————. 1908–1914. *Manuel d'archéologie préhistorique, celtique et galloromaine.* 4 vols. (*Archéologie préhistorique,* 1908; *Archéologie celtique ou protohistorique: Age du Bronze,* 1910; *Archéologie celtique ou protohistorique: Premier Age du Fer ou Epoque de Hallstatt,* 1913; *Archéologie celtique ou protohistorique: Second Age du Fer ou Epoque de la Tène,* 1914). Paris.

————. 1909. "Le culte du soleil aux temps préhistoriques." *Revue archéologique,* 4th s., 13, 1: 305–357.

Tim Murray

Howard Carter   *1874–1939*

*Beginning his career in Egypt as an illustrator and draftsman, Howard Carter
received on-site training by William Flinders Petrie and spent fifteen years
excavating before he discovered the magnificent tomb of Tutankhamun. Carter's
greatest gift to Egyptology and to posterity was not a monumental scholarly
work, but the eight years he spent organizing and supervising the work of a
large team of photographers, conservators, and illustrators who patiently cataloged and recorded the contents of the tomb of this minor pharaoh.*

Best known as the discoverer and excavator of the tomb of the Egyptian Pharaoh Tutankhamun, Howard Carter was born in Brompton
near Earl's Court, London, on 9 May 1874. He was the last of eleven
children of Samuel John Carter and Martha Joyce Sandys. His parents
were natives of Swaffam in Norfolk, and Carter was sent there as an in-
fant to be raised by his two aunts, Fanny and Kate. There is some mystery about the nature and extent of his formal schooling. Carter maintained that he had been privately educated because of his poor health. In
the most authoritative biography, T. G. H. James (1992, 7–8) concludes
that Carter most probably was educated in a dame school, with addition
of private tutoring possibly acquired in homes of the local magnates who
often employed his father to paint favorite relatives, horses, dogs, and
scenes from country life. Samuel John Carter was widely regarded as a
talented painter in this popular Victorian genre, acting as the principal
animal illustrator of the *Illustrated London News*. In later life Carter generously praised his father's artistry and drafting skills and acknowledged
that his own abilities in this area were sharpened by the on-the-job training received while doing small animal paintings for his father's clients.

The Amhersts, Newberry, and Discovering Egypt

There seems little doubt that Carter was set to follow his father's footsteps as an artist and illustrator when the opportunity arose to put his
skills to other uses. At the age of fifteen Carter began to visit Didlington
Hall, the country seat of William Amhurst Tyssen-Amherst (later first
baron Amherst of Hackney), which was about ten miles from Swaffam.
Again, details of Carter's early relationships with the Amherst family are
sketchy, but it is a fact that he was offered full-time employment at the
hall in 1891. What is significant about this association is that William

Howard Carter, 1936 (Corbis/ Hulton-Deutsch Collection)

Amherst was a noted collector of Egyptian antiquities and the Amherst collection was described as the most important private collection of its type in Great Britain during the nineteenth century. Carter later confirmed that his days spent among the relics of ancient Egypt "arroused my longing for that country—for the purity of her blue sky, her pale aërial hills, her valleys teeming with the accumulated treasures of Age" (quoted in James 1992, 10).

It is also significant that Lord Amherst was active in his support of the Egypt Exploration Fund, which had been set up in 1882 and was patronized by the popular travel writer and novelist Amelia Edwards. The primary purpose of the fund was to undertake excavation in the Nile Delta (an area usually associated with providing an archaeological illustration of places and events mentioned in the Bible). In the 1880s these excavations were carried out by Edouard Naville from Geneva and by WILLIAM FLINDERS PETRIE to much public acclaim, notwithstanding the poisonous relationship that inevitably developed between two excavators of such different interests and abilities. The fund flourished during the 1880s and accumulated sufficient surplus to allow it to tackle the pressing problem of creating an inventory of the monuments and antiquities of ancient Egypt before they were destroyed by time, vandalism, and theft. To this end in 1890 the fund established the Archaeological Survey of Egypt. Among its first recruits was Percy Newberry, a graduate of King's College, London, and a friend of the Amhersts.

Newberry had spent the first season of the survey tracing and copying the decoration of tombs at the site of Beni Hasan in Middle Egypt. Progress was slow, and when Newberry returned to Britain in early 1891, he managed to convince the supporters of the survey that an additional artist should be hired. Carter was introduced to Newberry at Didlington Hall around this time, and Lady Amherst's considerable influence with Newberry and the fund, when allied with Carter's evident skill as a draftsman and copyist, secured him employment by the survey at £50 per annum in October 1891. Before Carter could leave for fieldwork at Beni Hasan he was given the task of inking in the tracings from the first season; he also received rudimentary training in Egyptology at the British Museum from curator Alan Gardiner and the great expert in ancient Egyptian language, Frank Griffith. This accomplished, Carter set out alone for Egypt in September 1891 to join Newberry.

From Beni Hasan to Tutankhamun

In the event Newberry and his team quickly completed their work at Beni Hasan and moved about twenty miles south to record more rock-cut tombs at Deir el-Bersha. By this time Newberry, confident of Carter's artistic abilities and his commitment to detail, allowed him to introduce changes in the techniques of recording tomb decoration. Carter's naturalistic rendering of decoration in the tomb of Djehuti-hotpe set the standard for future work of this kind. Meanwhile, Flinders Petrie was beginning his first season at El-Amarna, the remains of the great city of Akhnaten, the late-eighteenth-dynasty pharaoh. At the completion of the survey's work at el-Bersha in early 1892, Carter joined Petrie at Amarna; Lord Amherst had, around the end of 1891, decided to go into partnership with Petrie, and Carter was to superintend the excavations. The Egypt Exploration Fund also supported Carter's involvement, impressed by the prospect of one of its junior workers being trained as an excavator by a man of unsurpassed field skills. Carter never forgot his debt to Petrie, and his deep respect for Petrie's expertise and learning is evident in his writing long after the first Amarna season ended in April 1892.

At that time one field season in Egypt in no way guaranteed a future in Egyptology. Carter, a man without independent means, worked at the whim of the fund, the financial state of which was determined by the unreliable interest of private benefactors. A further complication was the highly political atmosphere of Egyptology, with conflicts between French and British workers forming a prelude to later (more intense) conflicts with Egyptian interests. Despite his extraordinary first season, Carter had to wait until 1893 to return, when he joined Naville at Deir el-Bahari. During his six seasons at the site, Carter produced splendid and innovative renderings of the sculptured scenes and inscriptions in the temple of Queen Hatshepsut. These were published by the fund as *The Temple of Deir el Bahari* in six volumes between 1896–1908, and they represent what James regards as Carter's "greatest epigraphic achievement" (1992, 59).

Carter's rapidly growing proficiency as excavator and site manager, as well as illustrator and photographer, was recognized when he left the fund on 1 January 1900 to take up a new appointment as chief inspector of antiquities in Upper Egypt and Nubia, with his headquarters in Luxor. Given the fact that Carter was a practical rather than an academic Egyptologist, it seems clear enough that the director-general of the Antiquities

Service, Gaston Maspero, wanted an efficient administrator above all else. Carter's role was to safeguard the antiquities of the region and to supervise all archaeological work being undertaken south of the Valley of Qus. His range of activities was very broad and kept him busy: from installing electric light in the temple of Ramesses II at Abu Simbel, improving security of the tombs in the Valley of the Kings, to supervising excavations in Thebes and Aswan. During his time in Upper Egypt, which lasted until June 1904, Carter performed important conservation work at Kom Ombo, Edfu, Philae, and the Ramesseum, and he also put iron gates on many of the tombs in the Valley of the Kings (although these proved ineffective against determined tomb robbers).

Carter's new duties left him with little time to excavate, but what free time he had he spent in search of tombs in the Theban Hills. He methodically surveyed the main Valley of the Kings and the subsidiary side valleys, but before he could begin any serious long-term investigation, he needed funds. These were to be supplied by the American businessman Theodore Davis. Their collaboration resulted in the discovery and excavation of the tomb of Thutmosis IV in 1903. Later in the same year Carter applied his rapidly developing skills as an excavator of deep tombs to the uncovering of the tomb of Thutmosis I and Queen Hatshepsut.

Late in 1904, after five years in Upper Egypt, Carter changed places with J. E. Quibell and became the chief inspector of Lower Egypt. He held the post only briefly, and his eventual resignation was the result of a fracas at Saqqara on the night of 8 January 1905. A party of inebriated French tourists sought to enter the camp of Hilda Petrie, Flinders's wife, but meeting resistance, they retreated and continued drinking. Dissatisfied with the arrangements for their visit, they next sought entry to the monuments, and an already difficult situation rapidly deteriorated when the French tourists and the Egyptian guards (later joined by Carter) resorted to fisticuffs. There were dire consequences extending up to the highest levels of the Cairo administration. The root cause of the trouble was Carter's orders to the Egyptians to defend themselves against the French tourists, which resulted in injuries being sustained on both sides. In the Cairo of 1905, the fact that French citizens had been injured by Egyptians on the orders of an Englishman was simply unacceptable. Apologies had to be made and the matter covered up. Carter displayed extraordinary obstinacy in refusing to do so, despite the pleas of friends, supporters such as Davis, and government officials from both sides.

Carter was to suffer for his recalcitrance, and he was in effect demoted from his chief inspectorate and sent from Cairo to the town of Tanta in the delta. Maspero was tireless in his efforts to soothe the situation and to continue Carter's employment, but it was to no avail. By the end of the year Carter resigned from the service in a terse letter to Maspero:

> Sir,
> Owing to the late treatment I have received and the difficulties I now find while endeavouring to carry out my duties as Inspector in Chief in Lower Egypt in the Service des Antiquités, I beg herewith to submit my resignation (quoted in James 1992, 125).

Carter returned to painting and to Upper Egypt. Until early 1909 he supported himself as an archaeological illustrator and draftsman, executing his own watercolors, and acting as a guide for wealthy visitors to the Valley of the Kings. During this period he undertook commissions for Theodore Davis (especially the illustrations for the publication of the tomb of Yuia and Tjuiu), and the earl of Northampton. Despite this work, there can be no doubt that Carter's present situation was only marginally less uncertain than his future. But fate was to take a hand in his life in much the same way as it had during that meeting with Newberry at Didlington years before.

During several visits to Egypt, the earl of Carnarvon had developed a passion for Egyptology and decided that he would like to excavate in the Valley of the Kings. Lord Carnarvon's wish was communicated to Maspero, who fixed him up with a few rubbish mounds where he could do little damage. But soon Carnarvon tired of this, and Maspero was able to persuade him to hire Carter as his expert assistant. Carter joined Carnarvon's third season at Thebes in 1909, and one of the most productive partnerships in archaeology began.

Carter and Carnarvon

For the next five years Carter and Carnarvon worked in the Theban necropolis, which provided both of them with sustained experience and the chance to develop excavation systems that were of a high standard for the time. Carter's contribution to the publication of *Five Years Exploration at Thebes* (1912) during this period demonstrated that he had retained his undoubted skills as an illustrator while dramatically improving his abilities as an excavator. After three years of hard work, the relationship between Carter and Carnarvon had broadened and deepened into one of mutual respect. They also discovered a mutual passion for the collection of antiquities (James 1992, 152). While in the archaeological wilderness Carter had become an effective middleman in the antiquities trade, a skill (and interest) he was to develop for the rest of his life. At the conclusion of the first great Theban project, Carter sought new excavation opportunities for Carnarvon, immersing himself in the labyrinthine politics of Egyptian archaeology and once more straining his relations with Maspero.

Carter began to excavate the large delta site of Sakha/Xois in 1912, but work was abandoned after only a short period because of the infestation of the site by snakes. The party moved farther into the delta to Tell el-Balamun. That proved to be a more profitable experience, but in 1914 it too was abandoned when Carter and Carnarvon were granted the concession for the Valley of the Kings. This had been held by Theodore Davis since 1902, but after a series of great discoveries, he relinquished it, believing that the site had no more treasures to yield. Carter disagreed, and he was able to persuade Carnarvon to step in.

Carter began work clearing the tomb of the eighteenth-dynasty king Amenophis I in the spring of 1914. Although he knew that the tomb had been looted on several occasions, he was optimistic that more could be found, but there was a fairly insignificant reward for such considerable effort. In the end the excavations were overtaken by the First World War, as both Carter and Carnarvon turned their attention to other matters. In 1915 Carter joined the intelligence department of the War Office in Cairo as a civilian. Not much is known about his intelligence work during the war, but he certainly continued his other pursuits: As an archaeological illustrator, he published jointly with luminaries such as Alan Gardiner, he continued to deal in antiquities, and he maintained an active interest in the archaeology of the Valley of the Kings, which he would visit whenever the opportunity arose.

After the war, Carter continued to work Carnarvon's concession in the Valley of the Kings but without much success. During 1922 the politics of archaeology in Egypt drastically changed, partly because of the appointment of a new director of the Antiquities Service (Maspero had retired in 1913) but primarily because of the increasing political demands for Egyptian autonomy from British rule. Gone were the days of easy relationships between wealthy people who funded the excavations and government officials who helped them with the administration of antiquities laws. More and more time was spent bickering over permits and the division of excavated artifacts. This was to reach a new and more intense level when the tomb of Tutankhamun was found.

Almost mythic is the story of how Carter was determined to continue working in the valley despite disappointing results and how Carnarvon had gradually become disenchanted with the prospect of further work in the area. After the summer of 1922, it was understood that the partners would give it one last try. The workmen began to dig in front of the tomb of Ramesses VI in early November 1922. On the sixth Carnarvon received a cable from Carter:

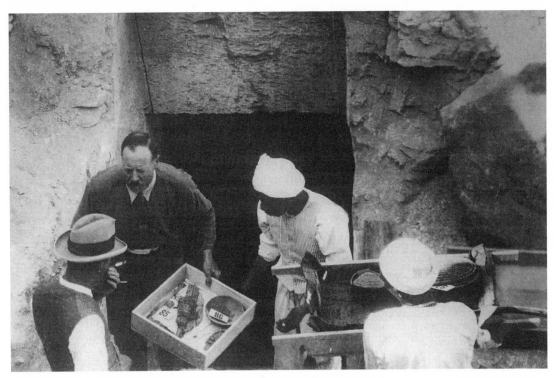

AT LAST HAVE MADE WONDERFUL DISCOVERY IN THE VALLEY. A
MAGNIFICENT TOMB WITH SEALS INTACT. RE-COVERED SAME FOR
YOUR ARRIVAL. CONGRATULATIONS. CARTER.

*Howard Carter
at the tomb of
Tutankhamun.
(Corbis / Underwood
& Underwood)*

Carter's long training in the practical business of excavating tombs,
as well as his undoubted skill in recording their contents, made him an
ideal person to undertake the task of clearing and documenting the newly
discovered tomb of Tutankhamun. But his lack of formal education, his un-
easiness about his social position, and his obstinacy and lack of diplomacy
(best exemplified in the business at Saqqara) were a powerful counterbal-
ance to his technical expertise. The revelation of Tutankhamun's tomb
completely transformed his life, from being an unknown journeyman excavator to a great archaeological discoverer. The experience of clearing the
tomb and cataloging the finds changed archaeology in Egypt forever, with
the decades-long strife between Carter and the Antiquities Service being
matched only by the tenacity of both sides (and the Egyptian nationalists)
in maintaining their interest in this most famous of archaeological sites.

Much has been written in recent years about the circumstances of
the discovery, which has served to debunk the famous story of the "curse
of the mummy," as well as raise very serious questions about the probity
of Carter, Carnarvon, and the Metropolitan Museum of New York City.
The gradual disclosure that the public story of discovery and clearance
of the tomb hid some significant activity on the part of Carter and
Carnarvon has only added to its fascination while detracting from the

reputations of two remarkable, though clearly flawed, men. However important that discussion may be, there are other equally important stories to tell about the excavation of the tomb and its contents.

Foremost among these is the great patience and skill displayed by Carter and his ability to attract others more skilled than he to work on the long project. The cataloging of the tomb and its contents is an extraordinary example of interinstitutional cooperation as photographers, drafting staff, illustrators, conservators, and others worked together for years at the tomb. Through the eyes of Carter's associates, a much clearer picture emerges of the impact the discovery made on the people who were engaged on site. Within a very short space Luxor teemed with people wanting to see the site and meet the discoverers, making actual work on the material next to impossible. Tensions existed between the excavators and the press, doubtless stemming from Carnarvon's decision to give the *Times* of London exclusive rights, to the chagrin of other newspapers, but there were also conflicts between the Carnarvons and staff members (including Mace) and between Carter and Carnarvon himself. Both characters and setting held the attention of the international media, and this interest only intensified when Lord Carnarvon fell ill and died from blood poisoning and pneumonia on 5 April 1923.

Carter became a very public person, entertained by royalty and much in demand on the public lecture circuit. Indeed he was so popular in the United States that he was able to purchase an annuity of £1,000 on the proceeds on his tour, thereby ensuring a comfortable retirement when the time came. But disagreements about the contents of and access to the tomb became particularly unpleasant on Carter's return to Egypt late in 1923. James (1992, 275–306) recounts his troubles at length; some were self-induced by his stubbornness and sensitivity to criticism, others were caused by petty jealousies and inevitable clashes of will in a fight for control over the future of the tomb and its treasures. After much behind-the-scenes activity between Carter's supporters and the director of the Antiquities Service, a compromise was reached and a new season of work on the tomb began. A letter to Carter from his associate Winlock provides a glimpse into the poor state of relations that existed between the protagonists:

> There is no use mincing words or trying to fool ourselves. In Cairo you have the reputation of being difficult. Some of this goes back to the old days and a long series of incidents in which you have not been sparing of the knocks . . .
>
> In short I believe that you stand about as follows:
> 1 They want you and your collaborators back.

2 They will give you a concession that is after all workable.

3 You must get the Carnarvon's renunciation.

4 You must convince them that they are totally wrong in their childish idea that you like to quarrel for the fun of insulting the Egyptian nation (quoted in James 1992, 319).

Although things never completely calmed down, from 1925 until February 1932 Carter was able to pursue the monumental task of clearing, cataloging, and conserving the tomb's artifacts. He also continued to work on his multivolumed popular account of the famous site, jointly authored with A. C. Mace. As it turned out, *The Tomb of Tut-ankh-Amen* was his only large-scale testimony to the excavation, a fact that is all the more regrettable when we consider the extensive notes, drawings, and discussions he left behind, which would have been an important resource for more detailed scholarly publication of the tomb.

After Tutankhamun

Carter's biographers are all agreed that he was not a great scholar and that in the absence of a collaborator such as Mace or Gardiner, the prospect of a major reference work on the tomb was indeed remote. On this basis it might be said that Carter's greatest gift to Egyptology (and posterity) was the discovery and patient cataloging of the contents of the tomb rather than any great and new insights into the nature of ancient Egyptian life. Certainly Carter's was all "on-the-job" training, admittedly under the guidance of archaeological and Egyptological giants such as Petrie and Griffith. After February 1932, when excavation on Tutankhamun's tomb was finally completed, Carter presumably had to come to terms with his own limitations. He spent much of his time in Luxor dreaming of discovering the tomb of Alexander the Great in the delta, and in London going about his business in the antiquities trade. He also experienced long periods of ill health and depression, probably an indication of the difficulty of his transformation from excavator and illustrator to the complete Egyptologist.

This inactivity might also explain why Carter acquired so few academic and public honors, certainly far fewer than the scale of his public fame should have almost guaranteed. Yale gave him a Doctor of Science degree and he was awarded Spanish and Belgian honors, but unlike such contemporaries as Sir Leonard Woolley, the discoverer of Ur in Mesopotamia, or Sir ARTHUR EVANS, he was overlooked by the British government and by British universities. The snub may have been related to Carter's educational deficiencies or to his social rank, but it may also have been a consequence of his persistent strife with bureaucracies, both Egyptian and British.

Howard Carter and a worker examine a coffin in the tomb of Tutankhamun in 1923. (Archive Photos)

Regardless, Carter's health critically failed, and he died in Kensington, London, of Hodgkin's disease on 2 March 1939. He was buried at Putney Vale Cemetery on 6 March in the presence of a small number of friends, associates, and family members. At his death he was comfortably well-off, surrounded by beautiful objects that clearly displayed his excellent taste, particularly in painting, antiquities, and rugs. Unfortunately his passing did not bring to an end his tumultuous relationship with the Antiquities Service, because among his effects were artifacts that could only have been illegally exported by Carter (or Carnarvon) from the tomb of Tutankhamun. Viewed in the best possible light, Carter may have taken them as compensation for all his troubles with the Egyptian authorities or may have been holding them for Carnarvon—but their existence nevertheless posed severe problems for the beneficiary and executors of his will. After delicate negotiations, the objects, which were in the possession of the king of Egypt after 1946, were finally returned to the Cairo Museum, finally bringing the shameful business to an end.

The greater part of Carter's professional records were presented to the Griffith Institute in Oxford, where they have been used by other scholars to bring the tomb of Tutankhamun to publication. Despite

Carter's limitations as a scholar (or indeed his shortcomings as a human being), no one should ever doubt his prodigious talent as an archaeological illustrator or as a patient, careful, and above all thorough excavator. Petrie was right in his assertion that Tutankhamun was indeed fortunate to have been found by Carter, but perhaps Carter was not so fortunate to have been made famous by Tutankhamun.

References
Primary
The principal Carter Archive is housed at the Griffith Institute, Ashmolean Museum, Oxford, UK.

Secondary
James, T. G. H. 1992. *Howard Carter. The Path to Tutankhamun.* London: Kegan Paul.

Newberry, Percy. 1939. Obituary. *Journal of Egyptian Archaeology* 25: 67–69.

———. 1949. *Dictionary of National Biography 1931–1940,* pp. 151–152. Oxford: Oxford University Press.

Reeves, Nicholas, and John H. Taylor. 1992. *Howard Carter before Tutankhamun.* London: British Museum Press.

Times (London). 3 March 1939 (obituary).

Winstone, H. V. F. 1991. *Howard Carter and the Discovery of the Tomb of Tutankhamun.* London: Constable.

Claudine Cohen

Abbé Henri Breuil   *1877–1961*

Translated from the French by Cynthia Hood

The French prehistorian Henri Breuil was a central figure in the field of world prehistory during the first half of the twentieth century. His main emphases were doubly oriented toward the chronology of prehistoric industries on the one hand and the study of Paleolithic art on the other. His work is contemporaneous in France with a period rich in debate and in discovery. During the pioneering years from 1859 to 1880, prehistory had emerged as a discipline; its subsequent institutionalization was also a key aspect of Breuil's career.

B orn in 1877 in Mortain, in the department of la Manche, Breuil entered into the great seminary of Saint-Sulpice in 1895. Abbé Guibert, his professor of natural science, introduced him to prehistory and the theory of evolution. Breuil's first scientific works were directed toward botany, but under Guibert's guidance, he became fascinated early on—his first works date from 1898—by archaeology: he initially took to describing and studying objects from the Bronze Age in museums or in private collections.

Beginning in 1896, he participated, in collaboration with Louis Capitan, in the excavation of the Neolithic site of Campigny. But it was the decisive encounter with French prehistorian Edouard Piette during a trip to Dordogne that turned his interest toward the "Reindeer Age" and prehistoric art. Breuil often acknowledged Piette as his true master and paid tribute to him as one "who applied a rigorous method and perseverance to the exploration of Pyrenean caves." Regardless, even if Breuil's work, in its practical and theoretical aspect, adopted certain ideas and observations from Piette, it also surpassed them in many ways. Piette's stratigraphy dealt with a limited territory in the southwest of France; Breuil extended it to multiple sites and regions. Piette's approach to art gave rise to complex nomenclature and a rather confusing chronology; in Breuil's hands, the method helped to found a chronology of Paleolithic art that used the periodization of prehistoric cultures as well as key concepts of style and cycle and ethnological comparison.

Breuil's work, both practical and theoretical, constituted an immense body of knowledge and marked a new stage after the first rudiments of the science were set forth in the last decades of the nineteenth

Abbé Henri Breuil.
(Copyright Museum
of Natural History)

century. However, it remains essentially a work of description and of classification. Abbé Breuil was more of a technician than a thinker. If he can be credited with having attempted the first synthesis on prehistoric cultures of Europe in terms of art and industries, his work does not display any true anthropological reflection. At the same time that the anthropologist Marcel Mauss was theorizing on the total human phenomenon, Breuil was content to describe and classify objects from the past. He never pursued a global conception of human beings, from either a philosophical or a metaphysical vantage point.

His status of priest (he was ordained in 1900) did not keep him from active research into prehistory, in the field or in theoretical reflection. Abbé Breuil belonged to a generation from the turn of the century that, after the massive rejection of "fossil man" by the Catholic Church in the name of revealed dogma, came to prehistory hoping to reconcile research on the evolution of man with religious beliefs. This was the movement to which Breuil's contemporary Pierre Teilhard de Chardin (1881–1955) also belonged. Teilhard, a Jesuit priest, directed important paleontological research in France and in China and tried to reunite evolutionary theory with theology by conceiving of the evolution of living beings as metaphysically oriented toward the appearance of humans, in whom the reunion of spirit and matter was realized. Breuil collaborated with Teilhard (a volume dedicated to the Paleolithic Age of China bears the signatures of Fathers Teilhard and Licent, Abbé Breuil, and the great anthropologist MARCELLIN BOULE). He was also associated for a long time in his anthropological research with fellow priests and archaeological scholars Abbé Kielmeyer, Abbé Bouyssonnie, and with Abbé Glory. Thus the milieu in France during the first third of the twentieth century was characterized by the coming together of priests with prehistoric scientists. The engagement of the ecclesiastical world in prehistoric archaeology is partly explained by the field's intellectual and spiritual challenge, but another reason is the financial freedom of the researchers, who were able to rummage, travel, and write at a time when institutional and university jobs in the discipline were still rare. However, Breuil's observations, descriptions, and archaeological speculations rarely betrayed his ecclesiastic grounding, except in his approach to Paleolithic art, where the influence of his religious convictions was most discernible.

The notoriety acquired by his first works earned Breuil the distinction, after graduation, of being named a professor at the University of Freiburg in 1905. In 1910, he became a professor in Paris at the Institute of Human Paleontology, created that very year thanks to the patronage of Prince Albert of Monaco. The first chair of prehistory of the Collège de France was established for him in 1929, and he became a member of the Académie des Inscriptions et Belles Lettres in 1938. Until 1961, the year of his death, Breuil was closely involved in all domains of human prehistory. His practical activities covered searches, summaries, and descriptions while his theoretical pursuits included the study of art and reflection on and interpretation of the archaeological and anthropological discoveries of his time. More than 800 publications resulted from this research.

Breuil and Paleolithic Classifications

During the second half of the nineteenth century, prehistorians focused on establishing a chronology of prehistoric time, to determine the stages of human evolution with regard to physical form, intelligence, and culture. Edouard Lartet (1801–1871) was the first to propose a periodization of the Paleolithic Age founded on successive modifications of fauna: the Mammoth Age followed that of the Great Bear, the Reindeer, and finally, in historic periods, the Aurochs.

Other schemes of periodization were produced during the course of the last decades of the century by Piette and GABRIEL DE MORTILLET. In the work of Mortillet especially, the evolution of cultures was envisioned according to a linear model similar to contemporary representations of biological evolution. It was with the critique and revision of this chronology that Breuil associated himself.

> Between the Mousterian industry, worked without bones and with lithic tools formed exclusively of short fragments, more or less ovoid or triangular, in various ways retouched, and the Azilian industry, which prolonged, on the threshold of the Neolithic period, the recent, expiring Paleolithic period, lies a particularly captivating period of human prehistory: the Age of the Reindeer, or, as Mortillet called it, the Solutreo-Magdalenian era. The innumerable variety of industrial forms, the lightness and finesse of the siliceous tool that diverts, almost whole, thin and stretched out strips judiciously adapted by skillful retouching to a thousand different uses, contrasts strangely with the range, so quickly run, of Mousterian points and scrapers. Bones, hardly used in earlier times, ivory, reindeer wood were extracted, from most of the deposits, tools, arms, ornamental objects which make us admire the

ingenuity of their inventors, and, often, defy our interpretations (Breuil 1907a, 1).

What were the characteristics, origins, and stages of evolution of these industries? These were exactly the questions that Breuil addressed during the early part of his career.

The Controversy of the Aurignacian Period

The initial research of the "young abbot" concentrated on the period that Lartet had defined as the Reindeer Age. One of the great intellectual battles that he led and that made him famous was his identification of an intermediate cultural stage between the Mousterian period and the Magdalenian period. The result was a revision in Mortillet's chronology, which had the Solutrean and the Magdalenian periods follow the Age of the Reindeer. According to Mortillet, "the Solutrean period would have first perfected stone work, then the Magdalenian period substituted for that largely bone work, and invented Fine Arts." Between these two periods, however, an industrial assemblage persisted, which was recognized and described by Mortillet but "whose mention was little by little erased." These were the Aurignacian industries.

In 1905, Breuil presented a paper titled "Essay on the Stratigraphy of Deposits in the Age of the Reindeer" before the first Prehistoric Congress of France, gathered in Périgueux. He first reminded his audience that Lartet had, from the earliest days of prehistoric archaeology, distinguished three successive stages of the Upper Paleolithic period: the "aurignac facies," which he considered as older; the stage "of the Laugerie-Haute type"; and the stage of the Madeleine. Breuil criticized Mortillet for having "inserted the first of these facies between the two others on theoretical grounds which were foreign to stratigraphy" (1905, 1). Instead, Breuil proposed to define, before the Solutrean stage, a "Presolutrean" period and a "specifically Aurignacian" level, characterized by a tool made of bone: "tips in ovoid or diamond-shaped contours, sometimes cracked at the bottom, sometimes . . . without this crack, many pointy bones, diverse smoothing instruments, sometimes flasks made of reindeer cannonbone, crude pins, ivory pearls, sticks and ribs decorated in hunting motifs, or in diverse elementary traits." Other features were produced by a tool made of flint:

> The Mousterian forms are not exceptional, as in Spy, Chatelperron, Isturitz, at the base of Bouitou. Burins are rare at the base and in several cases are badly characterised; toward the top of this layer . . . they take the shape of a well-defined type, a hooked end with, on one side, a sole rectilinear plane, and on the other a

series of parallel and very arched raised areas, often limited in their propagation by a little notch. . . . There are many special scrapers (the donkey back scraper of Reverdy), very thick, short, more or less planed to be streamlined; this type is . . . one of the best fossils of the Presolutrean era and is hardly found in the mid or superior strata from the Reindeer Age. The blades are very retouched; it's the retouching of beautiful Mousterian pieces, applied to make scrapers on the end of simple or double blades, pointed blades, etc. . . . But the retouching almost always involves the lateral edges of the instruments of this phase. Often, this retouching determines large notches on the edge (one or both), which are placed one opposite the other, in such a way as to produce "strangled" blades (1905).

It was Breuil who rigorously characterized this type of industry and who situated it in the sequence of industries of the Upper Paleolithic period: "The Aurignacian level, strictly speaking, is represented, with very light variations in detail, especially in the deposits of Spy (Belgium), Chatelperron (Allier), les Cottés (Vienne), les Roches (Indre), La Chaise (Charente), Gorges d'Enfer, Cro-Magnon, La Ferrassie (Dordogne), le Bouitou (Corrèze), Brassempouy (Landes), Tarté, Mérignac (Haute-Garonne) etc."

The text, published in 1907 in the *Revue Préhistorique* and titled "The Aurignacian Question: Critical Study of Compared Stratigraphy" definitively challenged Mortillet's schema by substituting new models. "If the clarity of a simplistic system has didactic advantages," Breuil wrote at the conclusion of his study, "it is incapable of distinguishing, among the diversity of facts, those which will give rise to more objective and more adequate views of what's real." Breuil added that one must not invoke in these models either the hypothesis "of a perfectly uniform and continuous development" or "the easy explanation of successive migrations." Rather, his alternative theory made room for the complexity of facts. Thus, the definition of an Aurignacian period was not merely an opportunity to add a new stage to the recognized and established sequence. It suggested a revision to the way one looked at the very evolution of Upper Paleolithic cultures: an evolution that must no longer be envisioned as a linear progressive succession, but as the development of parallel and branched lines. From this perspective, not only the indigenous progress of techniques intervened in evolution but also population inflows, bringing with them their cultural expressions.

The analysis that Abbé Breuil presented in 1907 threw down the gauntlet: "The stratigraphic situation of the Aurignacian period between the Mousterian period and the Solutrean period is one of the most certain facts of the Upper Paleolithic era" (1907b). At the same time that it challenged the continuity of evolution, the definition of the Aurignacian period inferred a methodological reflection that reinstated at the highest level of research the question of stratigraphy.

The Aurignacian controversy had resulted in a reassessment of the methods of prehistoric archaeology. The approach had been dominated by the morphological study of tools, practiced by archaeologists since the latter part of the preceding century. In stark contrast was Breuil's method, which followed the lines advocated by Lartet and Piette but was even more tied to geological stratigraphy and the identification of "marker fossils." "More than any other science," wrote Breuil in 1929, "stratigraphic geology is the basis for prehistoric studies, for it alone permits us, through the studies of soils which contain them, to distribute bones, the manufactured products that one finds there, in a successive order" (1929). This renewal of stratigraphy and the definition of "marker fossils" led to a fresh perspective on taxonomic categories of the Paleolithic period.

During the 1930s Breuil drew general conclusions from the reevaluation of Lower and Middle Paleolithic industries. On the one hand, he clarified the chronology, adding several new Paleolithic stages: the Clactonian (from the area Clacton-on-Sea), the Levallosian (from Levallois [Seine]), and the Tayacian (from Tayac [Dordogne]). On the other hand, he replaced the conception of a simple linear relationship. As the Chellean period was refined, it became the Acheulean period, which then progressed and was transformed into the Mousterian. During the 1930s Breuil proposed a new schema that, in his view, conformed more accurately with the evidence. For Breuil, two human groups had existed from earliest times. One made and used tools with two sides, the other relied on a fragmented tool. Consequently, Breuil deciphered the development of human industries according to two evolutionary, parallel traces: one was able to furnish the Abbevillian, Acheulean, and the Micoquian periods, the other the Clactonian, Languedocian, Levalloisian, Tayacian, and the Mousterian eras.

Breuil also revised the chronology of the Upper Paleolithic period (1937b). Assimilating contemporary anthropological themes to his reflection on prehistoric cultures, Breuil considered the populating of occidental Europe during the course of prehistory to be the result of invasions or migrations of successive waves of populations coming from the east and the south of the continent. Thus, the first cultures (Aurignacian) of the Upper Paleolithic era were not the result of an endogenous evolution of Mousterian cultures but instead marked a "social and industrial" change born of the importation of new traditions by *Homo sapiens* arriving from the east, who brutally replaced more primitive Neanderthal populations. If in the Upper Paleolithic era there were typological traits characteristic of the Mousterian—strip cutting, scrapers, and chisels, for example—they were, in Breuil's eyes, "degenerated Mousterian tools influenced by contact with tribes more frankly characterised as Aurignacian" (1912). These traits proved, not a gradual progression, but the significant impact of Aurignacian cultures on Mousterian traditions.

Similarly, the onset of the Solutrean period must be attributed, not to a local development, but to east European roots, as discerned in certain central European sites. Moreover, even if the Solutrean period was characterized by a high skill level in flint working, it included only a few bone industries, and thus it could not have evolved into the Magdalenian period, in which there was a mediocre working of flint but a bone industry of great quantity. The origin of the Magdalenians of western Europe must be found, not in localities of the Mediterranean basin, but in invasions from the northeast of Europe. Those cultures presented analogies to the industries of the northern plains, such as the Maszycka in Poland. Inspired by the anthropological hypotheses put forth by Testut (1889), in which the Chancelade man possessed characteristics similar to those of modern Eskimos, Breuil postulated that the Magdalenian populations could have originated northeast of Europe.

By 1930 these hypotheses together created an outline for the development of Paleolithic industries. It remained largely inspired on the one hand by anthropological theories on racial memberships and migrations and on the other by models of the linear evolution of industrial Paleolithic forms. Although the works of Denis Peyrony on the Perigordian era, of FRANÇOIS BORDES on Mousterian industries, and of ANDRÉ LEROI-GOURHAN on the Chattelperronnian period made important revisions to the classifications and filiations proposed by Breuil, the periodization of Paleolithic industries provided a framework for the study of prehistoric art.

Breuil and the Study of Paleolithic Art

In the 1860s, the idea took hold of an art created by humans who were contemporaneous with mammoths and the age of worked stone. One of the most brilliant proofs had been the discovery by Edouard Lartet, at the Madeleine in 1864, of an ivory mammoth plaque engraved with the figure of a mammoth. Between 1860 and 1870, a great quantity of movable Paleolithic pieces of art, engravings, and sculptures on bone, ivory, and antler wood had been exhumed at Massat (Ariège), at Bruniquel (Tarn and Garonne), in the region of Eyzies (Dordogne), at Laugerie-Basse, and

Breuil examines a rhinoceros frieze discovered with other paintings in 1956 in the Rouffinac caves. Controversy still rages as to whether these paintings are real or fakes. (AGIP)

at Lourdes (Basses-Pyrénées), and several years later at Brassempouy (Landes) and at Mas-d'Azil (Ariège). However, the authenticity of rupestrian (cave) painting remained to be confirmed.

At the turn of the century, the pace of discoveries quickened. Cave art at La Mouthe (Dordogne) was made public in 1895 and at Pair-non-Pair (Gironde) in 1896. In 1901, Abbé Breuil, Louis Capitan, and Denis Peyrony discovered in the valley of la Vézère, near les Eyzies, decorated caves of les Combarelles and of Font-de-Gaume; there, millennial concretions covered the engravings, proving their antiquity. The following year, Breuil, in the company of geologist Emile Cartailhac, rediscovered the decorated cave of Altamira (Spain) that, when first found in 1879, had been considered a trick and rejected as an authentic work of prehistoric art. The "Mea Culpa of a Skeptic," published by Cartailhac in 1902, signaled the recognition of Paleolithic cave art. It was also with Cartailhac that Breuil explored the cave of Niaux in the Ariège in 1906. He would also be one of the first to enter the cave of Lascaux after its discovery by four schoolboys in September 1940.

From 1902 Breuil was recognized as an international expert; as each new discovery came to light, he became the arbiter of authenticity, and it was he who carried out the plotting and examination of decorated caves. Breuil studied not only the rupestrian art of western Europe but also the decorated caves—Paleolithic and more recent—of southern Africa, the Sahara, Abyssinia, Asia Minor, and China. He published their descriptions in numerous monographs and in a synthesis, *Four Hundred Centuries of Wall Art,* which displayed only a portion of his collected materials. He was especially involved in reproducing, with remarkable precision and rigor, figures of almost all of the decorated caves, including the famous bison of Altamira, the frieze of the bison of Font-de-Gaume, and the closely interlaced figures from the cave of Trois-Frères. Throughout this copying process, which was executed either in pencil or watercolor, Breuil abandoned himself to the extraordinary task of decipherment. For decades, these reproductions, despite their occasional approximation or the inevitable bias in the interpretation that animated them, would be the only window to the pictorial works of the Paleolithic; after 1950, photographic processes permitted systematic reproductions, notably at Lascaux. Breuil's artistry remains today a delicious rendering of these art works by prehistoric human beings.

Paleolithic art was almost invariably about animals, and these representations—bison, horses, cows, bulls, reindeer, mammoths, woolly rhinoceroses, lions, bears, fish, birds—were often associated with geometric signs. Sometimes there were also images of human beings. Breuil tried to establish a chronology of rupestrian Paleolithic art by merging two essential notions: that of style and that of cycle.

The dating of the figures could be based on the study of the superimposition of the figures, similar to a palimpsest. Another basis was the study of styles, or the techniques of Paleolithic painting, engraving, and sculpting. This art appeared at the same time as modern humans (about 30,000 years ago) in a geographical area essentially limited to the southwest of France (Dordogne and the Pyrenean region) and in Spain to the Cantabrian region, with some extensions into the Parisian basin and the Rhône Valley. Breuil proposed a periodization in two successive cycles. The oldest, "Aurignaco-perigordian," began with shapeless lines and very crude animal representations and culminated around 15,000 years ago in the gigantic united red figures of Lascaux, with their black or sepia heads in "twisted perspectives"—that is, the body of the animal drawn in profile while the horns or antlers were represented facing front. Breuil speculated that there was an interruption during the Solutrean period, after which a second pictorial cycle, "Solutreo-magdalenian" began, typified by very simple black linear designs (at Altamira, les Trois Frères, le Portel, Niaux, les Combarelles). Its apogee occurred around 11,000 years ago with the polychrome figures, circled in black, of Altamira.

During the last decades of the nineteenth century, the first interpreters of movable prehistoric art—Emile Cartailhac, Gabriel de Mortillet, and Edouard Piette—had denied, in the name of a rationalist rejection of religion, that "primitive man" had the ability to use and recognize symbols, which they associated with religion. At the beginning of the twentieth century, several developments, including the expansion of ethnology, the clerical interest in prehistory, and the discovery of wall art, converged to give rise to the idea of a symbolic meaning behind Paleolithic art. The painted frescos and the rupestrian engravings seemed to hide secrets that demanded interpretation. Located in the depth of caves, they were difficult to access, and in some cases, there were few traces that anyone had been there. The theory emerged that they could have been sacred places, or "sanctuaries." Abbé Breuil saw in this art not only the fruit of artistic spontaneity but also a communal religious and magical expression, testifying to collective interests linked to the way of life of the great hunters of prehistory.

Using the method of ethnological comparison, Breuil took as his point of departure the African fertility rites and the customs of the Eskimos and Aboriginal Australians. The prehistoric animal drawings (the bison of Dordogne with exaggerated humps, males closely following females, sometimes gravid) seemed to be linked to rites of fecundity and to a "magic of game animal reproduction." Pictures of arrows piercing the sides of big animals (at les Combarelles or Montespan, or the bison of Niaux and of Bedeilhac), of bears vomiting blood, and of bison losing their intestines would be images of devotion: the "magic of destruction" or the "magic of hunting." The "tectifome" designs, whether or not they were superimposed on animal figures, would be symbolic drawings of traps or even of little huts, "residences of the spirits of ancestors in a narrow nook, apart from the rest of the cave." Finally, the human representations in the caves of Cougnac, Pech Merle, les Trois Frères, and even the well scene of Lascaux were interpreted as "witch" figures, heroes or gods presiding over the destiny of animals.

In particular, the representation of women in rupestrian and movable art seemed to point to the idea of fecundity, given their exaggerated sexual characteristics and the many signs of what Breuil interpreted as stylized sexual organs, such as vulvas. Breuil's analysis combined human representations and animal pictures. Thus the image of woman would necessarily be linked to the notion of desire and fecundity as well as to the rites of hunting, that is, to the preoccupation with immediate survival. As for masculine representations, the use of animal face masks would recall the ceremonies of the shamans and the celebration of mysteries and rituals modeled on contemporary peoples. "These are," according to Breuil, "the reflections of religious organisation, of complicated ideas that comparative ethnology alone can revive." Besides this religious aspect, Paleolithic art also revealed, in his view, the social structures of prehistoric humans. More recent art, such as that of the painted rocks of oriental Spain, "[permit] one to follow the natives of the time hunting, sometimes going to war, gathering honey, dancing, and even in their family life. We find there precious information on the cut of women's dresses, feather headdresses, men's elbow and leg ornaments, the form of bows and arrows, indeed quivers and baskets"(1937a, 17). Breuil was committed to tracing the relationships of Paleolithic art to its most recent manifestation in rupestrian Spanish and African art.

Conclusion

Breuil's work constituted in many ways an essential episode in the development of French prehistory. It was contemporaneous with a period extraordinarily rich in discoveries, notably of movable or rupestrian art. Consider, for example, Altamira, les Trois Frères, or Lascaux, which Breuil was the first prehistorian to explore and decipher. It was also a vital period with regard to the creation of interpretive frameworks and the diffusion of information to the general public. By Breuil's death in 1961, the scope of knowledge on prehistoric cultures, concerning Paleolithic industries as well as art, was immense. However, many concepts elaborated by Breuil had, even during his lifetime, given way to important revisions.

Breuil was engaged in significant debates over the periodizations and the evolution of Paleolithic industries: with Denis Peyrony in 1935 for the definition of Perigordian industries, a stage that he reluctantly accepted; and with Bordes on the question of the "bushing of [Mousterian] industries," during which he underscored his evidence with the introduction of new quantitative methods.

Concerning Paleolithic art, if Breuil had set out the chronological and methodological bases of his study, the deeper meaning of this art would be in conflict with Breuil's interpretations. Beginning in the

1960s, the works of André Leroi-Gourhan changed the chronology of Paleolithic art, leading especially to the rejection of the notion of cycle and the conception of the history of this art form as a linear development. Furthermore, in *The Religions of Prehistory*, published four years after Breuil's death, Leroi-Gourhan implicitly questioned the attribution of religious practices and beliefs to Paleolithic man and revised the ethnographic framework that Breuil had imposed for half a century. Regardless, Leroi-Gourhan had himself inherited, probably much more than he preferred to admit, a huge amount of descriptive material from Abbé Breuil. While Breuil criticized Leroi-Gourhan's "sexomaniac obsession," it was indeed Breuil who first stressed that representations of "vulvas" abounded in wall art and Breuil who had tried to understand, in more human terms than the researchers of the previous century, the life and mind of Paleolithic humans. In the field as in its self-reflection, Breuil's work opened the door to a better comprehension of prehistoric times.

References
Primary
Breuil, Henri. 1905. "Essai de stratigraphie des dépots de l'Age du Renne." *Premier Congrès Préhistorique de France*. Session de Périgueux.

———. 1907a. "La question aurignacienne, étude critique de stratigraphie comparée." *Revue préhistorique* 2, 6–7.

———. 1907b. *La question aurignacienne, etude de stratigraphie comparée.*

———. 1929. *La préhistoire, leçon inaugurale au Collège de France.* Paris.

———. 1937a. *La préhistoire, Leçon d'ouverture de la chaire de préhistoire au Collège de France, Revue des cours et conférences.* 30 December 1929 (2d ed. 1937).

———. 1937b. "Les subdivisions du Paléolithique Supérieur et leur signification." *Congrès International d'Anthropologie et d'Archéologie Préhistoriques.* Compte rendu de la XIVème session, 2d ed. Geneva.

Secondary
Testut, L. 1889. "Recherches anthropologiques sur le squelette quaternaire de chancelade, Dordogne." *Bulletin Anthropologique Lyon* 8: 131–246.

Douglas R. Givens

Sylvanus Griswold Morley

1883–1948

Frederic Ward Putnam's protégé and Alfred Tozzer's pupil, Morley spent many years surveying the archaeological sites of Central America. He became one of the most important Mayanists of all time through his discoveries and interpretations of Mayan glyphs and by bringing the Maya and their substantial achievements to the attention of the American public.

Sylvanus Morley was born on 7 June 1883. He was the eldest of six children, and with siblings Constance, Henry, Alice, Elinor, and Elizabeth, he enjoyed a happy and cohesive family life. His father, Benjamin, was an engineer and graduate of the Pennsylvania Military Academy at Chester, Pennsylvania, where he also taught chemistry and mathematics and served as the institution's vice-president. Morley's mother was the daughter of a Belgian language teacher and was also teacher of languages at the military academy. In 1894, Morley's father resigned his positions at the military academy and moved his family west to Romley, Colorado, where he bought part of the Mary Murphy Mine and became its operator (Brunhouse 1971, 14).

Morley's interest in archaeology became apparent by the age of fifteen with his reading of Lew Wallace's *The Fair God* and Rider Haggard's *Heart of the World*. Both works were about pre-Columbian Mexico. He also read pertinent articles in the *Encyclopedia Britannica* and William Prescott's *Conquest of Mexico*. Later, Morley began to correspond with Regis Chauvenet, a graduate of Harvard University and president of the Colorado School of Mines, about his archaeological interests (Brunhouse 1971, 15). Unable to answer fully the questions posed in Morley's letters, Chauvenet suggested that he contact FREDERIC WARD PUTNAM at the Peabody Museum of Archaeology and Ethnology (Harvard University). The result of this exchange was the recommendation that Morley read H. H. Bancroft's *The Native Races,* the most up-to-date synthesis of American archaeology at that time.

Before he had finished high school, Morley had already decided that he wanted to become an archaeologist. However, his father saw little remuneration in the field and enrolled his son in the Pennsylvania Military Academy, intending that he become a civil engineer. Morley's father died

Sylvanus Morley.
(Courtesy of Douglas
Givens)

in 1903, but the dutiful son continued his education and graduated as a civil engineer in 1904 (Brunhouse 1971, 15–16). Part of the training that Morley received at the academy was in the proper conduct of areal survey, a skill that he would apply in Edgar Lee Hewett's field school in the American Southwest.

An overpowering interest in archaeology still haunted Morley, and he succumbed to its fascination by entering Harvard to begin studies in anthropology. Living in a rooming house a short distance from the campus, Morley enjoyed the life at Harvard and the flavor of Cambridge without too much thought to the costs involved (AVK, 101). His aunt Virginia, a widow who had been left comfortably well-off at her husband's death, provided financial support during Morley's undergraduate years (Brunhouse 1971, 16).

Egyptology had first attracted Morley to Harvard, but under the influence of Putnam, his "archaeological mentor," Morley's attention turned from Egypt toward Yucatán. He made his first trip to Yucatán at Putnam's suggestion, and he finally severed his fascination with ancient Egypt by writing a paper in December 1904 on the deluge myths of Central America (Brunhouse 1971, 28). Subsequently, Harvard archaeologist Alfred Marsten Tozzer cultivated Morley's interest in Central America and narrowed his focus to the Maya. After his graduation from Harvard, the Archaeological Institute of America sent Morley to Yucatán to study linguistics, with funding for his trip provided by Charles Bowditch of the American Antiquarian Society. While there, he went to Chichén Itzá and visited pioneer Meso-American archaeologist Edward Thompson during some of his dredging operations at the Sacred Cenote, a large well that was supposed to be a site of human sacrifice. With this experience and also because of other travels throughout Yucatán, Morley abandoned linguistics and set a firm course for a career in archaeology.

Back at Harvard in 1905, Morley continued as Tozzer's student by taking his anthropology course covering Mayan archaeology. There he read Daniel Brinton's *Primer of Maya Hieroglyphics* and delved into aspects of glyph research, a subject that would become his forté throughout his professional life. Bowditch, a Mayanist himself, also encouraged Morley to study the Maya. (Bowditch would later establish in his name an endowed chair of Middle American and Mexican archaeology and ethnology at the Peabody Museum.)

Morley, A. V. Kidder, and Edgar Lee Hewett

Morley had been exposed to the field methods of the American Egyptologist George Reisner in his course on Egyptology at Harvard. However, his true education in the field came as the result of his participation in Hewett's "field methods school" in archaeology during the summer of 1907. By chance, Morley had read a notice in the spring issue of the university's student newspaper that three men interested in archaeology might be accepted to carry out a survey in the American Southwest. Having nothing to do that summer, Morley followed the instructions and presented himself at Tozzer's office. There he met ALFRED VINCENT KIDDER and John Gould Fletcher, his two companions in the field. Kidder would become Morley's life-long friend and gave him the nickname of Vay. Fletcher, a poet at heart, yielded to the heat and exhaustion and did not last the entire summer. Regardless, the three men embarked on an archaeological survey of the McElmo and Yellow Jacket Canyons, which straddled the Utah-Colorado border, as well as the Pueblo sites of Hovenweep, Mesa Verde, and Puyé (Givens 1992a, 14–16; Chauvenet 1983).

That summer Hewett provided no training in field methods for the trio, and Kidder credited Morley with their education in surveying skills.

> We would have to make our own map of the country as we went along, for we had none. As a matter of fact, no really good one existed, the government survey sheets for at least that part of the San Juan drainage being, as I later learned, very poor. Vay gave the mapping job to me, he would write the notes, I running the journal, all three of us would do the measuring, he and I the plans of structures.
>
> Fletcher, whose fingers were all thumbs, turned out, though willing, to be of little use except to hold one end of the tape. Said tape, supplied by Hewett was a 50-foot cloth one; I'd brought along a cheap pocket compass, Vay and I each had a kodak (AVK, 34).

In Kidder's view, Morley, not Hewett, was the real leader of the 1907 summer expedition. "Notwithstanding our primitive equipment, we did a pretty good job. But it was all due to Vay. He was an indefatigable worker, full of energy, invariably cheerful, whistling and singing as he stumbled about among the ruins. Very nearsighted, it was a miracle that he didn't break a leg or pitch himself over any of the cliffs to the very edges of which many of the little canyon-head pueblos clung. His example kept us going, in spite of the great heat, and various minor discomforts, the worst of which was the clinging of the swarms of flies (AVK, 43)."

Despite his participation in the survey, the archaeology of the American Southwest held no great fascination for Morley as it did for so many others. He still wanted to work in Mayan archaeology. However, from 1907 to 1914, Morley continued in Hewett's employ at the School of American Archaeology (later the School of American Research). He traveled to Mexico on occasion, which only increased his interest in the ancient Maya. In time he began to see that there was no future with Hewett, and he secretly harbored an ambitious plan to excavate Chichén Itzá, which had not been investigated with any degree of intensity since Tozzer in 1903 (Phillips 1955, 73). However, Morley knew that the modest budget of Hewett's School of American Archaeology could not afford the grand scheme he had conceived.

Morley and the Carnegie Institution

Morley's desire to make Mayan archaeology his life's work was heightened when, in 1912, he heard a rumor that the Carnegie Institution in Washington, D.C., was going to expand its activities into anthropology. Morley understood that the new effort would take the form of a department of Central American archaeology. The idea had actually been proposed in 1909, but the institution's executive committee had not been impressed by the specific plans for the venture, which had been drawn up by Hiram Bingham. Since 1900 Bingham, a historian, had been involved in investigations of Machu Picchu in Peru (Brunhouse 1971, 64), and his sensational accounts of his discoveries may have persuaded the committee that he was not the proper choice to spearhead their new project (Givens 1992b, 138). Moreover, Robert Woodward, president of the Carnegie Institution, was not convinced that an archaeology department was appropriate. He was heard to say that "archaeology exists to aid museums in the acquisition of collections, and since the Carnegie had no museums, archaeology was therefore not part of the Carnegie's mission" (Brunhouse 1971, 67). Ironically, the lack of museums gave the Carnegie Institution an edge over other organizations seeking to do archaeological work in foreign countries; no museum meant no place to house collections, thereby ensuring that archaeological materials would remain in the host country.

To be seriously considered by the Carnegie's executive committee, however, Morley would have to compete with two others who also had well-thought-out projects in mind. W. H. R. Rivers, A. E. Jenks, and Morley were to write position papers on the direction that the Carnegie Institution should take in getting its new anthropology program off the ground. Rivers's "Report on Anthropological Research outside America" stressed the urgency of ethnographic research among fast-disappearing native peoples and advocated Oceania as the area that would best relate important theoretical problems to the origins of American indigenous culture (Rivers 1913). In his "Report on the Science of Anthropology in the Western Hemisphere and the Pacific Islands" (1913), Jenks suggested a world clearinghouse for anthropology in the form of a research laboratory devoted to studies in ethnic heredity and environment. Morley's position paper, "Archaeological Research at the Ruins of Chichén Itzá, Yucatán," first reviewed the history of the Maya Indians and their civilization. His program of research included analyses of labor resources, climatic problems, and disease and the restoration of architectural remains (Morley 1913; Givens 1992b; Woodbury 1973). Using documentary and archaeological sources, he outlined the need for a twenty-five-year excavation program at a major site and presented detailed information on Chichén Itzá to justify its selection.

During the two years that Morley pursued the new Carnegie position, Hewett got wind of the "covert project" and confronted him about who he was really working for, "him or the Carnegie" (Givens 1992b, 16). Behind the scenes, Hewett also contacted the Carnegie's executive committee and led them to believe that Morley was the tool of Franz Boas, of Columbia University, and therefore could not be trusted to carry out the Carnegie's new venture into archaeology (SGM 1914, 19). Meanwhile, Morley waited for the decision of the executive committee. President Woodward was still not favorably disposed toward archaeology, in Central America or in any other location for that matter. Another factor delaying the acceptance of the Chichén Itzá project was the ever-worsening political situation between the United States and Mexico in the spring of 1914. American naval personnel had been arrested by Mexican authorities at Tampico, and President Woodrow Wilson ordered a naval bombardment and occupation of Vera Cruz. Morley was in Guatemala at the time, isolated from most of the outside world and from events to the north.

Finally, in May 1914 the executive committee of the Carnegie Institution judged Morley's proposal the best of the three and created a new department of Central American archaeology. The committee recommended that Morley be hired and put to work collecting information on existing materials of Central American archaeology until the political tensions between the United States and Mexico had subsided. In July Woodward wrote Morley that the job was his and asked him to come to Washington, D.C., for a conference. Morley was offered $200.00 in monthly salary to compile a bibliography of Central American antiquities until it was prudent to undertake fieldwork in Mexico. During the meeting, Morley spoke of finding stelae (stone calendars) in the Petén, in Guatemala, and about his interest in a book on Mayan chronology. Eventually the idea of a bibliography of antiquities was discarded in favor of a comprehensive volume on Mayan chronology.

Once Morley was notified that the position was his, he sent his resignation to Hewett, writing that this opportunity "promise[d] to . . . largely increase the sphere of [his] usefulness to American archaeology" (Morley to Hewett, 1 July 1914, ELH). In his response, Hewett blamed Carnegie's indecisiveness on the "Tozzer/Boas combination." However, Morley noted in his diary that Hewett never admitted "his own contra-activities" (SGM 1914, 17). Despite the obstruction of his former employer, Morley later acknowledged how much "he owed to Dr. Hewett's rugged training and how many of his accomplishments derived . . . from Hewett's direction" (Dutton 1988).

Mayan Fieldwork

In 1915 Morley began his long career of exploration and fieldwork with the Carnegie Institution. For a decade he searched and surveyed some of the most inaccessible parts of the Mayan territory, spending untold days traveling by mule and camping under miserable conditions, with ticks and flies his constant companions. All basic creature comforts were adversely affected by the jungle environment. Edward Thompson suggested that "Morley hated every minute of it, but he kept on because it was only by so doing that he could 'bring home the epigraphic bacon'" (1949, 294). When hearing references to the romance of the bush as a great frontier, Morley would respond by quoting an old-timer from Belize: "Anyone who says he likes the bush is either a bloody fool or a bloody liar" (ibid.).

Morley's expedition of 1916 indicated the dangers of fieldwork south of the U.S. border. Because of continuing bouts with malaria, which he had contracted during an earlier expedition, Morley took with him a medical doctor as part of his staff. He left New Orleans with the intention of making it to Guatemala. He visited Copán, Tulum, and Uaxactún, but wanted to reach Ococingo. After traveling over the highlands of western Guatemala, Morley almost lost his life. The Guatemalan army was guarding the border against incursions by Mexican bandits (Brunhouse 1971, 95). As his group was returning from Uaxactún, they were "mistaken for a party of revolutionaries and ambushed by a detachment of Guatemalan troops" (Thompson 1949, 294). The staff doctor and Morley's native guide were killed. Morley owed his life to the fact that a few minutes before the attack, a liana vine had caught and ripped off his glasses. He dismounted to pick them up and so was in the rear when the action began. With the sound of gunfire, the members of the expedition

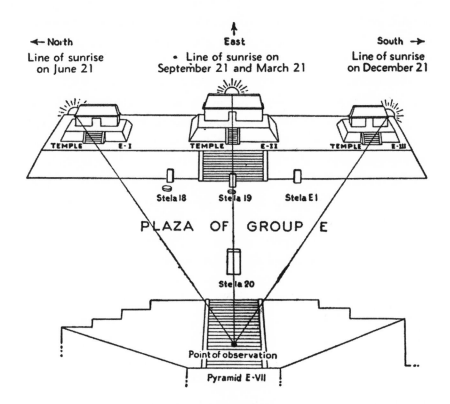

Morley's drawing of an astronomical plan of Mayan structures at Uaxactún, Guatemala. (From Grahame Clark, Aspects of Prehistory, *1970)*

← North
Line of sunrise
on June 21

↑ East
• Line of sunrise on
September 21 and March 21

South →
Line of sunrise
on December 21

TEMPLE E-I

TEMPLE E-II

TEMPLE E-III

Stela 18   Stela 19   Stela E1

PLAZA OF GROUP E

Stela 20

Point of observation

Pyramid E-VII

dove in to the forest on either side of the narrow trail and for hours lay hidden, fearing that any movement would bring another volley (ibid.). Morley and his party were forced to turn back at the border.

He traveled next to Copán, but his visit produced only a few ceramic fragments and a stela from A.D. 260. The artist WILLIAM HENRY HOLMES was part of the expedition to Copán, because Morley wanted him to draw a panoramic view of the site for the frontispiece of a volume on the inscriptions of Copán, which was nearing completion (Brunhouse 1971, 96). Morley also brought along Samuel Lothrop, a young Harvard student who was to make his own mark on American archaeology. Lothrop had worked with Kidder at Pecos Pueblo, New Mexico, in 1915. Now, as Morley's assistant, Lothrop prepared stone artifacts for photographing and sketching and learned from Holmes how to make panoramic drawings. Morley also traveled to the Mayan site at Tulum during this period.

World War I affected the conduct of Americanist archaeology in Central America as well as in the United States. Even before the United States entered the war, Morley and his colleagues, who were scattered over Central America, offered their services to the government. Under the guise of a scientist on a research trip, Morley worked for Naval Intelligence. After the declaration of war, Morley received a commission as an ensign and was formally attached to the Naval Coast Defense Reserve of the Navy Yard in Washington, D.C. He served for two years, retiring in March 1919 as a lieutenant, junior grade (Brunhouse 1971, 122).

Between 1919 and 1922, Morley spent most of his field seasons in the Petén looking for Mayan date inscriptions. He also visited Costa Rica and Guatemala to examine both public and private archaeological collections in order to understand the Mayan influence in those areas. Aside from ceramic materials, he found virtually no trace of ancient Maya in those countries (Brunhouse 1971, 148). During 1920, Morley took a brief hiatus in his fieldwork and went to Washington, D.C., to complete the proofs for his *Inscriptions of Copán* (1920). This was the first book to discuss in detail all the texts of a single site, and its publication played no small part in Morley's appointment as an "honorary citizen of Copán." It also led the Pennsylvania Military Academy to grant him an honorary doctoral degree. Later, the now-classic five volumes on *The Inscriptions of Petén* (1937–1938) earned him the Guatemalan Order of the Quetzal and the Loubat prize. Morley's other significant works demonstrated his natural ability to read glyphs from the most weathered stelae. His first book, *Introduction to the Study of the Maya Hieroglyphs* (1915), provided a synthesis of what was then known about Maya glyphs. In *The Supplementary Series in the Maya Inscriptions* (1916) Morley brought together drawings of all lunar glyphs, thereby allowing Teeple to solve the riddle of the lunar count.

Morley's available time for deciphering glyphs was seriously eroded by the constraints of field trips and lecture tours. However, he proved "the meanings of the so-called hotun and lahuntun glyphs, deciphered the winged Cauac glyph with its variants, and known glyphs." He consequently demonstrated that almost every Mayan monument was erected to "mark the close of a katun [a period of time in the Mayan calendar]or one of its quarters" (Thompson 1949, 295). Perhaps as important to Mayan archaeology as his scholarly work was his insistence that the public become aware of the achievements of the Maya. He delivered lectures throughout the United States and wrote popular articles on the Maya, such as the *National Geographic* piece on "Yucatán, Home of the Gifted Maya" (1936).

Morley's plan of making a thorough study of the Maya at Chichén Itzá was never realized; it was overtaken by his burning desire to find and decipher Mayan glyphs. Only a few years after the Chichén Itzá project had begun, some of the Carnegie officials began to have doubts about Morley's fieldwork. J. C. Merriam, president of the institution, complained that Morley was concerned primarily with the study of Mayan glyphs and the "glorification of the Maya as a premier civilization in Middle America" (Givens 1992a, 142). Morley, according to Kidder (AVK, 54), had little interest in administering the work at Chichén Itzá, either in terms of managing personnel or performing the mundane tasks of budgets and logistics. He was intent on collecting and arranging Initial Series inscriptions from as many Mayan sites as possible. In essence, Morley had left the project to its own devices and gone off in pursuit of his own research. As a result, the program was costing the Carnegie much more than had been estimated.

As early as 1925, the Carnegie Institution had begun considering making a change in the leadership of their Department of Central American Archaeology. Merriam asked Kidder, Clark Wissler, and James Breasted, all well-known archaeologists, to form an advisory committee to review the progress of their archaeology program. The following year Kidder received a formal appointment to the Carnegie staff, a preliminary indication that Morley's days at the helm of the archaeology department were numbered. To study the institution's current involvement in Central America and to make recommendations on better coordination, Kidder visited all the locations where Carnegie archaeologists were working. He then reported back to Merriam on the organizational changes needed to get the Chichén Itzá program back on track.

In 1928, the archaeologist Karl Ruppert took over the immediate supervision of the work at Chichén Itzá, and though Morley retained his title as director of the Yucatán program, his duties were restricted to oversight, research, and writing. Meanwhile, he corresponded with Merriam about a number of projects that should be undertaken, but his proposals were received without enthusiasm. Morley's field research, with its narrow focus, may have begun to seem old-fashioned; more innovative were the approaches that emphasized the interaction of diverse disciplines with archaeology (Brunhouse 1971, 277). The Carnegie Board of Trustees created a new administrative body, the Division of Historical Research, to coordinate their efforts in Central America and asked A.V. Kidder to serve at the director. The division's goal was to produce a cultural overview of the Maya, and its strategy regarding Mayan archaeology took into account Morley's perspective but also adopted Kidder's multidisciplinary approach. The closure of the Department of Central American Archaeology was not solely the result of Morley's administrative failure. In fact, it may have been due to the actions of another Carnegie representative—Dr. Thomas Gann, the department's unsalaried staff physician. MANUEL GAMIO had written to Merriam that Gann had violated Mexican law on antiquities by illegally removing from Mexico the famous Teotihuacan jade. In 1925, Kidder, then a member of Carnegie's advisory committee, learned from Merriam about the theft of the jade and that Merriam held Morley responsible for Gann's conduct: "I can't have Morley running his organisation [the Department of Central American Archaeol-

ogy] anymore. He gets a man like Gann into our staff. . . . I want you to take charge of our archaeological work" (AVK, 115). Morley's own version of events was recorded in his diary in 1923:

> After dinner and when we had come back to the hotel and were resting and chatting, Gann got up in a sort of self-conscious way—he had no coat on and said "do you notice anything about my back?" At first I did not but a closer examination revealed a flattish pad on the small of his back. He said, "do you remember that jade plaque that Wesson had?" I let him go no further. "Gann you Devil, did you buy it?" "Yes," he replied "even before we went to Yucatán." He carefully undid it from a cotton swathing inside of a Turkish towel that looked for all the world like a bustle, and there it was. It was beyond doubt the most magnificent piece of Maya jade I had ever seen both in colouring and execution. Gann had bought it . . . for $250.00 gold. It was the first piece of jade I have ever seen, and there is nothing in the Cenote jades to touch it (SGM 1923, 433–444).

Morley continued his pioneering work on Mayan glyphs until 1947, when he retired from the Carnegie's Division of Historical Research. That same year he became the director of the Museum of New Mexico in Santa Fe, a city that he had come to love over the years. However, his tenure was brief. He died of a heart attack on 2 September 1948 and was buried in Santa Fe.

Morley was not gifted as an administrator, but he was one of the most important Mayanists in the history of archaeology. A lifetime spent making glyph discoveries and interpreting them, in addition to bringing the Maya to the attention of the American public, was Morley's greatest gift to Americanist archaeology.

References
Primary
Archival collections directly cited in the text are identified as follows:

AVK: Alfred Vincent Kidder Papers, Harvard University Archives, Cambridge, MA.

ELH: Edgar Lee Hewett Papers, Museum of New Mexico, Santa Fe.

SGM: Diary of Sylvanus Griswold Morley, Sylvanus Griswold Morley Papers, Peabody Museum Archives, Peabody Museum of Archaeology and Ethnology, Harvard University, Cambridge, MA.

Morley, Sylvanus Griswold. 1913. "Archaeological Research at the Ruins of Chichén Itzá, Yucatan." In *Reports upon the Present Condition and Future Needs of the Science of Anthropology*. Washington, DC: Carnegie Institution of Washington.

————. 1915. *An Introduction to the Study of the Maya Hieroglyphs*. Bureau of American Ethnology Bulletin 57. Washington, DC: Smithsonian Institution.

————. 1916. "The Supplementary Series in the Maya Inscriptions." In *Holmes Anniversary Volume, Anthropological Essays Presented to William Henry Holmes in Honor of His Seventieth Birthday*. Washington, DC: Privately printed.

————. 1920. *The Inscriptions of Copan*. Carnegie Institution of Washington Publication 219. Washington, DC: Carnegie Institution of Washington.

————. 1936. "Yucatán. Home of the Gifted Maya." *National Geographic* 95: 591–644.

————. 1937–1938. *The Inscriptions of Petén*. 5 vols. Carnegie Institution of Washington Publication 16. Washington, DC: Carnegie Institution of Washington.

Morley, Sylvanus Griswold, and G. W. Brainerd. 1983. *The Ancient Maya*. 4th ed. Stanford, CA: Stanford University Press.

Secondary
Brunhouse, Robert L. 1971. *Sylvanus G. Morley and the World of the Ancient Maya*. Norman: University of Oklahoma Press.

Chauvenet, Beatrice. 1983. *Hewett and Friends (A Biography of Santa Fe's Vibrant Era)*. Santa Fe: Museum of New Mexico Press.

Dutton, B. 1988. Letter to Douglas R. Givens, 6 January.

Givens, Douglas R. 1992a. *Alfred Vincent Kidder and the Development of Americanist Archaeology*. Albuquerque: University of New Mexico Press.

————. 1992b. "Sylvanus G. Morley and the Carnegie Institution's

Program of Mayan Research." In *Rediscovering Our Past: Essays on the History of American Archaeology*. Ed. Jonathan E. Reyman. Aldershot, UK: Avebury Press.

Jenks, A. E. 1913. "On the Science of Anthropology in the Western Hemisphere and the Pacific Islands." In *Reports upon the Present Condition and Future Needs of the Science of Anthropology*. Washington, DC: Carnegie Institution of Washington.

Kidder, Alfred V. 1959. "The Diary of Sylvanus G. Morley." *Proceedings of the American Philosophical Society* 103, 6: 778–782.

Long, B., ed. 1950. *Morleyana (A Collections of Writings in Memoriam Sylvanus Griswold Morley, 1883–1948)*. Santa Fe: Museum of New Mexico and the School of American Research.

Phillips, P. 1955. "Alfred Marsten Tozzer, 1877–1954." *American Antiquity* 21, 1: 72–80.

Rivers, W. H. R. 1913. "Report on Anthropological Research outside America." In *Reports upon the Present Condition and Future Needs of the Science of Anthropology*. Washington, DC: Carnegie Institution of Washington.

Thompson, J. E. S. 1949. "Sylvanus Griswold Morley, 1883–1948." *American Anthropologist* 51: 293–297.

Willey, Gordon R., and Jeremy A. Sabloff. 1993. *A History of American Archaeology*. 3d ed. New York: W. H. Freeman.

Woodbury, Richard B. 1973. *Alfred V. Kidder*. New York: Columbia University Press.

Roberto Cobean and Alba Guadalupe Mastache Flores

Manuel Gamio   1883–1960

One of the first archaeologists to undertake stratigraphic excavations in North America, Manuel Gamio was also the director of the first multidisciplinary anthropological project in the Americas—an ethnographic and archaeological study of the Teotihuacan Valley. After a brief exile he returned to Mexico, where he directed several key government and international institutes devoted to improving the living conditions of contemporary indigenous groups.

In histories of archaeology, Manuel Gamio is credited, along with N. C. Nelson, with being the first archaeologist to make stratigraphic excavations in North America. However, considering also Gamio's contributions to New World anthropology, his innovative use of stratigraphy was but one of many important achievements. Most of his career was dedicated to social anthropology, or, more specifically, to what often is called "applied anthropology," which is distinguished by its instrumental focus. In Gamio's case, this was reflected in his attempts to improve the living conditions of Mexico's indigenous peoples. Gamio was part of the Homeric generation that produced the cultural renaissance in Mexico. This creative eruption, which began with the 1910 revolution, is most vividly represented in contemporary memory by the murals of Diego Rivera and José Clemente Orozco, yet it was the combined expression of thousands of artists, writers, intellectuals, and politicians, including such towering figures as the educator Jose Vasconcelos, the novelist Mariano Azuela, the general and future president Lázaro Cardenas—and Manuel Gamio, anthropologist, novelist, and sometime politician. Gamio's life and work have been the subject of a book-length biography (González Gamio 1987) and numerous biographical studies (for example, Comas 1974; Leon Portilla 1960; Matos Moctezuma 1972). This essay will be mainly devoted to his archaeological investigations.

Manuel Gamio was born in Mexico City on 2 March 1883 and died there on 16 July 1960. He studied at Mexico City's esteemed National Preparatory School, the alma mater of many Mexican intellectuals. After graduating in 1903, he briefly studied at the national School of Mining, then his father sent him to help administer a family plantation whose lands lay in the states of Veracruz and Puebla. Here he had his first extended contacts with an indigenous (Nahua) group. He learned their language and was appalled by their poverty and by the exploitation that

Manuel Gamio.
(Courtesy of
Arqueología
Mexicana)

kept them impoverished. He began writing short stories, not published until years later (1937), using fiction to describe the very real social problems of rural Mexico.

Returning to Mexico City in 1906, Gamio studied anthropology and archaeology at the National Museum for two years, his chief professor being Nicolas Leon (Matos 1983). In 1907 he published his first article describing and criticizing *derechos de capacitación,* a discriminatory tax passed down from Spanish colonial rule that many early-twentieth-century Mexican Indians were still forced to pay. In 1908 he did his first archaeological investigations at the site of Chalchihuites, Zacatecas. Part of his fieldwork was blocked by Leopoldo Batres, the inspector of archaeological monuments in Mexico, but Gamio obtained enough information to write a report (1910) and a thesis (Rivermar 1987). During the same period (1909) he made some preliminary nonstratigraphic excavations at Azcapotzalco in the west-central basin of Mexico, and he tried to associate the materials he obtained with indigenous groups from the fifteenth and sixteenth centuries (Bernal 1979, 159).

In 1909 Gamio received a scholarship to study anthropology at Columbia University and spent most of the next two years in New York City. His principal professor there, Franz Boas, became his friend and collaborator in a number of archaeological and anthropological programs over the years. Boas and his students at Columbia (especially A. L. Kroeber) were probably the most productive group of generalists in the history of anthropology. Boas's insistence on integrating archaeology with ethnology, linguistics, human biology, and the other fields of anthropology made a profound impression on Gamio and, as we shall see, inspired him to create the first interdisciplinary anthropological program in the Americas. During 1910 Gamio spent several months in Ecuador on an archaeological project directed by Marshall Saville of New York's Museum of the American Indian. The following year Gamio received an M.A. at Columbia with a thesis on the archaeology of Chalchihuites, Zacatecas. In 1912 he returned to Mexico and immediately began participating in the investigations of the recently founded International School of American Archaeology and Ethnography.

The staff of the International School included, among others, Eduard Seler (the first director), Boas, Harvard archaeologist Alfred Tozzer, Gamio, and George Engerrand, a French geologist and prehistorian. Boas began studying materials from the basin of Mexico in Mexico City's National Museum in an attempt to formulate a preliminary cultural sequence. On the basis of this work, he suggested that Gamio excavate once again at Azcapotzalco. Gamio's 1913 exploration of the famed mound at San Miguel Amantla (Azcapotzalco) constituted the first archaeological stratigraphy in Mesoamerica, but an unsolved mystery is which member of the International School staff originally introduced the idea of stratigraphic digging. The reports of Gamio (1913) and Boas (1911–1912) are unclear on this point. GORDON WILLEY and Jeremy Sabloff (1974, 215) suggest that the geologist Engerrand may have proposed the use of stratigraphy, a concept that had been well known in geology for many decades (Bernal 1979). Stratigraphic excavations were also fairly common in European archaeology by the end of the nineteenth century (Trigger 1989, 94–100), so there may have been multiple sources for Gamio's choice of technique. The culture sequence of Archaic (Formative)/Teotihuacan/Aztec that Gamio identified in his investigations was correctly ordered (if incomplete), as demonstrated by subsequent stratigraphic work in the basin of Mexico (Tozzer 1921, Kroeber 1925, Vaillant 1938, Armillas 1950).

In 1914 Gamio described the stratigraphic excavation technique in a manual entitled "Methodology Concerning the Investigation, Exploration and Conservation of Archaeological Monuments," published in the *Anales* of the National Museum. This work was typical of his interest in writing didactic texts; in fact, a significant portion of his vast bibliography was manuals and proposals for new methodologies in the social sciences. The same year he published a report on the excavations that he had directed in the center of Mexico City exploring sectors of the main plaza of Tenochtitlan, the Aztec capital.

The years 1916–1917 were extremely active for Gamio. He was named the director of the International School of American Archaeology and Ethnography (its last one, since the program ended in 1920) and produced important studies in archaeology, ethnology, and linguistics (Rivermar 1987). In 1916 Gamio published a very influential collection of essays on the political and social problems of Mexico entitled *Founding the Fatherland* (Forjando Patria), which included proposals for improving the lives of indigenous peoples. The work inspired many revolutionary intellectuals and political leaders, including two presidents, Venustiano Carranza (1911–1914) and Alvaro Obregon (1920–1924) (Gonzalez Gamio 1987, 47–48). Mexico at this time was essentially divided in a civil war between the conflicting revolutionary factions of Emiliano Zapata and of Pancho Villa and Francisco Madero. Not surprisingly, Gamio openly praised and supported Zapata, the revolutionary leader most concerned with the problems of Indian groups; Gamio was brave indeed to take this public stance because Zapata's movement was never popular among the politicians and generals of the Mexico City–based federal government.

In 1917 Gamio founded and was named the first director of a federal department of anthropology (Dirección de Antropología). Despite ongoing political upheavals, the department received sufficient resources to enable him to set up several research programs. The principal one, which constituted Gamio's crowning achievement as an archaeologist, was called "The Population of the Teotihuacan Valley," the first multidisciplinary anthropological project in the Americas. This work was nearly unique for its time and is still in many ways the most successful project of its kind ever conducted in Mesoamerica. In planning the methodology and theoretical framework of the program, Gamio obviously was strongly influenced by the integrated anthropological system of his teacher Boas, but even Boas, a rigorous multidimensional empiricist, never investigated a human society on the basis of so many different research fields as the Teotihuacan Valley project did.

Long before Gamio's time the ruins of Teotihuacan, located forty kilometers northeast of Mexico City, had been recognized as one of the great ancient Mexican cities abandoned centuries before the Spanish conquest. Previous to Gamio's project the most systematic studies of the archaeology of Teotihuacan had been done by Seler (1915). Gamio's program lasted five years (1917–1922) and involved investigations by over twenty scholars, some of whom (such as the archaeologists Ignacio Marquina and Hermann Beyer) distinguished themselves in their own programs years later. Even the regional focus of Gamio's project was an innovation. Until the 1940s, most archaeological excavations in Mexico concentrated on individual sites without researching the surrounding area, and few ventures combined ethnographic and archaeological studies.

In 1922, the Teotihuacan project reports were published in five volumes, and Gamio also wrote a doctoral dissertation for Columbia University based on this research. The scope of the reports is truly encyclopedic, and they still constitute an indispensable reference source for central Mexican anthropology and history. The full title offers insight into Gamio's lifelong approach to his work: *The Population of the Valley of Teotihuacan, the Environment in Which It Has Developed, Its Ethnic and Social Evolution, and Efforts to Achieve Its Betterment*. Despite the reference to evolution,

Gamio did not explicitly employ an evolutionary theoretical framework, though the volumes did empirically reconstruct the history of the people of the Teotihuacan Valley from pre-Hispanic times to the beginning of the twentieth century. The following list of subjects covered in the volumes illustrates the breadth and depth of Gamio's research program: the physical environment of the Teotihuacan Valley; the physical anthropology of the pre-Hispanic population; intellectual manifestations of the Teotihuacan culture; ancient architecture, sculpture, and ceramics; stratigraphy of the sites in the valley and geographical extension of the Teotihuacan culture; a comparison of Teotihuacan and Aztec civilizations; an ethnohistoric study of Aztec-period culture in the Teotihuacan Valley; Aztec antiquities (archaeological objects) in the Teotihuacan Valley; colonial geography, demography, ideas and customs, political and religious history, and economic organization; the Indian noble genealogies of Teotihuacan; indigenous codices and documents in Nahuatl (the Aztec language); sixteenth-century churches; colonial religious paintings and other works of art; and studies of the nineteenth-century population. On contemporary subjects, the reports included a census, physical anthropology (including diet and diseases), ethnography, folklore, schools and education, economic organization, agrarian problems, irrigation systems, agriculture and forests, botanical analysis of contemporary plants, geology of the Teotihuacan Valley, road systems, modern architecture, and linguistic study of contemporary Nahuatl speakers in the valley and indigenous place-names.

The first two volumes were primarily devoted to the archaeology of Teotihuacan. Gamio's most extensive excavations were concentrated in the Ciudadela plaza, where he restored the sculptured facades of the pyramid of Quetzalcoatl and dug stratigraphic pits that indicated a long, complex chronology for the ancient city. He also made numerous stratigraphic excavations in other areas of the urban zone, especially along the Street of the Dead (the central axis of the city) and in the main pyramid (the Pyramid of the Sun). Hermann Beyer presented an iconographic analysis of Teotihuacan art, while many of the architectural studies were done by Ignacio Marquina. The latter are of extraordinary quality and include a fine-scale topographic map of over two square kilometers of the city's central sector and many reconstructive drawings of specific buildings and ancient construction techniques. The volumes also contained excellent reproductions of Teotihuacan mural paintings and numerous illustrations of pottery, figurines, and lithics along with luxury objects (jade and marine shells) found in religious offerings. In the sections on architecture and artifacts, attempts were made to identify the probable sources in the Teotihuacan Valley for building stones and raw materials. The study

Excavations in Teotihuacan. (Foto Centro Regional del INAH en Pachuca, Hidalgo)

of the valley's geology by Pedro De Landero furnished one of the earliest descriptions of the important pre-Hispanic obsidian mines in the Otumba region, as well as chemical analyses of major rocks and minerals.

In the first volume, Gamio provided a thorough synthesis of the program's investigations and suggested that the ancient city of Teotihuacan recovered by archaeology was the Toltec city Tollan, as described in the indigenous central Mexican chronicles. (Later studies by Wigberto Jimenez Moreno [1941] and JORGE ACOSTA [1945] concluded that Tula in Hidalgo, not Teotihuacan, was the legendary Tollan.) Gamio discussed the ruins of Tula in some detail and correctly placed them chronologically after Teotihuacan. In the same essay, he presented a list of other major regions in Mexico where he believed the Department of Anthropology should organize similar multidisciplinary investigations of the local populations. Sadly, many of these areas were not studied until years later. As Eduardo Matos (1983) has observed, for various reasons Gamio's work at Teotihuacan was not followed by other comprehensive projects, and many of his lines of research lay dormant for nearly forty years. Then, in 1965, William Sanders started a long-term investigation of settlement patterns and cultural ecology in the Teotihuacan Valley and the rest of the basin of Mexico.

During the 1920s, in addition to the Teotihuacan program, Gamio initiated a series of important investigations into the early sedentary

Archaic (Formative) cultures in the basin of Mexico, excavating at Copilco and other sites and helping Byron Cummings (1933) start a key project at the early urban center of Cuicuilco. Also during this period, Gamio founded and edited the journal *Ethnos* (1920–1925), which published influential reports and essays by Gamio and others concerning the archaeology, ethnology, and contemporary problems of indigenous people of Mexico. Between 1924 and 1925 Gamio had a brief political career as undersecretary of public education in the administration of President Plutarco Elias Calles, but it ended disastrously. After denouncing government corruption in Mexico City newspapers, Gamio had to flee the country. He spent over two years in exile in the United States and Guatemala, during which time he began his famous studies of Mexican immigrant laborers in the United States, which became classics in sociology and applied anthropology (Gamio 1931). After his return to Mexico, and for the rest of his life, he was primarily occupied with the direction of several key government and international institutes devoted to improving the living conditions of indigenous groups. His most important contribution was as founder and director of the Instituto Indigenista Interamericano (the Inter-American Indian Institute) from 1942 to 1960. Gamio's work still exercises a profound influence on contemporary Mexican anthropology, and his vast academic production is documented in a biography by his granddaughter (Gonzalez Gamio 1987).

References
Primary
Gamio, Manuel. 1907. "Los derechos de Capacitación." In *Modern Mexico.* New York: Mes de Marzo.

———. 1909. "Restos de la Cultura Tepaneca." *Anales del Museo Nacional de México,* 3d s., 1: 233–253, 3 plates.

———. 1910. "Los monumentos arqueológicos de las inmediaciones de Chalchihuites, Zacatecas." *Anales del Museo Nacional de México,* 3d s., 2: 467–492.

———. 1911. "Informe sobre el reconocimiento de algunos vestigios de origen prehispánico existentes en la Hacienda de Zavaleta, Distrito de Chalco, Estado de México." *Boletín del Museo Nacional de México,* 83–85.

———. 1912. "La sucesión de tipos culturales en Azcapotzalco." *Escuela Internacional de Arqueología y Etnología Americanas* (1911–1912), 13, 14.

———. 1913. "Arqueología de Azcapotzalco." In *Proceedings of the XVII International Congress of Americanists* (1912), 180–187. London.

———. 1913. "Los prejuicios en la arqueología y la etnología." *Anales del Museo Nacional de México,* 3d s., 5: 41–49.

———. 1913. "Unidad cultural de Teotihuacán." *Anales del Museo Nacional de México,* 3d s., 5: 153–160.

———. 1914. "Los vestigios prehispánicos de la Calle de Santa Teresa (hoy Guatemala)." *Boletín de Educación,* 1, 1.

————. 1914. "Metodología sobre investigación, exploración y conservación de monumentos arqueológicos." *Anales del Museo Nacional de México,* 58.

————. 1916. *Forjando patria.* Mexico City: Porrúa.

————. 1920. "Las excavaciones del pedregal de San Angel y la cultura arcaica del Valle de México." *American Anthropologist* 22, 2: 127–143.

————. 1921. "Texto para el album de colecciones arqueológicas, seleccionadas y arregladas por Franz Boas." *Publicación de la Escuela Internacional de Arqueología Americana.* Mexico City: Imprenta del Museo Nacional, 46.

————. 1921. "Vestigios del templo mayor de Tenochtitlan, descubiertos recientemente. El Coateocalli." *Ethnos* 1: 8–12, 205–207.

————. 1922. *La población del Valle de Teotihuacán.* Mexico City: Talleres Gráficos de la Secretaría de Educación Pública.

————. 1924. "The Sequence of Culture in Mexico." *American Anthropologist* 26, 3: 307–322.

————. 1926. "The Indian Basis of Mexican Civilization." *Aspects of Mexican Civilizations.* Chicago: University of Chicago Press.

————. 1931. *Mexican Immigration to the United States: A Study of Human Migration and Adjustment.* Chicago: University of Chicago Press.

————. 1937. *De vidas dolientes* (From Pained Lives: Collection of Novels). Mexico City: Ediciones Botas.

————. 1945. "Considerations of Indianists Policy." In *The Science of Man in the World Crisis.* Ed. Ralph Linton. New York: Columbia University Press.

————. 1946. "La arqueología y el estudio de la cultura indígena actual." In *México Prehispánico,* pp. 847–851. Mexico: Editorial Hurtado.

————. 1952. "Informe sobre el proyecto que la UNESCO y el Instituto Indigenista Interamericano Desarrollan en el Valle del Mezquital." *Boletín Indigenista* 12: 6–18.

Secondary

Acosta, Jorge R. 1945. "La cuarta y quinta temporadas de excavaciones en Tula, Hgo. 1943–1944." *Revista mexicana de estudios antropológicos* 7: 23–64.

Armillas, Pedro. 1950. "Teotihuacan, Tula y los toltecas: Las culturas post-arcaicas y pre-aztecas del Centro de México: Excavaciones y estudios 1922–1950." *Runa* (Buenos Aires) 3: 37–70.

Bernal, Ignacio. 1979. *Historia de la arqueología en México.* Mexico: Porrúa.

Boas, Franz. 1911–1912. *Album de colecciones arqueológicas.* Mexico: Publicaciones de la Escuela Internacional de Arqueología y Etnología.

Comas, Juan. 1974. "Manuel Gamio en la antropología mexicana." *América indígena* 34, 4.

Cummings, Byron. 1933. *Cuicuilco and the Archaic Culture of Mexico.* Tucson: University of Arizona.

Goldschmidt, W., ed. 1959. *The Anthropology of Franz Boas.* Memoir 89. Menasha, WI: American Anthropological Association.

Gonzalez Gamio, Angeles. 1987. *Manuel Gamio: Una lucha sin final.* Mexico: UNAM.

Jimenez Moreno, Wigberto. 1941. "Tula y los Toltecas según las fuentes históricas." *Revista mexicana de estudios antropológicos* 5: 79–83.

Kroeber, Alfred L. 1925. "Archaic Culture Horizons in the Valley of Mexico." *University of California Publications in American Archaeology and Ethnology* 17: 373–408.

Leon Portilla, Miguel. 1960. "Algunas ideas fundamentales del Dr. Manuel Gamio." *América indígena* 20, 4.

Marquina, Ignacio. 1994. *Memorias*. Instituto Nacional de Antropología e Historia. Mexico City: Colección Biblioteca.

Matos Moctezuma, Eduardo. 1972. "Introducción." In *Manuel Gamio: Arqueología e indigenismo*. Ed. Eduardo Matos Moctezuma. SEP/Setentas, 24. Mexico City.

———. 1983. "Manuel Gamio." In *La población del Valle de Teotihuacan*, 1:vii-xxiv. Ed. Manuel Gamio. Mexico: Instituto Nacional Indigenista.

Rivermar Perez, Leticia. 1987. "En el marasmo de una rebelión cataclísmica." In *La antropología en México: Panorama histórico*. Ed. Carlos Garcia Mora. 2: 91–131. Mexico City: Instituto Nacional de Antropología e Historia.

Sanders, William T. 1965. *The Cultural Ecology of the Teotihuacan Valley*. University Park: Pennsylvania State University.

Seler, Eduard. 1915. "Die Teotihuacan-Kultur des Hochlands von Mexico." In *Gesammelte Abhandlungen zur amerikanischen Sprach- und Alterhumskunde*. Ed. Eduard Seler. 5: 405–585. Berlin.

Tozzer, Alfred M. 1921. "Excavations of a Site at Santiago Ahuitzotla, D.F., Mexico." *Bureau of American Ethnology* 74. Washington, DC.

Trigger, Bruce G. 1989. *A History of Archaeological Thought*. New York: Cambridge University Press.

Vaillant, George C. 1938. "A Correlation of Archaeological and Historical Sequences in the Valley of Mexico." *American Anthropologist* 40: 535–573.

Willey, Gordon R., and Jeremy A. Sabloff. 1974. *A History of American Archaeology*. London: Thames and Hudson.

H. T. Waterbolk

Albert Egges van Giffen   1884–1973

Best known for his skill as an excavator and the enormous quantity and wide chronological range of his excavations, Albert van Giffen accorded structure, periodization, and environmental data priority over archaeological finds at his excavations. A biologist before he became an archaeologist, van Giffen integrated natural science disciplines into archaeology.

> *Die Tatsachen bleiben, die Interpretation Schwankt.*
> —Albert Egges van Giffen, 1913

> *The antiquarian side of archaeology is antiquated, the empirical has replaced it.*
> —Albert Egges van Giffen, 1918

> *We shall only begin to understand the important cultures of the Pontic steppes, when van Giffen's methods are employed there.*
> —V. Gordon Childe, 1937

Internationally, the Dutch archaeologist Albert Egges van Giffen is best known for his skill as an excavator. Although his name is now connected only with the elegant "quadrant method" for the excavation of prehistoric barrows, one should not underestimate his influence on his fellow prehistorians during the 1920s and 1930s. In the archaeology of northwestern Europe, the excavations of the *terp* (dwelling mound) of Ezinge with its well-preserved houses and distinct succession of village plans, the barrows and urnfields of Harenermolen, Zeijen, Wessinghuizen, Vledder, and Laudermarke with their variety of peripheral structures, the megalithic tomb of Havelte, and the settlements of Fochteloo and Zeijen with their clear house plans and fences—all are classic for the novelty of the evidence and the clarity of documentation in drawings and photographs. In the late 1940s provincial-Roman archaeologists marveled at van Giffen's unraveling of the six wooden building phases of the *castellum* at Valkenburg on the Rhine. Medieval archaeologists appreciated his work on the famous Cistercian abbey of Aduard and the St. Walburg chapel in his home town of Groningen.

Van Giffen was a biologist by training, and his success as an excavator is explained by the rigorous application of biological methods. From courses in comparative plant anatomy he had learned that systematic combinations of horizontal, vertical, radial, or tangential sections must necessarily reveal the inner structure of the object under analysis. Earlier archaeologists had cleaned profiles for studying stratigraphy, and some

Albert Egges van Giffen. (Institute of Prehistory and Protohistory, University of Amsterdam, no. 84-682-P8)

had just begun to open up large areas for horizontal inspection of soil traces, but the deliberate and systematic combination of different sections was new. Van Giffen could therefore discover much more about the find circumstances, or what he called the "accompanying phenomena." Especially in his early work, the structure, periodization, and environmental data had priority over the archaeological artifacts. He even went so far as to say that the burial ritual, as evidenced by grave form and peripheral structure, would be more important for synthetic studies than the grave goods. When he did treat finds, he described and arranged them as if they were biological objects.

Van Giffen specialized in coastal geology and archaeozoology, but he always sought the expertise of paleobotanists, soil scientists, physical anthropologists, and chemists. His multidisciplinary approach to archaeology has served widely as a model and is a second major reason for his international renown. In his analytical descriptive methods and his ambition to produce high-quality, verified data, there is still discernible the mindset of a biologist trained in the early decades of this century. It was this attitude that distinguished van Giffen from his archaeological contemporaries.

On the national scene van Giffen's contributions were of paramount importance. He founded university institutes at Groningen (the Biological-Archaeological Institute, 1920) and Amsterdam (the Institute for Pre- and Protohistory, 1950). In 1947 he became the first head of the State Service for Archaeological Research. He was responsible for the archaeological collections of the provincial museums at Assen (1916–1954) and at Groningen (1917–1955), and he set high standards for the description and inventory of museum objects. At his Groningen institute he built up a large study collection. From 1929 to 1973 he was responsible for the protective governmental acquisition, maintenance, and restoration of megalithic tombs in the Netherlands. The quantity and chronological range of his excavations has ensured that his scientific legacy continues to play a major role in Dutch archaeology.

Van Giffen was born on 14 March 1884 in the village of Noordhorn, province of Groningen, where his father was a Protestant minister. As his father often changed parishes, mostly in the three northern provinces, young van Giffen got acquainted with the landscape, people, and regional languages of the area. He went to high school at Sneek and

Zutphen and enrolled in 1904 at the University of Groningen. His choice of biology over the theology of his father and grandfather might have arisen from an urge to be different and to follow his own path. Like many biology students of his day, van Giffen saw his future in one of the overseas research institutes in the Netherlands East Indies (now Indonesia). Archaeology came his way by accident.

His background would make van Giffen a typical "northerner," a stereotype that in the rest of the Netherlands stood for thoroughness, introversion, provincialism, and an unmistakable accent. However, van Giffen combined great personal charm with a strong will, a tireless capacity for work, an inventiveness in obtaining personal and financial support, and a perseverance in striving after his set goals, whether in scientific or organizational matters. Very few people could resist him.

Dutch Archaeology before van Giffen

Throughout the nineteenth century, national archaeology in the Netherlands was very much a Leiden affair. The city's dominance flowed from the foundation of the state Museum of Antiquities there in 1818 and the appointment of C. J. C. Reuvens as its first director and as professor of archaeology (Brongers 1976). Reuvens made a good start in developing Egyptian, classical, and Dutch archaeology. After his early death in 1835, the professorship was not continued. His successors as the museum director were either Egyptologists or classicists. At the beginning of the twentieth century, the museum was in the hands of A. E. J. Holwerda (1905–1919), and his son J. H. Holwerda (curator 1904–1919, director 1919–1939). Both had a background in classics. The later Holwerda had seen Carl Schurchhardt's excavations at Haltern and consequently had learned there to open up large areas and to recognize postholes. He brought new activity into the field of Dutch archaeology, and he was to play a dramatic role in van Giffen's career.

In the northern provinces, various circumstances had in the nineteenth century led to a considerable interest in archaeology (Waterbolk 1970). In Friesland the Frisians realized their antiquity as a people and began to study their language and archaeology. The *Fries Genootschap* [Frisian Society] was founded in 1827. The famous paper *Om nordiske oldsager og deres opbevaring* by the great Danish geologist and archaeologist C. J. Thomsen was translated in 1846 into Dutch to serve as a guide for collecting the remains of the glorious Frisian past. These remains came to light in quantity, for the earth of the *terps* in the coastal marshes was systematically dug away and used as fertilizer on the sterile peats and sands in the hinterland. In the province of Groningen, which many centuries ago had lost its Frisian language, the interest in archaeology had another source: the memories of the great storm floods of 1825. How old were the *terps,* and what could they say about living conditions in the past? In the uplands of Drenthe with its many *hunebedden* (megalithic tombs), barrows, and *legerplaatsen* (Celtic fields), the distant past had been a focus of interest ever since Johannes Picardt wrote his popular book *Antiquiteten* in 1660. In the course of the nineteenth century, the heathlands of Drenthe became private property, and large-scale plowing began, with the result that here, too, many antiquities were uncovered. Cabinets of Antiquities were founded in the provincial capital towns Leeuwarden (1855), Groningen (1846), and Assen (1855). The present provincial museums are their successors.

In Groningen a decisive move was made in 1906 by J. M. van Bemmelen (1830–1911), a retired professor of chemistry in Leiden who had been a school director in Groningen (E. H. Waterbolk 1969). His interest in the chemical properties of *terp* earth led him to write a summary review of the state of knowledge of the *terps.* Seeking comments, he sent a preprint of his paper to various specialists in the northern and western Netherlands, including J. H. Holwerda. Published in 1908, the paper concluded that a systematic *terp* excavation was urgently needed, before all *terps* had disappeared. As Holwerda did not feel ready to undertake such a project, a committee of learned people at and around the University of Groningen took over the initiative. Money was raised to employ a student to supervise the commercial digging going on at that time at Dorkwerd, a few miles from the town. In view of the importance of the geological aspects of *terp* research—there had been flooding in northwest Germany in 1905 and 1906—the committee's first choice was a student of geology. As this person was not available, they turned to the biology student van Giffen, who accepted immediately. Van Bemmelen invited him for a stay in his home in Leiden and brought him into contact with his advisers, including J. H. Holwerda.

The First Groningen Period (1908–1911)
Van Giffen started to work with incredible energy. He did not restrict himself to Dorkwerd but, to the astonishment of the committee, inspected all the *terps* at which there was commercial digging, both in Friesland and in Groningen. By accident he met the German geologist Heinrich Schütte, and together they visited the "living" dwelling mounds on the Halligen islands off the coast of Schleswig-Holstein. He studied *terp* sections, identified and leveled the subsoil, and collected archaeological and faunal remains. In 1910 he earned his master's degree and became assistant at the zoological laboratory.

His first published paper (van Giffen 1910) was devoted to the problem of sea-level changes. From observations on the base level of archaeologically dated *terps,* he concluded that the subsidence was much less than some German geologists, including Schütte, supposed. The topic was highly sensitive, for the German government had formally asked the opinion of the Dutch government. However, van Bemmelen, a member of the ad hoc committee set up by the Royal Netherlands Academy, incorporated van Giffen's results in his contribution, and that settled the matter. As early as 1910, the Holwerdas offered van Giffen a post in Leiden. On 1 January 1912, he was officially appointed as a keeper at the National Museum of Antiquities. He married Geertruida Klaziena Homan and settled at Oegstgeest near Leiden.

The Leiden Period (1912–1916/1917)

Soon after van Giffen's arrival in Leiden, many difficulties arose between him and the Holwerdas. Van Giffen had taken part in the Arentsburg excavations near the Hague in 1911, and he disagreed with the way his data had been altered to fit J. H. Holwerda's previous observations, a practice he regarded as pure fraud. Van Giffen also did not get the technical and financial support he had expected, and he was afraid that the younger Holwerda would succeed his father as director of the museum. On the other side, the elder Holwerda believed that van Giffen spent too much time on a "natural science" dissertation. He also felt that although van Giffen was not without talent, he lacked sufficient background in archaeology to justify his appointment to a permanent position at the museum.

Van Giffen pursued his rights to such a position with great vigor. When the university authorities did not give him complete satisfaction, he took his case directly to the responsible cabinet minister. Not until 1916 was a compromise reached. Van Giffen's complaints were formally rejected, but the budget of the zoological laboratory of the University of Groningen was expanded to allow the appointment of a permanent position as a keeper. Van Giffen left Leiden to return to field archaeology, since he had been requested by the Vereeniging voor Terpenonderzoek [Society for *Terp* Research] to excavate the *terp* of Wierhuizen, purchased by a sponsor for that purpose. The board of the society included members of the old Groningen committee, van Bemmelen's regional advisers, and a few regional members of the national parliament.

The Leiden period was not an entirely negative experience for van Giffen. He observed Holwerda's excavation of the Drouwen megalithic tombs, and on the museum's behalf, he excavated and published the Neolithic trackway of Buinen (van Giffen 1913), which posed the complexities of peat stratigraphy. He finished and defended his thesis *Die Fauna der Wurten* (van Giffen 1913). His projected second thesis on domestic animals never appeared, but he remained particularly fascinated with the problem of the philogeny of the domestic dog and, in a later publication, applied sophisticated statistical methods derived from genetics to canine bone measurements (van Giffen 1929). Van Giffen's program was already evident in the title of a public lecture in 1915: "Archaeology and Natural Science." It was during his time in Leiden that van Giffen conceived his ideas on the organization of archaeology in the Netherlands, which came to be realized after World War II.

Holwerda succeeded his father in 1919. He was successful as a museum man and as the author of semipopular books on archaeology. But his interpretations were not at the level of his international colleagues, and as an excavator van Giffen was far superior.

Toward Independence (1917–1922)

Van Giffen's formal appointment in Groningen started on 1 July 1917, when he was given full freedom to act, and the Groningen museum appointed him as an inspector of the department of prehistory and early history (1917). In Drenthe he became keeper of the prehistoric department of the museum (1916), and the *Drentsch Prehistorische Vereeniging* [Prehistoric Society of Drenthe] was reorganized so that it could fulfill the same role in Drenthe as the *terp* societies did in Friesland and Groningen. Van Giffen found a number of private sponsors among the well-to-do people of the region. In 1919 he received a formal request from the national government to report on the state of megalithic tombs. Since up to that time megaliths had been a Leiden subject, the request had very clear implications. In 1920 the university gave him a budget of his own, some personnel and a building—a former post office, which opened officially in 1922 (van Giffen 1922). He then began a period of intense excavation activity.

The excavations at Wierhuizen (1916, 1917) were not too successful. Van Giffen found the remains of wooden buildings at the base of the *terp*, but he was not yet able to interpret them correctly. However, the Godlinze *terp* (1919) revealed an interesting early-medieval cemetery (van Giffen 1920). In 1921 van Giffen began excavating the Frisian *terp* of Hatsum, which had yielded early Roman pottery and roof tiles. He continued his *terp* inspection tours but soon concentrated his excavation efforts on a new field of research in the sandy hinterland of the *terps* in Drenthe and in the Gorecht and Westerwolde parts of Groningen. In 1918 he excavated megalithic tombs at Havelte, Emmen, Bronneger, Exloo, and Valthe. Destroyed megaliths were the focus of attention at Valthe (1920) and Rijs (1922). In 1917, at the Zeijen barrows, van Giffen applied the quadrant method for the first time, followed by Eext

(1918), Zeijen again (1919), Weerdinge (1920), Annertol (1921), and Harenermolen (1921). The barrow of Harenermolen with its multiple peripheral structures was excavated according to the sector method (van Giffen 1924). At the urnfield of Wollinghuizen (1920), he discovered ring ditches surrounding the burials (van Giffen 1920). He also started the exploration of the *legerplaats* of Zeijen (1917) but did not yet recognize it as a Celtic field.

He also found time for more general publications. Van Giffen revised his views on the sea-level changes in a paper published by the National Society for Geology and Mining (van Giffen 1921). He summarized his *terp* research (van Giffen 1920) and initiated three series of regular excavation reports: the *Jaarverslagen* [Annual Reports] of the Vereeniging voor Terpenonderzoek (JVT), the Nieuwe Drentsche Volksalmanak (NDV), and in the Groningen museum (JGM).

By 1922 this series of excavations and publications had brought him national and international renown. Van Giffen had also built up and trained a staff of a foreman (J. Lanting), a draftsman (L. Postema), and an administrator-photographer (J. Dijkstra), all very capable and prepared to work just as hard as he was. At his excavations during the First World War he was also assisted by two Belgian internees.

Achievement and Recognition (1922–1934)

In the *terp* area, van Giffen decided to concentrate on Ezinge, where he succeeded in unraveling its true nature and history. At that time no one outside the Mediterranean world had presented a succession of house and settlement plans at one site. The excellent preservation conditions in the dung lagers of the Ezinge *terp* furnished a wealth of economic and environmental data, comparable to what the lake dwellings of Switzerland had yielded to archaeologists during the nineteenth century. A key element in his analysis was the discovery in 1930 of the principle of the three-aisled long house, a construction not unlike that of the historic farm buildings of Drenthe and lower Saxony. (The same principle had been independently found by the Dane Gudmunt Hatt in Jutland [Hatt 1928].) To distance himself from the commercial diggers, van Giffen had to buy the *terp* and finance the excavation by selling and transporting its earth. The *terp* society helped him with the initial investment, and funding became easier when he was allowed to use the government-paid labor of the unemployed (1932). At one time he had nearly 100 men at work. Visitors from all over the world came to see the excavations.

The plowing up of the heathlands of Drenthe and Westerwolde necessitated further field research there as well. Among the more important excavations were the megaliths of Buinen (1927); the barrows of

Balloo (1933, 1934), Odoorn (1929), Diever (1929), Hijken (1930), and Drouwen (1927); the barrows-cum-urnfields at Wessinghuizen (1927), with their beautiful timber circles and keyhole-shaped peripheral ditches; the urnfields of Wapse (1931), Laudermarke (1932), and Elp (1932); the *legerplaatsen* of Emmen (1927), Sellingen (1930), and Peest (1932); and the early-medieval cemetery of Wijster (1926, 1931) (van Giffen 1932).

At the request of the Frisian Society, van Giffen also excavated in Friesland: *terps* at Hatzum (1922, 1925), monastery of Smalle Ee (1923), and barrows and urnfields near Oosterwolde (1924, 1925, 1928). But in Friesland there was less cooperation with the regional authorities than in Drenthe and Groningen. The curator of the Frisian museum, P. C. J. A. Boeles, a strong-willed and capable man who had been a founding member of the *terp* society, would not let van Giffen roam too freely on his territory. Elsewhere in the Netherlands, van Giffen was active in the province of Overijssel (barrows at Holten and Stegerden, 1930), Gelderland (barrow at Epe, 1928; low mound at Ressen, 1927, 1928), Utrecht (Roman castellum at Utrecht, 1929; barrows at Baarn, 1926, 1927), north Holland (Neolithic settlement at Zandwerven, 1929), and Limburg (Rijckholt flint mines, 1923, 1925; Stein Neolithic settlement, 1930) (van Giffen 1925). Field activities abroad included excavations in Hungary (Bronze Age cemetery at Toszeg, 1923, 1928; Neolithic tell of Bodrogkeresztur, 1921) and Germany (various *terps;* barrows near Cologne, 1926, 1930).

The main results of Ezinge were made known to an international public by preliminary reports in German journals (van Giffen 1934, 1936). The work on the megaliths resulted in a lengthy publication, *De hunebedden van Nederland* (1925–1927), which contained precise drawings and photographs of all monuments, a description of his own excavations, and a review of the work done by earlier authors. The text volume was translated into English. The barrow and urnfield excavations were summarized in *Die Bauart der Einzelgräber* (van Giffen 1930), which is probably van Giffen's best-known book and was very favorably reviewed in all the leading international journals (Brunsting 1947). Along with these two major publications van Giffen continued to publish excavation reports in the JVT, NDV, and JGM series.

More recognition followed the international anthropological congress in 1927, including, in the same year, being made a chevalier in the French Legion d'Honneur. In 1929 he became a corresponding member of the *Deutsches Archäologisches Institut,* was elected in 1933 an honorary fellow of the Society of Antiquaries, and, at home, won a lectureship in prehistory and germanic archaeology (1930), the prize of mastership of

the *Maatschappij der Nederlandsche Letterkunde* [Netherlands Literary Society] (1931), and membership in the Royal Netherlands Academy of Sciences (1932).

Further Expansion (1934–1940)

After finishing Ezinge in 1934, van Giffen turned to other fields of interest: prehistoric settlement sites on the sandy soils, Roman fortresses, and medieval churches, monasteries, fortifications, and brickyards. He had come across such objects only in the course of his other activities, but now they became his major concern. Van Giffen excavated his first Iron Age three-aisled house on the sandy soil at Diphoorn (1934). Other such houses, complete with fences and palisades, were found at Zeijen (1934), Rhee (1935–1937), Fochteloo (1938, 1940), and Sleen (1937) (van Giffen 1958). This field of research would prove to be very fruitful in later years. Unfortunately, the increasing size and quantity of the excavations often meant a decrease in the time and attention available to van Giffen for the detailed recording of the field data. At some excavations only drawings on a large scale—1:100—were made. Roman *castella* were excavated at Utrecht (1936, 1938) and Cuyk (1937, 1938), churches at Bedum (1934) and Vriescheloo (1939, 1940), monasteries at Aduard (1939–1941), Klaarkamp (1940, 1941), and Rinsumageest (1939, 1940), town fortifications at Groningen (1934–1940), and brick-ovens at Erm (1938) (van Giffen 1968). Of his other excavations in Drenthe, mention should be made of the urnfield of Vledder (1937), a barrow and urnfield at Gasteren (1939), a trackway at Valthe (1936), and Neolithic flat-grave cemeteries at Sleen and Zuidwolde (1935).

The crowded excavation program continued unabated both at home and abroad: in Gelderland (barrows at Garderen, Millingen, Bennekom, 1935; Hoogsoeren, 1936) and Noord-Brabant (barrows at Hooge Mierde, 1934; Goirle, 1935; urnfield at Best, 1933, 1934). He went to Brittany to excavate a gallery grave at Kergunteuil (1939) and an early Bronze Age tumulus with rich grave finds at Lannion (1939) (Butler and Waterbolk 1974), and to Ireland to excavate a passage grave at Ballinoe (1937, 1938) (Groenman-Van Waateringe and Butler 1976). A major contribution to *terp* research was his excavation of an early-medieval *terp* at Leens (1939), where the houses were three-aisled as at Ezinge, but the walls were made of heavy layers of clay sods (van Giffen 1940).

Published papers included reports on the Vledder and Sleen urnfields in the German journal *Mannus* (van Giffen 1938) and a study on continental bell and disc barrows in the *Proceedings of the Prehistoric Society* (van Giffen 1938). From 1934 onward van Giffen had a special section of the NDV at his disposal for publishing short reports on his excavations in Drenthe. It is here that we find his reports on the settlement excavations at Zeijen and Rhee. He continued to publish in the JVT and the JGM.

Though van Giffen himself found little time to devote to the geological and biological aspects of archaeology, he made it a high priority to have specialists work for him. During his Ezinge studies, he had sought the paleobotanical expertise of Dr. W. Beijerinck, and his reports on the diatoms, seeds, and other plant remains of the *terp* proved the brackish character of the Ezinge environment (Beijerinck 1929). However, their cooperation was short-lived, so he enlisted the geologist M. M. Broekema to do some pollen investigations on the trackway at Valthe (1936) and the barrow at Odoorn (1937). Van Giffen was fascinated by the new perspectives that pollen analysis offered, as demonstrated by the work of Bertsch and Reinerth in the Federsee area in south Germany (Reinerth 1929, Bertsch 1931). Van Giffen also utilized the anatomy laboratory for work on human cremations and the Agricultural Research Station in Groningen for pedochemical analysis.

Van Giffen was now able to employ junior archaeologists to assist him, though often only on an unpaid and temporary basis. A number of these volunteers made their on mark in the profession, such as W. J. A. Willems, who wrote a doctoral dissertation on the pre-Roman urnfields in the southern part of the country (Willems 1935). Van Giffen's word was always law, so cooperation with him was not easy. In van Giffen's private life a major change took place. After nearly twenty-five years of marriage, he divorced his wife, Geertruida, and in 1938 he wed Guda Duyvis, a woman with private means who was self-educated in Mesoamerican archaeology.

The international honors kept coming. In 1936 van Giffen became an honorary member of the Society of Antiquaries of Scotland, and in 1938 he received an honorary degree from the University of Cologne. In 1939 his lectureship was turned into an extraordinary professorship.

War and Restoration (1940–1946)

When J. H. Holwerda retired as director of the Museum of Antiquities in 1939, the government decided to use the opportunity to end the Leiden-Groningen controversy. In 1940, a state commission was set up and included both van Giffen and Holwerda's successor, the Egyptologist Dr. W. D. van Wijngaarden. A Bureau for Archaeological Investigations was also established, located at Leiden and charged with the task of documenting archaeological monuments so that they could be listed for protection in new monuments legislation. The Leiden prehistorian Dr. F. C. J. Bursch became head of the bureau, and he tried to build up a state excavation service that was independent from the existing museums and university institutes. However, because he collaborated with the Germans, his appointment was terminated after the war.

The difficult economic conditions in the Netherlands immediately following the Second World War provided strong arguments for the establishment of a central institution, and on 1 January 1947, the Rijksdienst voor het Oudheidkundig Bodemonderzoek (ROB) [State Service for Archaeological Research] came into being (Van Es 1972). Many disparate elements came under its purview: the excavation departments of the Leiden and Nijmegen state museums, the excavation department of the State Service for Monuments Care, the remnants of Bursch's bureau, and the Biological-Archaeological Institute (BAI), which van Giffen had assumed charge of in 1941 (Reinders 1986). Van Giffen became the ROB's first head, combining this function with his Groningen professorship and his extraordinary professorship at Amsterdam. After thirty years, van Giffen's Leiden dreams of a centralized and professional archaeological service had come true.

Excavations continued during the war years. In 1940, the village of Valkenburg suffered damage from the war, and it opened the possibility of an excavation in the Roman *castellum* that van Giffen had discovered in 1914. In the years 1941–1943 and 1946–1952, van Giffen succeeded in unraveling the six wooden building phases that preceded the stone castellum. In Drenthe the German invaders started to build air strips on remaining stretches of heathland at Havelte (1943) and Zeijen (1944). In both areas van Giffen got permission to undertake rescue excavations of barrows. In the low-lying Holocene area of west Friesland (near Werver-shoof in the north of the province of Noord-Holland), van Giffen was asked in 1942 to excavate a series of Bronze Age barrows. These fascinated him because of the clear traces of plowing in their subsoil and because of the geological problems they presented: though lying below sea level, they were not covered by later sediments. His report, published in 1944, also explored general issues of prehistoric agriculture. Other wartime ex-cavations included a Roman bath at Heerlen (1941), a Hamburgian site at Gasselte (1942), an urnfield at Wedde (1942, 1943), a barrow with urn-field fragment at Erica (1944), and a bell-beaker barrow at Een (1944).

During this period, van Giffen published an important summary of his excavations in Drenthe (van Giffen 1943), a typology of peripheral urnfield structures (1941), and distribution maps of urnfields and Celtic fields in Drenthe (1941). Of special interest is his contribution to a sym-posium in 1941, in which he argued that Bronze Age barrows were built on a heather podzol (soil) profile, while Neolithic barrows were covered by such a profile. He concluded that there must have been an important environmental change, resulting in an expansion of heathlands.

Van Giffen continued to train significant numbers of students in the business of excavation and materials analysis. After the death of Postema (1940), H. Praamstra turned out to be a very capable successor. At Valken-burg R. Woudstra did most of the drawing. During the war Dr. H. Brunst-ing, a classical archaeologist by training, assisted van Giffen in Groningen. In the Zuider Zee polders P. J. R. Modderman was his assistant (1941–1945). He defended a doctoral thesis on his work in 1945 (Mod-derman 1945). Van Giffen managed to employ four student assistants in Groningen: T. H. van Andel (pollen analysis), H. Halbertsma *(terps)*, W. Glasbergen (Roman pottery), J. C. Gerritsen (Roman coins). I joined the team after the war as a successor to Van Andel, who left to finish his study in geology. Brunsting moved in 1945 to the Leiden museum. Finally, men-tion should be made of Dr. J. C. A. Böhmers, a specialist in paleontology and Paleolithic archaeology who had worked for the German occupying forces in Bohemia and Moravia and had in 1943 been forced upon the Uni-versity of Groningen by the German authorities. After a short period of in-ternment after the war, he was allowed to stay on at the institute.

The ROB Period (1947–1950)

Early in 1947 van Giffen held his ROB inaugural lecture in Amsterdam (van Giffen 1947). Later that year, the twenty-fifth anniversary of the opening of the Biological-Archaeological Institute (BAI) gave his friends, col-leagues, and students an opportunity to compile a Festschrift (Van Gelder et al. 1947). The twenty-eight contributions illustrated the newly achieved union of Dutch archaeology through the ROB and its cooperation with the natural sciences. Unfortunately, this harmony was not to last very long.

At first the ROB was based in the Hague, but in 1949 it moved to Amersfoort. As van Giffen stayed in Groningen, the daily affairs were in the hands of the deputy director Dr. P. Glazema, who came from the archaeological section of the old State Service for Monuments Care and had excavated many war-damaged churches in the southern part of the country. From the same service came J. G. N. Renaud, a specialist in castles and fortifications. In practice, documentation records of the site details and medieval archaeology were centered in Amersfoort, while the work on the older periods was directed by van Giffen in Groningen.

This division of labor was incompatible with the concept of an unified, integrated archaeological service, and it soon generated difficulties between van Giffen and Glazema, who had the support of the ministry. As head of the ROB, van Giffen was due to retire in March 1949. As a university professor, however, he had five years to go before mandatory retirement. Against his wishes, the ministry continued van Giffen's mandate only until 1 January 1950. It then issued a decree that specified the responsibilities of the various institutions, services, and museums and gave the ROB the task to carry out excavations to the exclusion of other groups, including the BAI. The BAI now became the central institution for the conservation and study of biological and anthropological materials, and Glazema was made its director (Van Es 1972).

During this commotion, the fieldwork continued. Van Giffen could not personally follow all the work in detail, but by short visits, telephone conversations, and reports, he kept track of the developments. In this period, he supervised the excavation of a large number of Bronze Age barrows in Noord-Brabant, barrows at Schaarsbergen (Gelderland province, 1947, 1948), the abbey churches of Egmond (Noord-Holland 1947) and Rijnsburg (Zuid-Holland 1949), and the early-medieval cemetery of Wageningen (Gelderland 1949). He spent a great deal of time at the excavation and publication of the Roman fortresses at Valkenburg, Utrecht, and Vechten (van Giffen 1948, 1950, 1955). The Bronze Age habitation in the low-lying areas of west Friesland (excavations at Grootebroek 1949) continued to puzzle him, and he sought expertise wherever he could.

The Groningen-Amsterdam Period (1950–1954/1956)

Van Giffen was not a man to quit after being forced to retire from the ROB. It was hard for him to see some of his former associates now working in what had become the enemy camp. After the Leiden-Groningen controversy of the 1920s and 1930s, there was now an even worse Amersfoort-Groningen struggle, and it was hard on all involved.

Working with those who had chosen to stay with him in Groningen, van Giffen continued to excavate where he could, ignoring the government decree of 1950 and relying (as in his younger years) on the support of regional museums and societies and his old university. These groups had not appreciated the centralizing maneuvers of the preceding years. At the University of Amsterdam, he had many supporters, and in 1950 he was able to establish a small society, the Institute for Pre- and Protohistory (IPP) (Glasbergen 1966). With his Amsterdam assistant J. D. van der Waals, he started excavations in and near the town of Amsterdam (1952, 1954, 1955) and continued excavations in west Friesland (1953).

In his home area in the north, van Giffen excavated early-medieval cemeteries at Aalden (1950) and Zweeloo (1952) (with a very rich "princess" grave, that is, the grave of an important female), an Iron Age barrow cemetery at Wijster (1952), a Neolithic/Bronze Age barrow field at Hijken (1952–1954), and Bronze Age barrows at Oudemolen (1950). Once more he achieved the spectacular: his excavation of the polygonal foundations of the St. Walburg chapel in the very center of the town of Groningen (1950, 1951). Van Giffen published summaries of his work on the Roman fortresses (van Giffen 1950) and on pre- and protohistoric houses (1954). In 1951 he founded a new journal, *Palaeohistoria,* which would become the main organ for the BAI. In 1950 van Giffen received the gold medal of the Society of Antiquaries.

As the first rumors of a new dating method based on radiocarbon reached the Netherlands, van Giffen urged a colleague, the biophysicist Hessel de Vries, to build a counting apparatus. In the years 1950–1951, 10 percent of the budget of the BAI was spent on buying materials for the physics laboratory (Waterbolk 1983). De Vries was at first reluctant, but he, too, could not resist van Giffen, and he soon became fascinated by the project. His method of gas counting replaced Willard Libby's original solid-carbon method of dating. Wood from a post under the St. Walburg church became one of the first international interlaboratory check samples.

In 1954 W. Glasbergen defended his thesis "Barrow Excavations in the Eight Beatitudes." In the same year I received my Ph.D. for a pollen analytical study, "Prehistoric Man and His Environment," and I became van Giffen's successor at Groningen. In Amsterdam van Giffen was twice reappointed for a year, before Glasbergen replaced him. At the museums of Assen and Groningen, van Giffen's activities ended in 1954 and 1955, respectively.

After Retirement (1954/1956–1973)

In 1955 van Giffen, who had been in charge of megalithic tombs in state care since 1929, was appointed "state adviser for the protection and maintenance of megalithic tombs and restored archaeological monuments." Although it was meant to be an honorary position, van Giffen soon made it a full-time job. He managed to find some personnel (including one of his retired foremen) and continued restoring all the Dutch megaliths, with small-scale excavations wherever he could find an excuse. He had much success with the building of an "instructive" megalithic tomb at Schoonoord, which was on the site of a largely destroyed true megalith and used the stones of another, partly destroyed megalith at Valthe (1959). He also restored some seventeenth-century earthen forts and, shortly before his death, a small part of the Zeijen Celtic field, which had been destroyed in 1944.

For the *terp* society van Giffen conducted some small-scale reconnaissance excavations in the Westergo part of Friesland (1954–1960). The archaeological remains from that area had seemed to differ from those in Groningen, and even during his Leiden period he had wanted to excavate the *terp* of Hichtum. But he did not finish his final report on Ezinge, as many had hoped he would.

In Groningen he completed his excavations of the St. Walburg church (1956, 1957) and wrote, together with H. Praamstra, a large report on it (van Giffen 1973) as well as summary papers on all their observations on the fortifications around the town of Groningen (van Giffen and Praamstra 1962, 1966). A preliminary paper on the Abbey of Aduard appeared in the *Bonner Jahrbücher* (1968).

Van Giffen moved to Zwolle, and after a relatively short illness, he died there in his ninetieth year on 31 May 1973.

Van Giffen's Professional Community

In his early work on coastal geology, Henrich Schütte was van Giffen's main teacher (van Giffen 1964). Though they disagreed in many respects and were separated by twenty years, they became friends. Schütte corrected the proofs of van Giffen's dissertation. In his zoological work, van Giffen was inspired by the much earlier studies of the Swiss archaeologist Rütimeyer (1862) on the fauna of the Swiss lake dwellings. He, too, believed that the comparative study of domestic animals might contribute to the solution of paleoethnological problems such as the origin of the Indo-Germans (van Giffen 1929). In his papers on the Neolithic and Bronze Age, he tried to find correlations between cultural phenomena and the skull types that had been defined by the physical anthropologists of his day, such as Bolk (1908). Unfortunately, excavations in the sandy soil produced at best silhouettes of a decayed body, so van Giffen could not contribute to the international discussion on this subject.

As a *terp* excavator, van Giffen had no mentors: he himself became the major authority. He was greatly admired by W. Haarnagel (Haarnagel 1974) and A. Bantelmann, and after World War II they took the lead in *terp* research in lower Saxony and Schleswig-Holstein, respectively. As a barrow excavator, he was far superior to his colleagues, even those in Denmark, as indicated by a comparison with the work of Peter V. Glob, who popularized the archaeological conclusions about the Danish bog bodies of Tollund and Granballe in his books *The Bog People* and *The Mound People*. Among those who admired van Giffen both for his skill as an excavator and his efforts to integrate natural-science disciplines into archaeology was Cambridge professor GRAHAME CLARK, who in 1930 had pioneered the cooperation of archaeology and pollen analysis in the fenlands together with H. Godwin (Clark 1939). For the periodization and interpretation of the megalithic tombs, barrows, and Celtic fields, Scandinavia was a source of inspiration. While Holwerda denied the existence of a separate Bronze Age in the Netherlands, van Giffen accepted the three-period system and applied the typology of OsCAR MONTELIUS to Dutch bronze artifacts. Megalithic tombs and their contents had their closest parallels in northern Germany, where Ernst Sprockhoff's megaliths studies were highly relevant to the classification of the Bronze Age in the Netherlands (Sprockhoff 1928).

For his timber circles, however, van Giffen had to look westward, to the henge monuments of Great Britain. V. GORDON CHILDE came in 1928 expressly to see the Bronze Age timber circles (van Giffen 1960). Some barrows with ditch and bank had their best parallels in Britain in the barrows and henge monuments at Avebury. Again other regions seemed to be responsible for the introduction of other phenomena: the early bell beakers from western Europe (Brittany), the Veluwe beakers and the linear pottery from central Europe, and other beaker forms from the northern lowland of Germany. Van Giffen repeatedly described the Netherlands as a peripheral, intermediate, and transit area for the main currents in European prehistory, which he illustrated in an often-reproduced map of the Netherlands (e.g., van Giffen 1943).

In his search for the origins of this great cultural diversity on Dutch territory, van Giffen had to resort to the international literature. In the library of his institute, he had all the major British, French, German, Austrian, and Danish journals. However, the very nature of the archaeological record in the northern Netherlands led him to look primarily to archaeological developments in Germany. As early as 1922 he had become close friends with Dr. K. H. Jacob-Friesen of Hanover, who actively took part in the excavations at Rijs (a destroyed megalith) and Hatsum (a *terp*), both in Friesland. Jacob-Friesen corrected the proofs of *Die Bauart der Einzelgräber* (van Giffen 1930). Van Giffen often used Jacob-Friesen's

1928 book *Grundfragen der Urgeschichtsforschung* (see van Giffen 1938). That van Giffen was strongly influenced by German archaeological thinking was particularly evident in the foreword to *Bauart*—which he dedicates *"verehrungsvoll Herrn Geheimrat C. Kossinna"*: "Erst wenn man die typischen Gräbercharaktere verschiedenen Stämmen und Völkern . . . zuschreibt, erst dann lernt man die Differenzen nach Bau und Inhalt . . . verstehen und würdigen." Soon, however, van Giffen seemed to sense that he was on dangerous ground. Invited in 1934 to present a paper on the *"Westgermanen"* at the "Zweites Nordisches Thing," he presented his Ezinge data and then wrote: "Diese Merkmale als Völker oder Stammeseigen zu prüfen und zu werten, überlasse ich zunächst der Fachwelt zur Beurteilung." This remark was interesting in view of the fact that the historian I. H. Gosses—van Giffen's Groningen colleague and a leading board member of the *terp* society to which van Giffen reported his research—delivered a slashing critique in 1935 of GUSTAF KOSSINNA's *Ursprung und Verbreitung der Germanen in vor-und frühgeschichtlicher Zeit.*

The problem of ethnic interpretation arose for van Giffen not only in the Neolithic and early Bronze Age. He first thought he could equate the urnfields with the Celts, but many finds pointed to the northeast, and some details of the burial ritual appeared to be of local origin. Van Giffen concluded that the problem could not be solved as long as there was little comparable research done in neighboring countries. He expressed less doubt with regard to Anglo-Saxon immigration, which he saw in the sunken hut settlement in the top layers of Ezinge, in the sporadic occurrence of such huts in the sandy heathland of Drenthe (Rhee, Schipborg), and in some pottery finds in the early-medieval cemeteries (e.g., van Giffen 1943). Unfortunately, a few objects in one of the Ezinge huts led him to a generalization that was contradicted by his own stratigraphic observations. The Anglo-Saxon *Haufensiedlung* appeared to consist of a drawing-room projection of sunken huts from many different levels. In reality, they were outhouses belonging to long houses that in the top layers of the *terp* were badly preserved (Waterbolk 1989a). In this van Giffen was the victim of a working hypothesis that meshed so well with current archaeological thinking that he did not stop to verify it. His interest in the "Saxons" made him a popular member of the Arbeitsgemeinschaft für Sachsenforschung, which was founded shortly after the war by northern German archaeologists and which did much to restore good professional relations among archaeologists all around the North Sea.

In his 1943 summary of his excavations in Drenthe, van Giffen argued that the present population of the area was the result of at least twelve consecutive immigrations. The ethnic identification of the archaeological cultures was for him an axiom from which he could not detach himself. After the war, in his Amsterdam lecture of 1947, van Giffen introduced the concept of the *cultureel streekdiagram* (regional cultural standard diagram). It was modeled after standard pollen diagrams, which summarized the regional vegetational development on the basis of a number of local diagrams, each representing only part of the total sequence. In the same way, van Giffen thought, a series of local archaeological stratigraphies could lead to a complete regional sequence. As a demonstration, he used his many observations near Zeijen in Drenthe. Standard pollen diagrams showed gradual changes without sharp breaks. From these works, it is apparent that van Giffen was leaning toward the idea that habitation continuity and cultural influence could both be established without migrations. However, he never returned to this theme in his later work. Instead, he concentrated on the Roman and medieval periods, not unlike many of his German colleagues in the period after the Second World War, and on the restoration and maintenance of Dutch megaliths.

References

For a complete bibliography see Bierma 1973. For an extended list of obituaries, etc., see Waterbolk 1976 and 1989. For the main dates on van Giffen's education and career see Lanting 1973. A list of his excavations (up to 1947) is published in Van Gelder et al. 1947. There are no specific text references to earlier papers by myself on van Giffen (Waterbolk 1973, 1976, 1989).

Primary

Van Giffen, Albert Egges. 1910. "Het dalingsvraagstuk der Alluviale Noordzeekusten, in verband met bestudeering der terpen." *Tijdschrift voor Geschiedenis, Land en Volkenkunde* 25: 258–294.

———. 1913. "De Buinerbrug en het steenen voetpad aldaar." *Oudheidkundige Mededelingen Rijksmuseum van Oudheden Leiden* 7: 51–90.

———. 1913. *Die Fauna der Wurten 1*. Teil. Proefschrift ter verkrijging van den graad van Doctor in de Plant- en Dierkunde, aan de Rijksuniversiteit te Groningen, op gezag van den Rector-Magnificus Prof. Dr. J. H. Kern, tegen de bedenkingen van de Faculteit der Wis- en Natuurkunde in het openbaar te verdedigen op 20 Juni 1913. Leiden (also publ. as: *Onderzoekingen, verricht in het Zoölogisch Laboratorium der R.U. te Groningen 3; and Tijdschrift der Nederlandsche Dierkundige Vereniging*, 2d s., 13, 1914: 1–167).

———. 1918. "Begin van een onderzoek van 'de zogenaamde voormalige Romeinsche legerplaats' en aangelegen grafheuvelveld te Zeijen." *Nieuwe Drentsche Volksalmanak* 36: 135–175.

———. 1920. "Een Karolingisch grafveld bij Godlinze." *Jaarverslagen Vereeniging voor Terpenonderzoek* 3–4 (1918–1920): 39–96.

———. 1920. "Het in April 1818 ontdekte en in October 1920 teruggevonden urnenveld met 'kringgreptumuli' bij den 'Pottenberg' onder Wollinghuizen, gem. Vlagtwedde." *Verslag Toestand Museum van Oudheden voor Provincie en Stad Groningen*: 33–59.

———. 1920. "Iets over terpen." *Jaarverslagen Vereeniging voor Terpenonderzoek* 3–4 (1918–1920): 7–31.

————. 1921. "Bikdrage tot de kennis van enkele geologisch-archaeologische verkenmerken in verband met het vraagstuk der bodemdaling in historischen tijd." *Verglagen Geologische Sectie Geologisch-Mijnbouwkundig Genootschap* 2 (1915–1919): 159–220.

————. 1922. *Het Biologisch-Archaeologisch Instituut en zijn Taak.* Rede, uitgesproken den 17 den Juni 1992 bij de officieele opening van het Biologisch-Archaeologisch Instituut aan de Rijksuniversiteit te Groningen. Groningen.

————. 1924. "Ein neolithischer Grabhügel mit Holzkonstruktion in Harendermolen, Gem. Haren, Prov. Groningen, Niederland." *Praehistorische Zeitschrift* 15: 52–61.

————. 1925. *De hunebedden in Nederland.* Text. 2 vols. Utrecht. English translation: 1927. *The Hunebeds in the Netherlands.* Part I. Utrecht.

————. 1927. *Atlas:* 2 vols. Utrecht.

————. 1927. "De Zuid-Limburgsche voorhistorische vuursteenindustrie tusschen Ryckholt en St. Geertruid (with an appendix by W.G.N. van der Sleen)." *Tijdschrift Koninklijk Nederlandsch Aardrijkundig Genootschap* 42: 481–507.

————. 1929. "On the Oldest Domesticated Animal and Its Significance for Palethnology." *Proceedings Koninklijke Academie van Wetenschappen* 32: 321–329.

————. 1930. *Die Bauart der Einzelgräber. Beitrag zur Kenntnis der älteren individuellen Grabhügelstrukturen in den Niederlanden.* 2 vols. Mannus-Bibliothek 44–45. Leipzig.

————. 1932. "Een germanaansch tempel of kapelrayon te Looveen bij Wijster, Gem. Beilen?" *Nieuwe Drentsche Volksalmanak* 50: 51–63.

————. 1934. "Ein Beitrag zur Germanenfrage im mittel- und westeuropäischen Grenzgebiete." *Zweites Nordischen Thing: Veröffentlichungen der Väterkunde* 2: 42–52. Bremen.

————. 1936. "Der Warf in Ezinge, Provinz Groningen, Holland, und seine westgermanischen Häuser." *Germania* 20: 20–47 (and in *Jaarverslagen Vereeniging voor Terpenonderzoek* 16–19 [1931–1935]: 1–8).

————. 1938. "Contintental Bell- or Disc-Barrows in Holland, with Special Reference to Tumulus I at Rielsch Hoefke." *Proceedings of the Prehistoric Society* 4: 258–271.

————. 1938. "Das Kreisgraben-Urnenfeld bei Vledder, Provinz Drente, Niederland." *Mannus* 30: 331–384.

————. 1940. "Een systematisch onderzoek in een der Tuinster wierden te Leens (with German summary)." *Jaarverslagen Vereeniging voor Terpenonderzoek* 20–24 (1925–1940): 26–115.

————. 1941. "De tijd van vorming van heidepodsolprofielen aan de hand van archaeologische waarnemingen." *Besprekingen over het Heidepodsolprofiel:* 12–23, gehouden op de bijeenkomst der sectie Nederland van de Intern. Bodemkundige Vereeniging op 18 en 19 April 1941. Groningen.

————. 1943. "Opgravingen in Drente tot 1941." In *Drente, een handboek voor het kennen van het Drentsche leven in voorbije eeuwen,* 391–564. Ed. J. Poortman. Meppel. (2d ed. Meppel, 1944).

————. 1944. "Grafheuvels te Zwaagdijk, gem. Wervershoof (N.H.)

(with an appendix by J. van der Spek)." *West-Friesland's Oud en Nieuw* 17: 121–231. (Reprint improved and augmented).

———. 1947. *Oudheidkundige perspectieven, in het bijzonder ten aanzien van de vaderlandsche prae-en protohistorie.* Rede, uitgesproken naar aanleiding van de aanleiding van het ambt van buitengewoon hoogleeraar aan de Universiteit van Amsterdam op 3 Februari 1947. Groningen (and *Een kwart eeuw oudheidkundig bodemonderzoek in Nederland,* 497–544. Gedenkboek A. E. van Giffen. Meppel).

———. 1948. "De Romeinsche castella in den dorpsheuvel te Valkenburg aan den Rijn (Z.H.) (Praetorium Agrippinae), I: De opgravingen in 1941 (with 14 appendices, among which VIa, Inheemsch aardewerk, by van Griffen)" *Jaarverslagen Vereeniging voor Terpenonderzoek* 25–28 (1940–1941): 1–316.

———. 1948. "Thermen en Castella te Heerlen (L.). Een rapport en een werkhypothese." *L'antiquité classique* 17: 199–236, Miscellanea Philologica, Historica et Archaeologica in honorem Huberti van de Weerd.

———. 1949. "Oudheidkundige aantekeningen over Drentse vondsten (XVI): Het Noordse Veld bij Zeijen, gem. Vries, opgravingen in 1944" (with an appendix by H. T. Waterbolk). *Nieuwe Drentse Volksalmanak* 67: 93–148.

———. 1950. "Inheemse en Romeinse terpen. Opgravingen in de dorpswierde te Ezinge en de Romeinse terpen van Utrecht, Valenburg (Z.H.) en Vechten" (with English summary by J. Gerritsen). *Jaarverslagen Vereniging voor Terpenonderzoek* 29–32 (1944–1948): 1–66.

———. 1951. "Oudheidkundige aantekeningen over Drentse vondsten (XVIII): De havelterberg en omgeving bij Havelte, gem. Havelte. Opgravingen in 1918, 1943, 1944 en 1946" (with collaborators) (with appendixes by H. T. Waterbolk and T. H. van Andel). *Nieuwe Drentse Volksalmanak* 69: 97–162.

———. 1955. "De Romeinse Castella in de dorpsheuvel te Valkenburg aan de Rijn (Z.H.) (Praetorium Agrippinae). II: De Opgravingen in 1942–1943 en 1946–1950" (with 11 appendixes). *Jaarverslagen Vereniging voor Terpenonderzoek* 33–37 (1948–1953): 1–209.

———. 1958. "Prähistorische Hausformen auf Sandböden in den Niederlanden." *Germania* 36: 35–71. (For the Dutch version see 1954.)

———. 1962. "Bijdrage tot de geschiedenis van de stad Groningen binnen de Diepen. I" (with H. Praamstra). *Groningse Volksalmanak:* 68–154.

———. 1966. "Bijdrage tot de geschiedenis van de stad Groningen binnen de Diepen. II" (with H. Praamstra). *Groningse Volksalmanak:* 1–243.

———. 1968. "Das St. Bernardus Kloster in Aduard (vorluaufige Mitteilung)." *Bonner Jahrbücher* 168: 307–314.

———. 1973. *De Groninger St. Walburg en haar ondergrond* (with H. Praamstra) (with an appendix by D. Bouvy). Koninklijke Nederlandse Akademie van Wetenschappen N.R. 78, afd. Letterkunde. Amsterdam.

Papers by A. E. van Giffen with Autobiographical Notes

Van Giffen, Albert Egges. 1960. "Herdenking van Vere Gordon Childe
(14 April 1892–9 October 1957)." *Jaarboek Koninklijke Akademie van
Wetenschappen* (1959–1960): 372–382.

———. 1964. "Erinnerung an Heinrich Schütte und seine wis-
senschaftliche Auswirkung (anlässlich seines 100). Geburtstages am
28. Dezember 1963." *Oldernurger Jahrbuch* 63: 121–124.

Secondary

Beijerinck, W. 1929. *De subfossiele plantenresten in de terpen van Friesland en
Groningen. I. Vruchten, zaden en bloemen.* Groningen.

Bertsch, K. 1931. *Paläobotanische monographie des Federseerieds.* Bibliotheca
Botanica 103.

Bierma, M. 1973. "Bibliography of the Published Works of A. E. van
Giffen." *Palaeohistoria* 15: 15–34.

Bolk, L. 1908. "De anthropologische samenstelling van de Nederlandsche
bevolking." In *Het Nederlandsche boerenhuis.* Ed J. H. Gallée.

Brongers, J. A. 1976. "Material for a History of Dutch Archaeology up to
1922." *Berichten Rijksdienst Oudheidkundig Bodemonderzoek* 26: 7–62.

Brunsting, H. 1947. "Het grafheuvelonderzoek." *Een kwart eeuw
oudheidkundig bodemonderzoek in Nederland:* 223–253. Meppel.
(Gedenkboek A. E. van Giffen.)

Butler, J. J., and H. T. Waterbolk. 1974. "La fouille de A. E. van Giffen
à 'La Motta.' Un tumulus de l'Age du Bronze Ancien à Lannion
(Bretagne)." *Palaeohistoria* 16: 107–167.

Childe, Vere Gordon. 1937. Sovietskaya Archeologiya No. 1 (Review).
Antiquity 11: 496–497.

Clark, J. G. D. 1939. *Archaeology and Society.* London.

Glasbergen, W. 1954. "Barrow Excavations in the Eight Beatitudes. The
Bronze Age Cemetery between Toterfout and Halve Mijl, North
Brabant." *Palaeohistoria* 2: 1–134 and 3: 1–204.

———. 1966. "De pre-en protohistorie van het I.P.P." *In het voetspoor van
A. E. van Giffen,* 1: 1–15. Groningen.

Glob, Peter. 1945. *Studier over den Jyske Enkeltgravskultur.* Copenhagen.

Gosses, I. H. 1936. "De groote Volksverhuizingen." *Tijdschrift voor
Geschiedenis* 51: 5–42.

Groenman-Van Waateringe, W., and J. J. Butler. 1976. (1977) "The
Ballinoe Stone Circle. With comments by G. Eogan & M. J. O'Kelly."
Palaeohistoria 18: 73–104.

Haarnagel, W. 1974. "Nachruf auf Prof. Dr. A. E. van Giffen."
Praehistorische Zeitschrift 49: 6–9.

Hatt, G. 1928. "To Bopladsfund fra Aeldre Jernalder, fra Mors og
Himmerland." *Aarbøger for Nordisk Oldkyndighed og Historie:* 219–260.

Jacob-Friesen, K.-H. 1928. *Grundfragen der Urgeschichtsforschung. Rassen
Völker und Kulturen.* Hannover.

Kossinna, Gustaf. 1928. *Ursprung und Verbreitung der Germanen in Vor- und
Frühgeschichtlicher Zeit.* Leipzig.

Lanting, J. N. 1973. "A. E. van Giffen's Education and Official Career."
Palaeohistoria 15: 13–15.

Modderman, P. J. R. 1945. "Over de wording en de beteekenis van het Zuiderzeegebied." Thesis, Groningen.

Picardt, J. 1731. *Korte beschrijvinge van eenige vergetene en verborgene Antiquiteten der Provintien en Landen gelegen tusschen de Noordzee, de IJssel, Emse en Lippe, waar bijgevoegd zijn Annales Drenthiae.* 2d ed. Groningen.

Reinders, H. R. 1986. "Scheepsarcheologie in Nederland, K.N.O.B."— *Congres: Verantwoord onder Water:* 15–40. Amsterdam/Zutphen.

Reinerth, H. 1929. *Das Federseemoor als Siedlungsland des Vorzeitmenschen.* Stuttgart.

Rutimeyer, L. 1862. *Die Fauna der Pfahlbauten der Schweiz.* Denkschriften der Allgemeinen Schweizerischen Gesellschaft der gesamten Naturwissenschaften 19.

Sprockhoff, Ernst. 1928. "Handbuch der Urgeschichte Deutschland." *Die Nordische Megalithkultur* 3.

Van Bemmelen, J. M. 1908. "Beschouwing over het tegenwoorsige standpunt onzer kennis van de Nederlandsche terpen." *Oudheidkundige Mededelingen Rijksmuseum van Oudheden* 2.

Van Der Waals, J. D. 1974. "Albert Egges van Giffen. Zijn werk in Drenthe." *Nieuwe Drentse Volksalmanak* 91: 9–19.

Van Es, W. A. 1972. [1974] "The Origins and Development of the State Service for Archaeological Investigations in the Netherlands." *Berichten Rijkscienst Oudheidkundig Bodemonderzoek* 22: 9–15.

Van Gelder, H. E., P. Glazema, G. C. Bontekoe, H. Halbertsma, and W. Glasbergen, eds. 1947. *Een kwart eeuw Oudheidkundig Bodemonderzoek in Nederland, Gedenkboek A. E. van Giffen.* Meppel.

Waterbolk, E. H. 1969. "Brieven over de aanloop tot de oprichting der Vereniging voor Terpenonderzoek." *Jaarverslag van de Verenging Voor Terpenonderzoek 51(= Vijftig jaren terpendonderzoek).*

Waterbolk, H. T. 1954. "De praehistorische mens en zijn milieu." Thesis, Groningen.

———. 1970. "Die Deutung der Wurten in historischer Sicht." *Probleme der Kustenforschung im sudlichen Nordseegebiet* 9: 1–12.

———. 1973. "A. E. van Giffen. Noordhorn 14 maart 1884–Zwolle 31 mei 1973." *Palaeohistoria* 15: 7–12.

———. 1975–1976. "Albert Egges van Giffen. Noodhorn 14 maart 1884–Zwolle 31 mei 1973." *Jaarboek Maatschappij Nederlandse Letter kunde Leiden:* 122–153.

———. 1983. "Thirty Years of Radiocarbon Dating: The Retrospective View of a Groningen Archaeologist." *Pact* 8: 17–27. (14 C and Archaeology: Symposium held at Groningen, August 1981.)

———. 1989a. "Ezinge." *Reallexikon der Germanische Altertlumskunde,* vol. 8.

———. 1989b. " 'Het was een mooie tijd, er viel wat te doen.' De archeoloog A. E. van Giffen (1884–1973)." In *Om niet aan onwetendheid en bargarij te bezwijken, Groningse geleerden 1614–1989,* 207–226G. Ed. A. van Gemert, J. Schuller tot Peursum-Meyer, and A. J. Vanderjagt.

Willems, W. J. A. 1935. "Een bijdrage tot de kennis der Vöör-Romeinsche urnenvelden in Nederland." Thesis, Amsterdam.

Douglas R. Givens

Alfred Vincent Kidder   *1885–1963*

Alfred V. Kidder raised the science of archaeology to a new interpretive level by combining ethnographic and excavation data. At Pecos Pueblo in New Mexico he carried out the first long-term, multidiscplinary project in North American archeology. As the premier archaeologist of the American Southwest Kidder proved that stratigraphy and ceramic analysis were major tools for charting cultural growth through time and space.

Alfred Vincent Kidder was born on 29 October 1885 in Marquette, Michigan, but moved with his family to Cambridge, Massachusetts, in 1892. Kidder's father befriended many of the best scientific minds of the day, including the geologists Raphael Pumpelly and Alexander Agassiz and the anthropologists Lewis Henry Morgan and FREDERIC WARD PUTNAM. Their influences on his father, and his influence in turn on his son, inspired a lifetime fascination with natural history that was first evidenced by Kidder's article on birds at the age of fifteen (Kidder 1901). Exploring his father's library, Kidder read George Catlin's *North American Indians* and John L. Stephens's *Incidents of Travel in Central America, Chiapas and Yucatan*. The library also contained complete sets of the annual reports of the Peabody Museum of Archaeology and Ethnology (Harvard University) and the Smithsonian Institution. At times, Frederic Ward Putnam would loan Kidder's father his own personal copies of the Peabody Museum's annual reports to be returned "when convenient" (AVK: 10). There can be little doubt that growing up in such an environment stimulated Kidder's interest in anthropology and archaeology.

After attending some of the best preparatory schools abroad and in Massachusetts, Kidder entered Harvard University in 1904 intent on becoming a medical doctor. However, his distaste for chemistry and mathematics ultimately necessitated a new career choice. In the summer of his junior year at Harvard, his search for other options brought him face to face with archaeology through his participation in Edgar Lee Hewett's field school. Kidder had read in a notice in the spring issue of Harvard University's student newspaper that three men interested in archaeology were needed to conduct a survey in the American Southwest. Being at a loose ends that summer, Kidder went to the office of Harvard professor of archaeology Dr. Alfred Marsten Tozzer, where he met fellow applicants SYLVANUS GRISWOLD MORLEY and John Gould Fletcher.

Alfred Vincent Kidder. (Courtesy Douglas R. Givens)

Morley and Tozzer would remain Kidder's life-long friends.

Hewett's so-called field schools did not actually provide formal training in archaeological field methods. Hewett merely pointed them to the geographic area in which the threesome were to undertake their archaeological survey. After six or seven weeks, Hewett would reappear on horseback to check on their progress. Thus the three men had to devise their own methods. Hewett's approach to field education was summed up in his book *Camp Fire and Trail:* "I have applied something that I learned on the waterfront of Lake Michigan when all the kids in the southern part of Chicago swam in the lake as a matter of inalienable right. I noticed one young leader who was obviously the boss of the waterfront. I observed that all the new recruits of the gang swam like a fish in a day or two. I said to this young ruffian, 'Who teaches these kids to swim so quickly and so well?' He said, 'I do.' 'Well, how do you do it?' 'Push 'em off the pier'"(1943, 149). Despite his sink-or-swim approach to instruction, Hewitt later became the first director of the School of American Archaeology in Santa Fe, New Mexico, which was subsidized by the Archaeological Institute of America.

At the end of Hewett's 1907 field season, Kidder and Morley had successfully surveyed and mapped a number of sites in Colorado and New Mexico. (Fletcher had left early because of heat exhaustion.) Kidder was so taken by his summer experience that, once back in Cambridge, he wrote to Hewitt about the possibility of participating in a second project: "I have talked matters over with my father and was of course delighted to find that he was entirely in sympathy with my desire to take up archaeology as a life-work. Is there a possibility of my working for the early part of next summer in Utah?" (ELH, 28 September 1907). Kidder graduated from Harvard in 1908 with a bachelor's degree in anthropology and spent another field season with Hewett.

In the fall of 1909, Kidder entered graduate school at Harvard to begin work on his doctorate in anthropology. In his studies under the Egyptologist George Reisner, Kidder received his first real training in field methodology; from the art historian George Chase, he received confirmation of his belief that ceramics were worthy of careful study and analysis by archaeologists. Chase's influence was apparent in Kidder's doctoral dissertation, which treated in detail the style and decorative motifs of Pueblo pottery (Wauchope 1965, 152). Kidder also had the opportunity to study under the great anthropologist Franz Boas, who was a visiting professor at Harvard for a term. He was thus exposed to Boasian "particularism" (the insistence on detailed, "particular" knowledge of any subject in order to fully understand it), but he did not embrace it as some of the professor's other students did. Kidder's summer excavations continued. In 1910, he participated in a project in Newfoundland, and in 1912 he excavated at historic Pueblo ruins in Gobernador and Largo canyons in New Mexico.

In 1914 Kidder received his Ph.D. in anthropology, with a dissertation entitled "Southwestern Ceramics: Their Value in Reconstructing the History of the Ancient Cliff Dwelling and Pueblo Tribes: An Exposition from the View of Type Distinction." The section dealing with the ceramics of the Pajarito Plateau in New Mexico was published by the American Anthropological Association in 1915. His dissertation suggested that ceramic materials could be used as a gauge of cultural development in the American Southwest, similar to what was being done by archaeologists at Old World sites in Europe, African, and Asia. For Kidder, two lines of inquiry should be followed in ceramic analysis: "the one technological, concerning itself with the quality of clay and methods of manufacture and burning; the other artistic, treating of the life-histories of design and their possible growth, changes and decadence" (Kidder 1914, 17). Kidder followed up his doctoral research through 1915 by collaborating with Samuel J. Guernsey to formulate an archaeological chronology of the southwestern United States.

Kidder at Pecos Pueblo, New Mexico

A. V. Kidder is perhaps best remembered for his pioneering approach to the study of Pecos Pueblo (1915–1924), an archaeological site in New Mexico southeast of Santa Fe and northeast of Albuquerque. With financial backing from the Peabody Museum and Phillips Academy in Andover, Massachusetts, Kidder undertook a study of this Pueblo site, which had been occupied in both prehistoric and historic times. Stratigraphic dating had first been applied to an archaeological site in the United States in 1914, at San Cristobal Pueblo, New Mexico, by Nels C. Nelson. Nelson dug arbitrary layers and then classified and recorded pottery shards by levels. Hoping to use stratigraphy to arrive at a site chronology, Nelson observed, "we were looking for someone to correlate all of this vast accumulation of data and to tell us what it really means" (Nelson 1914, 133). That someone was Alfred Vincent Kidder. The connection between potsherds and stratigraphic excavation would be the hallmark of Kidder's work at Pecos Pueblo, conducted on a massive scale. His use of stratigraphy not only introduced this method of relative dating to archaeology but also brought a sense of the spatial distribution of territory under the control of a specific prehistoric culture.

Moreover, Kidder established the value of stratigraphy to Americanist archaeology. As Roland B. Dixon, Harvard professor and friend of Kidder's, wrote: "Chronology is at the root of the matter, being the nerve electrifying the dead body of history. It should be incumbent upon the American archaeologists to establish a chronological basis of the precolumbian cultures, and the American ethnologist should make it a point to bring chronology into the life and history of the postcolumbian Indians" (1913, 577). However, as a method of establishing cultural chronology in the Americas, stratigraphy did not become an accepted tool of analysis until after 1920. The technique was conceived in Europe out of a geology in which vast gaps of time were recognized between the geological and cultural records. The American usage of stratigraphy (by, for example, WILLIAM HENRY HOLMES and Aleš Hrdlicka) did not successfully demonstrate the early existence of humankind. As a result, the stratigraphic method of chronology in Americanist archaeology was discredited (Willey 1968, 38).

Kidder had married Madeleine Appleton in 1910, and she devoted much time to potsherd analysis at Pecos Pueblo. The couple eventually had two daughters (Barbara and Faith) and three sons (Alfred III, Randolph, and James).

The first field season at Pecos (1915) was devoted to midden excavation. Here Kidder modified Nelson's stratigraphic approach at San Cristobal by making detailed descriptions of the nature of the refuse found in the Pecos middens, sketching the probable history of the refuse deposition, and specifying the methods employed in excavation. The deep middens permitted extensive stratigraphic investigation, which was one of the reasons Kidder chose that site. He continued to improve on Nelson's technique by the use of profile trenching, which furnished the first test of stratigraphy on a large scale in the Southwest. Each profile was examined for its natural strata, and potsherds found in those strata were given provenances according to their strata units. Kidder also marked with pegs and string the physical strata of the site to allow for ready recognition of the various levels during the ongoing excavations. Kidder's controlled provenances contained potsherds that were classified and tabulated, and he also employed the relative dating technique of seriation, whereas Nelson had not. Kidder's work during this initial field season reflected the influence of George Reisner, for Kidder adopted his methods by recognizing different types of debris that were likely to be found at a site (debris of occupancy or clearing) and by developing a cataloging system for recording artifact finds. Ultimately, Kidder's goal for the first season at Pecos was to obtain as much information as possible on the distribution of ceramic types in time and space, and he found evidence of culture contact in the trade goods uncovered in the middens.

The second (1916) and third (1917) field seasons at Pecos saw the continuation of the profile trenching operations. In 1916 Kidder began to reconstruct the ceramic occupation of the Pecos Pueblo site by establishing the stratigraphic chronology of various ceramic types. He was able to delineate the earliest residents of Pecos as evidenced by the black-on-white pottery. The glaze ceramics were made later by populations occupying the site after the black-on-white culture group. Kidder was unable to conduct the third field season at Pecos in person because of his enlistment in the United States Army at the outbreak of World War I. In his stead Carl Guthe of the University of Michigan, who had participated in the second field season at Pecos, continued the work, exploring sites down river from Pecos as well as to its west. Guthe surveyed many ruins on the upper Rio Grande and traced the northern limits of Pueblo culture by following it to its terminus in the San Luis Valley of southern Colorado (Kidder 1924, 24). Guthe then returned to Pecos and excavated the main ruin at the nearby site of Rowe for six weeks. It is not known if Kidder told Guthe to survey the Rowe ruins for ceramic remains that could be linked to Pecos stratigraphically, but Guthe did find extensive evidence of black-on-white pottery at the site.

Meanwhile, Kidder was in Santa Barbara awaiting induction. Receiving word that he would not formally enter the Army until August 1917, he decided to return to the Southwest during June and July. He went to Hopi country and lived at First Mesa with a sculptor named Emory Kopta. He also traveled around the area and found several Hopi religious shrines set on slabs of stone. He visited Second Mesa to see Piuteque, a refuge for Rio Grande indigenous people during the Pueblo Revolt of the 1690s. Kidder went there, as he said, "with my tongue hanging out, thinking that I was going to find some Rio Grande pottery—[but] it was all Hopi pottery, every bit of it. I couldn't find a single sherd. I have since found that it's true elsewhere. When a people move into a new place they take over the local culture, at least, in ceramics" (AVK, 14).

In Hopi country, Kidder first made use of ethnographic data from cultural anthropology. He read anthropologist Robert Lowie's assessment of archaeologist Jesse Walter Fewkes's analysis of Hopi traditions, which criticized Fewkes's failure to check the accuracy of what the Hopi told him. Later, Kidder would ask Elsie Clews Parsons to undertake an active study of the Jemez Pueblos, the descendants of the Pecos people. Kidder raised the science of archaeology to a new interpretive level by melding ethnographic and excavation data into a workable whole. This was in fact the methodological foundation of his pursuit of synthesis in American archaeology.

The Pecos fieldwork was at a standstill from 1917 until 1919 because of World War I. In 1920, the fourth field season continued with the unearthing of artifacts and burial remains, but Kidder felt he lacked adequate expertise in the analysis of human remains. This realization led him to take a first step in what became his multidisciplinary approach to the resolution of archaeological problems at Pecos. Kidder arranged for Dr. Earnest Albert Hooten to join him at Pecos; Hooten was then curator of physical anthropology at the Peabody Museum at Harvard. Many hundreds of human burials had been found during the previous field seasons, and Kidder thought it would be best for Hooten to see firsthand the field conditions under which the Pecos human remains were found and to assist in developing methods for their proper care (1924, 25). Hooten's presence at Pecos allowed Kidder to run a number of new trenches into the refuse-heap cemeteries on the east slope of the Pecos site. Through the work of Hooten and his collaborator T. Wingate Todd, the physical anthropology of the Pecos Pueblo not only provided the criteria for determining the age and sex of human osteological remains but also created an interest in the epidemiology of the populations living there (Hooten 1930, 13–32). Preliminary data were obtained concerning the population ratio of male and female, the average life span of the residents, and the diseases affecting the population. Hooten's work at Pecos was an early example of a physical anthropologist working alongside an archaeologist in the field, although Kidder had been aware of the importance of this discipline to archaeological fieldwork as early as 1908 (Kidder 1910).

Kidder was unable to excavate at Pecos in 1921 because his mother was ill, so he sent Carl Guthe to conduct a thorough study of pottery making among the Pueblo Indians in New Mexico. Guthe selected the Tewa Indians of San Ildefonso, a village on the Rio Grande north of Santa Fe. He spent several weeks there and recorded every step in the manufacture of pottery, from the digging of the clays to the firing of the completed vessels. The San Ildefonso studies were the first in a series of investigations into the techniques of pottery making; today they are considered an early venture into what is now called ethnoarchaeology. Kidder later asked Anna Shepard to analyze the physical properties of pastes, slips, and paints characteristic of Pecos pottery to gain a better understanding of its manufacture (Shepard 1942, Rohn 1973, 195).

Kidder at the Pecos mission church excavation. Bodies of mission priests were found under the mission floor. (From Douglas R. Givens, Alfred Vincent Kidder, *1992)*

In the sixth field season (1922) at Pecos Pueblo, the main quadrangle of the site was excavated. Particular attention was devoted to architecture, town growth, and the stratigraphy of the beds of early rubbish next to the building on the west side of the site. However, by the end of the summer of 1922, excavation at Pecos virtually ceased, and attention turned to surveying and investigating other archaeological sites in the general area, including one at Bandelier Bend across the Arroyo de Pecos from the main ruin. The pottery discovered there enabled Kidder to determine that the site had existed before Pecos Pueblo was founded.

In sum, Kidder brought his "pan-scientific" approach to the field of American archaeology by adopting a multidisciplinary strategy concerning the excavations and studies at Pecos Pueblo. He involved a physical anthropologist, an ethnographer, and colleagues from other sciences, directing their particular expertise and mode of analysis toward the solution of archaeological problems (Givens 1992, 29–76). Following principles of geologic stratigraphy, Kidder was able to link together area sites to Pecos Pueblo in both time and space. For the first time, a physical anthropologist (Hooten) analyzed human remains *in situ*. Some of the other fields contributing to Kidder's work at Pecos were chemistry, astronomy, agronomy, public health medicine, and engineering. Kidder provided two other important services to the developing science of Americanist archaeology. First, Pecos Pueblo was a training ground in field methods, and many well-known American archaeologists, including George Vailliant, Guthe, and Robert Wauchope, received their first field instruction from Kidder. Second, Kidder initiated the Pecos Conference, which became a forum for archaeologists to identify common field problems and discuss possible solutions. The Pecos Classification, which was based on differences in ceramics and their depth of deposit in archaeological sites, was developed during one of the conferences, and it was the first attempt to organize what was then known about southwestern prehistoric cultures (see Woodbury 1993 on the Pecos Conference).

A. V. Kidder was a dedicated cultural historian of the prehistoric Southwest and a superlative field archaeologist. He conducted the first long-term, multidisciplinary project in North American archaeology. Kidder's prominence in southwestern prehistory, which had a central place in North American archaeology overall, meant that he also had a major influence on the whole of Americanist archaeology. Kidder's work at Pecos Pueblo involved a number of methodological contributions to southwestern archaeology, both in field techniques and in interpretation. As a premier field archaeologist, Kidder viewed stratigraphy and ceramic analysis as major tools for charting cultural growth over time and place. The relative chronology of prehistoric Pueblo ruins was nearly ignored by southwestern scholars until Kidder popularized the use of stratigraphic dating there. Kidder ultimately hoped to piece together the story of Pueblo development through ceramics: to determine a sequence of local types and then, through the discovery of contemporaneous nonlocal types, to solve "the broader and more important problems of interarea chronology" (Kidder 1924, 45, 135).

The Carnegie Institution's Division of Historical Research
Before Kidder became involved in Mayan research through the Carnegie Institution, Central American archaeology had focused on the exploration and the description of sites and artifacts. Before 1914, some chronological ordering of data had been attempted for the Mayan lowlands, made possible by the translation of Mayan inscriptions and the

correlation of calendrical dates with those of the western calendar (Willey and Sabloff 1980, 113). In 1929 Kidder began the second half of his archaeological career by becoming the director of the Carnegie Institution's Division of Historical Research in Washington, D.C. Kidder now turned his attention for the most part to the Maya, but he continued to work on his Pecos Pueblo materials until 1958. However, his affiliation with the Carnegie Institution did not allow much time for fieldwork. He was now an archaeological administrator, planning investigations and directing the labors of other archaeologists on the staff.

Kidder's direction of the Division of Historical Research was patterned after his vision of a "collection of all pertinent sciences and their mutual input into the resolution of archaeological analysis and interpretation" (Kidder 1957, 72). In his view, the basic goal of archaeological work was to understand cultural development and the "development of the human race," and the only way to reach that goal was by using the insights of all sciences—social, natural, and environmental.

Now in charge of the Carnegie's Mayan projects, Kidder introduced his "pan-scientific"/multidisciplinary approach to resolve archaeological problems surrounding the Maya. Two months after becoming director, Kidder called for all Carnegie archaeologists to gather at Chichén Itzá, Yucatan, in January 1930. The purpose of the gathering was to provide a forum for new ideas about on-site fieldwork and analysis of recovered remains. From the beginning, it was Kidder's conviction that specialists such as as biologists, geologists, meteorologists, historians, comparative linguists, and medical doctors could be marshaled for a coordinated assault on archaeological issues arising from the Mayan projects. This approach would allow for "pooling of data, interchange of ideas, and . . . formulation of [a] combined attack upon problems of common interest" (Kidder 1930, 391; Givens 1989, 1–11).

In 1937 Kidder wrote that the individual archaeologist had been far too absorbed in the "tillage of his own little patches" and had failed to see the importance of what other disciplines could offer in the investigation of archaeological puzzles (Kidder 1937, 223). Although Kidder's multidisciplinary approach was never fully realized, it did succeed in collecting data about the Mayan habitat, agricultural base, technology, and living descendants. Before Kidder's tenure, lack of precedent might have kept such a detailed analysis from being undertaken.

Notable during Kidder's time at the helm of the Carnegie's Division of Historical Research was the use of aerial archaeology. Kidder and Charles A. Lindbergh worked jointly on the aerial discovery of Mayan sites throughout the Yucatan and in other locations and began to use the airplane as a tool to trace possible trade routes between Mayan cities.

Kidder's concern for information went beyond that gleaned from the discovery of Mayan artifacts. He employed his longtime friend Sylvanus G. Morley, who continued his groundbreaking work in the deciphering of Mayan hieroglyphs. One of his major contributions to the study of the Maya was his selection of Robert Redfield of the University of Chicago to head an investigation of folk cultures within the Mayan sphere of influence. Redfield's work was essentially nonhistorical and was concerned with the living descendants of the Maya studied in communities from Mérida to Chan Kom and the villages of Quintana Roo. Kidder's best-known personal contribution to Mayan archaeology was his excavation of the Kaminaljuyu mounds in Guatemala, undertaken at the request of the Guatemalan government. Finally, he was instrumental in nurturing the careers of two Mayan archaeologists: Anna O. Shepard and Tatiana Proskouriakoff. The former was extensively involved in the analysis of Mayan ceramics, and the latter, in the architecture of the Maya.

The second decade of Kidder's administration was not a period of archaeological progress at the division. Reductions in funding were beginning to be felt. Because of World War II, the Carnegie Institution was allocating more of its resources to the "hard sciences." At the same time, Dr. Vannevar Bush of the Massachusetts Institute of Technology assumed the reins of the Carnegie and quickly made it known that he was no friend of the humanities and the social sciences. Just before Bush closed down the Division of Historical Research, Kidder proposed to him that the institution underwrite the use of radiocarbon dating for archaeology. In 1950 Kidder retired from the Carnegie Institution, and the division ceased to exist in 1958.

A recurring theme in many of the division's publications on the Maya was Kidder's concern with the importance of the environment and its influence on human culture. He therefore implemented a concentration on environmental factors into his program of Mayan archaeology. He recognized that the environment within which a prehistoric culture existed put tremendous pressure on that culture. However, Kidder acknowledged that neither the historian nor the anthropologist had the expertise or the time to become conversant in environmental effects on culture. Regardless, his inclusion of this emphasis in 1953 was farsighted, since the archaeology of today considers this type of research routine for most field/site analysis.

From 1950 until his death in 1963, Kidder lived in Cambridge, Massachusetts, and his home was a gathering place for students as well as colleagues. While in retirement, Kidder also taught a graduate course in archaeology at the University of California at Berkeley.

Conclusion

Alfred Vincent Kidder's pioneering work at Pecos Pueblo originated and established many of the field methodologies now used in Americanist archaeology. Aside from this substantial achievement, Kidder is also remembered for writing the first overview of southwestern archaeology (*An Introduction to Southwestern Archaeology with a Preliminary Account of the Excavations at Pecos* [1924]), for his administration of the Carnegie Institution's program of Mayan archaeology, for his attempted synthesis of Mayan archaeology, and for his multidiciplinary approach to archaeological research. Kidder also formulated the first "scientific" classification system of analysis and explanation of archaeological remains in the United States. His Pecos Classification (1927) arranged potsherds according to family (method of manufacture, decoration, form), much like the Linnean taxonomic system did for botanical and animal types. During his long career, Kidder served as the mentor and counselor of many budding archaeologists, some of whom became well-known in the world of Americanist archaeology. As a reflection of the esteem in which he was and is still held, the Alfred Vincent Kidder medal was created by the Society for American Archaeology; it is awarded every three years to an outstanding Americanist.

Above all, Kidder exhorted archaeologists to tear themselves away from their excavations, take stock of their actions, and ask, "What have we learned thus far?" This expansive perspective was also evident in another of his recommendations: He urged his colleagues to leave a section of an excavation site untouched, thereby keeping it pristine for future advances in methodology or in explanatory insights.

References

A complete bibliography, both primary and secondary, of the writings of Alfred Vincent Kidder can be found in Wauchope 1965. The primary biographical sources (obituaries and biographies) of Kidder's life that the reader may wish to contact for further information are Givens 1992, Greengo 1968, Wauchope 1965, Willey 1967, and Woodbury 1973.

Primary

The Alfred Vincent Kidder Papers are on deposit with the Harvard University Archives, Pusey Library, Harvard University, Cambridge, Massachusetts. Additional archival materials also exist in Marquette, Michigan.

AVK: Alfred Vincent Kidder Papers, Harvard University
ELH: Edgar Lee Hewett Papers, Museum of New Mexico, Santa Fe

Kidder, Alfred Vincent. 1901. "A Bittern at Close Range." *Bird Lore* 3: 173.
———. 1907. Letter to Mr. Hewett from A. V. Kidder (28 September). Edgar Lee Hewett Papers, Santa Fe: Museum of New Mexico.

———. 1910. "Explorations in Southeastern Utah in 1908." *American Journal of Archaeology,* 2d s., 14: 337–359.

———. 1914. "Southwestern Ceramics: Their Value in Reconstructing the History of Ancient Cliff Dwelling and Pueblo Tribes: An Exposition from the Point of View of Type Distinction." Ph.D. dissertation, Harvard University.

———. 1924. *An Introduction to Southwestern Archaeology with a Preliminary Account of the Excavations at Pecos.* New Haven, CT: Yale University Press.

———. 1930. "Conference at Chichén Itzá." *Science* 71: 391–392.

———. 1937. "The Development of Maya Research." *Proceedings of the 2nd General Assembly, Pan American Institution of Geography and History, 1935.* Washington, DC (same paper in Spanish, pp. 226–234); also as U.S. Department of State, Conference Series 28, Publication 995.

———. 1957. *Reminiscences.* Audiotape transcriptions conducted by Gordon R. Willey, Fay-Cooper Cole, and J. O. Brew with Alfred Vincent Kidder, unpublished.

Secondary

Catlin, G. 1844. *Letters and Notes on the Manners, Customs, and Conditions of North American Indians.* London.

Dixon, R. B. 1913. "Some Aspects of North American Archaeology." *American Anthropologist* 15: 549–577.

Givens, Douglas R. 1989. "The Impact of A. V. Kidder on the Carnegie Institution and Americanist Archaeology." *Athenaeum Society Review* 5, 1:1 11.

———. 1992. *Alfred Vincent Kidder and the Development of Americanist Archaeology.* Albuquerque: University of New Mexico Press.

Greengo, R. E. 1968. "Alfred Vincent Kidder (1885–1963)." *American Anthropologist* 70: 320–325.

Hewett, Edgar Lee. 1943. "Making Archaeologists." Chapter 20 in *Campfire and Trail.* Albuquerque: University of New Mexico Press.

Hooten, E. A. 1930. "The Indians of Pecos Pueblo, A Study of Their Skeletal Remains." *Papers of the Phillips Academy, Southwestern Expedition* no. 4. New Haven, CT: Yale University Press.

Nelson, N. C. 1914. "Pueblo Ruins of the Galisteo Basin, New Mexico." *Anthropological Papers of the American Museum of Natural History,* vol. 15, pt. 1. New York.

Rohn, A. H. 1973. "The Southwest and Intermontane West." In *The Development of North American Archaeology.* Ed. James E. Fitting. New York: Anchor Books.

Shepard, A. O. 1942. "Rio Grande Glaze-Paint Ware: A Study Illustrating the Place of Ceramic Technological Analysis in Archaeological Research." In *Contributions to American Anthropology and History—Carnegie Institution of Washington.* Ed. Anna O. Shepard. Washington, DC: Carnegie Institution of Washington.

Stephens, J. L. 1841. *Incidents of Travel in Central America, Chiapas and Yucatan.* 2 vols. New York.

Wauchope, Robert. 1965. "Alfred Vincent Kidder, 1885–1963." *American Antiquity* 31, 2 (pt. 1): 149–171.

———. 1967. "Alfred Vincent Kidder." In *National Academy of Sciences Biographical Memoirs* 39: 292–322. New York: Columbia University Press.

Willey, Gordon R. 1967. "Alfred Vincent Kidder." In *National Academy of Sciences Biographical Memoirs* 39: 292–322. New York: Columbia University Press.

———. 1968. "One Hundred Years of American Archaeology." In *One Hundred Years of Anthropology,* pp. 29–53. Ed. J. O. Brew. Cambridge, MA: Harvard University Press.

Willey, Gordon R., and Jeremy Sabloff. 1980. *A History of American Archaeology.* 2d ed. New York: W. H. Freeman.

———. 1993. *A History of American Archaeology.* 3d ed. New York: W. H. Freeman.

Woodbury, Richard B. 1973. *Alfred V. Kidder.* New York: Columbia University Press.

———. 1993. *60 Years of Southwestern Archaeology: A History of the Pecos Conference.* Albuquerque: University of New Mexico Press.

Barry Cunliffe

Sir Mortimer Wheeler   *1890–1976*

Sir Mortimer Wheeler's formidable skills as an excavator, administrator, media personality, and public advocate for archaeology made him one of the most significant British archaeologists of the twentieth century. Although he made his reputation early through his excavations at Maiden Castle in England, Wheeler's work as director of the Indian Archaeological Survey, which occurred much later in his career, is of equal importance.

Robert Eric Mortimer Wheeler was born in Edinburgh in 1890 and died in London in 1976. His life spanned what can be regarded as the coming of age of archaeology, a development to which he contributed in no small part. The principal events of his energetic and colorful career are well known and have been dealt with in his autobiographical works (Wheeler 1955, 1966, 1976) and in more critical detail by his biographer, Jacquetta Hawkes (1982). A brief outline here will provide the basis for a consideration of the impact this giant had on his chosen discipline.

Wheeler's father was a journalist by profession and a classicist by training, and both pursuits had a lasting influence on the son. From Edinburgh the family moved first to Bradford and then to London, where, at the age of fourteen, Wheeler was set loose to "educate himself." Three years later, in 1907, he won a scholarship to University College to read classics, but he combined this course of study with classes at the Slade School of Art in order to satisfy his barely concealed ambition to become an artist. He gained his B.A. in 1910 and an M.A. in 1912 and faced the world at the age of twenty-two with a thorough training in classics, a lively writing style developed under his father's watchful tuition, and an awareness that his artistic skills, while not inconsiderable, were insufficient to provide a living. The foundation had been laid for the highly distinctive contribution that Wheeler was to make to the world of archaeology.

In 1913 he decided to apply for a postgraduate studentship, selecting for his research topic Roman pottery in the Rhineland, but at the end of the year he joined the Royal Commission on Historical Monuments for England as a probationary investigator. During the war he served with distinction with the Royal Artillery, leaving with the rank of major and having been awarded the Military Cross.

After a brief stint back with the commission, Wheeler embarked in 1920 on the first of four major creative tasks that were to occupy his

Sir Mortimer Wheeler. (Copyright British Broadcasting Corporation)

working life. He accepted the keepership of archaeology at the newly founded National Museum of Wales—a post that carried with it a lectureship in archaeology at University College, Cardiff. In the six years that he spent in the principality (becoming director of the museum in 1924), he revolutionized Welsh archaeology. He set the museum on a sound financial basis; directed with his wife, Tessa, a series of major excavations on Roman forts (Segontium 1921–1922, Brecon Gaer 1924–1925, and Caerleon 1926); and communicated the results of his researches to the general public through lectures and the publication of an exemplary guidebook, *Prehistoric and Roman Wales* (1925). His technical deftness as an archaeologist, his abilities as an administrator, and his brilliance as a communicator were developed and honed during this six-year apprenticeship.

In 1926 Wheeler moved to London to take up the keepership of the London Museum—an institution desperately in need of revitalization. His decision to turn down the newly created Abercromby Chair of Archaeology at Edinburgh shows clearly that he had, by this stage, consciously rejected a conventional academic career. In doing so he must also have been aware that only in London would he be able to manipulate the establishment to bring about the kind of revolution he was planning for his chosen discipline. His achievements during these London years were considerable. With accustomed energy he set the sorry museum to rights and published a series of catalogs that are still classics of their kind; *London and the Vikings* (1927), *London in Roman Times* (1930), and *London and the Saxons* (1935). (The fourth in the series, a medieval catalog, was produced in 1940 by his assistant John Ward Perkins.) But Wheeler's attention and persuasive skills were soon to be directed to the creation of the Institute of Archaeology at London University, which formally opened in April 1937.

During his London years Wheeler was busy developing his proficiency as an excavator in a series of carefully planned campaigns designed on the one hand to provide training for a new generation of young archaeologists and on the other to research the intriguing interface between Iron Age and Roman society in Britain. The first of these was undertaken in 1928–1929 at the Sanctuary of Nodens at Lydney in Gloucestershire (published 1932). Then followed an extensive campaign on the late Iron Age and Roman city of Verulamium, in southern England, during the four summers from 1930 to 1933 (published 1936). Tiring of the Roman world, Wheeler then turned to the massive hill-fort of Maiden Castle in Dorset, to which he devoted the summers of 1934–1937 (published 1943). Through all of these arduous programs of excavation, mounted annually for a decade, and during the equally time-consuming postexcavation analysis that followed, his wife, Tessa, was his constant partner. Together, by the end of the Maiden Castle campaign, they had developed the craft of excavation to a level it had never before reached.

Hitherto Wheeler had shown relatively little interest in European archaeology, but his work on the Iron Age of Dorset persuaded him to make a comparative study of adjacent areas of Brittany and Normandy. The rapid surveys and the test excavations that resulted in 1938 and 1939 showed to perfection his remarkable talents as an organizer and leader. His ability to frame an incisive research design and to see it through to completion was breathtaking. The report, finally published with his colleague Kitty Richardson in 1957, was a model of precise, uncluttered composition and is still unsurpassed as the standard work on the fortifications of northwestern France.

With the outbreak of war in September 1939, Wheeler, now forty-nine, threw himself into a second military career, eventually serving at El Alamein and Salerno and earning the rank of brigadier. While preparing for the Salerno landings at Algiers in July 1943, he received a cable inviting him, on behalf of the viceroy Lord Wavell, to accept the post of director general of the Archaeological Survey of India, a subcontinent then administered by the British. Wheeler accepted, subject to being allowed to lead his regiment in the initial stages of the Italian campaign, and in February 1944 he sailed for India.

India was to furnish the third and undoubtedly the greatest of his four Herculean challenges. Like the National Museum of Wales and the London Museum, the Indian Archaeological Survey was moribund, but the scale of the problem was altogether different. Not only was there a vast area of operations, but the considerable staff was largely untrained and totally demoralized. Moreover, in the closing years of the war, official support was necessarily restricted. Wheeler arrived with three prime objectives precisely formulated: to train a corps of Indians in modern standards of excavation and publication; to produce an annual publication of high academic standard; and to provide the skeleton of a sound chronological framework for Indian archaeology. With this program firmly in mind, Wheeler immediately initiated a rigorous six-month training school at Taxila; others were to follow. The first volume of the newly founded journal *Ancient India* appeared in 1946. Meanwhile, at Arikamedu, a trading station on the southeast coast near

Pondicherry, he established synchronisms with the Roman world and then extended the chronological boundaries in 1947 with excavations at Brahmagiri, Chandravalli, and Sisupalgar. On the other side of the continent Wheeler's work on the great citadel of Harappa significantly advanced the understanding of the Indus civilization.

His five-year appointment as director general was interrupted by Indian independence in 1947, and the turmoil of partition and the ensuing civil war made work impossible. In 1948 he left for England. He returned to the subcontinent on several subsequent occasions, acting as archaeological adviser to the government of Pakistan, directing a training school at Mohenjo-daro in 1950, and conducting a short campaign of excavation at Charsada near Peshawar

Back in England Wheeler became the part-time chair of the archaeology of the Roman provinces at the Institute of Archaeology, a position he held from 1948 to 1955. During this time he directed excavations at the Iron Age *oppidum* of Stanwick in Yorkshire in 1951–1952 (published 1954). But even at the age of fifty-eight, academic work provided an insufficient challenge for his unremitting energies, so in 1949 he accepted an appointment as part-time secretary to the British Academy.

The academy was the fourth of the decrepit institutions that Wheeler was to drag screaming into the modern world. For twenty years he served the academy faithfully, raising its profile and its prestige and never forgetting to put the interests of archaeology at the forefront. Through his efforts the British schools of archaeology abroad proliferated and flourished and funding for archaeological fieldwork increased dramatically. In this final period of service, Wheeler's influence and powerful presence pervaded all corners of the British archaeological scene.

Such are the bare bones of Wheeler's remarkable career, during which the torrent of energy he unleashed transformed his vocation. Before attempting to assess his contribution to the development of archaeology, we should try to understand something of Wheeler himself. He was a man driven by a thousand demons; endowed with tireless energy, he pushed himself and others without mercy. As fellow archaeologist Sir Max Mallowan so succinctly put it in his memorial address, Wheeler was "a man with a genius for organization, relentlessly, inflexibly driven to achieve his aim by a mechanism which enlisted the help of lesser mortals and compelled them to bow in his path" (Mallowan 1976). And yet this very chemistry, which in many could so easily have been disastrous, was nicely tempered with a touch of real creative genius. Wheeler was an artist but was still enough of a realist to know that, in the world of fine art, he could never achieve the heights that would have satisfied him. Instead, his undoubted abilities were put to good use in the archaeological illustrations that he so lovingly produced. He excelled even more as a writer, having been carefully schooled in the art by his journalist father. His prose is stylish, precise, and vivid, with a sense of drama never far away.

Above all Wheeler was a communicator—not just someone who could communicate well but possessing a passionate desire to do so in whatever medium was available, including letters to his friends, lectures, books, excavation reports, and, finally, television. And like all compulsive communicators, he needed an audience. It was for this reason that he produced his excavation reports with such enviable rapidity and at the same time made him crave the attention of young minds that he could train whether in the fields of Verulamium or the hills of Taxila. In later years he was never happier than when expounding the subtlety of the Acropolis to an adoring group of passengers on a Swan Hellenic cruise; the very act of communication provided intense satisfaction. Wheeler was indeed fortunate to discover archaeology at such an early age, for it offered infinite scope for arduous work, a ready and eager audience, and, suitably manipulated, a story line of inexhaustible fascination. One further point needs emphasis: Wheeler had a keen sense of order—not that of the collector content to sit and accumulate but of the person who cannot stand muddle. Disorder, be it a jumble of archaeological data or a moribund institution, had to be tidied and restructured before one could move on. Always there was the fun of doing a difficult job combined with the restlessness to find a new challenge: it was a dynamic that structured his life at all levels.

The British archaeological world of 1913 was depressingly mediocre. Lone scholars were pursuing their own somewhat self-indulgent lines of research, largely object-based, and for over a century there had been remarkably little by way of real advance except in the rather limited field of Paleolithic studies. The one bright star was the dramatic advance of field technique pioneered by General AUGUSTUS PITT RIVERS in the 1880s, but that had since dimmed without significant effect. Wheeler's early experiences with the Royal Commission on Historical Monuments, his participation as a student in the excavations at Wroxeter, and his field trip to the Rhineland impressed upon him the depths of the lethargy in which his chosen discipline was wallowing. The move to the National Museum in Cardiff in 1920 gave him the opportunity to put his own particular skills to work to change his world.

At the Roman fort at Segontium in 1921, Wheeler began to consciously develop the field technique for which he later became famous—known to the French even today as *Le système Wheeler*. The essence of the early work was to observe carefully the stratigraphy of a site, realizing that within it lay the key to historical development, and to present the sequence simply and graphically. In his autobiography he reproduced, not without some justifiable pride, a section through the *sacellum* of Segontium (Wheeler 1955, pl. 2). It had first been published in 1922, and he now dismissed it for its "certain crudity" but affirmed that "it has all the right stuff in it. . . . The whole bones of the matter are there . . . at the time our sections were unapproached anywhere for expressiveness and integrity." This was an entirely fair and by no means immodest claim, and it went to the very heart of Wheeler's philosophy—the story of a site could only be deduced through the understanding of the sequence of deposits, and the sequence was best appreciated and demonstrated in section. At the time he was developing these principles, there was more than a little novelty in them.

During his almost continuous campaign of excavation from the first year at Segontium in 1921 to the last year at Maiden Castle in 1937, Wheeler was refining the techniques of excavation, recording, and personnel management to arrive at the method that could best achieve the desired result of uncovering the sequence of deposits and retaining the artifacts within their stratified assemblages. At Maiden Castle the system was finally perfected. Excavation occurred within plotted grid squares separated by balks of soil. This method allowed a large labor force to be controlled while at the same time providing ample sections for study. The scheme was widely adopted and served well until its abandonment in Britain by the early 1960s (though in some parts of the world it is still utilized today). Its principal disadvantage was its focus on the vertical sequence rather than the horizontal; thus it tended to emphasize the linear "story" of a site rather than the spatial patterning of the activities carried out in successive phases of use. Even so, for the 1930s, the grid system was a significant step forward in archaeological field technique.

With it went a scheme for recording. Everything was planned accurately and in a detail seldom before achieved. All sections were drawn only after they had been carefully considered and interpreted, and an extensive photographic record was made, with the subjects being meticulously prepared to enhance their clarity. In addition, the finds were processed according to a carefully defined set of procedures that ensured that everything was cleaned, conserved, and identified to its context. The philosophy behind and practice of the fully developed Wheeler system was presented in the handbook *Archaeology from the Earth* (1954a), which remains one of the clearest and most inspiring introductions to field technique available. Although the technical aspects of excavation have changed considerably over the last forty years, the procedures devised by Wheeler have provided the unshakable basis from which innovations have sprung.

Central to Wheeler's philosophy was the obligation to train new generations of young practitioners in his methods, and from the outset, at Segontium, he welcomed students on his excavations. He wrote of emerging from the First World War deeply conscious of the loneliness of the survivor and thus of his enhanced responsibilities. "It became a mission . . . to gather the younger generation about me in all my field work, to inculcate it with a controlled enthusiasm, and to give it in the formative stage a sense of direction, or at least of the need for direction" (1954a, 67). Thereafter students, often coming from far-flung parts of the world, were accepted and instructed. From the earliest reports, the acknowledgments listed the names of individuals who went on to become highly productive professionals in their own right.

The need for systematic training was paramount in Wheeler's mind when he returned to London in 1926. As soon as the London Museum had been rehabilitated, much of his energy was devoted to creating the Institute of Archaeology, attached to University College, so that the techniques of archaeological fieldwork and research could be taught at postgraduate level. The embryonic institute came into being in 1934 with Wheeler as part-time lecturer, but it was not formally launched until 1937. Although Wheeler's concept of the scope of "archaeological science" was somewhat restricted, the institute offered incomparable training for those about to embark on an archaeological career. Moreover, it marked a complete break with the traditional university view of archaeology as an adjunct to history or the classics. As Wheeler was to affirm in his autobiography, the institute represented the culmination of his efforts, begun at Segontium, "to convert archaeology into a discipline worthy of that name in all senses."

If Wheeler's sense of isolation and mission was justified as he viewed the British archaeological scene in 1919, how much more so was it when he landed at Bombay in February 1944 to take up his appointment as director general of the Archaeological Survey of India. The staff was untrained, unmotivated, and unproductive. Aware that time was short, he furiously reorganized and put as top priority the training of fresh young converts. By October a school had been set up at Taxila where, for a grueling six-month period, sixty-one students from all over India learned the master's ways. As well as the techniques of archaeology, they came to know the meaning of work, since they began at 8:45 each morning, broke at 6:00, and reassembled at 9:00 in the evening for another lecture. The leadership that Wheeler exerted and the rigor of his discipline at Taxila and on subsequent excavations produced a highly efficient corps of assistants who, after his departure, were able to take charge of the discipline in independent India and Pakistan. Those six months at Taxila were time well spent.

Wheeler's desire to communicate was deeply rooted in his need for an audience, and in this his flamboyant personality and aptitude with words served him well. Even at the beginning of his career in Wales, he was already in command of the art, and he accepted wholeheartedly the truth of G. M. Trevelyan's dictum that "if historians neglect to educate the public, if they fail to interest it intelligently in the past, then all their historical learning is valueless except in so far as it educates themselves." For this reason he set himself the task of traveling throughout Wales to lecture to local amateur groups about their archaeology. The museum displays at the new National Museum and the guidebook *Prehistoric and Roman Wales* were expressly designed to be accessible to the nonspecialist. The compulsive vitality of *Prehistoric and Roman Wales* distinguished it entirely from the archaeological literature of the day, and the book was a precursor of the popular style that Wheeler soon mastered. The series of guidebooks that he inaugurated and for the most part wrote while at the London Museum was again a conscious effort to make the museum collections more widely available.

In his last year at Cardiff, he began to develop the press as a medium for popularizing archaeology. He had been intrigued by the enthusiasm with which the *Times* had pursued the stories surrounding the discovery of Tutankhamun's tomb. Thus he used a press conference to launch his proposed excavation of the Roman amphitheater at Caerleon, popularly known as "King Arthur's Round Table." The result was an almost immediate agreement with the *Daily Mail;* the paper would provide considerable funds for the project in return for exclusive coverage.

In his subsequent work at Verulamium and Maiden Castle, the weekly press conference became a normal part of site routine. In this way the excitement of the excavation in progress was communicated to a wide general public, who flocked to the site to enjoy regular tours and lectures and to buy postcards, interim reports, "and trivial oddments," such as beach-pebble sling stones, fragments of Roman tile, and Roman oyster shells. "In such multifarious ways can the present-day public be drawn to contribute directly or indirectly to archaeological research" (Wheeler 1943, 3). This deliberate policy of encouraging public interest set standards that were avidly followed by most directors of postwar excavations in Britain, and it is one of the reasons why archaeology enjoys such high regard in Britain today. However, Wheeler's conviction "of the moral and academic necessity of sharing scientific work to the fullest possible extent with the man in the street and in the field"(ibid.), although widely accepted by archaeologists today, was uncomfortably alien to an essentially inward-looking academic community in the 1920s and 1930s, when it was first put into practice.

Wheeler and students at an archaeological site in Wroxeter, England, 1958. (London Times/ B-35 / Archive Photos)

Wheeler's sense of style and of drama, together with his oratorical flair, made him a brilliant lecturer. Throughout his life in Britain and in India, he used this skill unsparingly, often to excellent effect—as when he harangued an unsuspecting group of Indian university vice-chancellors about the importance of developing archaeology in their universities. His larger-than-life performances charmed audiences and were exactly what was required in the early days of television. That Wheeler and television should find each other in 1952 was a happy accident for both, and the series of programs in which he appeared, titled *Animal, Vegetable, Mineral,* gave archaeology in Britain the greatest boost it has ever received. In 1954 Wheeler was voted "television personality of the year." Thereafter he and his discipline were in the forefront of public consciousness. Now in his early sixties with a distinguished career behind him, he could enjoy the public's adulation in the secure knowledge that with every appearance he was advancing the cause of archaeology.

Wheeler's skills as an administrator are legendary. There was nothing he relished more than being given a moribund organization to reinvigorate—the National Museum of Wales in 1920, the London Museum in 1926, the Archaeological Survey of India in 1944, and the British Academy in 1949. Each was a stage on which he could practice his skills, though it is perhaps notable that only in the case of the Institute of Archaeology did he actually build a stage from scratch. His most remarkable achievements were in India. "My immediate tasks," he wrote, "were threefold, to set my idling staff at headquarters to work, to see the problem on the ground throughout India and above all to meet every member of my staff, from Peshawar to Madras. The first of these tasks occupied a preliminary ten days" (Wheeler 1954a, 191). Still intoxicated from his wartime command, the brigadier was no doubt a startling figure to the "recumbent forms of peons" and the "little clusters of idle clerks." He could hardly have designed a more ideal challenge against which to pit his ferocious energies. The Indian adventure was a brief interlude of immense creativity and showed Wheeler's abilities as a leader and an administrator in stark relief, as he dealt mercilessly with incompetence, searched out and encouraged leadership potential, preached at every opportunity, and used his towering presence to bludgeon the government to do his will. It was all very simple—the problem was identified, the strategy set, the tactics deployed, and the object achieved. It was the procedure he used throughout his life.

Wales, London, and India were undoubtedly major accomplishments, yet it was probably as secretary of the British Academy that Wheeler was to make his greatest, though least visible, impact on archaeology as an academic pursuit. By restructuring and reviving the organization, he raised its prestige not only in the eyes of the academic world but in those circles of government from which finance flowed. Having shed its image as a senile gerontocracy, the academy took on new life, and with the greatly increased level of government funding that Wheeler had won, the organization moved into a more creative mode. It is hardly surprising that archaeological pursuits, particularly the development of British interests overseas, flourished under Wheeler's tireless patronage. Today the academy is the largest benefactor of British archaeological research at home and abroad.

An innovator in the field, an administrator, and a communicator, Wheeler can justifiably claim a prime place in the history of archaeology. However, as an academic his contribution is more difficult to assess, not least because the flamboyance of his personality has tended to overshadow and obscure his achievements. Moreover, by turning down the offer of the Abercromby chair at Edinburgh in 1926, he offended the sensibilities of those who considered a university professorship to be the pinnacle of one's career. Consequently, during his lifetime his academic work was occasionally denigrated by spectators watching from the sidelines. Today, with the perspective of time, it is possible to evaluate his contribution without the coloration of personal animosities.

Wheeler's great strength as a researcher was his clarity of vision: he was able to see what needed doing and to design a research strategy, at the appropriate scale, to achieve the desired ends. However, as a dedicated communicator, he needed a simple and direct story to tell, with the result that the *story* dominated his excavation reports and other writings. The problem was laid out, the strategy explained, and the solutions triumphantly paraded before the audience. There was little room for uncertainties or for consideration of the mass of background noise that inevitably emerged from a fieldwork campaign. His approach was that of the snappy entertainer rather than of the fastidious academic—he was a simplifier not a complicator. Yet he was not oblivious to the gray areas and subtleties of archaeological interpretation. Rather, he adopted this approach because he judged simple directness to be what the discipline most needed at that time.

The Maiden Castle report represents the epitome of his method. Many Iron Age hill-forts had been and were being dug into with minimal or confusing results. The work was too small-scale and was hampered by preconceptions and the obscurities in pottery typology. At Maiden Castle Wheeler tackled the problem on a grand canvas. Questions of sequence were settled at a stroke, fortifications were interpreted in military terms, areas of internal occupation were properly exposed for the first time, and the whole presented according to a simple historical narrative linked in its final stage to the Roman campaign of conquest. The report, despite contemporary criticism, was a masterpiece. A thorough present-day reworking of the records only emphasizes what complete control of the material Wheeler had. At a time when the discipline faces the problem of selecting data for publication, the decisions behind the publication of Maiden Castle are impeccable.

The work at Maiden Castle led to the consideration of the broader horizons of Brittany and Normandy in a search for comparative material. It soon became apparent what deplorably low standards of research existed in these regions, which inspired Wheeler's campaign of survey and trial excavation. Yet again, his clarity of vision was impressive, as was his almost impudent assurance that he could address the problem on the scale necessary to make a significant impact. If the questions asked and the simple "historical" answers given no longer seem relevant, the resulting publication of *Hillforts of Northern France* provided a compendium of material of immense value to continuing research. And what appeared in print is only a tithe of the rich harvest of notes and sketch surveys preserved in the notebooks—the only records of sites long since destroyed by agriculture.

In India Wheeler's question-asking approach to academic research was most effective, leading to the establishment of chronologies and synchronisms of lasting value. India had him at his creative peak, and his volume of the Cambridge History of India—*The Indus Civilization* (1950)—was his most significant contribution to scholarship. It shows him to be a synthesizer as familiar with the theories as he was with the facts.

To the subsequent generation of the 1970s and 1980s, nurtured on a diet of theory, Wheeler's many publications may seem simplistic, even naive, but that so many of them still have value as useful introductions to themes now infinitely more complex is a favorable comment on his judgment of what endures. Not an easy man to assess, his biographer Jacquetta Hawkes declared that he "lived life as an epic hero in an antiheroic age." Perhaps the most apt image was that offered by Mallowan in his memorial address: Wheeler was "a fire-breathing giant who bestrode the world like a colossus" (Mallowan 1976).

References
Primary
Wheeler, Robert Eric Mortimer. 1923. *Segontium and the Roman Occupation of Wales.* Y Cymmrodor 33. London.

———. 1925. *Prehistoric and Roman Wales.* Oxford: Clarendon.

———. 1926. *The Roman Fort near Brecon.* Y Cymmrodor 37. London.

———. 1927. *London and the Vikings.* London: London Museum Catalogue.

———. 1930. *London in Roman Times.* London: London Museum Catalogue.

———. 1935. *London and the Saxons.* London: London Museum Catalogue.

———. 1943. *Maiden Castle, Dorset.* London: Society of Antiquaries of London Research Committee Report.

———. 1953. "The Indus Civilization." In *Cambridge History of India Supplement.* 2d ed. 1960, 3d ed. 1968. Cambridge: Cambridge University Press.

———. 1954a. *Archaeology from the Earth.* Oxford: Clarendon Press.

———. 1954b. *The Stanwick Fortification, North Riding of Yorkshire.* London: Society of Antiquaries of London Research Report.

———. 1955. *Still Digging: Interleaves from an Antiquary's Notebook.* London: M. Joseph.

———. 1966. *Alms for Oblivion: An Antiquary's Scrapbook.* London: Weidenfeld and Nicolson.

———. 1976. *My Archaeological Mission to India and Pakistan.* London: Thames and Hudson.

Wheeler, Robert Eric Mortimer, and K. M. Richardson. 1957. *Hill Forts of Northern France.* London: Society of Antiquaries of London Research Report.

Wheeler, Robert Eric Mortimer, and T. V. Wheeler. 1932. *Report on the Excavation of the Prehistoric, Roman and Post-Roman Site in Lydney Park, Gloucestershire.* London: Society of Antiquaries of London Research Report.

————. 1936. *Verulamium: A Belgic and Two Roman Cities*. London: Society of Antiquaries of London Research Report.

Secondary

Hawkes, Jacquetta. 1982. *Mortimer Wheeler: Adventurer in Archaeology*. London: Weidenfeld and Nicolson.

Mallowan, Max. 1976. "Sir Mortimer Wheeler 1890–1976" (address given at St. James's Church, Piccadilly).

Bruce G. Trigger

Vere Gordon Childe   *1892–1957*

Gordon Childe was the most celebrated archaeological theorist and synthesizer of his generation and one of its foremost culture historians. He is the most widely read archaeologist of the twentieth century, and his ideas have remained a source of controversy as well as inspiration.

Culture-Historical Archaeology

Vere Gordon Childe was born in North Sydney, Australia, 14 April 1892, and died at Govett's Leap, New South Wales, 19 October 1957. Childe was the only surviving offspring of Stephen Henry Childe, a conservative Church of England minister, and his second wife, Harriet Elizabeth Gordon, both of whom had emigrated to Australia from England. Following his mother's death in 1910, Childe became estranged from his father. In 1913, he graduated from Sydney University with first-class honors in Latin, Greek, and philosophy. Childe grew up in the decades that witnessed the rise of the Australian Labour Party, and while an undergraduate he became a militant socialist.

In 1914, a Cooper graduate scholarship took him to Queen's College, Oxford, where John Beazley, the great expert on classical Greek pottery, became his tutor in classical archaeology. Childe began to investigate the origin of the Indo-Europeans, and his search for their homeland aroused his interest in European prehistoric archaeology. Though no copy of his B.Litt. thesis on "The Influence of the Indo-Europeans in Prehistoric Greece" (1916) is known to have survived, parts of it may have been incorporated into his book *The Aryans* (1926). At Oxford, Childe became a close friend of Rajani Palme Dutt, who was later a leading figure in the British Communist Party.

In 1916, Childe returned to Australia and became involved in anti-conscription and Labour politics, while supporting himself by teaching in a Queensland secondary school and for a time at Sydney University. Between 1919 and 1921, he was private secretary to John Storey, the premier of New South Wales. In 1922, he was appointed research and publicity officer in the Office of the Agent-General of New South Wales in London, but he was dismissed before the end of the year, following the defeat of that state's Labour government. In his only political book, *How Labour Governs* (1926), Childe revealed a deep distrust of parliamentary government, which was widespread at that time, although he rejected authoritarian doctrines.

Childe abandoned politics and resumed his interest in European prehistory. At the beginning Childe had to rely on private funds and money he earned by translating archaeological books into English. However, after 1925 an appointment as librarian for the Royal Anthropological Institute eased his situation. Throughout the 1920s, he visited archaeological sites throughout Europe, especially in the northern Balkans and the Carpathian basin, a little-studied area that he judged important as a corridor for the diffusion of innovations from the Middle East into northern and western Europe. Childe's familiarity with most European languages and his powerful visual memory gave him the ability to note and remember similarities among artifacts from all over Europe. In 1927, he joined with archaeologists from the Hungarian National Museum and Cambridge University in excavating the Hungarian Bronze Age Toszeg site.

The books that resulted from Childe's early research—*The Dawn of European Civilization* (1925), *The Aryans* (1926), and *The Danube in Prehistory* (1929)—were landmarks in the development of European archaeology. They replaced an already outmoded nineteenth-century evolutionary approach to archaeology with a culture-historical one. Like most social scientists of that era, Childe assumed that human beings were inherently conservative and that cultural change came about mainly as the result of diffusion and migration. Like most other archaeologists, he also tended to believe that the course of history was unpredictable and to account for the accomplishments of individual peoples in terms of ethnic and even racial stereotypes. While he credited the Indo-Europeans with a "peculiar vigour and genius," he described as an "inert mass" the prehistoric Danubians, whom he assumed were not Indo-Europeans. He also pronounced the "stagnant" megalithic cultures of western Europe to be unEuropean.

The greatest creative achievement of Childe's early work was his linkage of two concepts: He combined the idea of archaeological culture, which had been refined by the German prehistorian GUSTAF KOSSINNA as a device for tracing the histories of specific peoples in the archaeological record, with the diffusionism of the Swedish archaeologist OSCAR MONTELIUS, especially his belief that in prehistoric times technological skills had spread to Europe from their place of origin in the Middle East. Childe's views about diffusion were close to those of his Oxford mentors, ARTHUR EVANS and John L. Myers, who both stressed the creativity with which Europeans (especially Indo-Europeans) had made use of this introduced knowledge.

In 1927, Childe became the first Abercromby Professor of archaeology at Edinburgh University. He then organized the short-lived

League of Prehistorians as a popular alternative to the Society of Antiquaries of Scotland. Between 1928 and 1955, he carried out excavations at more than fifteen sites in Scotland and Northern Ireland and made sustained, if not entirely successful, attempts to unravel the Iron Age chronology of Scotland. He also published *The Prehistory of Scotland* (1935), which was intended to stimulate public interest in Scottish archaeology. Although he was not an innovative or even an exceptionally perceptive excavator, two of his projects were of methodological importance. He interpreted the internal furnishings of the Neolithic houses at Skara Brae in the Orkneys in terms of what was known about the social organization of rural houses in the Scottish Highlands and the Hebrides during the nineteenth century. This was one of the first studies to consider gender principles relating to the use of space. He also analyzed the relationship of megalithic tombs to arable land as a basis for estimating the size and distribution of the Neolithic population on the island of Rousay in Orkney. It is incorrect that Childe did not do fieldwork regularly, as some critics have contended.

Gordon Childe (back row, center) poses with workers at a dig. (Crown Copyright: Royal Commission on the Ancient and Historical Monuments of Scotland)

Economic Archaeology

Childe continued to produce cultural-historical syntheses, such as *Prehistoric Communities of the British Isles* (1940), but by the late 1920s, he had come to view the approach as a dead end. He doubted that the histories of particular ethnic groups could be reliably traced far back into prehistoric times or, even if they could, that such studies would reveal the most significant developments in human history. He regarded the culture-historical interpretation as prehistory's version of political history, which historians were abandoning in favor of social and economic perspectives. Childe sought to emulate the latter by searching for broad economic trends in prehistory. The results of this research were published in three books: *The Most Ancient East* (1928), *The Bronze Age* (1930), and *New Light on the Most Ancient East* (1934).

In the first of these books Childe stressed the development of agriculture as a crucial event in human history and the key element defining the beginning of the Neolithic period. Grafton Elliot Smith had expounded this view as early as 1915, as had the archaeologists Harold Peake and Herbert Fleure in the third volume of their series *The Corridors of Time* (1927). From Peake and Fleure, Childe also appears to have learned about Raphael Pumpelly's oasis hypothesis, which proposed that massive desiccation in the Middle East at the end of the last ice age had prompted people to domesticate plants and animals in order to feed the higher densities of human beings who crowded around the surviving sources of water. However, Childe contended that individual bands could have moved elsewhere or died out rather than develop agriculture. This formulation reflected the possibilism—the theory that in the past many possibilities existed for people to choose between—that was fashionable at that time among French and British geographers and ethnologists, including Childe's friend C. Daryll Forde.

In *The Bronze Age,* Childe studied the origins and spread of metallurgy and craft specialization. He believed, almost certainly incorrectly, that from the beginning metal casting required full-time, though initially itinerant, specialists who, along with prospectors and miners, became the first humans to function independently of any tribal affiliations. The adoption of metal tools resulted in a "double loss of Neolithic self-sufficiency," since it required communities to become dependent on craftsmen who were often unrelated to them and to develop extensive trade routes that would not be interrupted by periodic outbreaks of tribal warfare.

In *New Light on the Most Ancient East,* Childe argued that two earlier revolutions had been equivalent in their impact to the Industrial Revolution. These were the transition from food collecting to food producing and from self-sufficient agricultural villages to urban societies. Each revolution resulted in a more productive technology and was presumably followed by a massive increase in population. These technologies spread to Europe through migrations of surplus population, the exchange of manufactured goods for raw materials, and surplus craftsmen seeking employment in ever more remote hinterlands. The outcome was the emergence in Europe of Neolithic and Bronze Age societies that were very different from those that had developed in the Middle East.

Childe's interest in economic development in prehistoric times was rooted in the European, and especially the British, archaeology of the 1920s. Yet he advanced far beyond Smith, Peake, and Fleure in the consistency with which he applied an economic approach to the study of prehistory and in the scope of his formulations. Instead of positing that cultural change was a result of technological innovation, he began to see technological progress occurring within the context of broader economic and political patterns. This allowed him to explain how the same technological innovations could produce very different types of societies in Europe and the Middle East.

Childe's economic analysis inherently embodied a multilinear evolutionary perspective. Yet he was not primarily concerned with cultural evolution at this time. He maintained that "archaeology's revelations . . . disclose no abstract evolution but the interaction of multiple concrete groups and the blending of contributions from far-sundered regions." He continued to regard human beings as uninventive and relied heavily on diffusion and migration to explain cultural change. At the conclusion of *New Light on the Most Ancient East,* Childe stated that its main aim was to justify the "general doctrine of cultural diffusion." By moving toward a more materialistic account of cultural change, Childe was able to abandon the ethnic stereotypes that had featured prominently in his early work. Yet his materialism was far from complete. While he viewed some economic shifts as a response to environmental challenges, he interpreted much innovation in traditional culture-historical terms as a result of the spontaneous exercise of human intelligence to acquire greater control over the environment and make human life easier and more secure.

Evolutionary Archaeology
In 1935, Childe visited the Soviet Union for the first time. He met Russian archaeologists, toured museums, acquired new information about the prehistory of eastern Europe, and obtained some "typical Russian works on prehistory." During this period, Russian archaeology was undergoing unprecedented upheaval as a consequence of the attempt to bring it in line with Marxist principles. The main task assigned to archaeology was to interpret prehistoric times from the vantage point of historical materialism. Change was to be understood primarily in the context of social organization, not technology. And any change, including technological, was attributed to the development of contradictions

between classes and ultimately between the forces and relations of production. These contradictions were regarded as the dynamic forces that shaped human history. Archaeologists were called upon not only to describe archaeological remains but also to reconstruct the societies that had produced them. This required learning as much as possible about technology, social organization, and ideology from archaeological data. The charge of historical materialism encouraged archaeologists to study how people, especially ordinary people, had lived in prehistoric times. Attention turned to the excavation of settlements, campsites, and workshops, which were all classes of sites that Russian archaeologists had tended to ignore in the past.

Childe did not accept the entire program of Soviet archaeology. He admired how Soviet archaeologists sought to explain cultural change in terms of internal processes, and he was inspired by the potential value of a Marxist approach, but he rejected any unilinear scheme of social evolution. He also refused to stop viewing diffusion as a major means of cultural development and to abandon the emphasis that he placed on typology, which he saw as essential for constructing regional chronologies and tracing cultural influences between one region and another. By 1933, Childe had already begun stressing the importance of diffusionism as a corrective for Nazi racism, arguing that as a result of diffusion all humanity had benefited from innovations made by many different peoples around the world.

In the decade following his visit to the Soviet Union, Childe wrote three books dealing with cultural evolution, which had previously been of little significance in his writings: *Man Makes Himself* (1936), *What Happened in History* (1942), and *Progress and Archaeology* (1944). He also published a case study *Scotland before the Scots* (1946). The first two were written for the general public as well as for professional archaeologists and continue to be read by nonarchaeologists. In *Man Makes Himself,* Childe interpreted the archaeological record as evidence of a directional process whereby increasing scientific knowledge gave human beings greater control over nature and led to the formation of more complex sociopolitical systems. He later rejected these views as not being sufficiently different from conventional reasoning. In *What Happened in History,* he attempted in a more explicitly Marxist fashion to formulate explanations of cultural change that were focused not on technological knowledge as a prime mover but on the roles that social, political, and economic institutions played in bringing it about. Ironically, most of Childe's economic data were derived without acknowledgment from the two-volume *Wirtschaftsgeschichte des Altertums,* which the conservative German historian Fritz Heichelheim had published 1938.

In accordance with dialectical materialism, Childe viewed every society as containing within itself both progressive and conservative tendencies, coexisting in a relationship of dynamic unity as well as persistent antagonism. The tension provided the energy that in the long run brought about irreversible change. Hence every society bore the seeds of its own destruction and of a new social order. Even so, Childe still did not embrace unilinear change. He carefully documented the social and political differences between the city-states that had evolved in ancient Mesopotamia and the divine monarchy that had united Old Kingdom Egypt. He rather vaguely assigned these differences to divergent ways of controlling the agricultural surpluses that had developed in the course of these societies' transformation from tribal to class organization. Nor did he subscribe to the naive faith in the inevitability of progress that characterized many corrupted versions of Marxism. Writing under the threat of expanding Nazi power, Childe viewed the future bleakly. He feared that European civilization was about to collapse into a new dark age, but he argued that the archaeological record offered hope of humanity's gradual recovery from this disaster as from earlier ones. Nevertheless, his pessimism led him to make a novel contribution to a Marxist understanding of change: he offered a more detailed analysis of the social conditions that impede and reverse social progress than of those that promote it.

Childe argued that at any level of social development, but especially in early civilizations, entrenched hierarchies and inflexible systems of religious beliefs could slow or even halt social change. He distinguished between progressive and conservative societies. The former favored an expansion of productive forces and maintained a harmonious relationship among the means of production, social institutions, and the dominant system of beliefs; the latter possessed social and political elements that effectively blocked change. Childe believed that the ruling classes in the early civilizations sought to forestall any innovations that might threaten their hold on society. They accomplished this blatantly by physical coercion but more subtly by concentrating wealth in their own hands, exercising bureaucratic control over craftsmen, curtailing the pursuit of technical knowledge, and patronizing magic and superstition rather than science. They succeeded, however, only at the cost of making it difficult for their own societies to compete with more progressive ones. Childe thus ascribed important roles in shaping history to both economics and the superstructures of societies. Yet he was careful to qualify that, where the superstructure was dominant over the base, its influence could only be negative. Childe did not ignore the concept of class struggle in early civilizations or reject it as inapplicable to studies based on archaeological data. On the contrary, he found it was not useful for explaining such societies because their class struggles were blunted by highly effective political and religious techniques of social control. In his analyses of the classical civilizations, and in particular of the Roman Empire, he placed increasing emphasis on internal battles to seize wealth and power and on shifting patterns of political control.

Scotland before the Scots, based on lectures that he had given in Edinburgh in 1944, was Childe's most sustained effort to interpret archaeological data according to the Soviet developmental approach. He construed the archaeological record of Scotland (especially burial and settlement patterns) as evidence of increasing private ownership and political inequality. Childe argued that Marxist concepts could illuminate sociopolitical change in the past, and he contended that western archaeologists relied too heavily on diffusion and migration as explanations of change. Yet he affirmed that no one could account for the Neolithic period in Scotland without also accepting that a food-producing economy could not have evolved there until domesticated plants and animals had been introduced from the south.

Childe the Theorist

In 1946, Childe left Edinburgh to become professor of European archaeology and director of the Institute of Archaeology at the University of London, where he remained until he retired in 1956. In London, he had an opportunity through his teaching to influence and win the respect of a rising generation of professional archaeologists. Childe never married and appears to have been a lonely person. He had few close friends and much of his social life was centered around academic and political activities. Undergraduates seem to have been intimidated by his scholarship. In contrast, he found his students at the institute excellent company. Although Childe did less fieldwork after he left Scotland, this was a period of great scholarly productivity. Many of the ideas about methodology that he expounded in his lectures were given wider circulation in *Piecing Together the Past* (1956a). He also continued to produce revised versions of *The Dawn of European Civilization* (1927, 1939, 1947, 1950, 1957) and *New Light on the Most Ancient East* (1935, 1952).

As a result of his growing disillusionment with the quality of archaeological work being done in the Soviet Union, Childe abandoned Soviet archaeology as a principal source of inspiration and began to investigate the philosophical foundation of Marxism itself. He read widely in philosophy in a effort to acquire a more profound and less dogmatic understanding of Marxism as an analytical tool and to apply it to the study of archaeological data. Some of the conclusions he arrived at were challenging for archaeology but were so unrelated to the thinking of most archaeologists that they were generally ignored in his lifetime. The main theoretical writings that he produced during this period were *History* (1947), *Social Evolution* (1951), *Society and Knowledge* (1956b), and *The Prehistory of European Society* (1958a).

Like all Marxists, Childe regarded a historical approach as the basis for uniting all of the social sciences. He argued that the rules that account for human behavior, and human nature itself, changed as new forms of society developed. Hence the significance of any generalization could be established only in relationship to specific historical contexts. Because of this, human history was genuinely creative. It was capable of bringing into being novel and often unanticipated social orders and modes of human self-awareness. Yet he did not believe that progress was inevitable. Some societies remained static, while others might regress or even destroy themselves. Indeed, as a consequence of nuclear war, the whole of humanity might perish.

In Childe's view, a Marxist approach precluded the possibility of predetermined change. Functional constraints accounted for many similar features of social organization that appeared in unrelated cultures sharing analogous modes of production. Yet the specific features of cultures and of individual sequences of change were so much a product of the reworking of preexisting cultural patterns and of accidental cultural contacts that their precise nature could not be predicted. Childe argued, for instance, that the exact form of the British constitution in the nineteenth century could not be deduced from the capitalist mode of production alone.

In *Social Evolution,* Childe examined how environmental differences and highly variable antecedent cultural traditions had produced distinctive early Neolithic cultures in various parts of Europe and the Middle East, even though all these societies had adopted the same complex of domesticated plants and animals and the behavioral patterns that must have been associated with them. Even if every economic base ultimately had the power to shape a superstructure in accordance with its needs, equilibrium would still be out of reach, because the relationship between base and superstructure would continue to be disrupted by technological innovations, which tended to diffuse rapidly from one society to another.

Childe defined knowledge as shared mental approximations of the real world that permitted human beings to act, and he insisted that archaeologists treat artifacts as concrete expressions of human thoughts and ideas. He also argued that human beings adapted not to real environments but to their ideas about them, though an effective adaptation required a reasonably close correspondence between reality and perception. Tools fulfilled human needs, but these needs were not fixed. Consequently, the relative efficiency of any tool or process could not be measured by absolute criteria but only by chronological succession. Innovations and their applications to social needs also required new forms of thought and behavior, which ramified through whole societies. Advances in technology thus reflected not merely an increase in the volume of scientific information but the evolution of the total knowledge at the disposal of a society, including how human beings perceived themselves and their relationship to nature. Childe, however, was not a cultural relativist. He contended that the understanding of the world possessed by progressive societies continued to expand both geographically and temporally. He had no qualms about pronouncing industrial civilizations superior to all preceding societies because they provided a framework for a far greater number of activities.

Childe elaborated his theory of knowledge in terms of the Marxist dichotomy between true and false consciousness. True consciousness was characterized by the operational correspondence between views of reality and external reality itself. It was most obviously manifested in relation to technology. False consciousness, which occurred when there was no such correspondence, was apparent in the myths that all societies created to mask their technological inadequacies and that ruling classes used to disguise exploitation as altruism. The ultimate test of truth was operational. Simple technologies provided the basis for developing more complex ones, while false consciousness perished as social conditions changed; cherished religious beliefs then became mere folly or superstition or were forgotten completely. Childe believed that a more objective understanding of human behavior and society would allow people to control their social environment more humanely. He hoped that history and archaeology might together provide the foundation for a "science of progress" that would foster such objectivity, even if they could never become exact sciences. Childe accepted the idealist claim that the world to which human beings adapted existed in their own minds. Yet by insisting that the cultural equivalent of natural selection operates on the interface between a society and its environment and by maintaining the distinction between true and false consciousness, Childe remained a materialist and avoided a commitment to subjectivism and relativism, unlike R. G. Collingwood and many other British archaeologists of that period.

In *The Prehistory of European Society,* Childe, like many social anthropologists, treated society as the structural matrix that enabled individual items of culture to acquire their functional significance. He also maintained that functional constraints severely limited the range of variation in political systems, kinship behavior, and other forms of social relations. As a result, social structures tended to conform to a rather narrow range of types, while the specific forms of culture were far more variable. Childe had noted that religious beliefs, magic, and superstition left their mark on the archaeological record no less conspicuously than did technological knowledge. However, because the possible variations in magical and religious beliefs were infinite, Childe believed that the archaeologist had no hope of inferring their specific nature in the absence of written records or oral traditions. By contrast, the number of practical solutions to any technological problem was limited by material constraints that could be deduced with a high degree of accuracy by applying the laws of physics and chemistry. The study of prehistoric knowledge thus seemed restricted largely to technological matters and to be framed in terms of its practical results, not the subjective understandings of those who possessed it.

Nevertheless, as a Marxist, Childe also believed that the evolution and functioning of technology could only be grasped if archaeologists were able to reconstruct the social and political context in which they occurred. In the last years of his life, he searched for ways to infer that context. He was increasingly irritated and depressed by his inability to transcend the limitations of the typological method on which most of his life's work had been based. He apparently did not refer back to his pioneering studies of settlement patterns at Skara Brae and Rousay, nor did he note the beginning of settlement archaeology in the United States, which was marked by the publication of GORDON WILLEY's *Prehistoric Settlement Patterns in the Viru Valley, Peru,* in 1953.

At the end of his career, Childe was defeated not by disillusionment with Marxism as a research strategy but by what he saw as his own failure to devise new ways to carry his Marxist analysis of prehistory forward. He did not look for guidance to Soviet archaeology, having long since concluded that its domination by a totalitarian regime had led to intellectual bankruptcy. Convinced that the source of the problem was his own declining abilities rather than the intractable nature of the issues he was addressing, he was assailed by a fear that his creative life was over and by a growing dread of loneliness, helplessness, senility, and physical illness.

Childe retired a few months ahead of schedule in the summer of 1956, relinquishing the directorship of the Institute of Archaeology just before the institute moved into its new building on Gordon Square. He returned to Australia to visit old friends and the haunts of his youth. He delivered various lectures, finished *The Prehistory of European Society,* and wrote two papers that were later published as "Retrospect" (1958b) and "Valediction" (1958c). These papers reviewed his career in a detached manner and summarized his views about the current state of archaeology. On the morning of 19 October 1957, in the course of what seemed at the time to be his regular stroll, he fell 300 meters to his death at Govett's Leap in the Blue Mountains of New South Wales. A letter that he left behind, with instructions not to open it until 1980, made it clear that he had committed suicide.

Assessment

Largely as a result of the extraordinary sales of *What Happened in History,* Childe is probably the most widely read archaeologist of the twentieth century. In his lifetime his major works were translated into numerous languages. Although he became a professional archaeologist relatively late in life and his major works were published over a span of only thirty-two years, the scope of Childe's interests was prodigious. Few of his contemporaries were aware of the breadth of his work. Most European archaeologists acknowledged him to be the leading expert on the culture-history of prehistoric Europe. They tended to regard his evolutionary and philosophical works, not as another dimension of his scholarship, but as efforts at popularization. In the Soviet Union, where archaeologists had to treat Childe's left-wing political views with great circumspection, it was his early culture-historical works that were translated into Russian. These provided a model for the "ethnic" interpretations of the archaeological record that characterized Soviet archaeology in the 1940s and 1950s.

In the United States, Childe was regarded in the 1950s as one of the foremost cultural evolutionists of his time, largely on the basis of *What Happened in History.* Yet American archaeologists were deeply influenced by ethnologist and neo-evolutionist Julian Steward's characterization of Childe as a universal or unilinear evolutionist. The widespread acceptance of this misrepresentation of Childe's work resulted partly from a lack of familiarity with Childe's writings on European prehistory. Yet a careful reading of *What Happened in History* would have revealed that Childe's evolutionism was at least as multilinear as that of Steward. Childe himself viewed it as multilinear to the point of being historical.

As a result of the militantly anticommunist attitudes prevailing in the United States in the 1950s, Childe's Marxist tendencies were condemned, and his concepts of Neolithic and urban revolutions were criticized for misrepresenting the course of human history, which, according to then-accepted thought, was actually characterized by gradual and nondisruptive social change. Even the word *revolution* became taboo. In Mexico and Peru, however, Childe's evolutionary publications helped to strengthen indigenous movements to reconsider archaeology from a Marxist perspective.

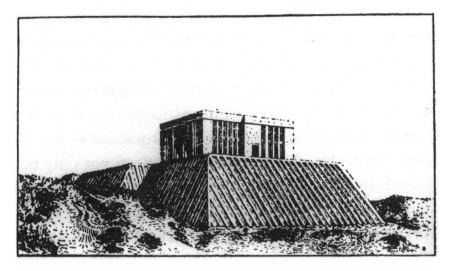

During Childe's lifetime, little attention was paid to his later writings about the nature of culture. He himself did not suggest any practical applications of these ideas to archaeological analysis. Yet these writings clearly adumbrated many of the cognitive and symbolic concerns of the postprocessual archaeology that emerged in the 1980s. What distinguished his approach was his commitment to materialism and his conviction that belief systems mainly played a role in resisting, rather than bringing about, social change.

Throughout Childe's life, the focus of his interest remained the prehistory of Europe and the Middle East. In particular, he was preoccupied with the uniqueness of Europe. In his early work, he interpreted this uniqueness as the result of a combination of Middle Eastern technological advances and the peculiar vigor and genius of the Indo-Europeans. In his last book, he attributed it to the fact that in Europe craftsmen and intellectuals had preserved their freedom of movement in a supratribal, and later a supranational, economy from the Bronze Age until modern times; by contrast, in Egypt and the Middle East they had quickly fallen under the control of reactionary state bureaucracies. In his effort to censure the impediments that the Iron Curtain had placed in the way of intellectual exchanges, and for which he appeared to hold the capitalist West entirely responsible, Childe the Marxist had produced a stirring encomium of free enterprise.

Despite his close contacts with archaeologists in the United States and around the world, Childe rarely compared developments in prehistoric Europe with what had happened elsewhere. Though he acknowledged that the fact that classic Maya had lacked metal tools was important for understanding the nature of all early civilizations, he did not attempt to draw any lessons from this observation. For Childe, the prehistoric cultures of Europe and the Middle East constituted the main stream of human history, while cultures found elsewhere were of secondary importance. There is no indication that he paid any detailed attention to other cultural sequences.

Soon after Childe's death, radiocarbon dating undermined the Montelian chronology on which most of his work had been based. In his "Retrospect," Childe recognized that his account of European prehistory might prove erroneous, but he expressed the hope that his interpretive concepts would constitute his most original and lasting contributions to archaeology. Most archaeologists' writings are antiquated within several decades of their deaths; it is thus an extraordinary testimonial to the vigor of Childe's scholarship that many of his works continue to raise questions and to inspire controversy and debate among both processual and postprocessual archaeologists.

References
Primary
Childe, Vere Gordon. 1925. *The Dawn of European Civilisation.* London: Routledge and Kegan Paul.

———. 1926. *The Aryans: A Study of Indo-European Origins.* New York: A. A. Knopf.

———. 1928. *The Most Ancient East: The Oriental Prelude to European Prehistory.* London: K. Paul, Trench, Trubner & Co.

———. 1929. *The Danube in Prehistory.* Oxford: Clarendon Press.

———. 1934. *New Light on the Most Ancient East: The Oriental Prelude to European History.* London: K. Paul, Trench, Trubner & Co.

———. 1935. "Changing Aims and Methods in Prehistory." *Proceedings of the Prehistoric Society* 1:1–15.

———. 1936. *Man Makes Himself.* London: Collins.

———. 1940. *Prehistoric Communities of the British Isles.* London: W. & R. Chambers.

———. 1942. *What Happened in History.* Penguin.

———. 1947. *History.* London: Cobbett.

———. 1949a. *Social Worlds of Knowledge.* Oxford: Oxford University Press.

———. 1949b. "The Sociology of Knowledge." *Modern Quarterly* 4: 302–309.

———. 1951. *Social Evolution.* London: Watts.

———. 1956a. *Piecing Together the Past.* London: Routledge and Kegan Paul.

———. 1956b. *Society and Knowledge.* London: Allen and Unwin.

———. 1958a. *The Prehistory of European Society.* London: Cassell.

———. 1958b. "Retrospect." *Antiquity* 32: 69–74.

———. 1958c. "Valediction." *Bulletin of the Institute of Archaeology* 1:1–9.

Secondary
Biographies and Major Studies
Green, Sally. 1981. *Prehistorian: A Biography of V. Gordon Childe.* Bradford-on-Avon: Moonraker.

McNairn, Barbara. 1980. *Method and Theory of V. Gordon Childe.* Edinburgh: Edinburgh University Press.

Trigger, Bruce G. 1980. *Gordon Childe: Revolutions in Archaeology.* New York: Cambridge University Press.

Other Studies

Allen, Jim. 1967. "Aspects of Vere Gordon Childe." *Labour History* 12: 5259.

Daniel, Glyn. 1980. "Editorial." *Antiquity* 54: 1–3.

Gathercole, P. 1971. "Patterns in Prehistory: An Examination of the Later Thinking of V. Gordon Childe." *World Archaeology* 3: 225–232.

———. 1980. "Childe's Early Marxism." In *Critical Traditions in Contemporary Archaeology.* Ed. V. Pinsky and A. Wylie. Cambridge: Cambridge University Press.

Makkay, J. 1991. "Gordon Childe (1892–1957) and Hungary." *New Hungarian Quarterly* 32: 107–114.

Pearce, W. J. 1988. "Vere Gordon Childe and American Anthropology." *Journal of Anthropological Research* 44: 417–434.

Piggott, Stuart. 1958. "Vere Gordon Childe, 1892–1957." *Proceedings of the British Academy* 44: 305–312.

Ravetz, A. 1959. "Notes on the Work of V. Gordon Childe." *New Reasoner* 10: 55–66.

Trigger, Bruce G. 1989. *A History of Archaeological Thought.* Cambridge: Cambridge University Press.

Sir Grahame Clark

Dorothy Garrod   *1892–1968*

Abbé Breuil's pupil, Dorothy Garrod used her detailed knowledge of the French Paleolithic to elucidate prehistory in territories beyond France and Europe. She was the first Disney Professor of Archaeology at Cambridge University to be a prehistorian, and she played a significant role in the emergence of world prehistory.

Dorothy Garrod made her greatest contribution to prehistory in her assertion that the cultural stages recognized by French archaeologists were only locally applicable and in fact largely reflected a sequence of cultural impulses that reached Europe from the outside (Thompson 1969). To understand even the French sequence correctly, it was necessary to explore the prehistoric sequences in territories beyond. This Garrod proceeded to do by concentrating her excavation work on different parts of southwest Asia. Her most notable theoretical statement was the presidential address of 1928 to the Prehistoric Society entitled (Garrod 1928c) "Nova et Vetera: A Plea for a New Method in Palaeolithic Archaeology," in which she urged the need for a phylogenic rather than geological approach to the classification of archaeological data.

Dorothy Annie Elizabeth Garrod was born in London in 1892. Her early adulthood was overshadowed by the First World War, in which all three of her brothers had lost their lives. She had come up to Newnham College, one of the first women's colleges at Cambridge, in 1913 to study history, and it is understandable that when she graduated in 1916, she obtained a class far below her natural abilities. After a brief spell in the Ministry of Munitions, she joined the Catholic Women's League to tend the wounded in France. Under considerable strain, she withdrew to convalesce in Malta, where her father was director of war hospitals, and it was there that she acquired her first taste for archaeology. When her father, Sir Archibald Edward Garrod, was appointed Regius Professor of medicine at Oxford, she decided to pursue her new interest by a course of study in anthropology under the supervision of social anthropologist R. R. Marret, rector of Exeter College. As a keen native of Jersey, Marret had for some years concerned himself with excavating La Cotte de St. Brelade, a paleolithic site that had recently yielded the teeth of a Neanderthal man in association with a Mousterian flint industry (Marret 1912, 1917).

Garrod earned her degree with distinction and become fascinated by Paleolithic archaeology. To qualify her for a career in this field, Marret sent her to Abbé HENRI BREUIL at the Institute of Human Paleontology in Paris. As Breuil's pupil she gained invaluable practical experience excavating Upper Paleolithic sites at La Quina, Les Eyzies, Isturitz, and Corrège in central France. She not only learned how to excavate cave sites but also familiarized herself with the system of classification devised by French prehistorians and completed by Breuil himself. The training she received, especially concerning the way French prehistorians subdivided the succession of cultures revealed by excavating the deposit of caves and rock shelters, was to stand her in good stead when she came to dig elsewhere. Yet her own life's work was to be determined by Breuil's comment in the final sentence of his definitive paper in 1912, in which he declared that Europe was after all only a peninsula of Africa and Asia (Breuil 1912).

On her return to Oxford, Garrod applied her detailed knowledge of the French sequence to classifying all available Upper Paleolithic material from sites in Britain, which, during the late Pleistocene, had been no more than a marginal extension of France. She did so with the encouragement of her mentor Breuil, whose interest in this subject was acute. Before the war the abbé had pressed W. J. Sollas, professor of geology at Oxford, to undertake a more complete and scientific excavation of the Upper Paleolithic deposits in Paviland cave on the south coast of the Gower peninsula in south Wales. Breuil even classified the material recovered by Sollas. Garrod's first book, *The Upper Palaeolithic Age in Britain* (1926), contained a preface written by Breuil, and Garrod went out of her way to acknowledge his assistance and to thank him for the valuable criticisms and suggestions offered during its preparation.

Breuil realized that if Garrod was to have a career as a prehistorian, the time had come for her to undertake original excavations of her own. There again he was able to help her from his own experience, and it was a mark of his confidence in her that he suggested she investigate the Devil's Tower, Gibraltar, at the southwest corner of Europe and within easy sight of Africa. His hope was that she might recover remains of Neanderthal man in association with a Mousterian culture, thus linking a particular fossil hominid with a particular technology. Garrod began digging at the Devil's Tower in 1925, and within five months she recovered remains of Neanderthal man in the context of a rich Mousterian industry and plentiful residue of a contemporary fauna. The full report of the discovery by a group of distinguished specialists (Garrod et al. 1928b) attracted widespread interest and established her reputation as an effective prehistorian. Her designation as the British representative at the Glozel Inquiry (held to investigate the provenance of the Glozel assemblage of artifacts, found in Allier, France, in 1924; now considered fraudulent, at the time this assemblage was claimed to provide evidence for an indigenous literate civilization in France before contact with the Greeks and Romans) in 1927 was a further indication of this regard.

As it happened, a find comparable to that at the Devil's Tower had just been made at the opposite end of the Mediterranean. Digging for the British School of Archaeology in Jerusalem, the English archaeologist Francis Turville-Petre had found a young Neanderthal adult in a Mousterian deposit in the Zettupeh cave by the Sea of Galilee (Turville-Petre 1927). The coincidence between these discoveries was not lost on Grant MacCurdy, founder and director of the American School of Prehistoric Research. The school had been established in 1921 with the prime object of introducing American students to the prehistoric archaeology of the Old World. For the first few years attention had been focused on Europe, but in 1926 the school's students visited Palestine and the site of Zettupeh, where Turville-Petre had found remains of Neanderthal man in the context of Mousterian culture. MacCurdy appreciated that the Galilee skull was the most easterly Neanderthal fossil known to date, and it occurred to him that the school might perform an important service to prehistory by testing how much farther east Mousterian culture had extended. Dorothy Garrod seemed the obvious person to undertake such a task.

Garrod made a preliminary visit to the Kirkuk region in Iraq and was able to demonstrate that the Mousterian reached as far as northeast Iraq (Garrod 1928b). With the support of the American school and the Percy Sladen memorial fund, she formed another expedition, whose members included Turville-Petre, in the autumn of the same year. Excavations at the cave of Hazar Merd not only confirmed the presence of the Mousterian but revealed an overlying Upper Paleolithic (Garrod 1930). Excavations at Zarzi confirmed the presence of an Upper Paleolithic level succeeded by microlithic industry. Between seasons, Garrod turned for the first time to Palestine, and in the cave of Shukbah in the Wady en-Natuf she found a microlithic industry that was distinctive because it covered an eroded breccia containing a Levalloiso-Mousterian industry, demonstrating continuous occupation and local development of technology (Garrod 1928a). In effect this inaugurated what was to be her most lasting contribution: the campaign of excavation undertaken with Theodore McCown between 1929–1934 in the Mount Carmel caves (Garrod and Bate 1937; McCown and Keith 1930).

In 1928, as she was beginning her work at Mount Carmel, Garrod delivered the presidential address to the Prehistoric Society, in which she explained why she was engaged in researches in southwest Asia and southeast Europe. The sequence of Paleolithic cultures worked out by French prehistorians and finalized by Abbé Breuil in his classic paper of 1912 was, she said, only valid for restricted parts of western Europe. She urged archaeologists to think of early cultures in the phylogenetic framework used by paleontologists rather than in narrow stratigraphic terms. Only some of the phyla used by French prehistorians originated in Europe, and in most cases they had emerged in adjacent or even quite remote territories. Consequently, the stratigraphic sequence established in Europe recorded in many cases no more than their European emergence or, more often, their arrival from outside. Accompanying her speech was a diagram, obviously incomplete, which emphasized the need to recover sequences from other parts of the world.

The excavation of the three cave sites of el-Wad, et-Tabun and es-Skhul at the Wady el-Mughara at Mount Carmel, Palestine, was sponsored by the British School of Archaeology in Jerusalem and generously funded by Sir Robert Mond and the American School of Prehistoric Research. Garrod served as director of the project, excavated two of the three sites herself, and was responsible for classifying all the artifactual evidence. Paleontologist Theodore McCown, who specialized in human remains, was appropriately in charge of the third site, since it yielded a veritable cemetery of Neanderthal people. Great care was taken in the collection of human and animal skeletal remains, and they were studied and published alongside cultural data. The value of the Mount Carmel excavations was immensely enhanced by the completeness and promptness with which the results were made available to scholars in fully illustrated and detailed volumes, the publication of which proved of enormous value to prehistoric archaeologists and human paleontologists (Rust and Wachholtz 1950).

The archaeological succession revealed by the Mount Carmel excavations was notable not merely for its range but also for its differences from that enshrined in French prehistory. Most significant was the occurrence within the Upper Acheulean of a level marked by blades, end-scrapers, and Chatelperronian (Early Aurignacian) points, indicating the presence of what in France would be classified as early Upper Paleolithic before the close of the Lower Paleolithic. Although in the early 1930s

Albert Rust had found a blade industry underneath levels containing Late Acheulean hand-axes at Jabrud in Syria, Garrod apparently had not read his summary account of 1933 and only took note of his full publication of 1950. The finds made by Garrod and Rust suggested that the phyla of blade cultures was already present in southwest Asia before the close of the Acheulean, which in Europe would be regarded as Lower Paleolithic. Garrod also found fossils of Neanderthal man in the context of Levalloiso-Mousterian artifacts, whereas in Europe those fossils occurred in connection with Mousterian industries. Quite plainly the pattern and sequence of cultures in the two regions differed markedly and demonstrated the essentially local character of the European sequence, which could no longer be accepted as a yardstick for southwest Asia, let alone for more distant parts of the Old World.

In 1936, Garrod gave an address as president of section H (the archaeological section) of the British Association, later published in edited form by the Prehistoric Society (Garrod 1938). Her phylogenetic research had already shown that only two of the cultures accepted as marking stages in the development of the Upper Paleolithic in France had in fact developed indigenously in Europe; namely, the Solutrean, which stemmed from central Europe, and the Magdalenian, which came from a Gravettian (Upper Aurignacian) source in southern France. All the rest were intruders that had originated outside Europe and spread into that continent. An industry of Chatelperronian character, introduced by an unidentified source, had in fact already penetrated Palestine before the close of the Lower Paleolithic and had apparently made its way into East Africa to form the so-called Kenya Aurignacian. On the other hand, the Aurignacian proper (Middle Aurignacian), which at Mount Carmel overlaid Levalloiso-Mousterian deposits and never reached Africa, must have spread to or from Europe by way of the Balkans. Its presence was revealed at Bacho Kiro in northeast Bulgaria in the course of excavations undertaken with J. Gaul and Bruce Howe (Garrod 1939). The Gravettian, which occurred as far west as the Pyrenees and Cantabria, had apparently spread into Europe from the Russian southern plains. Although perhaps rather late, the Upper Paleolithic industry that Garrod had encountered while excavating in Kurdistan probably belonged to the same dispersion. Like the Aurignacian, the Gravettian extended as far west as Spain and, as the Grimaldian, colonized the Italian peninsula. In summary, Dorothy Garrod was already able, despite the highly incomplete coverage by excavation, to show beyond doubt that the French sequence could hardly be accepted as reflecting indigenous development. On the contrary, it only reflected the order in which cultures—many of which had originated far afield—had appeared in France.

Garrod's researches in southwest Asia thus stressed that prehistory had to be pursued over widespread territories, far beyond those investigated by French prehistorians. Although she herself worked in a comparatively small part of the Eastern Hemisphere, her findings plainly pointed to the need to envision the subject on a worldwide scale. Evidence that she appreciated this is shown by the trouble she took to criticize Oswald Menghin's *Weltgeschichte der Steinzett,* published not many years previously and reviewed in a widely read British periodical (Menghin 1931). Although, as she pointed out, the basic distinction he made between his Protolithic (Lower and Middle Paleolithic) and his Miolithic (Upper Paleolithic and Mesolithic) was directly contradicted by her own work at Mount Carmel, she noticed Menghin's magnum opus because she realized that prehistory could only be comprehended if studied on a worldwide basis.

Garrod was elected to the Disney chair of archaeology at Cambridge in 1939, and she was the first recipient to have practiced prehistoric archaeology in the field. Her position seemed a perfect opportunity to dramatically advance the academic standing of the subject and to offer field training for university students. Unhappily, the outbreak of war dashed these prospects, and from 1942 to 1945, Garrod found herself as a WAAF (member of the Women's Auxiliary Air Force) interpreting air photographs of bomb damage at the Central Interpretation Unit in the Thames Valley. When academic activity resumed at Cambridge, the atmosphere was amenable to new initiatives. To the faculty of archaeology and anthropology, this meant developing the course of study into a degree course in prehistoric archaeology. Advancements in archaeology made it impossible for undergraduates to cover all fronts in the entire field. The solution was to require candidates to choose two concentrations from several options. Specialization was achieved by drawing on other faculties, notably classics, oriental, and Anglo-Saxon studies. As a field archaeologist, Garrod ensured that proper attention was paid to the methods used by archaeologists to obtain their primary data and to extract the maximum information by means of natural science. The history of archaeological endeavor was another required study. Above all, through a course in world prehistory, Garrod intended that students recognize their engagement with a subject that spanned the entire globe.

When Garrod took early retirement in 1952, she withdrew to France, the country where she had learned to become a prehistorian. She picked up her investigation of the rock shelter at Angles-sur-Anglin, Vienne, which she had begun in 1948 with Frech archaeologist Suzanne de Saint-Mathurin, and she continued this work until 1963. A special feature of the rock shelter, occupied during Magdalenian III times, was the low sculptured frieze that included figures of bison, horses, and ibex and detailed depictions of the sexual features of women.

Despite her involvement with the French rock shelter, Garrod was determined to press ahead with her researches in the Near East. In *The Stone Age of Mount Carmel,* she had noted the importance of strandlines for Quaternary chronology, and in 1954 she took the opportunity of inspecting the Pleistocene beaches of Lebanon in company with the archaeologist Père Fleish, who had distinguished three main levels. In 1956 she resumed excavations in the Near East, and in February of that year, she tested the stratigraphy of the Abri Zumoffen in southern Lebanon with the English archaeologist Diana Kirkbride. This work confirmed the presence of a stone-blade tool-making industry, which they termed Amudian (the Amudian period of stone tools occurred between the Acheulean and the Middle Paleolithic), underlying a Jabrudian (late Amudian) deposit with racloirs and bifaces (types of stone tools)(Garrod and Kirkbride 1961). Later that year she teamed up with G. Henri-Martin to examine the infill of a rock shelter at Ras el-Kelb, which had been rendered nearly inaccessible because of the construction of a road tunnel (Garrod and Henri-Martin 1961). They were nevertheless able to establish that the Levalloiso-Mousterian rested directly on the 6/8 meter terrace, the lowest of Père Fleisch's sequences. At the celebratory symposium held at Dusseldorf in 1956 to mark the centenary of the discovery of Neanderthal man, Garrod equated the flints from the lower horizon at Ras el-Kelb with those from Tabun C and observed that both had yielded remains of *Rhinoceros merckii* (Garrod 1962). She concluded that the younger stages of the Levalloiso-Mousterian in the region, and thus the fossils of Mount Carmel man, should be referred to as an early stage of the Würm glaciation of Europe.

Toward the end of her life, Professor Garrod summarized the paleolithic archaeology of Egypt and southwest Asia for the *Cambridge Ancient History* (Garrod and Clark 1965). The chronicle of southwest Asia was, with the exception of Albert Rust's work at Jabrud, largely the outcome of her own fieldwork and her collaborations. The earliest evidence for human occupation in the region was that afforded by the Early and Middle Acheulean industries from the bed of the Jordan, but her excavations provided the best evidence for the rest of the Old Stone Age. The first people to occupy the Mount Carmel region were makers of a Tayacian industry composed of choppers and rough flakes, lacking a retouch but exhibiting edges that showed signs of use. This was followed by a Levalloiso-Mousterian, the flake tools of which had been struck from prepared cores in the Levalloisian technique but shaped in Mousterian style. Overlaying this was a Late Acheulean industry with pear-shaped bifaces. The level above was an industry that included abundant retouched scrapers made on thick flakes with plain platforms, an industry resembling that discovered by Turville-Petre along with a fossil of Neanderthal man in Galilee. Garrod named this Jabrudian, in recognition of the pioneer work done by Rust. With regard to the Upper Paleolithic, Garrod recognized that the only site to provide a complete sequence in one section was that of Ksâr Akil in Lebanon, excavated by Ewing (Ewing 1942). At Mount Carmel, the earliest well-defined Upper Paleolithic, which nevertheless included some Levalloisian flakes, was called the Emiran after the Mugharet el Emireh in lower Galilee, which was dug by Turville-Petre and published after his death by Garrod herself (Garrod 1955). Next in succession were two levels, the earlier of which continued to display Levalloisian features and both of which (but particularly the later) showed strong Aurignacian affinities. The final Upper Paleolithic level was the Kebaran, an industry discovered by Garrod and McCown in 1930, excavated by Turville-Petre and Mrs. C. A. Baynes in 1932, and published by Garrod after both had died (Garrod 1954). The sequence established in Palestine by Garrod and her collaborators was rounded off by the Mesolithic Natufian, the uniqueness of which she had first stressed in 1932 and emphasized a quarter of a century later in her Reckitt lecture to the British Academy.

In her review of neighboring areas, Garrod emphasized the existence of regional differences. Although the evidence was still almost untapped for Anatolia, being confined to surface finds and the material from excavations in the Karian cave near Antalya, she suggested that the later prehistory of the region was closely linked with that from the Levant. Investigations in the Zagros region of Iran initiated by her excavations in the Sulaimanijeh region at Hazar Mard and pursued by American excavators revealed quite a different story. There the blade industry overlying Mousterian levels was of a distinct kind, termed Baradostian after the Baradost Mountains, and was succeeded by a discrete Zarzian culture marked by small notched and gravettelike blades connected possibly with southern Russia by way of the Caucasus and the valleys of the Zagros. The contrast with the sequence at Mount Carmel, which featured a strong Aurignacian element possibly derived from Central Europe, was obvious.

Garrod's review of North Africa was confined to Egypt. There the Acheulean of the 30 meter terrace of the Nile was succeeded by the Levalloisian. It was from this that the Sebelian of Upper Egypt and the Aterian of North Africa were derived. Elsewhere Garrod contended that the leptolithic blade tradition of southwest Asia had intruded into East Africa to produce the Kenya Aurignacian.

One immediate influence that Dorothy Garrod had on prehistory was in directing research away from Europe to western Asia. The challenge was promptly and vigorously taken up by American colleagues, notably by R. S. Solecki at Shanidar in northern Iraq (Solecki 1963) and by Carleton Coon in Iran (Coon 1964). A Cambridge prehistorian, CHARLES MCBURNEY, not only explored Iran and penetrated Afghanistan (McBurney 1964) but also later paid a lengthy visit to the Soviet Union. He gathered firsthand information about the evidence recovered by his Russian colleagues from the Black Sea to the Arctic zone and over much of Siberia, and that formed the subject of his Reckitt lecture to the British Academy (McBurney 1976). In the meantime McBurney had extended the problem presented by the early appearance of leptolithic industries in the Levant by excavating the great cave of Haua Fteah in Cyrenaica (McBurney 1967). He not only found leptolithic elements some 60,000 to 55,000 years old within a Levalloiso-Mousterian zone, but he revealed a new culture, which he termed Dabban, featuring backed blades, burins, and end-scrapers and dating back 40,000 to 15,000 years ago. McBurney had no doubt that these leptolithic elements must have come from southwest Asia, and it was thus appropriate that he dedicated his published account to Dorothy Garrod.

A new generation of American prehistorians adopted a more critical stance. Arthur Jelinek undertook excavations at the Tabun, and while substantially confirming the sequence established by Dorothy Garrod and Albert Rust, he preferred to account for early leptolithic intrusions as the outcome of movements of local populations rather than as the result of impulses from Europe. Many modern prehistorians would agree that, though Garrod was driven to excavate in southwest Asia in order to demonstrate the geographical limitations of the European sequence she had learned from Breuil, she was nevertheless too inclined to apply French terminology to the new material (Jelinek 1982). However, Polish professor J. K. Kozowski, who had continued with the exploration of the Bulgarian site of Bacho Kiro, conducted research with the aid of radiocarbon dating and found that her typologically based perception was in that case correct (Kozowski 1992). He concurred with a Balkan origin for the Aurignacian, which spread as far west as Iberia and ultimately reached the Levant by way of Bulgaria and presumably of Anatolia.

In view of what she aimed to achieve, it would have given Professor Garrod the greatest satisfaction to have attended the international conference held at Cambridge in 1988 (Mellars 1990, Mellars and Stringer 1989) to consider the origin of modern humans. The program included cultural evidence alongside the biological and the paleontological. Above all, it would have pleased her that the conference regarded the world as its stage, since she was one of those most responsible for the emergence of world prehistory.

References
Primary
Garrod, Dorothy A.E. 1926. *The Upper Palaeolithic Age in Britain.* Oxford: Clarendon Press.

————. 1928a. "Excavation of a Palaeolithic Cave in Western Judea." *Quarterly Statement Palestine Exploration Fund.*

————. 1928b. "Notes on Some Mousterian Finds in Spain and Iraq." *Proceedings of the Prehistoric Society of East Anglia* 5: 268–272.

————. 1928c. "Nova et Vetera: A Plea for a New Method in Palaeolithic Archaeology." Presidential Address to the Prehistoric Society. *Proceedings of the Prehistoric Society of East Anglia* 5: 260–267.

————. 1930. "The Palaeolithic of Southern Kurdistan: Excavations in the Caves of Zarzi and Hazar Merd." *Bulletin of the American School of Prehistoric Research* 60: 8–43.

————. 1932. "A New Mesolithic Industry: The Natufian of Palestine." *Journal of the Royal Anthropological Institute* 62: 257–269.

————. 1938. "The Upper Palaeolithic in the Light of Recent Research." *Proceedings of the Prehistoric Society* 4: 1–26.

————. 1939. "Excavations in the Cave of Bacho Kiro, North-East Bulgaria." *Bulletin of the American School of Prehistoric Research* 15: 46–76.

————. 1942. "Excavation of the Cave of Shukba, Palestine, 1928."
Proceedings of the Prehistoric Society 8: 1–20.

————. 1954. "Excavations at the Mugharet Kebara, Mount Carmel,
1931: The Aurignacian Industries." *Proceedings of the Prehistoric
Society* 20.

————. 1955. "The Mugharet el-Emireh in Lower Galilee: Type Station
of the Emireh Industry." *Journal of the Royal Anthropological Institute* 85:
141–162.

————. 1956. "Acheuléo-Jabroudien et pré-Aurignacien de la grotte
de Taboun (Mt. Carmel): Etude stratigraphique et chronologique."
Quarternaria 3: 39–59.

————. 1957. "The Natufian Culture: The Life and Economy of a
Mesolithic People in the Near East." *Proceedings of the British Academy:*
211–227.

————. 1962. "The Middle Palaeolithic of the Near East and the Problem
of Mount Carmel Man." Huxley Lecture 1962. *Journal of the Royal
Anthropological Institute* 92: 232–259.

Garrod, Dorothy A. E., and D.M.A. Bate. 1937. *The Stone Age of Mount
Carmel,* Vol. I. Oxford: Clarendon Press.

Garrod, Dorothy A. E., L. H. Dudley Buxton, C. Elliot Smith, and
D. M. A. Bate. 1928. "Excavation of a Mousterian Rock-Shelter at Devil's
Tower, Gibraltar." *Journal of the Royal Anthropological Institute* 58: 33–113.

Garrod, Dorothy A.E, and J. G. D. Clark. 1965. "Primitive Man in Egypt,
Western Asia and Europe." In *The Cambridge Ancient History.* Ed. Dorothy
A. E. Garrod and J. D. G. Clark. Vol. 1: 3–61. Cambridge: Cambridge
University Press.

Garrod, Dorothy A. E., and G. Henri-Martin. 1961. "Rapport preliminaire
sur la fouile d'une grotte au Ras el-Kelb." *Bulletin Museum Beyrouth* 16:
61–8.

Garrod, Dorothy A. E., and D. Kirkbride. 1961. "Excavations of the Abri
Zumoffen Palaeolithic Rock-Shelter in South Lebanon." *Bulletin Museum
Beyrouth* 16: 7–46.

Secondary

Breuil, Henri. 1912. "Les sub-divisions du paleolithique supérieur et leur
significant." *Compte Rendu XIVe Session Congrès Inernational d'Anthropologie
et d'Archaeologie Prehistoriques, Geneva*: 105–238.

————. 1922. "Palaeolithic Man at Gibraltar: New and Old Facts." *Journal
of the Royal Anthropological Institute* 52: 46–54.

————. 1979. *Four Hundred Years of Cave Art.* Transl. Mary E. Boyle. New
York: Hacker.

Clark, Grahame. 1989. *Prehistory at Cambridge and Beyond.* Cambridge:
Cambridge University Press.

Coon, C. S. 1964. *Cave Excavations in Iran, 1949.* Philadelphia: University
of Pennsylvania Monographs.

Ewing, J. F. 1942. "Preliminary Note on the Excavation at the Palaeolithic
Site of Ksâr Akil, Republic of Lebanon." *Antiquity:* 186–196.

Jelinek, A. J. 1982. "The Tabun Cave and Palaeolithic Man in the Levant."
Science 216: 1369–1375.

Kozowski, J. K. 1992. "The Balkans in the Middle and Upper Palaeolithic: The Gate of Europe or a Cul-de-Sac?" (See especially fig. 13.) *Proceedings of the Prehistoric Society* 58: 1–20.

Marret, R. R. 1912. *Archaeologia* 62: 450–480.

———. 1917. *Archaeologia* 67: 75–118.

McBurney, C. B. M. 1964. "Preliminary Report on Stone Age Reconnaissance in North-Eastern Iran." *Proceedings of the Prehistoric Society* 30: 382–399.

———. 1967. *The Haua Fteah (Cyrenaica) and the Stone Age of the South-East Mediterranean.* Cambridge: Cambridge University Press.

———. 1976. "Early Man in the Soviet Union. The Implications of Some Recent Discoveries." *Proceedings of the British Academy:* 3–55.

McCown, T., and A. Keith. 1937. *The Fossil Human Remains from the Levalloiso-Mousterian.* Volume II. Oxford: Clarendon Press.

Mellars, P., ed. 1990. *The Emergence of Modern Humans. An Achaeological Perspective.* Edinburgh: Edinburgh University Press.

Mellars, P., and C. Stringer, eds. 1989. *The Human Revolution. Behavioural and Biological Perspectives on the Origins of Modern Humans.* Edinburgh: Edinburgh University Press.

Menghin, O. 1931. *Weltgeschichte der Steinzeit.* Vienna: Anton Schroll. Reviewed by Clark, J. G. D. *Antiquity* 1931: 518–521.

Rust, A. 1933. "Beitrag zur Erkenntnis der Abwicklung der vorgeschictlicher kulturperioden in Syrien." *Prähistorische Zeitschrift* 24: 204–218.

Rust, A., and K. K. Wachholtz. 1950. *Die Höhlenfunde avon Jabrud (Syria).*

Solecki, R. S. 1963. "Prehistory in Shanidar Valley, Northern Iraq." *Science* 139: 179–193.

Thompson, G. C. 1969. "Obituary of Dorothy Annie Elizabeth Garrod, 1892–1968." *Proceedings of the British Academy* 55: 339–361.

Turville-Petre, F. 1927. "Researches in Prehistoric Galilee, 1925–1926." *Bulletin of the British School of Archaeology in Jerusalem.*

Richard B. Woodbury

William Duncan Strong   1899–1962

William Duncan Strong was an anthropological theorist and led a shift in archaeological emphasis from chronology to function. He was an early champion of the direct-historical approach and had a huge impact on North American Plains Indian as well as Central American and Peruvian archaeology.

William Duncan Strong (known to his friends as "Dunc") was, in the words of his eulogists, "one of the major figures in anthropology in the twentieth century, contributing as a field worker, a theorist, and a teacher" (Solecki and Wagley 1963, 1102). Strong was born in Portland, Oregon, 30 January 1899, the son of Thomas Nelson Strong, an attorney, and Mary Elizabeth Stone, both from New England. After graduating from high school he enlisted in the United States Navy in World War I and crossed the North Atlantic thirty times on convoy duty as a seaman, first class. When the war ended, he went to the University of California, Berkeley, earning his B.A. in 1923. His undergraduate interest was initially in zoology, particularly ornithology, but he shifted to anthropology, both ethnology and archaeology, mainly as a result of working for Alfred L. Kroeber, the founder and longtime head of the university's distinguished anthropology department. Strong analyzed and seriated the well-documented collections of pioneering archaeologist Max Uhle, whose digs in Peru under the sponsorship of the university early in the century had yielded significant material from individual Peruvian graves. This valuable experience influenced Strong's later career and began a lifelong friendship with Kroeber, who also affected Strong by his interest in all the subfields of the discipline.

Like others of his generation Strong received virtually no field training in archaeology, instead "learning by doing." He excavated with fellow student Julian Steward and W. E. Schenck in the Dalles region of the Columbia River, and in California he dug in Chumash Indian sites. It was not until 1940 that he returned to research on the archaeology of Peru. His 1926 doctoral dissertation, "An Analysis of Southwestern Society," was published the next year in the *American Anthropologist,* a considerable honor for a new Ph.D. graduate. The work combined ethnological and archaeological data to analyze the house-lineage-fetish complex from California to New Mexico. Strong included a chart entitled "Theoretical Reconstruction of Southwestern Society," with parallel

William Duncan Strong. (Courtesy of Ralph Solecki)

columns for societies from the Chumash of California east to Taos Pueblo in New Mexico, each showing key elements of social organization from early to late periods. It is an early example of Strong's skill at identifying similarities (and differences) across wide areas and over long periods of time and presenting them in concise and meaningful tabular form, an ability he would demonstrate again and again with many kinds of data. The article was immediately recognized as an important contribution both to anthropological theory and to culture history. Two years later the University of California published his "Aboriginal Society in Southern California," another major historical-ethnological-archaeological synthesis still regarded as a classic.

From 1926 to 1929 Strong was on the staff of the Field Museum of Natural History as assistant curator of North American ethnology and archaeology. While there he had the opportunity to go to Labrador for fifteen months with the Rawson-MacMillan subarctic expedition. Although he discovered a number of archaeological sites in northeastern Labrador that suggested an Indian-like occupation preceding the Eskimo, his main purpose was ethnographic research. He spent the winter with the Naskapi Indians, whose small nomadic bands roamed a vast bleak area and subsisted on hunting and fishing. Taking an active part in their hunting trips, sharing their diet, sleeping in their tents, and enduring the bitterly cold winter were experiences that Strong never forgot. He fascinated his friends and students years later with vividly remembered incidents and observations. His extensive diary and field notes, only partly in manuscript form at his death, are the basis for *Labrador Winter* (Leacock and Rothschild 1994), a remarkable personal memoir and scientific record of a way of life now vanished.

Among his coworkers at the Field Museum were Berthold Laufer (Ph.D. Leipzig 1897), an orientalist and scholar who had a significant intellectual influence on Strong; and Ralph Linton (Ph.D. Harvard 1925), assistant curator of ethnology and later a colleague at Columbia University. During his Chicago years Strong married Jean Stevens, a longtime friend. (A decade later they were divorced.)

In 1929 Strong accepted (after helpful consultation with Kroeber) an appointment as professor of anthropology in the University of Nebraska's Department of Sociology. Although he was there only two years, he made pioneering and fundamental contributions to the archaeology of the Plains. His previous experience in field archaeology had been limited, but he immediately began a highly successful summer program of archaeological research in Nebraska. At that time it was generally believed that human occupation of the Plains was relatively recent, although local amateur archaeologists had already provided limited evidence to the contrary by making carefully recorded artifact collections from prehistoric and contact-period village sites. For some locations, there were tentative tribal identifications. Strong immediately sought out these amateur scholars and benefited from their knowledge and collections, a cooperative relationship some "professionals" disdained then—and still do today.

Leading authorities on the Indians of the Plains, such as Kroeber and Clark Wissler of the American Museum of Natural History, believed that the equestrian hunters of historic times had been preceded only by small bands of prehorse nomadic hunters and foragers. From the research of the avocational archaeologists and his own surveys and excavations, Strong demonstrated that, to the contrary, there had been a long period during which agricultural villages were widespread on the Plains and maintained substantial ties to the farming villages east of the Plains. GORDON R. WILLEY, who has written a detailed portrait of Strong's career and personal life, commented that Strong's 1935 volume on Nebraska archaeology "had a revolutionary impact on both North American archaeology and ethnology . . . a telling demonstration of how archaeology could be an integral part of anthropology, providing us as it did a corrective for ethnological preconceptions" (1988, 75). It immediately confirmed Strong as a major American archaeologist as well as an anthropological theorist. Strong made effective use of the new "direct-historical approach," starting with historically documented village sites and working back to their prehistoric predecessors, thus establishing antecedents for some of the well-known Plains tribes, such as the Pawnee. In his Nebraska work as in later research, Strong saw history, ethnology, and archaeology (and also biological and linguistic anthropology, with which he was indirectly concerned) as interdependent; consequently, they should not be compartmentalized as separate "disciplines." Although Strong's position was diametrically opposed to that of Kroeber, they continued to be able to disagree as scholars and cooperate as friends.

Strong's primary responsibility at Nebraska was, of course, classroom teaching, and although not a polished lecturer, he was then as in later years a stimulating teacher who aroused enthusiasm in his students. As a former student and a colleague have observed, "Strong was a great teacher. He was not by any means a highly articulate and brilliant lecturer, although his classes were always interesting and filled with sound material. He did much of his teaching outside the classroom, in the laboratory and in the field, often by means of almost a master-apprentice relationship with some of his best students" (Solecki and Wagley 1963, 1106). Those at Nebraska who went on to distinguished careers in archaeology included John L. Champe, Preston Holder, and Albert C. Spaulding, all three of whom later earned Ph.D.'s at Columbia University under Strong. Waldo R. Wedel went to the University of California, Berkeley, for his Ph.D. but continued his interest in the Plains for the rest of his professional career, brilliantly developing the foundation that Strong had laid. Strong's attention to the Plains continued in future years, and at Columbia University he started several more students in Plains ethnology and archaeology, including Paul L. Cooper, Richard G. Forbis, Frank R. Secoy, and Carlyle S. Smith. Strong's research in Nebraska was a highly regarded beginning that inspired others to emulate it, not only there but in other Plains states where the precontact occupations had been similarly neglected. Few have so singlehandedly opened a door to concerted archaeological investigation of a major continental area.

Strong's next professional appointment came in 1931—senior anthropologist at the Smithsonian Institution's Bureau of American Ethnology, a position allowing full-time research in the field and in the office on problems of the incumbent's choice. The offer was made by Matthew Stirling, a friend from student days at Berkeley who was now chief of the bureau. In Washington, D.C., Strong continued his concern with the archaeology of the Plains, both through further excavation and by encouraging and cooperating with the work of others throughout the 1930s. He promptly completed *An Introduction to Nebraska Archeology* in 1932, though its publication was delayed until 1935. In 1946 he played an important role in the creation of the River Basin Surveys, which preserved a great wealth of archaeological material from sites being destroyed by the huge series of dams that the U.S. Army Corps of Engineers was building on the Missouri and other rivers.

Beginning in 1933, however, he developed an interest in quite a different area, Central America. He took part in an expedition to the Bay Island of Honduras, a hitherto largely neglected region that was peripheral to Mayan territory and had possible prehistoric connections to South America. With his usual sense of scholarly responsibility, by 1935 he had published a report on the joint research. He made a second and more extensive archaeological trip to Honduras in 1936, in company with archaeologists ALFRED KIDDER and A. J. Drexel Paul, which resulted in a preliminary chronology for an area where stratigraphic archaeology had been almost wholly lacking.

It is evidence of Strong's breadth of interest that in 1936 he was chosen as a member of a team of consultants to advise the new commissioner of the Bureau of Indian Affairs, John Collier, on the drastic changes required to make it responsive to the needs of Native Americans. Although Collier was derided by some as a visionary when he was appointed by Franklin D. Roosevelt, he successfully reversed the long-standing government policies of destroying all that was unique and traditional in Native American life. Strong, with his deep concern, as both ethnologist and archaeologist, for the American Indians, could feel satisfaction at his role in this achievement.

In 1937 Strong accepted a professorship in the Department of Anthropology of Columbia University, a position he occupied for the rest of his life. He combined teaching with continued fieldwork and writing. His courses were well prepared, with a content that was thoughtful and wide-ranging, and they were popular with both undergraduate and graduate students. They reflected his extensive reading of anthropology and archaeology, past and present; for example, he highly recommended a nearly forgotten classic, *Methods and Aims in Archaeology*, by W. M. FLINDERS PETRIE (1904) for its practical observations on archaeological research. Of one of his courses, "New World Origins and Continuities," Willey observed that "at that time, it was probably the best general survey course on North and Middle American archaeology that was offered in any university" (1988, 84). Strong also taught anthropological and archaeological theory and developed a very popular course on North American Indians (with his own observations on the Naskapi). "This particular course revealed him as an ethnologist as well as an archaeologist, but he had a way of viewing the two disciplines in concert, of wanting to see no barriers between them" (ibid., 85).

Solecki and Wagley (1963) list some thirty professional anthropologists who were Strong's students during his years at Columbia, most of them pursuing careers in North American or Latin American archaeology and ethnology, though a few directed their efforts toward the Pacific, the Near East, and elsewhere. This scholarly corps is eloquent testimony to Strong's leadership and inspiration as a teacher.

Ralph Linton was invited to join the Columbia faculty at the same time Strong was, and he became chair of the department the following year. His 1936 book, *The Study of Man,* was important for its exploration of the common ground among the theoretical camps of anthropology. Like Strong he wrote in clear, jargon-free prose that reached the general public as well as the specialist. The two of them greatly strengthened a department weakened by the retirement of founding anthropologist Franz Boas and composed to a considerable extent of his former students.

It was not long before Strong began to refocus on Peru. In the summer of 1940 he made an extensive trip there, visited important sites, and benefited greatly from time spent with Julio C. Tello, a world-renowned authority on Peruvian archaeology. However, in the next few years Strong would develop his own chronology and terminology for Peruvian prehistory, rather than relying on Tello's. On his return to Columbia in the fall, Strong started planning a long-term Peruvian research program. To better inform himself as well as others, he gathered a small group of graduate students, including Gordon R. Willey, for a seminar on Peruvian archaeology. Willey would become a colleague and friend and would soon make major contributions to Peruvian archaeology himself.

In 1941 Strong headed one of ten field parties in an ambitious, co-ordinated investigation of Latin American prehistory, organized by the private Institute of Andean Research, of which Strong was later president. Financial support came from the participants' affiliated institutions and from the federal Coordinator of Inter-American Affairs. Work was planned for lesser-known areas and was geared toward surveying and stratigraphic excavation rather than costly long-term architectural excavation. Strong decided to work at Pachacamac, a well-known site fomerly excavated by Uhle a few miles south of Lima, with his students Gordon Willey and John Corbett as assistants. Avoiding the Inca Temple 10, where Tello was working, they secured a long and crucial stratigraphic sequence in the site's enormous refuse heap. Work continued into 1942 at several other Peruvian locations, with emphasis still on establishing sound local and regional chronological sequences based on changing ceramic styles.

Strong published in 1943 the preliminary results of all ten of the institute's field projects as "Cross Sections of New World Prehistory." An important feature was his tabular presentation of cultural sequences in twenty regions from the southwestern United States to northern Chile, aligned to show contemporaneity as a basis for hemispheric comparisons. Besides the minutiae of sequences in individual regions, he was becoming increasingly interested in wide-ranging synthesis, built on these carefully developed regional chronologies. He looked forward to eventually moving beyond the New World regions he was currently correlating to worldwide comparisons. "When such comparative data are at hand the generalisations that will emerge may well revolutionise our concepts of culture history and culture process over the millennia" (Strong 1943, 41).

The remaining two decades of his career were marked by this dual concern with precise local and regional chronologies and broad comparisons. Strong was influenced in this by the work of his longtime

friend and colleague Julian H. Steward, whose early interest in archaeology had expanded to examining the parallels in cultural development of the world's major cultures from their simplest antecedents to the present time. Utilizing the tabular format again, Strong divided 5,000 years of New World prehistory into seven "epochs" with parallel columns for the sequences in each of nine regions (Strong 1951). Rather than depending mainly on distinctive ceramic styles, as had long been the practice in American archaeology, Strong defined his epochs by "(1) economic base, (2) the artistic level achieved, and (3) the political organisation, in so far as it can be envisaged" (Strong 1948, 101).

View of the Pachacamac from the Temple of the Sun looking toward the House of Cacique. (Reprinted from William Duncan Strong, Gordon Willey, and John M. Corbett, Archeological Studies in Peru: 1941–1942 *[1943])*

These broad comparisons and syntheses reflect the change that archaeology in the United States was experiencing at the time, moving from a primary concern with chronology to an increased interest in reconstructing the context within which changes occurred and in the functional interpretation of archaeological data. Strong was himself a pioneer in this shift in emphasis; his 1936 "Anthropological Theory and Archaeological Fact" urged that ethnology, archaeology, and history work together to improve the understanding of cultural growth and change and to test each other's hypotheses. No longer would chronology and areal distinctions be sufficient goals for archaeological research.

World War II interrupted Strong's archaeological teaching and research. In 1942 he became director of the Ethnogeographic Board, housed in Washington, D.C., in the Smithsonian Institution. It was a new, wartime federal agency, created to make available to the armed forces, particularly the Navy, information from anthropological sources—covering everything from details of the coral reefs around a Pacific atoll to the location of trails and passes in the mountains of Balkan countries to data on the customs of unfamiliar peoples. In 1945 Strong returned to New York, accompanied by Helen Richardson, whom he had met and married in Washington.

The next year, Strong joined with three colleagues, archaeologists Wendell C. Bennett of Yale University and Gordon R. Willey of the Bureau of American Ethnology, Smithsonian Institution, and social anthropologist Julian H. Steward of the Institute of Social Anthropology, Smithsonian Institution. Together they planned an innovative research project in Peru, which would focus on a single valley, the Virú, and study the geography and resources of the valley, human adaptation to the valley's environment over the full span of human occupation there, and the lifeways of its current inhabitants. This combined geographical and anthropological project became known as the Virú Valley Program and was under the sponsorship of the Institute of Andean Research. It soon added a number of scholars from other institutions to its fieldwork, including Allan R. Holmberg, Jorge C. Muelle, Junius Bird, and JAMES A. FORD. The program extended from 1946 through 1948 and produced notable publications of its results that significantly influenced future archaeological work in Peru. Strong's part, assisted by Clifford Evans, was to establish the basic archaeological chronology of the valley. Although the work of each field party was independent and self-contained, the program as a whole was organized to have immediate and frequent exchange of data and ideas, making the sum of the research program greater than its individual parts. The project became a highly regarded example of coordinated interdisciplinary research.

Strong and Evans published their report on the Virú chronology in 1952. That same year Strong conducted his last major field expedition, going again to Peru with two Columbia University students as assistants, Rose Lilien and Robert Stigler. They conducted survey and excavation in the Ica and Nazca valleys of the south coast. Willey called Strong's 1957 report on the research "a major contribution to Peruvian archaeological systematics," which clarified the relationships of several important and well-known cultural complexes through stratigraphy and ceramic analysis (1988, 95).

Strong's career was cut short by his sudden death on 29 January 1962. He received a number of honors, including appointment to Columbia University's Loubatt Professorship of Archaeology, which had been vacant since 1918. His active professional life was indicated by his presidency of the American Ethnological Society in 1941–1942 and of the Society for American Archaeology in 1955–1956. He was a fellow of the University Museum, University of Pennsylvania, and a research associate of the American Museum of Natural History. His fellow archaeologists selected him in 1954 for the Viking Fund Medal for Archaeology, "for pioneering research and stimulation of archeological projects," which notably included his 1927 "Analysis of Southwestern Society," his fieldwork and publications on Plains archaeology, and the first large-scale stratigraphic work in coastal Peruvian refuse deposits.

As the Viking medal citation might have added, Strong's research career was distinguished by his repeatedly demonstrated ability to move into an unfamiliar and poorly known area and quickly identify its key problems, promptly secure significant new field data (from both survey and excavation), derive fresh interpretations, both chronological and functional, and through his publications provide a solid foundation for his or others' future research. He was thus able to make substantial contributions to the archaeology of the United States Plains, Central America, and Peru. Another impressive trait was managerial. Though he could "rail at bureaucracy," as a friend said, he could also be an efficient and creative administrator, not only in the planning and execution of research in Nebraska and Peru and in directing the wartime Ethnogeographic Board, but also in the many years in which he served his turn as chair of the anthropology department at Columbia University.

In one sense Strong remained a lifelong naturalist, from his early interest in ornithology through his years of meticulous recordkeeping of the wildlife around his country retreat at Kent Cliffs outside New York City. Indeed, what guided his professional approach was the perception that humankind was part of the whole natural world, the biological and cultural aspects of human history being inseparable.

As an anthropological theorist, a leader in the shift of archaeological emphasis from chronology to function, and an early champion of the direct-historical approach, he could write optimistically but cautiously of the eventual establishment of cultural "laws" or worldwide regularities in economic, social, and cultural change. At the same time that he was extracting from ancient refuse heaps the myriad details of chronological change as seen through subtle differences in ceramics, he could see the dramatic centuries-long evolution of militaristic kingdoms or empires from tiny bands of foragers, scattered farming villages, and networks of prosperous small towns. He combined a romantic view of human cultural development with the scientist's practice of framing hypotheses, finding the data to test them, and reaching tentative conclusions on which future research could build. He left a lasting legacy for American archaeology in his pioneering research publications and in the distinguished roster of students who pursued careers in anthropological research largely as a result of his encouragement and example.

References
Primary

Strong, William Duncan. 1927. "An Analysis of Southwestern Society." *American Anthropologist* 29: 1–61.

———. 1929. "Aboriginal Society in Southern California." *University of California Publications in American Archaeology and Ethnology.* Vol. 26. Berkeley.

———. 1930. "A Stone Culture from Northern Labrador and Its Relation to the Eskimo-like Cultures of the Northeast." *American Anthropologist* 32: 126–144.

———. 1933. "The Plains Culture Area in the Light of Archaeology." *American Anthropologist* 35: 271–287.

———. 1935. "Archeological Investigations in the Bay Islands, Spanish Honduras." *Smithsonian Miscellaneous Collections* 92, 14.

———. 1935. "An Introduction to Nebraska Archeology." *Smithsonian Miscellaneous Collections* 93, 10.

———. 1936. "Anthropological Theory and Archaeological Fact." In *Essays in Anthropology Presented to A. L. Kroeber in Celebration of His Sixtieth Birthday.* Ed. R. H. Lowie. Berkeley: University of California Press.

———. 1940. "From History to Prehistory in the Northern Great Plains." In *Essays in Historical Anthropology of North America Published in Honor of John R. Swanton. Smithsonian Miscellaneous Collections* 100.

———. 1943. "Cross Sections of New World Prehistory: A Brief Report on the Work of the Institute of Andean Research, 1941–1942." *Smithsonian Miscellaneous Collections* 104, 2.

———. 1948. "Cultural Epochs and Refuse Stratigraphy in Peruvian Archaeology." In *A Reappraisal of Peruvian Archaeology,* assembled by Wendell C. Bennet. Memoirs of the Society for American Archaeology no. 4. Menasha, WI.

———. 1951. "Cultural Resemblances in Nuclear America: Parallelisms or Diffusion?" In *The Civilizations of Ancient America. Selected Papers of the XXIXth International Congress of Americanists.* Ed. Sol Tax. Chicago: University of Chicago Press.

———. 1957. "Paracas, Nazca, and Tiahuanacoid Cultural Relationships in South Coastal Peru." *Memoirs of the Society for American Archaeology* no. 13. Salt Lake City.

Strong, William Duncan, and C. Evans. 1952. "Cultural Stratigraphy in the Viru Valley, Northern Peru." *Columbia Studies in Archeology and Ethnology,* Vol. 4. New York.

Strong, William Duncan, A. Kidder II, and A. J. Drexel Paul, Jr. 1938. "Preliminary Report on the Smithsonian Institution–Harvard University Archeological Expedition to Northwestern Honduras, 1936." *Smithsonian Miscellaneous Collections* 97, 1. Washington, DC.

Strong, William Duncan, Gordon R. Willey, and J. M. Corbett, eds. 1943. "Archeological Studies in Peru, 1941–1942." *Columbia Studies in Archaeology and Ethnology,* Vol. 1. New York.

Secondary

Leacock, E. B., and N. A. Rothschild, eds. 1994. *Labrador Winter, The Ethnographic Journals of William Duncan Strong, 1927–1928.* Washington, DC: Smithsonian Institution Press.

Solecki, R., and C. Wagley. 1963. "William Duncan Strong, 1899–1962" (with complete bibliography). *American Anthropologist* 65: 1102–1111.

Willey, Gordon R. 1988. "William Duncan Strong (1899–1962)." In *Portraits in American Archaeology: Remembrances of Some Distinguished Americanists.* Albuquerque: University of New Mexico Press.

Roberto Cobean and Alba Guadalupe Mastache Flores

Jorge R. Acosta 1904?–1975

One of the most productive and influential Mexican archaeologists of the
twentieth century, Jorge Acosta carried out excavations at Tula, Monte Alban,
and Teotihuacan that were fundamental to the rediscovery of Mesoamerican
civilization.

Jorge R. Acosta was born in China in 1904 or 1908—various legal documents list different dates for his birth (Matos 1988). His father was the distinguished Mexican diplomat Alfonso Acosta Villalobos. As a youth and young man he studied for several years in England, first at the Seven Oaks School in Kent and then at St. Johns College, Cambridge (1924–1925), where he was a friend and classmate of the future Mayanist John Eric Thompson. Acosta's career as an archaeologist lasted nearly fifty years (1928–1975). He died in Mexico City on 5 March 1975.

In this brief essay, we will mainly concentrate on Acosta's investigations in Tula, the site of the ancient Toltec capital Tollan. This work was probably his central contribution to Mesoamerican archaeology. Both authors knew Acosta during the last decade of his life—a rather bitter period for him because his efforts at Tula and other sites were being severely criticized by Mexican and American archaeologists of the "younger generation." These scholars were reassessing the value of all previous investigations according to the Marxist or Binfordian "New Archaeology" canons, a development of the early twentieth century aimed at making archaeology more scientifc—now more often called processual archaeology. From this perspective, they were always encountering "serious" deficiencies. It is ironic that many of these same erstwhile critics have recently recognized the high quality of most of Acosta's work, and there are now books dedicated to him, tributes to the validity of his basic interpretations and conclusions, and projects to republish many of his key reports.

The list of sites and regions where Acosta did fieldwork is extremely impressive: Zacaleu, Guatemala; Mountain Cow, Belize (with John Eric Thompson); numerous locations in Michoacan; Monte Alban, Monte Negro, and other centers in Oaxaca; Chichén Itzá, Uxmal, Palenque, Tres Zapotes (Veracruz), Cholula, Ixcateopan (Guerrero), Tenayuca, and Teotihuacan. His most important investigations focused on three ancient cities, Monte Alban, Tula, and Teotihuacan, where he

Monte Alban—the main plaza of the Zapotec ceremonial city. (© American Museum of Natural History)

spent years doing research. In the course of other projects he discovered the famous mural sequence of drinking figures inside the Great Pyramid of Cholula, and at Uxmal (Yucatan) he directed an architectural restoration program that greatly influenced the theory and practice of cultural patrimony conservation in Mexico (Acosta 1958; Matos 1988). He discovered the ceremonial cave under the Pyramid of the Sun at Teotihuacan that probably played a key role in the founding and the general structural plan of that ancient city (Heyden 1981; Millon 1981). His restoration of the Palace of Quetzalpapalotl at Teotihuacan (Acosta 1964) has been considered excessive by some specialists, but it constituted a major success in making a 1,500-year-old building understandable for thousands of visitors.

Acosta's investigations in Oaxaca with Alfonso Caso and Ignacio Bernal during three decades were fundamental for the development of Mexican archaeology and produced several classic reports, including *The Ceramics of Monte Alban* (Caso, Bernal, and Acosta 1967). The decade of the 1940s, when Acosta directed his most consequential field seasons at Tula, was also a period of intense activity for him in Oaxaca, and he often served as the field director of Caso's program at Monte Alban. Even during this busy time, it is admirable that Acosta continued his custom of publishing his results very quickly, often during the same years when he did the fieldwork.

Acosta at Tula

On the basis of Acosta's work at Tula, his name can be added to the very short list of archaeologists who have rediscovered major ancient civilizations. The ruins at Tula in the modern Mexican state of Hidalgo were known to the Aztecs at the time of the Spanish conquest to be the site of the legendary Tollan, capital of the Toltec Empire during the tenth or eleventh century (Davies 1977). Aztec emperors and members of the royal dynasties of numerous other central Mexican states claimed to be descendants of the ancient Toltec kings, and the Aztec-period indigenous chronicles described the city of Tollan as a great center of cultural and artistic achievement. Because these accounts described a large, impressively constructed urban complex that at least superficially did not resemble the modestly sized ceremonial center at Tula, many early-twentieth-century archaeologists, including MANUEL GAMIO and George Vaillant, proposed that the nearby city of Teotihuacan with its immense pyramids was the legendary Tollan. By this time a considerable number of archaeological investigations had been done at Teotihuacan, but the only systematic studies at Tula were the excavations of the French explorer Desiré Charnay nearly fifty years earlier (1885).

During the 1930s the ethnohistorian Wigberto Jimenez Moreno (1941) analyzed the place-names of human settlements and geographical features mentioned in the chronicles (especially sixteenth-century accounts of the *Anales de Cuauhtitlan* and Fray Bernadino Sahagun) in connection with ancient Tollan, and he confirmed that most of these places were clearly identified with the area of Tula. Jimenez Moreno's conclusions were supported by archaeologists in Mexico's newly founded (1939) National Institute of Anthropology and History (INAH) and particularly by its first director Alfonso Caso. In 1940 Jorge Acosta was named head of the institute's excavation program at Tula and spent nearly twenty field seasons there. The 1940 field season was dedicated primarily to the excavation of numerous test pits and stratigraphic trenches in the main plaza and other sectors of the city. These investigations produced a preliminary ceramic sequence that clearly placed Tula's apogee after the decline of Teotihuacan and before the rise of the Aztecs (Acosta 1940). At the first roundtable conference of the Mexican Society of Anthropology in 1942, the theme was Tula and the Toltecs, and the definitive reports of Acosta (1941) and Jimenez Moreno (1941) provided the basis of discussion. After this conference, the majority of Mesoamerican archaeologists were convinced that Tula, Hidalgo, and not Teotihuacan was the city of Tollan described in the central Mexican chronicles.

The major part of Acosta's work at Tula was devoted to the excavation and restoration of many of the buildings on the main plaza. These were some of the best investigations of pre-Hispanic architecture ever conducted in Mexico, and most of the results were published in detail in the *Revista mexicana de estudios antropologicos* and the *Anales* of the Instituto

Nacional de Antropología e Historia. From the first, however, Acosta's research objectives went beyond mere architectural restoration. His studies concentrated on at least four problems: the cultural origins of Tula; the archaeological chronology for the main developmental stages of the city, from its beginnings through expansion, peak, decline, and postcollapse occupation; the correlation of archaeological phases with specific events described in the Toltec chronicles, especially the histories in the *Anales de Cuauhtitlan;* and iconographic interpretations of Tula's sculptures, including the identification of gods, historical figures (kings), and human figures who represented members of specific social classes or economic and political groups (warriors, priests, merchants, etc.). To some extent Acosta examined the urban plan of Tula through his excavations outside the monumental plaza, especially in a complex called Huapalcalco (1945) near Tula Chico, in the large ancient neighborhood on the hill called El Cielito (1941), and in the city's northeast sector at the circular pyramid called El Corral and its associated structures (1974). He also excavated a series of human burials in various parts of the city that were analyzed by physical anthropologists in unpublished reports stored in the INAH archives. Acosta's program at Tula functioned as field training for young archaeologists and anthropologists, several of whom (Alberto Ruz, Juan Valenzuela, Jose Luis Lorenzo, Felipe Montemayor, among others) went on to have notable professional careers. His chief assistant during the most important field seasons was Hugo Moedano, who wrote several key texts on Tula (1946, 1947) and served with distinction in various other archaeological projects before his death in his mid thirties.

In 1945 Acosta published the first detailed summary of Tula's archaeology based on findings from four seasons. He proposed a chronological sequence of five periods encompassing an early occupation before the city's Toltec expansion, to Spanish colonial settlements in the sixteenth century. This synthesis was the most accurate chronological system published at that time for what archaeologists call the late classic (A.D. 600–900) and the postclassic (900–1520) periods in the central Mexican highlands. Shortly afterwards Pedro Armillas (1950) adopted Acosta's classification as part of his thorough reconstruction of chronological and cultural phases in the basin of Mexico from Teotihuacan to the Aztecs, which is still commonly accepted by archaeologists.

Acosta proposed two pre-Aztec phases at Tula: an initial founding occupation called the Periodo Antiguo that was associated with a ceramic complex called Coyotlatelco; and a subsequent expansion and apogee of the city called the Periodo Reciente that had a ceramic assemblage dominated by orange-and-cream wares (especially a type

Acosta named Naranja a brochazos) as well as some important red-on-brown types. Using the ethnohistorical reconstructions of Jimenez Moreno, Acosta placed the first phase in the ninth century and the acme during the tenth and the eleventh centuries, with the city's destruction sometime late in the twelfth century. Recent radiocarbon and archaeomagnetic dates have confirmed most aspects of Acosta's chronology, with the exception that Tula's founding now dates to the eighth century (Cobean and Mastache 1989; Wolfman 1990; Austin Long, personal communication).

Acosta's correlation of the Coyotlatelco ceramic complex with the establishment of Tula was a crucial discovery, because previously archaeologists had been unsure of the chronological placement and cultural significance of the peoples using that pottery, except that they associated these groups with the abandonment of Teotihuacan (Acosta 1945, 1956–1957; Vaillant 1938). The Coyotlatelco complex had originally been defined by Harvard archaeologist Alfred Tozzer (1921), based on early stratigraphic excavations in the west-central basin of Mexico at Santiago Ahuitzotla, but his investigations did not clearly distinguish this pottery form early-classic Teotihuacan materials (Rattray 1966). Acosta identified several new types of Coyotlatelco-tradition pottery that have more recently been used as diagnostic elements for subdividing the early occupations at Tula into three separate phases (Cobean 1990).

Strangely, with the important exception of Armillas, many archaeologists during the 1950s and 1960s did not appreciate the cultural significance of Acosta's definitions of the orange-and-cream pottery types associated with Tula's apogee. The primary reference for this period continued to be George Vaillant's chronology, which emphasized different types, especially Mazapan red on brown, that were not common at Tula (Vaillant 1938). This bias was probably due to Vaillant's fame as a skilled analyst of cultural traditions and pottery groups, but as it turned out, his reconstructions of formative cultures, which he published in detail, were considerably better than his studies of late-classic and postclassic peoples, largely unpublished at his death in 1945. During the 1960s and 1970s, the settlement-pattern surveys of Sanders (1965) and Parsons (1971) in the basin of Mexico still employed Vaillant's ceramic typology to identify early postclassic sites contemporary with Tula. Yet as recent investigations have confirmed, Acosta's typology was substantially more accurate (McCullough 1966; Cobean 1978; Cobean and Mastache 1989).

It would be impossible to provide a detailed summary of Acosta's vast program of excavation and restoration of the main buildings on Tula's plaza, which he described in hundreds of pages of published reports and which have been outlined elsewhere (Cobean and Mastache

1988; Diehl 1989). His work concentrated on seven structures: the main pyramid (Pyramid C), the Pyramid of Tlahuizcalpantecuhtli, the main palace (called the Burned Palace), the great colonnade or vestibule, the Adoratory, Building 1 (a temple-palace complex), and Ball Court 1. Tula's ceremonial complex covered an area measuring 300 by 400 meters, which is only slightly smaller than the main plaza of Tenochtitlan, the Aztec capital (Matos 1986; Boone 1987). The ceremonial precinct initially seemed so unimpressive to archaeologists because its buildings had been badly damaged by fires at the time of the city's collapse (ca. 1150–1200) and then had suffered several centuries of looting by the Aztecs and the early Spanish invaders (Acosta 1956–1957; Nicholson 1971; Cobean, ed., 1994). Most of the facades and parts of the cores of the two main pyramids had been dismantled when the city fell at the hand of unknown groups—possibly the Toltecs themselves ritually destroying their most sacred structures in a manner similar to the destruction of monuments and buildings at the abandonment of other Mesoamerican centers, such as Teotihuacan (Millon 1981) and San Lorenzo Tenochtitlan, Veracruz (Coe and Diehl 1980).

Despite this devastation, there was much at Tula for Acosta to discover. For example, in just one of the three main halls of the Burned Palace, he found over 200 nearly complete stone panels sculpted with images of priests and warriors (Acosta 1956). Acosta published detailed descriptions, complete with maps, plans, and photographs, of the original damaged states of the buildings he later restored. Despite this, nearly fifty years later, it is still common to read or hear criticisms by archaeologists and architects that Acosta largely "invented" major structures at Tula such as the Burned Palace or the Pyramid of Tlahuizcalpantecuhtli. Anyone with sufficient patience can read Acosta's reports and easily determine which parts of Tula's buildings are original elements and which parts are restored.

Probably Acosta's most controversial reconstruction was the pyramid of the Atlanteans. This structure had been very badly damaged in pre-Hispanic times and seems to have consisted of three superimposed pyramids, the last of which had been almost totally destroyed (Acosta 1942–1944). The upper sections of the two earlier structures had been thoroughly dismantled, and a huge pre-Hispanic trench had been dug in the center of building's north facade. When Acosta excavated this trench, he found a hoardlike deposit of dismantled basalt sculptures, including the fearsome Atlantean warriors and four rectangular columns decorated with reliefs of elite armed figures.

Acosta decided to restore the upper section and stairway of the pyramid's second stage and to place the reassembled Atlanteans and the rectangular columns on its summit. His plan was partially based on similarities between this building and a recently restored Toltec pyramid that had been found in a much better state of preservation: the Temple of the Warriors at Chichén Itzá (Morris et al. 1931). The Temple of the Warriors was topped by rectangular columns that were very similar to the ones Acosta found buried with the Atlanteans at Tula. He proposed that the armed figures on the columns were portraits of Toltec kings. Each figure had a glyph or symbol near its head that he believed represented the person's name or lineage (Acosta 1956–1957). The identifying symbol for one figure was a feathered serpent, and Acosta concluded that this might be a portrait of Topiltzin Quetzalcoatl (Nahuatl for "our young lord the feathered serpent"), the legendary king of Tula who appeared in late pre-Hispanic indigenous chronicles as a hero of central Mesoamerican culture (Martinez del Rio and Acosta 1957; Nicholson 1957).

On the lower sections of the east facade of the pyramid, Acosta found fragments of a series of sculpted panels that probably originally covered the entire surface of the structure (Marquina 1964). These panels were decorated with reliefs of jaguars, coyotes, eagles, and other raptors as well as a composite creature with human, reptilian, and avian attributes. This figure represented Tlahuizcalpantecuhtli, a version of the god Quetzalcoatl who was associated with the planet Venus and rites of war and human sacrifice. Hence Acosta named the pyramid after Quetzalcoatl.

Acosta excavated parts of the largest pyramid at Tula (Pyramid C on the east side of the main plaza), but this structure was so damaged that he undertook only a limited consolidation of its facades and stairway. He mapped but did not excavate a huge pre-Hispanic trench that cut through the stairway and west facade of Pyramid C (Acosta 1961). This trench may well contain dismantled sculptures as its ancient counterpart did in the other pyramid. Following the early excavations of the French explorer Desiré Charnay (1885), Acosta discovered a sufficient number of basalt Atlantean fragments elsewhere near the plaza of Tula to suggest that Pyramid C also had a temple on its summit supported by Atlantean columns.

As Acosta's investigations advanced, he found an increasing number of similarities in architecture, iconography, and site planning between Tula and the much-later Aztec cities of Tenochtitlan, Tlatelolco, and Tenayuca. Consequently, he derived analogies from Aztec ethnohistorical and archaeological studies to reconstruct the general plan of Tula's ceremonial center and to identify the functions of specific buildings and sculpture complexes. For example, immediately to the north of the pyramid of the Atlanteans, he found hundreds of fragments of a sculpted panel sequence, which by reference to Aztec usage he identified as a Coatepantli or "serpent wall" that in Aztec cities defined the limits of the sacred space inside the main plaza (Acosta 1942–1944). Acosta and his workmen successfully restored what was left of Tula's Coatepantli, which displayed reliefs of giant serpents eating human skeletons. This ceremonial wall, the earliest discovered to date in Mesoamerica, probably served as the prototype for the serpent walls in the plazas of Aztec cities. Aside from the Coatepantli, Acosta identified other elements at Tula that constituted key aspects of Aztec monumental centers, including chacmool sculptures (anthropomorphic altars common in Mesoamerica) benches with friezes depicting processions of warriors and priests, sculptures of Atlanteans and standard-bearers, balustrades decorated with serpents, and I-shaped ball courts. These common features strongly suggested that Tula was the source for much of Aztec ceremonial art and architecture (Nicholson 1971). Recent projects at Tula have identified additional parallels with Aztec ceremonial elements, such as Matos's (1976) discovery of a Tzompantli (a platform for displaying the skulls of sacrificial victims) at a location in the plaza matching that where the skull rack at Tenochtitlan was situated.

In the colonnade directly south of the Pyramid of Tlahuizcalpante-cuhtli, Acosta and Moedano found benches with sculpted panels showing processions of elaborately dressed polychromed figures. The discovery constituted one of the best-preserved complexes of Toltec art at Tula (Acosta 1945; Moedano 1947). These friezes and the friezes on the benches in the Burned Palace were extraordinarily similar to the Aztec sculptured benches found near the main pyramid of Tenochtitlan (Beyer 1917; Matos 1986; Boone 1987).

The Burned Palace adjoining the west facade of the Pyramid of Tlahuizcalpantecuhtli was probably the most complicated structure that Acosta excavated and restored. He spent most of eight field seasons investigating this building, which covered over 5,400 square meters and included three large halls or meeting rooms, at least six smaller rooms with various functions (storerooms and ritual areas), and three large vestibules. The structure contained evidence of over 800 years of human occupation from approximately A.D. 900–1700, which furnished much of the data for his ceramic and cultural chronology of Tula. Its designation as the "burned palace" (Palacio Quemado) derived from its destruction by fire during the fall of Toltec Tula near the end of the twelfth century. Acosta also discovered a series of Aztec and early Spanish colonial occupations above the ruins of the Toltec structure, which complicated his interpretations of specific contexts because the later inhabitants had destroyed or altered parts of the original building.

The excavations in the Burned Palace uncovered hundreds of sculptured panels depicting warriors, priests, gods, possibly merchants, and abstract religious symbols that originally decorated the benches and walls of the main rooms. Acosta published drawings and photographs of the major classes of sculptures, but systematic iconographic studies of this material were begun only recently (Jimenez 1990). In the central great hall (Sala 2) of the palace, he found a series of important offerings and sculptures, including two basalt chacmools (the austere reclining human figures that inspired the twentieth-century English sculptor Henry Moore) and a badly damaged turquoise mosaic disk. Recent investigations by a Mexican government project in the same hall uncovered two additional Toltec offerings: another turquoise mosaic disk and an elaborate cut-shell mosaic ceremonial garment, both of which have been restored (Cobean, ed., 1994; Cobean and Estrada 1994).

After years of excavations, Acosta concluded that the Burned Palace did not function as a residence in Toltec times. He found no kitchens, dormitories, or other rooms or contexts within the structure to indicate that people had lived there. Instead he proposed that the main halls of the building served as assembly areas for councils of elders, warriors, and nobles and other governing bodies of the Toltec state. Aztec elite warrior councils met in similar halls with sculptured benches, as shown by excavations in Tenochtitlan (Matos 1986). A Mexican government project recently excavated another large building similar to the Burned Palace on the southern edge of Tula's plaza and concluded that this structure also probably functioned as a meeting hall for elite groups and was not a royal residence (Cobean 1994). Thus after nearly thirty years of fieldwork, the location of Tula's royal palaces is still unknown. Acosta, in preliminary reports, occasionally suggested that specific buildings on the plaza might have been royal residences, but in his actual digs, he never accumulated enough evidence to confirm his suppositions. Neither have the subsequent projects at Tula been able to solve the problem.

One of the structures that Acosta proposed as a royal palace was Building 1 (sometimes called the Palace of Quetzalcoatl) near the east facade of the Pyramid of Tlahuizcalpantecuhtli. Uncharacteristically, Acosta never published in detail his investigations of this building. Its complex history included at least seven construction phases and numerous changes in the main floor plans (Diehl 1989). Some of the final architectural modifications may have been done by the Aztecs, who reoccupied several buildings on Tula's main plaza. The plans that Acosta did publish for the probable Toltec stages of this structure showed a temple or ritual-area layout covering about 400 square meters and consisting mostly of one courtyard—a very small and simple building to have served as a royal residence (Acosta 1945, 1960).

The Adoratory, an altarlike platform in the center of Tula's plaza,

Aerial view of the
Temple of the Sun,
Teotihuacan.
(Corbis / Yann
Arthus-Bertran)

had been badly damaged by an exploratory trench that Charnay had dug through it in the 1880s. Acosta was nevertheless able to identify two construction phases and restored the earliest phase partly by reference to the better-preserved Toltec Platform of the Eagles at Chichén Itzá (Acosta 1945, 1964; Diehl 1989). He found a broken chacmool sculpture deposited between the first and second platforms.

The most successful reconstruction and consolidation that Acosta conducted at Tula was devoted to Ball Court 1 beyond the northern end of the plaza. The work occurred between 1940 and 1944, and nearly fifty years later it was still in stable condition despite exposure to the elements and tourists and minimal conservation (Cobean, ed., 1994). Probably the main reason for the limited damage was Acosta's restoration of the original pre-Hispanic drainage systems. He even found one large tunnel-like drain in the northwest corner of the building that was still functioning without repairs after a thousand years. Many parts of the ball court had been dismantled by the Aztecs, but Acosta was able to identify three superimposed structures and restore the final version of the building. There are two other nearby ball courts: Matos (1976) restored the large ball court on the west limit of the main plaza during the 1960s, and a small, apparently well-preserved ball court near the plaza's northeast corner has yet to be excavated.

Concluding Comments
Acosta published in 1957 a summary of many of his findings at Tula in the *Revista Mexicana de Estudios Antropologicos,* but at his death there

remained a number of unpublished reports on Tula, Monte Alban, and several other sites where he had worked. In his 1963 memoirs John Eric Thompson observed that his generation would probably constitute the last group of generalists in Mesoamerican archaeology. Jorge Acosta was a distinguished member of that generation, and no one has since taken his place. The scope of his contributions can be measured in an imprecise way by observing that only a modest sampling of his accomplishments has been described here. Similar essays could be written about his investigations at Monte Alban or Teotihuacan or in the Mayan area. No archaeologist today digs as much as he did, and no archaeologist attempts to investigate so many different cultures. The specialized archaeologists of the present achieve more scientific studies than their predecessors did, but it is nevertheless worth pondering why so many of the giants of the profession exist only in the past.

References
Primary

Acosta, Jorge R. 1930. "Las ruinas de Zacaleu." *Anales de la Sociedad de Geografía e Historia de Guatemala* 6, 4: 178–194.

———. 1931. *La civilización americana es originaria del Continente?* Resumen, XXIV. Mexico City.

———. 1939. "Exploraciones arqueológicas realizadas en el Estado de Michoacan durante los años de 1937–1938." *Revista mexicana de estudios antropológicos* (SMA), 3: 85–98.

———. 1940. "Bibliografía." *Boletín bibliografico de antropología americana* (Instituto Panamericano de Geografía e Historia, Mexico City): 274–275.

———. 1940. "Exploraciones en tula, Hidalgo, 1940." *Revista mexicana de estudios antropológicos* (SMA), 4: 172–194.

———. 1941. "Los altimos descubrimientos arqueologicos en Tula, Hidalgo, 1941." *Revista mexicana de estudios antropológicos* (SMA), 5: 239–243.

———. 1942. "La ciudad de Quetzalcoatl." *Cuadernos americanos* 2, 6: 138–146.

———. 1942. "Rasgos olmecas en Monte Alban." *Segunda Mesa Redonda: Mayas y Olmecas* (SMA): 55–56. Mexico City.

———. 1942–1944. "La tercera temporada de exploraciones arqueologicas en Tula, Hgo. 1942." *Revista mexicana de estudios antropológicos* (SMA), 6: 125–164.

———. 1943. "Los colosos de Tula." *Cuadernos americanos* 2, 6: 138–146.

———. 1945. "La cuarta y quinta temporada de exploraciones arqueologicas en Tula, Hidalgo." *Revista mexicana de estudios antropológicos* (SMA), 7: 23–64.

———. 1947. "El pectoral de jade de Monte Alban." *Anales del INAH,* 3: 17–26.

———. 1948. "Reseoa de Chimalacatlan de Florencia J. Miller." *Boletín bibliografico de antropología americana* (Instituto Panamericano de Geografía e Historia, Mexico City), 11: 210–212.

———. 1951. "Reseoa de la alfareria correspondiente al altimo periodo de ocupación nahua del Valle de México de James Griffin y Antonieta Espejo, 1947 y 1950." *Boletín bibliografico de antropología americana* (Instituto Panamericano de Geografía e Historia, Mexico City) 13, 2: 76–77.

———. 1953. "Reseoa de *Introduccion a la arqueología de Ignacio Bernal,*" 1952, *Yan,* 1, 74–76.

———. 1954. "Exploraciones arqueologicas efectuadas en Chichen Itza, Yucatan, 1951." *Anales del INAH* 8, 37–115.

———. 1956. "El enigma de los Chac Mooles de Tula." *Homenaje al Dr. Manuel Gamio:* 159–170. Mexico City.

———. 1956. "Resumen de los informes de las exploraciones arqueologicas en Tula, Hidalgo, durante las VI, VII y VIII temporadas, 1946–1950." *Anales del INAH* 8: 37–115.

———. 1956–1957. "Interpretacion de algunos de los datos obtenidos en Tula relativos a la epoca tolteca." *Revista mexicana de estudios antropológicos* (SMA), 14: 75–160.

———. 1957. "Resumen de los informes de las exploraciones arqueologicas en Tula, Hidalgo, durante las IX y X temporadas, 1953–54." *Anales del INAH* 9: 119–169.

———. 1958. *Nuevos ensayos de restauración en Uxmal,Yucatan.* Report, Archivo de la Coordinación Nacional de Antropología, Instituto Nacional de Antropología e Historia. Mexico City.

———. 1959. "Exploraciones arqueologicas en Monte Alban. XVIII temporada, 1958." *Revista mexicana de estudios antropológicos* (SMA), 15: 7–32.

———. 1959. "Tecnicas de reconstruccion." In *Esplendor del México antiguo,* 2, 501–518. Ed. Carmen Cook de Leonard and Julio Rodolfo Moctezuma. Mexico City: Centro de Investigaciones Antropológicas de México.

———. 1960. "Las exploraciones en Tula, Hidalgo, durante la XI temporada, 1955."*Anales del INAH* 11: 39–72.

———. 1961. "La doceava temporada de exploraciones en Tula, Hgo." *Anales del INAH* 13: 29–58.

———. 1961. "La indumentaria de las cariatides de Tula." *Homenaje a Pablo Martínez del Río,* 221–228. Mexico City: Instituto Nacional de Antropologia e Historia.

———. 1964. "La decimotercera temporada de exploraciones en Tula, Hgo." *Anales del INAH* 16: 45–76.

———. 1964. *El Palacio de Quetzalpapalotl.* Mexico City.

———. 1965. "Preclassic and Classic Architecture of Oaxaca." In *Handbook of Middle American Indians,* vol 3. Ed. Robert Wauchope. Austin: University of Texas Press.

———. 1972. "El epilogo de Teotihuacan." *Onceava Reunión de Mesa Redonda* (SMA). Mexico City.

———. 1974. "La piramide de El Corral en Tula, Hgo." In *Proyecto Tula*

(Primera Parte). Coord. Eduardo Matos. Instituto Nacional de Antropología e Historia Scientific Collection 121. Mexico City.

———. 1975. "La ceramica de Cholula." *Los Pueblos y los Señoríos Teocrático.*

———. 1993. *Excavaciones en Monte Negro, Oaxaca.* Instituto Nacional de Antropología e Historia. Mexico City.

Acosta, Jorge Rufier, and Hugo Moedano Kroeber. 1946. "Los juegos de pelota." *México prehispanico:* 365–384.

Acosta, Jorge Rufier, and Josefina Lomeli Quirarte. 1939. "Catalogo de los objetos encontrados en Monte Alban, Oax." *Congres International des Américanistes,* 27, 2: 136–142. Mexico City.

Martinez Del Rio, Pablo, and Jorge R. Acosta. 1957. *Tula,* Guía del INAH.Mexico City: Instituto Nacional de Antropología e Historia.

Secondary

Armillas, Pedro. 1950. "Teotihuacan, Tula y los toltecas: Las culturas post-arcaicas y pre-aztecas del Centro de México: Excavaciones y estudios 1922–1950." *Runa* (Buenos Aires) 3: 37–70.

Beyer, Hermann. 1917. *La procesion de los senores.* Report, Archivo de la Coordinación Nacional de Arqueología, Instituto Nacional de Antropología e Historia. Mexico City.

Boone, Elizabeth H. 1987. "Templo Mayor Research, 1521–1978." In *The Aztec Templo Mayor.* Ed. E. H. Boone. Washington, DC: Dumbarton Oaks.

Caso, Alfonso, I. Bernal, and J. R. Acosta. 1967. *La Ceramica de Monte Alban.* Mexico City: Instituto Nacional de Antropología e Historia.

Charnay, Desiré. 1885. *Les anciennes villes du Nouveau Monde.* Paris: Hachette.

———. 1978. "The Pre-Aztec Ceramics of Tula, Hidalgo, Mexico." Ph.D. dissertation, Harvard University.

Cobean, Robert H. 1990. *La ceramica de Tula, Hidalgo.* Mexico City: Instituto Nacional de Antropología e Historia.

Cobean, Robert H., ed. 1994. *Proyecto "Mantenimiento, conservacion y estudio de la Zona Arqueologica de Tula, Hidalgo."* Report, Instituto Nacional de Antropología e Historia. Mexico City.

Cobean, Robert H., and Elba Estrada. 1994. "Ofrendas toltecas en el Palacio Quemado de Tula, Hidalgo: Proyecto Tula 92–93." *Arqueología Mexicana* (INAH/Raices) 2, 6.

Cobean, Robert H., and Alba Guadalupe Mastache. 1988. "La excavacion monumental en Tula." In *La Antropología en México: Panorama Historico,* 6: 147–187. Ed. Carlos Garcia Mora and M. Del Valle Berrocal. Mexico City: Instituto Nacional de Antropología e Historia.

———. 1989. "The Late Classic and Early Postclassic Chronology of the Tula Region." In *Tula of the Toltecs.* Ed. D. M. Healan. Iowa City: University of Iowa Press.

Coe, Michael, and Richard A. Diehl. 1980. *In the Land of the Olmec: The Archaeology of San Lorenzo Tenochtitlan.* Austin: University of Texas Press.

Davies, Nigel. 1977. *The Toltecs until the Fall of Tula.* Norman: University of Oklahoma Press.

Diehl, Richard A. 1989. "Previous Investigations at Tula." In *Tula of the Toltecs*. Ed. D. M. Healan. Iowa City: University of Iowa Press.

Heyden, Doris. 1981. "Caves, Gods, and Myths: World-View and Planning in Teotihuacan." In *Mesoamerican Sites and World Views*. Ed. E. P. Benson. Washington, DC: Dumbarton Oaks.

Jimenez Garcia, Elizabeth. 1990. "La iconografía de Tula, Hidalgo." Licenciatura thesis, Escuela Nacional de Antropología e Historia, Mexcio City.

Jimenez Moreno, Wigberto. 1941. "Tula y los toltecas según las fuentes historicas." *Revista mexicana de estudios antropologicos* (SMA), 5: 79–83.

Marquina, Ignacio. 1964. *Arquitectura Prehispanica*. Mexico City: Instituto Nacional de Antropología e Historia.

Matos Moctezuma, Eduardo. 1976. *Tula: Guía*. Mexico City: Editorial Orto.

———. 1986. *The Great Temple of the Aztecs*. London: Thames and Hudson.

———. 1988. "Jorge R. Acosta." In *La antropología en México: Panorama Historico* 9: 45–52. Ed. Lina Odena G. Emes and Carlos Garcia Mora. Mexico City: Instituto Nacional de Antropologia e Historia.

McCullough, John. 1966. "Toltec Ceramics of the Lower Teotihuacan Valley." Report, Sixty-fourth Annual Meeting, American Anthropological Association, Denver.

Millon, Rene. 1981. "Teotihuacan: City, State and Civilization." In *Supplement to the Handbook of Middle American Indians*, 198–243. Ed. V. R. Bricker and J. A. Sabloff. Austin: University of Texas Press.

Moedano, Hugo. 1946. "Tollan." M.A. thesis, Escuela Nacional de Antropología e Historia, Mexico City.

———. 1947. "El friso de los caciques." *Anales del INAH* 2: 113–136.

Morris, E. H., J. Charlot, and A. A. Morris. 1931. *The Temple of the Warriors at Chichen-Itza, Yucatan*. Carnegie Institution of Washington Publication 406. Washington, DC: Carnegie Institution of Washington.

Nicholson, Henry B. 1957. "Topiltzin Quetzalcoatl: A Problem in Mesoamerican Ethnohistory." Ph.D. dissertation, Harvard University.

———. 1971. "Mayor Sculpture in Prehispanic Central Mexico." In *Handbook of Middle American Indians*, vol. 10. Ed. Robert Wauchope. Austin: University of Texas Press.

Parsons, Jeffrey R. 1971. *Prehistoric Settlement Patterns in the Texcoco Region*. Memoirs of the Museum of Anthropology, University of Michigan. Ann Arbor.

Rattray, Evelyn C. 1966. "An Archaeological and Stylistic Study of Coyotlatelco Pottery." *Mesoamerican Notes*, 7–8: 87–211.

Sanders, William T. 1965. *The Cultural Ecology of the Teotihuacan Valley*. University Park: Pennsylvania State University.

Thompson, John Eric S. 1963. *Maya Archaeologist*. Norman: University of Oklahoma Press.

Tozzer, Alfred M. 1921. *Excavations of a Site at Santiago Ahuitzotla, D.F., Mexico*. Bureau of American Ethnology Bulletin 74. Washington, DC: Bureau of American Ethnology.

Vaillant, George C. 1938. "A Correlation of Archaeological and Historical Sequences in the Valley of Mexico." *American Anthropologist* 40: 535–573.

———. 1941. *Aztecs of Mexico.* New York: Doubleday.

Wolfman, Daniel. 1990. "Mesoamerican Chronology and Archaeomagnetic Dating, A. C. 1–1200." In *Archaeomagnetic Dating.* Ed. J. L. Eighmy and R. S. Sternberg. Austin: University of Texas Press.

John W. Olsen

Pei Wenzhong   1904–1982

Pei Wenzhong was the founding father of Chinese paleoanthropology and Paleolithic archaeology. At Zhoukoudian he discovered the first remains of Homo erectus, *and the first stone artifacts in association with fossil humans in China, as well as evidence of the use of fire dating back more than 300,000 years.*

Pei (also P'ei Wen-chung or W. C. Pei) was born on 19 January 1904 in Fengnan County, Hebei Province, north China. Pei's contributions to Chinese archaeology over the course of his very long career are best understood in the context of the historical milieu in which his own education developed (Zhang 1983; An 1987; Zhang and Hu 1990). Pei's father, Pei Yanying, was a primary-school teacher whose active participation in local anti-illiteracy campaigns and educational reforms occupied much of his time. Historical documents also indicate that Pei Yanying took part in the Luanzhou uprising, a popular outpouring of sentiment against the increasingly imperialist presence of foreign countries in China and the retention of an essentially feudal system of social governance during the late Qing dynasty and early Republican period. Thus, from an early age, Pei Wenzhong was imbued with a philosophy that emphasized the need for both mass education and the wholesale reform of China's traditional social institutions. It was precisely this intellectual stance that predisposed Pei to become a leading figure in the restructuring of science in China following the foundation of the People's Republic in 1949.

Pei Wenzhong began his formal education in a traditional Chinese private school but soon transferred to the Kaiping Primary School in Tangshan, Hebei, where his father taught. His family's diminished financial resources precluded Pei's enrollment in one of the city's new high schools; he instead pursued his secondary education at the Third Provincial Normal School (now the Luanxian Normal School) in Luan County, Hebei. After graduation in 1921, he was admitted to Beijing University as a preparatory student. In 1923 he transferred to the Department of Geology and graduated with a major in paleobiology in 1927.

Pei's formative years were a period of dramatic internal struggle and social unrest in China. The failed social and economic reforms of the late nineteenth century contributed to the final collapse of the Qing dynasty

in 1911 and set the stage for nearly forty years of governmental insta-
bility and outright revolution. The most important changes to have
taken place within the Chinese intellectual community during that period were expressed in the philosophy of the May Fourth Movement,
which began on that date in 1919, primarily on the university campuses
in Shanghai and Beijing, and then spread to many other intellectual en-
claves in China. The May Fourth Movement was, among other things, a
reaction by Chinese intellectuals against the stagnant Confucian educational ideals of the past as well as the increasing domination of China by
foreign powers (mostly western European, North American and, to a
lesser extent, Japanese) in the realms of science, education, and economics. When the seventeen-year-old Pei Wenzhong arrived at Beijing
University to begin his studies in 1921, he found the campus deeply
embroiled in the fallout from the May Fourth Movement. The appreciation for social and educational reform passed on to him by his father
stood him in good stead, and he quickly became an active participant in
student strikes and other actions designed to express dissatisfaction
with the status quo, including the publication of newspaper articles as-
sailing government corruption and the lax attitude toward increasing
foreign ownership of Chinese property and territory. During his student years, Pei even published a short story in an alternative literary
journal, *Chenbao Fukan,* entitled "In the Midst of Battle," which attacked
the selfishness of China's early Republican warlords by pointing out the
extremely negative effect their internal bickering and warfare was hav-

ing on the Chinese people as a whole (Anonymous 1982). It is important to note that throughout his life Pei Wenzhong appreciated the need for balance in the development of science, by combining the training of highly specialized researchers and technicians with a strong program of mass education.

Simultaneous with his reformist activities, Pei pursued his studies at Beijing University. He attended lectures on literature given by such revolutionary figures as Qian Xuantong and Lu Xun (the latter of whom, it is said, read and praised Pei's *Chenbao Fukan* short story) and received a firm foundation for his subsequent specialization in geology under the guidance of Li Siguang.

After graduation, Pei was unable to locate permanent employment so, in the spring of 1928, on the recommendation of Weng Wenhao, director of the Geological Survey of China, he went to work in Hebei province at the site of Pleistocene fossiliferous fissures at Zhoukoudian (formerly Chou-k'ou-tien, Chou Kou Tien, or Choukoutien), where an international team of scientists had, since 1921, been endeavoring to uncover evidence of some of China's earliest human occupants. Beginning in 1929, Pei became field supervisor of the Zhoukoudian excavations and on 2 December of that year he made the most important discovery of his long career—the first skull of *Homo erectus* found on Chinese soil. This specimen, later known popularly as "Peking Man," formed the basis for a thorough reinterpretation of human evolution in East Asia.

At Zhoukoudian, Pei's intellectual development was influenced by such scholars as the Canadian anatomist Davidson Black, the American anthropologist Franz Weidenreich, and the French Jesuits HENRI BREUIL, archaeologist, and Pierre Teilhard de Chardin, geologist and vertebrate paleontologist. A remarkable aspect of Pei's character was that while his participation in the May Fourth Movement and related activities as a university student gave the impression of a nationalistic, revolutionary-minded young man fed up with the foreign exploitation of China and its people, he was able to work at Zhoukoudian in close association with these "outsiders" and others, including the Swedish archaeologist J. Gunnar Andersson. He seemed to recognize that not all foreign influence was pernicious and that one important avenue for China's development might be to expand its relatively brief history of intellectual contact with the West. The Zhoukoudian excavations from 1921 to 1937 became, in fact, a model not only of multidisciplinary science but also of multinational collegiality in which Chinese scholars including Pei and, most notably, his colleagues Yang Zhongjian (C. C. Young), Bian Meinian (M. N. Bien), and Weng Wenhao received due credit for their enormous contributions to the research project.

Pei's discovery of the *Homo erectus* cranium in Locality 1 at Zhoukoudian catalyzed his interest in China's Pleistocene prehistory; at age twenty-five Pei had embarked on the career path that he would pursue for the rest of his life. From 1929 to 1935, under his guidance, many important localities at Zhoukoudian were discovered and excavated. These included Locality 13, which has yielded what many believe are the earliest archaeological materials at the site (approaching one-half million years old); Locality 15, an early Upper Pleistocene fissure containing a rich Middle Paleolithic stone assemblage and vertebrate fauna; and the Upper Cave, which yielded some of the earliest human burials in China and a small artifactual assemblage in terminal Pleistocene sediments (Chang 1986, 41–50, 60–64). In 1932, under Pei's direction as field supervisor, a complex and successful alphanumeric grid system, truly remarkable for its day, was established at the Zhoukoudian site allowing excavators to maintain provenance control (Jia and Huang 1990, 81–91).

In July 1935 Pei interrupted his studies at Zhoukoudian to enroll at the University of Paris. He completed a doctoral dissertation in 1937 under the direction of Abbé Breuil and returned to Beijing in October, on the heels of the invading Japanese army, to take charge of the newly constituted Cenozoic Research Laboratory. During the difficult years from 1937 to 1948, Pei managed to continue his research on the Chinese Paleolithic and was simultaneously engaged by several universities, including both Beijing and Yanjing, to lecture on prehistoric archaeology. In 1948, Pei was inducted into the prestigious September Third Academic Society (Jiu San Xuehui), an influential organization with official Communist Party affiliations, and after Chinese liberation in 1949, he served on that society's central and standing committees.

From 1949 to 1953 Pei was head of the museums division of the Bureau of Social and Cultural Affairs under the Ministry of Culture in the new People's Republic of China. In 1954 he transferred to the Chinese Academy of Sciences and assumed the title of researcher in the academy's Institute of Vertebrate Paleontology and Paleoanthropology (IVPP), the successor to the Cenozoic Research Laboratory that Pei had headed for more than a decade after his return from Paris in 1937. Pei's primary task at the IVPP was the organization of the institute's paleoanthropology division and the development of research programs in both Paleolithic archaeology and human paleontology. In June 1956 Pei was elected to the Biology-Geology Section of the Chinese Academy of Sciences and was simultaneously promoted to first-level researcher. In 1963, he was appointed director of the Paleoanthropological Research Laboratory of the IVPP, and from 1979 until his death, he was chairman of the Beijing Natural History Museum. At the end of his life, he not only filled these positions but concurrently held honorary memberships in the Royal Anthropological Association (Great Britain, elected 1957), UNESCO's International Union of Prehistoric and Protohistoric Sciences (elected 1979), and the International Quaternary Association (elected 1982).

The course of Pei Wenzhong's academic career was profoundly influenced by both his traditional upbringing and his subsequent contact with the new breed of Chinese intellectuals who looked, in part, to the West for inspiration and guidance. Regrettably little is known of Pei's activities during his years in France. From his writings and those of his mentor Breuil, we are left with the merest impression of a serious, dedicated scholar anxious to reconcile his traditional cultural values with the more advanced scientific approaches of the West.

During his university years in Beijing, Pei seems to have been most interested in politics, literature, and journalism. His assignment to the Zhoukoudian excavations changed his life in that he was able, for the first time, to witness the complex interplay between the practicalities of fieldwork and the theoretical realm that guides such research. At Zhoukoudian, Pei actively participated in fieldwork and honed his skills in prehistoric archaeology through voracious reading and close, continual contact with leading Chinese and foreign scientists involved in the project, particularly Li Ji (Li Chi) and Pierre Teilhard de Chardin. Pei's role as field director at Zhoukoudian in the short period from 1929 to 1935 resulted not only in his discovery of the first remains of *Homo erectus* there but also in the discovery of the first unequivocal stone artifacts in association with fossil humans in China and evidence of the use of fire dating back more than 300,000 years.

Pei's analysis of simply chipped flakes of quartzite discovered in 1930 in Locality 1 led him to conclude that Peking man was indeed a tool user. This assertion, later confirmed by Breuil, was outlined in a landmark 1931 publication, "Notice of the Discovery of Quartz and Other Stone Artifacts in the Lower Pleistocene Hominid-bearing Sediments of the Choukoutien Cave Deposit." This article, the first to establish a link between fossils of *Homo erectus* and stone artifacts in China, was also the first independent achievement in Paleolithic research made by a Chinese scholar. Its publication drew attention to the potential contributions of China in resolving the relationship between the Zhoukoudian hominids and their Indonesian cousins (the remains of so-called Java man or *Pithecanthropus* discovered by Eugene Dubois in 1891); it also signaled the beginning of a new era in Chinese archaeology—one in which Chinese scholars were recognized by the world scientific community as being fully capable independent researchers. No doubt it was the combination of Pei's remarkable skills as director of excavations at Zhoukoudian as well as the more than two dozen academic papers and three monographs published by him between 1929 and 1935 that brought him to the attention of Henri Breuil and convinced him to take Pei on as his doctoral student in Paris.

The initial body of publications generated by Pei Wenzhong before his departure for France represented an astounding array of archaeological subjects (An 1987, 282–283; Zhang and Hu 1990, 383–384). He described the human and other vertebrate fossils from Zhoukoudian (1929, 1933), analyzed the stone assemblage from that site (1931), published one of the world's first descriptions of modified bone from an archaeological context (1932), introduced the term *Mesolithic* into Chinese archaeology (1935), and expanded his area of interest into the Neolithic (1934). These were only a few of the important papers released during this critical period.

During the 1950s, a time of structural reorganization and growth in the People's Republic, Pei Wenzhong developed the first coherent chronology for the north Chinese Paleolithic (Pei 1955, 1959). Clearly influenced by his typologically focused training in France, Pei subdivided the Chinese Paleolithic into three phases: Early (represented by Localities 1, 13, and 15 at Zhoukoudian), Middle (represented by the Shuidonggou and Salawusu [Sjara-osso-gol] sites in north-central China, an assemblage Pei labeled "Ordos Culture"), and Late (represented by the Upper Cave at Zhoukoudian and the Dingcun site in Shanxi). In his writings there was evident a gradual evolution in his largely typological focus, one in which the effects of raw material variability and tool function begin to play an increasingly important role in defining prehistoric cultures. Pei nurtured a lifelong fascination with the arid plateau encompassed by the *hetao* or great bend of the Yellow River (called *ordos* by the area's local Mongolian-speaking inhabitants) in north-central China. As late as the mid-1960s, he was still pursuing fieldwork in the Ordos region and refining his conception of what synchronic artifact variability meant in terms of archaeological definitions of culture.

It would be a false oversimplification to suggest that Pei Wenzhong's contribution to science was limited to his replication of essentially European archaeological method and theory in a Chinese context. The impact of the May Fourth Movement, his association with foreign scholars at Zhoukoudian, and his doctoral education in France all shaped his thinking on the proper course of archaeological investigation. Pei's earliest independent scholarly treatises, dating to the 1930s, clearly indicated the influence of his contact with western colleagues as well as his own ability to detect the unique characteristics of Chinese prehistory.

Pei Wenzhong did not simply seek to apply a western European (mostly French) Paleolithic typology to Chinese materials without modification. He recognized that such factors as the availability and selection of raw materials and the techniques of manufacturing made direct comparison of the European and Chinese Paleolithic impossible. Through time, Pei's perception of large-scale typological variability in the Paleolithic coalesced into a theory of cultural pluralism that focused on both geography and environmental factors to explain the differences he saw in the earliest prehistoric record of the West and China (P'ei et al. 1933).

The exploration of the Upper Pleistocene Dingcun (formerly Tingts'un) localities in Shanxi province during the 1950s (1955, 1958) afforded Pei Wenzhong a perfect opportunity to further refine his conception of the Chinese Paleolithic and its relationship to contemporaneous industries elsewhere. Pei also pointed out the fundamental ways in which the Dingcun Middle Paleolithic industry varied from its northern China predecessor, the Lower Paleolithic remains from Zhoukoudian Locality 1. Thus, by the end of the 1950s, Pei had begun to grapple with the complex problem of diachronic and synchronic variability in Paleolithic assemblages and to offer explanations for such variation in the Chinese case.

The excavation of Guanyindong (Guanyin Cave) in Guizhou Province, southern China, in the mid-1960s provided Pei and his colleagues with abundant new evidence for the complexity of the Chinese Paleolithic (Pei et al. 1965). Because it was derived from a controlled excavation rather than haphazard survey or the result of amateur collection, the Pleistocene Guanyindong lithic assemblage furnished the first unequivocal evidence of substantial synchronic variability within the Chinese Paleolithic. The analysis of the Guanyindong materials laid to rest the anachronistic notion that the Chinese Paleolithic was some great homogeneous entity exhibiting little or no variation through time or across space. Pei and his colleagues, in reference to Guanyindong, stated that "it is almost impossible to compare such a stone tool assemblage with those found so far in Europe . . . and it is very difficult to see common characteristics shared by Guanyindong and Zhoukoudian" (Pei et al. 1965, 277). The assertion clearly echoed Pei's notions concerning cultural pluralism and the necessity of understanding Chinese prehistoric sequences on their own terms rather than as watered-down or aberrant derivatives of a western European Paleolithic tradition.

Pei's contributions to the development of archaeological theory in China were balanced by his continuing attention to the practical acquisition of basic data. Throughout his professional career, Pei Wenzhong was a consummate field worker. A record of more than half a century of

A skull of "Peking man," half-free from its prehistoric bed of rock in Dragon Bone Hill, is prepared for final removal by four scientists with picks, 1936. (© The American Museum of Natural History)

field studies documents Pei's work in regions ranging from Inner Mongolia and Gansu in the north to Guizhou and Guangxi in the south. These expeditions not only generated much of the information on which the current understanding of early Chinese prehistory rests, but they also provided opportunities for the training of most of China's cadre of professional paleoanthropologists through the 1970s.

One distinguishing characteristic of Pei's approach to research was his refusal to simply comply with conventional wisdom in the interpretation of the archaeological record. The discovery of the first simply flaked quartzite tools at Zhoukoudian in the 1930s immediately generated controversy over their anthropogenic versus natural origin. Pei was among a small vanguard of early-twentieth-century archaeologists who relied heavily on an explicitly experimental approach to solve questions such as this, and his doctoral dissertation was devoted to developing and applying the experimental and analytical methodology necessary to distinguish human artifacts from stones chipped by natural processes (eoliths). An extension of his earlier analysis of bone fragments from Zhoukoudian (Pei 1932), this work encapsulated Pei Wenzhong's whole approach to understanding the past—interpretation of the archaeological record through prudent application of experimental studies and the replication of prehistoric technologies.

It is a great tragedy that the irrational xenophobia that defined official Chinese science from the late 1950s through mid-1970s effectively denied Pei Wenzhong his proper place in the annals of modern archaeology. Until recently he was remembered solely in the context of his admittedly impressive though nonetheless now outdated studies at Zhoukoudian. His researches later in life into the Neolithic and even dynastic archaeological record of China—in particular, his systematic studies of the ancient ceramic and bronze vessel forms termed *ding* and *li*—were equally impressive though virtually unknown outside China (Zhang and Hu 1990, 384–386). Pei Wenzhong, unlike many of his contemporaries who had also received their advanced degrees abroad, suffered no grievous injury to self or property at the hands of zealots during the excesses of the so-called Cultural Revolution of the late 1960s, yet his government's policies nonetheless effectively isolated him from the world community of archaeologists during the most productive years of his life (Zhang 1983).

Pei Wenzhong died on 18 September 1982 in Beijing at the age of seventy-nine following a protracted illness. He was entombed in a simple crypt immediately behind the site museum, near Locality 1, at Zhoukoudian.

References
Primary

P'ei, W. C. (also Pei, W. Z.). 1929. "An Account of the Discovery of an Adult *Sinanthropus* Skull in the Chou Kou Tien Deposit." *Bulletin of the Geological Society of China* 8, 3: 203–205.

————. 1931. "Notice of the Discovery of Quartz and Other Stone Artifacts in the Lower Pleistocene Hominid-Bearing Sediments of the Choukoutien Cave Deposit." *Bulletin of the Geological Society of China* 11, 2: 110–146.

————. 1932. "Preliminary Note on Dome Incised, Cut, and Broken Bones Found in Association with *Sinanthropus* Remains and the Lithic Artifacts from Choukoutien." *Bulletin of the Geological Society of China* 7, 1: 105–111.

————. 1935. "On a Mesolithic [?] Industry of the Caves of Kwangsi." *Bulletin of the Geological Society of China* 14, 3: 393–412.

————. 1955. "Palaeolithic Cultures of China." *Kexue Tongbao* 1: 30–45 (in Chinese).

————. 1958. "The Mammalian Fauna from Locality 103 at Dingcun, Shanxi." *Gushengwu Xuebao* 6, 4: 359–374 (in Chinese).

P'ei, W. C., ed. 1959. "Palaeolithic Research in Chinese Academy of Sciences." In *Science in China during the Past Decade. Palaeontology,* 115–125. Beijing: Science Press (in Chinese).

P'ei, W. C., and C. C. Young. 1934. "On a Collection of Yangshao Cultural Remains from Mienchihhsien, Honan." *Bulletin of the Geological Society of China* 13, 2: 305–318.

Pei, W.Z, and S. S. Zhang. 1985. "A Study on the Lithic Artifacts of *Sinanthropus.*" *Palaeontologia Sinica,* n.s. D, 168, 12 (in Chinese with English abstract).

P'ei, W. C., D. Black, P. Teilhard de Chardin, and C. C. Young. 1933. "Fossil Man in China." *Geological Memoirs Geological Society of China,* Series A, 11.

Pei, W. Z., Z. X. Yuan, Y. P. Lin, Y. Y. Zhang, and Z. T. Cao. 1965. "Report on Excavations in Guanyin Cave, Qianxi County, Guizhou." *Gujizhuidongwu yu Gurenlei* 9, 3: 275–278 (in Chinese).

Secondary

An, Z. M., ed. 1987. *Pei Wenzhong: Collected Writings on Prehistoric Archaeology.* Beijing: Cultural Relics Press (in Chinese).

Anonymous. 1982. "Profoundly Cherishing the Memory of the Celebrated Scientist, Comrade Pei Wenzhong." *Acta Anthropologica Sinica* 1, 2: frontmatter (in Chinese).

Chang, K.-C. 1986. *The Archaeology of Ancient China.* 4th ed. New Haven, CT: Yale University Press.

Jia, L. P., and W. W. Huang. 1990. *The Story of Peking Man.* Beijing: Foreign Languages Press: Hong Kong: Oxford University Press.

Zhang, S. S. 1983. "'Productive, Like a Silkworm, Until the End of His Days'—Profoundly Cherishing the Memory of Professor Pei Wenzhong." *Shiqian Yanjiu* 1, 2: 182–184 (in Chinese).

Zhang, R. M., and X. C. Hu, eds. 1990. *Collected Scientific Papers of Pei Wenzhong.* Beijing: Science Press (in Chinese).

Stephen Williams

James Bennett Griffin   1905–1997

James B. Griffin's contributions to the archaeology of eastern North America were equaled only by his interest in cultural interactions between areas. A pioneer of the use of carbon–14 dating in North America, Griffin helped to establish a radiocarbon dating lab at the University of Michigan that would serve as the major source of New World dates for over twenty years.

During the past fifty years there have been few individuals in the field of American archaeology whose scope of interest and breadth of personal study has approached that of James B. Griffin. He covered the country from the Rocky Mountains on the edge of the Great Plains to the Atlantic Coast, from the southern edge of Canada to peninsular Florida, with actual visits to the locales and research institutions and vicariously through the myriad students that he trained. With this immense background of data translated into a series of significant and broad-scale syntheses, he affected the way all archaeologists involved in this large territory organized their own research findings (Griffin 1946, 1952a, 1967a). At this time his basic terminology of the cultural periods has, for better or worse, been almost universally adopted across this continental space, with some local variations.

Griffin's goals were always larger than mere culture-historical integrations, although his forays into that realm were very influential. The earliest work of this sort (Griffin 1946) included in the title the words "continuity" and "change," signaling his interest in cultural process, and though often neglected by later scholars, there were many significant paragraphs dealing specifically with social, economic, and political aspects of the cultures and sites that he had reviewed and put in chronological order (ibid., 75–93; see *contra* Taylor 1949, 82–90). From early on he also repeatedly examined the connection of prehistoric remains to the historically recorded tribal units—"ethnohistoric" concerns, as they are now termed (Griffin 1937, 1943, 1960).

A cardinal rule of his investigations was to obtain as much firsthand knowledge of the sites and artifacts that he was writing about as he could. In the search for broad expertise he traveled extensively in North America and Mexico and also studied materials in Europe and the Soviet Union. Although sometimes characterized as an armchair scholar, Griffin as a young man had substantial field experience in survey and exca-

James Bennett Griffin. (Chase Photographs, courtesy of Steve Williams)

vation. Some of these activities have only recently been published (Griffin 1991).

His interest in spatial expanses, larger than the eastern United States and including the American Southwest, Mexico, and even Siberia, stemmed from his fundamental emphasis on interareal interactions. This analytical perspective was reflected in a number of papers on such subjects as chronological correlations between the American East and Southwest (Griffin 1956) and between North America and Siberia (Griffin 1970), and purported Mesoamerican connections with the southeastern United States (Griffin 1947, 1967b, 1980).

For his database in these studies, he carefully investigated museum collections as well as the holdings of amateur (avocational) archaeologists. He always believed that "you have to *see* the data" whether it was housed in museums in Moscow, Leningrad, and Irkutsk or in the multitude of varied artifacts collected by local interested parties. People brought their favorite "rocks" and shards to the museum in Ann Arbor to show Griffin, or invited him to their homes, both humble farmhouses and palatial plantations, to look at their treasures. His eidetic memory for nearly every potsherd or arrowhead he had ever seen abetted this methodology, and age did not appreciably dim those abilities.

Two other attributes characterized Griffin's intellectual stance. First, he was always open-minded about new methods of analysis. In fact, he helped pioneer the use of carbon–14 dating in North America. His compilation of the dates and his explication of their meaning for the prehistory of the eastern United States, published in the "Cole Volume," a Festschrift for Professor Fay-Cooper Cole (Griffin 1952b), was one of the first attempts to apply the new technique. In 1949 he assisted a Michigan colleague, physics professor H. R. Crane, in establishing a radiocarbon-dating laboratory in Ann Arbor, which would thereafter serve as a major source of New World dates for nearly twenty years. In addition, Griffin became involved with Professor A. A. Gordus in the "sourcing" through laboratory analysis of obsidian, a widely traded mineral among prehistoric and classic peoples, and he wrote on the significance of its aboriginal distribution (Griffin 1965). Fifteen years later he was honored with the Fryxell Award from the Society for American Archaeology for his contribution to this special area of intersection between the physical sciences and archaeology.

Griffin's other outstanding attribute was his generosity in sharing his knowledge with others; no one ever showed him an artifact at a scientific meeting without getting a careful and useful reply. He was an inveterate attendee of national and regional conferences, and he was always available to assist students and young scholars in every way—on strictly archaeological questions as well as general advice on jobs, papers, and research. He taught for thirty-two years in the anthropology department at the University of Michigan, and he was also a visiting professor at four other institutions. His impact on the profession is revealed by the fact that when he retired in 1975, it took two Festschrift volumes to accommodate his numerous scholarly well-wishers.

James Bennett Griffin was born in Atchison, Kansas, on 12 January 1905, the son of Charles Bennett Griffin and Maude Bostwick Griffin. His father was a railroad man, with a New Hampshire background. Young Griffin lived in Kansas for seven years, followed by a two-year stay in Denver, Colorado. There he made fondly remembered visits to the Denver Museum of Natural History (Griffin 1985c). In 1914, the family moved to Oak Park, Illinois, where his father had a permanent position with the Rail Joint Company. This was to be Griffin's formative setting. He went to the local schools, and one of his boyhood friends was Wendell C. Bennett, who became a great Andean/South American archaeologist.

In the fall of 1923, at the age of eighteen, Griffin enrolled at the University of Chicago in a two-part, six-year program in their School of Business Administration and Law School. He obviously had in mind a career in the "real world," not academia. However, by the middle of his sophomore year, he switched to the social sciences and took two introductory courses in anthropology with Professor Fay-Cooper Cole. He received a Ph.B. in general social science in March 1927, but a career in business was still in his thoughts. He took a position in a training program for junior executives with Standard Oil of Indiana. When his time was spent more in pumping gas than learning management skills, Griffin became disenchanted with the business world.

In the fall of 1928 he decisively switched to academia when he enrolled as a graduate student in anthropology at the University of Chicago. The next four-and-a-half years were filled with academic courses taught by Cole, Edward Sapir, and Robert Redfield, among others, and with summer field experiences. In 1930 he received his M.A. in anthropology with a thesis written under the direction of Redfield on "Mortuary Customs in the Western Half of the Northeast Woodland Area" (Griffin 1985c, 2). During the summer of 1929, Griffin was supervised by Wilton M. Krogman in an archaeological survey in Adams County, Illinois (Griffin 1934), and an excavation at the Parker Heights

Mound near Quincy, Illinois (Griffin 1991). His long-term association with the Hopewell culture began the following summer (1930) when he dug at the Morton site near Lewiston, Illinois, under the direction of Cole and his assistant Thorne Deuel. His codiggers in the program, which was subsidized by the anthropology laboratory in Santa Fe, New Mexico, were J. O. Brew, Dorothy Cross, Rita Hahn, and Harold Driver and University of Chicago graduate students Fred R. Eggan and Richard D. Morgan. Only Hahn did not continue in the field, making this a remarkably successful training program for would-be archaeologists.

Finally, in the summer of 1931, Griffin himself led a field party in the excavation of late Algonkian and historic Delaware sites in the Upper Susquehanna Valley, Bradford County, Pennsylvania, for the Tioga Point Museum (Griffin 1931, 1985c). He was hired to continue the work the following summer, but state funds were vetoed by the governor. The Great Depression had arrived.

Another crucial turn in Griffin's academic path was awaiting. In the fall of 1932, while registered as a graduate student at Chicago, he was offered a three-year graduate fellowship, funded by Eli Lilly, at the University of Michigan, where Dr. Carl Guthe was developing an innovative program in American archaeology. His Chicago professors had nominated him for this rare opportunity. In February 1933 he moved to Ann Arbor, where he would spend his entire academic life, and began his appointment as "fellow in aboriginal North American ceramics." Although this new direction would dominate his professional life, he was still intellectually influenced by other trends that were "updating" North American archaeology. In May 1932, attending as a graduate student a small meeting of archaeologists in Chicago, he heard W. C. McKern set forth his "midwestern taxonomic classification" (a way of describing archaeological sites in the Midwest, where there was little deep-refuse stratigraphy, in both time and space); Griffin would later apply this methodology in his classic *Fort Ancient Aspect* volume (Griffin 1943). In late December 1934 he went to the organizational meeting for a national society for American archaeology, and he was one of the thirty-one signatories of its founding constitution (Griffin 1985b).

His fellowship at Michigan required that he complete his doctoral program by 1936, and he met the deadline with a dissertation that focused on the ceramics from the Norris basin in Tennessee, excavated under the direction of William C. Webb (Griffin 1938). He had studied these materials (1934–1935) in the Michigan Ceramic Repository established by Guthe. By the spring of 1936, he had received his degree and started a family: on Valentine's Day, he married Ruby Fletcher in the University of Chicago chapel. They later had three sons, John, David, and James.

The years between 1936 and 1941 were busy for the freshly minted Ph.D.; he became a research associate and associate curator in charge of the Ceramic Repository in the Museum of Anthropology at the University of Michigan. With this responsibility he began his lifelong investigation of eastern archaeology, characterized by specimen study and frequent travels to conferences and museums. At a meeting held in his research office in 1937, he helped to found the Southeastern Archaeological Conference in conjunction with JAMES A. FORD, then a graduate student at Michigan (Griffin 1985c, 6–7). He also formulated the preliminary synthesis (Griffin 1941) that became the intellectual background for his seminal paper on "Cultural Continuity and Change" delivered at the American Anthropological Association meeting in Andover, Massachusetts, in 1941 (Griffin 1946).

During World War II, he remained in Ann Arbor, teaching economic and political geography in a military training program at the university. In 1945 he was finally made an associate professor of anthropology with regular teaching responsibilities. His title at the museum was upgraded to director in 1946, shortly after the departure of his mentor Guthe to another position. In 1941 Griffin had teamed up with Ford at Louisiana State University and Philip Phillips of Harvard's Peabody Museum to undertake extensive field survey and archaeological testing in the Lower Mississippi Valley. This continued through the war (1940–1947), and the major monograph (Phillips et al. 1951) that resulted from this work has become a classic. Griffin's focus was on the ceramics, but he contributed significantly to the volume's synthetic aspects as well.

Over the next twenty-five years (1950–1975), Griffin continued to build his record of accomplishments from his base in Ann Arbor. He became a full professor in 1949, and his teaching and extensive involvement with graduate students increased as the Museum of Anthropology and the department became one of the principal training grounds for North American archaeologists in the country. Griffin extended his professional sphere through visiting professorships, at the University of California, Berkeley, the University of Colorado, Florida State University, and Louisiana State University. He also spent six months in Mexico in 1946, an academic year in Europe (1953–1954), a summer in Mexico and the Southwest (1955), three months in the USSR (1961–1962), and a Fulbright term in Denmark (1963), where he taught the first North American archaeology course at the University of Copenhagen. In his service to the profession, he was president of the Society for American Archaeology in 1951–1952, and in 1957 the society voted to award him the Viking Fund Medal for Archaeology for his achievements.

Griffin's fieldwork definitely diminished over the years. During the

Griffin examining the contents of the central burial pit in 1964 in Grand Rapids, Michigan. (Copyright University of Michigan Museum of Anthropology)

1950s he led a two-season program in the American Bottom, Illinois (Griffin 1951). In 1963–1964 he supervised the excavations at the Norton Mound group in Grand Rapids, Michigan, as well as at sites in the Flint and Saginaw areas. In 1966–1967 he helped a group of his students undertake an important field research program in Missouri—the Powers Phase project (Price and Griffin 1979). He believed that this venture could go beyond test-pitting and deal with entire-site occupations (Griffin 1985c, 15–16) as some of his students had desired to do.

Some of his noteworthy contributions to the literature included his three segments of the Festschrift for his Chicago professor Fay-Cooper Cole, which he also edited (Griffin, ed., 1952). In the summary chapter of this volume, he expounded his second major synthesis of eastern prehistory, dealing with the nature and scale of the social units discussed (Griffin 1952a, 354–355). His final comprehensive effort would be his article for *Science* magazine in 1967, though his ability to compose cogent overviews was apparent in contributions to various other volumes (Griffin 1978a, 1978b, 1985a). Despite his frequent characterization as only a "ceramic specialist," Griffin in fact covered a very broad range of periods and topics in his many works—from paleoindian times to the historic, and from climatology to dating techniques.

As his active academic career came to a close with his retirement in 1975, he was accorded many richly deserved honors: membership in the National Academy of Science (1968), an honorary doctor of science degree from Indiana University (1971), and awards as Henry Russell Lecturer (1972) and for distinguished service (1976) from the University of Michigan. At age seventy, Griffin took his leave from teaching and was feted at the Midwestern Archaeological Conference in October 1975 (Williams 1976) and at the annual meeting of the Society for American Archaeology in May 1976. The two-volume Festschrift (Cleland 1976, 1977) contained forty-two contributions, making another landmark in American archaeology. After retirement, Griffin continued to live in Ann Arbor doing research and writing historical reviews; his wife died in 1979. In 1984 he received a Regents Fellowship appointment at the National Museum of Natural History, Smithsonian Institution, in Washington, D.C., so he relocated there (with a fine alliance with Mary DeWitt Griffin) and remained associated with the institution for over ten years. In 1990 the Michigan Literary College named him one of ten distinguished professors of recent years.

Griffin's career trajectory was very straightforward, much like the man himself. He discovered the field of anthropology as an undergraduate, made a modest try at business, and then turned to academia for the rest of his life. He was very comfortable in those surroundings, confident of his own abilities and able to achieve his professional objectives. He was not a scatterbrained academic but was instead practical, forthright, and both politically and socially astute. He was a good administrator, well known for his ability to fight for the interests of his department and discipline. His successes at the university spanned more than forty years, and part of his legacy was an endowment to assist future students in the field of southeastern American archaeology. Although often reserved in his contacts with students, he had a wry sense of humor, which could emerge unexpectedly, such as in lectures. He had an old-fashioned propensity for telling people how to behave, but he never dictated what or how one should think. The deep respect in which he was held by his students and his colleagues needs no repetition here.

Griffin's legacy to American archaeology was significant. First, there was his strong published record of basic research, integrative reports, and synthetic overviews, totaling more than 260 items. Second, he affected the personal and intellectual lives of scores of students and scholars. By 1975, he had guided more Ph.D. candidates to their degree than anyone else in the department.

Finally, Griffin set a standard of academic behavior that is worthy of emulation today. He never ascribed excellence without due cause, and he never suffered fools gladly. If he saw or heard some "outrageous nonsense" being touted, he was wont to strike it down. He did, however, have a fine-tuned ability to evaluate new data and new ideas critically, and his numerous book reviews, which were well-balanced but truthful, were evidence of this. All serious students of the archaeology of eastern North America must acknowledge Griffin's contribution—whether their area is woodland influences on the western Plains or on the mid-Atlantic coast or the question of Iroquoian origins in the Great Lakes region. Griffin covered an unequaled range of subjects in space and time, and he knew the literature of his whole area as well as the people who did the actual work. In that sense, given the deluge of publications and researchers today, he was the last of a kind.

References
Primary

Biographical materials on Griffin are drawn primarily from personal acquaintance with the subject and from three autobiographical pieces (Griffin 1976, 1985b, and 1985c).

Griffin, James B. 1931. "The Athens Excavations." *Society for Pennsylvania Archaeology Bulletin* 2: 3.

———. 1934. "Archaeological Remains in Adams County, Illinois." *Illinois State Academy of Science* 2: 97–99.

———. 1937. "The Archaeological Remains of the Chiwere Sioux." *American Antiquity* 2: 180–81.

———. 1938. "The Ceramic Remains from the Norris Basin, Tennessee. An Archaeological Survey of the Norris Basin in Eastern Tennessee." Ed. W. S. Webb. *Bureau of American Ethnology Bulletin* 118: 253–358.

———. 1941. "A Preliminary Synthesis of Eastern United States Archaeology." Abstract: *Society for American Archaeology Newsletter* 2, 2: 33–34.

———. 1943. *The Fort Ancient Aspect: Its Cultural and Chronological Position in Mississippi Valley Archaeology.* Ann Arbor: University of Michigan.

———. 1946. "Culture Change and Continuity in Eastern United States Archaeology." *Papers of the R. S. Peabody Foundation for Archaeology, Andover* 3: 37–96.

———. 1947. "The Archaeological Zone of Buena Vista, Huaxcama, San Luis Potosi." With Wilfrido du Solier and Alex D. Krieger. *American Antiquity* 12: 15–33.

———. 1951. "The Central Mississippi Valley Archaeological Survey, Season 1950: A Preliminary Report." With A. C. Spaulding. *Journal of Illinois State Archaeological Survey,* n.s., 1 :74–82.

———. 1952a. "Culture Periods in Eastern United States Archaeology." In Griffin, 1952b: 352–392.

———. 1952b. "Festchrift for Professor Fay-Cooper Cole." In *Archaeology of Eastern United States.* Ed. James B. Griffin. Chicago: University of Chicago Press.

———. 1956. "The American Southwest: A Problem in Cultural Isolation." *Society for American Archaeology, Memoir* 11: 59–127.

———. 1960. "A Hypothesis for the Prehistory of the Winnebago." In *Culture in History: Essays in Honor of Paul Radin.* Ed. Stanley Diamond. New York: Columbia University Press.

———. 1965. "Hopewell and the Dark Black Glass." *Michigan Archaeologist* 11: 115–155.

———. 1967a. "Eastern North American Archaeology." *Science* 156: 175–191.

———. 1967b. "Mesoamerica and the Eastern United States in Prehistoric Times." In *Handbook of Middle American Indians,* 4: 111–131. Ed. G. F. Ekholm and Gordon R. Willey. Austin: University of Texas Press.

———. 1970. "Northeast Asian and Northwestern American Ceramics." *Proceedings of the Eighth International Congress of Anthropological and Ethnological Sciences* 3: 327–230.

———. 1976. "A Commentary on Some Archaeological Activities in the Mid-Continent, 1925–1975." *Mid-Continental Journal of Archaeology* 1, 1: 5–38.

———. 1978a. "Late Prehistory of the Ohio Valley." In *Handbook of North American Indians* 11: 547–559. Ed. William C. Sturtevant. Washington, DC: Smithsonian Institution.

———. 1978b. "The Midlands and the Northeastern United States." In *Ancient Native Americans.* Ed. J. D. Jenning. San Francisco: W. H. Freeman.

———. 1980. "The Mesoamerican-Southeastern Connection." *Early Man* 2, 3: 12–18.

———. 1985a. "Changing Concepts of the Prehistoric Mississippian Cultures of the Eastern United States." In *Alabama and the Borderlands,* pp. 40–63. Ed. R. R. Badger and L. A. Clayton. Tuscaloosa: University of Alabama Press.

———. 1985b. "The Formation of the Society for American Archaeology." *American Antiquity* 50: 262–271.

———. 1985c. "An Individual's Participation in American Archaeology." *Annual Reviews of Anthropology* 14: 1–23.

———. 1991. "The Parker Heights Mound at Quincy, Illinois, Appendix 3." In *The Kuhlman Mound Group and Late Woodland Mortuary Behavior.* Ed. Karen A. Atwell and Michael D. Conner. Kampsville Archeological Center Research Series 9: 276–291.

Griffin, James B., ed. 1952. *Archaeology of Eastern United States.* Chicago: University of Chicago Press.

Phillips, Philip, James A. Ford, and James B. Griffin. 1951. *Archaeological Survey of the Lower Mississippi Alluvial Valley, 1940–1947.* Papers of the Peabody Museum, no.25. Cambridge, MA: Harvard University.

Price, James E., and James B. Griffin. 1979. *The Snodgrass Site of the Powers Phase of Southeast Missouri.* Anthropological Papers 66. Ann Arbor: Museum of Anthropology, University of Michigan.

Secondary

Cleland, Charles E., ed. 1976. *Culture Change and Continuity: Essays in Honor of James Bennett Griffin.* New York: Academic Press.

———. 1977. *For the Director: Research Essays in Honor of James B. Griffin.* Anthropological Papers 61. Ann Arbor: Museum of Anthropology, University of Michigan.

Taylor, Walter W. 1949. *A Study of Archeology.* American Anthropological Association Memoir 69.

Williams, Stephen. 1976. "Reflections from the Lower Valley." *Mid-Continental Journal of Archaeology* 1, 1:101–103.